Counseling Psychology
Second Edition

Counseling Psychology
Second Edition

Charles Gelso
University of Maryland

Bruce Fretz
University of Maryland

THOMSON

WADSWORTH

Australia • Canada • Mexico • Singapore • Spain • United Kingdom • United States

Publisher	Earl McPeek
Acquisitions Editor	Brad Pothoff
Developmental Editor	Lisa Hensley
Market Strategist	Katie Matthews
Project Editor	Claudia Gravier
Art Director	David Day
Production Manager	Serena Sipho

ISBN: 0-15-507156-4
Library of Congress Catalog Card Number: 00-105660

Wadsworth Group/Thomson Learning
10 Davis Drive
Belmont CA 94002-3098
USA

For information about our products, contact us:
Thomson Learning Academic Resource Center
1-800-423-0563
http://www.wadsworth.com

For permission to use material from this text, contact us by
Web: http://www.thomsonrights.com
Fax: 1-800-730-2215
Phone: 1-800-730-2214

Printed in the United States of America
10 9 8 7 6 5

PREFACE

From the time of our graduate school days in the 1960s to the publication of the first edition of *Counseling Psychology* in 1992, we were troubled by the absence of a beginning text in our field. It appeared to us that every field within psychology had specialized books for students being introduced to the science and practice of the field—except the field that we studied, practiced, taught, and cared most about, counseling psychology.

At the time, there were numerous books on the activity of counseling, and such books were typically used as the texts in beginning courses in counseling psychology. As a result, both students and some professionals mistakenly confused counseling, the activity, with counseling psychology, the profession, considering the two synonymous. There were no texts devoted exclusively to the field of counseling psychology.

So the book filled a void in counseling psychology specifically and the field of psychology more generally. It also filled a personal need of ours as we taught advanced undergraduate and beginning graduate courses in counseling psychology. We have been heartened by how *Counseling Psychology* has been received by the field over the years, and pleased by what we think the book has contributed.

FEATURES OF THIS TEXT

This text is one of few, if any, to provide a comprehensive overview of counseling psychology—its professional practices and issues, its interventions, its science and research, and its basic concepts. Although this text should prove useful to experienced counseling psychologists, as did its predecessor, our focus is the student commencing his or her study of counseling psychology, be that student at the beginning graduate or advanced undergraduate level. For usage at the undergraduate level, the book is suitable for the upperclass student who has already completed a number of psychology courses.

The second edition is divided into three parts. In Part 1, we introduce the reader to the field of counseling psychology—its defining features and relationships to other specialties within and outside of psychology, its historical background and development, and its scientific and research bases. We explore new developments in the profession to deal with the changing world of health care; key concepts in being an ethical professional; and vital elements in becoming multiculturally competent as a counseling psychologist.

In Part II, the focus is on fundamental issues in individual counseling and psychotherapy, including both the essential ingredients of counseling and overviews of the three primary theoretical perspectives in the field—psychoanalytic, cognitive–behavioral, and humanistic–experiential. Part II concludes with the historically controversial topic of diagnosis and assessment, with an eye toward how assessment uniquely relates to counseling psychology. Part III reviews theory, research, and practice in several key intervention areas: career psychology, career interventions, couples and family interventions, therapeutic group work, prevention and outreach, and consultation. This set of key intervention areas encompasses and illustrates the unifying themes of counseling psychology, which are described in Chapter 1.

Despite the book's fundamental purpose as a useful comprehensive text, portions of *Counseling Psychology* are also applicable to other courses in the field. For example, Part I may be combined into a package suitable for courses on professional issues in counseling psychology. Likewise, Part II, and much of Part III, as well as Chapter 6 on multicultural counseling, could be incorporated into courses covering topics such as theories and techniques of counseling and therapy or courses introducing the student to the counseling process.

NEW TO THIS EDITION

It would be an understatement to say that things have changed a lot since the appearance of the first edition. Counseling psychology has moved forward substantially as a science and a profession. The number of doctoral programs has increased significantly; the quantity and quality of theoretical and empirical work has improved markedly; and the specialty itself hold a much stronger place within the discipline of psychology than it ever did. Along with this strengthening of counseling psychology, major social, intellectual, and professional changes have occurred over the past decade. Because of these substantial changes it seemed clear that *Counseling Psychology* needed revision.

In this second edition, we have sought to update thoroughly our material. As with the first edition, our intent is to provide an overview of counseling psychology—its professional practices and issues, its interventions, its science and research, and its basic concepts. We have aimed to be comprehensive, while at the same time, providing enough depth to make the material intellectually stimulating. Some of the most significant revisions and additions are:

- New developments in the profession to deal with the changing world of health care
- Updated research findings on all key counseling interventions and topics
- Key concepts in being an ethical professional
- Emerging developments in the major theories of counseling psychology, for example, career development, multicultural, and counseling theories
- Vital elements in becoming multiculturally competent as a counseling psychologist
- Current issues in the scientific study of counseling psychology practices.

ACKNOWLEDGMENTS

In certain ways, revising a book is much harder than writing the original. One constantly grapples with questions of what to add, what to omit, and what to change. Ms. Suzanne Friedman, who read and commented on nearly every chapter, has aided us enormously in this process. Suzanne was in the unique position of using the first edition as an undergraduate student, a graduate student, a teaching assistant, and an instructor! Thus, she was able to provide feedback from each of these perspectives. We are also grateful to Dr. Jean A. Carter, who gave feedback on several chapters from the vantage point of a psychotherapist as well as a leader in the field of counseling psychology. Our special thanks to Ms. Helen Palmer, Pitkin County (Colorado) Library for her efficient processing of countless interlibrary loan requests. We want to express our gratitude to Dr. Lisa Hensley, our editor at Harcourt, who abiding enthusiasm, encouragement, and suggestions greatly benefited us. Special thanks are due to Claudia Gravier project editor, for her support and wisdom in helping bring the project to completion. We would also like to thank David Day, art director; and Serena Sipho, production manager, for their excellent work on this project. We are particularly grateful to those individuals, who reviewed all or part of this manuscript including Heather Servaty, Radford University; Tammi Vacha-Haase, Western Michigan University; Alex Szollos, Millersville University; Saundra Tomkinson-Clark, Rutgers University.

In this second edition, we have tried to provide an updated overview of counseling psychology that is evenhanded, accurate, and "objective." You, the reader will of course be the ultimate judge of that.

C. J. G.

B. R. F

BRIEF TABLE OF CONTENTS

TABLE OF CONTENTS

Chapter 5
On Being an Ethical Psychologist   130

Chapter 6
Competent Counseling in a Culturally Diverse Society   152

Chapter 12
The Third Force: The Humanistic–Experiential Approach   361

Chapter 17
Systems in Action: Family and Couples Intervention   546

C H A P T E R 1

COUNSELING PSYCHOLOGY: AN INTRODUCTION TO THE FIELD

This book is devoted to counseling psychology, one of the major specialties within the broad science and profession of psychology. In this book we shall explore what counseling psychology is about—its central interventions and practices, its practitioners, and the job arenas in which counseling psychology is practiced. We shall examine both the scientific and the professional aspects of counseling psychology, while maintaining the view that science and research are, have always been, and always will be vital and necessary elements of this field. Finally, we shall take an in-depth look at the professional issues, problems, and beliefs that characterize the specialty.

On a personal note, this book has been written by two counseling psychologists who have practiced counseling psychology throughout their professional careers. You will not get a wholly impartial picture of the specialty and its issues and practices, simply because we, the authors, are steeped in the field, value it, and are strongly committed to its growth and development. We believe that counseling psychology has something special to offer to both its practitioners and the public, and you will certainly detect this viewpoint in the pages to come. Nonetheless, we have done our best to present the facts of the specialty in a clear, precise, and unbiased way.

STRUGGLE, GROWTH, AND DIVERSITY

In providing a general introduction to the specialty of counseling psychology and its development, three concepts are highly pertinent: struggle, growth, and diversity. The field has labored to clarify its identity, to distinguish itself from other specialties and fields within and outside of psychology, and indeed to maintain itself as a separate and independent specialty within psychology.

There have been times in the life span of counseling psychology in which the specialty seemed to flag. For example, one indication of the health of a professional field is the number of accredited training programs it offers and the changes in this number over the years. Within the first decade of the specialty's life (in the 1950s), there were approximately two dozen doctoral training programs accredited by the American Psychological Association (APA). These programs provided training at the doctoral level and offered degrees such as doctor of philosophy (Ph.D.) and doctor of education (Ed.D.). Following the first decade, however, the growth appeared to stop as the number of programs remained stable for several years and those in other related specialties such as clinical psychology increased markedly. In the early 1970s, the number of accredited programs even diminished slightly (dropping to 19 in 1972). During this time, the specialty was showing signs of stress and strain: Was it really distinctive enough to maintain itself as a separate entity? Did it have a broad enough appeal to attract a sufficient number of the best students to its doctoral programs? Was it viewed in sufficient esteem within the psychological community that its graduates could compete successfully in the job markets of their choice?

Any field, specialty, or profession must endure constant flux if it is to avoid stagnation and must struggle with issues involved in defining and enhancing itself. Countering these early difficulties, during the past two decades counseling psychology has managed to resolve some of its most serious problems and has grown considerably, showing many signs of strength and vitality. For example, over 70 doctoral training programs are now accredited by the APA.[1] This figure reflects a growth rate of greater than 60% since the mid-1980s, a rate that exceeds most other major fields in psychology. The strength and vitality of counseling psychology is also evidenced in the field's increased voice within the broader field of psychology and the American Psychological Association (Watkins, 1994), as well as notable accomplishments in both science and practice (Davis, 1996).

One aspect of the specialty that has been a part of it since its beginnings and has, if anything, increased in recent times, is its diversity. Counseling psychologists can be found working in a wide range of job settings and performing an even wider range of activities within them. In fact, some have suggested that counseling psychology is the most diverse of all of the specialties in psychology. Ivey (1979), for example, contends that:

> Counseling psychology needs to declare itself for what it is—*the most broadly based applied specialty of the American Psychological Association*. Our practitioners focus on the broadest array of professional psychological activities of any specialty. The counseling psychologist has the greatest array of possible interventions to assist client development and works with populations from infants through seniors in an almost infinite array of settings (p. 3) (italics in original).

In a book on applied specialties in psychology, Fretz (1985) begins the counseling psychology chapter by presenting a wide range of job activities and settings for psychologists and asking his readers to guess which kind of psychologist performed all the jobs in each of the settings. Interestingly, all of the jobs have been filled by counseling psychologists and are seen as highly appropriate for these professionals. (We shall present information on job functions and settings later in this chapter.)

In addition to implementation of a wide range of activities and interventions, there is another way in which counseling psychology has reflected diversity: its attention to cultural diversity and to the role of culture and diversity (e.g., racial–ethnic, gender, sexual orientation) in our society, in the profession, and within counseling interventions. Counseling psychology has been a leader within the field of psychology in its incorporation of multicultural and diversity concerns into its training, science, and practice. Examples of such attention may be seen in recent issues of *The Counseling Psychologist* devoted to multicultural counseling (Fischer, Jome, & Atkinson, 1998); multicultural counseling training (Kiselica, 1998); and gay, lesbian, and bisexual affirmative training (Croteau, Bieschke, Phillips, & Lark, 1998). Attention to cultural and individual diversity is also fully evident in the model training program created jointly by the Division of Counseling Psychology (Division 17) of APA and the Council of Counseling Psychology Training Programs (Murdock, Alcorn, Heesacker, & Stoltenberg, 1998). For example, as part of this model program, it is stated that:

---

[1]This number includes six departments in which counseling psychology is accredited jointly with school and/or clinical psychology as what are called "Combined Professional–Scientific Psychology" programs.

The specialty of counseling psychology has had a central role in the establishment of diversity as an important domain in professional psychology. Consequently, students in counseling psychology are taught to take a systemic, person–environment approach to understanding the psychological development of the individuals to whom assessment and intervention services are offered. Within such a framework, the interaction of factors such as culture, ethnicity, gender, sexual orientation, socioeconomic status, physical ability, and the unique characteristics of the individual are given special attention. Further, an emphasis is placed on understanding of personal values and belief systems within the framework of the individual's culture (p. 669).

Clearly, counseling psychology is diverse, and diversity is one of its major assets. However, clear and easy self-definitions and rich heterogeneity do not go hand in hand. It is not surprising that counseling psychology has had difficulty defining itself over the years.

At this point it is important to note that, within the diversity we have discussed, there have always existed several general roles and unifying themes in counseling psychology. Although it may seem at times that the specialty is so broad as to have no boundaries, and thus no identity, we believe that the general roles and unifying themes to be discussed below have always served to lend coherence and identity to the field.

Defining Features of Counseling Psychology

Throughout the history of counseling psychology, three roles have been central: the remedial, the preventive, and the developmental. (Probably the first to articulate these systematically were Jordaan, Myers, Layton, & Morgan, 1968). The individual importance of the roles has varied over time, yet all three have been significant in lending counseling psychology self-definition.

The *remedial* role entails working with individuals or groups, to assist them in remedying problems of one kind or another. As noted by Kagan, Armsworth, Altmaier, Tanney, and Vasquez (1988), remedial interventions may include personal–social counseling or psychotherapy at an individual, couples (e.g., marriage counseling), or group level. Crisis intervention and various therapeutic services for students requiring assistance with unresolved life events, are additional examples of work at the remedial level.

In remedial work, we take the view that something is awry, something needs to be "fixed," or some problem needs to be resolved in the individual, couple, or group. The problem(s) may be specific or general, at the surface level of personality or more deep-seated, and/or current or long-standing. As will be discussed later in this chapter, most counseling psychologists devote more time to this role than to the others; the frequency and popularity of individual counseling and psychotherapy are evidence of the role's prominence (Watkins, Lopez, Campbell, & Himmell, 1986). Nevertheless, the two remaining roles are viewed as vital to the specialty.

The *preventive* role is one in which the counseling psychologist seeks to "anticipate, circumvent, and, if possible, forestall difficulties that may arise in the future" (Jordaan et al., 1968, p. 1). Preventive interventions may focus on what are called "psychoeducational programs" aiming to forestall the development of problems or events.

In a university counseling center, one of the principal employers of counseling psychologists, preventive interventions may entail classes or workshops designed to impact a large number of students, for example, drug prevention programs, date-rape seminars for students, or suicide prevention programs for residence hall counselors and university personnel (Kagan et al., 1988). In a business or industrial setting, the preventive role is exemplified by consultations held with the company on matters such as team building, supervisor–staff relationships, management assessment and development, communication enhancement across departments, and so forth. As you can see from these examples, the specific form of the preventive activity differs for various settings. The key feature is to help clients make changes in their personal and interpersonal environments to minimize the occurrence of problems (Fretz, 1985) and forestall remedial work.

The third general role of the counseling psychologist is referred to as the *educative-developmental* role, the purpose of which is to "help individuals to plan, obtain, and derive maximum benefits from the kinds of experiences which will enable them to discover and develop their potentialities" (Jordaan et al., 1968, p. 1). Examples of the educative–developmental role might include various skill training interventions, couples groups formed to enhance relationships, growth groups, various workshops or seminars, and so forth. Another example might be a study skills class for college students aimed at making good students even more effective (rather than remedying ineffective academic behavior).

In the developmental role, the focus is on enhancement. We teach skills or enhance attitudes that facilitate dealing with inevitable, everyday problems and that maximize effectiveness or satisfaction. Obviously, the distinction between the developmental and preventive roles is often subtle—a matter of degree rather than kind. The key feature of the developmental role is that when performing it we are going beyond prevention, and are involved in enhancement.

We have been addressing the three general roles of the counseling psychologist as if each activity involved only one of the roles. Thus, the reader might now think, for example, that individual therapy or counseling is remedial, consultation with residence hall counselors is preventive, and couples' enhancement workshops are developmental. This is far from the truth. Most or perhaps all activities combine the three roles in one way or another. The difference is the point of emphasis. For example, when working in individual counseling with a client suffering from anxiety that interferes with job performance, the primary role of the counseling psychologist may be remedial, but the preventive and developmental roles will also be present. The counselor seeks to prevent more-debilitating disorders and to actualize the client's potential. Indeed, one of the distinguishing features of the counseling psychologist is his or her consistent attention to the three roles, and to the preventive and developmental, even when working with clients suffering from severe problems.

Unifying Themes

Although the three roles discussed above help to clarify what counseling psychology is and does, they do not show how it is distinguished from other fields. However, there have always existed certain themes that serve to bring together the diverse and sometimes disparate elements and activities of the profession and to differentiate it from related fields and specialties within and outside of psychology.

The first theme is the focus on intact, as opposed to profoundly disturbed, personalities. Although it appears that greater numbers of counseling psychologists have increasingly worked with more disturbed clients (Corazzini, 1997), it is also true that counseling psychologists (relative to practitioners in other fields, such as clinical psychology and psychiatry) more often work with clients who are closer to the normal range of functioning (see, for example, Hayes' [1997] analysis of the problem severity of clients seen in 31 counseling centers throughout the United States). Despite great variability in the range of clients with whom counseling psychologists now work, these practitioners often deal with clients who have "problems in living"; with individuals in the normal–neurotic rather than psychotic range; and with clients who function well but would like to improve.

In the earlier years of the specialty, it was often stated that counseling psychologists worked only with "normal" people. Given the increased number of counseling psychologists in private practice of therapy (who work with the same client population as practitioners from other fields; see later section) and the greater levels among disturbances of students now seen at college and university counseling centers (e.g., Corazzini, 1997), that statement no longer seems accurate. Although present-day counseling psychologists continue to be vitally interested in the concept of normality and well-functioning, some do most of their work with the severely disturbed, and most spend at least some of their time working with such persons.

At the same time, when considering the range of interventions offered by counseling psychologists, and when contrasting counseling psychology with other fields (e.g., clinical psychology, psychiatry), it is clear that counseling psychology devotes relatively more of its energy to clients closer to the normal range, and to the issue of psychological health and wellness (e.g., Lightsey, 1996). Thus the focus on intact personalities remains a unifying theme of the specialty.

When discussing level of severity of client problems, it is important to note that the term "client" is used here in its broad sense, since counseling psychology interventions include much more than counseling and psychotherapy. Although counseling and therapy are clearly very central activities, other key interventions include consultation, training, guidance, teaching, supervision, research, administration, and so forth. Many of these will be examined in various parts of this book. In any event, considering the clients we serve and the interventions we offer, it is easy to see how the preventive and developmental roles discussed earlier fit quite naturally into the work of the counseling psychologist.

The second unifying theme is the focus on people's assets and strengths, and on positive mental health, *regardless* of the degree of disturbance. Many years ago, in a classic paper by Super (1955), this emphasis on assets was referred to as a focus on hygiology (or health), rather than on psychopathology (or sickness). Super noted that even when working with the severely disturbed, the counseling psychologist tended to look for strengths and build on them. The underlying assumption is that even profoundly disturbed persons have strengths, assets, and coping abilities and that it is valuable to work with these.

Tied to this emphasis on the positive is a "point of view" characterized by hopefulness and optimism, based on the belief that

> individuals can change, can lead satisfying lives, can be self-directing, and can find ways of using their resources, even though these may have been impaired by incapacitating attitudes and feelings, slow maturation, cultural deprivation, lack of opportunity, illness, injury, or old age (Jordaan et al., 1968, p. 2).

How is this philosophical emphasis on the positive, and on assets and strengths, put into practice? In part, it is an assumption and attitude that we carry with us and convey to our clientele. In addition, the focus on strengths is operationalized in numerous ways. When counseling psychologists do career counseling with very disturbed clients, they are expressing the belief that the client has coping abilities that can be built upon that will allow him or her to make use of the counseling. When counseling psychologists work in an inpatient setting and develop an empathy training program for disturbed patients, they are building on these patients' resources. And when counseling psychologists empirically study healthy aspects of personality, they are expressing their involvement in this second unifying theme. The reader is encouraged to think of other examples of how this emphasis on strengths may be manifested. Suffice it to say for now that, whenever the counseling psychologist is functioning in the educative–developmental role, she or he is focusing on strengths and assets.

The third unifying theme of counseling psychology is an emphasis on relatively brief interventions. Thus, counseling psychologists typically view counseling as one of their primary activities, and this intervention is, by definition, relatively brief. To clarify what we mean by the term *brief,* it will help to contrast what we call *counseling* with a closely related term, *psychotherapy.* Some psychologists view these two terms as representing the same process, but we think the terms can be differentiated at least in the extreme, and that it is useful to do so.

Although exact numbers (e.g., numbers of counseling sessions) are of course arbitrary, we think of interventions up to about 12–15 sessions as constituting counseling, whereas interventions beyond that point are psychotherapy, or "therapy" as it is commonly called. In further differentiating counseling and therapy, we subscribe to the model suggested by Brammer, Abrego, & Shostrom (1993). In that model, at the extreme ends of the continuum, the two activities differ. At one extreme, work that is supportive seeks to educate, and focuses on situational problems and problem-solving at a conscious level, with normal individuals, is aptly called counseling. At the other end of the continuum, interventions that seek to reconstruct personality, include depth analysis, and analytically focus on subconscious processes with more troubled individuals, are best labeled psychotherapy. In the broad middle-range of this continuum, when the interventions contain a mixture of the factors just described, the terms *counseling* and *psychotherapy* imply one and the same process.

Having discussed the terms counseling and psychotherapy, let us now return to the issue of duration of treatment. We have said that counseling psychologists view counseling as defined above as a central part of their work (cf. Fitzgerald & Osipow, 1986). Further, although counseling psychologists certainly conduct psychotherapy, the kind of psychotherapy that has been seen as central to the counseling psychology tends to be short-term. (The reader is referred to Leona Tyler's [1961] early discussion of brief therapy as especially suited to counseling psychology.) Again, although exact figures would be arbitrary, generally interventions of up to 6 months' duration would be considered short-term therapy.

In recent years many social and economic factors have combined to create a climate in which short-term treatment is strongly favored and, in fact, is mandated by many managed-care companies (discussed in Chapter 4). Although we do not see brief therapy as a panacea or indeed as always appropriate (see Seligman, 1996), it often is a highly effective format (Gelso, 1992; Steenbarger, 1992). Given their long-standing focus on brief treatments, counseling psychologists are in a good position to work successfully within the current climate, while also working to change the climate toward one in which each client receives the most suitable treatment, be it short term or longer term.

The fourth unifying theme of counseling psychology is an emphasis on person–environment interactions, rather than an exclusive focus on either the person or the environment. Although the specialty has been criticized for not paying enough attention to the environment portion of the person–environment interaction in actual practice (as opposed to writing about practice; see Ivey, 1979), counseling psychology has since its inception carefully considered the impact and role of the situation in the client's life (whether the client is an individual, group, organization, etc.). Consequently, theories that have placed an extreme emphasis on *intrapsychic* explanations of behavior have not on the whole been attractive to counseling psychologists. The interest in person–environment transactions is also evident in the attention paid over the years to activities such as consultation, outreach, and environmental modification (Gallesich, 1985; Howard, 1993; Ivey, 1979; Meade, Hamilton, & Ka-Wai-Yuen, 1982).

The fifth and final unifying theme is an emphasis on educational and career development of individuals and on educational and vocational environments. Along with educational psychologists, counseling psychologists have contributed significantly to the study of academic performance and problems. An early example of this is the work of Robinson and his students on the development of effective study methods and treatments (Robinson, 1970). In the career development area, counseling psychologists both study vocational choice and development and provide services to enhance career development and treat vocational problems. For some counseling psychologists, career counseling and development is the heart of counseling psychology and is its most distinctive area of research and practice (e.g., in contrast to personal counseling or therapy, an activity counseling psychologists share with many other professionals). These psychologists are concerned that practitioners are no longer making career counseling a central enough part of their work and are not as interested in it as they ought to be or used to be (Fitzgerald & Osipow, 1986; Watkins et al., 1986).

Although career counseling does represent less of the worktime of counseling psychologists than, for example, personal counseling or therapy, graduate training in career counseling continues to be strong (Birk & Brooks, 1986; Schneider, Watkins, & Gelso, 1988; Watkins, 1994). Further, counseling psychologists continue believe that they should be competent in career counseling and assessment (Holahan & Yesenosky, 1992); and they do devote time to career and educational interventions, particularly when working in educational settings, such as counseling centers. In keeping with our fifth unifying theme, Watkins (1994) asserted that one of the major trends in counseling psychology was that

> [t]he vocational arm of the specialty continues to be a significant part of who we are, continues to provide rich fertile opportunities for practice and research, and continues to thrive and flourish within counseling psychology (p. 322).

A Perspective on Definition and Identity

From what we have presented thus far, it can be seen that counseling psychology is that specialty within psychology that tends to focus on research, assessment, and interventions on and with clients who have relatively intact personalities; that is, people who are not profoundly disturbed, but instead are closer to the "normal range," than typically treated clients, for example, by psychiatrists or clinical psychologists. Also, the specialty tends to pay close attention to individual's assets and psychological strengths—even when those persons are profoundly disturbed. The central interventions of the specialty tend to be brief and varied, for example, counseling, therapy, guidance, training, consultation, outreach, teaching, and so forth. Throughout the life of counseling psychology, particular attention has been paid to person–environment interactions and to educational and vocational development and environments.

It is important to stress that the roles and themes discussed in the preceding sections represent central tendencies. In particular, while the unifying themes help solidify counseling psychology's identity and clarify its distinctiveness in relation to other fields within and outside of psychology (examined later in this chapter), it must be understood that there is great variability around these central tendencies, and that probably few, if any, individual counseling psychologists fit each theme perfectly in their career. In fact, individual practitioners vary greatly regarding the extent to which, and the ways in which, the themes fit their practice. One practitioner may, for example, do mostly long-term therapy with deeply troubled clients, but still consider herself as practicing counseling psychology because she pays close attention to the healthy aspects of her clients' personalities, does a good deal of career counseling within the context of her psychotherapy, and is very attentive to the person–environment interactions in her clients' development. Another counseling psychologist may work largely with relatively normal clients, conducting a variety of workshops and consulting with business organizations on, for example, how to improve the leadership sensitivity to worker concerns and ways of reducing violence in the workplace. His work is largely within a preventive and developmental framework.

Given the above complexity, what determines whether one is a counseling psychologist and whether one is doing counseling psychology? Just as in any field or profession, the answer to such questions must be complex. We offer that whether one is a counseling psychologist is determined by the interaction of the five unifying themes in his or her professional life. Given proper credentialing in the specialty (discussed in next section), the practitioner may perform a wide range of activities and be legitimately considered a counseling psychologist doing the work of counseling psychology.

TRAINING, JOB SETTINGS, AND ACTIVITIES

In this section, we shall look at the kind of graduate training required to be a counseling psychologist, where counseling psychologists work, and the typical job activities in which they are involved.

How and Where Are Counseling Psychologists Trained?

Unlike numerous psychological and educational–vocational counselors who work with a master's degree, the counseling psychologist is trained at the doctoral level. It is strongly recommended that the doctorate (usually a Ph.D.) be earned from a university training program accredited by the APA. Such accreditation influences several factors that are typically quite important to the professional life of the counseling psychologist: how readily he or she can become licensed as a psychologist in the state in which he or she practices; the range of psychologist positions in which he or she is employable; whether or not he or she can become a member of several important organizations, for example, the National Register of Health Service Providers in Psychology; how likely his or her clients are to obtain insurance payments when being treated on a private basis. Although in the past many counseling psychologists received their doctoral degrees in nonaccredited programs, it has become increasingly important and now the standard practice for graduates to be trained in APA-accredited programs.

As of this writing, there are some 71 counseling psychology doctoral training programs that are APA accredited. Although the number of accredited programs increased dramatically during the 1980s, the number of programs seeking accreditation in the past few years has leveled off. Accreditation patterns suggest that the list of accredited programs will, as in other areas of professional psychology, continue to grow at a slow but steady rate.

Characteristics of Training in Counseling Psychology
We have been focusing thus far on the question of APA accreditation for doctoral programs. But what are the main features of these programs? And what is the nature of training in counseling psychology?

To begin with, most doctoral programs are organized so that students will need about 5–6 years to complete graduate study. Also, in most programs students either earn a master's degree on the way to the doctorate or have already earned the master's prior to admission to the doctoral program.

Doctoral training programs in counseling psychology are located either in colleges of education or departments of psychology, and these two settings often differ with respect to whether or not the master's degree is required or expected before admission to the doctoral program. In departments of psychology, students are typically admitted to the doctoral program regardless of whether they have earned a master's. If they do not already have that degree, they usually earn it on the way to the doctorate. In many programs located in colleges of education, on the other hand, students must first get a master's degree and then apply for admission to the doctoral program. Some of these programs also consider it desirable for the student to gain work experience in the counseling field before being admitted to a doctoral program. These issues (experience, master's before admission) being somewhat controversial; students contemplating a career in counseling psychology should think through the pros and cons in deciding about which programs to apply to.

Counseling psychology programs in colleges of education and those in departments of psychology are extremely similar in nearly all other important respects. Significantly, the overall quality of training in psychology generally and counseling psychology specifically is equivalent in the two settings (see Birk & Brooks, 1986). Further, within the broad field of psychology, it has been resolved unequivocally that where graduate programs were administratively housed was essentially unimportant (Resolutions Approved by the National Conference, 1987).

Another main feature of training in counseling psychology is that the scientist–practitioner or scientist–professional model is seen as the basic training model in the field. (Note that the terms *practitioner* and *professional* are used interchangeably.) Thus counseling psychology training at the doctoral level seeks to prepare students both to practice psychology (e.g., conduct counseling) and to perform research. Although the scientist–practitioner model may be somewhat less prominent in applied fields of psychology in general than it has been in the past (see Resolutions Approved by the National Conference, 1987), in counseling psychology this model of training appears to be as prominent as ever. Thus, at the aforementioned Georgia Conference (counseling psychology's third national conference), the following statement on training was approved:

> We acknowledge the balance of science and practice will vary across programs, their faculty and students. Some counseling psychologists may not publish research, some may never consult or evaluate programs, and others may neither teach nor offer direct therapeutic services; but all are expected to have education and training which will provide them with entry level professional competencies in research, therapeutic practice, teaching and other skills of our discipline (Meara, Schmidt, Carrington et al., 1988, p. 369).

In chapters 2 and 3, we shall take a further look at the scientist–practitioner model of training in counseling psychology. In terms of the main features of training that we have been discussing, the point to be made here is that throughout graduate education, students are expected to learn about and conduct both scientific research and counseling psychology practice. Three or four years of coursework are

TABLE 1.1.   Percentage of Counseling Psychologists in Various Job Settings.

Setting	Percentage
College or university (includes departments of psychology, counseling psychology, educational psychology, etc.)	35.2
Independent practice	20.1
College or university counseling center	17.2
Hospital (includes general, psychiatric, and VA hospital)	7.4
Clinic (private and HMO clinic, community mental health center)	4.4
Other human service (includes nursing home, rehab facility, etc.)	4.2
Government (military, criminal justice system, federal government, etc.)	2.1
Schools and other educational settings	2.1
Medical schools	1.7
Business and industry	.9
Other	4.5
Not specified	.1

Source: Adapted from *1995 APA Directory Survey* (APA Research Office, 1995). Note that the percentages of participants employed at counseling centers and other human service settings are extrapolated from the 1998 APA Survey.

followed by an internship, ordinarily a full-time one-year experience in which the student receives in-depth supervised training in a service setting such as a university counseling center, community mental health center, or medical hospital. During the last phase of training, and what for many is the end point of their program, the student completes a doctoral dissertation. This is a major piece of scientific research aimed at advancing knowledge in the field. The student works closely with a research advisor, typically a faculty member in his or her counseling psychology program, in developing the project.

Where Do Counseling Psychologists Work?

Over the years, a number of surveys have been conducted on counseling psychologists, examining where they work and what they do. Most of these surveys have sampled members of the Division of Counseling Psychology (Division 17) of APA, and have yielded consistent findings. The largest samples are derived from the surveys done by the APA's Research Office. Table 1.1 presents data of job settings from a recent APA survey that included 2,151 members of Division 17 who were employed full time (APA, 1995).

As you can see, over a third of the participants were in the category College and University (over 90% of these are faculty members and a few are administrators). Also, approximately 17% were employed in college and university counseling centers. Thus over 50% of this large sample had their primary jobs in higher education settings.

Of the remaining job settings, the only one that stands out in terms of the percentages is Independent Practice. A fifth of the sample had their primary employment in independent practice. The remainder of the sample were spread across a wide range of settings.

We should note that these results compare very closely to data gathered in the 1980s (e.g., Fitzgerald & Osipow, 1986; Watkins et al., 1986). When we compared the recent APA surveys (APA, 1995, 1998) with others over the years, several trends become apparent. First and perhaps foremost is the great diversity of employment settings demonstrated in each and every survey. Throughout, a few settings are shown to employ the majority of counseling psychologists, while the remaining professionals are spread out among many others.

Second, over the years a remarkably stable proportion of counseling psychologists have been employed in higher-education settings. From the time of the first analysis by Dreese (1949), one-half or more of the participants sampled have found their primary employment in this setting, either as a faculty member, counseling center practitioner, or administrator. Within the higher-education setting, the percentages filling such jobs have also appeared to remain stable.

Two changes in employment patterns deserve comment at this point. The first of these represents a trend over many years, whereas the second is much more recent. Regarding the first trend, a steady decline has occurred over the years in the percentage of counseling psychologists who have their primary employment in VA medical centers. Historically the VA has been a primary employer of counseling psychologists. In fact, as shall be discussed in Chapter 2, the VA was instrumental in the development of counseling psychology as an independent and separate specialty in psychology. In the first occupational analysis of counseling psychology, Dreese (1949) found that 19% of his sample worked at VA centers. In Samler's analysis in the early 1960s, however (Samler, 1964), this number dropped to 9%, and in Fitzgerald and Osipow's analysis (1986), the number declined further, to less than 3%. The most recent analyses have suggested that this figure has stabilized (e.g., APA, 1998; Gaddy, Charlot-Swilley, Nelson, & Reich, 1995).

On the other side of the ledger, the percentage of counseling psychologists who are employed primarily as independent practitioners has increased markedly in recent years. For many years, the number of counseling psychologists who chose private practice as their primary career hovered around 5%. In the late 1970s and early 1980s this began to change, so that by the mid-1980s greater numbers of counseling psychologists had as their primary job setting private practice than counseling centers, the traditional practice setting for the specialty (Fitzgerald & Osipow, 1986; Watkins et al., 1986). At that time, that fact that younger counseling psychologists who were sampled were even more likely to seek private practice careers suggested that the trend would continue. And, in fact, during the 1990s, there did appear to be a further increase in the numbers of counseling psychologists in private practice (Gaddy et al., 1995; Holahan & Yesenosky, 1992). Further, there is reason to believe the figures reported on the percentage of counseling psychologists in private practice (and other practice settings, as well) in most studies are underestimates (APA, 1998; Gaddy et al., 1995). This is because, as noted earlier, most surveys have looked at job settings of counseling psychologists who were members of

Division 17. The sizable number who are *not* members of this division of APA are more likely to be in practice, and less likely to be in academic positions. It is not clear just how large is the percentage of all counseling psychologists whose primary job setting currently is private practice, but the number could represent well over one-third of the field (see the APA, 1998, for the *1997 Directory Survey*).

At the same time, it is also not clear whether the trend toward private practice will continue, given the stresses and strains of this job setting in the current economic climate (see Chapter 4 for discussion). Our best guess is that the private practice figures will decline somewhat or at least level off in the near future.

It is important that beginning students and professionals alike recognize the trends and data discussed above, and that doctoral training programs incorporate these data into their planning. Division 17, which was once considered a home for academics only, has made serious efforts in recent years to increase its relevance to counseling psychologists in practice settings, while maintaining its long-standing relevance to college- and university-based counseling psychologists.

What Do Counseling Psychologists Do?

Probably the most fundamental and clear finding from job analyses is that counseling psychologists are involved in performing an extensive range of jobs (APA, 1995, 1998; Fitzgerald & Osipow, 1986; Watkins et al., 1986). Just as their job settings are highly diverse, so are their actual job activities. For example, sizable numbers of counseling psychologists devote at least a portion of their work time to each of the following: counseling and psychotherapy (individual, group, couples/family); consultation; psychological testing, assessment, and evaluation; research and writing; teaching, training, and supervision; and administration. When one considers the specific activities incorporated under each of these general job categories, as well as the various job settings in which the activities are carried out, one can appreciate the rich diversity of activities within counseling psychology.

Within the context of this diversity, the activity performed by the greatest number of counseling psychologists for the greatest amount of time is counseling in general and individual counseling in particular. (Here we include psychotherapy under the general category "counseling.") When we piece together findings from earlier, more comprehensive studies (Fitzgerald & Osipow, 1986; Watkins et al., 1986) with surveys conducted in the 1990s (APA, 1998; Holahan & Yesenosky, 1992), the primacy of counseling is entirely clear and consistent. Earlier data (Fitzgerald & Osipow, 1986), which is still very likely applicable today, indicates the percentages of counseling psychologists involved in six different counseling modes: personal adjustment counseling (80.1%), individual vocational counseling (70.9%), long-term psychotherapy (69.2%), couple and family counseling (58.4%), group counseling (49.3%), and group vocational counseling (36.2%). These findings are also consistent with those of Watkins and colleagues, which indicated that individual treatments were the most frequently performed of the counseling activities.

In addition to the numbers of counseling psychologists who perform various activities, Watkins and colleagues and Fitzgerald and Osipow looked at the percent-

Primary and Secondary Self-views of Counseling Psychologists.   TABLE 1.2.

	Primary		Secondary	
Self-view	*n*	%	*n*	%
Clinical practitioner	330	47.7	131	19.2
Academician	197	28.4	103	15.1
Administrator	79	11.4	100	14.7
Consultant	40	5.8	136	19.9
None	25	3.6	34	5.0
Researcher	17	2.5	68	10.0
Other	2	0.3	36	5.3
Supervisor	2	0.3	74	10.8
Total	692	100.0	682	100.0

Source: Reprinted from Watkins et al. (1986).

age of respondents' work time devoted to the different job functions. Both research teams found that counseling psychologists typically devote about 25% of their time to counseling activities, more time than is devoted to any other single activity or cluster of activities.

Fitzgerald and Osipow also found that the majority of their respondents were involved in: research (67% of the respondents), the supervision of counseling (70%), teaching and training (75%), administration (68%), consultation (71%), and writing/editing (65%). Of these activities, the median percentage of work time devoted was greatest for teaching/training (19%), followed closely by research combined with writing and editing. The total percentage of time devoted to these two sets of activities is 15%. (Note that Fitzgerald and Osipow separated research from writing and editing, whereas we believe they are better placed into one broad category, "research.") The percentages of work time devoted to the remaining activities are as follows: consultation, 10%, administration, 10%, and supervision 9%. The job activity percentages presented by Fitzgerald and Osipow closely approximate data gathered in more recent surveys (APA, 1995, 1998). The Fitzgerald and Osipow survey, though, used more refined and relevant categories of job activities.

Given the job activities of counseling psychologists, one might ask, as did Watkins and colleagues (1986), how professionals in this specialty view themselves. For example, what percentage of counseling psychologists view themselves primarily as practitioners? What percentage view themselves secondarily as clinical practitioners? What percentage view themselves primarily or secondarily as consultants? academicians? researchers? administrators?

As seen in Table 1.2, in the Watkins et al. sample of nearly 700 members of the Division of Counseling Psychology of APA, most respondents viewed themselves as either clinical practitioners (47.7%) or academicians (28.4%). Few claimed as *primary* any of the other roles listed by Watkins et al. The respondents' *secondary* self-views, however, seemed more spread out, with 10% or more seeing their secondary self-view as either that of clinical practitioner, academician, administrator, consultant, supervisor, or researcher. Thus, although most counseling psychologists see themselves primarily as either practitioners or academics, most also have secondary self-views, and these reflect the variety of roles that are played.

Changes in Job Activities Over the Years.

Have things changed in terms of what counseling psychologists do? Is the specialty different in this way from when it emerged as an independent specialty nearly 50 years ago? The answer must inevitably be yes and no. Let us try to clarify why.

Just as has always been true, counseling and related activities (therapy, assessment, interviewing, etc.) are engaged in by a sizable proportion of counseling psychologists. Things have changed, however, in that when one compares the review by Samler (1964) to analyses by Watkins and colleagues and Fitzgerald and Osipow, as well as the most recent APA data (1995, 1998), it is clear that a greater percentage of counseling psychologists appear to be involved in a wider variety of counseling interventions than ever before. For example, in the early 1960s, about a quarter of the counseling psychologists did counseling as their main activity. In looking at data gathered in the 1980s and 1990s, it appears clear that significantly more than 25% of current counseling psychologists do counseling as their main activity. Remember, well over 60% are in practice settings (see Table 1.1) and for nearly 50% the primary self-view is as clinical practitioner (see Table 1.2).

In contrast to Fitzgerald and Osipow, however, we do not interpret these changes as indicating that the specialty is becoming increasingly service-oriented and decreasingly research-oriented. To begin with, it is inevitable that as the specialty graduates more and more counseling psychologists, the percentage holding service positions will increase. After all, we cannot simply train counseling psychologists to be academicians because of the finite number of academic posts available, and because the training, by definition, focuses on teaching students to *practice* counseling psychology, not merely to study it.

When comparing earlier to more recent studies, there does appear to be a substantial increase in the numbers of counseling psychologists who call what they do "psychotherapy." In earlier times, that activity appeared to be the sole province of clinical psychologists (within psychology). In more recent times, counseling psychologists have joined the large number of professionals from several fields (psychiatry, psychiatric social work, clinical psychology, etc.) who perform therapy as a part of their clinical practice. Although not fully documented, it does appear to us that, given the specialty's historical and current emphasis on brevity, the psychotherapy performed by counseling psychologists has tended to be short term, even before brief treatments were required by managed-care companies for insurance reimbursement (see Gelso & Johnson, 1983; Tyler, 1961).

As increased numbers of counseling psychologists have become focused on personal counseling and psychotherapy in recent years, some observers have suggested that the centrality of the vocational side (e.g., vocational psychology and career counseling) has been eroding simultaneously. Samler's (1964) earlier review, however, indicates this was also the case 35 or so years ago. It seems to us that if vocational psychology and vocational counseling were ever *the* foundation of counseling psychology, that may have been in the earliest days of the specialty; soon after, a host of other activities were added to form the core of the field.

Moreover, as noted earlier, training in career counseling continues to be strong, and has not declined in quality or amount in recent years (Birk & Brooks, 1986; Schneider et al., 1988; Watkins, 1994). It does appear that, when forced to state a preference, counseling psychologists prefer to do personal counseling or therapy more than career counseling. But it appears equally true that career counseling continues to be engaged in by most practitioners, and that practitioners view this activity as important to their identity as counseling psychologists (Fitzgerald & Osipow, 1986; Holahan & Yesenosky, 1992).

Finally, rather than seeing the specialty as becoming less oriented toward research and science, we see the research emphasis being a major thread of continuity in the specialty from its beginnings to the current time. As we enter the twenty-first century, it appears that the research role of the counseling psychologist is as strong as ever (Gelso, Betz, Friedlander, Helms et al., 1988; Rude, Weissberg, & Gazda, 1988; Watkins, 1994), and that as a continuation of the 1990s, there is an increased commitment to making the scientist–practitioner model work (see Heppner, Carter, Claiborn, Brooks et al., 1992; Watkins, 1994).

COUNSELING PSYCHOLOGY AND OTHER SPECIALTIES AND FIELDS: DISTINCTIVENESS AND OVERLAP

Within the broader discipline of psychology, there are a number of applied specialties that overlap considerably with each other and thus with counseling psychology. The specialties most closely related to counseling psychology are clinical psychology, industrial/organizational psychology, school psychology, and community psychology. These specialties are referred to as "applied" because each seeks, in its own way, to apply principles of psychology to the solution of human problems. The lack of clear and concise boundaries among these specialties is inevitable because they rely essentially on the same training and education in basic core areas of psychology. Further, all employ similar assessment and intervention procedures in their attempts to solve human problems. At the same time, each specialty has some distinctive foci.

In comparing counseling psychology to other fields and specialties within and outside of psychology, it is useful to keep in mind the unifying themes of counseling psychology as discussed earlier: (1) the focus on intact personalities, or problems and clients closer to the "normal" part of the range; (2) attention to assets and strengths, even when working with the severely disturbed; (3) implementation of relatively brief interventions; (4) emphasis on person–environment interactions; and (5) emphasis on educational and career development of individuals and on educational and vocational environments.

The specialty most often compared to counseling psychology is that of clinical psychology. The latter is the largest of the applied specialties in psychology. Despite much overlap in training, job activities, and job settings of counseling and clinical psychologists, there are notable differences. Historically as well as currently, clinical psychology has concerned itself with the study and treatment of abnormal or maladaptive behavior (Garfield, 1985). Although clinical psychologists do not ignore people's assets or strengths, relatively greater attention has typically been paid to underlying pathology rather than health (Norcross, Sayette, Mayne, Karg, & Turkson, 1998). Perhaps as a consequence, clinical psychologists have tended to implement treatments of longer duration, more often called psychotherapy (of a longer-term nature) than counseling. Attention to educational and vocational development and environments has not been a central part of the clinical psychologist's work. Because of the focus on psychopathology, clinical psychologists are much more likely than counseling psychologists to be found in work settings that focus on the severely disturbed, for example, inpatient psychiatric settings and mental hospitals; they are much less likely to be found in educational settings, for example, university counseling centers (Gaddy et al., 1995; Strauss, 1997).

Although significant differences remain between counseling and clinical psychology, and will likely continue to remain (Norcross, Sayette, Mayne, et al., 1998), the two specialties have moved closer together over the years. In the 1980s, for example, Garfield (1985) noted that clinical psychologists were more likely than in past years to work with the less disturbed and pay attention to assets. Likewise, as we have noted earlier, counseling psychologists increasingly conduct psychotherapy.

In attempting to define themselves and their specialty, counseling psychologists have most often focused on the similarities and differences between themselves and clinical psychologists. Perhaps this is because of the major overlap in the area of counseling/psychotherapy, an activity that holds broad appeal to both specialities (as well as to other fields). In fact, though, there are similarities with other specialties that seem about as great.

The specialty of *community psychology* focuses on person–environment interactions as they promote psychological health and cause disturbances. Community psychology tends to move "beyond the individual to deal with broad problems of mental health and human relations in community settings" (Iscoe, 1997, p. 117). Although this specialty is more difficult to cleanly and neatly define than perhaps any in psychology, its general goal is "broadly . . . concern . . . with clarifying the complex interrelationships between individuals and their social environment, and with the discovery and implementation of more effective ways of coping with the stresses of modern life" (Spielberger & Stenmark, 1985, p. 75). Through a wide variety of interventions, community psychologists seek to help broader systems, institutions, communities, and so forth, change so that they facilitate psychological well-being.

In contrast to either counseling or clinical psychologists, community psychologists are more likely to be involved in consulting on issues of organizational development, on community development and social change, with school systems, on community mental health planning and administration, on social policy analysis, and so forth (see Iscoe, 1997). They are indeed concerned with clinical and counseling activities but not nearly so much as clinical and counseling psychologists.

Counseling psychology and community psychology overlap considerably in their attention to the environment side of person–environment interaction. This is most clearly seen in the counseling psychologist's role in consultation and outreach (see chapters 18 and 19). Also, both fields emphasize preventive and developmental roles in intervention. The counseling psychologist, however, is more likely to be concerned with direct counseling or psychotherapeutic interventions and with problems of educational and vocational development and choice.

A third specialty that overlaps with counseling psychology is *school psychology*. This specialty has been defined by Bennett as "the application of knowledge and skills to the prevention or solution of problems children face in learning what society deems essential for success" (1985, p. 129). Bennett goes on to note the overlap between school psychology on the one hand and counseling, clinical, and industrial/organizational psychology on the other but stresses that their key difference lies in the concern of school psychologists for children, adolescents, and college students "in their world of work, the school setting." School psychologists do consultation, counseling, and assessment with students, parents, and teachers, with the aim of furthering the educational process; for example, helping children learn more effectively and enhancing emotional adjustment. It should be noted, though, that in recent years, school psychologists have moved into a wider range of roles and job settings; for example, vocational rehabilitation facilities, behavioral medicine programs, day treatment and residential facilities (see Poland, 1997; Talley & Short, 1994).

The overlap between counseling and school psychologists is especially great when counseling psychologists work in elementary and secondary schools (more typically the setting for the school psychologist) and when school psychologists work in higher education (more typically the setting for the counseling psychologist). Even in these settings, it appears that the school psychologist is more likely to be involved in educational and psychological assessment of students (e.g., to determine which factors are impeding effective learning), whereas the counseling psychologist is more often involved in counseling efforts with students and their families. Essentially, though, the major differences between these two specialties is in work setting and all that leads to. The school psychologist is primarily employed in elementary and secondary schools; the counseling psychologist is found in the variety of settings discussed earlier.

The final applied specialty within psychology that will be contrasted to counseling psychology is industrial/organizational (I/O) psychology. Siegel (1985) defines I/O psychology as "the science of behavior applied to persons in industrial and other organizations. Its objective is to enhance organizational effectiveness" (p. 207). Moreover, I/O psychologists, as Siegel notes, are centrally involved, in one way or another, in the assessment and enhancement of employee, supervisory, and managerial performance. As Tenopyr (1997) notes, the traditional core of activities of the industrial psychologist revolves around personnel selection; appraisal of employees' job performance; job analysis to determine what the job duties are and what employee knowledge, abilities, and skills are necessary to do each job; and the development of assessment centers, that are "collections of simulated work situations in which employees are observed to determine job abilities" (Tenopyr, 1997, p. 186). There are important differences between the traditional industrial and the organizational roles of the I/O psychologist. Tenopyr indicates that the industrial role emphasizes the assessment and improvement of individual behavior (e.g., work performance), whereas the organizational role focuses on whole organizations (e.g., a company's purchasing department). The organizational role may be subsumed under a newer subfield of I/O psychology called "organizational development" (Tenopyr, 1997).

In comparing I/O and counseling psychology, a major area of overlap becomes evident: the concern with career and vocational development and environments. Counseling psychologists study career development in all settings and have sought to develop theories of what makes people gravitate toward certain fields, what interferes with their deciding on a suitable career path, and which treatments facilitate career development. I/O psychologists are more interested in the work and worker–performance aspect of career functioning. When working within business and industrial settings, both types of psychologists perform similar functions. The differences are a matter of degree rather than kind. Overall, the counseling psychologist is more likely to work with individuals in a counseling context, whereas the I/O psychologist is more inclined to study and intervene at a broader organizational level. The counseling psychologist is probably more invested in overall individual emotional adjustment; the I/O psychologist in organizational as well as individual work performance and its impediments.

Like the counseling psychologist, I/O psychologists deal with relatively intact personalities and are concerned in a very basic way with person–environment interactions. Both specialties are involved in organizational consulting. The counseling psychologist, on the whole, however, is basically more involved in therapeutic interventions, again at the level of the individual.

A Perspective on Similarities and Differences: Counseling Psychology's Distinctiveness

Counseling psychology has struggled to define itself and the ways in which its identity is unique. It has sought to clarify its distinctiveness within applied psychology specialties. At times critics—especially from within counseling psychology—have lamented the lack of clear differences, and have even suggested that, because of the lack of distinctiveness of its own, counseling psychology should be merged with other fields.

However, arguments about the lack of distinctiveness of the specialty seriously overlook the fact that virtually all of the applied specialties in psychology overlap. The in-depth descriptions of applied specialties in psychology by Altmaier and Meyer (1985) and more recently Sternberg (1997), substantiate that each specialty overlaps considerably with every other one. Counseling psychology is by no means unique in that.

At the same time, each specialty differs from every other one in certain ways. To be sure, no specialty in applied psychology can lay exclusive claim to a given activity (e.g., counseling, consulting) or setting. Yet each has its particular areas of emphasis, its particular foci, and settings in which it is more often found than are other specialties. To reiterate, the five unifying themes of counseling psychology lend this specialty its distinctiveness, although not in some simple, linear way. Counseling psychology may differ from one specialty, for example, clinical psychology, in relation to certain of these themes; but differ from another specialty, for example, school psychology, in relation to others of the five themes. Counseling psychology's distinctiveness derives from its embodiment of all five of the unifying themes. Although each specialty that we have summarized (and others, e.g., applied neuropsychology, health psychology) overlaps with counseling psychology on one or more of these themes, taken together, no other specialty reflects these themes to nearly the extent that counseling psychology does.

Counseling Psychology versus Fields Outside of Psychology

Although there are a number of fields outside of psychology that are involved in similar activities to those of counseling psychology, there is a fundamental difference between these fields and counseling psychology. Counseling psychologists, from the beginnings of the specialty, have been psychologists first and "counselors" second. That is, professionals in this specialty are trained in basic areas of psychology and seek to apply theories and principles of psychology to their professional activities and interventions. The three fields outside of psychology proper that are most closely related to counseling psychology are psychiatric social work, psychiatry, and the general counseling profession (often referred to as counselor education or mental health counseling). Let us briefly discuss each of these.

Psychiatric social workers generally complete a 2-year master's degree program, referred to as Master of Social Work (MSW) degree. Ordinarily, the first year of their program is academic and the second entails closely supervised work in an agency. Many psychiatric social workers, like counseling psychologists and others, conduct counseling and psychotherapy and are often found in private practice settings. In hospital and clinic settings, psychiatric social workers work on health-care teams. They may specialize in the intake process, consult with other agencies, do family counseling, and develop social histories on patients (Brammer, Abrego, & Shostrom, 1993). Professionals with MSWs rarely conduct research, do not perform psychological testing, and do little educational and vocational counseling.

Psychiatrists are physicians (medical doctors) who have gone on to specialize in psychiatry. This specialty is concerned with the diagnosis and treatment of severe emotional disorders and in this way is probably most closely related to clinical psychology among the applied psychology specialties. As MDs, psychiatrists are responsible for medical–psychological interventions, such as the prescription of drugs. They overlap with counseling psychologists, and a number of other specialists, in conducting counseling and psychotherapy. The brand of therapy they conduct is often the same or similar to counseling psychologists, although psychiatrists are more likely to take a psychodynamic and psychoanalytic perspective in their work than are counseling psychologists.

The final field we shall cover is perhaps the most similar of all to counseling psychology. The counseling profession (also termed counselor education or mental-health counseling) probably adheres to the same unifying themes as counseling psychology. Counselors are found in a wide range of job settings and may function as school counselors, rehabilitation counselors, employment counselors, college counselors, or community counselors. Many counseling positions require a master's degree rather than a doctorate.

In addition to differences in the level of training, counseling psychology, to a greater extent than the general counseling profession, subscribes to the scientist–practitioner model of training and practice. Because of this, the counseling psychologist receives more training in research and the scientific aspects of psychology.

Also, the counseling psychologist is extensively trained as a psychologist, with required graduate-level coursework in several core areas (e.g., biopsychology, learning) of the discipline of psychology. In contrast, although students who pursue degrees in counseling may take many psychology courses, expectations about which psychology courses they take, as well as how many, vary greatly from training program to training program. The combination of extensive study in the discipline of psychology with acquisition of the skills needed to be both a psychological practitioner and a scholarly investigator provides counseling psychologists with a broader array of competencies and career choices.

SUMMARY

A specialty within the science and profession of psychology, counseling psychology has struggled to establish itself firmly as a distinct profession that exhibits growth, strength, and vitality. Diversity is a key aspect of this field, which encompasses an extensive range of activities and positions, as well as a central focus on human and cultural diversity.

Throughout the history of counseling psychology three roles have been most central: the remedial, the preventive, and the developmental. Carried out in various settings, the three roles are combined in most activities performed by counseling psychologists.

One can distinguish five unifying themes in counseling psychology: (1) a focus on intact as opposed to severely disturbed personalities, (2) attention to people's assets and strengths regardless of degree of disturbance, (3) emphasis on relatively brief interventions, (4) attention to person–environment interactions rather than an exclusive focus on either the person or the environment, and (5) emphasis on educational and career development and environments. These themes help bring together the diverse aspects of the specialty and clarify how counseling psychology is differentiated from other specialties within and outside of psychology. Despite their defining character, the five themes represent no more than central tendencies. Counseling psychology practitioners differ considerably in the extent to which they subscribe to each particular theme.

Counseling psychologists are trained at the doctoral level, usually earning a Ph.D. from a counseling psychology training program accredited by the American Psychological Association. Their training typically adheres to the scientist–practitioner model, whereby the student is educated to be a scientist and researcher as well as a counseling practitioner.

Counseling psychologists work in a wide range of job settings, the most frequent being higher education (in academic departments and counseling centers) and independent practice. Likewise, counseling psychologists perform a wide array of professional activities. Individual personal and vocational counseling and therapy are the most commonly conducted, but a sizable percentage of counseling psychologists also frequently perform many additional activities and interventions. In terms of self-views, most counseling psychologists see themselves as either practitioners or academicians.

Comparing and contrasting counseling psychology to other applied specialties within psychology, such as clinical psychology, community psychology, industrial/organizational psychology, and school psychology, serves to delineate the unique characteristics of each. Likewise, common ground can be found between counseling psychology and fields outside of psychology, such as social work, psychiatry, and the general counseling profession, though substantial differences exist.

REFERENCES

Altmaier, E. M., & Meyer, M. E. (1985). *Applied specialties in psychology.* New York: Random House.

American Psychological Association (APA). (1995). *1995 APA Directory Survey.* Compiled by APA Office of Research. Washington, DC: Author.

APA. (1998). *1997 APA Directory Survey.* Compiled by APA Office of Research. Washington, DC: Author.

Bennett, V. C. (1985). School psychology. In E. M. Altmaier and M. E. Meyer (Eds.), *Applied specialties in psychology* (pp. 129–154). New York: Random House.

Birk, J. M., & Brooks, L. (1986). Required skills and training needs of recent counseling psychology graduates. *Journal of Counseling Psychology, 33,* 320–325.

Brammer, L. M., Abrego, P. J., & Shostrom, E. L. (1993). *Therapeutic counseling and psychotherapy* (sixth ed.). Englewood Cliffs, NJ: Prentice-Hall.

Corazzini, J. G. (1997). Using research to determine the efficacy and modes of treatment in university counseling centers. *Journal of Counseling Psychology, 44,* 378–380.

Croteau, J. M., Bieschke, K. J., Phillips, J. C., & Lark, J. S. (1998). Moving beyond pioneering: Empirical and theoretical perspectives on lesbian, gay, and bisexual affirmative training. *The Counseling Psychologist, 26,* 707–711.

Davis, K. L. (1996). Defining questions, charting possibilities. *The Counseling Psychologist, 24,* 144–160.

Davis, K. L. (1997). Emphasizing strengths: Counseling psychologists. In R. J. Sternberg (Ed.), *Career paths in psychology* (pp. 93–116). Washington, DC: APA.

Dreese, M. A. (1949). A personnel study of the Division of Counseling and Guidance of the American Psychological Association. *Occupations, 27,* 307–310.

Fischer, A. R., Jome, L. M., & Atkinson, D. R. (1998). Reconceptualizing multicultural counseling: Universal healing conditions in a culturally specific context. *The Counseling Psychologist, 26,* 525–589.

Fitzgerald, L. F., & Osipow, S. H. (1986). An occupational analysis of counseling psychology: How special is the specialty? *American Psychologist, 41,* 535–544.

Fretz, B. R. (1985). Counseling psychology. In E. M. Altmaier and M. E. Meyer (Eds.), *Applied specialties in psychology* (pp. 45–74). New York: Random House.

Gaddy, C. D., Charlot-Swilley, D., Nelson, P. D., & Reich, J. N. (1995). Selected outcomes of accredited programs. *Professional Psychology: Research and Practice, 26,* 507–513.

Gallesich, J. (1985). Toward a meta-theory of consultation. *The Counseling Psychologist, 13,* 336–354.

Garfield, S. L. (1985). Clinical psychology. In E. M. Altmaier and M. E. Meyer (Eds.), *Applied specialties in psychology* (pp. 19–44). New York: Random House.

Gelso, C. J. (1992). Realities and emerging myths about brief therapy. *The Counseling Psychologist, 20,* 464–471.

Gelso, C. J., & Johnson, D. H. (1983). *Explorations in time-limited counseling and psychotherapy.* New York: Columbia University, Teachers College Press.

Gelso, C. J., Betz, N. E., Friedlander, M. L., Helms, J. E., Hill, C. E., Patton, M. J., Super, D. E., & Wampold, B. E. (1988). Research in counseling psychology: Prospects and recommendations. *The Counseling Psychologist, 16,* 385–406.

Hayes, J. A. (1997). What does the Brief Symptom Inventory measure in college and university counseling center clients? *Journal of Counseling Psychology, 44,* 360–367.

Heppner, P. P., Carter, J. A., Claiborn, C. D., Brooks, L., Gelso, C. J., Fassinger, R. E., Holloway, E. L., Stone, G. L., Wampold, B. E., & Galassi, J. P. (1992). A proposal to integrate science and practice in counseling psychology. *The Counseling Psychologist, 20,* 107–122.

Holahan, W., & Yesenosky, J. M. (1992). Subgroups within Division 17: Divisiveness or opportunity for cohesion? *The Counseling Psychologist, 20,* 660–676.

Howard, G. S. (1993). Ecocounseling psychology: An introduction and overview. *The Counseling Psychologist, 21,* 550–559.

Iscoe, I. (1997). Reaching out: Community psychologists. In R. J. Sternberg (Ed.), *Career paths in psychology* (pp. 117–132). Washington, DC: APA.

Ivey, A. E. (1979). Counseling psychology—the most broadly based applied psychology specialty. *The Counseling Psychologist, 8*(3), 3–6.

Jordaan, J. E., Myers, R. A., Layton, W. C., & Morgan, H. H. (1968). *The counseling psychologist.* Washington, DC: American Psychological Association.

Kagan, N., Armsworth, M. W., Altmaier, E. M., Dowd, E. T., Hansen, J. C., Mills, D. E., Schlossberg, N., Sprinthall, N. A., Tanney, M. F., & Vasquez, M. J. T. (1988). Professional practice of counseling psychology in various settings. *The Counseling Psychologist, 16,* 347–365.

Kiselica, M. S. (1998). Preparing Anglos for the challenges and joys of multiculturalism. *The Counseling Psychologist, 26,* 5–21.

Lightsey, O. R. (1996). What leads to wellness? The role of psychological resources in well-being. *The Counseling Psychologist, 24,* 589–736.

Meade, C. J., Hamilton, M. K., & Ka-Wai-Yuen, R. (1982). Consultation research: The time has come, the walrus said. *The Counseling Psychologist, 10*(4), 39–52.

Meara, N. M., Schmidt, L., Carrington, C., Davis, K., Dixon, D., Fretz, B., Myers, R., Ridley, C., & Suinn, R. (1988). Training and accreditation in counseling psychology. *The Counseling Psychologist, 16,* 366–384.

Murdock, N. L., Alcorn, J., Heesacker, M., & Stoltenberg, C. (1998). Model training program in counseling psychology. *The Counseling Psychologist, 26,* 658–673.

Neimeyer, G. J. (1994, August). *Council of counseling psychology training programs 1994 survey of doctoral programs.* Report presented at the Annual Convention of APA, Los Angeles.

Norcross, J., Sayette, M., Mayne, T., Karg, R., & Turkson, M. (1998). Selecting a doctoral program in professional psychology: Some comparisons among Ph.D. counseling, Ph.D. clinical, and Psy.D. clinical psychology programs. *Professional Psychology: Research and Practice, 29,* 609–614.

Poland, S. F. (1997). Pathways to change and development: The life of a school psychologist. In R. J. Sternberg (Ed.), *Career paths in psychology* (pp. 165–184). Washington, DC: APA.

Resolutions Approved by the National Conference (1987). *American Psychologist, 42,* 1070–1084.

Robinson, F. P. (1970). *Effective study* (4th ed.). New York: Harper & Row.

Rude, S. S., Weissberg, M., & Gazda, G. M. (1988). Looking to the future: Themes from the Third National Conference for Counseling Psychology. *The Counseling Psychologist, 16,* 423–430.

Samler, J. (1964). Where do counseling psychologists work? What do they do? What should they do? In A. S. Thompson and D. E. Super (Eds.), *The professional preparation of counseling psychologists: Report of the 1964 Greyston Conference.* New York: Columbia University, Teachers College Press.

Schneider, L. J., Watkins, C. E., & Gelso, C. J. (1988). Counseling psychology from 1971 to 1986: Perspective on and appraisal of current training emphases. *Professional Psychology: Research and Practice, 19,* 584–588.

Seligman, M. (1996). The effectiveness of psychotherapy. *American Psychologist, 50,* 965–974.

Siegel, L. (1985). Industrial and organizational psychology. In E. M. Altmaier and M. E. Meyer (Eds.), *Applied specialties in psychology* (pp. 207–238). New York: Random House.

Spielberger, C. D., & Stenmark, D. E. (1985). Community psychology. In E. M. Altmaier and M. E. Meyer (Eds.), *Applied specialties in psychology* (pp. 75–98). New York: Random House.

Steenbarger, B. N. (1992). Toward science–practice integration in brief counseling and therapy. *The Counseling Psychologist, 20,* 403–450.

Sternberg, R. J. (Ed.). (1997). *Career paths in psychology.* Washington, DC: APA.

Strauss, B. S. (1997). Treating, teaching, and training: Clinical psychologists in hospitals. In R. J. Sternberg (Ed.), *Career paths in psychology* (pp. 133–150). Washington, DC: APA.

Super, D. E. (1955). Transition from vocational guidance to counseling psychology. *Journal of Counseling Psychology, 2,* 3–9.

Talley, R., & Short, R. (1994). A wake-up call to school psychologists from school psychologists. *The School Psychologist, 48,* 1, 3, 15.

Tenopyr, M. L. (1997). Improving the workplace: Industrial/organizational psychology as a career. In R. J. Sternberg (Ed.), *Career paths in psychology* (pp. 185–196). Washington, DC: APA.

Tyler, L. (1961). *The work of the counselor.* New York: Appleton-Century-Crofts.

Watkins, C. E. (1994). On hope, promise, and possibility in counseling psychology or some simple, but meaningful observations about our specialty. *The Counseling Psychologist, 22,* 315–334.

Watkins, C. E., Lopez, F. G., Campbell, V. L., & Himmell, C. D. (1986). Contemporary counseling psychology: Results of a national survey. *Journal of Counseling Psychology, 33,* 301–309.

2

DEVELOPMENT OF THE PROFESSION

This chapter describes the emergence of counseling psychology as a profession. We shall first examine the roots of the profession as found in changes in both American society and in the discipline of psychology during the late 1800s and early 1900s. Then, within a broad developmental framework, we shall look at how the profession of counseling psychology has matured since its formal establishment in the 1940s. Finally, we shall describe both the continuities and changes of recent years that have resulted in a vigorous profession of counseling psychology for the twenty-first century.

ROOTS OF THE FIVE UNIFYING THEMES

An interesting exercise for a beginning counseling psychologist is to trace the academic heritage of his or her instructor or advisor. The profession is sufficiently young that it is usually possible to find out who one's advisor's advisor was, his or her advisor, and so forth, back at least to the formal beginnings of the profession in the 1940s (and in many cases, to trace the lineage back to some of the progenitors in the first half of the century, and in a few cases, back even to the nineteenth century). As Alex Haley illustrated in his work on the roots of African Americans (1976), understanding heritage gives deeper and even new meaning to life in the present. Themes and traditions that link past and present can also help make sense out of what at times may seem scattered and chaotic. We shall explore the roots of counseling psychology by examining how the five unifying themes reviewed in Chapter 1 (assets and strengths, person–environment interactions, educational and career development, brief interactions, and intact personalities) grew out of distinctive social movements, historical events, and disciplinary developments in the late-nineteenth and early-twentieth centuries.

Assets and Strengths

It is now more than a century since persons with mental illness were seen as possessed by demons and hopelessly incurable. Insane asylums were the best life could offer to those who became mentally ill. Then, in the mid-nineteenth century, what is now known as the "mental health movement" became well established. Under the leadership of Dorothea Dix (1802–1887) in 1848, New Jersey built a hospital (rather than an asylum) for the mentally ill. At this point in history, the mental health movement sought to provide more humanitarian custodial care for the mentally ill; there was still little expectation for cures. Several decades later, a new level of understanding concerning the role of assets and strengths in working with mental problems was reached via the work of Clifford Beers (1876–1943). His book, *A Mind That Found Itself* (1908), represents a critical turning point in the public's awareness that persons with mental problems could recover and that, even in the depths of depression or other problems, they had strengths that could be utilized to help them make that recovery. Freud's significant contributions to therapeutic treatment served to further enhance the viewpoint that many persons with mental health problems had the potential for moving beyond their difficulties; that is, they were not incurable.

Another major step forward in mental health ideology was the establishment of a psychological clinic by Lightner Witmer at the University of Pennsylvania early in the twentieth century. His clinic was devoted to working with children who had learning or behavioral problems in contrast to those yet described as insane or mentally disturbed. Such a clinic helped the public understand that persons other than those identified as mentally ill could be helped by therapeutic intervention. In one sense, Witmer's clinic is the precursor of thousands of mental health clinics and counseling centers that now exist throughout this country. Although the clinic's operations were largely remedial, the concept that children could be helped to function more effectively served to lead counseling psychology to focus more on potential development of the individual rather than on deficits that must be overcome.

Person–Environment Interactions

To understand the theme of person–environment interactions in counseling psychology, we must first explore the roots of psychology's measurement of persons, then the "discovery" of the critical role of environment, and then, finally, how the two are interactively bound in the creation of human behavior.

Essential to the approach of psychologists in understanding behavior (in contrast, for example, to the approaches of philosophers and theologians) is the incorporation of the methods of empirical science as developed in the physical and natural sciences in the eighteenth and nineteenth centuries. According to these methods, psychological phenomena can and must be measured.

Thus one of the first tasks of early psychologists (and still a major task of all psychologists today) was to develop means of measuring psychological processes and behaviors—now referred to as *psychometrics.* Psychology's roots in the area of measurement may be traced back to the work of Galton (1822–1911) and his quest for understanding differences among people by applying quantitative methods. J. M. Cattel (1860–1944) continued this study of individual differences, using much of what he had learned in Wilhelm Wundt's (1832–1920) laboratory established in Leipzig in 1879. Shortly thereafter, Binet (1857–1911), in France, established the first intelligence test, further expanding the measurement of differences in persons.

The combination of these psychometric developments with the vocational guidance movement, described in the next section, helped launch psychology as a profession in the first half of the twentieth century. The mass use of tests for occupational selection in World War I and World War II provided further stimulus. By the late 1920s, leading psychologists of the day expressed hopes that aptitude testing would soon be the answer to many of the educational and vocational problems faced by society (Hull, 1928).

Even in those halcyon days of aptitude/intelligence testing during World War I and the postwar boom years of the 1920s, there were those who were beginning to see that limits existed to what could be accomplished through measurement of differences only in persons. In 1935 Lewin provided his now (but mostly not well recognized until the 1960s) classic explication of the concept that behavior is a function of both the person and the environment. In Lewin's (1935) view, predictions of what persons will do, no matter how much information one has about aptitudes or skills, will always be limited unless information about the environments in which persons function is also considered.

Psychologists have increasingly come to understand that they cannot simply ask the questions "What kind of person will succeed as a dentist?" or "Which kind of client problem will benefit from psychotherapy?" outside of an environmental context. One type of individual may be an effective leader of one kind of organization (environment) but not of another. The critical factor is the *interaction* between the person and the environment. Not only do environments affect persons, persons also affect environments. Claiborn and Lichtenberg (1989) have elaborated the history of interactional thought in psychology, and more specifically within counseling psychology.

Even in one-on-one counseling, "environments" will differ and change according to who constitutes a dyad (similar versus different gender, race, etc., of client and counselor) and how the counseling progresses. Clients who change their behaviors produce variable environments. Organizational psychologists have become increasingly aware that environments do not exist in a vacuum but rather are defined by the sum of the people who compose them (Schneider, 1983). Unlike the predominantly person-oriented strategies developed in the middle decades of the twentieth century, the research and counseling interaction strategies of the twenty-first century will be heavily influenced by interactional and systems approaches.

Educational and Career Development

The transition from the nineteenth to the twentieth centuries also saw the beginnings of the vocational guidance movement, one of the profession's most visible roots (and, in the view of many, the taproot of counseling psychology). In today's technological age, with literally thousands of jobs to choose from, many requiring highly specialized training, it may be difficult to realize that over 100 years ago the majority of young people did not really consider career choices. Most followed in their parents' occupational footsteps, whether that be farmer, bootmaker, or seamstress. With the many new and different jobs created by the Industrial Revolution, it became increasingly clear that not only were there career choices to be made but also that certain kinds of work required specific skills and training.

The social reformer Frank Parsons saw the need to develop what would today be called a career counseling service. In 1908 he established his vocations bureau in Boston to guide individuals through a three-step process he developed, which still serves as the foundation of most current career counseling. Parsons's three steps involve acquisition of

> (1) a clear understanding of [oneself], [one's] aptitudes, abilities, interests, ambitions, resources, limitations and their causes; (2) a knowledge of the requirements and conditions of success, advantages and disadvantages, compensation, opportunities, and prospects in different lines of work; (3) true reasoning on the relations of these two groups of facts (Parsons, 1909, p. 5).

The vocational guidance movement quickly incorporated much of the psychometric tradition as a way of providing information about individual aptitudes, abilities, and interests. In subsequent years, the need for occupational classification of literally millions of men in the two world wars was answered in large part by the methods of the vocational guidance and the psychometric movements.

Of even greater significance for the development of counseling psychology was the response of these movements to the American Depression in the 1930s:

> The economic depression of the 1930's added a new current to the stream of history. Large scale unemployment highlighted vocational guidance as a job placement activity as well as educational function. The Minnesota Employment Stabilization Research Institute experimented with psychological tests, occupational information, and retraining as methods of getting adult workers back into the labor force. Then many private and public vocational counseling centers, together with the United States Employment Service, quickly took over the research and counseling methods developed in this pioneer project (Super, 1955, p. 4).

In chapters 14 and 15 we shall see how the vocational guidance movement continues to foster some of the major unique research and theoretical and practical contributions of counseling psychologists.

Brief Interactions

Until the 1930s, treatments based on humanitarian (not to be confused with humanistic) viewpoints emanating from the late-nineteenth century mental health movement were limited largely to the psychoanalytic perspective and were lengthy and intensive. Then E. G. Williamson and Carl Rogers each developed very different perspectives on counseling and psychotherapy. As a leading figure in the development of college student personnel services, Williamson (1939) dealt with the full range of problems of personal living and other nonacademic problems that students bring to large universities. He developed a process of focused, goal-oriented counseling to help students adjust to their environment. In addition to his own writings (see *How to Counsel Students*), he was the mentor for several generations of counseling psychologists who further researched and developed his brief, active, focused counseling in the various university counseling centers established across the country after World War II to meet the educational, vocational, and personal counseling needs of the thousands of veterans then returning to college.

During the same time period, mostly as a reaction against his psychodynamic training in child clinical psychology, Carl Rogers developed his phenomenological, client-centered approach to counseling. His now classic book on counseling and psychotherapy (Rogers, 1942) had a tremendous impact on shifting the focus of the then-emerging specialty of counseling psychology from assessment and diagnosis to counseling and psychotherapy. Evidence that such a shift had taken place was clearly manifested in the decade after Rogers's book was published: "[The] early 1950's saw the publication of ten books on counseling methods and only three had retained their exclusive diagnostic and assessment emphases" (Whiteley, 1984b, p. 5).

Intact Personalities

It was only in the 1960s and afterward that the profession of counseling psychology, and indeed psychology at large, began to fully recognize the distinctive importance and relevance of developmental stage models produced by Piaget (1952), Erikson (1959), Perry (1970), and Kohlberg (1984). During the past 30 years, counseling psychologists have given increasing attention to these developmental models for the understanding they provide about normal developmental crises and transitions, all of which are accompanied by threats to well-being as well as opportunities for growth.

The "translation" of these theoretical concepts into the work of counseling psychologists may be seen in two distinctive bodies of literature in counseling psychology. The first encompasses the movement known as *deliberate psychological education,* and includes the initial major work by Mosher and Sprinthall (1971). These researchers outline the many ways in which counseling psychology can promote psychological development of all adolescents, not just those seeking personal counseling. As teachers, consultants, and counselors, counseling psychologists can create conditions that reduce the number of psychological casualties likely to occur during the adolescent years (Wagner, 1996).

The second body of literature based on developmental aspects of intact, normal persons focuses on human adaptation to transition (Schlossberg, 1981) as well as intervention strategies for coping with transitions (Brammer & Abrego, 1981). Later work (Matheny, Aycock, Pugh, et al., 1986) analyzes coping with stress. All these studies discuss interventions for persons acknowledging need for help in coping with both everyday and transitional situations but who are not sufficiently distressed to require counseling or therapy. Gibson and Brown (1992) have reviewed more recent developments on coping with life transitions.

In these five brief sections, we hope we have shown how each of the five unifying themes of counseling psychology is clearly linked to developments in the early-twentieth century (or even before) in both psychology as a discipline (e.g., psychoanalysis, developmental theory) and in society at large, such as the Industrial Revolution, war, and depression. We now turn to an exploration of the formal organizational steps of the psychological specialty that came to be identified as counseling psychology.

Coming of Age: Stages in the Development of the Profession

In this section we shall see how, and most important from our perspective, why counseling psychology became an identifiable profession in the years immediately following World War II. Some of the factors leading to the creation of the profession during that time continue to contribute to its present vitality. In elaborating the events of each of the past six decades, we shall use a broad developmental model, including the terms *infancy, childhood, adolescence, young adulthood,* and *maturity.* (Note that, from this point forward, the terms *profession* and *specialty* will be used interchangeably. The term *specialty* usually denotes a specific discipline within the profession of psychology. Yet, in most ways, the level of autonomy and organization of the various specialties allows them to be classified as professions.)

Infancy: The 1940s

Sociologists studying professions specify that for a group of workers to constitute a profession they must form governing organizations that establish educational and service standards and thereby create the conditions necessary for autonomous functioning. The psychologist Erikson (1959) emphasized autonomy as a major task for the period of infancy. The beginning autonomous organizational steps for counseling psychology were set in motion during the 1940s, even though the official written record of many of these initial steps did not appear until the early 1950s.

The beginnings of organized counseling psychology can be found in the "psychological foxholes" (Scott, 1980) of World War II. During that time, almost every person with any training as a psychologist became involved in some way with assessment activities, either for selection and training of military personnel or for psychological diagnosis of military casualties. Thus there were collections of psychologists in every major military installation throughout the country and even sometimes abroad. During the war years, an increasing number of psychologists who were involved in selection and training began to see the need for an organization that would respond to their specific interests, outside the realm of psychiatric hospitals.

In the rapidly expanding divisional structure of the American Psychological Association (APA) immediately following World War II, these interests became represented by a new division, that of the Division of Counseling and Guidance. Founded in 1946 by E. G. Williamson and John Darley, it joined the increasing number of applied divisions then being added to the APA, for example, those of clinical psychology, consulting psychology, industrial psychology, educational psychology, and school psychology. Whiteley has provided extensive original source material (1980) and descriptions (1984a, b) of the details of these early organizational developments, including meeting places, agenda, persons involved, and so forth.

Let us raise a twofold question not often addressed in these historical descriptions: Why did persons interested in counseling choose to affiliate with psychology and why did psychology choose to include counseling? Many prospective counselors still choose to practice outside the profession of psychology. Others have felt the need for a connection to the empirical and psychometric traditions of psychology. It is this grafting of counseling onto empirical roots that helps explain the greater commitment of counseling psychologists, as compared to counselors in general, to the scientist–practitioner model of training and functioning.

On the other side of the coin, why did psychology include counseling as a division? As already noted, in the beginning, clinical psychologists concentrated on assessment and diagnosis primarily in psychiatric hospitals; the focus on counseling and therapy did not develop for *any* psychologists until the 1950s. Industrial psychology began as the study of what is known today as human factors and engineering psychology. (The emphasis on organizational behavior now seen in industrial/organizational [I/O] psychology was largely a development in the 1960s.) The emergence of counseling psychology filled a perceived vacuum within psychology between industrial psychology and clinical psychology: the study and treatment of normal personality functioning and development, which was not yet represented by any applied division.

Despite the overlaps and shared heritage with generic counseling on the one hand and other applied psychology fields on the other, in the over 50 years of its history counseling psychology has continued to be linked to both. During that time, probably more than half of those who identify themselves as counseling psychologists have also maintained membership in either a major counseling organization (e.g., American Counseling Association, formerly known as the American Personnel and Guidance Association) or a more clinically oriented psychology division (e.g., the APA Division 12, Division of Clinical Psychology or Division 29, Psychotherapy). Although these dual associations have sometimes caused tensions, the maintenance of breadth of perspectives is one of the sources of the profession's vitality. As suggested in Moore's (1970) sociological study of professions:

> The plight of the professional is that extreme specialization radically narrows
> those significant others with whom he can carry on job-centered social discourse.

> Here, once more, the importance of identification with a broader calling is
> apparent, even if common interests are in some measure nostalgic rather than
> strictly contemporary (p. 83).

Another perspective on this post–World War II emergence of counseling psychology has been provided by Schmidt (1977) in his examination of why the specialty developed and has remained strongest in the United States. Schmidt draws a parallel between our society's commitment to change—specifically change wrought through scientific technology—and counseling psychology as a process of change that builds on the empirical findings of the science of psychology. Schmidt also notes the high degree of mobility in our culture coupled with the emphasis on achieving self-improvement. Counseling psychologists have provided both the social support needed to cope with changed environments as well as the technical assistance for launching personal careers. After World War II, millions of veterans, who had been dislocated for several years from their home communities, were expected to forge ahead in new careers for which they typically had little or no preparation. From this perspective, in 1945–1950, counseling psychology was a profession "waiting to happen."

Childhood: The 1950s

If the 1940s are counseling psychology's infancy, where it began to take steps toward autonomy, the 1950s encompass the stages of childhood when it had to demonstrate its ability to stand and be recognized as an independent entity. The exciting times of "let's get organized" had to give way to a period of sustained development that would establish the foundation of systematic knowledge needed to maintain a profession. The first of these major steps was addressed by the Northwestern Conference in 1951, the first major conference for the profession of counseling psychology. Key leaders of the Division of Counseling and Guidance met at Northwestern University August 29–30, 1951; they prepared formal definitions of the roles and functions of counseling psychologists. They proposed standards for practicum training, research training, and the content of core psychology courses. Final versions of these statements were originally published in the *American Psychologist* (APA, 1952) and were reprinted in Whiteley's (1980) *The History of Counseling Psychology.*

Although there have been two subsequent conferences addressing many of the same definitional and curriculum issues, and innumerable position papers published about these topics, it is of interest to reread many of those original statements for their timelessness. Although surveys of the actual training practices and employment locations of counseling psychologists have documented a number of changes over the years, the applicability of many of the initial statements is truly remarkable. Consider the following definition of roles and functions:

> The professional goal of the counseling psychologist is to foster the psychological development of the individual. This includes all people on the adjustment continuum from those who function at tolerable levels of adequacy to those suffering more severe psychological disturbances (APA, 1952, p. 176).

The impetus for setting training standards at the very beginning of the specialty derived mostly from the interests of the Veterans Administration (VA) in employing counseling psychologists. The VA had created the job title of counseling psychologist to function in the Division of Medicine and Neurology, outside of the psychiatric division where clinical psychologists normally practiced, in order to provide counseling services for the full range of general medical and surgical patients. The standards of training and practice established at the Northwestern Conference were used to set VA employment standards. The VA has remained, throughout the history of counseling psychology, a major employer of counseling psychologists. These same training standards also served as the foundation for the creation of a diplomate in counseling psychology from the then newly created American Board of Examiners in Professional Psychology and in the establishment of program accreditation procedures by the APA Doctoral Education Committee.

Hammering out these position statements also led the pioneers of counseling psychology to realize their increasing connections to the discipline of psychology; in 1952 the decision was made to change the discipline's title from "counseling and guidance" to "counseling psychology."

Through the wisdom and initiative (though some colleagues of the time probably thought foolhardiness) of four young counseling psychologists—Milton E. Hahn, Harold G. Seashore, Donald E. Super, and C. Gilbert Wrenn—in the 1950s a major new empirical journal was launched to address publication needs in the same areas that the division of counseling and guidance had been established to fill—the *Journal of Counseling Psychology*. The idea of putting a journal into practice, of course, required considerable funds. Wrenn describes the journal's economic origins as follows.

> We established a list of probable stockholders who would represent various dimensions in counseling, each to be asked to buy a limited number of shares at $50 a share. None was to have over ten shares even if he was foolish enough to want to risk that much money . . . for it was clearly stated that this was a risk investment. . . . The response was remarkable. I found an early list of 28 prospects . . . there were 19 of the 28 who had become stockholders—and I am not even sure that we invited all on this particular list (Wrenn, 1966, p. 486)!

The first volume of the *Journal of Counseling Psychology* was published in 1954; it has since become the most important empirical journal in counseling psychology. Because of the excellence it achieved over its first decade of publication, it was actively sought by the APA for inclusion in its set of journals and has been published by them since 1967. The journal is today one of the most selective of the APA publications and has more paid subscribers than any other journal published by the APA. A fascinating perspective on the journal's first 25 years, including its antecedent social and political conditions (1946–1956) as well as its subsequent impact on the profession of counseling psychology, has been prepared by Pepinsky, Hill-Frederick, and Epperson (1978). More recent outstanding achievements of the *Journal of Counseling Psychology* may be found in four articles commissioned by the journal in recognition of the centennial of APA in 1992. The purpose of these articles was [to provide] critical examination of how knowledge in certain core areas of psychology has been used by counseling psychologists, how counseling psychologists have transformed and modified that knowledge for their purposes, and what has been the impact, if any, of counseling psychologists' knowledge base on these core areas of scientific psychology (Richardson & Patton, 1992, p. 3).

All four of these articles will be cited in this and/or later chapters in this text.

Adolescence: The 1960s and 1970s

Because counseling psychologists work with adolescents who have significant and prolonged identity problems, perhaps it is fitting that the profession itself seems to have had to endure a long period of self-searching with regard to its identity. Barely before the ink was dry on some of the documents of the 1950s that created counseling psychology as an organized and autonomous profession, some writers were raising questions about the identity of the specialty. The 1960s and early 1970s were a time of significant self-doubt among the leadership in the profession. Growth leveled off in both membership of the division and number of accredited programs.

Whiteley (1980) brought to light previously unpublished papers that had been written in the early 1960s regarding the "decline" of counseling psychology (Berg, Pepinsky, & Shoben, 1980), and another concluding that counseling psychology "presently has only a weak potential for growth" (Tiedeman, 1980, p. 126). Other articles during this period cited low-level prestige of counseling psychologists as compared to clinical psychologists. The strains were not just around declining growth but also about future directions. Because the 1950s had seen an increase in the counseling and psychotherapy activities of both counseling and clinical psychologists (based on much of the work of Rogers), some counseling psychologists were proposing that it was time for a merger of these specialties. Others, vehemently opposed to the remedial therapeutic emphasis in clinical psychology, identified more with the emergence of community psychology and its emphasis on prevention and developmental activities. For almost every paper that criticized the profession, others in the profession arose to prepare counterarguments (e.g., Tyler, Tiedeman, & Wrenn, 1980).

The division responded by organizing a second conference to reexamine its self-definition and the standards it had originally set at the Northwestern Conference. In the Greyston Conference of 1964, many concerns were aired extensively. The majority of participants endorsed the Northwestern statements. Recognizing changing times and contexts, the conference included in the introduction to its specific recommendations (Thompson & Super, 1964) the following statement.

> The conferees further recognize that counseling psychologists have significant overlapping interests with the related specialties of clinical, educational, industrial or personnel, and school psychology. The great majority, but not all, subscribe to the statement that counseling psychology has a special substance and emphases requiring preparation in a number of didactic as well as practicum courses that are not necessarily included in the preparation of other psychologists. This special substance consists of the educational and vocational and, less

distinctively, the familial and community environments of the individual, of the psychology of normal development, and of the psychology of the physically, emotionally, and mentally handicapped; the special emphases are on the appraisal and use of assets for furthering individual development in the existing or changing environment (pp. 3–4).

Perhaps as is true in the developmental phase of adolescence, these publicly manifested aspects of self-doubt and confusion were hiding, or at least overshadowing, the ongoing accomplishments of counseling psychologists that were building upon the foundations established in previous decades. Both theoretical and empirical developments in the area of career psychology were expanding and growing with considerable practical impact, for example, new assessment instruments and new types of interventions. Research on how to train counselors to provide the necessary and sufficient conditions in psychotherapy was building so rapidly that, by the end of the 1960s, counseling psychology researchers were among those who were most often identified (Bergin & Garfield, 1971) for research on training.

Continuing the linkage with mainstream psychology, developments in experimental analysis of behavior were being translated into counseling theory and practice most notably by Krumboltz and Thoresen (1969). Perhaps the clearest manifestation of the continued growth of the conceptual as well as empirical expertise of the profession was the establishment, at the end of the 1960s, of *The Counseling Psychologist,* a journal dedicated to stimulating professional dialogue about important theoretical and conceptual issues of the day. John Whiteley, founder and first editor (1969–1984), developed the format of having each issue dedicated to one or sometimes several major conceptual articles on a single topic, followed by a set of reactions from other counseling psychologists and professionals. This "dialogue" format has clearly withstood the test of time—more than 30 years later, it remains the primary format of the journal. The topics of the journal (see Heppner [1999] for a full listing of major topics during the years 1969–1998) serve as a quick survey of the major topical interests of each decade, from early issues on client-centered, behavioral and vocational counseling to more recent issues on wellness, multicultural counseling, qualitative research, and social cognitive models of training. *The Counseling Psychologist* has become a widely read and cited journal far beyond the profession of counseling psychology: "[T]he number of citations of major contributions has increased in the past 11 years . . . across almost 90 journals within psychology, more than 120 from a wide range of other disciplines, and almost 50 international journals" (Flores, Rooney, Heppner, Browne, & Wei, 1999, p. 93).

By the 1970s, although the identity problem of counseling psychology was still not fully resolved (Are any of us absolutely sure of who we are?), the character of the identity issue shifted from pessimism about whether the field should exist to how it should be defined in relation to others. The task of the 1970s seems to have been to find out how counseling psychology would relate to all of those other professions with which it shares so many aspects.

In terms of the number of APA-approved training programs, the beginning of the 1970s saw the nadir of the profession. However, since that time, the growth in number of accredited programs has been phenomenal by any standard—an over

200% increase in the past two decades. Significant developments in the setting of standards for credentials in professional psychology were a major factor in this growth. With an increasing number of states developing procedures for the licensing of psychologists in the 1960s, plus the more widespread inclusion of mental health benefits in health insurance policies, there were a series of questions raised for all of psychology about which kinds of training qualified persons for licensure as psychologists as well as for providing health care service. Conferences sponsored by the National Register of Health Services Providers in Psychology and the APA, attended by psychologists from all specialties, resulted in greater specifications regarding the curriculum and the identity of the programs (see Chapter 4 for further details).

Most important for counseling psychology, these standards recognized that psychological training might take place in a variety of settings other than psychology departments, for example, colleges of education, colleges of business and management, colleges of medicine, or freestanding schools of psychology. The formal recognition that psychology programs could exist in colleges of education (long the home of many programs in counseling and guidance), coupled with the new requirement for identification of the programs as *psychology* programs (if the graduates were to be eligible for licensing as psychologists), had an immediate impact on many programs that were formerly identified as "counseling and guidance" but that had for years graduated persons who considered themselves trained as counseling psychologists.

Many programs moved as expeditiously as possible to make whatever changes were necessary to their curriculum, faculty, and resources to receive accreditation by the APA. This rapid growth brought new political strength and, at the end of the 1970s, counseling psychology was regaining, within the APA, some of the representation and leadership roles that it had had in the 1950s but that had waned over the 1960s and early 1970s. The leadership of the Division of Counseling Psychology and the newer organization of the Council of Counseling Psychology Training Program Directors found itself, for the first time in the profession's history, in continual dialogue with the leaders of clinical, school, and I/O psychology, as well as professional leaders in the American Personnel and Guidance Association for the purpose of developing an understanding of both overlapping and distinctive roles. Heppner, Casas, Carter, and Stone (in press) interviewed, in the late 1990s, many of the persons involved in the leadership of these various organizations; they have provided not only historical facts, but also intriguing perspectives on the pertinent political developments in professional psychology during the 1970s and 1980s.

Young Adulthood: The 1980s

The decade of the 1980s began with the publication of two collections of papers, one set looking to the year 2000 (Whiteley & Fretz, 1980), the other to "The Coming Decade" (Whiteley, Kagan, Harmon, Fretz, & Tanney, 1984). Both sets of papers addressed how the profession would develop for coming generations of counseling psychologists.

The most tangible indicators of the emerging maturity of counseling psychology were the publication of the profession's first comprehensive handbooks, *Handbook of Counseling Psychology* (Brown & Lent, 1984) and *Handbook of Vocational Psychology* (Walsh & Osipow, 1983b); and the beginning of two book series, *Advances in Vocational Psychology*, edited by Walsh and Osipow, and the Brooks/Cole series in *Counseling Psychology*, edited by Whiteley and Resnikoff (1983a).

Also, during this decade, three reviews of counseling psychology published in the *Annual Review of Psychology* (Borgen, 1984; Gelso & Fassinger, 1990; Osipow, 1987) covered a broad array of topics, indicating the growing diversity of the field. Borgen (1984) noted that "the discipline teems with vitality and resolve" (p. 597). Osipow (1987) examined its strengths, especially in the areas of career counseling and vocational developments. Gelso and Fassinger (1990) applauded the accomplishments of the 1980s, observing that many of the methodological and conceptual recommendations of earlier reviewers and critics had been incorporated by researchers.

Two "firsts," again reflecting the confidence that comes with maturity, enabled the profession to look at some nontraditional research methodologies. For the first time ever, the *Journal of Counseling Psychology* published a special issue dedicated entirely to the topic of research design (October 1987). *The Counseling Psychologist* also published (in January 1989) a special issue on alternative research paradigms, with special attention to the teaching of them.

The emerging maturity of the profession was also indicated in the recognition accorded counseling psychology by other specialties and organizations. At some time during the 1980s, almost every major board and committee in the APA was chaired by a counseling psychologist, as were the boards of related credentialing organizations, for example, the National Register of Health Service Providers in Psychology, the American Board of Professional Psychology, and the American Association of State Psychology Boards.

Responding to long-standing calls for a third national conference on Counseling Psychology, the Georgia Conference was held in April of 1987. Despite having less government and foundation support than either of the prior conferences, over 180 psychologists attended this working conference. They formed five different task groups to prepare recommendations in the areas of training and accreditation, research, organizational and political structures, public image, and professional practice in various settings. Each group's recommendations for the development of the profession may be found in the July 1988 *The Counseling Psychologist*.

Rudd, Weissberg, and Gazda (1988) summarized the common themes of the conference discussions as follows.

> First, we are scientist–practitioners. . . . Discussion[s] of identity . . . include counseling psychology's emphasis on "positive mental health . . . adaptive strategies . . . empowerment of individuals." . . . Also mentioned was what might be termed the counseling psychologist's *scope of vision*, the attention to promotion of mental health at the level of groups and systems as well as individuals, to development across the entire life span, to adjustment and satisfaction in vocational as well as personal spheres, and to prevention and enhancement as well as remediation (pp. 425–426).

Their closing observation was the reaffirmation, seen in all the task groups, of the importance of viewing people and behavior in the context of cultural variables such as ethnicity, gender, age, and sexual orientation. The conference participants promoted a diversity of roles but remained passionately committed to the viability of the unifying themes.

Maturity: The 1990s and Beyond

By the end of the 1980s there was a sense of meaningfulness in what had been accomplished that permitted greater receptivity to diversification within the profession in terms of work setting, theoretical orientation, gender, race, lifestyle, and so forth. Rather than fighting the problems of diversity and feeling compelled to choose to go one way or the other (e.g., remedial/therapeutic versus developmental/educational), counseling psychologists were embracing diversity and finding strength in it. Naomi Meara, president of the Division of Counseling Psychology for 1989, chose the theme "unified diversity" for the annual convention (Meara, 1990). Even though counseling psychologists engage in many different roles in many different settings, they share a unity of perspective and ideology.

In the final part of this chapter we describe both the definitional and organizational changes of recent years that have resulted in counseling psychology becoming, at the beginning of the new millennium, an even more vigorous and rigorous "clearly identified psychological specialty whose scientist–practitioners engage in a wide variety of activities including research, education and training; and a full range of psychological services in the areas of assessment, treatment, and evaluation" (Meara & Myers, 1998). A revised archival description of the specialty of counseling psychology, reflecting contemporary parameters of professional practice, was approved and published by the American Psychological Association in 1999 (APA, 1999).

CONTINUITIES AND CHANGES FOR THE NEW MILLENNIUM

We believe the essence of the vitality of counseling psychology at the beginning of the twenty-first century can be captured by describing a set of four continuities from our earlier history, along with four changes in the 1990s in the vision for, and structure of, the Division of Counseling Psychology (Division 17). The remainder of this chapter explores these continuities and changes.

The Scientist–Practitioner Model: Enduring the Tests of Time

From the initial founding conference at Northwestern in 1951 through the third conference in Atlanta, Georgia, in 1987, the training model that has been endorsed by the profession of counseling psychology is the scientist–practitioner model. From the earliest days this choice has been and continues to be controversial. We hope it is clear to the reader, by this point, that keeping the "scientist" part of counseling psychology is *the* central reason for some counselors to have a home in psychology. "First, we are scientist–practitioners" (Rudd, Weissberg, & Gazda, 1988, p. 424).

What is the scientist–practitioner (also known as scientist–professional) model? Stated simply, it is a model of training requiring that professionals master both the helping, practitioner roles and the methods of investigative science. Such professionals can ask the questions that will help establish, maintain, and enhance the body of specialized knowledge needed to make contributions to the welfare of all individuals and society.

As one often finds out in interdisciplinary staff meetings, many persons trained to do counseling in psychiatry, social work, and other counselor training programs typically do not know how to design investigations for questions like "Is what we are doing effective?" or "How does counseling work?" or "Can counseling be made more effective for these kinds of clients?" Similarly, persons trained exclusively in research methodology, who may have tremendous sophistication in terms of research design but lack training and experience in actually conducting counseling, may have extraordinary difficulties in asking and answering the questions in ways that are meaningful to practitioners. As recognized in the inaugural definition of the profession, "counseling psychologists can make unique contributions to psychological knowledge *because* their counseling experience provides an especially fruitful opportunity to formulate hypotheses. It is therefore essential to maximize their research training" (italics added, American Psychological Association, 1952, p. 180).

Concerns of professional psychologists about both the time and energy demanded by the scientist–practitioner model, as well as its effectiveness, led some *clinical* psychologists to develop, during the past three decades of the twentieth century, professional schools of psychology and the Doctor of Psychology (Psy.D.) degree. These programs are generally far more focused on professional practice, and less on research skills and achievements, although there are some professional programs in psychology that are quite similar to more practice-oriented traditional clinical programs. Within *counseling* psychology, the emphasis has remained on how to implement the scientist–practitioner model more effectively (Bernstein & Kerr, 1993), rather than separating the two. As further described in Chapter 3, Gelso (1993) and colleagues have addressed both the theory and empirical bases for creating research training environments that lead to greater integration of science and practice.

Diversity of Scope of Practice

From the very beginnings of counseling psychology, the range of professional activities and settings in which counseling psychologists practice has been widely diverse, even though in the early decades of the profession the majority of counseling psychologists were located in university settings. However, during the last three decades of the twentieth century, a rapidly increasing number of counseling psychologists became involved primarily in some type of independent practice: some focused on therapy, some on consultation, some on career interventions. With this increasing diversity there emerged a struggle for the "soul" of counseling psychology. Some of the advocates of each diverse practice and research domain felt that not enough attention was being given to their concerns by the profession. As further described below in the section on changes, counseling psychology was fortunate to have leaders who worked to encourage developments in all of these domains, in both the definition and structure of the profession of counseling psychology. Diversity of scope of practice was conceptualized as a strength, rather than a weakness so that each domain could feel affirmed, rather than as a "stepchild" of the profession. The changes of the 1990s, described later in this chapter, have provided a strong continuity for embracing diversity of scope of practice, requiring effective leadership and the shared goodwill of all counseling psychologists. "We need to carefully plan and nurture the intellectual diversity within our specialty every bit as carefully as we build and strengthen the ties that bind us together as counseling psychologists" (Howard, 1992, p. 428).

Attending to the Diversity of Clientele

A recent president of the American Psychological Association asked us why counseling psychologists have emerged as the strongest leaders, in all of psychology, of multicultural research and practice. In one sense, we were startled by the question— counseling psychologists have been increasingly addressing the concerns of special populations since 1970 (see Heppner et al., in press; Meara & Myers, 1998). Our fumbling response to the question would not have been highly rated by faculty grading comprehensive exams! While the accomplishments of counseling psychologists in the development of knowledge and practice bases for multicultural counseling are described in Chapter 6, here we want to note that this continuity of concern rests on our heritage of attention to both individual differences in assets and strengths (Betz & Fitzgerald, 1993; Dawis, 1992) and to person–environment interactions—"special populations" exist largely because of environmental discrimination and oppression. Helping individuals in special populations achieve their potential has required that counseling psychologists develop both new methodologies for psychological assessment and interventions, as well as organizational structures to support such developments. The former will be more fully explored in chapters 6 and 13, the latter in the section below on organizational changes.

Division 17: The Tie That Binds

As noted earlier in this chapter, the *formal* beginnings of counseling psychology coincided with the establishment of divisions within the APA immediately after World War II. In one sense, then, it seems that the Division of Counseling Psychology would have to be one of the continuities of the profession, otherwise the profession might cease to exist. From the perspective of all the diversity of interests, scope of practice and special populations addressed by contemporary counseling psychologists, one might ask why the Division of Counseling Psychology remains such a vital and increasingly active force within the APA. After all, with over 50 divisions in the APA, does not each counseling psychologist find his or her specific interests better addressed by a more narrowly focused division? In fact, many counseling psychologists are also members of other divisions within the APA (one can belong to any division for which one meets eligibility requirements). Yet, for those who have been trained as, or develop practices as, counseling psychologists, Division 17 provides a unique connectedness through the ideological context of the unifying themes described in Chapter 1. What is that evidence for connectedness? In the 1990s, Division 17 consistently had, among all divisions of the APA, one of the highest per-capita attendances at APA conventions; its hospitality suite programs and social hours quadrupled in number between 1985 and 1998. Hurst (1989), in his presidential address titled "Counseling Psychology—A Source of Strength and Pride in the Ties that Bind" described 11 ties, perhaps best summed up in "we celebrate our diversity within our core of inner sameness" (p. 158).

Division 17: New Structures for the New Millennium

The four continuities just described have been complemented by four equally powerful changes in the past decade. We begin our description of these four changes with a focus on the *structure* of Division 17. While the division's very existence served as a source of continuity, meeting the increasingly diverse needs of the members of the division called for a radical new structure to address emerging problems (Carter & Davis, in press).

By the late 1980s, many counseling psychologists had concerns that (1) their diverse interests were not being met, (2) the division was not sufficiently proactive within the APA, and (3) there were too few opportunities for new and energetic counseling psychologists to become active participants in the affairs of the division. During the early 1990s, the executive board of the division met together for many extra hours and, in a special retreat, to develop a structure that would address all of these concerns. Four vice-presidencies were created to facilitate more proactive leadership of the division within the APA as well as support professional development for Division 17 members in the areas of Science, Professional Practice, Diversity and Public Interest, and Education and Training. The new structure also provided for Sections, Special Interest Groups and Special Task Groups. Sections were to be reserved for those interest groups that could enroll and sustain a significant number of members and provide their own programs and conferences. The new structure has been successful beyond anyone's expectation. Within 5 years of the establishment of this new structure, there were six interest groups that had met the stringent criteria for becoming a section: Counseling Health Psychology; Ethnic and Racial Diversity; Independent Practice of Counseling Psychology; Lesbian, Gay, and Bisexual Awareness; Society for Vocational Psychology; and Section on Women. As of this writing, there are 12 additional Special Interest Groups ranging from Children and Adolescents to Prevention and Public Interest to Qualitative Methods. "It is doubtful that the early leaders of the division could have foreseen the multifaceted, complex, efficient, and well-managed organization that has resulted from their initiatives" (Meara & Myers, 1998, p. 19).

Inclusiveness for Practitioners

Despite the fact that the scientist–*practitioner* model of training has always been the formally endorsed model for training counseling psychologists, up through the 1980s, those who chose to practice outside of academic settings—that is, in independent practice—often felt excluded from active roles within the Division of Counseling Psychology. Practitioners often felt they were regarded as second-class citizens and that their concerns about changes in the health care system were not being adequately attended to by the leadership of the profession. Fortunately, for the well-being of the future of counseling psychology, a few counseling psychologists who were in independent practice worked actively and effectively both within the Division of Counseling Psychology, and in other parts of the APA, to see that critical issues were addressed. These issues included items like the definition of health service providers for qualifying reimbursement by Medicare, generic versus specialty licensing, and so forth (see Chapter 4 for other professional issues). By 1988 Division 17 had established an Ad Hoc Committee on Independent Practice to assure that practitioners' issues received adequate attention. Heppner and colleagues (in press) provide further details of the work of this committee which, during the reorganization of Division 17 described above, became the responsibility of the Vice President for Practice. Thus, in the reorganization, practitioners had achieved a parity with science, education, and training, and diversity and public interest. As further evidence of clearer recognition for practitioners, in 1994, the John Black Award was created, supported by Consulting Psychologists Press to recognize outstanding contributions to professional practice by a Division 17 member. Perhaps most symbolic of this rapid development of inclusiveness for independent practice, within Division 17, was the election of the division president for the year 2000. For the first time in the history of the division, the person who was elected president (Dr. Jean Carter) was one whose entire career was focused on independent practice.

Expanding Proactive Leadership

While the two changes just described rapidly matured during the 1990s, the next two changes we describe are really just getting under way, even though both have histories of nascent development in the 1980s. During the early years of counseling psychology, there were only a few counseling psychologists involved in leadership roles of the APA; the few who served in key positions such as executive officer (John Darley) or as president of the APA (Leona Tyler). Until the late 1970s, counseling psychologists' focus within the division, as compared to a broader focus within the profession of psychology, was not particularly problematic, although it certainly limited other psychologists' and health professionals' awareness of the potential contributions of the profession. As more fully explored in Chapter 4, by the late 1970s a number of critical issues had emerged regarding licensing, specialty definitions, and other such issues. It then became vital for the voice of counseling psychologists to be more fully heard within the profession of psychology as well as in health care and educational institutions.

Consider just one example of the kinds of problems that can emerge if attention to leadership outside of the immediate specialty is not carefully nurtured: in the late 1970s, there was a brief period when representatives from counseling psychology were excluded from the APA Committee on Accreditation even though about 20 counseling psychology programs were then being regularly reviewed for accreditation. Strong reactions to this situation by the leadership of Division 17 marked the beginning of a major change in the roles of counseling psychologists in many psychological and credentialing organizations. In fact, in the last two decades of the twentieth century, the number of counseling psychologists who served as chair of the APA Committee on Accreditation or as presidents of the National Register of Health Service Providers in Psychology, the American Board of Professional Psychology, and the Association of State and Provincial Psychology Boards far exceeded what would be predicted based on the number of counseling psychologists, as compared to clinical psychologists, served by these organizations. Moreover, by 1998, seven of the 14 members of the APA Board of Directors had received their doctoral training in counseling psychology programs (Heppner et al., in press). By 1999, there was an unprecedented number of counseling psychologists serving in the APA Council of Representatives, its primary legislative body. These counseling psychologists had been elected by a broad range of colleagues outside of counseling psychology, in a wide range of divisions and state associations.

However, in our view, the greater potential of the profession of counseling psychology will be achieved only by more counseling psychologists serving in the highest levels of organizations and government *outside of psychology*. Fortunately, a small handful of counseling psychologists are paving the way as top-level executive administrators in the Veterans Administration and managed care organizations; moreover, the first psychologist elected to the U.S. Congress (Ted Strickland) is a counseling psychologist. Counseling psychologists in such leadership roles can bring to these major social agencies the understandings of the profession regarding individual differences in strengths and assets, person–environment interactions, and ways to encompass cultural diversity. We want our readers to aim for high positions in the leadership of our government, health care agencies, and educational institutions, as well as becoming effective scientist–practitioners in the profession of counseling psychology.

Globalization of Counseling Psychology

Of all the changes we have reviewed here, globalization is the most still-to-be developed one. Although Fretz established an International Forum in *The Counseling Psychologist* in 1985, over the years there have been fewer contributions to this forum than to others. In the late 1990s, co-editors were established for the International Forum, charged with enlarging the number and scope of its contributions. Moreover, while there have long been informal liaisons between Division 17 and counseling psychologists in a few other countries, in more recent years formal liaison relationships have been established with 16 different countries from every continent except Antarctica! What is needed now is a strategic plan for how counseling psychologists in the United States can develop more frequent relationships and exchanges with counseling psychologists in these many other countries. Such connectedness can serve to enhance the research and practice of all counseling psychologists and to extend the benefits of our core values to our increasingly global society.

As we come to the conclusion of this chapter on the Development of the Profession and as we consider the potential of the current vigor and vitality of the profession of counseling psychology, we wish to echo the joys, challenges, and possibilities inherent in the title of Howard's (1992) *Journal of Counseling Psychology* centennial contribution: "Behold Our Creation! What Counseling Psychology Has Become and Might Yet Become."

SUMMARY

Although the formal, written history of counseling psychology is now just passing the half-century mark, the roots of the profession lie in sociocultural and disciplinary developments of the late nineteenth and early twentieth century. Changes in lifestyles and work, two world wars, and the Great Depression created the need for a new helping profession—counseling psychology was a profession "waiting to happen." Conceptual developments in psychology and mental health care formed the foundation for the research and practice of the emerging profession and served to delineate its five unifying themes.

The mental health movement of the nineteenth century led to changes in society's perspective on mental illness, revealing that not only could "insanity" be cured but also that the problems of daily living can be alleviated by drawing on the unique set of assets and strengths each individual possesses.

Psychology's long and distinguished history on measurement of human behavior laid the foundation for counseling psychology's emphasis on person–environment interaction. Without measurement there can be no science. Equally important to the development of this emphasis was the much slower recognition and subsequent measurement of the effects of environment on human behavior. Within the various disciplines of psychology, too often those assessing personality have ignored the work of those studying environmental influences, and vice versa. Psychologists in applied practice have gradually realized, perhaps sooner than basic researchers, that behavior is not only a function of individual differences and environment but that the two have a reciprocal relationship. Persons affect environments just as environments affect persons. Only now are research and intervention strategies being developed that truly incorporate this interactive thinking.

The profession's emphasis on educational and career development has perhaps the clearest lineage—the vocational guidance movement, established at the beginning of the twentieth century to assist persons in the transition from the world of agriculture to the world of work created by the Industrial Revolution. This movement continues as counseling psychologists assist workers in the changing work world resulting from today's technological revolutions.

Because counseling psychology was created to respond to the psychological needs of persons that did not have to be hospitalized, primary emphasis was given to theoretical developments advocating brief treatment. Both directive (Williamson) and nondirective (Rogers) models of counseling, developed in the late 1930s and 1940s, provided a springboard for the development of myriad time-limited strategies during the second half of the twentieth century. Conceptualizations of cognitive developmental theorists complemented the work of personality theorists on how intact humans process interpersonal and environmental experiences, promoting research and interventions for prevention of psychological adjustment problems and for helping persons move through transitions with a minimum of disruption and a maximum of new opportunities.

The formal steps of establishing an autonomous specialty within psychology occurred in the 1940s. The 1950s saw the profession through its "childhood" stages, with the establishment of sets of standards, accredited programs, employment designations, and a major research journal. The "adolescence" of counseling psychology coincided with the turbulent 1960s and 1970s, during which American society itself struggled with identity problems in relation to sociopolitical issues like the Vietnam War and the civil rights movement. Counseling psychology wrestled with its own increasingly diffused identity, encompassing remedial counseling and therapy, prevention, career psychology, and so forth. Despite efforts toward mergers and "hostile takeovers," in the 1970s the profession was ready to build upon its foundation and to define itself. Though sharing interests with other specialties and professions, it possessed a unique core of emphases. A new journal, numerous accredited programs, and affiliation with professional organizations all helped propel the profession toward the highly productive 1980s—impressive years in terms of highly visible accomplishments—handbooks, book series, task forces, and conferences, all representing increased vitality and promising continued growth and development.

The ever greater vitality and productivity of the profession of counseling psychology in the 1990s is most succinctly captured in four continuities from our past, complemented by four effective changes in the structure and vision of the profession, changes that address the society and professional world in which we all now find ourselves. Our connectedness has been enhanced by the continuities of the scientist–practitioner model, embracing the diversity in the scope of our practice, and the diversity of the clientele we serve, and in recognizing the core values that bind us together. The responsiveness of the profession to changing times is found in a dynamic new structure for the Division of Counseling Psychology, its expanded inclusiveness of practitioners, its expanded leadership roles in psychology, health care organizations and government agencies, and in its nascent development of a more global profession of counseling psychology for the twenty-first century.

REFERENCES

American Psychological Association (APA), Division of Counseling and Guidance. (1952). Recommended standards for training counseling psychologists at the doctoral level. *American Psychologist, 7,* 175–181.

APA. (1999). Archival description of counseling psychology. *The Counseling Psychologist, 27,* 589–592.

Beers, C. W. (1908). *A mind that found itself.* Garden City, NY: Longman, Green.

Berg, I. A., Pepinsky, H. B., & Shoben, E. J. (1980). The status of counseling psychology: 1960. In J. Whiteley (Ed.), *The history of counseling psychology* (pp. 105–113). Monterey, CA: Brooks/Cole.

Bergin, A. E., & Garfield, S. L. (1971). *Handbook of psychotherapy and behavior change.* New York: John Wiley & Sons.

Bernstein, B. L., & Kerr, B. (1993). Counseling psychology and the scientist–practitioner model: Implementation and implications. *The Counseling Psychologist, 21,* 136–151.

Betz, N. E., & Fitzgerald, L. F. (1993). Individuality and diversity: Theory and research in counseling psychology. *Annual Review of Psychology, 44,* 343–381.

Borgen, F. (1984). Counseling psychology. *Annual Review of Psychology, 28,* 257–278.

Brammer, L. M., & Abrego, P. J. (1981). Intervention strategy for coping with transitions. *The Counseling Psychologist, 9*(2), 19–35.

Brown, S. D., & Lent, R. W. (Eds.). (1984). *Handbook of counseling psychology.* New York: John Wiley & Sons.

Carter, J. A., & Davis, K. L. (In press). Revitalizing the division: The reorganization of Division 17. *The Counseling Psychologist.*

Claiborn, C. D., & Lichtenberg, J. W. (1989). Interactional counseling. *The Counseling Psychologist, 17,* 355–453.

Dawis, R. V. (1992). The individual difference tradition in counseling psychology. *Journal of Counseling Psychology, 39,* 7–19.

Erikson, E. H. (1959). Identity and the life cycle. *Psychological Issues, 1,* Monograph 1.

Flores, L. Y., Rooney, S. C., Heppner, P. P., Browne, L. D., & Wei, M. (1999). Trend analyses of major contributions in *The Counseling Psychologist* cited from 1986–1996. *The Counseling Psychologist, 27,* 73–95.

Gelso, C. J. (1993). On the making of a scientist–practitioner: A theory of research training in professional psychology. *Professional Psychology: Research and Practice, 24,* 468–476.

Gelso, C. J., & Fassinger, R. (1990). Counseling psychology. *Annual Review of Psychology, 41,* 355–386.

Gibson, J., & Brown, S. D. (1992). Counseling adults for life transitions. In S. D. Brown and R. W. Lent (Eds.), *Handbook of counseling psychology* (2nd ed., pp. 285–314). New York: John Wiley & Sons.

Haley, A. (1976). *Roots.* Garden City, NY: Doubleday.

Heppner, P. P. (1999). Thirty years of *The Counseling Psychologist*: 1969–1999. *The Counseling Psychologist, 27,* 5–13.

Heppner, P. P., Casas, J. M., Carter, J., & Stone, G. L. (In press). The maturation of counseling psychology: Multifaceted perspectives, 1978–1998. In S. D. Brown and R. W. Lent (Eds.), *Handbook of counseling psychology* (3rd ed.). New York: John Wiley & Sons.

Howard, G. S. (1992). Behold our creation! What counseling psychology has become and might yet become. *Journal of Counseling Psychology, 39,* 419–442.

Hull, C. L. (1928). *Aptitude testing.* Yonkers, NY: World Book.

Hurst, J. C. (1989). Counseling psychology—A source of strength and pride in the ties that bind. *The Counseling Psychologist, 17,* 147–160.

Kohlberg, L. (1984). *Essays in moral development.* New York: Harper & Row.

Krumboltz, J. D., & Thoresen, C. E. (1969). *Behavioral counseling.* New York: Holt, Rinehart & Winston.

Lewin, K. (1935). *A dynamic theory of personality: Selected papers.* New York: McGraw-Hill.

Matheny, K. B., Aycock, D. W., Pugh, J. L., Curlette, W. L., & Cannella, K. A. S. (1986). Stress coping: A qualitative and quantitative synthesis with implications for treatment. *The Counseling Psychologist, 14,* 439–549.

Meara, N. (1990). Science, practice and politics. *The Counseling Psychologist, 18,* 144–167.

Meara, N. M., & Myers, R. A. (1998). A history of Division 17 (Counseling Psychology): Establishing stability amid change. In D. A. Dewsbury (Ed.), *Unification through divi-*

sion: *Histories of the divisions of the American Psychological Association.* Volume III (pp. 9–41). Washington, DC: American Psychological Association.

Mischel, W. (1968). *Personality and assessment.* New York: John Wiley & Sons.

Moore, W. E. (1970). *The professions: Roles and rules.* New York: Sage Publications.

Mosher, R. L., & Sprinthall, N. A. (1971). Psychological education: A means to promote personal development during adolescence. *The Counseling Psychologist, 2*(4), 3–84.

Osipow, S. H. (1987). Counseling psychology: Theory, research and practice in career counseling. *Annual Review of Psychology, 28,* 257–278.

Parsons, F. (1909). *Choosing a vocation.* Boston: Houghton Mifflin.

Pepinsky, H. B., Hill-Frederick, K., & Epperson, D. L. (1978). The *Journal of Counseling Psychology* as a matter of policies. *Journal of Counseling Psychology, 25,* 483–498.

Perry, W. (1970). *Forms of intellectual and ethical development during the college years.* New York: Holt, Rinehart & Winston.

Piaget, J. (1952). *The language and thought of the child.* London: Routledge & Kegan Paul.

Richardson, M. S., & Patton, M. J. (1992). Guest editors' introduction to the centennial articles. *Journal of Counseling Psychology, 39,* 3–6.

Rogers, C. R. (1942). *Counseling and psychotherapy.* Boston: Houghton Mifflin.

Rudd, S. S., Weissberg, N., & Gazda, G. M. (1988). Looking to the future: Themes from the third national conference for counseling psychology. *The Counseling Psychologist, 16,* 423–430.

Schlossberg, N. K. (1981). A model for analyzing human adaptation to transition. *The Counseling Psychologist, 9*(2), 2–18.

Schmidt, L. (1977). Why has the professional practice of psychological counseling developed in the United States? *The Counseling Psychologist, 7*(2), 19–20.

Schneider, B. (1983). On the etiology of climates. *Personnel Psychology, 36,* 19–39.

Scott, C. W. (1980). History of the division of counseling psychology: 1945–1963. In J. M. Whiteley (Ed.), *The History of Counseling Psychology* (pp. 25–40). Monterey, CA: Brooks/Cole.

Super, D. E. (1955). Transition: From vocational guidance to counseling psychology. *Journal of Counseling Psychology, 2,* 3–9.

Thompson, A. S., & Super, D. E. (Eds.). (1964). *The professional preparation of counseling psychologists. Report of the 1964 Greyston Conference.* New York: Bureau of Publications, Teacher's College, Columbia University.

Tiedeman, D. B. (1980). Status and prospect in counseling psychology: 1962. In J. M. Whiteley (Ed.), *The history of counseling psychology* (pp. 125–132). Monterey, CA: Brooks/Cole.

Tyler, L., Tiedeman, D., & Wrenn, C. G. (1980). The current status of counseling psychology: 1961. In J. M. Whiteley (Ed.), *The history of counseling psychology* (pp. 114–124). Monterey, CA: Brooks/Cole.

Wagner, W. G. (1996). Optimal development in adolescence. *The Counseling Psychologist, 24,* 360–399.

Walsh, W. B., & Osipow, S. H. (Eds.). (1983a). *Advances in vocational psychology.* Vol. 1. Hillsdale, NJ: Lawrence Erlbaum.

Walsh, W. B., & Osipow, S. H. (Eds.). (1983b). *Handbook of vocational psychology.* Vols. 1–2. Hillsdale, NJ: Lawrence Erlbaum.

Whiteley, J. N. (Ed.). (1980). *The history of counseling psychology.* Monterey, CA: Brooks/Cole.

Whiteley, J. N. (1984a). Counseling psychology: A historical perspective. *The Counseling Psychologist, 12*(1), 3–109.

Whiteley, J. N. (1984b). A historical perspective on the development of counseling psychology as a profession. In S. G. Brown and R. W. Lent (Eds.), *Handbook of counseling psychology* (pp. 3–55). New York: John Wiley & Sons.

Whiteley, J. N., & Fretz, B. R. (Eds.). (1980). *The present and future of counseling psychology.* Monterey, CA: Brooks/Cole.

Whiteley, J. N., Kagan, N., Harmon, L. W., Fretz, B. R., & Tanney, F. (Eds.). (1984). *The coming decade in counseling psychology.* Alexandria, VA: American Association for Counseling and Development.

Williamson, E. G. (1939). *How to counsel students.* New York: McGraw-Hill.

Wrenn, C. G. (1966). Birth and early childhood of a journal. *Journal of Counseling Psychology, 13,* 485–488.

CHAPTER 3

RESEARCH AND SCIENCE

In this chapter we focus on the topics of science and research in counseling psychology. The chapter is divided into four sections. In the first, the concept of "scientist" within the scientist–practitioner model is explored. We seek to answer the question "What does the 'scientist' part of the scientist–practitioner model really mean?" Different levels of "being a scientist" are examined.

Whereas the first section tends toward the philosophical, the second and third sections are more practical. Our aim is to help the reader understand approaches to counseling psychology research and some key issues in research. We have intentionally sought to go beyond the beginning survey course, gearing the material to the student or professional with some background in psychological research, but little or no background in counseling psychology research. The second section presents four research strategies commonly used in counseling psychology research, whereas in the third section, two focal points of intervention research are discussed and differentiated: The process and the outcome of counseling psychology interventions.

The chapter concludes with a perspective on research in counseling psychology and a discussion of the relevance of research to practice. In this final section, Gelso's "bubble hypothesis" is suggested as a useful way of thinking about the advantages and disadvantages of different research strategies and of the many decisions the researcher must make about the methods used in any given study. We also explore the concept of research relevance, with an emphasis on what the counseling psychology practitioner should and should not expect from research. Finally, some often ignored complexities of the idea of relevance are explored, and ways in which research can be highly relevant to practice are discussed.

THE "SCIENTIST" PART OF THE SCIENTIST–PRACTITIONER MODEL: WHAT DOES IT MEAN?

Earlier we discussed the scientist–practitioner model of training and practice in counseling psychology. We noted that from the beginnings of the specialty, this model has been seen as crucial to sound progress in our understanding of all of the activities in which counseling psychologists are involved (e.g., counseling, assessment, consultation, etc.) and the phenomena that counseling psychologists study (e.g., career development).

Within the scientist–practitioner model, students are trained (more precisely, educated) so that they will be scientists as well as professional practitioners. And a vital element of this scientific training is learning how to conduct scientific research. Because research is so vital in this model and in the field, before proceeding further, we shall offer answers to the questions "Why, in fact, is scientific research so important to counseling psychology?" and "Why not just practice what we believe to be true from our personal experiences with clients and human beings more generally?"

Without the benefits of scientific checks and rigorous scientific tests of our favorite hypotheses, we run the risk of creating magical solutions or cures that are more products of our fantasies and personal needs than of reality. Along this same line, without scientific research and theory, we shall very likely develop treatment approaches that are only products of our biases and prejudices. In the last analysis, counseling practice, in the absence of controlled tests of the efficacy of that practice, is doomed to limited effectiveness at best and harmfulness at worst. Research allows us to check whether our beliefs and theories hold up under controlled conditions and, just as important, whether we are in fact having the effects (e.g., on our clients) that we think and hope we are. In this way, science helps us to continually improve practice.

Along with helping the counseling psychologist check and study his or her theories and treatments, scientific research can have a still more proactive effect. Not only can we find out if our research hypotheses hold up under controlled conditions, we can also create new knowledge and theories through research. Research findings virtually always lead to new directions for the researchers, suggest new ideas and theories, and point to ways in which treatments may be modified so as to become more effective. In these ways, scientific research and the findings emanating from it are always exciting—at least a portion of what turns up is almost always new!

Do the above formulations imply that all counseling psychologists should be involved in science and research? Should the counseling psychologist who, for example, is working full time as a private practitioner, make empirical research a part of his or her workday? Is it enough for the practitioner to think scientifically? to be a consumer (i.e., reader of) rather than a producer of scientific theory and research? These important questions lead us to a discussion of what the "scientist" part of the scientist–practitioner model really means.

Although the scientist–practitioner model has been around for a long time, there has never been a great deal of agreement or clarity about what the terms of the model mean and how they are to be actualized, both in graduate education and in the worklives of counseling psychologists (or psychologists in other specialties). Defining just what is meant by being a scientist within this model is more complicated than might first appear. Thus there are several meanings to the concept of "scientist" and several ways in which the concept is manifested in practice.

From the time of the Northwestern Conference in 1951, it has been suggested that, at a minimum, "being scientific" means having the "ability to review and make use of the results of research" (APA, 1952, p. 179). Thus the counseling practitioner should be able to understand research and apply research findings to his or her practice. We might view this as the first level, or minimal level, of functioning as a scientist–practitioner.

A second way in which the counseling psychologist is to be a scientist is in the way he or she goes about thinking of practice as well as the manner in which he or she conducts counseling psychology practice. With respect to one's thinking, the practitioner follows what is perhaps the most fundamental tenet of the scientific attitude: Think critically and be sufficiently skeptical. Thus, one is to think critically about theories, one's own and others, rather than just accept them. Also, when one reads research studies, one is to think critically. When new approaches are suggested in the literature, the practitioner does not simply swallow them; he or she is duly skeptical. After careful examination, approaches may be tried out tentatively.

In terms of the manner in which the practitioner conducts his or her practice, for example, in his or her work with clients, a scientific process is followed. In counseling, the counselor sifts through material the client presents and forms hypotheses about (1) what the client's problem is, (2) how best to intervene, and (3) the ways in which the client might respond to various interventions. The counselor then puts these hypotheses to the test in practice, and the hypotheses are subsequently revised as a result of the client's response. These steps continually recycle throughout the therapeutic work.

This adherence to a critical thinking style and to a scientific process in one's work may be viewed as a second level of functioning within the scientist–practitioner model. The scientific process, as used in counseling, was first systematically articulated many years ago by Pepinsky and Pepinsky (1954) and has been an important part of the scientist–practitioner model since then (see Howard [1986] for an interesting version of the "counselor as personal scientist" model).

Many scholars in the specialty believe that the "scientist" part of the scientist–practitioner model means or ought to mean much more than being able to review research, apply research findings to practice, and carry out one's practice in a scientific way. In effect, they call for a third level of functioning within the scientist–practitioner model. Whiteley (1984), for example, is a leading spokesperson for a more demanding view of the scientist–professional model of training. He suggests that, at a minimum, training at the doctoral level in counseling psychology should teach students to "formulate hypotheses, and to conduct original inquiry" (p. 46), as well as to review and make use of research.

In fact, at the doctoral level, students are now and have always been taught to "formulate hypotheses and conduct original inquiry." What Whiteley and others are implying is that not only should students be taught this, there should also be an expectation that they actually do empirical research as part of their subsequent careers, regardless of whether they are in academic settings, independent practice settings, or other settings. In this sense, being a scientist–practitioner means being involved in research as well as counseling practice throughout one's career, although individual counseling psychologists will of course differ greatly in just how much of their work time is devoted to research.

In sum, the concept of "scientist" within the scientist–practitioner model refers to each of the three levels just discussed (see Heppner, Kivlighan, & Wampold, 1999). Although the counseling psychologist functions as scientist at each and any level, we suggest that the field will benefit most if the individual actualizes all three levels. The counseling psychologist must be able to understand research and be able to apply it to practice although, as shall be proposed later in this chapter, the application of research to practice should rarely if ever be direct. The counseling psychologist should also think scientifically and carry out practice in a scientific fashion. Finally, if the field and our clients are to profit maximally, the counseling psychologist should conduct scholarly work as part of his or her career. Note that we here use the term *scholarly work* rather than *research, empirical research,* or *science.* Scholarly work is the broadest and most inclusive of these terms and, as we shall see, expecting that counseling psychologists will do scholarly work is more realistic than expecting that they will do empirical research, regardless of their work settings. To make sense of this suggestion, we first need to clarify further our use of the terms *research, science,* and *scholarly work.*

Research, Science, and Scholarly Work

As part of the Third National Conference on Counseling Psychology (referred to as the Georgia Conference), the Committee on Research (Gelso, Betz, Friedlander, Helms et al., 1988) grappled with the similarities and differences among three related concepts: research, science, and scholarly work. Too often these terms are used interchangeably, and without clarification, in the counseling psychology literature. In discussing the scientist–practitioner model and the role of research in counseling psychology, it is important to differentiate them.

As noted by Gelso and colleagues (1988), empirical research is done within the broader context of science. In such research, the investigator ordinarily imposes controls so that his or her observations will lead to nonbiased conclusions about the phenomena under study. Usually—but not always—there is a degree of quantification in counseling psychology research. The purpose of research, as discussed by Gelso et al. (1988), is to contribute to a body of knowledge that, together with theory, comprises the scientific endeavor.

Note here that theory, as well as research, is part of the scientific endeavor. Too often in counseling psychology and other specialties and fields, the fact that theory and research go hand in hand in science is forgotten (Gelso, 1996). In producing hypotheses, theories provide the subject matter that research studies seek to test (of course, theories themselves vary greatly in how formally, coherently, and comprehensively they are stated). In turn, research results serve to revise and refine theoretical hypotheses. This reciprocal process has been referred to as "the cycle of scientific work" (Strong, 1991, p. 208).

Of the three concepts (research, science, and scholarly work), science is the hardest to define clearly and simply. That is because science is many things. Not only does science consist of theory and research, as discussed above, it can also be seen as an attitude, a method, and a set of techniques. (See Heppner, Kivlighan, & Wampold [1999], Howard [1985], and Rychlak [1968], for clear and interesting elaborations.) For present purposes, science may be viewed as an attitude and method that places a premium on controlled observations, precise definitions, and repeatability or replicability. The scientist controls variables to rule out competing explanations; he or she clearly defines terms, operations, and procedures so that other scientists may understand what is meant and to be able to replicate the investigation. In order for a scientific theory or research finding to be accepted as valid, the events or phenomena being observed must be replicable. The value placed on control, precision, and replicability in science applies to both scientific theory and scientific research.

As indicated by Gelso and colleagues (1988), scholarly work or activity is the most general of the three concepts (research, science, and scholarly work), including intellectual activities that may go well beyond what we ordinarily consider as science, for example, philosophical inquiry, historical analysis, and thoughtful but nonquantified and minimally controlled analyses of counseling cases. We may define scholarly work as a disciplined and thoughtful search for knowledge and understanding. Although it may not include the degree of control, precision, and replicability characteristic of science, the search for knowledge inherent in scholarly work is nonetheless disciplined.

Scholarly Work and the Counseling Psychologist

A key point to this discussion of research, science, and scholarly work is that when we discuss the scientist side of the scientist–practitioner model in counseling psychology (and other applied specialties in psychology), we are concerned first and foremost with training effective scholars—individuals who thoughtfully and creatively seek to understand phenomena in counseling psychology, who seek to understand deeply, and who communicate that understanding to others, for example, in written papers and conference presentations. It is within this intellectual context, as Gelso et al. (1988) proposed, that we promote graduate students' functioning as scientists and empirical researchers.

Let us now return to the discussion of what ought to be expected from the scientist side of the scientist–practitioner model. To recapitulate, we looked at three ways in which being a scientist within the model is manifested: (1) reviewing and applying research findings to one's practice, (2) thinking scientifically and carrying out one's work scientifically, and (3) actually doing research as part of one's career—regardless of one's job setting.

The expectation that the counseling psychologist be able to review and apply research is the least demanding of the three courses, whereas the expectation that he or she actually do research is the most demanding. Is this latter expectation realistic and viable? Not really. On the one hand, as affirmed by many observers (e.g., Gelso, 1979a, b, 1993; Gelso & Lent, 2000; Heppner et al., 1999; Magoon & Holland, 1984; Whiteley, 1984), there is, and probably will always be, an ongoing need for more and better research in counseling psychology. Faculty who train counseling psychologists should do everything possible in the training situation to promote students' continuing their research after obtaining the doctorate.

Yet, on the other hand, it is also true that many counseling psychologists are in work settings (e.g., community mental health settings, private practice settings) in which carrying out empirical research is extraordinarily difficult. Also, some counseling psychologists (no matter how inspiring or competent their doctoral training) simply do not have the inclination or perhaps enough of the kinds of abilities needed to do empirical research. Many of these people can do very effective scholarly and scientific work other than empirical research. Thus, for example, developing theories and treatment approaches, and publishing these in the professional literature, can be highly scholarly, and contribute significantly to science as well as good practice. One who writes conceptual articles that are not based on research—clinical theory papers, hypotheses developed from individual cases, and so forth—effectively satisfies the dictates of the scientist side of the scientist–professional model. Such activities are more viable than empirical research in some settings.

In summary, scholarly and scientific work should be a part of the counseling psychologist's job activity, regardless of job setting. The particular kind of such work that is done will depend on a host of factors, most notably, the job demands and facilities of the specific setting and the inclinations and abilities of the individual counseling psychologist.

In regard to setting, those who work in university settings, especially in academic departments, will have the most favorable climate and the most concretely facilitative environment for the conduct of empirical research. Those who work in private practice and other agency-type settings will typically have the fewest practical and psychological facilities for doing research. Unless they are exceptionally motivated and/or are able to collaborate with colleagues in more favorable settings (e.g., universities), research will not get done. But, again, scholarly work can and should be contributed by counseling psychologists in all settings.

INVESTIGATIVE STYLES: A TYPOLOGY FOR RESEARCH

Although we have been discussing scholarly activities that are viable alternatives to empirical research within the scientist–practitioner model, it needs to be underscored that empirical research has always held a highly prominent place in counseling psychology. Because of its importance to the specialty, the next two sections of Chapter 3 are devoted to some key research issues in the field: (a) a classification of research approaches and (b) the distinction between process and outcome research in counseling. The student of research methodology knows that there are a great many key issues in counseling psychology research, as well as in psychological research in general. One could devote many pages to topics such as selection of criteria, the use of control groups, reliability and validity of measurements and instruments, statistical issues, and so on. Rather than examine topics such as these in a superficial manner (as would be necessary in a book that covers the entire specialty of counseling psychology), we have chosen to focus on two topics (research approaches, and the process/outcome distinction) that seem fundamental to understanding counseling psychology research. At the same time, in the course of the discussion, some of the most important issues in counseling research should become

TABLE 3.1.   A System for Categorizing Types of Research.

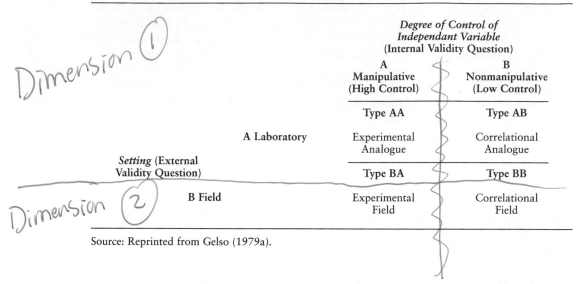

Dimension ①

Dimension ②

		Degree of Control of Independant Variable (Internal Validity Question)	
		A Manipulative (High Control)	B Nonmanipulative (Low Control)
Setting (External Validity Question)	A Laboratory	Type AA — Experimental Analogue	Type AB — Correlational Analogue
	B Field	Type BA — Experimental Field	Type BB — Correlational Field

Source: Reprinted from Gelso (1979a).

apparent. Also, references to in-depth work on some central issues in counseling research will enable the reader to pursue these topics more fully. (Heppner et al.'s [1999] book on counseling research provides a comprehensive treatment of the entire range of counseling research issues.)

In the present section, we discuss a way of classifying counseling research that should aid the reader in understanding counseling psychology research generally. As one of the authors had earlier suggested (Gelso, 1979a, b), and as has been empirically verified (Ponterotto, 1988; Scherman & Doan, 1985), one can classify most counseling research into four basic types or approaches. Each of these four types has its own advantages and disadvantages, and it is important for the student of counseling psychology research to understand these.

To arrive at the four types of research in question, it is useful to think of counseling research as existing along two basic dimensions. One of these dimensions reflects the degree to which the experimenter or researcher controls or manipulates the independent variable (the variable or variables that are considered to have the experimental effect). As you can see in Table 3.1, we can divide studies into those that are manipulative (high control of the independent variable) or nonmanipulative (low control).

Note that in Table 3.1 this dimension of Degree of Control is termed an internal validity question. That is because the extent to which the researcher manipulates or controls the independent variable relates very closely to how internally valid the study is—how clearly we can say that the variable(s) we presume to be producing the experimental effect, and not other variables, are the ones that are in fact having that effect.

The second dimension of counseling psychology research is simply labeled Setting in Table 3.1. As you can see, there are basically two different settings, one being the laboratory and the other the field. Laboratory studies are usually simulations of the activity they are studying; whereas in field studies, the researcher examines the actual activity (e.g., counseling) in its natural setting.

Whereas the first dimension, as discussed above, related directly to internal validity, this second dimension relates to external validity—the extent to which one can generalize the findings from this particular study and this particular sample to the actual activity and population of interest. For example, if one studied career counseling with a sample of college students, the question of external validity would ask to what extent the findings could be generalized to career counseling, as practiced outside of the experiment, for example, in actual college counseling centers. Generally, studies done in field settings are high on external validity (one can generalize from them), whereas those done in laboratory settings contain some problems with external validity. These issues shall be explored more fully as we examine the types of research below. (The reader is referred to Cook and Campbell [1979] for a classic work on internal and external validity issues in research.)

As is evidenced in Table 3.1, when one combines the two levels of the Degree of Control dimension (manipulative and nonmanipulative) with the two levels of the Setting dimension (laboratory and field), four types of research, or investigative styles, result. Before examining how each of these operates in counseling psychology research, it should be underscored that categorization systems such as these are inevitably simplifications. In the real world of counseling psychology research, studies usually vary in the extent to which they represent a given type, and often studies are mixtures of the four types. Yet such simplifications can be very useful in understanding the strengths and weaknesses of different approaches.

Research Strategy AA: The Experimental Analogue

The first investigative style, the experimental analogue, is considered experimental because the researcher has full control over the independent variable (in counseling, for example, the treatment, who gets it, and when). The researcher controls the independent variable (IV) ordinarily through assigning subjects to different treatments randomly and determining when the treatments are offered. Thus, for example, in a therapy study, the researcher may randomly assign clients who visit an agency to different types of treatments and perhaps to a control group for whom treatment is delayed. The groups receiving different therapies are compared to each other and with the delayed treatment control group. Alternatively, the researcher may conduct what is called a within-subjects experiment in which the subject gets each of two or more different treatments, with the order in which he or she receives them being determined randomly (called counterbalancing order).

If assignment to groups was random, and if all treatments were offered at equivalent times, the researcher is in a good position to conclude that the experimental effects were due to the treatments and not to other extraneous variables. Such a conclusion is likewise warranted if the client or subject received each treatment, and the order in which they were offered was alternated among subjects. In other words, the experimental control allows for strong causal inferences. If you manipulate IVs in a highly controlled situation and find changes in the dependent variables (those being affected) that follow the manipulation, you can safely conclude that it was the IV that had the effect.

So far we have been discussing how the experimental analogue is experimental. These comments reflect general thinking in psychology and other fields about what constitutes an experiment and what kinds of conclusions an experiment permits. The experimental analogue, however, is also an analogue of something we are interested in studying. That is, the analogue does not study the activity directly in a real-life situation; rather it studies the activity by analogy—in one way or another, by approximating or simulating the activity.

Analogue research within counseling psychology most often studies an intervention. This intervention may be any of a wide range of activities or treatments in which the counseling psychologist is involved. Some examples of these are counseling, psychotherapy, consultation, guidance, assessment, supervision, training, and teaching. Again, the intervention is not studied as it actually is or naturally occurs, but instead as it is approximated by the researcher. Also, it should be understood that the typical analogue examines some aspect of the intervention rather than the entire intervention.

In the context of a given intervention, the experimenter may study the effects of any of an almost infinite array of independent variables and an equally wide range of dependent variables. Among the manifold aspects of counseling, for example, one can study the effects of (1) counselor techniques, behavior, personality, appearance, intentions, or style; (2) numerous client characteristics; and (3) different kinds or characteristics of treatments. In a like manner, the researcher may examine the effects of such variables on various client and counselor behaviors, perceptions, reactions, and so on. Here we can look at how the independent variable(s) affects some aspect of the client's behavior, some aspect of the counselor's behavior, some aspect of their interaction, or all these.

Let us be more specific about how experimental analogues are carried out. Basically, there are two kinds of analogues: the audiovisual (AV) analogue, and the quasi-intervention (Q-I) analogue. In the AV analogue, to use an example from counseling, the subject is typically (a) presented with a stimulus tape or film (although at times only written stimuli are used); (b) asked to assume the role of counselor or client; and (c) asked for different responses at various points in time. The tape or film usually displays a client, a counselor, or both. The researcher has complete control over what transpires on the tape or film.

An example of an AV analogue was an experiment by Jones and Gelso (1988). These experimenters wanted to find out if a particular class of counselor response (an interpretation) is preferred by clients when delivered in a tentative as compared to an absolute manner. College student–subjects, who were asked to psychologically place themselves in the role of the client, listened to audiotapes of a counselor making one or the other type of interpretation at three points in a session. Thus, the counselor noted to the taped client what she viewed as the causes of the client's problems (an interpretation), and she did this in either a tentative or an absolute manner. Unbeknownst to subjects, the roles of taped counselor and client were played by counseling graduate students.

The student–subjects were randomly assigned to listen to either the tentative or the absolute interpretations. After listening to three segments of an interview (each containing one counselor interpretation), the students then evaluated the counselor and counseling. Generally, the counselor and counseling were rated as more effective when counselor interpretations were tentative rather than absolute. Note that the study also looked at whether a particular client characteristic (labeled as "resistance") affected the kind of interpretations subjects preferred. This variable had no detectable effect.

How does the AV analogue, as exemplified above, compare to the second kind, the quasi-intervention (Q-I) analogue? In the Q-I analogue, one or more interviews are actually held, and the activities that transpire may vary greatly in how closely they approximate the actual intervention being studied. To continue our use of counseling as an example of the intervention being studied, in the Q-I analogue, characteristics such as the following are displayed typically: (a) one or more interviews are held in which (b) counseling is approximated to one degree or another, and (c) a confederate client or counselor exhibits behaviors or characteristics that are prearranged or predetermined by the experimenter and are (d) systematically varied in order to (e) assess their effects on certain behaviors of the client–subject, the counselor–subject, or their interaction.

In past decades, Q-I analogues often only remotely resembled counseling. For example, rather than discussing real problems, students recruited from psychology courses were often asked to role-play problems, while counselors behaved according to some prearranged script. Thus counselors might behave in a planfully expert versus inexpert manner in order to assess the impact of expertness on the subject–clients' perceptions of the counselor during a 15-minute "counseling session." The problems of generalizing findings from studies such as this to actual counseling were considerable, to say the least. Because of concerns about the artificiality of such analogue methods, in recent years investigators have tried to devise more realistic Q-I analogues.

An example of an analogue experiment that is high on realism was the study conducted by Heaton, Hill, Peterson, Rochlen, and Zack (1998). In recent years, there has been growing attention to different methods of working with clients' nightdreams during counseling (e.g., Hill, 1996). Heaton and colleagues sought to determine if a therapist-facilitated dream interpretation session had a more positive impact on clients than did a self-guided session, using a model of dream interpretation that had been recently developed (Hill, 1996). Clients were university students who were recruited through class announcements and fliers posted in the psychology department of a mid-Atlantic university. Rather than being assigned randomly to one or the other of the two dream interpretation conditions, participants received *both* conditions (a within-subjects design), one week apart, with the order in which they received the conditions counterbalanced.

The counselors who conducted the therapist-facilitated sessions were counseling doctoral students who received several hours of training in the Hill dream interpretation method. In the self-guided session, clients followed the step-by-step approach presented in Hill's (1996) dream interpretation manual. Sessions lasted for 90–120 minutes in each condition. After each session, clients completed several measures aimed as determining what they gained and their evaluations of the sessions. One month later, clients were asked to evaluate each of the two types of sessions.

TABLE 3.2.   An Experimental Analogue Study That Is High on Realism.*

Independent Variable	Experimental Condition	Order of Treatments (One Week Apart)		Dependent Variable
		First	Second	
Therapist versus self-guided dream interpretation	1	Therapist facilitated	Self-guided	Client rated: preference understanding
	2	Self-guided	Therapist facilitated	insight mastery gains

Source: Heaton et al., 1998.

———

*Clients were assigned randomly to the two different treatment orders.

Although the self-guided session was viewed by clients as effective, the therapist-facilitated session was evaluated even more positively. Clients preferred therapist-guided sessions. They reported deeper involvement and greater insight during these sessions, and greater application of this insight to their lives.

The dream interpretation (either therapist-facilitated or self-guided) was the "real thing." So what makes this an analogue? The client–subjects were recruited for an experiment and were not seeking treatment. Also, the researchers telephoned the clients before each session to remind them of their appointments and encourage them to come to sessions prepared to discuss a recent, salient dream. In the real world of counseling practice, dream interpretation nearly always occurs within ongoing counseling; and when a dream is dealt with, the client does not alternate between therapist-facilitated and self-guided interpretation sessions. Thus, although the treatment in this study was the real thing, the many conditions surrounding the experiment made it more a simulation of dream interpretation work as it naturally occurs in counseling.

Evaluation of the Experimental Analogue in Counseling Psychology Research.

The laboratory analogue has a number of strengths and weaknesses that must be kept in mind when conducting and reviewing research. On the positive side, it permits precise control of variables in a tightly controlled setting. Relatedly, the researcher is able to isolate some very specific variables for study, as in the Jones and Gelso (1988) study of counselor interpretation.

Not only can specific variables be isolated and tightly controlled, the experimenter can also manipulate variables to an extent that is not possible in actual counseling. Thus, in actual counseling conducted in, for example, a counseling center, the researcher could not possibly have counselors limit or modify their behavior with clients in a way that prohibits them from doing the best job possible. Contrary to the Jones and Gelso (1988) experiment, for example, actual counselors could not be restricted to a certain number of interpretations and their interpretations limited to only certain kinds, even when that seemed ineffective or clinically unwise. The researcher cannot manipulate variables as freely in the real world of counseling because of ethical considerations. Ethics must of course always be an issue in considering experimental control.

Probably the most fundamental strength of the experimental analogue is that because it tightly controls and manipulates, it allows for strong causal inferences. If an experimental effect occurs, we can have a high degree of confidence that the effect was *a function of the independent variable(s)* and not due to other extraneous factors.

As in all research strategies, though, all is not methodologically well with the experimental analogue. In a certain way, its very strengths are its weaknesses. In isolating specific variables, and in rigorously controlling them, we violate nature, so to speak. To isolate a variable, that variable must be pulled out of its natural context. Again using Jones and Gelso's (1988) experiment as an example, interpretation was essentially the only kind of response made by the counselor in the taped vignettes. This response was carefully isolated, and was manipulated in that different subjects heard different kinds of interpretations.

By contrast, in the real world of counseling, counselor interpretations are offered in a broader context, which includes a range of other counselor responses, numerous client responses, and a client–counselor relationship that has developed. When we isolate variables in an analogue, the effects of that variable may be assessed in and of themselves, but we cannot know if they would occur in a like fashion in the real world. In this way, internal validity is enhanced at the expense of external validity.

To maximize experimental control, laboratory research inevitably simplifies the phenomena it studies. As implied above, the whole package is not studied, but only portions of its contents. The question about this is always, "Have we simplified too much—such that the findings are not really relevant to the treatment we sought to study?" In counseling psychology there is currently a great deal of sensitivity to this issue, and analogue researchers are seeking to develop simulations that are as realistic as possible.

Despite attempts to make analogues as realistic as possible, it should be clear that there will always be an artificiality to them—by their very nature. Because of this artificiality, and the attendant problems of generalizing analogue results to real-life counseling, the ultimate usefulness of the laboratory analogue has come under close scrutiny in recent years. The merits of this approach have been debated, hotly at times (e.g., Forsyth & Strong, 1986; Gelso, 1979a, b; Gelso & Fassinger, 1990; Goldman, 1979; Heppner et al., 1999; Stone, 1984). Some believe that research by analogy is not of particular value and might best be done away with or conducted only under very special circumstances. Indeed, whereas in past years, many experimental analogues appeared in leading counseling research journals (e.g., 27% from 1978–1982 in the *Journal of Counseling Psychology (JCP)*; Scherman & Doan, 1985), the number has reduced rather dramatically in recent years.

We believe there is still a valuable place for the experimental analogue in counseling psychology research. It is one's research question, above all, that should dictate the research approach taken (Heppner et al., 1999), and for some questions, the experimental analogue is an excellent strategy. For many questions, an analogue experiment is the best approach, and for some it is the only viable method. Some studies, again because of the questions being asked, require the tight control and precision allowed for by the analogue. Also, for ethical reasons, there are many important questions that simply could not be studied in real-life counseling. Moreover, as long as their inherent limitations are appreciated and efforts are made to produce sound simulations and enhance their realism, experimental analogues will continue to serve an important role in the counseling psychology research literature.

Research Strategy AB: The Correlational Analogue

The correlational analogue, our second research approach, is similar to the experimental analogue in that it is an approximation or simulation of some intervention situation. Also, the correlational analogue does not ordinarily occur in a real-life intervention setting but rather in a laboratory setting that itself is a simulation of the natural intervention setting.

It should be noted that even when the correlational analogue (or the experimental one, for that matter) occurs in a natural setting, for example, a university counseling center office, it is *still* an analogue. That is because, although the actual physical setting may be naturalistic, real-life counseling as it typically occurs is not being investigated.

The correlational analogue is unlike the experimental analogue in that the design is correlational rather than experimental. It is correlational in nature because independent variables are not manipulated; random assignment (of subjects to treatments, for example) does not occur. Essentially, the researcher does not have full control of who receives which experimental condition at what time. What does happen in the correlational analogue is that the researcher examines how two or more variables are related to one another in a controlled context. An almost infinite array of variables may be studied in this manner, although it is important that the selection of variables be guided by some theory or sound reasoning (and preferably both).

It must be underscored here that the AB strategy's *correlational* aspect in no way relates to the type of statistics used to analyze the data in a study. One may use correlational statistics (e.g., correlation coefficients) in experiments; and, likewise, the researcher may examine the differences between means for different groups in a correlational study. Correlational and group difference statistics are essentially interchangeable mathematically. Our use of the terms *correlational* and *experimental* pertain strictly to the experimental operations used—to the extent to which variables are isolated, manipulated, and controlled.

The fact that the AB strategy is correlational has profound implications for what we may conclude about the findings. Specifically, we may conclude that variables are systematically interrelated, but we cannot draw strong causal inferences. We cannot know what causes what. For example, if a researcher finds that, after a 30-minute interview, degree of counselor empathy is closely related to whether or not interviewees would want to be counseled by that person (should they desire counseling), we cannot know that empathy caused the wish to see the counselor. It is equally plausible that subjects who would want to be counseled possess qualities that counselors easily empathize with.

The axiom that "correlation does not imply causation" underlies an interesting paradox in psychological research. As a result of correlational findings, we cannot infer causality based on our methodology; yet we can, and in many cases should, *theorize* about what causes what and, further, we can use correlational research to test theories about what causes what. In testing the theory, for example, that counselor empathy is causally related to clients' wish to be counseled by the counselor in question, a correlational study will support the theory in that, if we find the hypothesized relationship, the theory has *escaped disconfirmation* (a relationship was, in fact, found to exist).

Let us examine an example of a correlational analogue. Latts and Gelso (1995) studied whether counselors' (a) awareness of how their own personal conflicts and issues played into their counseling (called *countertransference awareness*) and (b) use of counseling theory in their counseling combined to affect (c) how they responded to a videotaped actress portraying a client–survivor in a date rape scenario. The "client" in the video "described the details of her attack as well as her emotional reactions, including fear, depression, and self-blame" (p. 409). During six predetermined pauses in the tape, the therapists (doctoral students in counseling and clinical psychology) responded as they would to a real client who described this experience. Counselors' verbal responses were then rated for whether they approached or avoided the client's feelings and thoughts.

It was found that counselors who were high on countertransference awareness *and* the use of a theory in their work exhibited the highest approach (appropriate involvement) and least avoidance responses (emotional distancing) to the "client." Counselors who were low in countertransference awareness but high on use of a theory displayed the highest avoidance responses. Can we conclude that low awareness of countertransference, when joined with using theory in counseling, *caused* avoidance responses to the taped client? Based on this correlational design, certainly not. It is equally plausible that some other variable (e.g., counselor defensiveness) causes certain counselors to not be aware of their own countertransference, to use theories to maintain distance from emotions, and to avoid intense client feelings, for example, in sexual abuse situations. Awareness of countertransference feelings, use of a theory, and approach–avoidance do appear to be interrelated, but it cannot be determined what causes what from this correlational design. On the other hand, from the results of this study, we can offer *a meaningful theory* of how these variables are related causally, a theory that is at least clinically reasonable and compatible with the actual results.

Evaluation of the Correlational Analogue in Counseling Psychology Research.

The correlational analogue generally is not discussed as a research strategy or approach in itself. Writers sometimes mistakenly assume that analogues are by definition experimental. This assumption confuses control of the context of a study with control of the independent variables. As we have seen, the correlational analogue is indeed one of the approaches to counseling psychology research.

In terms of limitations, the correlational analogue, as an analogue of an intervention or situation, shares many of the problems of the experimental analogue, such as artificiality and external validity (generalizability). On the other hand, because we are not isolating and manipulating specific independent variables, the correlational analogue may be more realistic than the experimental analogue.

An example may help clarify how this increased realism is possible. Suppose you wanted to study in a laboratory context the relationship of counselor expertness to clients' self-exploration. In an experiment, you might arrange for counselor–confederates to behave in expert or inexpert ways. Client–subjects would be assigned randomly to the expert or inexpert condition and asked to discuss some role-played problem in a 30-minute interview. This study is low in realism because counselors are required to behave in arranged ways and clients are asked to role-play. In fact, in experiments such as this, the "inexpert" counselor has been required to behave so ineffectually that she or he was less expert than would be conceivable in the real world (even granting that some counseling can be pretty awful). Now, contrast this with a correlational analogue in which, during a 30-minute session, counselors behave naturally while students recruited to participate in a counseling study discuss a real problem (which is ethically permissible because the counselors are doing their best). Trained raters could evaluate expertness and these ratings could be related to subjects' self-exploration during the session (using whatever statistics best fit the specifics of the study). This approach is correlational in that the independent variable (counselor expertness) is not manipulated, and obviously what transpires is a more realistic approximation of counseling than in the experiment.

The trade-off for the increased realism that is permitted in the correlational analogue is the inability in this strategy to make strong causal inferences. The correlational analogue is ordinarily far more controlled than the correlational *field* study (discussed later), but it is nonetheless correlational.

At this point in time, few studies appearing in counseling journals are correlational analogues. Yet the AB strategy has some strengths that make it highly valuable. It allows for greater control (e.g., of the context) than the field study, greater realism than the experimental analogue, and perhaps greater convenience than any other strategy. In terms of convenience, for example, Latts and Gelso (1995) would have had to devote an enormous amount of time and effort to study the relation of counselor awareness of countertransference feelings, use of theory, and approach–avoidance with rape survivors, or in fact with any other client problem, in real-life counseling. Indeed, it is not clear whether it is even possible to conduct such a study on real-life counseling (which may account for why so little research was done over the years on therapist countertransference until laboratory analogues were used to study this complex construct). Also, the lessened control in actual counseling would have increased the likelihood that the relationships uncovered in this study would have been masked by other uncontrolled factors.

Finally, although correlational analogues are not frequently used in and of themselves, correlational components are often incorporated into experiments. Thus many studies have a correlational and an experimental component. Ruelas, Atkinson, and Ramos-Sanchez (1998), for example, did an interesting study that examined Mexican American and European American students' evaluations of counselors' effectiveness under four experimental conditions. These four conditions varied in terms of how much responsibility counselors attributed to clients for causing and for quitting their cigarette smoking habit. Each student read one of the four contrived transcripts in which counselors differed from one another in these responsibility attributions. The correlational component in this study was the Mexican American students' adherence to both Mexican and North American values, attitudes, and behavior (called acculturation). It was found that the four experimental conditions (varied on responsibility attributed to the client) did not differ in their effect on participants' evaluations of the counselor. However, Mexican American students' evaluations of the counselor were positively related to adherence to Mexican values, attitudes, and behavior (the correlational component). The more the participants adhered to Mexican values and so forth, the more positive were their perceptions of the counselor under all of the experimental conditions. (Note that in the earlier discussed Jones and Gelso [1988] experiment, the correlational component was client resistance.)

Incorporating a correlational component into an experimental analogue can be a powerful way of taking advantage of the strengths of both approaches. The advantages of this procedure have been discussed in greater detail in Heppner et al. (1999).

Research Strategy BA: The Field Experiment

The third type of investigative style is called the *field experiment*. As you can see in Table 3.1, the Type BA study is manipulative; the researcher has full control (or nearly so) over the independent variable—who gets which experimental treatment, when. Random assignment of subjects to groups or treatments occurs.

The term *field* implies that the intervention being observed is the real-life activity itself. For example, if one is interested in studying the effects of consultation, the field experiment would examine actual consultation. Typically, the term *field* also implies that the study occurs in the natural setting of the intervention. In counseling or therapy, that setting might be a counseling center, a community health center, or a psychology department clinic. The basic feature of the field experiment, as we use this term, though, is that the real-life activity under study is being carried out (rather than an approximation of it) in a context that is not artificial.

In counseling psychology research, the field experiment usually investigates the effects of some intervention(s). When the Type BA study does look at the effects of interventions it is called an *outcome study*. Such outcome studies will frequently compare the effects of an intervention on subjects randomly assigned to one or more treatment groups and a control group, to treatment groups and more than one control group, or to treatment groups with no control groups.

There are many methodological and ethical issues surrounding the use of control groups in experimental field research in counseling psychology. To begin with, methodologically, control groups or modified controls are usually necessary in order to assure that the treatment(s) had an effect. For example, if we compare two methods of training and find that one is superior to the other, without a control group we cannot know if both had a desirable effect, neither had such an effect, or, in fact if one or both had a deleterious effect.

On the other hand, if subjects or clients must wait for some extended time period in a control group before receiving treatment, the likelihood increases that they will either decide against professional help or seek help elsewhere. The latter, especially, presents the researcher with serious methodological concerns. But what about the ethics in such situations? Is it ethical to delay treatment? What about under conditions in which the evidence is substantial that a given treatment is effective? Or when the potential client experiences some urgency in terms of the need for the intervention?

These are complex and vexing questions that cannot be answered simply or in the abstract. Each study needs an assessment of the appropriateness of control groups; the liabilities must be weighed against the benefits, both of using and not using control groups. Because of some of the methodological and ethical issues in the use of traditional control groups, alternative methods of forming and carrying out controls have been suggested and deserve consideration: established treatments as quasi-controls, time-abbreviated waiting periods as controls, and approximations of random assignments to control groups (see Gelso, 1979a).

Two different field experiments exemplify the BA research strategy. Worthington and his colleagues (Worthington, Hight, Ripley, Perrone, Kurusu, & Jones, 1997) conducted an experiment in which a certain type of couples–marital counseling was evaluated. The treatment was called "Strategic Hope-focused Relationship-Enrichment Counseling" (SHRC). This counseling seeks to help couples enhance intimacy, resolve differences, and make commitments. Couples were assigned randomly to five weekly sessions of SHRC or to a control group in which participants completed three written assignments with no feedback, but a promise of treatment after the study ended. The counselors received special training in SHRC and followed the guidelines prescribed in a manual. Directly after counseling ended and three weeks later, it was found that couples receiving SHRC reported greater changes in satisfaction with their relationship (based on several measures) than did those in the control condition. The degree of positive change in the counseled couples was as much as that found in prior studies in which the counseling was of longer duration.

In an earlier field experiment, Gelso, Spiegel, and Mills (1983) wanted to find out how time-abbreviated individual counseling compared to regular counseling (in which a time limit is not established). Clients seeking counseling at a university counseling center were assigned randomly to one of three conditions: 8-session time limit, 16-session time limit, no time limit. Clients were told of the time limit during their first session. It was found that at 1 month and 18 months after counseling had ended, clients in the regular treatment reacted slightly more favorably than those in the time-limited treatments. This tendency to react more favorably to the regular counseling was especially notable for clients who were in the lower half of psychological adjustment when they began treatment. For those who were in the upper half, however, time-limited counseling was reacted to as positively as was time-unlimited counseling.

In comparing the two field experiments, we can see that in both there was random assignment of clients to treatment conditions. Worthington's couples intervention study compared one treatment and a control group. Gelso et al. did not use a traditional control group but instead compared two treatments to an established treatment. Both experiments examined outcomes directly after treatment ended and a time later, an important ingredient of outcome research. The Gelso and colleagues' (1983) study incorporated a *client factor* into the design in that the different counseling approaches were compared for students who were initially above and below the midpoint on psychological adjustment.

The inclusion of a client factor into field experiments moved a step toward what is perhaps the most prominent and by now established trend in counseling psychology research: going beyond simply asking if a given treatment is better than no treatment, toward finding out who the intervention works best with, under what conditions, at what times, and when offered by what types of interveners. The importance of going beyond the broad question of "Does it work?" and, in effect, looking at the conditions under which a given intervention succeeds was perhaps first pointed to in counseling psychology by Krumboltz (1966) over three decades ago. This more refined and complex set of questions has been referred to as the "who, what, when, and where" question by one of the authors (Gelso & Fassinger, 1990). Earlier, Fretz (1981) discussed the need to address questions at this level in career intervention research. Although studying these questions is now the key in field experiments, there will always be room for the general "does it work" question, especially when studying a new treatment, such as the couples–marital intervention designed by Worthington and his colleagues.

An Evaluation of the Field Experiment in Counseling Psychology Research.

Because it is a controlled experiment in a field setting, the BA research strategy combines scientific rigor with clinical relevance. Its rigor stems from the fact that because of random assignment and the related ability to determine who gets what experimental condition, at what times, the field experiment can be well controlled. On the other side of the ledger, the clinical relevance is high, or at least is capable of being high, because the BA strategy investigates actual interventions or other phenomena in field settings in which these activities occur. As implied earlier, field experiments can be especially effective strategies if they incorporate additional independent variables; that is, additional to the primary treatment variable. These added variables are in practice often aspects of the client, the counselor, the intervention, the intervention situation, and so forth. No one experiment can look at more than a few factors; but the inclusion of one or more in addition to the main independent variable allows the experiment to move toward addressing the "who, what, when, where" questions that are so important.

Despite the positive features, the BA strategy is not without its limitations. A major difficulty is that field experiments are simply *very hard to do*. There are many practical problems in carrying out controlled experimentation in a field setting. For example, if a researcher plans to do an intervention study in a university counseling center, assigning clients randomly to different treatment groups, pretesting clients, posttesting clients, following them up, and perhaps assigning clients to control group conditions—all create concerns in the agency setting. Not only are ethics an ever-present issue, but if the experiment is not well organized, the research can also create administrative difficulties in agency settings.

In addition to being difficult to accomplish in many applied settings, the field experiment is limited in that it tends to examine global variables. When offering actual interventions to recipients who are in an actual client role, it is often not possible to inspect specific variables that are elements of the treatment. For example, in the Jones and Gelso (1988) analogue experiment discussed earlier, the researchers could readily isolate one specific counseling technique (interpretation) for examination. In a field experiment, it would not be possible to offer counseling to clients, with the implicit promise that counselors are doing their very best, and then provide a treatment that was only a fraction of the promised intervention.

Because field experiments ordinarily examine global variables, and laboratory studies are able to inspect specific variables (in a more precise manner), it can be extremely valuable for researchers to use both approaches in studying particular phenomena. In this manner investigative styles can be combined in a way that most effectively advances knowledge.

Because of its many desirable features, a sizable number of BA studies have appeared in leading counseling journals over the years (Scherman & Doan, 1985). Due to the field's emphasis on studying phenomena in their natural settings (Gelso & Fassinger, 1990), in the previous edition of this book, we had forecast that the percentage of field experiments in counseling psychology would remain high in the 1990s. However, that has not been the case. For reasons to be discussed in the next section, experimental work has declined in recent years, and correlational research has increased.

Research Strategy BB: The Correlational Field Study

The last investigative style is the most commonly used of the four approaches. Although exact figures are not available, we would estimate that well over half the studies now published in counseling journals employ the BB strategy. As we shall see, the correlational field study is also the most varied and multifaceted of the research approaches.

What are the defining features of the correlational field study? Its most basic elements are that it is nonmanipulative and occurs in a field setting. The researcher does not seek to control the "when" and "to whom" of exposure to experimental conditions—no random assignment to treatments is attempted. As regards setting, either the BB strategy takes place in the setting in which the phenomena being studied naturally occur or there is no attempt to simulate treatments or situations, or both. Overall, the correlational field study aims to look at relationships between and among variables as they occur naturally.

As noted in examining the correlational analogue strategy, the fact that the BB strategy is correlational has nothing whatsoever to do with the kinds of statistics used to analyze the data. The researcher conducting a correlational field study may analyze his or her data with correlational statistics (e.g., correlation coefficients), group difference statistics (e.g., analysis of variance), or in fact may not use statistics at all. As will be discussed further below, counseling psychology researchers are becoming increasingly interested in qualitative analyses, wherein data are analyzed linguistically and logically rather than statistically. Again, the key in the BB strategy is that the researcher studies the relationships between and among variables, as they occur naturally.

Whereas the three research strategies discussed earlier typically (not always) examine the effects of some intervention (e.g., counseling, consultation, training, supervision), or elements of an intervention, the correlational field study may or may not focus on interventions. It may, and often does, study the interrelationships between and among characteristics of the person, for example, between personality and behavior, thoughts and feelings, interests and choices, and so forth.

An example of a central content area in counseling psychology in which the BB strategy is most frequently used is vocational psychology or what is called the "psychology of career development" (see Chapter 14). Some of the fundamental questions being addressed in this large and important area of study are: "What factors underlie the choice of a career? How do people develop career maturity? What factors influence some individuals to have satisfying, stable careers and others to have unhappy and unstable ones? What are the causes, effects, and correlates of career indecision?" As you can see, these questions do not directly involve interventions. Also, although the questions point to causes and effects, the research most often done to address the questions is correlational. This is because the research studies personal characteristics, usually as the independent variables, and one cannot ordinarily manipulate experimentally qualities that are an inherent part of a person.

In attempting to understand the BB research strategy, it is important to examine its connection to what is usually called *naturalistic research*. It is common for observers of the research scene to view correlational field research and naturalistic research as one and the same, almost by definition. This view is incorrect. Although naturalistic research is invariably correlational field research, the reverse may or may not be true. What are the characteristics of naturalistic research? In a classic paper, Tunnell (1977) clarifies that there are three independent dimensions of naturalness: natural behavior (part of the person's existing behavior and not instigated by the researcher), natural setting, and natural treatment (an event the subject would have experienced with or without the research).

Artificiality can occur along any of the three dimensions pointed to by Tunnell. Consider the fairly common practice in correlational field research of testing subjects at several points. To begin with, when we use a test of our making, we are imposing categories on the subject's responses, and that intrudes on naturalness (i.e., the categories prevent subjects from responding as they would naturally). The process of repeatedly testing subjects also intrudes on the natural flow of behavior. So a correlational field study may be very "nonnaturalistic" in certain ways—or it may be fully naturalistic.

As in the correlational analogue, the correlational aspect of the BB strategy has great consequences for what we may conclude about its findings. Namely, although we may conclude that the variables are systematically interrelated, we cannot conclude, *on methodological grounds,* that they are causally related. Also as noted earlier, however, we certainly may and should make causal interpretations on theoretical and subject matter grounds. The reader is referred to a thoughtful piece by Neimeyer and Resnikoff (1982), in which these authors discuss a procedure, called "analytical induction," for drawing causal inferences from correlational data. In effect, the researcher using analytical induction searches for "control groups" in the natural world.

Let us now look at some examples of published studies using the Type BB strategy. A study by Hill, Carter, and O'Farrell (1983) has become a classic because, unlike virtually all counseling psychology studies preceding it, this investigation examined counseling with a single client. The authors intensively studied the case of a 20-year-old college senior who received 12 sessions of counseling for which a duration limit was established at the beginning of the work. The client, called Sue, was involved in extensive testing as part of the research. She took a battery of psychological tests before counseling; completed a session evaluation after each session; was tested again early in the treatment; and completed posttesting 1 week, 2 months, and 7 months after ending counseling. Sue also kept a diary during the counseling. With her permission, sessions were audiotaped, and a small undergraduate honors class observed all sessions via a one-way mirror. The counselor also completed a number of evaluation measures. As you can see from this brief summary, this research could hardly be considered naturalistic, although it clearly was a correlational field study in that no variables were manipulated and real-life counseling was involved.

The researchers found that the client improved up to the 2-month follow-up but relapsed at 7 months. They suggested that the relapse was because counseling did not last long enough for this client. Also, as one part of the work, Hill and colleagues found that counselor interpretations occurred more frequently in sessions rated as "the best" (vs. "the worst"). From this they made causal inferences; that is, interpretations had desirable effects on client self-exploration.

Given the correlational nature of the study, was it appropriate for the researchers to conclude that the relapse was because counseling did not last long enough? to conclude that interpretations have a desirable effect? On strictly methodological grounds, it clearly was not appropriate to assert or imply these causal inferences. Yet these researchers drew on a variety of data and theoretical sources to arrive at their causal statements. Thus, causal inferences were made on theoretical and subject matter grounds, which we maintain is appropriate as long as it is clear that this is what is being done.

A second study is perhaps more typical of the BB strategy. Based on prior theory and research, Dunkle and Friedlander (1996) hypothesized that certain personality characteristics, as well as therapists' level of counseling experience, would be related to their clients' assessments of the quality of the working alliance between therapist and client. Seventy-three therapists completed measures of self-directed hostility, the quality of their social support network, and their degree of comfort with intimacy; one client of each therapist completed a measure of the quality of their working alliance. As predicted, the greater the self-directed hostility in therapists, the weaker their working alliance with their clients; on the other hand, the

Characteristics of Alternative Research Methods Compared
to Those of Traditional Methods.

TABLE 3.3.

Alternative Research Methods	Traditional Research Methods
1. *Qualitative:* Observations are made and interpreted in words; that is, verbally and linguistically. Research seeks underlying, subjective meanings.	1. *Quantitative:* Observations are transformed into numbers and expressed mathematically. Results are analyzed statistically.
2. *Molar:* Broad and general patterns studied.	2. *Molecular:* Specific and precise behavior studied.
3. *Naturalistic:* Research does not impose categories or disrupt natural behavior.	3. *Experimental:* Research isolates variables, imposes categories, and disrupts natural behavior.
4. *Idiographic:* Focus on individual; N = 1, or small sample studies.	4. *Nomothetic:* Focus on general patterns; large sample studies.
5. *Field:* Research conducted in natural context.	5. *Laboratory:* Research is an analogue done in laboratory.
6. *Subjective:* Attention to internal processes and meanings for the individual person.	6. *Objective:* Attention to external processes and to exterior behavior of persons.
7. *Nondeterministic:* Views subject as active agent who guides own behavior; has goals, intentions, and so forth, that cause actions.	7. *Deterministic:* Subject seen as passive recipient of stimuli; behavior caused by external stimuli.

stronger social support networks and greater comfort with interpersonal closeness in these therapists were indicative of better working alliances. Contrary to prediction, therapists' level of counseling experience was not related to the strength of their working alliances. Because of the correlational methodology, Dunkle and Friedlander were careful not to draw conclusions about what caused what, but they did offer interesting theoretical ideas about how the therapist factors (e.g., self-directed hostility) might contribute to poorer alliances.

Alternative Methodologies and the BB Research Strategy.
At the beginning of this section, we noted that the correlational field study was at once the most commonly used strategy and the most varied and multifaceted. The vast differences between the single-case approach of Hill et al. (1983) and the study by Dunkle and Friedlander (1996) on two very different topics give the reader a glimpse at the varied nature of research designs within the BB strategy. Yet these studies only hint at the multifaceted nature of correlational field research.

Over the past two decades in counseling psychology, there has been a gradually building dissatisfaction with traditional research approaches, and a corresponding interest in alternatives to traditional approaches (Borgen, 1984; Gelso & Fassinger, 1990; Heppner et al., 1999). This interest in alternative approaches has been substantial enough to be labeled a movement. Virtually all of the approaches to research that have been suggested as a result of this "alternative methodologies movement" fit squarely within the category of correlational field study. Essentially all seek to study humans in their natural context, and examine relationships among variables nonmanipulatively.

What approaches to research are being advocated? Which are being "reacted against"? Table 3.3 contains what appear to be the primary characteristics of the movement as well as the characteristics being opposed. The left-hand column presents and defines the terms that reflect the alternative methodologies movement, whereas the right-hand column gives the terms characterizing traditional psychological research.

We want to emphasize two points about the material in Table 3.3. First, the concepts in the two categories, alternative and traditional, are presented to accentuate the differences. Few of the advocates of the alternative approaches suggest that traditional methods are not valuable. They say that different approaches are needed to supplement, not supplant, traditional methods. Second, although there are many different approaches to research within the alternative methods movement, the term and approach that has come to embody this movement is *qualitative research*. The decade of the 1980s was marked by numbers of conceptual papers advocating alternative approaches in counseling research (e.g., Hoshmand, 1989; Howard, 1984, 1985; Neimeyer & Resnikoff, 1982; Patton, 1984; Polkinghorne, 1984). By the 1990s actual research studies using qualitative methods began to appear in leading counseling journals, and presently have become both valued and common.

There are many specific approaches to research that can be grouped under the qualitative category (see Heppner et al., 1999, Chapter 10; Highlen & Finley, 1996; Morrow & Smith, 2000). Despite differences among these approaches, common to all of them are the features listed in the left-hand column of Table 3.3. A particular qualitative approach that is now in wide use in counseling is the Consensual Qualitative Research (CQR) method devised by Hill, Thompson, and Williams (1997).

An example of a qualitative study using the CQR method is that by Hayes and colleagues (Hayes, McCracken, McClanahan, Hill et al., 1998). These researchers wanted to find out the causes and triggers of therapist countertransference (CT), and how CT is manifested during counseling sessions. In order to do so, Hayes and colleagues studied transcripts of eight expert therapists' responses to questions about their CT that were asked after each therapist completed sessions of time-limited therapy. Based on their reading of these transcripts, Hayes et al. selected all instances of CT (defined as therapist reactions stemming from his or her unresolved intrapsychic conflicts). The researchers found that CT occurred in 80% of the sessions that were studied and, using a consensus method, they also determined that virtually all specific CT reactions could be placed into three general domains: the *origins* of CT in the therapists' lives; the *triggers,* or the events in therapy that elicited CT; and CT *manifestations,* or how CT was exhibited by the therapist in the hour. These findings were arrived at by the research team's reading transcripts, reaching consensus on what responses represented CT, and also coming to agreement on how therapists' responses about CT could be categorized. Most important, rather than determining which categories of CT to study in advance, as is typical of quantitative research, the investigators allowed the categories to be determined by their therapist–participants' responses to open-ended questions about their CT during sessions. Thus these categories emerged from the data rather than from the investigators' hypotheses.

An Evaluation of the Correlational Field Study.

Given the movement toward qualitative methodologies, which are carried out largely with correlational field strategies, the Type BB study may be more popular in counseling psychology today than ever before. Indeed, it has many strengths. More than any strategy, the correlational field study allows for the simultaneous study of many variables. At the same time, this strategy permits a relative lack of interference with natural processes of the phenomena being studied. By definition, also, the BB strategy occurs in the field rather than the laboratory. Kiesler (1971) sums up these strengths nicely when he states that this type of research "represents a more comprehensive strategy, potentially dealing with multiple variables, thus bowing toward the admitted complexity of real-life events" (p. 55).

From the perspective of alternative methodologies, correlational field research allows for the methods given in the left-hand column of Table 3.3. More than other strategies, it permits (and in certain ways facilitates) research that is qualitative, molar, naturalistic, idiographic, in the field, subjective, and nondeterministic. It should be noted that the BB strategy does not stipulate any of the alternative methodology concepts. In other words, the BB strategy in no way *requires* the research to be idiographic and naturalistic, but it permits the research to be such.

Perhaps the main overall strength of the correlational field study is its external validity. This is especially true when the BB strategy moves toward the naturalistic side of the continuum. The more we study natural behavior and events in natural settings, the more clearly we can generalize the results to the real world, which is, after all, what our theories are about. On the negative side, external validity is usually gained at an expense, and that expense is *internal validity*. In the correlational field study, as indicated, we cannot determine what is causing what, on methodological grounds. This is especially so as the strategy moves toward the naturalistic side. In fact, as the correlational strategy increasingly incorporates concepts of the alternative methodologies movement (e.g., qualitative research), causality becomes increasingly less clear. (To wit, some qualitative researchers would suggest that it can never be determined how variables may be related causally.) To reiterate, though, under appropriate conditions, causal inferences may be made on thoeretical and subject matter grounds.

PROCESS AND OUTCOMES OF COUNSELING PSYCHOLOGY INTERVENTIONS

One key way of differentiating counseling psychology research pertains to whether the focus is on the process of one or more interventions or on the effect or outcome of the intervention. The distinction between process and outcome has had a long history in the area of counseling or therapy research (Hill & Corbett, 1993). In this section, we clarify the distinction and summarize some central findings and issues in the area of counseling outcomes.

Process Research

Process generally refers to what happens during an intervention (e.g., counseling, therapy, consultation), usually in terms of counselor behaviors, client behaviors, and the interaction between client and counselor (Hill & Corbett, 1993; Lambert & Hill, 1994). As Hill and Corbett clarify, the behavior being studied can be either overt or covert (e.g., thoughts, internal reactions, inner experiences). Studies of the process of counseling have been occurring for many decades (see Robinson, 1950), and a large literature has developed. An excellent review of current findings is presented in Hill and Williams (2000).

Although much research has been done on personal counseling and therapy process, very little has been done on the process of other interventions. We know little, for example, about the process of career counseling, the process of consultation, or the process of teaching certain skills. Process research on these interventions is likely in the years ahead.

Outcome Research

Whereas process research focuses on what goes on (e.g., during a counseling hour), outcome research examines the results or effects of particular treatments. The researcher may study outcomes that represent a step toward the changes that are desired and/or the desired effects themselves. An example of a step toward the desired change might be the client's expressing feelings more openly during sessions at the end of treatment than the beginning. Outcomes at this level may be referred to as *proximate* outcomes because they approximate a desired effect, but they do not actually measure that effect. Outcomes that actually measure the effect that is sought can be referred to as *distal* or *ultimate* outcomes (e.g., specific behavior change being sought, increase in appropriate expression of feeling outside of treatment). Finally, outcome measurement usually occurs directly after treatment ends, and at follow-up. Such follow-ups may take place anywhere from a few weeks to many months, and at times years, after the intervention ends.

Over the years, there have been virtually hundreds of outcome studies (usually field experiments) on the effects of well-known psychological treatments, for example, individual personal and career counseling, psychotherapy, group counseling and therapy, and couples counseling. A method called metaanalysis has been devised to allow researchers to quantitatively integrate the results of large groups of individual studies, so that we could get a picture of the effects of given treatments. Throughout this book we shall point to the effects of different treatments that are discussed. As an overall statement, it may be noted that the established psychological treatments have, in general, been found to be effective. For large-scale, integrative reviews of studies on the outcomes of different psychological treatments, the reader is referred to the following: individual counseling and therapy—Lambert and Bergin (1994); marital and family counseling—Alexander, Holtzworth-Munroe, and Jameson (1994); career counseling—Whiston, Sexton, and Lasoff (1998); group therapy—Bednar and Kaul (1994).

The Issue of Empirically Validated or Empirically Supported Treatments

In recent years, the counseling and psychotherapy field has been faced with a deep paradox in the area of counseling outcomes. On the one hand, it has become clear that counseling and therapy, on the whole, are efficacious. This fact has been repeatedly supported over many years (Lambert & Bergin, 1994). Additionally, research evidence supports the idea that, on the whole, the established theoretical approaches to counseling (e.g., psychoanalytic, humanistic, cognitive–behavioral) (see chapters 10, 11, and 12) seem to be about equally effective (Wampold, Mondin, Moody, Stich et al., 1997). Thus, it appears that (a) counseling in general is effective, and (b) the established treatments do not differ in their general efficacy. On the other hand, a movement has occurred that assumes that some treatments are more demonstrably effective than others, and seeks to select and publicly list these specific treatments. The empirically validated treatments' movement has sought to create a list of specific treatments that have been found through research to be effective for specific problems, with the idea that those treatments would receive priority in graduate training and insurance reimbursements.

This movement emanated from Division 12 (Clinical Psychology) of the APA. Spawned partly by the wish to present to governmental agencies and insurance companies lists of psychological treatments of proven effectiveness, and also partly by the fear that psychotherapy would be left out of rapidly emerging practice guidelines in favor of psychopharmacological agents that are no more effective (Elliott, 1998), Division 12 established a task force to create the list (Chambless, 1996; Task Force, 1995). Although it may seem obviously worthwhile to spell out which of our treatments have been validated by research, the effort to create a list has been deeply controversial.

The sources of the controversy are many, but some of the arguments against the creation of a list of validated treatments seem most telling. The most fundamental arguments focus on the criteria used for validation. First, the criteria for validating treatments require that these treatments be manualized. Thus, therapists would conduct treatment according to a written manual, which many believe inhibits creative advances and ultimately hinders effectiveness. As Blatt (1995) suggests:

> We run the risk that treatment manuals can become mechanistic cookbooks which do violence to the complexities of the therapeutic encounter. To put it another way, painting by numbers may produce a painting, but it is not a work of art. Nor is it a way to inspire students to become artists or to teach them the subtleties of painting (p. 75).

A second fundamental difficulty with the list is that the criteria require the use of specific treatments. This would tend to disfavor the efforts to provide theoretically integrative treatment. Third, the criteria clearly favor treatments and studies that address specific client problems or diagnoses. Many therapies, for example, humanistically and psychodynamically based, were not developed to treat specific problems and are not studied in the context of specific client problems or disorders. In other words, these therapies seek to treat a range of problems and diagnostic groupings. The requirement that treatments be validated for specific problems also ignores the fact of "comorbidity" (i.e., most clients do not have single, specific problems).

Given the criteria for so-called validation, it is not surprising the large majority of treatments on the original list produced by the Task Force fit clearly within the behavioral and cognitive approaches. These approaches fit very well with the criteria. A consequence of the particular criteria used for validation has been that a number of major theory-based treatments that have been empirically supported in studies using criteria relevant to those theories will likely never get on the list.

We expect that the movement toward listing and publicizing the psychological treatments that have been empirically supported will continue. There are many advantages to clarifying the extent to which treatments are, in fact, supported by research. At the same time, because of the problems described above, we suspect that some key changes will occur in this movement. At a simple semantic level, the term empirically *supported* is now favored by many over the term empirically *validated,* since the latter implies a degree of definitiveness that is scientifically unwarranted. More important, it is likely that the criteria for support or validation will be broadened and further refined to allow for a wider range of types of research, as well as client selection and treatment approaches that allow for fairer evaluation of many different theories. Division 17 has created a task force aimed at formulating a counseling psychology perspective on identifying empirically supported interventions (Wampold, 1998). For further material on the empirically supported treatment movement, the reader is referred to excellent summaries by Elliott (1998) and Waehler (1998).

The Integration of Process and Outcome

Although we have discussed process and outcome research as if these were very different procedures, many researchers are now seeking to link the two in single studies. Thus, in recent years there has been an increase in studies examining how the process of counseling psychology interventions is related to the outcomes—of a given hour, of a series of sessions, or of treatment as a whole. An example of a study that connects process to outcome is that by Patton, Kivlighan, and Multon (1997). These researchers examined how client resistance and transference, client–counselor working alliance, and therapist techniques unfolded over the course of counseling, were related to each other, and were predictive of a range of treatment outcomes in brief, psychoanalytic counseling.

Research is also addressing client and counselor factors that contribute to the process and the outcomes of counseling. For example, one may investigate, as did Dunkle and Friedlander (1996), the extent to which a counselor personality variable (e.g., comfort with interpersonal intimacy) will predict the development of a client–counselor working alliance over the course of treatment (process) or the researcher can assess how such a personality variable related to a client change due to counseling (outcome).

The linking of process to outcome, and of client and counselor factors to process and outcome, helps us address the "who, what, when, where" question as earlier described. These linkages represent the growing edge of counseling psychology research.

THE BUBBLE HYPOTHESIS AND THE SEARCH FOR CLINICAL RELEVANCE

In this final section of the chapter, we offer a perspective on psychological research in general and counseling psychology research in particular. The aim is to clarify how each and every piece of research or, more broadly, approach to research possesses inevitable weaknesses and, especially, to demonstrate *the inevitable connection between the weaknesses and strengths of all studies and research approaches.* In addition to presenting this research perspective, the final section explores the issue of the relevance of research to counseling practice—the ways in which research may be relevant, the costs of relevance, and the consumer's role in making research relevant to practice. These issues are presented to show that the concept of relevance is complex and that the problem of perceived low relevance of research to practice does not have simple solutions.

One need only be involved in a tiny amount of research to begin to see what is so obvious to the experienced scientist—that each and every study is highly imperfect and that each contains some inevitable flaws. Each broad research approach also has strengths and weaknesses. Although one begins to see the inevitability of this with a little experience, what may be less clear is that weaknesses cannot be eliminated and that each attempted solution to methodological problems and shortcomings *in itself* causes another set of problems.

As a way of illuminating the phenomena discussed in the above paragraph, Gelso (1979a, b) coined the term *bubble hypothesis*. This concept likens the research process to a sticker on a car windshield. Once a bubble appears in the sticker, it is impossible to eliminate it. Pressing the bubble simply causes it to pop up in another place. Each attempted solution causes a problem to appear elsewhere.

In order to clarify how the bubble hypothesis operates in counseling research methodology, Gelso (1979b, p. 62) offers two propositions:

> a. Immutable trade-offs exist with respect to the choices the researcher must make in each and every phase of the research process. These trade-offs are most apparent in critical general areas such as the basic selection of a design, the choice of criteria, sampling procedures, decisions about the scope of the project, etc.
>
> b. Solutions to problems of design themselves create problems, such that the partially subjective, partially objective choices as regards matters of design need to be based on formulations about which problems are least (and most) injurious

to the research endeavor, the generation of knowledge in which the investigator is most interested.

In effect, every choice we make with respect to how we design a study entails a trade-off; every decision we make to solve one or a set of methodological problems, in itself, causes another problem or set of problems. Consider how the bubble hypothesis might apply to the four investigative styles already discussed, to the strengths and weaknesses of each.

As but one example of the application of the bubble hypothesis to the general area of research methodology, one can examine what has been called the "rigor–relevance issue" in counseling psychology research (Gelso, 1985). The term *rigor* usually implies that a study is tightly controlled—high on internal validity. That is, the design of the study allows an ample degree of certainty that the independent variables, rather than other extraneous variables, are what produce the changes in the dependent variables. In other words, we have a good idea of what is causing what. Of the four research strategies discussed earlier, the one that is strongest in terms of internal validity is the AA strategy: the experimental analogue.

In the experimental analogue, the researcher attains rigorous control at the expense of relevance. The greater the control, the less the operations of the study reflect what happens in real life—the less natural the procedures. In other words, *we attain internal validity at the expense of external validity.*

To solve the problem of low external validity (low generalizability to the real world of whichever phenomenon we study) we can conduct a fully naturalistic version of the correlational field study. Obviously, in this case we have the greatest possible external validity, since nothing is tampered with by the experimenter—he or she simply observes and records what is happening, for example, in counseling. As discussed earlier, this external validity is gained at a cost. We now have proportionately reduced the ability to make sound causal inferences about what is causing what.

The reader is encouraged to think through how these trade-offs exist with respect to other aspects of methodology. In so doing, he or she may begin to wonder if we can ever advance knowledge and improve our research techniques. As all research is flawed, should we just give up and settle for inferior studies? How is knowledge advanced if problems are inevitable in every study and approach?

Our answers to the above questions are optimistic and positive. Despite the inevitable limitations, we can and should design studies to answer most effectively the questions being asked. Even in the face of the bubble hypothesis, knowledge may indeed be advanced by studying topics from a variety of vantage points, each with its own sets of problems. To use an example discussed earlier, in studying the effects of the counseling technique called *interpretation,* a number of different analogue studies (e.g., the Jones & Gelso [1988] analogue experiment) may be combined with various field studies (e.g., Hill et al.'s [1983] correlational field study of a single case), each with its own set of methodological problems. Convergent findings from these studies (again, each with its own set of weaknesses) allow us to have confidence that knowledge has been advanced reliably. The key concepts here are *continued study* (or programmatic research, as it is called), the use of a *variety of methods,* and the *convergence of findings under conditions of methodological diversity.*

In recent years in counseling psychology and other applied psychology specialties, great concern has been expressed that our research is not sufficiently relevant to our practice. Some critics have attacked research, especially experimental research, as being irrelevant because of an obsession with control and quantification (Goldman, 1978, 1979). Others have proposed that the problem of low relevance is due to the fact that traditional research models view humans as passive recipients of stimuli, whereas counseling practitioners see humans as active agents whose goals, plans, and intentions determine their behavior (see Howard, 1985). This profound difference in the image of humans held by scientists versus practitioners, according to Howard and others, makes for a poor fit between science and practice—thus the low relevance of research to practice.

The belief that research should be highly relevant to practice is perhaps most clearly expressed in what was called the "test of relevance" a number of years ago by one of the leading researchers in the field (Krumboltz, 1968). According to Krumboltz's test of relevance, for any piece of research to be worthwhile, it must have an effect on what counselors do in their practice. Research that does not affect what counselors do is seen as "academic calisthenics" (Krumboltz & Mitchell, 1979, p. 50), and, by implication, probably should not be published in counseling psychology journals.

Although there is debate within the field as to just how relevant research typically is to practice (see, for example, the more positive views of the Georgia Conference as evidenced in the report by Gelso et al., 1988; and Heppner & Anderson's 1985 discussion of the many areas in which counseling psychology research has aided practice), and how relevant it *ought* to be, most researchers and practitioners do believe we should continually work on relating research to practice.

In seeking to make research relevant to counseling psychology practice, however, we encounter certain difficulties that need to be understood. In fact, we may be faced with a dilemma in the search to enhance clinical relevance. The kind of research that is most clearly relevant has been discussed by Gelso (1985) as *experience-near research*. In experience-near research, the questions being studied closely approximate those raised in practice (e.g., in counseling); the theory from which the research originates closely approximates the counselor's experience of what goes on in counseling; the methodology of the research closely approximates counseling; and the constructs being studied closely approximate those used in practice. Examples of the most experience-near research are the uncontrolled and unquantified case study in counseling, and counseling itself as a research method (as is popular in psychoanalysis—where analysis itself is seen as a research model).

The problem with experience-near research, and the source of the dilemma noted above, is that as we move more in that direction we become increasingly less sure of what causes what in the research and of how the findings generalize to other samples. That is because of the lack of control and quantification, and because experience-near research tends to focus on the individual (as in the case study). *Experience-far research*, on the other hand, is better controlled, and does allow for clearer explanations about what causes what. (The tightly controlled experimental analogue tends to be the prototype of the experience-far study.) Yet, as we move in the direction of experience-far research, perceived relevance is diminished. The research tends to capture less of the fullness, richness, and vitality of the intervention experience. We again are faced with the bubble hypothesis; experience-near (relevant) and experience-far (rigorous) research both have costs. And we cannot optimally advance knowledge and improve practice by simply doing research that has the greatest perceived relevance (experience-near research).

Despite these inevitable limitations, research can still be profoundly important to practice. It can help the practitioner think more clearly and in a less biased way about his or her practice, and organize his or her ever-changing personal theory about whatever processes he or she is involved in (e.g., consultation, teaching, therapy). In this way research is relevant, but *indirectly rather than directly relevant to practice*. One should not expect to apply research findings, even those based on experience-near research, directly to one's practice. Rather, findings help one refine one's theory of practice and think more clearly about that practice. When the issue of relevance is considered in this way, experience-far research is seen as highly relevant (indirectly) to practice.

In addition to the issue of indirect relevance, research can be made relevant to practice only if the practitioner is an *active agent* in the process. All too frequently consumers of research expect to be able to read journals and have the relevance of the research strike them, without having to actively work at seeing the relevance. This passive approach is doomed to failure. If the reader is going to be able to use empirical research in practice, he or she must approach the reading with the notion of *finding what is relevant*. That is, the reader needs to take the attitude that he or she is going to look for what is relevant and actively think about how a given study may apply to practice. When one takes this active approach to reading research, it is striking to see just how many applications most pieces of research have.

SUMMARY

Scientific research is vitally important to counseling psychology. It allows us to test our theories and improve them. Without scientific research, we would simply be acting out our biases in counseling psychology practice, and in the final analysis such practice would be ineffectual.

Within the scientist–practitioner model, three levels of being a scientist were explored: (1) reviewing and applying research findings to one's practice, (2) thinking and carrying out one's work scientifically, and (3) doing research as part of one's career. All three levels are important for the practicing counseling psychologist to be involved in, although many counseling psychologists have neither the physical facilities nor the inclination to do traditionally defined empirical research. Instead, these practice-oriented psychologists can and should do scholarly work, which is a broader concept than empirical research. Scholarly work may include research but also includes other intellectual activities aimed at advancing knowledge.

In terms of counseling psychology research strategies, four prominent *research strategies* were explored in depth. These four strategies result from combining two dimensions: setting (field or laboratory), and degree of control of the independent variable (high or low control). The resulting strategies are labeled (1) the experimental analogue, (2) the correlational analogue, (3) the experimental field study, and (4) the correlational field study. Each of these four strategies has notable advantages and disadvantages. Combining strategies in certain ways may advance knowledge in the field maximally.

Within the strategy labeled "correlational field study," the *alternative methodology movement* was explored. This complex and important movement is being advanced by scholars who are opposed to what they view as an overuse of traditional experimental methods. Alternative approaches are advocated, for example: qualitative research, naturalistic approaches, and research focusing on the individual. This emphasis on alternative methodologies is benefiting the field and will continue to do so. As a bottom-line principle, the approach that should be taken in a given study is determined by the research questions the investigator seeks to answer.

Regarding the focus of research, the distinction between *process* and *outcome* research was examined. Process research focuses on what goes on during an intervention, whereas outcome research focuses on the effects of interventions. In recent years, many findings have emerged about the processes of counseling interventions. Regarding outcomes, a variety of forms of counseling (e.g., group, individual) have been found on the whole to be effective, and it appears that the major current therapies are about equally effective. At the same time, there has been a movement to specify and list the particular psychological treatments that are indicated by research to be effective. This movement, called the *empirically validated treatments* movement, has been controversial for several reasons. Although the current criteria used to provide support will likely be broadened in the years to come, the concept of clarifying which interventions are supported by research will likely endure. The growing edge of intervention research is represented by the linking of the process of interventions to their outcomes, and by the connecting of client and counselor factors to both process and outcome.

Gelso's *bubble hypothesis* serves as a way of clarifying the inevitable advantages and disadvantages of every research strategy and of demonstrating how each decision the researcher makes about the design of a study contains a cost. The most basic features of this perspective on research are that inevitable trade-offs exist about choices the researcher must make at all stages of research and that solutions to problems of design create other problems. In effect, all studies are flawed to some extent. Knowledge is most powerfully advanced by the continuing study of a given topic through the use of a variety of methods, each with different methodological limitations.

Regarding the issue of *relevance,* counseling psychology researchers must continually work on connecting their research to practice. In keeping with the bubble hypothesis, however, a trade-off exists with respect to relevance. The most clearly relevant research, called *experience-near,* is also often the least rigorous and controlled. The field needs a balance of experience-near (relevant) and *experience-far* (controlled) research. It should be emphasized, though, that research is rarely directly relevant to practice. Rather, it is indirectly relevant and aids practitioners by helping them to think more clearly, reduce bias, and refine personal theories of practice. Finally, if research relevance is to be perceived by the consumer, he or she must take an active approach to discovering the relevance of a given piece of research.

REFERENCES

Alexander, J. F., Holtzworth-Munroe, A., & Jameson, P. B. (1994). The process and outcome of marital and family therapy: Research review and evaluation. In A. E. Bergin and S. L. Garfield (Eds.), *Handbook of psychotherapy and behavior change* (4th ed., pp. 595–630). New York: John Wiley & Sons.

American Psychological Association (1952). Recommended standards for training counseling psychologists at the doctorate level. *American Psychologist, 7,* 175–181.

Bednar, R. L., & Kaul, T. (1994). Experiential group research. In A. E. Bergin and S. L. Garfield (Eds.), *Handbook of psychotherapy and behavior change* (4th ed., pp. 631–663). New York: John Wiley & Sons.

Blatt, S. (1995). Why the gap between psychotherapy research and clinical practice: A response to Barry Wolfe. *Journal of Psychotherapy Integration, 5,* 73–76.

Borgen, F. H. (1984). Counseling psychology. *Annual Review of Psychology, 35,* 579–604.

Chambless, D. L. (1996). In defense of dissemination of empirically supported psychological interventions. *Clinical Psychology: Science & Practice, 3,* 230–235.

Cook, T. D., & Campbell, D. T. (1979). *Quasi-experimentation: Design and analysis for field settings.* Chicago: Rand-McNally.

Dunkle, J. H., & Friedlander, M. L. (1996). Contribution of therapist experience and personal characteristics to the working alliance. *Journal of Counseling Psychology, 43,* 456–460.

Elliott, R. (1998). Editor's introduction: A guide to the empirically supported treatments controversy. *Psychotherapy Research, 8,* 115–125.

Forsyth, D. R., & Strong, S. R. (1986). The scientific study of counseling and psychotherapy: A unificationist view. *American Psychologist, 41,* 113–119.

Fretz, B. R. (1981). Evaluating the effectiveness of career interventions [Monograph]. *Journal of Counseling Psychology, 28,* 77–90.

Gelso, C. J. (1979a). Research in counseling: Methodological and professional issues. *The Counseling Psychologist, 8*(3), 7–35.

Gelso, C. J. (1979b). Research in counseling: Clarifications, elaborations, defenses, and admissions. *The Counseling Psychologist, 8*(3), 61–67.

Gelso, C. J. (1985). Rigor, relevance and counseling research: On the need to maintain our course between Scylla and Charybdis. *Journal of Counseling and Development, 63,* 551–553.

Gelso, C. J. (1996). Applying theories in research: The interplay of theory and research in science. In F. T. L. Leong and J. T. Austin (Eds.), *The psychology research handbook* (pp. 359–368). Thousand Oaks, CA: Sage.

Gelso, C. J., Betz, N. E., Friedlander, M. L., Helms, J. E., Hill, C. E., Patton, M. A., Super, D. E., & Wampold, B. E. (1988). Research in counseling: Prospects and recommendations. *The Counseling Psychologist, 16,* 385–406.

Gelso, C. J., & Fassinger, R. E. (1990). Counseling psychology: Theory and research on interventions. *Annual Review of Psychology, 41,* 355–386.

Gelso, C. J., & Lent, R. W. (2000). Scientific training and scholarly productivity in counseling psychology. In S. D. Brown and R. W. Lent (Eds.), *Handbook of counseling psychology* (2nd ed.). New York: John Wiley & Sons.

Gelso, C. J., Spiegel, S. B., & Mills, D. M. (1983). Clients' and counselors' reactions to time-limited and time-unlimited counseling. In C. J. Gelso and D. H. Johnson (Eds.), *Explorations in time-limited counseling and psychotherapy* (pp. 14–62). New York: Columbia University, Teachers College Press.

Goldman, L. (Ed.). (1978). *Research methods for counselors.* New York: John Wiley & Sons.

Goldman, L. (1979). Research is more than technology. *The Counseling Psychologist, 8*(3), 41–43.

Hayes, J. A., McCracken, J. E., McClanahan, M. K., Hill, C. E., Harp, J. S., & Carozzoni, P. (1998). Therapist perspectives on countertransference: Qualitative data in search of a theory. *Journal of Counseling Psychology, 45,* 468–482.

Heaton, K. J., Hill, C. E., Peterson, D. A., Rochlen, A. B., & Zack, J. S. (1998). A comparison of therapist-facilitated and self-guided dream interpretation sessions. *Journal of Counseling Psychology, 45,* 115–121.

Heppner, P. P., & Anderson, W. P. (1985). On the perceived non-utility of research in counseling. *Journal of Counseling and Development, 63,* 545–547.

Heppner, P. P., Kivlighan, D. M., & Wampold, B. E. (1999). *Research in counseling* (2nd ed.). Pacific Grove, CA: Brooks/Cole.

Highlen, P. S., & Finley, H. C. (1996). Doing qualitative analysis. In F. T. L. Leong and J. T. Austin (Eds.), *The psychology research handbook* (pp. 177–192). Thousand Oaks, CA: Sage.

Hill, C. E. (1996). *Working with dreams in psychotherapy.* New York: Guilford.

Hill, C. E., Carter, J. A., & O'Farrell, M. K. (1983). A case study of the process and outcome of time-limited counseling. *Journal of Counseling Psychology, 30,* 3–18.

Hill, C. E., & Corbett, M. M. (1993). A perspective on the history of process and outcome research in counseling psychology. *Journal of Counseling Psychology, 40,* 3–24.

Hill, C. E., Thompson, B. J., & Williams, E. N. (1997). A guide to conducting consensual qualitative research. *The Counseling Psychologist, 25,* 517–572.

Hill, C. E., & Williams, E. N. (2000). The process of individual therapy. In S. D. Brown and R. W. Lent (Eds.), *Handbook of counseling psychology.* New York: John Wiley & Sons.

Hoshmand, L. (1989). Alternate research paradigms: A review and teaching proposal. *The Counseling Psychologist, 17,* 3–80.

Howard, G. S. (1984). A modest proposal for a revision of strategies for counseling research. *Journal of Counseling Psychology, 31*(4), 430–442.

Howard, G. S. (1985). Can research in the human sciences become more relevant to practice? *Journal of Counseling and Development, 63,* 539–544.

Howard, G. S. (1986). The scientist–practitioner model in counseling psychology: Toward a deeper integration of theory, research, and practice. *The Counseling Psychologist, 14,* 61–105.

Jones, A. S., & Gelso, C. J. (1988). Differential effects of style of interpretation: Another look. *Journal of Counseling Psychology, 35,* 363–369.

Kiesler, D. J. (1971). Experimental designs in psychotherapy research. In A. Bergin and S. Garfield (Eds.), *Handbook of psychotherapy and behavior change* (pp. 36–74). New York: John Wiley & Sons.

Krumboltz, J. D. (Ed.). (1966). *Revolution in counseling: Implications of behavioral science.* Boston: Houghton Mifflin.

Krumboltz, J. D. (1968). Future directions for counseling research. In J. Whiteley (Ed.), *Research in counseling.* Columbus, OH: Merrill.

Krumboltz, J., & Mitchell, L. K. (1979). Relevant rigorous research. *The Counseling Psychologist, 8*(3), 50–52.

Lambert, M. J., & Bergin, A. E. (1994). The effectiveness of psychotherapy. In A. E. Bergin and S. L. Garfield (Eds.), *Handbook of psychotherapy and behavior change* (4th ed., pp. 143–189). New York: John Wiley & Sons.

Lambert, M. J., & Hill, C. E. (1994). Assessing psychotherapy outcomes and process. In A. E. Bergin and S. L. Garfield (Eds.), *Handbook of psychotherapy and behavior change* (4th ed., pp. 72–113). New York: John Wiley & Sons.

Latts, M. G., & Gelso, C. J. (1995). Countertransference behavior and management with survivors of sexual assault. *Psychotherapy, 32,* 405–415.

Magoon, T. M., & Holland, J. L. (1984). Research training and supervision. In S. Brown and R. Lent (Eds.), *Handbook of counseling psychology* (pp. 682–715). New York: John Wiley & Sons.

Morrow, S. L., & Smith, M. L. (2000). Qualitative research methods. In S. D. Brown and R. W. Lent (Eds.), *Handbook of counseling psychology* (3rd ed.). New York: John Wiley & Sons.

Neimeyer, G., & Resnikoff, A. (1982). Qualitative strategies in counseling research. *The Counseling Psychologist, 10*(4), 75–86.

Patton, M. J. (1984). Managing social interaction in counseling: A contribution from the philosophy of science. *Journal of Counseling Psychology, 31*(4), 442–456.

Patton, M. J., Kivlighan, D. M., & Multon, K. D. (1997). The Missouri psychoanalytic counseling research project: Relation of changes in counseling process to client outcomes. *Journal of Counseling Psychology, 44,* 189–208.

Pepinsky, H. B., & Pepinsky, P. N. (1954). *Counseling theory and practice.* New York: Ronald Press.

Polkinghorne, D. E. (1984). Further extensions of methodological diversity for counseling research. *Journal of Counseling Psychology, 31,*(4), 416–429.

Ponterotto, J. G. (1988). Racial/ethnic minority research in the *Journal of Counseling Psychology:* A content analysis and methodological critique. *Journal of Counseling Psychology, 35,* 410–418.

Robinson, F. P. (1950). *Principles and procedures of student counseling.* NY: Harper.

Ruelas, S. R., Atkinson, D. R., & Ramos-Sanchez, L. (1998). Counselor helping model, participant ethnicity and acculturation level, and perceived counselor credibility. *Journal of Counseling Psychology, 45,* 98–103.

Rychlak, J. F. (1968). *A Philosophy of science for personality theory.* Boston: Houghton Mifflin.

Scherman, A., & Doan, R. E. (1985). Subjects, designs, and generalizations in volumes 25–29 of the *Journal of Counseling Psychology. Journal of Counseling Psychology, 32,* 272–276.

Stone, G. L. (1984). In defense of the artificial. *Journal of Counseling Psychology, 31,* 108–110.

Strong, S. R. (1991). Theory-driven science and naive empiricism in counseling psychology. *Journal of Counseling Psychology, 38,* 204–210.

Task Force on Promotion and Dissemination of Psychological Procedures. (1995). Training in and dissemination of empirically validated psychological treatments: Report and recommendations. *The Clinical Psychologist, 48,* 3–23.

Tunnell, G. B. (1977). Three dimensions of naturalness: An expanded definition of field research. *Psychological Bulletin, 84,* 426–437.

Waehler, C. A. (1998, August). *The EVT movement in professional psychology: A short history.* Paper presented at the 106th Annual Convention of the APA, San Francisco, California.

Wampold, B. E. (1998, August). *EVTs in counseling psychology: Guiding rationale for principles.* Paper presented at the 106th Annual Convention of the APA, San Francisco, California.

Wampold, B. E., Mondin, G. W., Moody, M., Stich, F., Benson, K., & Ahn, H. (1997). A meta-analysis of outcome studies comparing bonafide psychotherapies: Empirically, "all must have prizes." *Psychological Bulletin, 122,* 2–3, 215.

Whiston, S. C., Sexton, T. L., & Lasoff, D. L. (1998). Career-intervention outcome: A replication and extension of Oliver and Spokane (1988). *Journal of Counseling Psychology, 45,* 150–165.

Whiteley, J. M. (1984). A historical perspective on the development of counseling psychology as a profession. In S. Brown and R. Lent (Eds.), *Handbook of counseling psychology* (pp. 3–55). New York: John Wiley & Sons.

Worthington, E. L., Hight, T. L., Ripley, J. S., Perrone, K. M., Kurusu, T. A., & Jones, D. R. (1997). Strategic hope-focused relationship—enrichment counseling with individual couples. *Journal of Counseling Psychology, 44,* 381–389.

CHAPTER 4

PROFESSIONAL PSYCHOLOGY IN A CHANGING WORLD

The convergence of new economic, demographic, and technological developments in the 1990s brought revolutionary changes to the career patterns and practices of all professional psychologists. Indeed, all health care providers—physicians, nurses, social workers—as well as clinical, school, and counseling psychologists are finding the "old ways" of the latter half of the twentieth century must be replaced with new ways in the twenty-first century in order to have the variety of opportunities and satisfying careers that health care professionals have had in the past.

In this chapter we shall examine the developments of the late-twentieth century that have had so great an influence on the shaping of health care professions. We identify not only the "old ways" that now seem less viable but, importantly, the opportunities that the "new ways" bring. We feel fortunate that counseling psychology, as described in the previous three chapters, is especially well suited to meet the challenges of the new truly international technological world in which we live.

There are three major sections in this chapter devoted to the economic, demographic, and technological changes that have had significant impacts in recent years. While all three forces have affected career development of psychologists, the economic changes are examined in terms of their effects on how health care is presently provided in our society. We look specifically at how changes in health care have affected both providers of psychological services and their clients. These changes have presented not only new challenges, but also new opportunities for those counseling psychologists who have prepared themselves for the world of industrialized health care. In the second major section, we shall review demographic changes (1) in our society, (2) in psychology, and (3) in enrollments in graduate programs related to counseling psychology; these changes are having effects on both traditional and new opportunities for careers in counseling psychology. In the third section, technological changes are examined primarily in terms of how professional education—doctoral and postdoctoral—will be delivered and how such education will be valuable in attaining the most useful credentials for professional psychologists in the coming decades.

Whereas the past chapters 1–3 focused almost exclusively on counseling psychology, this chapter encompasses those issues that are affecting all of professional psychology, even though we often focus on specific implications for counseling psychologists. Many national and state psychology organizations are already acting to provide leadership in developing the most effective strategies for coping with the challenges of ongoing economic, demographic, and technological changes. Not all of the problem areas identified in this chapter can be fully resolved in the next few years. We have tried to identify areas where the next generation of counseling psychologists, along with other professional psychologists, will have to assume active roles to achieve the full potential of our profession.

INDUSTRIALIZATION OF HEALTH CARE

> Price consciousness had ceased to be a functioning force regulating the market, since benefits were expansive and the consumers (patients) of services were no longer the payers. Neither was quality a strong market force, since little or no organized information was available about the comparative quality of behavioral health care providers and the services they provided (Freeman & Trabin, 1994, p. 13).
>
> After 200 years as a cottage industry, health care is industrializing. The supply–demand control of health care's goods and services has shifted from the practitioner to industrial interests (Cummings, 1995, p. 13).

Each of the late-twentieth century developments indicated by these quotes, that is, first "runaway" health care costs—costs far beyond the nation's average rate of inflation—and then the shift of control of health care from practitioners to industrial interests, occurred in larger economic contexts that will be affecting how all health care, including psychological services, will be delivered in the foreseeable future. Understanding these economic contexts is, we believe, a key to functioning as an effective counseling psychologist in contemporary society.

Enduring Economic Forces Create Lasting Changes

As we explain in the following paragraphs, the economic forces that are described are not temporary or cyclical glitches that will soon pass, allowing a return to the previous ways of "doing business" in American society. Equally true, the problems of inflation in health care costs are not problems that have a "fix" that has not just yet been found. Several value dilemmas have emerged with the development of modern health care that make inflationary costs an inherent element. Difficult and often painful fiscal and ethical decisions will have to be made continually throughout the future.

Globalization: Competition Means Fewer Dollars, More Accountability

It is probably not much of an exaggeration to say that a great many Americans over age 30 still have a very limited understanding of how globalization is affecting their lives. While most believe they can define the term, they would be hard pressed to describe how globalization has affected them directly or even indirectly. Yet, it most assuredly has. The difficulty in understanding the term for those born prior to 1970 is entirely comprehensible. We (the authors included) grew up in a time when the

United States was experiencing unprecedented growth economically and taking its place as the leader of the free world. University student enrollments were doubling and tripling in size; therefore, new faculty and counseling center psychologist positions were also growing rapidly. Community and government-supported mental health clinics were being developed in small towns as well as in large cities. Graduate training programs in mental health were being well supported by a variety of governmental agencies, for example, Veterans Administration, National Defense Education Act. Given all these developments, it is understandable that this period was also the time when counseling psychology became well established in universities and as health care providers.

While America remained the "leader of the free world," the rest of the world did not remain unchanged. As more and more countries fully recovered from the ravages of World War II, and developed their own modern economic structures, the United States found itself with significant competition in the production of even its most valuable products such as airplanes, computers, and other products of sophisticated technology. Profits fell so tax revenue declined. With less income in state and federal treasuries, support of many governmental services declined significantly, especially in areas such as education and health. As one key example, state-funded support for public universities prior to the 1990s often equaled up to 50% of a state university's budget; by the mid-1990s that figure had declined to average 30% (in the state of Colorado, state support in 1999 provided only 7% of the University of Colorado budget). Universities found themselves having to justify teaching loads and other operational costs and, for the first time in the history of most universities, had to begin closing some departments and colleges. "Downsizing" has reached universities as well as automobile manufacturing, telecommunications, banking, and other production and service industries. Another trend has been an increase in mergers in order to reduce overhead costs and remain competitive with companies in other parts of the world where labor and/or other costs, such as real estate, are often significantly lower than in the United States. Stockholders and business executives demand far more information on costs and revenues, often seemingly placing more importance on "return on investment" than on the value the service might have for the community. Hopefully it is now clear that globalization of the world's economies has brought lasting effects to how business is conducted in any sector, especially when stockholders or taxpayers are reviewing costs. We may not at all like the fact that health care, and increasingly education, have become businesses, but as long as employers, insurance companies, or taxpayers are paying the bills for such services, business principles will be a major factor in the delivery of health care.

Inherent Inflationary Forces in Health Care Costs

Along with the economic factors associated with globalization, modern health care has some intrinsic factors that make controlling costs very difficult at best. Before the emergence of highly technological clinics and hospitals, the costs of a visit to an emergency room or even a brief hospitalization were often manageable within many family budgets, or, since services were mostly personnel such as nurses and aides rather than highly expensive equipment, costs could be adjusted without too much difficulty to an affordable level. Now a very different situation prevails. Clinics and hospitals are full of expensive equipment that must be paid for. To avoid litigation, "defensive medicine" means that numerous technological tests are completed to ensure that all possible injuries or problems are diagnosed. By the 1990s, a routine visit to an emergency room could easily cost 10 or more times what it cost in the 1970s, a degree of inflation far beyond that already prevailing in society at large.

In the age of "routine" heart surgery and organ transplants, how many transplants should be given to an 8-year-old? an 80-year-old? How many therapy sessions should be provided for a chronically mentally ill person? for an unhappy but productive worker? for a college student who cannot decide on a career or what to do about a seeming inability to form any lasting interpersonal relationships? In short, in both physical and mental health we have the capacity to provide far more extensive help, both in diagnostics and treatments, than can be afforded by everyone without doubling or tripling the high percentage of our gross national product already spent on health care. In earlier times, health care was typically rationed in a hidden way in that poor people received only the care available in publicly, and often poorly, funded clinics. As a society, we have tried to correct the worst of those practices, but now that health care is routinely more expensive than ever, how can we afford to pay for providing all available treatments for each health care problem?

Emergence of New Forms of Organized Health Care

In the past 20 years psychologists have been confronted by an ever increasing and changing array of types of health care organizations. Each new type of organization has its own implications for how a psychologist becomes a provider in that organization, how clients are acquired, how cases are managed, and how finances are managed. Whole new vocabularies and sets of acronyms in health care have emerged: capitation, carve-outs, PPOs, MCOs, RGPs. Both Drum (1995) and Freeman and Trabin (1994) have provided excellent concise descriptions of the evolution of new forms of organized health care, comparisons between them, and their differential impact on the practice of behavioral health care. Here we summarize the major themes of this evolution.

Drum (1995) helpfully summarizes the many kinds of recently evolved health care into three major categories. His first category is actually not a new form of health care, but rather the form that existed for much of the last half of the twentieth century and is most familiar to the generations of psychologists who began their practice prior to the 1990s. Insurance companies provided payments to any appropriately licensed or credentialed health service provider for services to any client covered by the insurance company, up to any specified limits in benefits. Sometimes insurance coverage reimbursed clients just 50% of the provider's costs, sometimes as much as 80%, and reimbursements continued for some specified number of sessions per year. Reimbursement for up to 50 sessions was typical, but the number varied greatly depending on the insurer. Which therapist the client saw and how many sessions were completed was determined solely by discussion between the therapist and the client. The terms "fee for service" by "any willing provider" (appropriate provider credentialing/licensing assumed) described this kind of practice; psychologists with such practices considered themselves in "private practice." They were self-employed, acquired their clients through a variety of referral systems and simply arranged for an office in which to see clients, then billed the clients or their insurance company directly. If clients had not exceeded limitations in their coverage, their psychologists could be assured that the agreed upon percentage of their fee would be paid by the insurance company.

This rather full description of the way things used to be is provided in order that new and aspiring psychologists can understand older psychologists' very strong negative emotional reactions to the new forms of health care that have emerged. In every new form (e.g., managed care organizations [MCOs], preferred provider organizations [PPOs]), the organization has become directly involved in provider–client relationships in four ways. First, in determining whether or not the client is even permitted to seek psychological services (referral from a primary care physician may be necessary; the primary care physician is then identified as the "gate keeper"). Second, in determining which health care provider the client may see (as compared to a client choosing whomever he or she would like to see). Third, in setting the fee for service (as compared to the provider setting the fee). Fourth, in determining how many sessions will be paid for, typically determined by the diagnosis, rather than by the number of sessions the provider and client feel are necessary. Summarily, health care providers thus lose immense amounts of autonomy in terms of who their clients will be, how they will be treated, who pays, and how much.

Returning to Drum's (1995) descriptions, he refers to his second category of health care systems as "first generation carve-out systems." To understand this category we need to explain the transition from the term "mental health treatment" to "behavioral health care." Prior to the 1980s, benefits for psychological treatment were most often described as mental health inpatient and outpatient benefits. There had long been concern that the term "mental health" was inappropriate for the increasing variety of services covered, ranging from treatment of addictions, stress, and psychosomatic disorders to the more stereotypical "mental illnesses" such as depression, psychoses, and neuroses. To contrast all these kinds of problems with those of more clearly organic illnesses and injuries, the term "behavioral health" came into use. Because behavioral health care was typically provided by professionals other than physicians, and because determining diagnoses and treatment plans in behavioral health was far more controversial than in medicine and surgery, a number of insurance companies chose to "carve out" behavioral health care into a separate organizational entity from the one they used for medical and surgical benefits. While some such "carve outs" still exist, the problems related to this lack of integration of behavioral and medical health care quickly became apparent for both clients who had to go to separate practices for medical as compared to behavioral services, and for providers who found interdisciplinary collaboration impeded by the separate bureaucracies. As Drum (1995) describes, providing a full continuum of health care was soon identified as more effective for both clients and providers. In his third category of emerging health care systems, there is an integration of facilities (e.g., hospitals and clinics) with providers (e.g., physicians, nurses, behavioral health care providers). This development is the reason why hospitals and/or large health care corporations are "buying" or partnering with already existing clinics and psychology practices. By these medical and behavioral health care entities merging together as a single corporate entity, "A full continuum of seamless care can be provided"

(Drum, 1995, p. 7) in a more cost-effective manner than has previously been available. In short, the economic forces to merge have come to health care!

How the Practice of Psychology Is Affected

In this section we provide descriptions of several changes in the practice of psychologists related to the developing industrialization of health care. These changes have a number of implications for contemporary training of counseling psychologists; after we review the emerging changes in the practice of psychology, we discuss some needed new developments in training. While the preceding sections may have seemed applicable only to those counseling psychologists who wish to work in professional practices outside of universities or clinics, it is essential to understand that future employment opportunities for all psychologists providing therapeutic services may increasingly be through health care corporations. Although it used to be true that the majority of counseling psychologists were employed by universities and clinics, the number of those positions has been declining somewhat not only because of the lower level funding of *public* health and educational institutions (discussed earlier in this chapter), but also because there is an increasing trend for governments to "privatize" services such as precollege education, welfare, corrections, and health. Psychologists in a variety of mental health clinics across the country have been given notice that their employment may be terminated if current negotiations are completed for contracting county or state health services to a private for-profit corporation. Some psychologist positions might then become available with the corporation that takes over the clinic; however, there is seldom any assurance that the providers—psychologists, social workers, doctors, or nurses—will have a position in the new corporation. All providers have to apply and compete with other applicants. Many government leaders have become convinced that a private for-profit agency may provide adequate services at less cost than government-run agencies. Even among both private and publicly supported universities, some have already outsourced their health services; that is, the university contracts with a private agency to provide the health care services (Shea, 1995). These developments keep even those counseling centers still run by a university paying close attention to costs of professional services. If a university administration comes to believe that it can save significant amounts of money by outsourcing its infirmary or counseling center, it may well do so. Because such developments are still largely under exploration, it is too early to make any firm predictions; however, we believe it is likely that in the coming years there will be fewer government-supported (federal, state, local) positions for psychologists but more opportunities in health care corporations. Therefore, at least some of the impacts of new forms of organized health care described in the following paragraphs are likely to apply to the majority of counseling psychologists. Even those counseling psychologists who are in full-time academic positions should understand these issues since the majority of graduate students they are teaching will enter professional practice positions (see Chapter 1).

Financial Impact

The financial effects of the industrialization of health care for providers, whether physicians or psychologists, vary greatly according to the level of experience of the provider. Some senior psychologists who, prior to the 1990s, had developed large client-based practices, have found that many current and potential clients have had their insurance plans shifted to managed care organizations. When these managed care organizations placed limits both on the number of reimbursable sessions and the amount paid per session, it was not unusual for senior psychologists to experience a 30% drop in income. On the other hand, the emergence of health care companies desiring to create panels of providers of psychology services, at the best rates possible, has meant that newly licensed psychologists could almost immediately find patients, rather than take the 2–5 years typically needed to build a full practice in earlier times. Therefore, newer psychologists have often experienced far less financial impact than more senior psychologists. The impact of these effects has also varied greatly by geographic area. In the early 1990s, some areas, like the far western states, experienced the development of large managed care organizations much faster than did the Midwest. However, by the late 1990s, some form of managed care programs covered the majority of insured persons in nearly every state.

Because of the numerous concerns regarding eligibility for treatment, privacy of records, and the like (described further in a later section), some clients choose not to use insurance coverage for their psychological services. Therefore, in large cities with affluent populations and/or when a psychologist is willing to adjust the fee to amounts the clients can pay themselves, a counseling psychologist might well have a full practice of clients with a financial impact far less than a 30% reduction.

Focus of Practice

Managed care has had a significant impact on the focus of psychologists' practice. In the earliest forms of managed care that emerged, some companies imposed a limit of just 3–6 sessions before the psychologist–provider had to make special, time-consuming requests for extensions, that were often denied. Such limits were in stark contrast to the average of 8–12 sessions that most clients had received under previous coverage, with some clients taking 20–50 or more sessions to regain a satisfactory level of functioning. Brief therapy quickly became the primary type of intervention that prevailed, even though in many cases neither the client nor the therapist felt the therapeutic work was satisfactory within the allowed number of sessions. Counseling psychologists felt this shift somewhat less painfully than other psychologists since their training and experience in counseling had often included more brief therapy and counseling. While there has been considerable controversy about the effectiveness and ethical appropriateness of brief therapy for so many clients, a large number of continuing education programs were developed and offered throughout the 1990s to assist psychologists, who had had no training in counseling and brief therapy, to reorient their practices.

Provider Panels and Provider Profiling

Since industrialized health care organizations control costs in whatever ways possible, they usually limit the number of providers of each type who they will reimburse. Unlike earlier times, when any qualified provider could be reimbursed for services, now a provider of health care usually has to be "on the panel" of a specific company in order to have professional services reimbursed by that company.

A client covered by that company can seek reimbursable services only from one of those providers on the company's panel. In some cases, during the transitions of the 1990s, clients who were seeing psychologists who were not part of the panels of the corporations that took over the clients' insurance, had to terminate the relationship and begin seeing a new therapist. If such clients wished to stay with their prior therapist, they had to be responsible for the full costs. The effects of these developments for psychologists was that they might have to apply to six or more companies to be assured of being on all the panels that included coverage for the clients they wanted to continue seeing. Even after the psychologist had completed sometimes lengthy documents and incurred the expenses of providing documentation of degrees, licenses, and so forth, a health care company could well decide that the applicant psychologist did not offer services that were any different from psychologists already on the panel and would therefore deny the psychologist's application. Note that this denial had nothing to do with the level of competence of the psychologists, but rather the kinds of services offered. When a psychologist was not accepted on a panel, he or she could no longer be reimbursed for any service given to clients covered by the company that had not accepted him or her on its panel of providers. Shueman, Troy, and Mayhugh (1994) provide an excellent overview of the important parameters of a network such as geographic coverage and provider mix, as well as strategies that will facilitate counseling psychologists becoming part of, maintaining, and improving provider panels.

As another way of controlling costs, health care corporations have also initiated the practice known as "provider profiling." For this profiling, a company examines its records for a particular psychologist for factors such as how many sessions the psychologist typically provides for each client, how many requests are made for extensions, for psychological testing, and so forth. After such profiling began, psychologists whose practices were not oriented primarily toward brief therapy sometimes found themselves being dropped from panels. In some cases, these decisions were reversed after a psychologist was able to provide adequate diagnostic and treatment plan information to justify their "profiles" (one psychologist with a well-established reputation for effectively treating borderline personalities was routinely exempted by several companies from requesting extensions until after 20 sessions of treatment). However, the sometimes seemingly arbitrary procedures that were used in excluding providers from panels became the basis of some of psychologists' legal challenges to managed care (see later section). Unfortunately, in the early stages of these developments, psychologists themselves often had little or no data on their own typical patterns of treatment, and no data on quality of outcomes related to length of treatment. Even as late as the mid-1990s, Phelps, Eisman, and Kohout (1998) found fewer than 25% of all independent practitioners reported using any formal measures for assessing clinical outcomes with their patients.

New Issues for Clients

As old forms of health insurance were replaced by new forms of health care organizations, clients suddenly encountered several disturbing factors. Most widely discussed, for all types of health care services, has been clients' loss of freedom in choosing the providers they want to see. In some cases, such as in health maintenance organizations (HMOs), there is no coverage at all for seeing any provider not in the company, except for emergency care. Other plans have developed that allow clients to seek services from providers who are not on established panels if the client agrees to a higher self co-pay and/or far more extensive limits to reimbursable treatment. In essence, clients have been faced with either significant loss of freedom of choice of provider or maintaining some freedom at a higher personal financial cost.

Moreover, since these new health care corporations now regularly examine both diagnoses and treatment plans for each of their covered clients, privacy issues have become a significant concern. Who will see the information that counselors and psychotherapists have to submit to the corporation in order to justify reimbursement? What controls are there on release of such information to employers or other agencies, especially regarding therapeutic progress? In earlier decades, this information never went beyond the therapist's office unless legally subpoenaed. Psychologists now have the responsibility of informing their clients about this loss of privacy.

Psychology's Role in Legal Challenges to Managed Care

By the late 1990s the public had made clear to its legislators that it believed that the industrialization of health care was often resulting in inferior and inadequate care. A survey by the American Psychological Association in 1998 indicated that more than three-quarters of Americans wanted Congress to pass a law enabling consumers to sue their managed-care insurers when the companies' cost-containment measures lead to negligent treatment decisions (Sleek, 1998a). While the early 1990s saw unfettered capitalism at work in health care—squeezing out maximum profits by reducing quality and controlling access—the late 1990s saw the very rapid emergence of legislation to address these growing concerns. The legal actions ensuing from the early 1990s are well reviewed in Chapter 5 of Lowman and Resnick (1994). By the mid-1990s, negative articles in the news media regarding managed care outnumbered positive articles by a ratio of 5:1. By the end of 1997, 20 states had passed new laws "designed to protect consumers from inappropriate managed-care abuses" (Sleek, 1997, p. 22). The passage of an increasing number of laws has begun to provide some of the needed correctives to the earlier abuses of the era of unfettered capitalism in the health care of the early 1990s. Companies with the worst records soon found their profits badly eroded by dissatisfied consumers and providers, some of whom pursued legal actions.

Emerging Quality Management by Psychologists

Although it has been a painful educational process, professional psychology learned from the recent upheavals in health care organization that there are significant and unique ways in which psychologists can contribute to the betterment of all types of health care, not just psychological care. In the next three sections, we describe ongoing developments in psychology that have the potential to make new forms of organized health care both more humane and effective for clients, and more respectful of psychologists' professional judgments. We must note, however, that each of these ongoing developments proceeds with considerable debate within the profession. Some psychologists are sure that the industrialization of health care will fall on its face due to client complaints and legal developments and that psychologists should not participate in making industrialized health care more humane.

Other psychologists believe that, for the economic reasons cited earlier in this chapter, industrialized health care is here to stay and that we owe it to the public and to ourselves to use psychological knowledge to make contemporary health care as humane and effective as possible. In our sections on developing practice guidelines, defining and measuring outcomes, and effective health care administration, we describe ways in which counseling psychologists can contribute to improving the quality of contemporary health care. We then describe the kinds of training that will enable counseling psychologists to make such contributions.

Developing Practice Guidelines

There has long been immense variability in what treatment techniques are used and how long clients are treated, despite having similarly diagnosed problems. One psychologist might wish to have 25 sessions to treat a problem another psychologist says can be effectively treated in six sessions. It should not therefore be surprising that one of the key developments during the early phases of the industrialization of health care was the establishment of "review criteria" for use by health care companies to determine what amount of care was reasonable. From these review criteria emerged the first "practice guidelines." Such guidelines basically state two things: what techniques should be used to treat a client with a given diagnosis, and how many sessions should be allowed to complete treatment. Shueman, Troy, and Mayhugh (1994) provide a concise description of some early missteps and misuses of the first practice guidelines. When properly developed, practice guidelines are based on the best available empirical evidence regarding appropriate measures for the diagnostic, acute, and maintenance phases of treatments. Since psychologists, among health care professionals, are typically those best trained in research, we have had the opportunity to provide leadership not only in the development of practice guidelines for psychological services, but also in educating physicians and other health care providers regarding the critical components of high quality empirical evidence.

Despite the significant leadership roles of many psychologists in the development of practice guidelines, the guidelines regarding psychological problems and treatments have generated considerable controversy. Questions are often raised about the reliability and validity of much of the empirical literature on which the guidelines are based and the conclusions that are drawn. Munoz, Hollon, McGrath, et al. (1994) provide an excellent example of the range of concerns that can be fairly raised when practice guidelines for a given diagnostic category are first issued. The Board of Professional Affairs of the APA has prepared a Template for Developing Guidelines to improve development, dissemination, and use of practice guidelines. This document represents what might be described as a reasonable compromise agreement between those who believe guidelines are the "devil incarnate" and those who believe the development of empirically based practice guidelines is long overdue if we are to ensure that our clients receive the best available, most cost-effective treatment, regardless of who pays for it.

A continuing concern about practice guidelines relates to an overreliance on them by health care organizations, who do not recognize the immense variability presented by any individual case, regardless of the impressiveness of the empirical data about treatment procedures and outcomes for the total population of any group of patients. Here again, psychologists have tried to help both health care corporations and providers understand appropriate use.

> If used properly, then, these new practice guidelines neither prescribe nor provide "recipes" for treating individual patients or clients. . . . What practice guidelines do, in effect, is to require that a provider who wishes to deliver services which differ from what scientific evidence suggests would be effective provide a reasonable justification for his or her treatment plan (Shueman, Troy, & Mayhugh, 1994, p. 157).

Defining and Measuring Effective Outcomes

One of the most notable positive developments that has come with the industrialization of health care is more attention to issues in assessing and measuring the outcomes of health care, both physical and behavioral. While outcome research is discussed in several chapters in this book (e.g., chapters 3, 15), in this section we highlight two areas of outcome research that have become valued contributions by psychologists in the new era of organized health care. One of these lines of research is the study of effectiveness related to duration and kind of treatment, the foundation for the kinds of practice guidelines just described. The other area of research is the study of cost savings from having psychological treatment provided to many medical patients who go to physicians with problems the patients believe are medical problems but which have significant behavioral health components. When savings in total health care costs are made because psychological services have been used to supplement medical services, the savings are usually referred to as the "medical offset" of psychological services. At the end of this section, we therefore focus on psychologists' current and potential contributions in the development of more effective assessments of client satisfaction and outcome. Such improvements can assist health care corporations in collecting data that can be valuable to both the clients and stockholders of the corporation.

For over 40 years psychologists have been the most active mental health professionals in the development of research on the outcomes of counseling and psychotherapy. By the 1980s, with the era's increasing emphasis on accountability and cost effectiveness, much of this research was directed toward a comparison of brief or time-limited therapy with longer-term therapy. Counseling psychologists were key contributors to the early developments of such research; some of the first carefully conducted comparisons may be found in Gelso and Johnson (1983). Steenbarger (1994) provides a comprehensive review of much of the more recent research revealing that the effectiveness of brief therapy, while often positive, was also mediated by a variety of client, therapist, and contextual mediators. Howard, Lueger, Maling, and Martinovich (1993) find from their meta-analyses that, while brief therapy can be quite effective in having patients say they feel better, attaining actual changes in symptoms and quality of interpersonal functioning typically require longer treaments. Thus, serious challenges emerged regarding the almost total reliance of many managed care organizations on group data regarding the efficacy of brief psychotherapy. Many clients may indeed feel significantly better after 3–6 sessions, but large numbers of clients will neither feel nor be functioning better after such treatment. Seligman and Levant (1998), in a very large study published in *Consumers' Report,* also provide evidence that "long-term therapy works much better than short-term therapy; no particular modality of therapy or medication exceeds any other for any disorder; and insurance limits on choice and duration of therapy predict worse outcome" (p. 212). Cost savings may be illusory if clients have to return to treatment a short time after completing their first set of sessions. Miller (1996) captures much of the controversy in his article "Time-Limited Brief Therapy Has Gone Too Far: The Result Is Invisible Rationing." Psychologists, as the most well-trained researchers of behavioral health outcomes, will continue to have much to contribute to refining the relationship of outcomes of counseling and psychotherapy to "dosage"; that is, number and kinds of sessions.

Turning now to consideration of "medical offset" research, by as early as the 1970s, significant data had been accumulated indicating that providing psychological interventions for many medical patients results in sufficient reductions in general medical services to more than pay for the costs of the psychological services. During the past few decades there have been several government and privately sponsored research projects investigating the extent of medical offset. Cummings (1993) has been a leader in summarizing this research and, based on his accumulated data and expertise in this area, was central in the development of some of the earliest behavioral health care corporations.

Like the data on brief therapy, there was somewhat of an oversimplification in initial applications of these data and principles. As Fraser (1996) describes, the amount of dollars gained by medical offset is greatly affected by the client population studied. If the consumers are elderly patients or those with many psychosomatic concerns or chronic illnesses such as diabetes and hypertension, then the medical offset will probably be quite significant; however, with a population of healthy working-age individuals, there may be no medical offset obtained since few of these individuals are frequent users of any kind of medical care. Moreover, if psychological interventions are offered to the poorest and most underserved of our population, they may actually be referred for more medical treatment than they otherwise would have sought, thereby causing a "negative" medical offset; that is, psychological treatment increases their other medical costs. As with our studies of outcomes of therapy, we are learning how to fine-tune the results to make clear to health care corporations how to achieve the most cost-effective mix of services.

Beyond the study of outcomes of treatments, psychologists' skills in using standardized assessment techniques, as well as in developing customized reliable and valid measures, are contributing to the evaluation of health care. Quirk, Strosahl, Kreilkamp, and Erdberg (1995) have provided a unique example of how personality assessment can be a valuable tool in expediting cost-effective favorable outcomes in a managed care practice. In the evaluation of health care, psychologists can be quite helpful in the development of more reliable, valid, and informative measures of client satisfaction. Health care companies and managers of employee benefit programs often rely heavily on measures of satisfaction from their client–users (patients and their families) in determining what kinds of changes and innovations to make in the coverage they provide (McCall-Perez, 1993).

Effective Health Care Administration

Psychologists, both by their professional training and their concern for human welfare have, in the emerging health care organizations, significant opportunities to assist in the development of more "humane" organizations and in the creation of rewarding new career opportunities. We describe two types of activities in which psychologists are now becoming increasingly engaged: (1) in consulting with company executives who make decisions about how to manage their health care benefits, and (2) in taking on a variety of administrative roles, as compared to psychological service provider roles, within newly developed health care organizations.

The role of consultant to health care corporations is a role that the profession of psychology has had to promote. Psychologists active with APA's Business of Practice Network (BOPN) would like to help health care corporate executives develop and offer health care plans that address both their business concerns and quality of care issues for clients. Regretfully, these psychologists have learned that many executive officers of health care corporations typically do not trust them, believing that all psychologists want is to resist oversight and "milk the benefits" (McGuire, 1998, p. 24). A number of managed care executives have stated to us that psychology has been the most difficult profession to deal with in developing new health care organizations. While some psychologists are very proud of that distinction, believing that we must resist these new developments, such a position makes it very difficult for BOPN to achieve its goal of creating more humane health care corporations. McGuire (1998) reports also on another effort of psychologists to improve the future of corporations by offering courses in MBA programs designed to "show future leaders how an awareness of psychology can enhance management of the most valuable resource in business—people" (p. 24).

Patricelli and Lee (1996) describe a range of employer-based innovations in behavioral health benefits that provide a wide array of opportunities for psychologists to serve as consultants or as executive officers in practices or corporations. As Shueman (1997) notes, those managed care companies which are most concerned about quality operation are "more and more delegating responsibilities for utilization review and quality management to multidisciplinary behavior group practices with which they contract" (p. 555). Psychologists in these settings are then personally involved in setting up and supervising the gatekeeping and utilization review procedures that frequently proved to be aversive to psychologists. Often the concern about gatekeeping was about who was doing it and how it was done (e.g., a nonprofessional clerk consulting a manual to see how much service was allowed for a given diagnosis, without regard for complicating aspects of a given case). When the process of gatekeeping can be seen as professionally handled, providers will be far less upset.

Training Models: New Attitudes, Skills, and Knowledge

Despite all the upheavals of the 1990s in how health care was delivered and financed, and despite requests by new psychologists regarding their needs in graduate training for "information about marketing, the medical culture, alternatives to long-term psychotherapy, integrated delivery models, interdisciplinary teams, and the ethical and legal implications of managed care" (Phelps, et al., 1998, p. 36), we find, even as we write this, that graduate education remains relatively unchanged. "Psychology, if you look at the field, is a remarkably changing, dynamic discipline. Psychology, if you look at the graduate school curriculum is a static discipline" (Stricker, 1997, p. 20). During the past decade a number of recommendations for modifications in training have been developed and promulgated. Here we briefly summarize major components that current graduate students should look for in the curriculum of their own training programs. These components are presented in the categories of needed new attitudes, skills, and knowledge.

> Over the past decade I have retrained literally hundreds of psychiatrists, psychologists, social workers and counselors in a 130-hour module over a 2-week period and observed that for retraining to be successful, there must be significant changes in the practitioners' attitudes and belief systems (Cummings, 1995, p. 10).

Troy (1994) believes the most needed attitude change is for professionals' valuing accountability, not only to health care corporations, but also to other professionals and to the public's well-being. He is also the clearest spokesperson in psychology regarding the value of interdisciplinary functioning. Psychologists have for decades, especially in independent practice, worked essentially in a professional vacuum, with interactions with other professions limited to referrals and an occasional consultation. In the emerging integrated health care systems, psychologists will have significant opportunities and responsibilities largely to the extent that they work closely with other health care providers, from primary care physicians to cardiac specialists to social workers. Such collaboration needs to be seen as the most effective way to plan treatment rather than as a "necessary evil" for working within organized health care. Thus, there are two basic attitudes that have not been part of traditional professional psychology training or practice, but which need to become part of contemporary training: (1) an explicit appreciation of both the business and public welfare needs for ongoing accountability in all phases of our professional services, and (2) an explicit appreciation of the values of interdisciplinary professional functioning for the most effective services for our clients.

The "new" skills that are needed in the era of industrialized health care are fortunately least new for most counseling psychologists. Many of the skills we mention here, and that are identified by writers concerned with appropriate training for professional psychology in today's world (e.g., Belar, 1995), are already part of doctoral level counseling psychology training programs. However, these skills as currently taught are often not well focused on the current needs of new professionals. For example, assessment skills need to be focused as much on the planning of cost-effective treatment as they are on information for diagnoses and/or feedback to the client. Strategies for accountability are merely an application of basic assessment and research skills that are part of every doctoral program. Yet few graduates have ever had training or practice in applying these assessment and research skills directly to their own professional services or to a group practice.

Case management has rarely been taught in psychology; some version of it is more typically part of the curriculum in social work. Yet psychologists now need to master the concept that cost-effective services will require some careful planning at the time treatment is begun and during the treatment process. Explicit strategies for combining assessments with diagnoses, then with goal-setting, then with development of treatment plans to reach those goals, then with both process and outcome evaluation strategies need to become a routine part of counseling psychologists' training and practice. The elements for all these steps are usually within a psychology training program; what is missing is training and practice in how to combine and apply them to individual cases as part of a management strategy.

Skills in brief therapy as the primary mode of intervention are more typically part of the training of counseling psychologists than other professional psychologists. Even in some counseling training programs, however, there is the view that brief therapy is "second class"; that is, if resources were available, all clients would be seen longer. The shift that is needed is to a perspective that brief therapy may be the first choice with a wide range of clients if we are to meet our obligations for accountability.

Turning from skills to the knowledge now needed to be acquired in training programs, some reflection on the preceding sections of this chapter should make the key knowledge components self-evident. Each of the needed skills just described has a knowledge base that should be part of the coursework. Ideally, the coursework will provide many examples of how the knowledge underlying these skills is readily adapted to the strategies needed for professional functioning in current health care practices. Everything we have covered in this chapter thus far is also a critical part of the knowledge base for understanding the new perspectives that counseling psychologists should have in order to find a full range of satisfying and fulfilling career options in the world of industrialized health care. Even though we have provided numerous references throughout this chapter, we need to note that health care practice is evolving rapidly; it will remain advisable for counseling psychologists in training, as they plan their choices of courses and practica (see also Chapter 7), to consult the most recent articles and books that include information on changes in the world of health care. Journals such as *Professional Psychology: Research and Practice,* and *The Counseling Psychologist* provide readers with an ongoing array of current viewpoints and surveys.

CHANGING DEMOGRAPHICS: NEW OPPORTUNITIES

By the year 2000, the demographics of both the society at large, and the profession of psychology itself, had changed radically from the time of the development of professional psychology following World War II. These changes have provided new opportunities for both broader representation of our society in the profession of psychology as well as for the development of more effective psychological services for all segments of our society. As will be explored more fully in Chapter 6, diversity in our society and in our profession, however, call for some new perspectives and new roles. In this section we first briefly describe the developing demographic changes in our society, especially how those changes affect contemporary clientele of psychological services. We then review the demographic changes of the past few decades in the mental health professions in terms of gender, diversity, and size. The explosion of enrollments in mental health programs—especially at the master's level—combined with industrialized health care's emphasis on using lowest cost credentialed professionals for as much service as possible, contributed to growing concern in the 1990s as to whether doctoral-level psychologists were being "over-produced." After our review of the resulting debate, we explain why it is believed that no serious action is required to reduce enrollments in doctoral programs in counseling psychology.

Our discussion of this supply-and-demand debate will be a logical segue to the other part of this major section on changing demographics: changes in global economics are resulting in changes in the concept of "career" for *all* professions. Fortunately, with both counseling and I/O psychologists among the leading thinkers and researchers on career patterns, there is already much information on how counseling psychologists can best take advantage of the new meanings of career in the twenty-first century. Opportunities from all of these new perspectives will be enhanced by ongoing public information campaigns to address some "underselling" of psychology in the past. We will therefore describe how the APA and state organizations are moving forward on these issues.

Clientele of the Twenty-First Century

No matter where psychologists work in the coming decades, the one sure change they will encounter, compared to the generations of psychologists who preceded them, is that they will be working with an "older" population (not necessarily "old," but at least older). College and university students are no longer typically age 18–22; they now include many returning students for retraining or new degrees as well as many students who, often for financial and/or experiential reasons, are spreading out their degree work over six or more years. The largest bulge in our demography are the "baby boomers" who were born in the decades after World War II; they are now entering the retirement years. Moreover, their parents—the group over age 85—is the fastest-growing segment of our population because of improvements in longevity. Since early in the 1990s, Medicare has included psychologists as reimbursable health care providers for those over age 65; therefore, the Medicare populations will be a fast-growing clientele for psychologists who have the skills for working with them.

The other major demographic change that many psychologists will encounter, especially if they practice in large cities or in any of the coastal regions of the United States, is a much more ethnically diverse population of clients. In many coastal states, ethnic minority groups are already a plurality of society. In Chapter 6 we will review the well-needed explosion of material on multicultural counseling, a literature that can provide the effective foundations for counseling psychologists to serve these growing, often underserved segments of our population.

Changing Demographics in the Mental Health Professions

Gender and Diversity in Psychology: How Big a Change?

In the past 30 years there has been a major change in gender of psychologists, but only small changes in their ethnic diversity. Looking first at gender changes, in the 1990s 40% of all psychologists were women, whereas in 1970 only 20% were women. It may be interesting to note that during that same period, women's representation in medicine changed from 9% to 36%, and in dentistry from 1% to 32%. By the early 1990s, two of every three graduate students in psychology were female; in many professionally oriented programs like clinical and counseling psychology, four of every five graduate students were female. While some psychologists feared that the profession would lose prestige, earning power, and autonomy as more women entered the field (as had accounting, pharmacy, dentistry, and medicine), a careful and comprehensive study (Martin, 1995) yielded no significant data to support this fear.

There is, however, other evidence in numerous reports to the legislative body of the APA (the Council of Representatives) that psychology as a profession still has more work to do to achieve gender equity. Despite the major gender changes in constituency of psychology organizations, leadership positions in the journals and boards of the profession have remained disproportionally male. In counseling psychology, in recent years the record has been significantly better with the gender of officers and editorial appointments proportional to gender representation in the Division of Counseling Psychology.

The data on ethnic diversity in psychology is in every way less positive. While the 1970s brought significant gains in enrollments in graduate training programs, only a handful of programs throughout the country had achieved greater than 10% minority enrollment by the 1990s, even though the proportion of ethnic minorities in many college and university graduating classes approximated 20%. The first Ph.D.s from the diversity initiatives of the 1970s brought in the 1980s the first significant representation of ethnic minorities to psychology faculties, with "significant" having to be defined as 1% to 3% of all faculty as compared to the prior modal figure of 0%. Unfortunately, by the year 2000, the number of minority faculty in psychology had not increased over these small percentages from the 1980s. Moreover, even relative to their small representation within the profession, ethnic minorities are underrepresented in leadership positions in psychology. As with gender diversity, counseling psychology again has become a model exception; in the late 1990s the Executive Board of the APA Division of Counseling Psychology had a higher proportion of ethnic minorities than the overall membership of the division. As will be further explored in Chapter 6, counseling psychologists have become identified as key leaders, within all of psychology, for the development of multicultural research and practice.

Explosion of Enrollments in Mental Health Programs

The profession of psychology grew rapidly during the last three decades of the twentieth century, with a 300% increase in the number of licensed psychologists. During that same period, the number of licensed or certified mental health counselors increased to over 130,000, a number greater than the combined numbers of all licensed psychologists and psychiatrists (Cummings, 1995). Glueckauf, Frank, Bond, and McGrew (1996) report that there are now over 8,000 master's-level graduates *each year* from the 800+ universities that offer master's programs related to mental health counseling; such programs may be called master's degrees in counseling, in psychology, in family therapy, and so forth. By comparison, there are approximately 2,400 new doctoral-level psychologists per year graduating from the combination of all Ph.D. and Psy.D. psychology training programs, including school and clinical psychology as well as counseling psychology.

The Master's Degree in Psychology: The Ambivalence Continues

> Psychology's failure to find a place for the master's level practitioner has resulted in the formation of a subdoctoral psychotherapy profession that now has statutory recognition in almost all of the 50 states. The APA has continued to recognize, through the annual publication of a directory (Graduate Study in Psychology), over 500 terminal master's programs in psychology . . . (Cummings, 1995, p. 13). The number of schools awarding master's degrees in psychology jumped by 12 percent between 1985–86 and 1991–92. . . . This growth has not been accompanied by formal quality checks and guidelines, Fox said. "There is an absence of uniformity of master's curricula and a need for better definition of master's level training" (Murray, 1995, p. 47).

These two quotes capture the essence of some of the more recent concerns related to over 50 years of ambivalent treatment of master's degrees in psychology. (In this discussion, the term "master's degrees in psychology" refers to those master's degrees awarded by departments of psychology, and not to degrees in counseling awarded by departments of counseling, human development, and so forth.) Repeated calls for accreditation of psychology master's training programs have always been rebuffed by major professional psychology organizations that argue that since the beginning of organized specialties in applied psychology, the expectation has been that the doctoral degree is the only level acceptable for independent practice. Many established psychologists believe that the progress that psychology has had in obtaining hospital privileges, being approved as Medicare health care providers, and gaining prescription privileges, has been possible only because the doctoral degree is the "entry" level for degree for independent practice of psychology (Sleek, 1995). Those holding such views will, of course, object to any developments that give more recognition to masters' degree programs whether it be training program accreditation or licensing of its graduates as psychologists.

However, without accreditation of psychology master's degree training programs, immense variation in quality continues. Some programs are just 1-year long with almost no supervised experience, others are 2-years long and incorporate as much supervised practicum experience as some doctoral-level programs. Universities have long supported master's programs because, compared to doctoral programs, the far larger class sizes of these programs and fewer requirements for

supervision generate tuition money and graduate student assistantships for doctoral-level students. Many doctoral programs are aware that if they closed down
their master's-level programs, they would lose both faculty and graduate assistant-
ship positions.

In 25 states that issue some type of license for a master's-level psychology graduate, unsupervised independent practice is not allowed (except in Vermont and West
Virginia as of the time of this writing) and the title of these practitioners must be
something like psychological associate or psychological examiner. Because calls for
licensing of master's-level *Psychology* graduates to practice independently within
psychology have been rejected by the majority of states, the past three decades saw
the emergence of legislation for certification or licensing of *mental health counselors*. Many graduates of master's-level programs in psychology now choose to become certified or licensed as mental health counselors since they then do not have
to practice under the supervision of a doctoral-level psychologist. Throughout the
past 50 years, various associations of psychology master's degree graduates have
been formed, which then advocate for more adequate recognition within professional psychology, then wither as they lose repeated battles for such recognition. In
some cases they have developed certification procedures for master's-level psychologists, but such procedures have not typically resulted in increased practice opportunities as compared to certification or licensing as a mental health counselor. In our
view, the emergence of a well-established profession of mental health counseling
with its own examination, certification, and licensing procedures, and increasing
recognition as service providers in federal and state mental health legislation, has
doomed efforts for finding something more than the ongoing "second-class citizen-
ship" for a terminal master's degree in psychology. Departments that have *both*
master's and doctoral degree programs should be extraordinarily explicit with their
students regarding what the master's degree will lead to. If the master's degree program provides training that fulfills local state requirements for certification as a
mental health counselor, then the master's degree recipient will have a reasonable
range of career options. If, on the other hand, the master's degree program does not
meet the state's stipulations for certification or licensing as a mental health counselor, then students should know that completing only the master's degree will yield
few job opportunities and, at best, "associate," often nonvoting membership in
most psychology organizations.

Supply and Demand for Doctoral Psychologists: An Issue or Nonissue?

The following quotes may be alarming; it is also likely that similar ones will continue to appear in psychological newsletters and publications. The primary purpose
of this section and, indeed, the remainder of this chapter, is to provide the more
calming context of relevant information and ongoing developments in professional
psychology that address issues raised in these quotes.

> Cost-containment measures and the reduction of excess capacity in the health
> care system are essential if health care is to remain affordable. Given this and
> the fact that bachelor's and master's level health and mental health practitioners

(e.g., nurses and social workers) are educated to provide some counseling services in health and mental health settings at generally lower cost than doctoral-trained providers, reimbursement for psychological services may move toward the lowest acceptable provider charge. Therefore, it would be prudent for education and training programs to assess current and future needs for practitioners, and to use this information to guide both admissions policy in current programs and, more important, to determine if new programs are needed (Glueckauf et al., 1996, p. 30).

Is psychology training students for jobs that don't exist? (Hersch, 1997, p. 191).

The concerns reflected in these quotes were exacerbated in the mid-1990s by clear evidence that there was an inadequate number of APA-accredited internships available for all the doctoral-level students who had reached the internship level. Oehlert and Lopez (1998) provide the most comprehensive report of the problems that emerged as graduate enrollments continued to grow faster than the number of accredited internships. The same economic forces that were described earlier in this chapter were affecting various hospitals and clinics such that few new internships were being created. This small growth in number of internships simply did not match the growth in numbers of students in doctoral programs. Even a small incongruence in a given year rolls over to create a continuing problem as persons denied an internship one year apply again the following year, adding to an already too large number of applicants for available slots. Oehlert and Lopez (1998) conclude that about 300 students will be caught in what they call the "bottleneck" of too few accredited internship positions each year for the foreseeable future. While they recommend a number of short-term possibilities for increasing supply or reducing demand, as Stricker (1997) so well articulates, the fact that doctoral programs, internships, employers, and licensing boards all operate independently of one another, allows each to dodge responsibility for oversupply at any one point in the training and professional development sequence. A national conference convened by the Association of Professional Psychology Internships in late 1997 attempted to address both the "large picture" supply-and-demand factors in professional psychology as well as the "bottleneck" regarding internship training. Most pertinent to the latter issue was the passage of resolutions that accreditation of a doctoral program should include an examination of the percentage of its students obtaining an internship at the time they qualify, and then subsequently find employment. The clear implication of this resolution is that training programs should ensure that they do not accept more students for training than they can find placements for in internships or postdoctoral employment. Some programs may now take a more active role in working with internships to obtain additional positions for their students; others may decrease the number of students they accept.

Counseling psychology students have been less affected by the internship bottleneck for two reasons: (1) since the 1970s there has been a growing number of internships within university counseling centers that have been a natural niche for counseling psychology doctoral interns; (2) most counseling psychology programs have a smaller number of students than professional Psy.D. programs. These counseling psychology programs can more easily find intern placements for 6–8 students a year compared to finding slots for 25–40 students a year from a Psy.D. program.

Because some of the bottleneck effect will probably continue for a number of years, graduate students at the time of first applying to graduate school should seek out specific information from any program to which they are applying regarding the percentage of students who are delayed in completing their degrees because they were unable to obtain an accredited internship on schedule.

Regarding the broader issues of supply and demand, even the authors of the above quotes had to note that there was no evidence of any increasing unemployment of psychologists. VandenBos, DeLeon, and Belar (1991) provide an extensive rebuttal of all of the concerns about oversupply expressed by Robiner (1991), concluding that "his assumptions, analysis, and scope are far too limited" (p. 446). At worst what can be said is that psychologists who wish to devote most of their time to general psychotherapy might find they are paid little more than master's-level therapists from social work or mental health counseling programs. On the other hand, counseling psychologists who become prepared to participate in the kinds of initiatives described earlier in this chapter's section on "Emerging Quality Management by Psychologists" will have many new opportunities for challenging positions that call upon their doctoral-level skills and remunerate them accordingly.

The most tangible outcome of the articles and conferences held in the 1990s regarding supply and demand was a much more active role of the APA in publicizing information on new types of career opportunities for both current psychologists as well as psychologists in training. A public information campaign has also been undertaken in order to enlarge the scope of the public's views of the potential contributions of psychologists. Further information on these initiatives appears in the next sections.

Changing Career Patterns in the Profession of Psychology

New Meanings for "Career" in the Twenty-First Century

It was not unusual throughout the twentieth century for a broad segment of the workforce—from semiskilled plant workers to managers to professors to chief executive officers—to work for a single company throughout their 30 to 40 working years. (This text's authors have had only one primary employer since receiving their doctoral degrees.) Bank presidents to hospital directors to university presidents often came up through the ranks to the top-level positions in a company. No longer! The economic forces of the past few decades, as described earlier in this chapter, combined with the emergence of the technological information age, have brought a rapid end to that frequent pattern of single employer histories.

Many skilled positions in manufacturing plants have simply disappeared, requiring those workers to find new kinds of employment. Downsizing from company mergers and cutbacks have sent thousands of mid-level managers and executives in search of employment in new companies. Many service professions, including universities, now hire a greater proportion of their staff on a part-time basis (from 22% to 41% for universities between 1970 and 1995), mostly to limit their long-term commitments but also to reduce the costs of providing employee benefits since part-time employees are often ineligible for costly health and retirement benefits. Current projections are that most college graduates will work for approximately seven or eight different employers during their expected 40 working years. Murray (1998a) quotes counseling psychologist Leong in an article titled "Notion of a Life-Long Career Is Now a Thing of the Past" as saying "The notion of career is shifting to mean many different forms of work life."

New Niches for Doctoral Psychologists

When you combine the issues of changes brought to the practice of psychology by the industrialization of health care with the emerging trends from the new concept of career for all workers in our society, you will reach an inescapable conclusion: There is a need for some new conceptualizations of a career in psychology. Consider the recommendations found in Murray (1998c): "Flexibility is key to a successful career." Flexibility is described as developing new skills to practice throughout one's working years, working contractually or part-time to break into new settings, and focusing on areas of opportunity. Such a perspective is almost the complete antithesis of "career" as the same position held with the same employer for several decades.

We repeat only briefly what has already been said in the section on new skills needed in the era of industrialized health care, yet noted again and again in every article about new niches for psychologists: "[P]sychologists in every work setting are seeing a rising demand for applied research . . ." (Murray, 1998b). "Data sources reveal that traditional training in the content and methods of psychology provides a good foundation to respond to changing demands in current settings and roles as well as creating and succeeding in nontraditional settings and roles" (APA, 1997, p. 2). The *APA Monitor* is leading the way with specific information and articles on how traditionally trained psychologists can develop new career niches (Psychology graduates develop career niches, 1998) and how some universities are restructuring their programs to prepare students for a range of atypical, yet challenging and fulfilling careers (Murray, 1998b).

For counseling psychologists there are three specific niches that should be noted; all three are of importance in the foreseeable future and all have implications for both pre- and postdoctoral training choices. The first concerns the role of a psychologist as a key participant in primary medical health care. With 60%–70% of visits to primary care physicians prompted by stresses that are often only temporarily alleviated by drugs, which in themselves may create other problems, there are growing opportunities for collaboration with primary care physicians, pediatricians, OB-GYNs, and family practice physicians to develop cost-effective interventions with the psychologist as the primary provider of treatment following appropriate primary care intake (which might well be completed by a physician's assistant [PA]). Hersch (1995) provides detailed examples of such collaborative arrangements. Broskowsi, Marks, and Budman (1981) provide an even broader range of conceptualizations for psychologists in the development and evaluation of psychological practice in integrated medical service delivery settings. Psychologists have often been viewed far more positively by primary care physicians than by psychiatrists and welcomed for their development of specialized programs ranging from smoking cessation and weight control to recovery from cardiovascular disease, cancer, and diabetes.

A related development under way is that of prescription privileges for psychologists. There have now been several graduates of the Department of Defense's 2-year postdoctoral training program in psychopharmacology for military psychologists; these psychologists now have prescription privileges within the military system. Klusman (1998) reports on the positive evaluations of this program by physicians as well as other health professionals. At that time, legislation to grant psychologists the right to prescribe had been proposed in six states; while none were approved initially, bills reentered in subsequent years have reached higher levels of consideration. Gutierrez and Silk (1998) provide an excellent overview of the history of the intra- and interprofessional controversies that have accompanied the development of the APA's position of support for prescription privileges for appropriately trained professional psychologists. Because such training will almost assuredly remain an intensive 2-year postdoctoral program, it is expected that only a limited number of psychologists will seek to take on this role. Such training is open to doctoral-level counseling psychologists. It should be noted that, to the extent there is an increased privatization of public health, opportunities for all psychologists who have obtained prescription privileges will increase greatly since they will typically provide prescriptions less expensively than physicians and psychiatrists.

The last niche we describe is currently the most unfilled niche. When Seligman served as president of the APA in 1998, he made a call to action for more study on human strengths. He lamented that social scientists "have come to view courage, perseverance and good cheer as illusory, defensive and inauthentic negative states, while weaknesses like depression, greed and lust are genuine" (Sleek, 1998b, p. 11). Every defining feature we identified in Chapter 1 impels counseling psychology toward development of research and *practice* related to human strengths. Counseling psychology has a long history of a periodic research attention to healthy personality (e.g., Heath, 1965; White, 1973). Gelso and Fassinger (1992), in their APA centennial contribution to the *Journal of Counseling Psychology,* identified the development of the healthy self as counseling psychology's "unfilled promise"; they describe some of the kinds of research and theory that yet need to be developed. More recently, an issue of *The Counseling Psychologist* was devoted to "What Leads to Wellness? The Role of Psychological Resources in Well-Being" (Lightsey, 1996). All of these articles have been concerned primarily with the research bases of the facilitation of effective functioning and, in some cases, identification of some practical implications. What we have not yet accomplished is the development of intervention strategies to promote those very factors that we identify as most health protecting and promoting. We have done well in developing remediation programs, like smoking cessation; less well in developing prevention programs, like promoting optimism. Osipow's (1977) "law" still holds: "Remediation drives out prevention in the form of counseling intervention where the two are present in the same agency" (p. 94). We will describe in Chapter 18 and Chapter 19 some developments that provide foundations on which to build more active careers in counseling psychology for this relatively unfilled niche.

Correctives for the "Underselling" of Psychology

Most nonpsychologists have very foggy ideas about the nature of our discipline. Many are still confused about the difference between psychologists and psychiatrists, and when they do find out they are all too likely to accept the negative definition that medicine has pinned on us. We are the ones who do not have MDs and cannot prescribe drugs (Peterson, 1996, p. 7).

The even harder truth to face from this statement is that most of the public thinks of us "only" as something like psychiatrists and concerned with mental health. Every effort psychologists have made to move into the primary health care area has been slowed down, but fortunately not stopped, by the perception that we are *only* mental health care providers.

Janda, England, Lovejoy, and Drury (1998) provide recent evidence of less than positive attitudes of the public toward psychology as a discipline.

> In two samples, one of the general population and one of college faculty, both psychology and sociology were rated as having made less important contributions to society and as having less expertise than biology, chemistry, medicine and physics (p. 140).

Peterson (1996) has concisely articulated how we do indeed "shoot ourselves in the foot" when it comes to describing ourselves to the public:

> We're a profession, but we aren't really a profession, we're a science. We do research, but most of us don't actually do any research. We aren't really scientists, we aren't really professional, we're scientist–professionals. . . . We're sort of like scientists, but we aren't general scientists; we're local scientists. What we do isn't exactly research, it's disciplined inquiry" (p. 7).

Zytowski, Casas, Gilbert, Lent, and Simon (1988) articulate specifically for counseling psychology the fact that the public simply does not have a distinct image of counseling psychology. While this fact is not a significant handicap for counseling psychologists continuing to fill those roles they have long been in, for example, counseling centers, the lack of a distinct public image does make it more difficult to move into new areas, many of which we have described above as essential for the development of new opportunities for counseling psychologists if there is to continue to be a wide range of challenging and fulfilling roles. Lent (1990) notes, somewhat despairingly, that unless the profession can generate enough support for active "self-promotion" (and those who select counseling psychology as a profession are not typically those who strongly value self-promotion), it is unlikely that the public will soon perceive counseling psychology's unique potential.

Now for some good news after the above three discouraging paragraphs! By the late 1990s, the APA had a number of public awareness initiatives that were being funded at $1 million per year, with these funds supplemented by contributions from various state psychological organizations. These states work with the APA to design the ad campaigns that they believe will be most helpful; target populations may be health care providers, business executives, radio listeners, and so forth. There have also been grants to a national radio show to promote the public's knowledge of scientific psychology, and funding of a program to improve journalists' understanding of scientific psychology. These initiatives require the involvement of many psychologists as well as media and public relations experts; counseling psychologists, as Lent (1990) notes, must become active participants in these initiatives if we are to maximize the new opportunities that have come with the changing world of the twenty-first century.

New Developments and Technologies for Postdoctoral Education and Credentialing

The last decade of the twentieth century brought significant changes in both the concept of postdoctoral education in psychology and, given the emergence of new electronic technology, in the forms in which that education is to be obtained. In this section we first describe three major reasons why far more attention is being given to postdoctoral education. An understanding of these reasons helps explain why *accredited* postdoctoral programs first emerged in the 1990s and may continue to gain in importance in the coming decades as an integral part of the training of professional psychologists. Equally important will be the understanding that completion of even a formal postdoctoral program will only be the first step in postdoctoral education throughout one's career. Fortunately, emerging technologies will make such "continuing education" (a term that has, as we will explain, unfortunately gained some ill-repute!) much more easily and effectively obtained.

In the final section of this chapter we explore how new developments in health care have affected the kinds of credentials counseling psychologists should attain in order to have the most rewarding and satisfying careers. Licensing as a professional psychologist remains a necessary step, but is increasingly becoming an insufficient credential. We provide a brief historical context of licensing in psychology as well as a description of the new kinds of credentials that are increasingly valuable in contemporary health care settings. Lastly, we explain how current technology can greatly facilitate the attainment of these credentials.

While all of the material presented in this section reflects some ongoing professional issues and new developments in the profession of psychology, it also has direct applications for career planning for counseling psychologists. This section therefore includes a description of many of the implications of these new developments for how counseling psychologists might choose from various educational and credentialing options. Whereas all of Chapter 7 is focused on the more "advisory" aspects of career development of counseling psychologists, the material included here provides supplemental information especially pertinent to career development after a doctoral degree in counseling psychology is completed.

Why a Doctoral Degree Is Not Enough

The heading for this section may be distressing since even completing the doctoral degree may seem like an arduous and long process to most readers. The good news is that each of the three reasons why a doctoral degree is not enough can now be more easily addressed than in past years. The three reasons relate to (1) past deficiencies in the monitoring of quality of postdoctoral supervised experience, (2) the emergence of specialization within psychology, and (3) the rapidly changing world in which we live. Although the problems in these areas affect all psychologists, we have focused our discussions on the specific aspects most pertinent for counseling psychologists.

A long-standing problem in professional psychology has been the very uneven quality of supervision that new psychologists have received as part of their qualifications for licensure as psychologists. This variation in quality is most directly related to large variations in state licensing laws regarding required postdoctoral supervised experience. Some states, for example, require 2 years of postdoctoral supervision, some just 1 year. Some states specify how many hours of service and supervision are required; some only require a licensed psychologist to report that he or she supervised the new professional without providing any evidence of how much, if any, actual face-to-face interaction the supervisor had with the supervisee. Obviously, such latitude has resulted in some new professionals never really receiving any actual supervision during their first year of postdoctoral work experience. At the other extreme, some new psychologists have received intensive additional training in postdoctoral residencies where they may have had as much as 8 hours a week of formal training and 5 hours a week of individual supervision of their caseload. Despite these variations, both new professional psychologists could meet some states' requirements for postdoctoral supervised experience. State licensing boards have been reluctant to enter into the long and contentious processes that would make experiential requirements more uniform; many psychologists feel that the quality cannot be legislated because boards do not have the personnel or time to monitor the quality of supervision. As we will explore in the next section, accredited postdoctoral residencies are one way to address this issue without getting into changes of state licensing laws and regulations.

A second major reason for the emergence of more attention to postdoctoral education relates to the emergence of specialization within psychology. Until the late 1970s, specialization within psychology usually referred only to the four "specialities" that had emerged at the end of World War II: counseling, clinical, school, and industrial (later called industrial/organizational [I/O]). As the profession continued to mature, more specialized areas such as neuropsychology, behavioral psychology, health psychology, forensic psychology, and so forth, began to emerge and sought recognition both for their training programs and in credentialing. Yet until the 1990s the APA had accreditation procedures only for the original four. Although there remains some ongoing discussion about the extent to which training in these various specialities can and should be taught at the doctoral degree level compared to the postdoctoral level, there has been no debate about the appropriateness of having postdoctoral training and supervision in these new specialty areas. In fact, by the 1980s a number of postdoctoral residencies focused on areas such as neuropsychology and health psychology were already well established in a number of hospitals (Wiens, 1993).

Finally, the third reason for increased attention to postdoctoral education is found both in the section above on "New Meanings for 'Career' in the Twenty-First Century" and in an examination of the impact of managed care on the practice of psychology. The rapidly changing economics and technology of this new century will continue to result in changes in how and where services are provided. No matter how up to date a training program may be today, it is unlikely that its graduates will be practicing in much the same way 25 years from now. Consider, for example, that the Internet with its Web pages, which provide so much of our information now and new possibilities for managing our lives (e.g., purchasing, banking), as well as our continuing education, as described below, did not even exist when the first edition of this book was written less than a decade ago! A mature profession will ensure that there are ample opportunities for its maturing members to develop the knowledge and skills needed to remain valued and contributing professionals in a changing world.

> Changing demands and economic stress evident in all aspects of our workplace underscore the importance for all psychologists to remain vigorous players, able to adjust readily to new questions and ways of answering them. It has become abundantly clear that it is no longer feasible to think of educating a workforce able to meet the demands of the discipline within the boundaries of a doctoral degree program. Moreover, this lifelong learning we have so long espoused must now be more visible, formal and systematic to ourselves and others because of the demands it must meet and the rapidity with which these demands are expected to change (APA, 1995, p. 4).

Emergence of Accredited Postdoctoral Residencies

Various kinds of postdoctoral programs in psychology have been in existence since the late 1950s, and their merits debated at many training conferences over the years (Kaslow, McCarthy, Rogers, & Summerville, 1992; Wiens, 1993). Wiens (1993) was able to identify nearly 400 training sites offering some sort of postdoctoral education in over 50 applied and research settings, ranging from aging to women's health. The majority of these sites trained just one postdoctoral student at a time and over two-thirds were offered in medical centers. Wiens (1993) charitably describes the high degree of variability in these nearly 400 settings by stating "It is not known how many of these training opportunities would qualify as 'programs' of postdoctoral study" (p. 421).

While a goodly number of the oldest postdoctoral programs were oriented toward the development of research skills, an increasing number of them, during the final decades of the twentieth century, were designed to provide advanced training in professional psychology, sometimes fairly generalized training, other times very specialized training in focused areas like neuropsychology, health psychology, or psychoanalysis. Concerns about quality control in these practice-oriented postdoctoral programs, combined with a desire for the profession of psychology to have a way of ensuring more quality control in postdoctoral experiences used to qualify for licensure in psychology, led to the development of formal standards and procedures for accreditation of postdoctoral programs. From the early 1990s until 1997, representatives from most of the long-standing credentialing and accrediting organizations in psychology, along with representatives of developing organizations of postdoctoral specialty groups such as neuropsychology, behavioral, family, and health psychology, worked with the APA Committee on Accreditation to formulate postdoctoral accreditation standards and procedures. When the APA formally adopted these standards, the programs to which they were applied were identified as APA-accredited postdoctoral residencies (APA, 1996). Postdoctoral training programs can seek to become accredited postdoctoral residencies in either advanced general professional psychology or in specialty practice areas within professional psychology, for example, neuropsychology, psychoanalysis. In the initial year that accreditation of postdoctoral residencies was offered, two were approved. Many others seeking accreditation were too small to meet the accreditation criteria; ongoing developments in such programs, as well as in the formulation of the accreditation procedures, make it difficult to predict how quickly there will be a significant number of accredited postdoctoral residencies.

It is important to note—especially for counseling psychologists—that completion of a postdoctoral residency is not now, or expected to become in the near future, a requirement for beginning a career in counseling psychology. For psychologists who wish to specialize beyond a more traditional area like counseling or clinical psychology, there may well develop the expectation that one will complete a postdoctoral residency in a specialized area like health psychology or neuropsychology. It should also be noted that there may be some distinct advantages (even though not required or even expected) for counseling and clinical psychologists to complete one of the postdoctoral residencies in general (as compared to a specialty residency) professional psychology. As the number of accredited postdoctoral residencies increases, it is likely that some states will change their licensing regulations to recognize an accredited postdoctoral residency as automatically fulfilling postdoctoral experience requirement. Therefore, any counseling psychologist who completes such a residency will not need to seek further documentation regarding the kinds of services provided, and amount and kinds of supervision received during the first years of his or her career, in order to meet a state's postdoctoral experience eligibility requirements for licensing. There may also be developments like most selective employers giving preference to those who have completed an accredited postdoctoral residency, just as happened in the 1980s when several major employers of psychologists, such as the Veterans Administration, began requiring that applicants for psychology positions must have completed an APA-accredited predoctoral internship. Stewart and Stewart (1998) provide a concise review of other implications for psychology graduate students, as well as recommendations for securing and completing postdoctoral training. While the postdoctoral residency will add 1–2 years to the "formal" training period in professional psychology, it is important to note that such residencies do not often add any time needed to obtain licensure as a psychologist since a postdoctoral residency more than fulfills the postdoctoral experience requirements required by most states.

Tangentially related to the emergence of accredited postdoctoral residences is the ongoing debate about whether the predoctoral internship should remain at that level or be moved to the postdoctoral level (Murray, 1997). Currently, APA-accreditation criteria require that the internship be completed prior to the granting of the doctoral degree. Some psychologists have been arguing for moving the internship to the postdoctoral level. Interns could then, like intern physicians, be identified as doctors. Reimbursement for professional services in hospitals and health care companies might then be easier to achieve. Another argument in favor of the move is that an intern who has already completed all the doctoral degree requirements could then dedicate all of his or her time and energy to the internship rather than also trying to complete a dissertation and/or other predoctoral requirements. Arguments against the move are concerns about a training program's loss of control over the selection and completion of an internship appropriate to the prior training of the student. Also, what controls would there be against exploitation of a new professional psychologist who has to have supervised training to obtain licensure yet no longer has advocates from a training program? Much of this discussion about the placement of the internship began and evolved in the same time period as the development of accredited postdoctoral programs. Counseling psychology program directors have taken the position that the internship should remain at the predoctoral level. Now that accreditation of postdoctoral residencies is in place, it seems unlikely that the internship will be moved to postdoctoral status as well. Whatever develops regarding such placement, it is very important to note that whether the internship is predoctoral or postdoctoral does not change the length of time needed for completing training as a professional psychologist; the impact of a change, in most cases, would be limited simply to the order in which doctoral requirements were completed.

Quality Improvement in Continuing Education

> How do we maintain the high-level, sophisticated, and consistently competent workforce of psychologists necessitated by this changing world? . . . Given the value psychology places on lifelong learning, and its part in the socialization (whether formal or informal) of most graduate students across all areas of study, it came as a surprise, at least to these authors, how little is known about where, when, how or with what support this learning is to occur (APA, 1995, p. 5).

These authors were diplomatic! After more than 30 years of experience with continuing education (CE) as part of the requirements for continued licensing of psychologists in many states, the discipline of psychology, which promotes itself as a research-based profession, has very little empirical data on the effectiveness of the techniques or outcomes of such education. The anecdotal evidence, that is, the personal experience of many psychologists who have completed some continuing education programs, is not very favorable. In fact, significant concerns about the educational value of many offerings, combined with the bureaucratic problems in monitoring compliance has led a number of states to reduce or even abandon any CE requirements. The range of requirements across states is astounding. In some states, CE requirements mandate attending and passing very specifically focused courses, for example, dual relationships, AIDs, as offered by a very limited number of approved sponsors. In other states, CE requirements are largely self-reports of convention sessions attended, books read, and so forth. At either extreme of this range, rarely is there any prior assessment of participants to determine if the program they are taking is addressing any of their own educational weaknesses. Until recently, it was a rare occasion when programs included reasonably well-constructed evaluations of what participants learned; still today it is extraordinarily rare for participants to receive any feedback evaluating the strength of their performance at the completion of the CE program. Given these conditions, it is easy to understand why many psychologists have viewed CE as more the fulfillment of a requirement as compared to a desirable part of their own career development.

In our view, CE can easily be "fixed" by applying to ourselves the very skills we outlined earlier in the chapter related to good case management. As noted in the report of the National Conference on Postdoctoral Education and Training in Psychology (APA, 1995), we need to have (1) strategies for individualized self-assessment of each of our own strengths and weaknesses, (2) strategies for reviewing the range of interventions available to address our weaknesses, (3) ways of choosing an appropriate intervention and evaluating our own progress, then finally (4) strategies for reiterating these steps so that our next CE efforts build on a new assessment of what is our next weakness to address. Emerging electronic technology makes all of this realizable; we no longer have to wait until we can go to a specific location and take a 1-day course. Self-assessments for all of the needed areas of attention, as listed above, as well as in various specialized intervention areas, could be developed and reside in electronic files for any psychologist to access confidentially. Online CE options of varying intensity and style could then be chosen in accordance with self-assessment scores obtained. The range of options today through CD-ROM, teleconferencing, online services, simulations, branching, and so on can make CE truly "user friendly." Whatever CE option is chosen will ideally conclude with an outcome evaluation that provides feedback—has the psychologist attained an adequate level of knowledge and/or skill or is further work indicated? We are optimistic that the quality of CE will be greatly enhanced in the coming years and that it can become a desirable part of our ongoing career development, providing intrinsic satisfaction as well as extrinsically valuable credentials.

Credentialing of Psychologists

Licensing of Psychologists: Necessary But Not Sufficient

Psychologists, like lawyers, medical doctors, and many other professionals, are subject to some form of licensure in every state. Because professions, by definition, include high levels of training in a specific kind of expertise, it is a reasonable assumption that the public cannot readily make informed decisions about whether the services being offered are of adequate quality. Licensure enables a state to regulate the use of the title of the profession and legally define the activities that constitute its practice. Psychology licensure laws typically include definitions of what training and supervised experience are necessary to be eligible for licensure, required examination procedures, definitions of the scope of practice, and what sanctions apply to people who violate specifics of the licensing regulations. In many state psychology licensing laws, the ethical standards of the APA are included as part of the legal responsibilities of the psychologist.

Fretz and Mills (1980) provide a review of decades of controversy surrounding the need for and development of psychology licensing laws, primarily in the 1960s.

Although a few psychologists were in independent practice from the beginnings of clinical and counseling psychology in the 1940s, the vast majority of such psychologists in earlier decades were employed in hospitals, clinics, and university settings where licensure was not viewed to be necessary. With the emergence in the late 1960s of health insurance policy reimbursements for some counseling and psychotherapy, there was a rapid increase in the number of psychologists seeking licensure. This increase occurred because such reimbursements were often limited to, as in medicine, licensed professionals.

The psychology license laws that were developed in the 1950s and 1960s had very broad definitions about who could be eligible for licensing as a psychologist. Many persons had become licensed as psychologists had completed degrees in over 30 graduate programs other than those in psychology, for example, law, divinity, public health, guidance, family studies. In those early years there were also no differences in the licensing procedures for someone who had completed a research doctorate, in sensation and perception, for example, and someone who had completed a doctorate in counseling, school, or clinical psychology. In order to address the great variations in states' requirements for licensure, the APA and the National Register of Health Service Providers in Psychology held two credentialing conferences in the 1970s that resulted in recommendations that have continued to affect significantly requirements both for accreditation of training programs and licensing of psychologists.

These recommendations included a far more restrictive definition of the educational backgrounds that could be submitted to licensing boards for eligibility for licensure. However, if appropriate educational requirements were included, there was flexibility about the location of the training. Of major importance for counseling psychology was the recommendation that "the program, wherever it may be administratively housed, must be clearly identified and labeled as a psychology program. Such a program must specify in pertinent institutional catalogs and brochures its intent to educate and train professional psychologists" (Wellner, 1978, p. 33). It then became possible for many programs in counseling and guidance, that wished to train counseling psychologists as well, to make the curricular changes necessary for a formal transition to psychology training programs. In fact, the more than 100% increase in the number of APA-accredited programs in counseling psychology from the early 1970s to the late 1980s was directly related to this change. The majority of the newly approved programs were formerly counselor education or counseling and guidance programs in colleges of education.

Another issue in psychology licensing has been the desire for more unified examination procedures. Despite the existence of numerous licensing laws in psychology since the 1960s, it was not until the 1990s that all states and Canadian provinces required license-eligible psychologists to achieve a specified minimum score on the Examination for Professional Practice in Psychology (EPPP), a standardized exam that has been developed and administered by the Association of State and Provincial Psychology Boards (ASPPB). There remains much variation in the required passing score, one of the reasons that reciprocity of licensing between states remains very limited; that is, a psychologist licensed in any given state will very likely have to go through extensive new application and possibly examination procedures when moving to another state. Moreover, even though the EPPP has been subject to many revisions over the years to bring it into congruence with what the profession believes is most essential for competent functioning as psychologists, there remains much controversy as to what is the desirable balance of content areas, for example, how much on basic knowledge about principles of biopsychology as compared to applied ethics as compared to principles for assessment/diagnosis. Various studies of performance of graduates of psychology programs on the EPPP exam predictably find that graduates of programs who had higher Graduate Record Examination (GRE) scores, before entering graduate school, also attain higher scores on the EPPP (Yu, Rinaldi, Templer, Colbert, et al., 1997). However, also correlated with higher GRE entrance scores are such factors as smaller programs with more faculty per student and the granting of the Ph.D. degree as compared to the Psy.D. degree; therefore all these factors are also significant predictors of higher EPPP scores.

The variations in state laws regarding amount of supervised experience required and the minimum acceptable score on the EPPP, plus the fact that licensing laws are continually being challenged and revised, makes it extremely difficult to advise anyone regarding what exactly will be needed to become licensed. Few of us know what state we will be living in 10 years from now. Even once licensed in one state, there is very limited mobility of licensure between states because of variations in requirements. In recent years, efforts have been made for greater reciprocity and some states and Canadian provinces have entered into the "agreement of reciprocity" developed by ASPPB. That organization has also developed a Certificate of Professional Qualification in Psychology to aid in mobility; however, each state retains autonomy as to whether it will recognize reciprocity agreements or the ASPPB certificate. Psychologists who have some of the credentials described in the next section, for example listed in the National Register of Health Service Providers in Psychology or who become board certified by the American Board of Professional Psychology, will find it an easier process to complete licensure in a new state, than those without such credentials. In summary, there are still many variations in state requirements for licensing as psychologists, and it is unlikely that these variations will ever disappear; it is valuable to note that students who receive their doctoral degrees in APA-approved counseling psychology programs and then complete internships and postdoctoral residencies accredited by the APA, will clearly have the least difficulty meeting licensing eligibility requirements in any state or province.

All of this section has focused on licensing as psychologists. As noted earlier, licensing of a variety of master's degrees in mental health areas has emerged in the past couple of decades. Space limitations do not permit describing all the kinds of master's level credentials and licensing currently available in over 40 states. A great deal of information about such licensing can be obtained from the American Counseling Association (see Chapter 7 for more information on, and an address for, this organization); Wallace and Lewis (1998) provide extensive information on preparing for certification as a professional counselor.

Generic or Specialty Licensing?
Another ongoing issue in psychology is whether licensing should be generic or specialty based. A generic license can be granted to a biopsychologist as well as a coun-

seling psychologist. As noted earlier in this chapter, this was the form of all the early licensing laws in psychology. By the late 1960s, insurance companies that were then beginning to provide reimbursements for psychotherapy provided by licensed psychologists, raised very legitimate concerns about the training and experiential backgrounds of some psychologists. Should a licensed psychologist whose doctoral training was as a researcher in sensation and perception, and who had never taken courses or supervised practica in assessment or counseling, be eligible for reimbursement for providing psychological services to clients? It was for this reason that the APA and the American Board of Professional Psychology collaborated, in the early 1970s, in establishing the National Register of Health Service Providers in Psychology (NR). The primary goal of the NR was, and remains, to provide insurers, governmental agencies, health care organizations, as well as individual consumers, a listing of licensed psychologists who have met specified criteria in education, training, and supervised experience as health service providers, as compared to merely having a doctoral degree in some aspect of psychology.

Only after a psychologist is licensed can he or she be considered for listing in the NR; counseling psychologists who have completed APA-accredited training programs and internships, and received supervised postdoctoral experience in accord with the licensing requirements in the state in which they are practicing, will typically meet all criteria for listing in the NR. Moreover, to address this issue within states about distinguishing health service providers from all other psychologists licensed in the state, 14 states have developed regulations identifying health service providers as a separate category, using the NR as the primary procedure for identifying health service providers.

Just as the NR was emerging, several states attempted to develop an alternative to generic licensing by developing specialty licenses. Since the only officially recognized specialties at that time were those of counseling, clinical, school, and I/O, some states attempted to set up different licenses for those groups. However, because of the high degree of overlap that has emerged among the first three of these specialties, there were numerous problems in maintaining differential criteria for separate licenses. While candidates might have earned different degrees, the overlap in their professional training and the completion oftentimes of exactly the same internship programs, created numerous legal entanglements such that specialty licensing was typically abandoned within a few years of its creation. Even now that more specialities are gaining official APA recognition, for example, health psychology, psychoanalysis, it is not likely that specialty licensing will emerge any more than it has in medicine. Physicians can earn board-certified status in specialties, but their license to practice is still a general license to practice medicine. Psychology licensing will probably remain generic with many states having some designation for distinguishing health service providers. More specialized training will likely be recognized by the kinds of credentials described in the next section, rather than by licensing.

The preceding discussion leads to the final issue to be discussed in this section—what has come to be called the "small c clinical" problem. In most fields of health care, the term "clinical" has often been the adjective used to distinguish the provision of health care services as compared to other roles; for example, clinical medicine as compared to research medicine, clinical social work (trained in therapy) as compared to social work case management for aid to dependent children or other social programs. In a number of instances over the years, the word *clinical* has been incorporated into state or federal legislation with the intention that it apply to health service providers as compared to others. Because psychology has, since World War II, had counseling and school programs, as well as clinical programs, producing health service providers, there have been times when counseling and school psychologists encountered some temporary difficulties in qualifying for positions or reimbursements described as available to "clinical psychologists" even though the intended reference in the legislation or rules was all health service providing psychologists. In every known case where state and federal statutes referred to clinical psychologists, without differentiation from counseling and school psychologists, it was eventually determined that the use of *clinical* was intended to refer to health service providers and not just to graduates of clinical psychology programs.

As additional specialities and proficiencies in the 1990s wished to use the adjective *clinical* (e.g., clinical child psychology), the APA, in 1998, declared a moratorium on the further use of the term "clinical" as an adjective in describing specialities or proficiencies. The APA has also worked closely with the leadership of counseling psychology to ensure, when the term "clinical" is intended to refer to health service providers, that it not be used in any discriminatory way. One example of the kind of clarifications that the APA has helped make may be found in the rules for reimbursement of psychologists under the Medicare Act. This act, when it was established in the early 1990s, used the term "clinical psychologist" at all places where reference was made to psychologists. Because of some problems this term created for counseling psychologists working with elderly clients, counseling psychologists worked with the APA to achieve a clarification in Medicare rules such that they now specify:

> [A] clinical psychologist is an individual who (1) holds a doctoral degree in psychology; and (2) is licensed or certified, on the basis of the doctoral degree in psychology, by the State in which he or she practices, at the independent practice level of psychology to furnish diagnostic, assessment, preventive, and therapeutic services directly to individuals (*Federal Register*, p. 551).

Specialty Credentials

Over the years a number of credentials have been developed to provide professional psychologists with attainment of advanced levels of training, experience, and competence. Drum and Hall (1993) provide an excellent overview of the developments psychology has made in self-regulation and the setting of professional standards in accreditation and credentialing in order to achieve and maintain quality assurance. In this section we first describe those that have been developed by and for psychologists; at the end of the section we describe how ongoing issues about new credentials are being monitored.

The credential most widely held by professional psychologists (after licensing as a psychologist, which is a prerequisite for every credential discussed here) is listing in the National Register of Health Service Providers of Psychology (NR), or its Canadian equivalent, the Canadian Register of Health Service Providers in Psychology. As described in the preceding section, these registers were developed to identify which generically licensed psychologists have had appropriate training and supervised experience to qualify as health service providers. The NR is used now not only in designating health service providers in many states, but also by managed care companies. For example, Pacific Care Behavioral Health Inc. gives preference to those psychologists listed in the NR for becoming part of their provider panels; Magellan, a major health care corporation, uses the NR for verification of credentials of psychologists who apply to be providers.

The oldest form of specialty recognition in psychology is the American Board of Professional Psychology (ABPP). Founded in 1947, congruent with the establishment of the first applied specialties, that is, counseling, clinical, and industrial (later called I/O) psychology—it was established to recognize the highest levels of attainment in the specialty, requiring a rigorous examination process which, when successfully completed, resulted in the award of a diplomate in the specialty. For a variety of reasons, very few psychologists in the first 40 years of ABPP completed the diplomate requirements. In the late 1980s all the application and examination issues that psychologists had raised over the years were carefully addressed by the Executive Board of the ABPP. Also, recognizing the emergence of new specialities within psychology, the ABPP created procedures for becoming board certified in behavioral, clinical neuropsychology, family, forensic, health, and psychoanalysis as well as the older specialities of counseling, school, clinical, and I/O psychology. For each of these specialties there are now standardized examination procedures that a psychologist may take at the completion of 2 years of supervised practice in the specialty, of which 1 year may be predoctoral. For example, a recent graduate of a counseling psychology program who completes a predoctoral internship and 1 year of supervised postdoctoral experience in a setting for, and supervised by counseling psychologists (and has become licensed as a psychologist), could become an applicant for the Diplomate in Counseling Psychology. Awarding of the diplomate entitles the psychologist to be identified as "board certified," a term that is widely used and recognized in medicine, and therefore a valuable credential for recognition by hospitals and other health care organizations.

One of the newest credentials in psychology emerged because of ongoing issues in defining what actually constitutes a specialty in psychology. Because of the desire of the profession to control proliferation of what might be called specialties, a credential was developed called a Certificate of Proficiency. Procedures for obtaining such a certificate have been developed by a new board within the APA, the College of Professional Psychology. As of this writing, the only certificate offered is the one for treatment of alcohol and other psychoactive substance abuse disorders. Just what distinguishes a proficiency from a specialty? To address this issue, the APA created a Commission for the Recognition of Specialties and Proficiencies in Professional Psychology. The commission began its work in 1995 and has, for example, given official recognition as specialties to Clinical Health Psychology, Psychoanalysis, and Child Clinical Psychology, whereas gerontology and biofeedback have been recognized as proficiencies. A focused area like biofeedback will probably always remain a "proficiency," whereas an area like gerontology might, in a decade or two, and after the development of a specific body of research-based knowledge and practice, become, like child clinical psychology, a specialty rather than a proficiency. Any area that becomes recognized as a proficiency may work with the APA College of Professional Psychology to develop and refine examinations for evaluating applicants for a Certificate of Proficiency. These certificates certify the acquisition of the knowledge and skills associated with competent practice in the proficiency. Any licensed psychologist can, given appropriate training and experience, apply for any and all of the certificates offered by the college. It is expected that, as additional proficiencies are recognized by the APA, additional certificates will be developed.

There are ongoing issues in the field of psychology as to which credentials should be developed and recognized by the profession. The Council of Credentialing Organizations in Professional Psychology (CCOPP) was created in 1996 in order to ensure that the development of any new procedures for accreditation or credentialing of psychologists meets the quality of standards of existing procedures and is coordinated with the participating groups in order to both facilitate the career progress of professional psychologists and to provide the public with clear information about the meaning of each credential.

Credentialing Processes for Industrialized Health Care

> Despite professionals' ambivalence about credentialing, payers and the public clearly believe in it. As the health care system rapidly moves from open-panel, fee-for-service arrangements to limited-panel, managed care arrangements, provider selection criteria will become even more stringent. Managed Care Organizations (MCOs)—including Preferred Provider Organizations (PPOs), network managers and HMOs—try to sell their products on the basis of two factors: cost and quality. Since "quality" in health care has proven so difficult to advertise based on the *outcomes* of care, those who assemble networks usually resort to asserting quality based on the *inputs*—i.e., the providers' credentials. It will become increasingly important to providers to possess widely respected credentials (Stromberg & Ratcliff, 1995, p. 3).

While Mickelsen (1996), as well as Stromberg and Ratcliff (1995) address some of the importance of specialized credentials in managed care, beyond being licensed as a psychologist, the question of which credentials are most important is not easily answered. What can be said is that for panels of providers with significant roles in hospitals, hospital privileges as a psychologist may be most important. For panels with little interaction with hospitals, however, such privileges may be largely irrelevant. If a panel needs specialists in substance abuse, then a credential in this area may be most important. Stromberg and Ratcliff (1995) advise, "pay attention to maintaining your credentials" (p. 9). At the beginning of one's career, the broader the range of credentials, the more opportunities one will have for joining provider panels.

Technology and Seamless Credentialing

In this closing section we can finally return to the potential positive impact technology can have on the career development of psychologists in the twenty-first century. In the section on quality improvements in continuing education, we have already outlined how current technology can greatly facilitate completion of the assessment, intervention, and evaluation stages of more individualized quality continuing education. We next describe some of the equally facilitative possibilities for credentialing in psychology. Then we shall describe what organizations of professional psychology, aided by the coming generation of more computer savvy counseling psychologists, must do to make these possibilities a reality.

For almost every new credential, psychologists must begin anew the process of completing a multipage application form requesting transcripts, confirming supervision received, and obtaining certificates indicating credits earned in courses or programs two, three, or even five years ago. The entire process is entirely too reminiscent of multiple applications to graduate school and for internships. Those latter processes in themselves are unnecessarily redundant. While there might be some merit to the argument that there is some intrinsic value in the first gathering of data on professional accomplishments, and the development of essay responses for some parts of internship applications, certainly there is no intrinsic merit to reiterations of the same material. Moreover, much of the material gathered for an internship application is subsequently needed for licensing, specialty credentials, and applications to provider panels of health care corporations. Similarly, after completing the doctorate and internship, information on completion of continuing education programs, especially when appropriately individualized, will be part of the "portfolio" of information needed for those same purposes.

Those readers already comfortable with even the most basic uses of computers, beyond word-processing, can see implicit in the previous sentences the need for a uniform psychology credential form that would have, in an electronic format, an agreed upon set of "prompts" for recording—from the very beginning of graduate education—appropriate information on courses and practica, extending on then through the additional items needed regarding supervised professional experiences for applying to predoctoral internships, postdoctoral residencies, and the full range of specialized psychology credentials. With such an electronic file, then, for example, the application to become eligible for the examination to become board certified in psychology (by the American Board of Professional Psychology) would require simply a few minor additions to the personal electronic files that a counseling psychologist had been accumulating since the first year in graduate school; a file that had already served for applying for internships, gaining licensure, and so forth. When applying to join the provider panel of a health care corporation, all of the necessary information would already reside in an electronic file.

Why doesn't the uniform psychology credential form exist? Why is there no uniform application blank for internships? Why must there be redundant paper applications for licensing as psychologists in almost every state? for most specialty credentials in psychology (National Register excepted)? for most health care provider panels? The answers in some ways are complex, but mostly it is a failure of effective inter- and often intraorganizational collaboration. Progress is also slow because of the generational gap between newly graduating professional psychologists and psychologists in these organizations' leadership positions. Many, but certainly not all, of these leaders have little experience in using computers beyond word-processing and email, as compared to younger psychologists who are heavy users of technology both for obtaining and recording information. While the Council of Credentialing Organizations in Professional Psychology shares the perspective that all psychologists would be well-served by the seamless credentialing a "uniform psychology credential form" would allow, there are as yet no working groups in place to begin the negotiations with the numerous accrediting and credentialing organizations that must be involved. The fulfillment of the goal of seamless credentialing will most likely rest with the leadership that emerges from the graduates of doctoral psychology programs in the coming decade.

Summary

During the closing decades of the twentieth century, much of the control of health care in the United States shifted from the providers themselves (physicians, psychologists) to newly developed health care corporations. In this chapter we described the long-lasting economic forces that brought about these changes and their implications for the practice of psychology. Counseling psychologists whose careers fall largely outside university settings will find new challenges in the focus of their practice, in how to ensure income commensurate with a doctoral degree, and in dealing with health care corporation provider panels and provider profiling. We described how much of the traditional training in counseling psychology can be adapted easily to prepare graduate students not only to cope with these challenges, but also to be prepared to take advantage of the opportunities that are emerging for psychologists in developing quality management within health care corporations. The fundamentals of doctoral-level education in counseling psychology provide the basics for contributing to the development of practice guidelines, defining and measuring effective outcomes, and enhancing the humaneness and effectiveness of health care administration.

Changing demographics in the United States are resulting in an increasingly diverse society. We noted that counseling psychologists have become, and will need to continue to be, leaders in the development of research and training in multicultural competence. Regarding changes in demographics in the profession, we described how counseling psychology is leading the profession in terms of providing more leadership opportunities for both women and ethnic minorities. We described why we believe that the emergence of the profession of licensed mental health counselor will mean that the profession of psychology will continue to regard master's degrees in psychology as second-class citizens; students who wish to become practitioners and to pursue only a master's degree, as compared to a doctoral degree, should be careful to choose master's degree programs that fulfill the local state's requirements for being a certified or licensed mental health counselor. We also described why we believe that there is no supply-and-demand crisis for doctoral level counseling psychologists, especially for those who attend to the issues described in this chapter regarding how to meet the challenges and opportunities that have come from the industrialization of health care.

The final part of the chapter described the issues underlying changes in post-doctoral education and credentialing. First, we explained why accreditation of post-doctoral residences has emerged. Second, we described how modern technology can address long-standing concerns about the quality of continuing education in psychology. Finally, we described both some old and new issues underlying various kinds of licensing and professional credentials in psychology. The chapter concluded with a challenge for the coming generation of counseling psychologists to help attain the vision of "seamless" credentialing within the profession of psychology.

REFERENCES

American Psychological Association (APA). (1995). *Education and training beyond the doctoral degree.* Madison, CT: International Universities Press.

APA. (1996). *Guidelines and principles for accreditation of programs in professional psychology.* Washington, DC: Author.

APA. (1997). *Task force on training: Challenges of changing workplace/marketplace* (Report to Council of Representatives). Washington, DC: Author.

APA. (Annual). *Graduate study in psychology* (Directory). Washington, DC: Author.

Belar, C. D. (1995). Collaboration in capitated care: Challenges for psychology. *Professional Psychology: Research and Practice, 26,* 139–146.

Belar, C. D. (1998). Graduate education in clinical psychology. *American Psychologist, 53,* 456–464.

Broskowski, A., Marks, E., & Budman, S. H. (1981). *Linking health and mental health.* Beverly Hills, CA: Sage Publications.

Cummings, N. A. (1993). The successful application of medical offset in program planning and in clinical delivery. *Managed Care Quarterly, 2,* 1–6.

Cummings, N. A. (1995). Impact of managed care on employment and training: A primer for survival. *Professional Psychology: Research and Practice, 26,* 10–15.

Drum, D. J. (1995). Changes in the mental health service delivery and finance systems and resulting implications for the National Register. Register Report, 20 (3), 4–10.

Drum, D. J., & Hall, J. E. (1993). Psychology's self-regulation and the setting of professional standards. *Applied & Preventive Psychology, 2,* 151–161.

Federal Register. (1998, April 23). Vol. 63, No. 78.

Fraser, J. S. (1996). All that glitters is not always gold: Medical offset effects and managed behavioral health care. *Professional Psychology: Research and Practice, 27,* 335–344.

Freeman, M. A., & Trabin, T. (1994). Managed behavioral health care: History, models, key issues, and future course. Rockville, MD: U.S. Center for Mental Health Services.

Fretz, B. R., & Mills, D. H. (1980). *Licensing and certification of psychologists and counselors.* San Francisco: Jossey-Bass.

Gelso, C. J., & Fassinger, R. E. (1992). Personality, development, and counseling psychology: Depth, ambivalence, and actualization. *Journal of Counseling Psychology, 39,* 275–298.

Gelso, C. J., & Johnson, D. H. (1983). *Explorations in time-limited counseling and psychotherapy.* New York: Teachers College Press.

Glueckauf, R. L., Frank, R. G., Bond, G. R., & McGrew, J. H. (Eds.). (1996). *Psychological practice in a changing health care system.* New York: Springer Publishing.

Gutierrez, P. M., & Silk, K. R. (1998). Prescription privileges for psychologists: A review of the psychological literature. *Professional Psychology: Research and Practice, 29,* 213–222.

Heath, D. H. (1965). *Explorations of maturity: Studies of mature and immature college men.* New York: Appleton-Century-Crofts.

Hersch. L. (1995). Adapting to health care reform and managed care: Three strategies for survival and growth. *Professional Psychology: Research and Practice, 26,* 16–26.

Hersch, L. (1997, July/August). Is psychology training students for jobs that don't exist? *The National Psychologist,* 191–192.

Howard, K. I., Lueger, R. J., Maling, M. S., & Martinovich, Z. (1993). A phase model of psychotherapy outcome: Causal mediation of change. *Journal of Consulting & Clinical Psychology, 61,* 678–685.

Janda, L., England, K., Lovejoy, D., & Drury, K. (1998). Attitudes toward psychology relative to other disciplines. *Professional Psychology: Research and Practice, 29,* 140–143.

Kaslow, N. J., McCarthy, S. M., Rogers, J. H., & Summerville, M. B. (1992). Psychology postdoctoral training: A developmental perspective. *Professional Psychology: Research and Practice, 23,* 369–375.

Klusman, L. E. (1998). Military health care providers' views on prescribing privileges for psychologists. *Professional Psychology: Research and Practice, 29,* 223–229.

Lent, R. W. (1990). Further reflections on the public image of counseling psychology. *The Counseling Psychologist, 18,* 324–332.

Lightsey, O. R. (1996). What leads to wellness? The role of psychological resources in well-being. *The Counseling Psychologist, 24,* 589–735.

Lowman, R. L., & Resnick, R. J. (Eds.). (1994). *The mental health professional's guide to managed care.* Washington, DC: American Psychological Association.

Martin, S. (1995, January). Field's status unaltered by the influx of women. *APA Monitor, 9.*

McCall-Perez, F. (1993, November/December). The voice of the customer in managed behavioral health care. *Behavioral Healthcare Tomorrow,* 20–24.

McGuire, P. A. (1998, June). "Missionaries" connect business with practice. *APA Monitor,* 24.

Mickelsen, R. A. (1996). Credentialing: Legal supplement on managed care credentialing. *National Register Report, 22*(2–3), 15–27.

Miller, I. J. (1996). Time-limited brief therapy has gone too far: The result is invisible rationing. *Professional Psychology: Research and Practice, 27,* 567–576.

Munoz, R. F., Hollon, S. D., McGrath, E., Rehm, L. P., & VandenBos, G. R. (1994). On the AHCPR depression in primary care guidelines. *American Psychologist, 49,* 42–61.

Murphy, M. J., DeBernardo, C. R., & Shoemaker, W. E. (1998). Impact of managed care on independent practice and professional ethics: A survey of independent practitioners. *Professional Psychology: Research and Practice, 29,* 43–51.

Murray, B. (1995, April). Master's program growth spurs educational concerns. *APA Monitor,* 47.

Murray, B. (1997, November). Support increases for moving the internship. *APA Monitor,* 32.

Murray, B. (1998a, May). Notion of a life-long career is now a thing of the past. *APA Monitor,* 35.

Murray, B. (1998b, May). Schools urge students toward atypical career. *APA Monitor,* 38.

Murray, B. (1998c, June). Flexibility is key to a successful career. *APA Monitor,* 38.

Oehlert, M. E., & Lopez, S. J. (1998). APA-accredited internships: An examination of the supply and demand issue. *Professional Psychology: Research and Practice, 29,* 189–194.

Osipow, S. H. (1977). Will the real counseling psychologist please stand up? *The Counseling Psychologist, 7*(2), 93–94.

Patricclli, R. E., & Lee, F. C. (1996). Employer-based innovations in behavioral health benefits. *Professional Psychology: Research and Practice, 27,* 325–334.

Peterson, D. R. (1996). Making psychology indispensable. *Applied & Preventive Psychology, 5,* 1–8.

Phelps, R., Eisman, E. J., & Kohout, J. (1998). Psychological practice and managed care: Results of the CAPP practitioner survey. *Professional Psychology: Research and Practice, 29,* 31–36.

Psychology graduates develop career niches. (1998, January). *APA Monitor,* 1, 28–29.

Quirk, M. P., Strosahl, K., Kreilkamp, T., & Erdberg, P. (1995). Personality feedback consultation to families in a managed mental health care practice. *Professional Psychology: Research and Practice, 26,* 27–32.

Robiner, W. N. (1991). How many psychologists are needed? A call for a national psychology human resource agenda. *Professional Psychology: Research and Practice, 22,* 427–440.

Seligman, M. E. P., & Levant, R. F. (1998). Managed care policies rely on inadequate science. *Professional Psychology: Research and Practice, 129,* 211–212.

Shea, C. (1995, April 7). Rx for student health? *The Chronicle of Higher Education,* A35–36.

Shueman, S. A. (1997). Confronting health care realities. *Professional Psychology: Research and Practice, 28,* 555–558.

Shueman, S. A., Troy, W. G., & Mayhugh, S. (Eds.). (1994). *Managed behavioral health care.* Springfield, IL: Charles C. Thomas.

Sleek, S. (1995, January). Managed care sharpens master's-degree debate. *APA Monitor,* 8.

Sleek, S. (1997, November). State initiatives curb abuses of managed care. *APA Monitor,* 22.

Sleek, S. (1998a, June). Americans want the right to sue for negligent care. *APA Monitor,* 25.

Sleek, S. (1998b, April). Behavioral researchers call for more study on human strengths. *APA Monitor,* 11.

Steenbarger, B. N. (1994). Duration and outcome in psychotherapy: An integrative review. *Professional Psychology: Research and Practice, 25,* 111–119.

Stewart, A. E., & Stewart, E. A. (1998). Trends in postdoctoral education: Requirements for licensure and training opportunities. *Professional Psychology: Research and Practice, 29,* 273–283.

Stricker, G. (1997, Summer). Slouching toward the millennium. *APPIC Newsletter, 4,* 19–25.

Stromberg, C., & Ratcliff, R. (1995). *A legal update on provider credentialing* (The Psychologist's Legal Update #7). Washington, DC: National Register of Health Service Providers in Psychology.

Troy, W. G. (1994). Developing and improving professional competencies. In S. A. Shueman, W. G. Troy, and S. L. Mayhugh (Eds.), *Managed behavioral health care* (pp. 168–188). Springfield, IL: Charles C. Thomas.

VandenBos, G. R., DeLeon, P. H., & Belar, C. D. (1991). How many psychological practitioners are needed? It's too early to know. *Professional Psychology: Research and Practice, 22,* 441–448.

Wallace, S. A., & Lewis, M. D. (1998). *Becoming a professional counselor* (2nd ed.). Thousand Oaks, CA: Sage Publications.

Wellner, A. M. (Ed.). (1978). *Education and credentialing in psychology.* Washington, DC: American Psychological Association.

White, R. W. (1973). The concept of the healthy personality: What do we really mean? *The Counseling Psychologist, 4*(2), 3–12.

Wiens, A. N. (1993). Postdoctoral education-training for specialty practice. *American Psychologist, 48,* 415–422.

Yu, L. M., Rinaldi, S. A., Templer, D. I., Colbert, L. A., Siscoe, K., & VanPatten, K. (1997). Scores on the Examination for Professional Practice in Psychology as a function of attributes of clinical psychology graduate programs. *Psychological Science, 8,* 347–350.

Zytowski, D. G., Casas, J. M., Gilbert, L. A., Lent, R. W., & Simon, N. P. (1988). Counseling psychology's public image. *The Counseling Psychologist, 16,* 332–346.

CHAPTER 5

ON BEING AN ETHICAL PSYCHOLOGIST

Evolving Discourse on Ethics

Ethical Training

Ethical Standards, With Illustrations of Unethical Behaviors

1. General Standards

2. Evaluation, Assessment, or Intervention

3. Advertising and Other Public Statements

4. Therapy

5. Privacy and Confidentiality

6. Teaching, Training Supervision, Research, and Publishing

7. Forensic Activities

8. Resolving Ethical Issues

Ethical Dilemmas

What does it require to be an ethical psychologist? We deliberately examine ethical issues, principles, and standards *before* presenting the fundamentals of counseling and psychotherapy. Fully attending to the well-being of our clients is more than a matter of using good counseling techniques. What are psychologists' professional obligations beyond using good techniques? Are there rules governing what psychologists can and cannot do? should and should not do? This chapter is designed not only to acquaint readers with current ethical standards that are to be observed by all psychologists, but also to gain an appreciation of the limits of such codes in resolving all ethical situations and in ensuring that all professionals act in ways that are beneficial to clients, colleagues, and our society.

Why are ethical standards needed? On what basis have the current standards been chosen? Are these standards sufficient for adequate protection of the public and the promotion of human welfare? The major issues underlying these questions are identified in the first section of this chapter. The chapter's second section provides a brief review of the literature on the limited outcomes of training in ethics in past decades along with some suggestions of what might need to be added to such training to improve its effectiveness.

In the third section, we provide examples and commentary on 14 behaviors that typify violations of the APA Ethical Principles of Psychologists and Code of Conduct (1992). Our examples are drawn from among the *least* sensational violations of ethics; they have been chosen to increase sensitivity beyond the media-emphasized ones such as sexual exploitation and breaching of confidentiality. The fourth section explores the concept of ethical dilemmas compared to specific behaviors that can be identified as "ethical" or "unethical." These situations present difficult challenges to psychologists since there can be no simple right or wrong action to take in such situations. The final section of this chapter looks at some of the problems and difficulties that have been discovered regarding psychologists' implementation of ethical standards and codes of conduct.

It is our hope that readers' integration of these sections' theoretical, applied, and empirical contexts will enable them to achieve the aspirations of Meara, Schmidt, and Day (1996) in their treatise on virtue ethics.

> Reflections upon and increased understanding of the moral domain (its theories, principles, virtues, and other constructs) in the context of professional codes,

changing mores, multicultural communities, and intellectual and technological advances provide ways to improve one's ethical decisions, policies, and character (p. 70).

EVOLVING DISCOURSE ON ETHICS

In a society strongly predicated on observance of individual rights, the very fact that a profession develops a code of ethical standards that mandates some behaviors and forbids others may seem "un-American." Yet most of the major service professions in our society have developed codes of ethics in the twentieth century. Since a profession is by definition a group that has "expertise and competence not readily available to the general public" (Biggs & Blocher, 1987, p. 3), the public is not usually very knowledgeable about what constitutes competent professional behavior. The concept of being professional thus includes a trust that members will monitor their own and other members' professional behavior so that competent services are provided to the public. Notice both elements: Professionals are to be competent in their services, and it is their responsibility to see that fellow professionals provide competent services. When persons contact a physician, attorney, or psychologist, they typically do not know what is best for them (other than that they need help); otherwise they would not be contacting a professional. It can be argued that the marketplace principle *caveat emptor* (let the buyer beware) does not apply to human services as it does to products like clothes or refrigerators. Counseling psychologists, like all mental health professionals, have supreme responsibility to the public trust. Persons seeking help from them are troubled and vulnerable and, consequently, are especially subject to exploitation and manipulation. Client trust is one of the most valuable commodities of the profession, but too often ethics are considered only after a problem arises.

The need for some set of standards for professional ethics has been widely recognized by most professionals; the development of such codes has proved to be quite controversial. Pope and Vetter (1992) have provided a concise and informative history of the development of the APA's current ethical standards, highlighting especially the attempt of the profession of psychology to use its own empirical methodology to develop both a responsible and responsive set of standards. Since the publication of the APA's first ethics code in 1953, there have been four extensive revisions. Despite the existence of ethics codes for these many years, plus an APA committee to monitor ethical compliance since 1938, and evidence that ethics codes are being taught more explicitly now than in the past (see next section), the past few decades have seen a significant increase in the number of ethical charges and complaints; moreover "serious mistrust of professionals has escalated dramatically" (Meara et al., 1996, p. 4). This mistrust is especially pervasive among ethnic minority Americans (Ibrahim, 1996; Payton, 1994).

> Thus it appears that effective self-regulation entails more than clearly written, widely disseminated, frequently taught and strictly enforced ethical codes. What appears to be necessary is a membership capable of making sophisticated judg-

ments about which course of action may be ethical in situations in which no one behavior seems entirely ethical or unethical (Welfel & Lipsitz, 1984, p. 31).

What more is necessary beyond a code of ethics? Beginning in the 1980s, an ever increasing number of psychologists began attending to both the conceptual and implementation issues for developing a profession that could gain and maintain the full trust of the public. All of these efforts have generated immense amounts of controversy. In this brief overview, we can identify only a few of the concerns. Extensive exploration of these concerns may be found in both Meara et al. (1996) and Kitchener (2000).

Many of the conceptual controversies can be tied back to very basic philosophical issues about the nature of humans. Attempts to increase our understanding of what is needed to be a more ethical profession by counseling psychologists such as Biggs and Blocher (1987), Jordan and Meara (1990), and Meara and colleagues (1996) call upon both classic philosophers (e.g., Aristotle and Kant), as well as contemporary writers on moral development (e.g., Kohlberg and Gilligan). Contrasts of philosophical dialectics such as deontological and teleological principles, absolutism, and relativism, underlie many of the contemporary controversies.

> Psychologists have certainly become more daring in questioning the value base of their work, but their commitment to articulating moral visions remains tenuous at best. Psychologists find themselves in the paradoxical position of talking more about values and knowing less about what to do (Prilleltensky, 1997, p. 517).

At the most fundamental level, an ethical psychologist understands what it means to be a moral person; all the authors cited in this paragraph provide foundation material for the development of this fundamental level even if there remains much controversy about how to ensure that all psychologists behave ethically.

When current APA ethical standards are presented later in this chapter, it will be evident that the standards address quite specific behaviors, often listing behaviors that psychologists should not engage in. For example, "psychologists do not engage in sexual harassment" (APA, 1992, p. 1601) or "psychologists do not promote the use of psychological assessment techniques by unqualified persons" (APA, 1992, p. 1603). As the introduction to the standards indicates, "[t]he Ethical Standards set forth enforceable rules for conduct as psychologists" (APA, 1992, p. 1598). While such enforceable standards are important in setting minimum thresholds of acceptable behavior, and making it more possible to legally enforce the standards if any psychologists violate them, such very specific statements leave unaddressed at least two major problems. One of these problems relates to ethical dilemmas, dilemmas that are not the result of a psychologist's inappropriate actions, but rather most often from conflicts between what a client desires and (a) a counselor's values, (b) laws (e.g., a mother of children being abused by her husband may not want the abuse reported to any authorities), or (c) injustices in the client's environment that could well increase the client's distress if he or she pursues his or her desires (e.g., revealing a gay sexual identity to one's military commanding officer). Ways of coping with such dilemmas will be a major section later in this chapter.

The other issue not addressed by existing standards is that of the character of psychologists. Kitchener (2000) cites the metaphor of putting good seed in bad soil; will ethical training of a flawed character result in a deformed sense of ethical behavior? While, for most of the twentieth century, character was virtually ignored as an aspect of being ethical, in the past few decades almost all major writers have devoted far more attention to the topic (Beauchamp & Childress, 1994; Kitchener, 2000; Meara et al., 1996). Meara and colleagues (1996) propose that the best way to enhance the ethical standing of the profession of psychology is by increasing the attention we give to character and virtue: "Virtue ethics focus on the ideal rather than the obligatory and on the character of the agent or professional rather than on the solving of specific ethical dilemmas" (Meara et al., 1996, p. 47). In this provocative treatise published in *The Counseling Psychologist,* they identify the virtues that should serve as the fundamental foundation of a psychologist's ethical behavior. Meara and colleagues describe four virtues: prudence, integrity, respectfulness, and benevolence. While none of these writers or others claim these virtues to be an exclusive set of pertinent virtues, they are the most widely supported ones.

> Prudence . . . involves appropriate restraint or caution, deliberate reflection upon which moral action to take, an understanding of the long-range consequences of the choice made, acting with due regard for one's vision of what is morally good, and a knowledge of how present circumstances relate to that good or goal (Meara, et al., 1996, p. 39).

For a definition of integrity, Meara et al. (1996) turn to Beauchamp and Childress: "Moral integrity, then, is the character trait of a coherent integration of reasonable stable, justifiable moral values, together with active fidelity to those values in judgment and in action" (Beauchamp & Childress, 1994, p. 473). Regarding respectfulness, Meara et al. (1996) write

> respectfulness means that we, as professional psychologists, respect (i.e., provide special attention, deference, or regard to) individuals or communities on and in the terms they themselves (not the professionals) define. The critical question is how others wish to be respected" (p. 44).

They follow their definition with examples of what it means to be respectful of clients who may come from a culture quite different from that of the counselor. Finally, benevolence:

> To label an individual as benevolent means that [that] person can be distinguished by wanting to do good . . . We believe that benevolence is important if psychologists and the profession of psychology are going to achieve the goal of contributing to the common good (p. 45).

Thus, benevolence involves actions not only concerning clients, but also to the profession's social responsibility. "[P]rudence and integrity are most closely related to the goal of competence. . . . respectfulness and benevolence further the goals of developing a psychology sensitive to multiculturalism and providing for the common good" (p. 47).

Should the criteria for selection as a graduate student in psychology include assessment of character? If so, how is it to be assessed? How much of each virtue is needed? Obviously, difficult questions to answer. Can a person without high amounts of such virtue learn to become an ethical psychologist? Are there risks of creating a "deformed" sense of ethics if training is provided to one without virtue? While such questions have not been definitively addressed, in recent years, there has been increased attention devoted to the outcomes of training in ethics. The results of those studies are reviewed in the next section.

ETHICAL TRAINING

"Researchers have found evidence of poor ethical awareness, limited skills in interpreting the Ethical Principles . . . , and a good deal of unwillingness to carry out ethical action even when known" (Welfel, 1992, p. 187). This quotation makes the title of this section slightly ambiguous—is the section about how to provide training in ethics or is it a judgment of whether that training is done ethically? Welfel (1992) provides a comprehensive review of what little we do know empirically. Somewhat unfortunately, until the 1979 revision of the APA standards for accreditation of psychology graduate programs mandated formal training in ethics, most programs had no formal coursework in ethics. "The sentiment among many psychology educators at the time was that ethical behavior was almost fully determined by moral character, which was established and essentially unchangeable by adulthood" (Welfel, 1992, p. 182), yet assessment of moral character was not a formal criteria for admittance to graduate programs.

After the introduction of ethics courses in many programs during the 1980s, the earliest positive results were that both faculty and students *believed* they were reasonably well prepared to deal with ethical dilemmas (Wilson & Ranft, 1993). Welfel (1992) found, however, that more behaviorally oriented outcomes were often lacking. She organized her review of the research on difficulties in accomplishing more positive outcomes in ethics courses according to Rest's (1984) four components of moral behavior. This is an especially appropriate framework to use since Rest has specifically spelled out how this model applies to the training of counseling psychologists. His first component is to be able to identify which situations call for ethical decisions, that is, to be morally sensitive. While this element sounds extraordinarily self-evident, the data say otherwise. Rest (1984) comments:

> Typically, professional education is so focused on the technical aspects of the job that students . . . are "professionally socialized" not to look for moral problems or to recognize moral issues in their work. The students . . . do not expect that they are an inevitable part of professional life and are usually ill-prepared to know how to approach a moral problem when one does smack them in the face (p. 21).

Welfel's review nearly a decade later continued to find that in every study designed to assess students' sensitivity to ethical issues, whether by using transcripts of counseling sessions or case presentations, nearly half of the psychology graduate students surveyed did not perceive the inherent issues. When prompted that there was an ethical issue, there were still many students who could not identify it. Even when such testing is done after providing the students with traditional training in ethics, only very modest improvements in ethical sensitivity have been obtained. Psychologists who serve on licensing boards and ABPP examination committees also find limited ethical sensitivity a continuing concern, even though the psychologists taking the exams obviously know they are being scrutinized. Obviously, training in ethics needs continued modification to increase levels of psychologists' sensitivity to some of the more subtle ethical situations.

Rest's (1984) second component of moral reasoning, that is, what ought to be done, has typically been assessed by examining the ability of students to know what to do when faced with a particular ethical dilemma. Welfel's (1992) review of studies found, on the positive side, that those who had had training in ethics usually attained significantly higher scores than those who did not; on the negative side, nearly half of the students who had had training were still unable to make appropriate applications of psychology's ethical standards. The research data related to Rest's third and fourth principles, related to deciding what one intends to do and strategies for implementing appropriate actions, indicate the need for more examination of how psychologists can be helped, both in training and by professional colleagues, in their implementation of ethical standards. Throughout the 1980s there was increasing evidence that students of psychology—and professional psychologists as well—were sometimes unwilling to carry out what they knew were appropriate actions for given ethical violations. Now researchers are beginning to look at what the reasons are for these cases of noncompliance by psychologists; for example, the fact that "evidence" of many violations is ambiguous, an unwillingness to get involved in "messy" situations with colleagues, fear of legal ramifications, and so forth. How can psychologists be helped to address such difficult, uncomfortable, anxiety-producing situations so that as much attention is devoted to implementation as to understanding? What are the critical professional socialization experiences that need to occur to improve the ethical functioning of *all* professional psychologists? These are the challenges we need to face together as professionals, faculty, and students so that we can be proud of how the profession of psychology serves the public.

ETHICAL STANDARDS, WITH ILLUSTRATIONS OF UNETHICAL BEHAVIORS

Every psychologist is expected to be fully acquainted with, and willing to comply with, the APA's *Ethical Principles of Psychologists and Code of Conduct* (1992). These standards may be applied to both psychologists and *students* of psychology by state psychology boards, courts, and other public bodies. (One complimentary copy of the APA's *Ethical Principles of Psychologists and Code of Conduct* may be requested by each reader by writing to the American Psychological Association, 750 First Street, NE., Washington, DC 20002. Specific information on how states and provinces use such standards, monitor compliance, and adjudicate violations may be found in Bass, DeMers, Ogloff et al., [1996].) In this section, each of the eight parts (see numbers 1–8 in sections below) of the APA's ethical standards will be illustrated by one or more examples of a violation. After stating the violation, an abbreviated quotation from the most applicable standard will be provided as well as pertinent commentary. (The three-digit number by the cited standard is the reference number in the 1992 APA Code of Conduct; some of the violations provided could be cited as violations of several standards; however, in order to keep the discussion of each violation concisely focused, only one key standard is presented with each of the violations.)

We have deliberately avoided choosing the most highly sensationalized and publicized violations such as predatory sexual relationships and fraudulent billing (e.g., a psychologist billing an insurance company for a greater number and/or length of sessions than was provided to an insured client); rather, we have chosen examples that reflect the ethical problems typically created by impulsive and unthinking (or at least poorly thought through) actions by psychologists, the far more prevalent source of ethical violations (Packard, 1997). Since only a few of the 102 standards can be explored in this chapter, readers are encouraged to become acquainted with numerous other examples of ethical violations and dilemmas found in publications such as those by Pope and Vetter (1992) and Koocher and Keith-Spiegel (1998). An acquaintance with a broad range of such examples is critical to increasing one's sensitivity to the presence of ethical situations, a sensitivity that, as reviewed in the preceding section, is embarrassingly low among graduate students in psychology training programs.

1. General Standards

Violation: Psychologist A is asked by the chief executive officer (CEO) of the company that employs him to provide psychological evaluations of several candidates being considered for promotion to a vice-presidency. The CEO indicates that the only persons he wants evaluated, from among all those nominated, are the men, since he will not consider any females as vice-presidential candidates. Psychologist A agrees to conduct the psychological evaluations only on the men.

> **1.10.** *Nondiscrimination:* In their work-related activities, psychologists do not engage in unfair discrimination based on age, gender, race, ethnicity, national origin, religion, sexual orientation, disability, socioeconomic status, or any basis proscribed by law (APA, 1992, p. 1601).

Psychologist A, by agreeing to test only the male nominees, colluded in discriminatory actions against women, even though there are a number of alternatives, within both the ethical obligations and legal rights of the psychologist, which the psychologist could have chosen rather than collude with the CEO's discriminatory action.

Violation: Psychologist B accepts and begins working in a position at a mental health clinic where many of her clientele are children from a Native American community. Psychologist B has had no prior experience or training in working with Native Americans or with children.

> **1.08.** *Human Differences:* Where differences of age, gender, race, ethnicity, national origin, religion, sexual orientation, disability, language, or socioeconomic status significantly affect psychologists' work concerning particular individuals or groups, psychologists obtain the training, experience, consultation, or supervision necessary to ensure the competence of their service, or they make appropriate referrals (APA, 1992, p. 1601).

Psychologist B could have ethically accepted this position if she arranged to seek supervision of her work until she had completed appropriate training.

Violation: Psychology professor C, well known for her research and practice with victims of sexual abuse, is asked by one of her advisees to become her primary internship supervisor as well. The intern will be working on her dissertation during the internship. Professor C agrees to serve as both advisor and supervisor.

> **1.17.** *Multiple Relationships:* (a) . . . A psychologist refrains from entering into or promising another personal, scientific, professional, financial, or other relationship with such persons if it appears likely that such a relationship reasonably might impair the psychologist's objectivity or otherwise interfere with the psychologist's effectively performing his or her functions as a psychologist, or might harm or exploit the other party. (b) Likewise, whenever feasible, a psychologist refrains from taking on professional or scientific obligations when preexisting relationships would create a risk of such harm (APA, 1992, p. 1601).

While there is apparent logic in the intern wanting supervision from an established expert in her area of both research and practice, such dual roles are fraught with dangers to the objective performances of both the professor and the intern and, perhaps more important, to the quality of their working relationship. Since the psychologist would need to be in an evaluative role in two very different contexts—that is, evaluating the dissertation, evaluating the intern's performance—there could well be conflicts that would arise in one area that would then "spill over" into evaluation or performance in the other area. Slimp and Burian (1994) identify the many often regrettable consequences of the prevalence of multiple role relationships that occur in internships. While there may be cases where specialized expertise, and/or rural locations make such dual relationships almost unavoidable, such relationships should be entered into only after the superiors of both parties in the relationship (e.g., director of internship, chair of psychology department) have all been informed of, and given their consent to, the establishment of a dual relationship.

Violation: Psychologist D, who was in the midst of litigation regarding divorcing his wife of 12 years and custody of their four children, began canceling nearly 40% of his scheduled appointments week after week, saying some unexpected developments precluded him from coming to the office. Some clients whom he did see were overheard telling other clients that Psychologist D seemed very preoccupied and had fallen asleep during some of their recent sessions.

> **1.13.** *Personal Problems and Conflicts:* (b) . . . psychologists have an obligation to be alert to signs of, and to obtain assistance for, their personal problems at an

early stage, in order to prevent significantly impaired performance (APA, 1992, p. 1601).

Psychologists are persons too! They do at times encounter difficulties in their personal lives and/or become overburdened with their workloads. Sherman and Thelen (1998) are among the most recent to document "Distress and professional impairment among psychologists in clinical practice." Fortunately, in the past few years there has been an increase in the number of research articles and continuing education programs that focus on ways to prevent and ameliorate some of the stresses inherent in our professional roles as psychologists (Coster & Schwebel, 1997; Kramen-Kahn & Hansen, 1998; Mahoney, 1997), focusing on the rewards our work bring as well as the stresses. Sherman and Thelen (1998) recommend that training programs "should be proactive in preparing trainees for coping effectively with distress and impairment" (p. 84).

2. Evaluation, Assessment, or Intervention

Violation: Psychology Professor E, who teaches career development at a community college with 60% minority students, 30% of whom have English as a second language, offers them the opportunity to come in and use his personal computer to take a computer-assisted academic aptitude test developed for and normed with traditional university students. The students receive a sheet interpreting their results which, the professor tells them, can be of use in helping them decide whether or not they have the ability for education beyond the community college level. They do not have any further contact with Professor E to discuss the results.

> **2.04.** *Use of Assessment in General and With Special Populations:* (c) Psychologists attempt to identify situations in which particular interventions or assessment techniques or norms may not be applicable or may require adjustment in administration or interpretation because of factors such as individuals' gender, age, race, ethnicity, national origin, religion, sexual orientation, disability, language, or socioeconomic status (APA, 1992, p. 1603).

Psychologist E not only used an assessment instrument that was developed and normed on a population that differed radically from the one he was teaching, he also did not meet with the students to discuss how their results might well have been affected by their ethnic and language background. These results were at best of dubious value regarding any assessment of the students' potential for continuing college-level education.

3. Advertising and Other Public Statements

Violation: A popular radio announcer tells Psychologist F how impressed she is with the progress her son has made in the program the psychologist developed for children with mild learning disabilities. Psychologist F tells her that he would be glad to waive any fees for her son's further participation if she would talk about the "good results" from his program on some of her radio programs.

3.05. *Testimonials:* Psychologists do not solicit testimonials from current psychotherapy clients or patients or other persons who because of their particular circumstances are vulnerable to undue influence (APA, 1992, p. 1604).

If Psychologist F wanted some publicity for his program, he should have followed the usual procedures for purchasing advertising time on the radio. It would not have been inappropriate for Psychologist F to ask the radio announcer how best to arrange for such a purchase but any further involvement of the announcer would be inappropriate in accordance with standards regarding both multiple relationships and advertising.

4. Therapy

Violation: Psychologist G is asked by the president of the company that employs him to provide employee Jones with some counseling to "get him out of his plateau." Psychologist G invites employee Jones to have coffee with him in his office and subsequently continues to invite him in for "coffee" during which time the psychologist shapes the sessions into ever more personal counseling sessions.

4.01. *Structuring the Relationship:* (a) Psychologists discuss with clients or patients as early as is feasible in the therapeutic relationship appropriate issues, such as the nature and anticipated course of therapy, fees, and confidentiality (APA, 1992, p. 1605).

By Psychologist G not making clear to employee Jones that he had been requested to be of assistance to him, he was actually deceiving Jones regarding his (the psychologist's) intent when inviting him for coffee. Such deception would almost inevitably lead to an eventual betrayal of trust with damaging implications for the client, the psychologist, and the profession of psychology.

Violation: Psychologist H has a home page with information on treatment for sexual dysfunction, an area in which he has appropriate training and supervised experience; he provides an option for respondents to e-mail questions. Psychologist H then responds to the questions with what he believes are appropriate responses.

4.02. *Informed Consent to Therapy:* (a) Psychologists obtain appropriate informed consent to therapy or related procedures, using language that is reasonably understandable to participants. The content of informed consent will vary depending on many circumstances; however, informed consent generally implies that the person (i) has the capacity to consent, (ii) has been informed of significant information concerning the procedure, (iii) has freely and without undue influence expressed consent, and (iv) consent has been appropriately documented (APA, 1992, p. 1605).

Kulynych & Stromberg (1998) provide an excellent description of emerging legal and ethical concerns related to the use of telecommunication in psychological practice. Regarding informed consent, they note ". . . in cyberspace, anonymity often is the norm, and a psychologist may be prevented from verifying the age, affect, demeanor and possibly the legal capacity of the patient" (p. 15). Minor children could well be accessing the psychologist's home page and submitting e-mail questions. At this point in time, legal experts advise limiting telecommunications to existing online information only, and not to provide individualized advice in response to personal inquiries since there is no adequate way to determine that a responsible adult has provided informed consent for therapeutic procedures.

5. Privacy and Confidentiality

Violation: Psychologist I shows the counseling center receptionist the results of an IQ test he has recently given to one of his clients, noting that the client obtained the highest IQ score he had ever seen.

> 5.03. *Minimizing Intrusion on Privacy:* (b) Psychologists discuss confidential information obtained in clinical or consulting relationships, or evaluative data concerning patients, individual or organizational clients, students, research participants, supervisees, and employees, only for appropriate scientific or professional purposes and only with persons clearly concerned with such matters (APA, 1992, p. 1606).

Though the psychologist might have thought he was not sharing anything damaging, but rather something quite complimentary, any information obtained in professional relationships is to be treated confidentially. Sharing such information, with identity of the client not concealed, is always limited to those with a "need to know" even if it is complimentary, humorous, or particularly instructive.

Violation: Psychologist J was asked by an accounting firm president to provide substance abuse counseling to one of the firm's junior executives. After 3 months of treatment have been completed, the firm president requests treatment records before he will make payment for the psychologist's services. Psychologist J refuses to provide the records but does provide a progress report prepared in consultation with the client. The president finds this unacceptable and has the firm's attorney issue a subpoena for the records; Psychologist J then submits the record to the firm's president.

> 5.05. *Disclosures:* (a) Psychologists disclose confidential information without the consent of the individual only as mandated by law, or where permitted by law for a valid purpose, such as (i) to provide needed professional services to the patient or the individual or organizational client, (ii) to obtain appropriate professional consultations, (iii) to protect the patient or client or others from harm, or (iv) to obtain payment for services, in which instance disclosure is limited to the minimum that is necessary to achieve the purpose (APA, 1992, p. 1606).

Why was Psychologist's J action an ethical violation when a subpoena had been issued? This example provides the opportunity to make two vital distinctions: one, there is a difference between a court order and a subpoena; any lawyer may request a subpoena (Stromberg, 1993); two, privilege belongs to the patient, not to the psychologist; therefore, even in response to a subpoena the psychologist needs to consult the client (and possibly the client's attorney) before responding to the subpoena. Even though the president of the firm believed he was entitled to the records since he was paying for the therapy, he could not really justifiably request more than evidence that treatment was necessary and being provided. Additional communications between the therapist and the client remain privileged communications (Knapp & VandeCreek, 1997).

6. Teaching, Training Supervision, Research, and Publishing

Violation: Psychologist K invites students to take part in an experiment she describes as an investigation of various modes of group discussion. Once students have begun participating in the experiment, in some of the groups they are urged by group leaders to reveal their most pressing personal problem; those participants who are reluctant to do so are assured "we're all friends here who want to help one another."

> **6.15.** *Deception in Research:* . . . (b) Psychologists never deceive research participants about significant aspects that would affect their willingness to participate, such as physical risks, discomfort, or unpleasant emotional experiences (APA, 1992, p. 1609).

Psychologist K neither fully informed students nor took safeguards to protect their welfare when they were essentially manipulated into revealing personal problems to others in their groups. There are only a very limited number of circumstances, as outlined in sections (a) and (c) of Standard 6.15, in which deception is permitted in research.

Violation: Psychologist L asks a graduate student to work with him on developing a research project, then has the graduate student collect the data, run the analyses, and prepare a report of the results. When Psychologist L prepares a manuscript for publication based on the research report, he lists himself as sole author and acknowledges the contribution of the graduate student only in a footnote.

> **6.23.** *Publication Credit:* (b) Principle authorship and other publication credits accurately reflect the relative scientific or professional contribution of the individuals involved, regardless of their relative status (APA, 1992, p. 1609).

The involvement of the graduate student in almost all phases of the research, as well as the primary responsibility for data collection, analyses, and reporting, merits at least co-authorship credit, possibly even primary authorship. Psychologist L should have made clear from the outset of their working relationship how the work of the graduate student would be recognized and that the level of this recognition would be relative to the student's contributions to the research.

7. Forensic Activities

Violation: At the request of the attorney for complainants, Psychologist M completes an extensive battery of psychological tests on three participants in an age discrimination lawsuit. Only a few of the test results show any significant evidence of adjustment problems; most results fall within the normal range. The attorney requests that reports be prepared limiting the information to those tests that yielded evidence of adjustment problems. Psychologist M prepares the reports in accordance with the attorney's request.

> 7.04. *Truthfulness and Candor:* (a) In forensic testimony and reports, psychologists testify truthfully, honestly, and candidly and, consistent with applicable legal procedures, describe fairly the bases for their testimony and conclusions (APA, 1992, p. 1610).

Requests from attorneys to provide only the information most supportive of their case is typical, rather than exceptional. Standard 7.04 had to be added to the standards particularly because of this practice. Psychologists must often educate attorneys about the limits to the reliability and validity of assessment procedures and our obligations for full, candid, and truthful disclosure, before the attorneys decide whether and how they want psychologists involved with their cases.

8. Resolving Ethical Issues

Violation: Psychologist N becomes aware that a colleague, Psychologist Z, frequently invites his clients to go out to dinner with him and, on several occasions, has invited them to go on weekend trips with him. Psychologist N speaks with Psychologist Z and indicates concern about Z's violation of the standard (1.17) regarding multiple relationships. Z argues that taking these clients out is part of the treatment they need for learning how to develop effective friendships. Subsequently, Psychologist N hears from several different sources that Z engages in sexual relationships with some of these clients. Psychologist N takes no further action after the initial expression of concern to Z.

> 8.05. *Reporting Ethical Violations:* If an apparent ethical violation is not appropriate for informal resolution under Standard 8.04 or is not resolved properly in that fashion, psychologists take further action appropriate to the situation, unless such action conflicts with confidentiality rights in ways that cannot be resolved. Such action might include referral to state or national committees on professional ethics or to state licensing boards (APA, 1992, p. 1611).

As noted earlier in this chapter, psychologists are often reluctant to take the step of reporting violations to ethics committees or licensing boards even though they know an ethical violation has been committed. Like Psychologist N, they more willingly attempt an informal resolution, but when that fails, they hesitate to take on the next step because of its potential for long-lasting complications in working relationships and possible legal ramifications. Yet, it must be clearly noted, such in-action is derived from self-protection, rather than protection of the welfare of clients of psychologists. Therefore, *not* reporting a known ethical violation is actually an ethical violation in itself and can result in censure or more severe penalties if the psychologist who failed to report the violation does not cooperate with licensing boards' and/or ethics committees' inquiries about a colleague's unethical behavior.

ETHICAL DILEMMAS

We use the term "ethical dilemmas" to describe those situations in which taking any action or even taking no action is going to violate at least one or more ethical princi-ples. In this section we explore the kinds of ethical dilemmas that are all too often en-countered in the everyday practice of psychology (see Sharkin [1995] for a very useful description and analysis of ethical dilemmas that frequently occur in university coun-seling services). We then explore the most useful approaches to analyzing, and then taking action, in these difficult situations. Consider the following situations.

A. A client tells the counselor that he wants to commit suicide, and has a plan to do it, but does not want the counselor to tell anyone. The client has thought about it carefully and has decided that this is his "best" choice. He refuses all the counselor's attempts to have him consider alternatives. Sensing the counselor's concern and sus-pecting that she might commit him, he threatens to sue for breach of confidentiality if she tells anyone about his plans. (This scenario assumes that the counselor and the client have not previously discussed limits to confidentiality.)

B. The only female counselor in a rural county's mental health center has a list of eight persons who have been waiting up to 3 months for counseling. A new client comes to the clinic in a highly agitated state of depression and insists on seeing a fe-male counselor because "no men are to be trusted." The female counselor suspects that if this client is not treated promptly, she is at risk for either a psychotic break-down or possibly suicide. Yet if the counselor begins seeing her at this time, she would be making other clients, who were referred earlier though are less disturbed, wait several more weeks or months. There are no practical referral resources avail-able because the next nearest female counselor is 125 miles away.

C. "The counseling psychologist concerned with the increase in cases of bulimia re-ported in university counseling centers decides to compare the effects of a cognitive–behavioral intervention with a pharmacological treatment in a controlled study. He considers using a wait-list control group and a placebo group but is aware that the use of the placebo group will involve deceiving subjects and the use of a wait-list group will involve refusing some individuals treatment for several months" (Kitchener, 1984, p. 43).

In both counseling and research settings, counseling psychologists often find them-selves between a rock and a hard place. Although such situations typically get far less media attention than ethical violations such as dual relationships, misrepresentation of credentials, and inappropriate public statements, it is the dilemmas, rather than the violations, that help us most clearly understand the limitations of ethical codes in solving ethical problems.

Kitchener (1984, 2000) has usefully articulated the relationship of existing ethical standards to "principle ethics" when faced with these dilemmas. In her "decision tree," a psychologist would first ask whether the current APA ethical standards indicate how one should proceed. For most of the dilemmas, like those cited above, two or more conflicting courses of action would be recommended. How can we simultaneously respect a client's wishes if that means allowing a client to harm himself or herself or others? When confronted with such dilemmas, Kitchener (1984, 2000) provides for counseling psychologists a very useful explication of principle ethics. She describes not only how principle ethics underlie the development of APA ethical standards, but also, the necessity to return to these fundamental principles to determine how to proceed when ethical dilemmas present themselves. By understanding these basic principles, psychologists gain a better understanding of what ethical values are in conflict and can therefore make a more informed choice about what and why any one given ethical standard may have to be violated. Kitchener's (1984) description of five basic principles, drawn from earlier versions of the work of Beauchamp and Childress (1994), remains the most concise presentation of a set of principles highly pertinent for psychologists and is therefore presented here. Extensive material on the definition, origins and usefulness of each of these principles may be found in Kitchener's most recent book (Kitchener, 2000).

> Autonomy . . . includes the right to act as an autonomous agent, to make one's own decision, to develop one's own values . . . [and] includes respecting the rights of others to make autonomous choices, even when we believe they are mistaken, as long as their choices do not infringe on the rights of others. . . .
>
> Nonmaleficence . . . not causing harm to others, includes both not inflicting intentional harm nor engaging in actions which risk harming others. . . . seeing nonmaleficence as fundamental suggests that if we must choose between harming someone and benefiting that person, another, or society, our stronger obligation, other things being equal, would be to avoid harm. . . .
>
> Beneficence . . . doing good to others is critical to ethical issues in psychology and especially counseling psychology. . . . the term "helping profession" underlines this obligation. . . .
>
> Justice . . . in order to live together with minimal strife, people must develop rules and procedures for adjudicating claims and services in a fair manner. . . . considerations of equal need are particularly relevant to the issue of how to distribute scarce psychological services. . . .
>
> Fidelity . . . involves questions of "faithfulness," promise-keeping, and loyalty. Issues of fidelity arise when individuals enter into some kind of a voluntary relationship (e.g., counselor–client, husband–wife, supervisor–supervisee) . . . [T]he issue of fidelity seems especially critical in psychology because issues like truthfulness and loyalty are basic to trust . . . it is particularly vital to client–counselor, research–participant, supervisor–supervisee, and/or consultant–consultee relationships. All are dependent on honest communication and the assumption that the contract on which the relationship was initiated, obliges both parties to fulfill certain functions (Kitchener, 1984, pp. 46–51).

The example of the suicidal client at the beginning of this section represents a conflict between the principles of autonomy and beneficence. If interventions are made to protect him from harming himself, his dignity and worth as an autonomous person have been "violated" since his wishes to act in accordance with his own plan are not being honored by the psychologist. On the other hand, if no effort is made to intervene, then there is great risk that the welfare of the client will not be protected, assuming "protecting the welfare" means keeping him from suicide. As Beauchamp and Childress (1994) note, in our society principles of beneficence usually outweigh those of autonomy in these dilemmas, the justification for this being that clients are being protected from harms that would result from their illness, immaturity, or psychological incapacitation rather than a fully rational, mature judgment.

In the example concerning the highly agitated depressed woman, a conflict between the principles of justice and nonmaleficence is illustrated. Since the principle of justice is based on the presumption that all people are equally deserving, one could argue that treatment of them should be on a "first come, first served" basis. However, in this particular case, not to provide treatment to the agitated client seems to contribute to potential harm to the client, that is, to maleficence.

Ideally, in a just society, there would be adequate resources for all individuals. However, such availability of resources is all too rare, especially in rural settings, and this kind of dilemma is an almost daily occurrence. University counseling centers oftentimes find themselves in similar situations near the end of semester when huge waiting lists may develop since there are far more clients wanting services than the staff can provide. At such times, many agencies develop some policies that recognize that some needs are greater than others; distribution of services then is based on this differential assessment of needs, thereby redefining the basis of justice.

In the third example, concerning research on bulimia, the conflict is between the principle of nonmaleficence (do no harm by eliminating the waiting list and so avoid refusing some individuals treatment for several months) with the principle of beneficence (the research potentially could make significant contributions to determining the most effective treatment for bulimia). Making decisions about research projects, as well as whether to use any given treatment when there is little or no research to support its benefits, has to include, in the reasoning process, a careful consideration of whether or not the potential benefits of the research project outweigh the "costs" suffered by those treated with placebos or not treated at all (if on a waiting list).

These examples are just a few of the many illustrations that could be offered in how to use principle ethics when confronted with an ethical dilemma. Which principles can be honored and which one(s) must be "violated"? Such an analysis is critical in accomplishing the third step in Rest's (1984) model of moral behavior; that is, selecting, from among competing values, the one to act on. In the final section of this chapter we will return to the fourth step of Rest's model: that of executing and implementing what one intends to do.

Ethical Dilemmas Created by Laws

The passage of several laws in the past two decades has added to the complexity and urgency of several types of ethical dilemmas. Many states now have laws regarding "duty to warn or protect"; that is, if a client discusses in therapy the intent to cause harm to another person through actions such as assault or infection with AIDS, the psychologist must take appropriate action to protect the intended victim. "Duty to report" laws require, for example, that when a psychologist has any first-hand knowledge of child abuse, such abuse must be reported to appropriate social service authorities. Thus, in one sense, the laws create ethical dilemmas since, if the psychologist fulfills legal obligations, client confidentiality will be breached. However, in another sense, while the laws create a perceived dilemma, they prescribe exactly what must be done. The laws are clear that confidentiality must give way to protection, autonomy must be sacrificed for beneficence. Since the nature of laws regarding duty to warn and duty to report vary greatly from state to state, psychologists need to become fully cognizant with these kinds of laws in any states in which they practice. Failure of the psychologist to act expeditiously when confronted with these situations can lead to the imposition of criminal penalties on the *psychologist* or becoming a defendant in a civil suit, or wrongful death. Detailed descriptions of the origins and development of each of these types of laws, and cogent legal advice for all psychologists, are provided by Stromberg, Schneider, and Joondept (1993) regarding duty to warn, and by Stromberg (1993) regarding duty to report.

Ethical Dilemmas Created by Personal Values

Some ethical dilemmas occur primarily because each of us has our own set of personal values, some of which may conflict with those of our clients. Each of us had an upbringing that provided us with cultural norms, some derived from ethnic backgrounds, some from religious backgrounds. These values affect not only personal views about how we should manage our own lives with respect to such issues as what constitutes masculinity, femininity, sexual relationships, appropriate roles within a marriage, and the like, but also the range of options we can comfortably consider with our clients. During the first half of the twentieth century, proponents of both traditional Freudian analytic and Rogerian client-centered perspectives argued that therapy and counseling needed to be value-free. After years of struggle to keep therapy neutral, there was a growing consensus, best captured by Corey, Corey, and Callanan (1979):

> Since we believe that counselors' values do inevitably affect the therapeutic process, we also think it's important for counselors to be willing to express their values openly when they are relevant to the questions that come up in their sessions with clients (p. 85).

Can one be an effective therapist for a client who wishes to have an abortion if the therapist believes that abortion is always wrong? Can one be an effective therapist for a gay client who wishes to pursue an interracial adoption when the therapist believes children should not be raised by gay parents and/or only by parents of their own race? The issue is clearly not whether it is acceptable for psychologists to have such personal views—the introduction to the APA Ethics Code (APA, 1992) clearly states "This Ethics Code applies only to psychologists' work-related activities"

(p. 1598). Thus the issue is how to be sure that our personal values do not interfere with the welfare of our clients. The first challenge for us is to be fully conscious of the values we hold—a greater challenge than many of us realize until we have been confronted with how we have many implicit values that conflict with the values of, for example, those of persons from other cultures, religions, and worldviews (see Chapter 6). The second challenge is the one noted above by Corey and colleagues (1979): a willingness to express these values openly with our client and explore together how they affect the therapeutic relationship and the options for the client to consider, including the option of working with another therapist who may feel more comfortable and effective in aiding the client explore all available options.

IMPLEMENTING ETHICAL DECISIONS

Recall that Rest's (1984) fourth component of moral behavior is the execution and implementation of what one decides is the ethical course of action. In the late 1980s and early 1990s, there was increasing evidence that large numbers of psychologists would not actually implement what they knew to be appropriate ethical actions. Bernard, Murphy, and Little (1987) were among the first to document that nearly half of all practicing psychologists surveyed would not do what they thought they should do. ". . . it is easier (i.e., more expedient) not to report the inappropriate professional behavior of another, thus avoiding possible confrontation and time away from one's practice" (Smith, McGuire, Abbott, & Blau, 1991). These last authors were among the first to study which factors influenced ethical compliance. One of their key findings was that compliance was far more likely when laws as well as ethical standards applied to the situation, for example, cases of sex with clients, child abuse reporting, insurance fraud. Other research is under way to determine possible demographic, training, and personality traits, as well as competing concerns, that affect psychologists' willingness to comply with ethical standards.

The finding of Smith and colleagues (1991) regarding greater compliance when laws are involved has the disadvantage of increasing the pressure on legislatures to develop even more laws, rather than having the profession be a self-regulating one. Having an increased number of professional behaviors subject to laws also leads to greater distrust of the profession of psychology as well as to increased legal and malpractice costs for all psychologists. Clearly it would be desirable to have more voluntary compliance with existing standards so additional laws do not become necessary.

Psychology as a profession has seemed somewhat reluctant to directly confront the evidence on its members' lack of compliance, especially regarding the failure of psychologists to report unethical behavior on the part of other psychologists. As described in our section on standards and illustrations of ethical violations (see case of Psychologist N), a psychologist not reporting an ethical violation that he or she has observed is an ethical violation in itself, yet there are very few instances where psychologists have been formally charged and reprimanded for lack of reporting others' ethical violations. It is worth noting, somewhat regretfully, that the commentary on the APA Ethics Code provided by Canter, Bennett, Jones, and Nagy

(1994), which includes a chapter on "Learning the Process of Ethical Decision Making," does not include, in its seven steps, issues in the implementation of appropriate ethical decisions. All psychologists would do well to review the research on "bystander intervention" (Darley & Latane, 1968) and understand that feeling the weight of responsibility to respond is a concept that is as applicable to ethical situations as it is in "need for help" situations.

What does it require to be an ethical psychologist? Knowledge such as we have covered in this chapter has proved necessary but not quite sufficient for the highest levels of public perception as a fully trustworthy, self-monitoring profession. In the coming years we will do well to focus more research on how to ensure that the profession will be perceived as a highly trustworthy one by the public. From the various writers cited in this chapter we will certainly want to look at selection procedures, predoctoral training—including supervised experience in identifying and responding to ethical dilemmas—continuing education for resolving new types of ethical dilemmas that emerge, and how to provide more "user friendly" collegially supported professional socialization and monitoring for each other.

SUMMARY

As professionals serving persons in troubled and turbulent situations, counseling psychologists need to keep ethical considerations at the highest level of awareness. Psychologists, along with philosophers and biomedical ethicists, have an ongoing discourse about how best to ensure that the public is well served by our professions. There is healthy debate about the roles of character (virtues) and training in how to achieve our goals of being a more fully trusted profession by the public. There needs to be continued research on the development of more effective training programs to improve psychologists' identification of ethical situations and then choosing and implementing appropriate actions.

In providing 14 illustrations of the eight major sections of the current APA ethical standards, our purpose was to sensitize readers to the frequent ethical implications of many professional behaviors. Many ethical violations result from behaviors that are carried out with good intentions. Violations often result simply from psychologists not giving full consideration to the ethical implications of their behaviors.

Ethical dilemmas are situations that are not easily responded to using only the APA ethical standards. These dilemmas occur in situations in which honoring one ethical standard unavoidably results in violation of one or more other principles. For example, a counselor's wanting to maintain confidentiality about a client's communications in counseling sessions about a wish to kill someone, might lead to significant bodily harm to another person. Psychologists' understanding and use of principle ethics, as well as applicable laws and personal values, is the primary way to deal with these dilemmas. Finally, the implementation of, and compliance with, ethical standards often requires that psychologists recognize the weight of responsibility, even though that responsibility may bring stress to oneself and collegial relationships.

REFERENCES

American Psychological Association (APA). (1992). Ethical principles of psychologists. *American Psychologist, 47,* 1597–1613.

Bass, L. J., DeMers, S. T., Ogloff, J. R. P., Peterson, C., Pettifor, J. L., Reaves, R. P., Retfalvi, T., Simon, N. P., Sinclair, C., & Tipton, R. M. (1996). *Professional conduct and discipline in psychology.* Washington, DC: American Psychological Association.

Beauchamp, T. L., & Childress, J. F. (1994). *Principles of biomedical ethics* (4th ed.). New York: Oxford University Press.

Bernard, J. L., Murphy, M., & Little, M. (1987). The failure of clinical psychologists to apply understood ethical principles. *Professional Psychology: Research and Practice, 18,* 489–491.

Biggs, P., & Blocher, D. (1987). Foundations of ethical counseling. New York: Springer.

Canter, M. B., Bennett, B. E., Jones, S. E., & Nagy, T. F. (1994). *Ethics for psychologists.* Washington, DC: American Psychological Association.

Corey, G., Corey, M. S., & Callanan, P. (1979). *Professional and ethical issues in counseling and psychotherapy.* Monterey, CA: Brooks/Cole.

Coster, J. S., & Schwebel, M. (1997). Well-functioning in professional psychologists. *Professional Psychology: Research and Practice, 28,* 5–13.

Darley, J. M., & Latane, B. (1968). Bystander intervention in emergencies: Diffusion of responsibility. *Journal of Personality and Social Psychology, 8,* 377–388.

Ibrahim, F. Z. (1996). A multicultural perspective on principle and virtue ethics. *The Counseling Psychologist, 24,* 78–85.

Jordan, A. C., & Meara, N. M. (1990). Ethics and the professional practice of psychologists: The role of virtues and principles. *Professional Psychology: Research and Practice, 21,* 107–114.

Kitchener, K. S. (1984). Intuition, critical evaluation and ethical principles. *The Counseling Psychologist, 12*(3), 43–55.

Kitchener, K. S. (2000). *Foundations of ethical practice, research and teaching in psychology.* Mahwah, NJ: Lawrence Erlbaum.

Knapp, S., & VandeCreek, L. (1997). Jaffee V. Redmond: The supreme court recognizes a psychotherapist–patient privilege in federal courts. *Professional Psychology: Research and Practice, 28,* 567–572.

Koocher, G. P., & Keith-Spiegel, P. (1998). *Ethics in psychology* (2nd ed.). New York: Oxford University Press.

Kramen-Kahn, B., & Hansen, N. D. (1998). Rafting the rapids: Occupational hazards, rewards, and coping strategies of psychotherapists. *Professional Psychology: Research and Practice, 29,* 130–134.

Kulynych, J. J., & Stromberg, C. (1998). Telecommunication in Psychological Practice (Legal Update #11). *National Register Report, 24,* 9–18.

Mahoney, M. J. (1997). Psychotherapists' personal problems and self-care patterns. *Professional Psychology: Research and Practice, 28,* 14–16.

Meara, N. M., Schmidt, L. D., & Day, J. D. (1996). Principles and virtues: A foundation for ethical decisions, policies, and character. *The Counseling Psychologist, 24,* 4–77.

Packard, T. (1997, August). *An interactive model for ethical decision making.* APA convention, Chicago.

Payton, C. R. (1994). Implications of the 1992 ethics code for diverse groups. *Professional Psychology: Research and Practice, 25,* 317–320.

Pope, K. S., & Vetter, V. A. (1992). Ethical dilemmas encountered by members of the American Psychological Association. *American Psychologist, 47,* 397–411.

Prilleltensky, I. (1997). Values, assumptions, and practices. *American Psychologist, 52,* 517–535.

Rest, J. R. (1984). Research in moral development: Implications for training counseling psychologists. *The Counseling Psychologist, 12*(3), 19–29.

Sharkin, B. S. (1995). Strains on confidentiality in college-student psychotherapy: Entangled therapeutic relationships, incidental encounters, and third-party inquiries. *Professional Psychology: Research and Practice, 26,* 184–189.

Sherman, M. D., & Thelen, M. H. (1998). Distress and professional impairment among psychologists in clinical practice. *Professional Psychology: Research and Practice, 29,* 79–85.

Slimp, P. A. O., & Burian, B. K. (1994). Multiple role relationships during internship: Consequences and recommendations. *Professional Psychology: Research and Practice, 25,* 39–45.

Smith, T. S., McGuire, J. M., Abbott, D. W., & Blau, B. I. (1991). Clinical ethical decision making: An investigation of the rationales used to justify doing less than one believes one should. *Professional Psychology: Research and Practice, 22,* 235–239.

Stromberg, C. (1993). *Privacy, confidentiality and privilege.* (The Psychologist's Legal Update Number 1). Washington, DC: National Register of Health Service Providers in Psychology.

Stromberg, C., Schneider, J., & Joondept, B. (1993). *Dealing with potentially dangerous patients.* (The Psychologist's Legal Update Number 2). Washington, DC: National Register of Health Service Providers in Psychology.

Welfel, E. R. (1992). Psychologist as ethics educator: Successes, failures, and unanswered questions. *Professional Psychology: Research and Practice, 23,* 182–189.

Welfel, E. R., & Lipsitz, N. E. (1984). The ethical behavior of professional psychologists: A critical analysis of the research. *The Counseling Psychologist, 12*(3), 31–42.

Wilson, L. S., & Ranft, V. A. (1993). The state of ethical training for counseling psychology doctoral students. *The Counseling Psychologist, 21,* 445–456.

CHAPTER 6

COMPETENT COUNSELING IN A CULTURALLY DIVERSE SOCIETY

Enhancing Intervention Strategies for Culturally Diverse Clients

Ethnic Similarity of Counselors and Clients

Counselor Knowledge of Ethnic Cultures

Modifying Conventional Forms of Treatment

Interactions of Counselor and Client Culture Statuses

"Return" of the Scientist–Practitioner

Summary

References

Numerous researchers agree that the single most important reason both for the underutilization of mental health services by ethnic minority clients and for the high dropout rates are [sic] the inability of psychotherapists and counselors to provide culturally sensitive/responsive therapy for the ethnic minority client (Essandoh, 1996, p. 131).

Preparing Anglos for the Challenges and Joys of Multiculturalism (Kiselica, 1998, p. 5).

I submit that political correctness, guilt, and paternalistic attitudes are self-serving and less appropriate motivators for developing a philosophical basis for multicultural training, whereas humanitarianism, changing demographics, interest in diversity, and welfare of society are altruistic and more appropriate motivators. . . . inappropriate motivations may lead to inappropriate learning objectives and possibly even inappropriate instructional strategies (Atkinson, 1994, p. 301).

In the 1990s there was an explosion of literature in counseling psychology on the development of strategies for providing competent counseling to the increasingly diverse clientele we encounter in our society. As the quotations at the beginning of this chapter indicate, passionate, yet healthy, dialogues have developed regarding both the individual and collective responsibilities of all mental health professionals. This chapter focuses on the many ways in which counseling psychologists are developing the conceptual and empirical bases for effective strategies to respond to the long unmet needs of countless individuals in our society who have (and indeed still often do) experienced discrimination and oppression based on physical characteristics (e.g., race, disability) and/or lifestyle (e.g., sexual orientation, religious beliefs). The extensive work of counseling psychologists in this domain has earned the profession recognition by other specialties in psychology as a national leader in the development of effective standards and strategies for multicultural counseling.

The first section, of the six sections in this chapter, provides a brief overview of the immense changes in the meanings and importance of cultural diversity in recent decades compared to the first 40 years in professional psychology. The factors that underlie those changes are also the basis for the new standards and models for training and practice that are explored in the remainder of this chapter. The new developments have not come without controversies; the second section of the chapter explores ongoing controversies about the appropriate scope of definitions for terms such as multicultural, cultural diversity, race, ethnicity, and minority.

The third through fifth sections of this chapter provide an overview of the conceptual and empirical developments in the three major areas of multicultural training of counseling psychologists: counselor self-understanding, knowledge of client cultures, and development of multicultural counseling skills. Within the past two decades, numerous journal articles and books have been published that provide new perspectives and research on each of these topics. The sixth and final section of this chapter describes key strategies of ongoing research for enhancing the effectiveness of counseling interventions for culturally diverse clientele. From a review of this literature, prospective counseling psychologists should then comprehend the range and kinds of competencies that must be developed and implemented to ensure ethical and competent research and practice in the culturally diverse world of the twenty-first century.

THE TRANSITION FROM SPECIAL INTEREST TO FOURTH FORCE

Jackson (1995) provides a succinct historical review of the literature in multicultural counseling, from a dearth of literature on the topic prior to the 1960s to the exponential increase in every decade since that time. By the 1990s, training in and practice of multicultural counseling were more frequently, than any other topic, the focus of major contributions to *The Counseling Psychologist,* the primary conceptual journal of the profession. While many counseling psychologists remain concerned that a great deal more progress is needed to have a truly multicultural profession, this emphasis in *The Counseling Psychologist,* along with the election of many more culturally diverse leaders in the profession, the emergence of a Section on Racial and Ethnic Diversity in the Division of Counseling Psychology, and the evidence of higher levels of commitment to multicultural training (Quintana & Bernal, 1995), all indicate that issues of cultural diversity have moved *from* the status of an elective course or interest group primarily for racial and ethnic minorities *to* at least a dimension (Essandoh, 1996) that requires the attention of all counseling psychologists, no matter what their own cultural background. Pedersen (1999) has documented how multiculturalism has become a "fourth force" in psychology, complementing the earlier three forces of the twentieth century; that is, the psychodynamic, behavioral, and humanistic explanations of human behavior.

What happened in the latter decades of the twentieth century to bring about such a radical change in attention to cultural diversity? Two factors can be cited. First is the changing demographics in our society (already described in Chapter 4), with some parts of the United States already having a "majority" of previously labeled "minorities." Of far greater impact, at least for the beginnings of more serious attention to cultural diversity in the 1960s, was the fact that social changes, begun in the 1950s, for the first time brought significant numbers of racial and ethnic minorities into contact with psychologists. Too easily forgotten is the fact that until the desegregation of schools and universities began in the late 1950s, and the passage, in the mid-1960s, of policies and funds for the creation of community mental health centers, most counseling psychologists rarely encountered racial or ethnic minority clients. Economic and political strategies of the times created de facto segregation that kept African Americans, Hispanics, and Native Americans isolated in separate communities, attending separate schools and colleges, and excluded from most mental health services other than mental hospitals. As the process of desegregation of schools and colleges progressed, and as a large number of community mental health centers were established in some of the country's least well-served areas, mental health practitioners began to come in contact with significant numbers of culturally diverse clients.

This increased contact, beginning largely in the 1960s and continuing to the present, has led to an ever-increasing array of evidence of the more limited effectiveness psychologists have with culturally diverse clientele in almost every role: in making accurate psychological assessments and diagnoses, in providing effective counseling and, in research, in achieving predictions and explanations of behavior that are as statistically significant for the culturally diverse as for Anglo middle-class populations. Essandoh (1996) cites many of the key studies from the 1980s and 1990s showing the underutilization and high drop-out rates of ethnic minority clients. Hall (1997), Sue (1998), and Sue and Sue (1999) all cite inadequacies in current psychological research in determining what works as well for ethnic minorities as for the Anglo majority. This accumulating evidence, while clearly noted by those whose work was focused on the culturally diverse, only very slowly began to get the attention of the mental health professions. Jackson (1995) reviews the slow progress of the professional organizations in attending to the issues. By the late 1970s, psychology training programs began admitting larger numbers of culturally diverse graduate students. While the percentage of such students was most typically then still only somewhere between 3%–10% of the total graduate student enrollment, this percentage often represented a very large increase over past minority enrollments. Yet even these new students found themselves in largely unchanged curricula, learning about many explanations of human behavior and strategies for intervention that did not at all relate to everything they had learned while growing up in their home communities. Often, at the request of students who found large gaps in the available curricula, programs began to include one or more courses on cultural diversity. Typically, these courses were taught by adjunct faculty since none of the full-time faculty had the knowledge, skills, or inerests to teach such a course. Few graduate students, prior to the late 1980s, had any extensive exposure to a base of knowledge or set of intervention skills that had been built upon empirical findings from studies of culturally diverse clientele.

Curriculum changes accelerated greatly in the final decades of the twentieth century. The combination of the demographic changes and the inescapable evidence of the shortcomings of traditional training and intervention practices finally began to have a serious impact. By the early 1990s, nearly half of all counseling programs required a multicultural course and most had additional electives (Hills & Strozier, 1992). Yet even these developments left issues of cultural diversity more as a special interest elective than as a pervasive contextual concern. The major focus for the April 1993 issue of *The Counseling Psychologist* was a series of papers devoted to issues of multicultural research and counseling by Anglo Americans. How can progress be made, many authors asked, if multicultural competency remains an elected special interest rather than a minimal competency that is infused throughout the curriculum in both didactic and experiential training? In recent years, increasing attention has been given to asking how multicultural training is provided in each graduate training program and the strengths and weaknesses of various approaches (Reynolds, 1995).

Writers of the 1990s also spelled out how the growing movement of "fourth force" status for multicultural issues in counseling psychology has greater ethical implications than the earlier psychodynamic, behavioral, and humanistic forces. While it is part of the foundation of the training of all counseling psychologists to understand the potential contributions of each of these latter three forces, it has been argued that there are fewer risks of harm to clients in not attending to one of these three than there are in not attending to issues of cultural diversity (see Hall, 1997). As will become evident in the final two sections of this chapter, principles and guidelines for multicultural competence now extend to every area of practice and research of counseling psychologists.

SOME DEFINITIONS: ONGOING CONTROVERSIES

What is included when using the terms "multicultural," "cultural diversity," and "minority"? When should one use the word *race* as compared to the word *ethnicity*? There are ongoing controversies in response to these questions, with some counseling psychologists passionately arguing one position, whereas other counseling psychologists just as passionately argue for a contrasting position. In this section we explore these various positions on definitions and why there are such strong feelings about how the terms are used. Understanding these definitional concerns provides some of the fundamentals counseling psychologists need to begin to explore their own culture as well as the culture(s) of those they work with in their research and practice.

Before moving into the more controversial terms, it may be useful to provide a working definition of *culture* as the word is used in this chapter: ". . . culture is a learned system of meaning and behavior that is passed from one generation to the next" (Carter & Qureshi, 1995). Note several key words in that definition: culture is learned, meanings are affected by culture, behavior is affected by culture. That behavior is affected by culture probably seems self-evident; however, much less self-evident, especially in the majority population, is an understanding that the meanings we ascribe to things vary significantly according to one's culture. Finally, because culture is learned, one can study what has been learned in one's own culture as well as what has been learned in another's culture. These last few sentences provide key assumptions for much of what is covered in the next two sections: for counselors, as well as clients, change is possible! Now, on to some controversial terminology.

"Multicultural counseling is counseling that takes place between or among individuals from different cultural backgrounds" (Jackson, 1995, p. 3). Jackson's broad definition of multicultural counseling is now a commonly used, even if controversial one. When used in its broadest sense, multicultural counseling then includes an African American male counseling an African American female, an Asian American counseling a Hispanic, a visually impaired counselor counseling a wheelchair-bound client, a heterosexual counseling a bisexual, an Anglo 25-year-old counseling an Anglo 85-year-old. What is the concern with such inclusiveness? Helms (1994) says it best: "[A] decided disadvantage of the all-inclusive, pluralistic, or multicultural perspective was that it permitted the mental health specialties to shift their attention away from an analysis of the impact of racial factors on the therapy process" (p. 162). As both Helms (1994) and Jackson (1995) elaborate, the roots of the attention now given to multiculturalism are found largely in the racial civil rights movements of the late 1950s to early 1970s. The identification of discrimination, oppression, and neglect of basic health, education, and welfare services experienced by African Americans led, especially in the 1960s, to "a composite consideration of the mental health concerns of members of various racial (e.g., Asians and Blacks), cultural (e.g., Latinos and women), and ethnic groups (e.g., various Native American tribes or nations)" (Helms, 1994, p. 162). As will be further elaborated in the definitional issues regarding the words *race* and *ethnicity*, significant concerns remain that many of the unique and potent issues regarding race in U.S. society receive insufficient attention when the word *multicultural* is so broadly encompassing.

On the positive side of this broad definition of *multicultural* is a growing realization, in the society at large, and especially in the mental health professions, that numerous individuals from many backgrounds experience discrimination in striving for educational and work opportunities as well as incur the painful psychological effects of societal oppression, all based only on their group membership (e.g., age, race, ethnicity, gender, sexual orientation, religious beliefs, physical disability).

In the earliest years of attention to multicultural counseling, the term "minority counseling" was the most commonly used. As already noted, first attention to multicultural issues came out of the racial civil rights movements. The word *minority* has long been used in our society for those who "because of physical or cultural characteristics, are singled out from the others in society in which they live for differential and unequal treatment" (Wirth, 1945, p. 347). As the scope of definition of *minority* expanded in ways described in the previous paragraph, the word, of course, became a misnomer: women were already not a statistical minority even in the 1960s; changing U.S. demographics, as reviewed in Chapter 4, also meant that in many geographic areas, racial and ethnic groups were no longer statistical minorities. Thus in the 1970s the term "culturally disadvantaged" came into vogue.

Yet the *disadvantaged* part of this term had for many implications of deficiency, even if the term was well intentioned to indicate that such individuals had been deprived of many of the opportunities enjoyed by other citizens. Therefore, "culturally disadvantaged" was quickly replaced by "culturally diverse," which remains the most frequently used term today.

For similar reasons, the 1960s term "minority counseling" evolved into cross-cultural counseling. There were two important implications in this evolution. First, the issues to be considered went beyond those of a majority group counselor working with a minority group client; that is, there were issues also to be considered when counselors and clients came from different minorities, or when the counselor was from a minority group. Second, "[b]y shifting the focus away from minority groups exclusively, these terms challenged majority group counselors to become aware of the role that their own cultural assumptions played in their interactions with clients" (Jackson, 1995, p. 11).

In the 1980s, the term "cross-cultural counseling" evolved into "multicultural counseling" for at least two reasons. First, "cross-cultural" had long been a sociological term referring to the study of international ethnic groups, and therefore led to some confusion when the primary focus was intended to be on American ethnic groups. The word *multicultural* came into use to distinguish a focus on American ethnic groups as compared to cultures from other countries. Second, because so many counselors and clients belonged to more than one culturally diverse group (e.g., Asian American hearing-impaired male, fundamentalist Christian female, biracial bisexual male, African American female), *multicultural* made clear that the issues from more than two cultures could often be involved in the research and practice of counseling psychologists.

Turning now to some more controversial terms: What are the differences in meaning for the words *race* and *ethnicity*? Does one subsume the other? Are both words needed? Once again, there are opposing viewpoints maintained by different counseling psychologists, as well as psychologists from many other specialties. Addressing issues of defining *race* first: when Yee, Fairchild, Weizmann, and Wyatt (1993) published their article on "Addressing Psychology's Problems With Race," it was soon followed by eight diverse passionate reactions (see pp. 40–47 in *The American Psychologist* [January 1995]), some arguing that *race* should no longer be a categorical variable in psychology, others arguing just as strongly, but for incredibly diverse reasons from the biological to the psychological, why *race* needed even more concerted attention as a variable in psychological research and practice. There is much evidence that what is labeled *race* in many studies may not be defined reliably: is *race* self-defined by those being studied or counseled and, if so, what is the race given by someone with an Asian American father and an African American mother? Or is race determined by some biological marker such as skin color or eye shape and, if so, how reliable are the categorizations when, for example, someone has naturally blond hair and what are called Mongoloid facial features (Rushton, 1995)? In many studies with *race* as a category, *race* has been confounded with *social class* as a descriptive and/or explanatory variable. This questionable reliability of how race is determined, as well as the recognition that it is really more a socio-political than a biologically defensible term, is what leads many to argue for its elimination as a category for further study.

On the other side are authors such as Eisenman (1995) and Helms (1992) who provide persuasive arguments that eliminating *race* as a category for study would actually lead to more racial discrimination and to less awareness on the part of the Anglo majority about their own ongoing contributions to discrimination. Their well-articulated strong concerns about why race needs continued focused attention in psychologists' research and practice apply not only to the continuance of *race* as a category, but also to its differentiation from *ethnicity*.

Phinney (1996) attempted to address much of the messiness in the use of the word *ethnicity:* ". . . ethnicity is a complex multidimensional construct that, by itself, explains little" (p. 918). She used the term "ethnic group" to refer only to members of nondominant groups of non–European origin, and encompassed *race* within that definition since her definition of *ethnic group* referred almost exclusively to persons of color, for example, African Americans, Asian and Pacific Islander Americans, Latinos, and Native Americans. "The term race is avoided because of wide disagreement on its meanings and usage for psychology. . . . biologists find more differences within so-called racial groups than between them" (p. 918). Phinney's (1996) focus did allow her to build a case for recognizing that *ethnicity,* as a category of psychological study, confounded issues of ethnicity as culture, ethnicity as identity, and ethnicity as minority status. As we explore in the next two sections, all of us, including Anglos, have both a cultural and a racial identity. What varies tremendously is the strength, saliency, and meaning of *culture* and *racial identity* for each of us.

In response to Phinney's (1996) distinctions, Helms and Talleyrand (1997) argued that "Race is not ethnicity." However poorly *race* might be defined, they find it a less fuzzy construct than *ethnicity,* which "seemingly has no real meaning apart from its status as a proxy for racial classification or immigrant status" (p. 1246). Some years before Phinney's work, Cook and Helms (1988) recognized that when words like *diversity* and *ethnicity* were being used, the primary focus was on visible racial ethnic groups (VREGs), the same groups Phinney encompassed in her attempts to clarify what we mean by American ethnic groups. One of the less discussed aspects of this controversy is that, because *race* is such a sociopolitical term in our society, with heavy negative overtones, many persons who are comfortable being identified as part of a distinct ethnic group are not comfortable being identified as from a distinct racial group. In short, there is no clear consensus about when to use *race* and when to use *ethnicity*. Both researchers and practitioners need to maintain cognizance of the multiple and often confounding ways in which these words are used.

All of the issues confounding definitions of *race* also impact definitions of *racism,* the final term to be discussed in this section. Ridley (1995) fortunately devotes an entire chapter to the definition of *racism;* his more behavioral approach overcomes much confusion and contradictions he has found in the literature on racism. Moreover, his entire book is designed to help counseling psychologists overcome being what he calls "unintentional racists": ". . . many well-meaning counselors should discover that, despite their best intentions, they are unintentional racists" (Ridley, 1995, p. xiv). Developing self-understandings about racism and other biases and stereotypes is the focus of the next section. Therefore, Ridley's (1995) definition of *racism* provides a fitting segue:

> Racism is any behavior or pattern of behavior that tends to systematically deny access to opportunities or privileges to members of one racial group while perpetuating access to opportunities and privileges to members of another racial group. . . . This definition consists of five key features: a variety of behaviors, systematic behavior, preferential treatment, inequitable outcomes, and nonrandom victimization (Ridley, 1995, pp. 28–29).

The five key features are each well elaborated and illustrated in his book; his work can serve as the foundation for all of us to become more responsible citizens as well as ethical counseling psychologists.

COUNSELOR SELF-UNDERSTANDING

> Counselors bring to counseling their own personal experiences, beliefs, values, and expectations. These, in turn, affect the ability of counselors to accurately perceive, comprehend, and integrate into treatment the idiographic meanings clients attach to their own experiences. If counselors' unexamined personal agendas block perceptual schemata, they may ignore, distort, or underemphasize incoming cultural information to the detriment of the client. This mishandling of cultural information can occur even after years of training and professional practice (Ridley, Mendoza, Kanitz, Angermeier, & Zenk, 1994b, p. 131).

Ridley and colleagues go on to state that an accurate understanding of culturally diverse clients' perceptual schema requires "self-analytic counselors, who ferret out private agendas and actively work to eliminate their prejudicial or stereotypic perceptions of culturally different clients" (p. 131). This last quote underlies the basis for this section: counselor self-understanding. Simply knowing about other cultures has yielded only limited gains in counselor effectiveness in working with culturally diverse clientele (Enns, 1993; Thompson, Worthington, & Atkinson, 1994). Counselor self-understanding of his or her own culture is just as essential as understanding a client's culture, especially as one's own culture has created, for a counselor, prejudicial (biased) or stereotypical perceptions.

One of the earlier approaches to facilitating counselor self-understanding was the use of consciousness-raising groups. Such groups were initially developed primarily in response to empirical data on sexism in psychotherapy. As Enns (1993) reviews, while such groups were often valued by participants as positive and supportive experiences, empirical outcomes seldom included behavioral or lifestyle changes. The use of consciousness-raising groups regarding racism received less empirical attention; the technique has had some very limited application in other areas of cultural diversity such as sexual orientation and disability. In some ways, it might be argued, consciousness-raising, regardless of its focus, makes participants more aware of prejudices and unintentional behaviors, leading first to discomfort and then often to defensiveness. Such groups were often focused on developing awareness and not on providing an environment that enabled participants to undertake significant behavioral changes.

An important development related to these early struggles in helping counselors increase their own awareness about culture, especially the struggles of majority counselors to become aware of, and change their own racist behaviors, was the development of the concepts of Anglo racial identity (Helms, 1995) and Anglo racial consciousness (Rowe, Behrens, & Leach, 1995). (As will be described in the next section, development and application of racial identity concepts and measures for various persons of color preceded the development of Anglo racial identity theory.) Over the past two decades, there has been accumulating evidence that what Helms calls "White Racial Identity Ego Statuses and Information-Processing Strategies" and what Rowe and colleagues (1995) call "types of White racial consciousness," do affect multicultural counseling competencies (Ottavi, Pope-Davis, & Dings, 1994). Even more important, there is now evidence that appropriate training can facilitate counselors' development of more sophisticated and sensitive statuses (Neville, Heppner, Louie, Thompson et al., 1996).

In attending to issues of counselor self-understanding, racism has received the most concerted attention by counseling psychologists for at least two reasons. One, there is, of course, continuing evidence of racism's ongoing pernicious effects in society related to any one of our contemporary social problems (e.g., AIDs, income discrepancies); two, issues of racism have proved to be some of the most highly charged discomforting areas for counselors to deal with when attempts are made to help counselors understand the impacts of their own behaviors (Kiselica, 1998). The training and research strategies that have been pursued regarding how counselors can cope with their own racism can, in many ways, be "translated" for use in helping counselors understand many of the biases, stereotypes, and unintentional behaviors that are part of their heritage in growing up in the United States. Because of this potential for broader application, combined with the importance in addressing racism as the area that has proved most resistant to societal change, the remainder of this section provides brief descriptions of the development of measures and interventions for racial identity/awareness and the usefulness of such statuses in facilitating self-understanding.

While ongoing controversies remain about the precise and differential meanings of various terms used in describing types of "White Racial Identity Ego Statuses" (Helms, 1995) as compared to Rowe and colleagues' (1995) types of "White racial consciousness," either of their models of racial awareness provide useful illustrations of both (1) the range of functioning of Anglo persons, and (2) a perspective on the progression counselors need to make to move away from avoidance of racial material and toward complex and effective management of racial material. The authors involved in developing these models also recognize that persons typically do not function exclusively in just one type or stage. Helms (1995) points out that for most Anglos, one status most often governs the person's racial reaction (that status is then labeled "dominant"), whereas the person may be able to react in other ways if any other racial identity ego statuses are accessible. The clear implication is the need to help counselors make more statuses accessible. Helms' six statuses of "White Racial Identity," along with their corresponding information-processing strategies indicated after each slash are, from least to most mature: contact/obliviousness, disintegration/suppression and ambivalence, reintegration/selective perception and negative out-group distortion, pseudoindependence/reshaping reality and selective perception, immersion-emersion/hypervigilance and reshaping, autonomy/flexibility and complexity. Self-descriptions from Anglo persons' fitting each of these categories are provided in Helms (1995).

Rowe and colleagues' (1995) Anglo racial consciousness types are based on considerations of (1) willingness to explore racial/ethnic issues, and (2) commitment to taking a position about such issues. Their seven categories, from least to most mature, are: avoidant, dissonant, dependent, conflictive, dominative, integrative, reactive. Like Helms, Rowe et al. (1995) have developed an empirical measure to help Anglos assess where they are developmentally in their Anglo racial awareness. In the final section of this chapter, where the research on enhancing multicultural counseling effectiveness is discussed, these measures form one part of a growing body of critical research in understanding what matters most. These measures have already been used, for example, for comparisons of Anglo racial identity among faculty and students, with implications for the extent and kinds of interventions that will be necessary to help students develop more commitment to exploration and more complex ways of dealing with racial material (Pope-Davis, Menefee, & Ottavi, 1993).

Ridley (1995), Kiselica (1998), and Leong and Santiago-Rivera (1999) have all contributed to understanding some of the challenges and resistances encountered in developing the self-awareness needed for multicultural competence. Often, despite counselors not having any overt prejudicial attitudes, actions and behaviors occur in counseling sessions that are indeed biased and stereotypical and therefore significantly impede the development of trusting relationships. Kiselica's (1998) article is helpful mostly for the emotionally supportive aspects found in his description of discomforts he encountered in exploring highly charged areas of diversity. Ridley's (1995) work is quite helpful conceptually in his identification of eight defenses. He clearly explains that these defenses, like most psychological defenses, are typically used quite unconsciously. His eight racially related defenses are especially helpful in understanding what he calls "unintentional racism," as compared to overt or covert intentional racism. The eight defenses are: color blindness, color consciousness, cultural transference, cultural countertransference, cultural ambivalence, pseudotransference, overidentification, and identification with the oppressor. While we have space to describe just one of these defenses, readers may want to consult Ridley (1995) for his very useful and understandable explanations and illustrations of the other seven. Here we describe the defense of color consciousness:

> . . . the opposite of color blindness . . . based on the premise that the client's problems stem essentially from being a minority. . . . The color-conscious counselor places too much on the color of the client, while overlooking the client's contribution to the presenting problem (Ridley, 1995, p. 68).

Leong and Santiago-Rivera (1999) provide other examples of challenges to self-awareness that arise from quite normal and typical socialization processes. Of the six challenges they describe, perhaps most unexpected are their explications of the pitfalls in multicultural understanding presented by the social psychological forces of false consensus and the workings of the attraction–selection–attrition framework.

False consensus is the well-documented process of seeing one's own behavior as most typical and assuming that, under the same circumstances, others would react in the same way. What has often been called Eurocentric thinking is not necessarily an overt philosophical position, but rather often just false consensus operating—the way I think is what a normal person would think! Regarding attraction–selection–attrition frameworks, organizational psychologists have recently shown that one of the reasons organizations often find it extremely difficult to institute change is that new members keep being selected who are like those present and those that do not fit well quickly leave. Thus getting new perspectives on how people think or how to do things differently is greatly impeded.

To achieve any behavioral change where defenses and social psychological processes are used quite habitually and unconsciously, it is essential to develop both awareness *and* alternative coping strategies. While there has been at least an implicit consensus in the profession of counseling psychology that counselor self-understanding must be part of the preparation for becoming multiculturally competent, there has not been much published literature on what are the most effective strategies for facilitating that self-understanding. Various responses to Kiselica's (1998) article, all found in the January 1998 issue of *The Counseling Psychologist,* add both student and faculty perspectives to the necessary affective and conceptual components of training for facilitating counselor self-understanding, including key roles that faculty must now fulfill. Perhaps the clearest message in the articles in that issue of *The Counseling Psychologist,* is that whatever strategies for developing counselor self-awareness are initially provided must be followed up with continued attention by mentors and supervisors. Such continued attention and encouragement are often necessary to ensure that counselors-in-training continue the often discomforting experience of exploring the effects of their own behaviors as critical factors in all phases of relationships with clients, from assessments, to treatment plans, to treatment interactions.

KNOWLEDGE OF CLIENT CULTURES

One of the earliest and most extensive responses to Wrenn's (1962) criticism of the counseling profession as being "culturally encapsulated" was the development of literature focused on the cultures of specific ethnic groups. The assumption was that if counselors knew more about the unique value structure, behavioral patterns, and ongoing life experiences of individuals from minority cultures, counselors would be able to be more empathic with them. This culturally sensitive empathy was expected to overcome some of the cultural mistrust that leads culturally diverse clients to avoid or prematurely terminate counseling relationships. Therefore, during the 1970s numerous articles began to appear that focused primarily on significant cultural factors for African Americans and women, the two groups initially most involved in civil rights movements of the 1960s. By the 1980s, similar articles and book chapters emerged for all four major groups of American ethnic minorities; that is, Asian American, Hispanic, and Native Americans as well as African

American, and for nonethnic minorities such as women, handicapped, and gays/lesbians. Sue and Sue (1999), Ponterotto, Casas, Suzuki, and Alexander (1995), and Pedersen, Draguns, Lonner, and Trimble (1996) all include more recent examples of chapters focused on specific ethnic minorities. Microtraining Associates in North Amherst, Massachusetts, provides up-to-date audiotapes of experts speaking on cultural considerations for counseling with Latinas, Native Americans, African Americans, and Asian Americans. Atkinson and Hackett (1988) provide chapters focused on the nonethnic minorities. In recent years, several of the major treatises in *The Counseling Psychologist* have also focused on increasing cultural awareness for nonethnic minorities, for example, feminist counseling and therapy (January 1993); lesbian, gay, and bisexual affirmative training (September 1998); and male identity, including gender role conflict (May 1998).

The rapid growth of such literature soon presented two issues for counseling psychologists: (1) Does a focus on the culturally specific overshadow important universal issues that all humans encounter in psychological adjustment? (2) How can any one counselor possibly become knowledgeable about such a comprehensive array of material, and be able to use such material effectively with so many different ethnic and nonethnic clients?

The first question has best been addressed by comparing the strengths and weaknesses of etic (universalist) and emic (culture specific) approaches. Ridley, Mendoza, and Kanitz (1994b) have perhaps the most concise review of these approaches for counseling psychologists, clarifying that the etic approach does not mean ignoring culture. "Etic theorists either create new multicultural counseling theories and techniques that are universally applicable across cultures . . . or they extract the universal aspects from traditional counseling theories and techniques and create modified versions of these for use in multicultural counseling" (p. 240). Fischer, Jome, and Atkinson (1998) also focus on "universal healing conditions in a culturally specific context" (p. 525), providing an extensive integration of the research literature on critical components of effectiveness in psychotherapy with what has been learned about healing in diverse ethnic cultures. Such integrations provide the foundations that all counseling psychologists need to maintain a balance of etic and emic approaches in conceptualizing and treating culturally diverse clients (further discussed in the final section of this chapter).

The second issue that has arisen is how to deal with the huge quantity of material now available regarding many racial, ethnic, and nonethnic minorities. No counseling psychologist can have comprehensive knowledge for each and every ethnic group. In the next three sections of this chapter we identify four kinds of knowledge, rather than specific facts, that should be considered when conducting assessments, interventions, or research in multicultural settings: (1) within-group differences in racial identity and acculturation, (2) worldviews, (3) beliefs about psychological problems and therapeutic processes, and (4) the problem of over- and underdiagnosis.

Within-Group Differences

Some of the greatest advances of the late twentieth century in the conceptual and empirical foundations of multicultural competence were probably stimulated by *misuse* of culturally specific information. Majority, or using Wrenn's (1962) term, "culturally encapsulated counselors" often seized upon newly published information about a culturally diverse group in formulating diagnoses and treatment plans, to the almost total exclusion of everything that had been learned previously about principles of diagnosis and treatment. Such cultural overgeneralization was, of course, just as harmful, if not more so, than ignoring culture (Casas, 1984). Clients who felt treated as an undifferentiated group member, as compared to an individual, could well feel demeaned as well as not understood. Cultural mistrust was surely not addressed. The axiom that "a little knowledge is a dangerous thing" was never more appropriate! Fortunately for the profession, this unintentional misuse of cultural knowledge by majority counselors, as well as issues that emerged for minority counselors working with clients from either their own or other minority groups, all led to helpful developments in the concepts of "racial identity" and "acculturation" as critically important components of differences *within* each culture. Understanding the components of such concepts is a critical first step in any consideration of the applicability, to a given individual, of any of the culturally specific knowledge found in the readings cited above.

Racial Identity

While there are clearly some shared conceptual bases for the constructs of both racial identity and acculturation, the next topic in this chapter, there are also some meaningful unique origins and implications to be explored for each concept. The concept of "racial identity" was already discussed in the section on counselor awareness, specifically Anglo racial identity. The work of Helms (1990) and her predecessors initially focused on African American racial identity. As she began to look at how counseling relationships were affected by African American racial identity, it became quickly apparent that Anglos also had within-group variations concerning race issues that affected therapeutic relationships. Students of other ethnic groups, largely mentored by Helms, also developed racial identity measures that could be used with other visible racial–ethnic groups, all of whom had some overlapping, yet distinctive, experiences with being persons of color in American society. Helms (1995) reviews both the distinctive and converging conceptual and measurement developments of these scales and indicates many of the possible uses in enhancing multicultural research and practice. In contrast to the statuses listed in the previous section regarding Anglo racial identity, Helms finds a different configuration of statuses for people of color. The statuses, as listed in Helms (1995), from least mature and avoiding racial material to high levels of integration of personal and socioracial concerns (along with their corresponding information-processing strategies listed after each slash), are: conformity/selective perception and obliviousness to socioracial concerns; dissonance/repression of anxiety-provoking racial information, immersion-emersion/hypervigilance toward racial stimuli and dichotomous thinking, internalization/ flexibility and analytic thinking, integrative awareness/flexibility and complexity. Looking especially at the information-processing strategies for each status makes almost self-evident that clients in different statuses would be expected to have very different reactions to a counselor incorporating cultural material in the relationship. If, for example, a counselor brings up the matter of racial differences between a client and his roommate, one African American client might say he never even thought about it (obliviousness of conformity stage) to another who might say that the race difference was the source of all his problems (immersion-emersion).

Closely related to Helms' (1995) work is the development of biracial identity for those whose parents are from different racial groups. Kerwin and Ponterotto (1995) provide a good summary of overlapping and distinctive developments in understanding and assessing biracial identity. Turning to identity development based on culture other than race, Gelso and Fassinger (1992) provide a concise overview of generalization of racial identity models to other cultural identity models. Perhaps the greatest developments of this type are models of gay and lesbian identity development. While the measurement aspects of such identity are not nearly as well developed as in racial identity, again it is not difficult to understand that clients who are at quite different stages of the coming-out process might vary greatly in how they respond to a counselor's exploration of sexual identity.

Acculturation

Atkinson and Thompson (1992) have provided an excellent summary of the evolution of the study of acculturation, studied first by sociologists, then by psychologists in understanding the kinds of stress culturally diverse individuals encounter in trying to adapt to what are often two quite different sets of values and worldviews (see next section). For many decades, the primary interest of sociologists had been in how immigrants became assimilated into the dominant Anglo culture. Such terms as acculturative stress and "marginal man" were used to describe the social and psychological problems persons encountered as they tried to manage the differences in their culture of origin and the dominant Anglo culture. As Atkinson and Thompson (1992) concisely review, psychologists began to appreciate that acculturation was often more than a matter of assimilation; in fact, to become assimilated in the dominant culture created lasting stresses with one's culture of origin, often cutting off valuable sources of psychological support from family and community.

Studies of acculturation among both Hispanics and Native Americans led to the development of the alternative term "biculturalism." Then, LaFromboise, Coleman, and Gerton (1993), in their review of the theory and research on biculturalism, make a case for talking about "second culture acquisition" instead of biculturalism. Their research suggests at least five different levels of second culture acquisition, with persons at each level having quite different feelings about, and reactions to, the dominant culture. Their five levels are: assimilation, acculturation, alternation, multiculturalism, and fusion. At the highest level of their continuum, persons interested in fusion endeavor to see how some unique factors in their own culture might be combined with some elements of the dominant culture to enhance quality of life for members of either or both cultures. For example, are there healing practices in some Native American or African American cultures that would enhance the quality of traditional Western medicine? Are there spiritual traditions in some cultures that can help Anglos make their lives less stressful and depressing?

Over the past few decades, studies of acculturation (including biculturalism and second culture acquisition) of Hispanics, Native Americans, Asian Americans, and recently arrived immigrant groups, have resulted in the identification of the varied and often unique coping strategies used by these individuals. From these studies, various schemas for coping with diversity have been conceptualized (e.g., Coleman, 1995) and measures developed for assessing which type of acculturation individuals are engaged in (see Paniagua [1998] for identification of 14 such scales).

These advances in conceptualizations and measures of racial identity and acculturation have been major contributions of counseling psychologists in helping counselors from all backgrounds understand the heterogeneity of attitudes and behaviors related to culture-specific information. When reading the next two sections, where major categories of culture-specific information are identified, the reader should always keep uppermost in mind that the ways in which to use such information (not *whether* or not to use it, but rather *how* to use it), both in appraising an individual, and in developing a therapeutic working alliance, will be significantly affected by the client's racial identity and/or type of acculturation.

Differing Worldviews

In Chapter 8, the concept of empathy will be introduced and discussed as the most well-researched concept in developing a therapeutic relationship. A key component of Rogers's (1957) classic definition of empathy is sensing "the client's private world" (p. 98). How does a counselor sense the client's private world when that world is viewed in so many different ways from how the counselor views the world? What if the client's fears or views of the spirit world or definitions of *family* are completely outside of the experience of the counselor? "There is consensus in the counseling profession that to understand a client's frame of reference for the counseling process, and to meet the client's needs and expectations in therapy, the counselor must accurately assess the client's worldview" (Grieger & Ponterotto, 1995). The purpose of this section on "Differing Worldviews," and the next one on "Beliefs about Psychological Problems and Therapeutic Processes" is to alert the reader to frequent differences in the ways majority counselors view the world compared to the views of many clients from culturally diverse backgrounds. The types of differences discussed are in a sense a checklist for counselors to review before working with a culturally diverse population with whom they have not had prior training and experience.

The history of the development of the concept of "worldview" as a vital component of multicultural competence has been well articulated by Trevino (1996). She reviews not only the wide range of relevant dimensions (e.g., locus of control, interpersonal relationships, time orientation) and the development of assessment measures of worldview, but also then describes a model for counselors to use when working with clients whose worldviews are very different from those of the counselor. "The essential point is that counselors and clients work together to discover more viable ways of understanding and interacting with the world in order to facilitate change" (Trevino, 1996, p. 207). Neither cultural viewpoint is denied or given precedence. Rather, there is a collaborative search by counselors and clients, from their different worldviews, to determine various options for change that might address clients' concerns.

There are five dimensions on which differences have frequently been found between the worldviews of clients from American ethnic minority backgrounds and/or recent immigrants compared to the worldviews of majority counselors. For each of these five dimensions we have developed some questions for counselors to ask themselves about their clients' worldviews.

Views About Family

What is the relationship of the self to the family, that is, is the self secondary to the family in importance? If so, then many decisions and behaviors will be "controlled" by explicit and/or implicit family expectations rather than by clients' own preferences. The majority culture in America expects, indeed values, a level of independence from family that is rarely shared by any of the ethnic minority cultures. Counselors can be extraordinarily nonempathic with clients if they do not truly comprehend the importance of "saving face" or "being shunned" by one's home community.

Cooperation Versus Competition

Is personal success seen as harming one's friends since they cannot join in the success? Do products of group efforts seem intrinsically more valuable than those done individually? Again, the majority culture in America emphasizes a more independent, competitive mode of learning and performance than the modes typical in many cultures, most especially the Native American and African American cultures. Choices of goals and behaviors that seem quite logical and desirable for majority counselors may seem truly alien and threatening for some ethnic minority clients.

Time Orientation

How important is the past compared to the present? the present compared to the future? For some ethnic minority cultures, both the exigencies of the present time, combined with an orientation more toward "being" in the present compared to "becoming" something in the future, yields a present time emphasis that may frustrate majority counselors seeking to make linkages to past and or future times.

Communication Styles

How much of communication is accomplished by words compared to implicit messages in shared experiences (Hecht, Andersen, & Ribeau, 1989)? Are there certain nonverbal behaviors (e.g., eye contact), which have significantly different meanings in a minority culture compared to the majority culture? For example, is lack of eye contact from a client indicating anger or shame? Does a client's low level of self-disclosure indicate lack of trust, an inability to label feelings, or an assumption that the counselor must already know what the client is feeling? Two different clients exhibiting the same *behaviors* may have quite different *intentions* regarding what they want to communicate.

Locus of Control

How much of life is "fate" compared to self-controlled? Just how much can one control what happens in life? And, to whatever degree an individual can control what happens in life, what are the components of that control? Is the control achieved, for example, by pleasing the right gods or by developing self-efficacy? Obviously, individuals' views on this dimension significantly affect whether or not they will even seek counseling; and if they do, what expectations will be held for what both counselor and client must do. These kinds of expectations are further explored in our next section.

Beliefs About Psychological Problems and Therapeutic Processes

Perhaps the most immediately crucial part of clients' worldviews as counseling begins are clients' beliefs about the causes of their psychological problems, what implications the problems will have for themselves and their relationships with family and friends, and their beliefs about how they can best be helped. Worldviews regarding each of these areas are strongly affected by clients' racial identity and acculturation (Atkinson, Thompson, & Grant, 1993; Leong, Wagner, & Tata, 1995; Paniagua, 1998); therefore, care must be taken before automatically assuming, for example, that an ethnic minority client will believe evil spirits are a major cause of the problem. As Paniagua (1998) points out, while beliefs in spirits and hexes are more prevalent among American ethnic minorities than among the majority culture, such beliefs are by no means universal or even typical within a given minority group.

Regarding beliefs about sources of problems, client beliefs should be ascertained regarding (a) whether the problem is seen as internally caused (e.g., mood swings, phobias, lack of impulse control) or externally caused; and (b) if externally caused, is the problem caused by someone (e.g., spouse, coworker), a situation (e.g., discrimination at work), or by unseen forces. It should be self-evident that variations in these beliefs about causes of a problem will have a significant effect on all the other areas mentioned in the next paragraphs as well as on the steps the counselor must take to establish a working alliance and therapeutic relationship with the client.

What guilt, fears, and stigma are associated with the client admitting that he or she has a problem and has to seek professional help? Is the client experiencing being in a state of sin or being the target of an evil eye? Does the client fear that family and other interpersonal relationships will be affected negatively if others become aware that the client is seeing a counselor? Does the client have significant doubts about whether the counselor can be helpful and worries about whether counseling might leave him or her in a worse state? Leong and colleagues (1995) provide a comprehensive review on how race and ethnicity affect clients' help-seeking, citing typical fears and concerns held by African Americans, Hispanic Americans, and Asian Americans.

What are clients' expectations about how therapy works? Clients who are recent immigrants or have been raised in very traditional African, Hispanic, or Native American cultures may well think of healing processes in terms of their culture's traditional healers (a medicine man/woman, a shaman). How much does the client view the therapeutic process as something done to/for him/her compared to a collaborative process? Are there expectations that the counselor will work to change the client's life situation, for example, dysfunctional family, housing discrimination?

FIGURE 6.1.   **Three-dimensional model for counseling racial/ethnic minorities.**

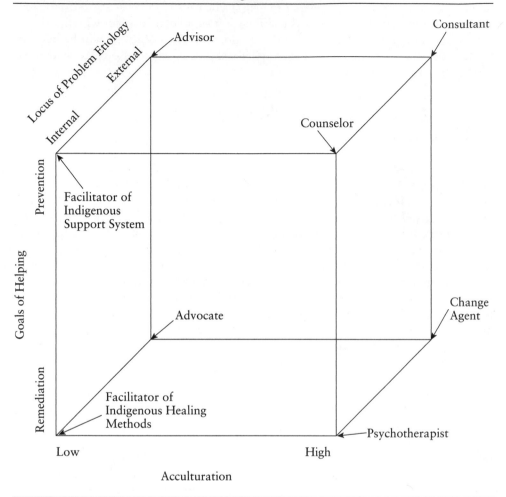

From Atkinson, Thompson, and Grant (1993). Used by permission.

Atkinson and colleagues (1993) provide a three-dimensional cube model for what roles might work most effectively, depending on client beliefs about (a) whether the problem is internally or externally caused, (b) level of acculturation to the majority culture, and (c) client goals (see Figure 6.1). The eight roles resulting from the inter-sections of the three dimensions are: facilitator of indigenous healing methods, facilitator of indigenous support system, advisor, consultant, advocate, change agent, counselor, psychotherapist. Atkinson and colleagues recognize that many of the roles they describe are not traditional counseling psychologist roles, yet clearly explicate how all eight possible roles need to be considered if we are to greatly increase our effectiveness in working with a full range of culturally diverse clients.

Over- and Underdiagnosis

The previous three sections have focused on major issues to consider when working in multicultural settings: within-group differences, worldviews, and beliefs about sources of problems and healing processes. In this section, the focus shifts to what counselors do with their knowledge of clients, most especially problems counselors often create for themselves in their *unintentional* misuses of cultural knowledge. The misuses are described as two kinds of overdiagnosis and two kinds of underdiagnosis. In one sense, this material on diagnosis could be part of Chapter 13 on the Science and Practice of Assessment. However, since there is now accumulated evidence about problems with diagnoses and treatment planning specifically related to use of cultural knowledge about clients, the problems are addressed here as part of the knowledge that counseling psychologists must have in order to become multiculturally competent (Ridley, Li, & Hill, 1998).

The first of the two kinds of problems described as "overdiagnosis" is the matter of counselors pathologizing culturally determined behavior. Without awareness of some of the worldviews described above, and by possible misinterpretations of psychological test results that have limited cultural validity (see Chapter 13), counselors often make the mistake of diagnosing pathology when the problems the client is experiencing are a result of the cultural environment in which they live. Ridley (1995) summarizes much of the evidence showing that African American students—more than any other group—are likely to be mislabeled as learning disabled or emotionally handicapped; Paniagua (1998) reviews some of the evidence of misdiagnosis of psychopathology when minority clients talk about communicating with spirits. While there are indeed some minority clients with learning and/or emotional disabilities, extreme care must be taken to separate which behavior is a reflection of client culture compared to idiosyncratic; that is, individualized dysfunctional behaviors.

A second type of overdiagnosis relates to counselors' overgeneralization of cultural knowledge (Casas, 1984). Overdiagnosing occurs primarily as a result of attributing too much of clients' adjustment difficulties to discrimination, oppression, and acculturation stress. Somewhat ironically, whereas counselors without training in multicultural issues may well underdiagnose the importance of such factors (see next paragraph), counselors who do have multicultural training may well be too quick to assume that clients self-perceptions and considerations of options are more determined by external forces in society than by internal dynamics. Obviously, either an over- or underemphasis in the consideration of client experiences with oppression and acculturation will lead to serious problems in establishing effective therapeutic relationships. In the case of overdiagnosing effects of acculturation, clients may well feel a lack of empathy from the counselor for their problems as they are experiencing them and, indeed, some critical internal dynamics of the client may not be addressed in the work of counseling if the counselor has overgeneralized cultural factors.

Turning next to underdiagnosis, there are again two types to consider. First and most simply, underdiagnosis may occur if adequate attention is not paid to issues of discrimination, oppression, and acculturation stress in understanding the origins of clients' problems. If the focus in counseling is kept primarily on internal dynamics, and critical cultural factors are ignored, even though the client might well feel empathically responded to, both client and counselor may experience extreme frustration as the client tries to make behavioral changes. Atkinson and colleagues (1993) provide three excellent examples in which the clients' presented problems initially appeared to derive from an internal source, yet the problem was eventually found to be caused by past experiences of discrimination or oppression. Unless these issues become part of the work of counseling, such clients find it nearly impossible to overcome their feelings of stress and abnormality.

> [A] Mexican-American student may manifest feelings of inadequacy . . . because teachers have systematically (although perhaps unconsciously) given her negative feedback. . . . An African-American man may express feelings that the counselor labels paranoid when in reality they are justifiable reactions of cultural mistrust to a social environment that is insensitive at best and dangerous at worst. . . . an Asian-American man may feel insecure about his new management role because throughout his life people have overlooked his interpersonal skills and rewarded his computational skills (Atkinson et al., 1993, p. 260).

A second kind of underdiagnosis occurs when cultural knowledge is inappropriately used to dismiss critical therapeutic issues. Unlike underdiagnosis that comes from counselor lack of awareness of culture, as just described in the preceding paragraph, this second kind of underdiagnosis occurs when counselors believe that all or part of a client's problems are a "natural" part of their culture and cannot therefore be treated by usual therapeutic practice. Perhaps the most poignant example of such underdiagnosis is not attending to spouse abuse of a Hispanic woman because the counselor assumes that what is happening is what can be expected from a machismo husband. While machismo may affect how the problem can be addressed in counseling, it does not negate the presence of a serious problem. Paniagua (1998) notes that in some literature there is a tendency to refer persons with culturally related syndromes (e.g., possession by evil spirits) to folk healers rather than to therapists. While there may be cases where collaborative work with folk healers may be quite useful, simply referring out such clients may overlook serious cognitive or emotional problems that need to be addressed.

In the preceding sections, we reviewed two major components of the tripartite conceptualization of multicultural competence: attitude (counselor self-understanding) and knowledge (of client cultures). We now turn to the final component, multicultural counseling skills.

DEVELOPMENT OF MULTICULTURAL COUNSELING SKILLS

We define *multicultural counseling skills* as "integration of cultural considerations into intervention planning, goal setting, diagnosing, and treatment selection" (Ridley et al., 1994b, p. 126). How does one acquire such skills? There are ongoing, increasingly well-informed dialogues about the content of training for developing such skills as well as when, how, and where to implement such training. An exploration of some of the consensus that appears to be emerging will be the core of this section, allowing the reader to make informed inquiries about multicultural skills training available in his or her own potential or current graduate training program.

In this section, we describe the principles and guidelines that have been developed to ensure the attention of all counselors and therapists to the special issues inherent in therapeutic work with culturally diverse clientele. Since these guidelines include counselor self-awareness and knowledge of client culture, as well as specific skills, they could well have been presented at the beginning of this chapter. We have deliberately chosen to present these guidelines at this point so that the reader already has a well-developed perspective on the self-understanding and knowledge fundamentals that serve as the foundations for these principles and guidelines.

After reviewing conceptual and implementation issues in multicultural training, we provide a brief review of the measures that have been developed to assess multicultural counseling skills. Such measures have become increasingly important in evaluating the effects of training programs as well as determining counselors' readiness for engaging in therapeutic relationships with culturally diverse clientele.

Principles and Guidelines

Counseling psychologists have been foremost among all psychologists in developing principles and guidelines for counseling and therapy with culturally diverse populations. The earliest such developments were by the Committee of Women in the Division of Counseling Psychology. This committee developed a consensus document (Principles Concerning the Counseling and Therapy of Women, 1979) which received, throughout the 1980s, a large number of adoptions and endorsements from other divisions within the APA and other mental health organizations. While the tripartite division of self-awareness, knowledge, and skills was not in the 1970s so well used as it is today, the components of all three are clearly evident in the 13 principles that were developed. Three of the principles are given here as illustrations of the tripartite model. Self-awareness: "Counselors/therapists are aware of how their personal functioning may influence their effectiveness in counseling/therapy with women clients" (Principles Concerning the Counseling and Therapy of Women, 1979, p. 22). Knowledge: "Counselors/therapists are knowledgeable about women, particularly with regard to biological, psychological and social issues which have impact on women in general or on particular groups of women in our society" (p. 22). Skills: "Counselors/therapists ascribe no pre-conceived limitations on the direction or nature of potential changes or goals in counseling/therapy for women" (p. 22). This last item may seem a bit obscure to contemporary readers; however, even as late as the 1970s, many counselors were still discouraging, or at least not supporting (Betz, 1989), women who wanted to pursue professional careers and/or independent lifestyles.

While more recent guidelines for multicultural counseling competence (cited in the next paragraph), in one sense encompass counseling with women, as one of many culturally diverse groups, Fassinger and Sperber-Richie (1997) document that

TABLE 6.1.   Seven Skills Competencies in Culturally Appropriate Intervention Strategies.

1. "Culturally skilled counselors are able to engage in a variety of verbal and nonverbal helping responses . . . They are not tied down to only one method or approach to helping, but recognize that helping styles and approaches may be culture-bound . . ."

2. "Culturally skilled counselors are able to exercise institutional intervention skills on behalf of their clients . . ."

3. "Culturally skilled counselors are not averse to seeking consultation with traditional healers or religious and spiritual leaders and practitioners . . ."

4. "Culturally skilled counselors take responsibility for interacting in the language requested by the client and, if not feasible, make appropriate referrals . . ."

5. "Culturally skilled counselors have training and expertise in the use of traditional assessment and testing instruments. They not only understand the technical aspects of the instruments but are also aware of cultural limitations . . ."

6. "Culturally skilled counselors should also attend to, as well as work to eliminate, biases, prejudices, and discriminatory contexts in conducting evaluations and providing interventions, and should develop sensitivity to issues of oppression, sexism, heterosexism, elitism, and racism . . ."

7. "Culturally skilled counselors take responsibility for educating their clients to the processes of psychological intervention, such as goals, expectations, legal rights and the counselor's orientation . . ."

from Arredondo et al., 1996, pp. 70–73.

some specific cultural issues related to working with women are still often overlooked. Therefore, study of the 1979 principles concerning the counseling and therapy of women, and the documented research underlying each principle (Fitzgerald & Nutt, 1986) ideally should continue to be part of the multicultural training of all counseling psychologists, both men and women.

Throughout the 1970s, counseling psychologists concerned with counseling of ethnic minorities also collaborated on the development of a position paper on cross-cultural counseling competencies. A first set of guidelines was published in *The Counseling Psychologist* in 1982 (Sue, Bernier, Durran, Feinberg et al., 1982). Over the years, these guidelines have been revised and operationalized with helpful rationales and examples (Arredondo, Toporek, Brown, Jones et al., 1996). As of 1999, the Division of Counseling Psychology had formally endorsed these latest guidelines and was developing a strategic plan to assure that the competencies noted in these guidelines would be appropriately implemented in training programs, accreditation criteria, and professional credentialing procedures. (These competencies are intended to expand both the training and implementation aspects of the only other published guidelines on working with culturally diverse populations; i.e., those published by the Office of Ethnic Minority Affairs of the American Psychological Association: *Guidelines for Providers of Psychological Services to Ethnic, Linguistic, and Culturally Diverse Populations* [1993]).

The most helpful document for counseling psychologists to consult initially is that of Arredondo and colleagues (1996). They provide concise explanatory statements for the multicultural competencies they outline in terms of (a) attitudes and beliefs, (b) knowledge, and (c) skills in each of three areas: counselor awareness of own cultural values and biases (9 competencies), counselor awareness of client's worldview (7 competencies), and culturally appropriate intervention strategies (15 competencies). Because we have already reviewed many of the fundamentals of the attitudes and beliefs (self-understanding), as well as knowledge, components of multicultural competence, we list in Table 6.1 only slightly abbreviated versions of the seven skills competencies (as compared to attitudes and beliefs and knowledge competencies) in the category of culturally appropriate intervention strategies.

Multicultural Training Models: Conceptual and Implementation Issues

Evolving Status of Multicultural Training in Counseling Psychology

If the metaphorical question "Is the glass half-empty or half-full?" applies to any-thing in counseling psychology, the status of multicultural training has to be the prime example. Hills and Strozier (1992), in their review of the status of multicul-tural training in the 1980s, reported "[A]lthough most respondents agreed in prin-ciple with the need for expanded training and clinical experience in multicultural issues, their actual course and practical offerings did not mirror this attitude" (p. 43). When Ponterotto (1997) compared his survey results to those of the prior 10 years, he concluded that there had been notable progress in at least the development of curriculum related to multicultural training and in inclusion of research training and opportunities, but far less progress in incorporating multicultural training in counseling practice and supervision. Pope-Davis, Reynolds, Dings, and Nielson (1995) found that counseling psychology students received greater amounts of coursework, training, and multicultural supervision than did clinical psychology students; however, the differences were significant mostly because there was so little multicultural training in clinical programs, not because of extensive amounts in counseling psychology. Is the glass half-full or half-empty?

The deficits in multicultural supervision found by Ponterotto (1997) are also reflected in the findings of Mintz, Bartels, and Rideout (1995). They find that the psychology interns they surveyed "reported mediocre preparation for counseling ethnic minority clients" (p. 316). Incorporation of a multicultural focus in practica and internships has no doubt been slowed by the fact that 70% of the current gen-eration of supervisors has had no formal training in dealing with multicultural is-sues (Constantine, 1997). Almost every survey finds that training programs believe that these are transitional times in which they are continuously engaged in improv-ing available multicultural training and supervised experience (Quintana & Bernal, 1995; Speight, Thomas, Kennel, & Anderson, 1995).

Conceptual Models of Training

It has been much easier to agree on the need for training in multicultural compe-tence than on what the content of such training should be. Until the beginnings of the integrative developments of the 1990s (described in the next few paragraphs), both the content and processes of training varied immensely from program to pro-gram, and even within programs from one year to another. For many students, rela-tionships were unclear, for example, between development of self-awareness about culture and how that awareness should affect counseling practice. Or, once students learned about Native American culture, how should their counseling strategies be modified, if at all? Students might learn a long series of "dos" and "don'ts" for each different culture, for example, be fairly direct with Native American clients, pay increased attention to extended family with African American clients, and so forth. Such lists increase the risks of counselors engaging in the kinds of overgeneralizations of culture described above; moreover, how many separate lists of "dos" and "don'ts" can a counselor be expected to remember?

Fortunately, in the 1990s two kinds of integrative conceptualizations began to appear that hold promise for a more comprehensible perspective on multicultural counseling in the years to come. While it is too early in the development of these conceptualizations to have any of them emerge as "the one," these integrative developments are providing a better focus for research on both the effectiveness of training in, and the practice of, multicultural counseling.

The first of these integrative movements to be described relates primarily to the development of skills in incorporating attention to universal–etic, culture specific–emic, and individual–idiosyncratic factors. We have already reviewed the problems of overgeneralization of culture that emerged from the first developments in multicultural counseling with their emphasis on cultural awareness and cultural knowledge. Yet, simply a shift back to traditional universal factors would be just as erroneous; in fact, the errors of the past led to developments of multicultural counseling: culturally diverse clients whose culture is not acknowledged and/or incorporated in a therapeutic relationship terminate prematurely. Leong (1996), in building the case for his integrative model, has one of the best articulations of the problems of focusing too narrowly on any one of the three perspectives reflected in the saying that "Every person is in certain respects: (a) like all other persons (etic), (b) like some other persons (emic), and (c) like no other person (idiosyncratic)." While noting the progress that had been made on identifying intragroup differences within a given culture (see previous discussion of racial identity and acculturation), Leong pointed out that these models have failed to account for "the existence and constant interplay of all three levels of human personality in a complex and dynamic fashion" (Leong, 1966, p. 201). Carter and Qureshi (1995) also emphasize the need for understanding the interplay of these factors, not just simultaneous existence. As these and similar models are developed and further illustrated with actual cases, it can be hoped that more general principles and therapeutic strategies can be extracted to replace the culture specific "dos" and "don'ts" technique lists.

The second kind of integration is an outstanding exemplar of the scientist–practitioner model of counseling psychology. Several multicultural leaders, also dissatisfied with the fragmentary nature of much multicultural training and its lack of established relationships to either theoretical or empirical bases, have focused on integrations that bring together some long-established theoretical perspectives in psychology with what we have learned from the early developments of multiculturalism. Two major examples of such integrations appeared in *The Counseling Psychologist* (Ridley et al., 1994a; Fischer et al., 1998).

Ridley and colleagues (1994a), in their reexamination, operationalization, and integration of multicultural training, called on the well-established literature on the principles of effective instruction in order to provide a framework for multicultural training. They generated a matrix of 10 learning objectives by 10 instructional strategies. Each learning objective (e.g., cultural empathy, ability to critique existing counseling theories for cultural relevance, knowledge of within-group differences) was accompanied by relevant literature demonstrating the need for including this learning objective in multicultural training. Their 10 instructional strategies (e.g., participatory learning, modeling/observational learning, introspection) were all illustrated by examples from multicultural counseling training programs. Their model provided the best "map" of multicultural training that had ever been presented. Although it did not provide a great deal of information and strategies on "how" all the learning objectives can be achieved, it did show "all the places one needs to go to [or] touch base with" in the process of becoming multiculturally competent.

Whereas the Ridley and colleagues' (1994a) integration called on the psychological literature on effective instruction, Fischer and colleagues (1998), for their integrative model, called on the psychological literature on common factors of effective psychotherapy and healing. They also addressed (1) concerns noted in the first part of this section regarding tensions between etic and emic considerations in working with culturally diverse clientele, (2) the "somewhat fragmented and sometimes particularist literature" (Fischer et al., 1998, p. 540) of multicultural counseling, and (3) how five prior models of multicultural counseling (e.g., Helms, 1995; Leong, 1996) might become more unified using their common factors approach.

From their review of the literature on common factors of effective psychotherapy, considered from both Western and transcultural approaches, Fischer and colleagues identified four essential components of effective multicultural counseling: the relationship, shared worldview, client expectations, and ritual or intervention. After building their case for how each of these four can rest upon significant results obtained from the study of both traditional and multicultural counseling, they conclude:

> [T]he counselor needs (continually) to hypothesize what he or she can do, within the context of the client's unique culture, to enhance the therapeutic relationship, to facilitate convergence in worldview, raise the client's expectations, and implement culturally relevant interventions. We believe that psychologists can best serve culturally different clients by applying their knowledge of common factors in a cultural context (Fischer et al., 1998, p. 566).

Finally, these authors also spelled out specific research implications for each of the four common factors; the results of such research will be extraordinarily helpful in identifying the strengths and weaknesses of the model. By way of summarizing this section, the very positive conclusion is that there are now several fairly comprehensive integrative models one can utilize for multicultural training, all of which represent significant advances over accumulating fragmentary and unintegrated experiences of and knowledge about diverse cultures.

Implementation Issues

Beyond the issues of which essential multicultural counseling skills are to be learned, there are also issues about when, how, and where to incorporate training in these skills. There has been a healthy ongoing dialogue (e.g., Reynolds, 1995) about issues such as whether multicultural content should be covered in a single course or by modules in several courses, at beginning or advanced levels, taught by "majority" or "minority" faculty, and so forth. While the fine points of such dialogues should be primarily the concern of faculty who need to know how to implement the highest quality multicultural training, consensus has been emerging for several implementation issues. These consensus views are based more on experiential reports than on any firm data (see next section); yet we believe that in these transitional times, as programs are seeking to enhance their multicultural training, it is valuable for students to be aware of consensual trends as to what makes training most effective.

Perhaps the clearest consensus that has been reached is that both *a course* (or courses) on multicultural counseling and *infusion of multicultural concerns* into most of the curriculum of a counseling psychology training program are essential. Experience has shown that a single course often left participants not only with inadequate exposure to all of the essential components of competent multicultural counseling but also with the perspective that cultural diversity was a separate specialized interest.

Much has also been learned about faculty and students' perceived values of having instructors of multicultural counseling from diverse backgrounds. While students from "majority" backgrounds sometimes differ from students from "minority" backgrounds regarding the desirability of having "majority" compared to "minority" instructors, all can agree that there are advantages to having instructors from *both backgrounds* involved in multicultural instruction. The broader the range of faculty who are involved in aspects of teaching multicultural counseling, the greater will be the perception of students that multicultural counseling is an integral part of being a counseling psychologist. Similarly, courses that include students from a diverse variety of cultural backgrounds are usually experienced as far more stimulating and meaningful than those classes that are highly homogeneous, whether that homogeneity is primarily Anglo, or primarily students of color.

A final set of implementation issues concerns timing of the various aspects of a multicultural counseling curriculum. Once again a consensus has been emerging that counselor self-awareness about one's own culture is clearly fundamental to being able to make effective use of whatever knowledge and skills are taught regarding other cultures. A natural corollary position to this observation is that self-awareness training should begin very early in the program so that the knowledge and skills infused in other parts of the curriculum can be meaningfully understood and applied by students as they proceed through their programs. Finally, far more attention is now being given to ensure that there is follow-through in practica and internship so that all students have well-supervised experiences (Brown & Landrum-Brown, 1995) in applying multicultural knowledge and skills with a broadly diverse range of clientele.

Assessing Multicultural Competence of Counselors

LaFromboise, Coleman, and Hernandez (1991) diplomatically confront counseling psychologists with a "notable" deficiency in research regarding the effectiveness of training in multicultural counseling. Their review of investigations of the effectiveness of such training indicates that almost every such study included only traditional global measures of counseling effectiveness; the studies lacked measures assessing the cultural sensitivity and competence of the counselors. Such a lack was at least understandable given that measures of multicultural competence had not been developed; however, investigations of effectiveness of multicultural training could hardly be conclusive without such measures. For example, if the measure of effectiveness of training in a multicultural program is the same as the measure of effectiveness for a generic or traditional program, how does one know that the multicultural component had any effect? Or, in a study with clients, if client ratings are obtained only on global measures of satisfaction and perceptions of counselors, how can it be known whether clients were helped by culturally sensitive interventions?

LaFromboise and colleagues were among the first to develop a measure that could address some of these issues. During the early 1990s, three other groups of investigators also initiated the development of measures of multicultural competence. All four measures are briefly described in the next two paragraphs. Before making use of any of these measures, counseling psychologists would do well to consult Pope-Davis and Dings (1995), who provide an excellent conceptual and empirical review of the first three measures discussed below, all of which are counselor self-report measures compared to the supervisor rating scale developed by LaFromboise and colleagues (LaFromboise et al., 1991).

The earliest of the self-report measures was the Multicultural Awareness–Knowledge–Skills Survey (MAKSS) (D'Andrea, Daniels, & Heck, 1991). Note from its title that this survey has three scales based on the tripartite model of the Sue and colleagues (1982) report on multicultural competence. (In fact, all four measures discussed here relied on that report for their initial development of items.) The MAKSS consists of 60 items, with 20 items each for the awareness, knowledge, and skills areas. Counselors respond to each item on varying 4-point scales; for example, Very Limited to Very Aware for an item like "At this point in your life, how would you rate your understanding of the impact of the way you think and act when interacting with persons of different cultural backgrounds?"; or Strongly Disagree to Strongly Agree for an item like "In the early grades of schooling in the United States, the academic achievement of such ethnic minorities as African Americans, Hispanics, and Native Americans is close to parity with the achievement of Anglo mainstream students." These two sample items indicate not only the varying response format but also the fact that some items are self-descriptions, whereas others are items that could be scored right or wrong. Pope-Davis and Dings (1995) review some of the assets and limitations of this mixture of items.

Sodowsky, Taffe, Gutkin, and Wise (1994) developed the Multicultural Counseling Inventory (MCI) using factor analyses to develop a brief yet comprehensive measure of the various domains within multicultural competence. Their factor analyses of responses from hundreds of graduate students yields four factors with varying number of items: multicultural counseling skills (11 items), multicultural awareness (10 items), multicultural counseling knowledge (11 items), and multicultural counseling relationship (8 items). The relationship scale compared to the multicultural counseling skills scale, refers to "the counselor's interactional process with the minority client such as the counselor's trustworthiness, comfort level, stereotypes of the minority client, and world view" (Sodowsky et al., 1994, p. 142.) Counselors are asked to indicate how accurately each of the 40 items describes them using a 4-point scale ranging from Very Inaccurate to Very Accurate.

The Multicultural Counseling Awareness Scale-Form B (MCAS-B), developed by Ponterotto, Rieger, Barrett, and Sparks (1994) was also developed factor analytically. The final 42 items in their scale yield just two factors: (1) knowledge and skills (28 items), and (2) awareness (14 items). Like the MAKSS and the MCI, the MCAS-B is a self-report measure; the counselor responds to each of the items on a 7-point rating scale (Not at All True to Totally True) indicating "the truth of each item as it applies to you." As Pope-Davis and Dings (1995) review, all three of these measures have been developed with reasonable attention to standards of reliability and validity. Validity has been addressed, in most cases, by showing that students who receive some training in multicultural training do attain somewhat higher scores. More research needs to be conducted to determine whether the lack of more impressive gains by students on some of these scales indicates that (a) the scales are not adequately measuring what students have learned or (b) the training programs are not helping students make significant gains in multicultural competence. Also problematic are the low intercorrelations of these three scales that supposedly measure the same kinds of outcomes. It is not unusual during the early stages of test development to have scales with the same names yielding significantly different information (see Chapter 13); however, in order to increase the validity of these developing measures, researchers will have to determine more precisely just what the different scales are measuring. Another major limitation of the validity of these three self-report scales will be taken up after a brief description of the LaFromboise et al. (1991) supervisor-completed scale since that scale shares the same limitation in validity.

The Cross-Cultural Counseling Inventory-Revised (CCCI-R)(LaFromboise et al., 1991) includes 20 items on which the supervisor rates a counselor's demonstration of a particular competency on a 6-point scale ranging from Strongly Disagree to Strongly Agree. Factor analyses of the responses of many supervisors, as well as counselors who were asked to rate videotaped counselors conducting sessions with culturally diverse clients, yielded three factors that were then labeled (a) cross-cultural counseling skill (10 items like "aware of own cultural heritage; values and respects cultural differences"), (b) sociopolitical awareness (6 items like "elicits variety of verbal and nonverbal responses; appreciates social status of client as an ethnic minority"), and (c) cultural sensitivity (4 items like "presents own values to client; demonstrates knowledge about client's culture"). The CCCI-R has had less extensive use in evaluating multicultural training programs primarily because it requires that a supervisor observe and rate students, obviously not nearly as efficient as the three self-report measures described above. On the other hand, the CCCI-R does have the distinct advantage of being closer to a measure of behavioral competence since a supervisor has to observe a manifestation of cultural competence as compared to the counselor simply self-reporting that he or she feels competent regarding a particular scale item.

None of the measures has had extensive use in assessing actual performance of counselors with culturally diverse clients. Yet to be determined is whether counselors who are rated higher on the scales have more effective counseling outcomes with culturally diverse clients than do counselors who rate lower on these scales. There are many theses and dissertations that can be completed in the coming years, all of which could make significant contributions to improved assessment of both the outcomes of multicultural training programs and the outcomes of culturally sensitive counseling (Pope-Davis & Coleman, 1997).

Before leaving this topic of assessment of multicultural competence, the radically different approach of Coleman (1996) should be noted. Frustrated with the inadequacies of existing measures for demonstrating whether counselors in training had achieved adequate levels of multicultural competence, he proposed the use of portfolio assessment. Just as artists and architects have long prepared portfolios of their work, counselors could, for example, (a) prepare videotapes of their work with culturally diverse clients, (b) write a proposal for a culturally relevant intervention, and/or (c) design a program for an agency/setting in which the counselor is working/has worked that maximizes access to treatment by culturally diverse clients. The portfolio would also need to include evidence of counselors' effectiveness, for example, clients' ratings of the counselor, an agency's approval of the conceptual design of a new program, and so forth. Coleman values not only the clearer evidence such a portfolio provides, as compared to the results of current measures of multicultural competence, but also the encouragement and feedback that preparation of such a portfolio provides for the student. "Portfolios have also been useful at encouraging individuals to (a) be more self-reflective about their learning, (b) take greater ownership of the learning process, and (c) show what they have learned to others" (Coleman, 1996, p. 219). While portfolios can indeed be a valuable asset in designing the training and evaluation of individual counselors, their disadvantage is that they cannot be used easily in research investigations involving numerous clients and counselors, such as reported in the next section.

ENHANCING INTERVENTION STRATEGIES FOR CULTURALLY DIVERSE CLIENTS

> [I]nvestigators have been remarkably consistent in offering recommendations or suggestions for improving the relationship between therapists and ethnic-minority clients . . . (a) more ethnic therapists who presumably are bilingual or are familiar with ethnic cultural values should be recruited into the mental health field, (b) students and therapists should acquire knowledge of ethnic cultures and communities, and (c) traditional forms of treatment should be modified because they are geared primarily for mainstream Americans (Sue & Zane, 1987, pp. 37–38).

These conclusions of Sue and Zane, from their review of research in the 1970s and early 1980s on counseling practices with ethnic minority populations, have been cited repeatedly as the basis both for the kinds of multicultural training described in earlier sections of this chapter and for increasingly sophisticated programs of research on how counseling services for culturally diverse clientele can be enhanced. In this final major section of this chapter, we review the significant progress that has been made in understanding the components of effective multicultural counseling and some of the most pressing research that yet needs to be conducted. The three recommendations in the quotation that opens this section have led directly to programs of research described in the next three subsections. As fine examples of the scientist–practitioner model, two additional types of research on effective multicultural counseling are now in progress, building on the findings of the earlier programs of research. "Fourth force" multiculturalism, invigorated by active scientists–practitioners, promises even greater progress in the coming decade in counseling psychologists' attainment of cultural competence.

Ethnic Similarity of Counselors and Clients

Atkinson and Lowe (1995) have appropriately noted that recurring national policy recommendations calling for the training of more ethnic minority counselors is built on the assumption that ethnic minority clients will be able to form more effective therapeutic relationships with ethnic minority counselors. For more than two decades, researchers have investigated (1) the preferences of ethnic minority clients for ethnic minority counselors, (2) ethnic minority clients' ratings of counselor credibility in relation to minority and nonminority status of counselors, and (3) outcomes of counseling for ethnic minority clients when counselors were ethnic minority compared to nonethnic minority. In all three of these categories of research, significant evidence has accumulated for every American ethnic minority that ethnic similarity is related to more positive results, for example, ethnic minority clients prefer ethnically similar counselors (Coleman, Wampold, & Casali, 1995) and, even more crucial to effective counseling outcomes, are less likely to terminate counseling prematurely when their counselor is of similar ethnicity (Atkinson & Lowe, 1995).

While most studies of this kind yield significant main effects for similarity, they also often yielded evidence of considerable variation in the responses of the ethnic minority clients, with some feeling very strongly about having ethnically similar counselors, others having little if any concern for such matching. As will be discussed below, it soon became apparent that clients' own racial identity acculturation style, and level of cultural mistrust all affect the importance of ethnic similarity. Moreover, a very recent study has found counselor skills and similarity in personality traits more critical than ethnic similarity (Vera, Speight, Mildner, & Carlson, 1999). The "good news" from such findings is the possibility that culturally competent nonminority counselors can indeed have effective therapeutic relationships with minority clients.

Counselor Knowledge of Ethnic Cultures

While much professional training of counseling psychologists has been redesigned to ensure counselor knowledge of ethnic cultures, there have yet been no direct studies that counselors with such knowledge have more positive outcomes with ethnic minority clients (Atkinson & Lowe, 1995). As noted above in the discussion of the measures of multicultural competence, most validity studies have focused simply on whether or not counselors saw themselves as better informed and more ready to provide multicultural services. In one sense, this lack of direct correlation between amount of knowledge a counselor has and his or her effectiveness in counseling is less important than the question of whether or not the counselor is using this knowledge in the counseling relationship and, if so, is the counseling more effective? The next section includes more positive results of this kind.

Modifying Conventional Forms of Treatment

Atkinson and Lowe (1995) review three types of research focusing on whether modifying traditional forms of treatment can yield improved outcomes for ethnic minority clients. Their first category is identifying conventional counseling strategies that are effective with ethnic minority clients; the focus of most such research has been comparing (1) directive versus nondirective counseling techniques, and (2) level of counselor self-disclosure versus nondisclosure. Most, but not all, studies have found ethnic minority clients prefer counselors who use more directive counseling techniques; there has been no consistent patterns of results regarding level of counselor self-disclosure.

The second kind of research Atkinson and Lowe (1995) review examined the effects of counseling in which the counselor clearly attends to cultural concerns. The results are extremely positive. Studies completed with African Americans, Asian Americans, and Mexican Americans provide

> . . . a clear-cut case for cultural responsiveness as a counseling strategy for building credibility with ethnic minority clients. There is also evidence that culturally responsive counseling results in greater client willingness to return for counseling, satisfaction with counseling, and depth of self-disclosure (Atkinson & Lowe, 1995, p. 403).

Such results provide a compelling rationale for attention to building the cultural knowledge base of counselors; counselors cannot attend to cultural concerns if they are not aware of them!

The final category reviewed by Atkinson and Lowe (1995) includes studies of the effectiveness of incorporating indigenous beliefs and techniques in the counseling process; Sue (1998) refers to such research as ethnic-specific services. Research of this kind is quite heterogeneous and ranges from, for example, including culturally specific examples in a substance abuse program (e.g., Afro-centric religious traditions as part of a 12-step recovery program) or serving tea instead of coffee to Chinese clients or including an indigenous healer in planning and implementing a psychological treatment program. The outcomes of such studies have been less impressive than those reported in the previous paragraph where counselors attended to cultural concerns as a focus of the discussions in counseling. However, the results do suggest that ethnic minority clients do find such modifications attractive and are more likely to seek services from agencies that have such programs and are less likely to drop out of counseling prematurely. There is no evidence, however, that the eventual outcomes of counseling are greater for clients who are in such programs compared to those who receive traditional counseling, provided the clients complete counseling (Sue, 1998).

Interactions of Counselor and Client Cultural Statuses

As noted in the discussion of the research on effects of ethnic similarity of counselor and client, clients' ratings of the importance of having a counselor of their own ethnicity were highly varied: "The fact that racial identity development, acculturation and cultural mistrust play such an important role in client/participant expectations for, and reactions to, counseling reinforces the need for counselors to recognize both cultural influences and individual differences" (Atkinson & Thompson, 1992). Models are very slowly beginning to emerge that incorporate such within-group differences in the study of how to attain more significant outcomes for multicultural counseling. This refinement of research strategies, based on the results of previous research, along with observations from actual counseling as to what is affecting client reactions to counseling, exemplifies the scientist–practitioner model in action.

Helms (1984) was the first researcher to provide counseling psychologists with a clear model of how individual differences within ethnic minority groups of clients, as well as within counselors—be they majority or minority—could be utilized interactively to enhance the effectiveness of multicultural counseling. Since Helms's own research is focused on racial identity, her interaction model, briefly described here, focuses on within-group differences in racial identity; however, the conceptual model could easily be adapted to any other within-group difference shared by counselors and clients, for example, differences in acculturation. By referring back to the separate sets of statuses of racial identity described earlier in this chapter, for Anglos and people of color, and recalling that they were presented from least to most complex, and from least to most mature, Helms points out that if a client is at a more advanced status in his or her racial identity than the counselor is in his or her racial identity, then one can expect that the client will experience considerable frustration and possibly even a worsening of his or her psychological distress.

Helms theorizes four types of relationships based on pairings of counselor and client racial identity statuses: parallel, crossed, progressive, and regressive. Parallel relationships occur when counselor and client are in similar statuses of complexity; crossed relationships occur when counselor and client are at diametrically opposite statuses (e.g., a counselor in immersion status, a client in reintegration status). A progressive relationship is the most promising since the counselor is at a more complex, mature status than the client, providing opportunity for significant client growth in his or her own racial identity status with resulting increased self-confidence. Regressive relationships are just the opposite: the client has a more complex and mature racial identity status than the counselor; the counselor experiences much anxiety; the client feels the counselor is not able to be helpful and prematurely terminates. In her 1990 book, Helms provides examples of all of these pairings; she also identifies common affective issues, typical counselor strategies, and probable outcomes related to each type of pairing.

Although all these possible matchings make it somewhat difficult to conduct comprehensive research on this model, all of the initial studies yielded significant results for at least some of the predicted outcomes (Helms, 1990). The model has tremendous logical appeal as a way to understand and utilize within-group differences. Such developments, along with the results reviewed in the previous three subsections, clearly indicate that future research on strategies to enhance the effectiveness of multicultural counseling must incorporate within-group variations in experimental designs and/or as statistical moderator variables.

"Return" of the Scientist–Practitioner

While Helms has focused on within-group cultural differences in developing a new model for enhancing multicultural competence, two other models also emerged that provide opportunities for counseling psychologists to use both their scientist and practitioner skills to attain greater understanding of how to integrate the various components of multicultural practice. Both Leong (1996) and Fischer et al. (1998) exemplify the best traditions of our scientist–practitioner model by building not only on the results of multicultural research but also on the existing theoretical and empirical literature in other areas of psychology. Leong (1996) has called on social psychological theory on complementarity and cognitive psychological theory on complexity and mindfulness to provide an integrative model that seeks to comprehend the dynamics of the balance in effective multicultural counseling, of etic, emic, and individual considerations. Leong recognizes that he has provided a framework that now needs to be tested by counselors and clinicians.

> [I]t would be important for researchers to formulate and test hypotheses about the effects of the proposed dynamic sequences on the cross-cultural counseling relationship and the associated outcomes. We need more research that analyzes when clients and therapists shift between levels and what antecedents and consequences are associated with these shifts. Effective cross-cultural counseling and psychotherapy will depend significantly on the use of an integrative and complete model as opposed to unidimensional models that use only one of the three dimensions of human experience (Leong, 1996, p. 208).

Fischer and colleagues (1998), as noted earlier in this chapter, have called on the research on common factors of effectiveness in psychotherapy in order to address the

> . . . problems with both the etic and emic approaches to multicultural counseling. . . . Our thesis was that common factors found in conventional psychotherapy and in healing across cultures, combined with a thorough knowledge of cultural context, can serve not only to frame the extant multicultural counseling literature but also to inform multicultural practitioners, educators and researchers in the future (p. 578).

They also provide well-crafted research questions which, if pursued, can lead to a better understanding of what strategies lead to more effective multicultural counseling outcomes.

Whereas the emphasis in multicultural issues in the 1970s and 1980s was on long-overdue attention to the impact of culture on therapeutic relationships, and on the need for counselors to break out of their encapsulation and come to understand much more about their own culture and that of their clients, within the past few years there has been increasing attention paid to how to integrate the knowledge gained from those years with other knowledge bases in psychology. Sue (1998), in his review of what is basic to our continued search for cultural competence in psychotherapy and counseling, captures the overarching strategy counseling psychologists need to utilize to pull together the many strands of awareness, knowledge, and skills we have reviewed in this chapter:

> There probably are some skills that are beneficial to have in cultural competency—characteristics or skills that cut across cultures. . . . I believe one of these characteristics is scientific mindedness. By scientific mindedness, I am referring to therapists who form hypotheses rather than make premature conclusions about the status of culturally different clients, who develop creative ways to test hypotheses and who act on the basis of acquired data (Sue, 1998, p. 445).

SUMMARY

Multiculturalism has emerged as a fourth force in counseling psychology as research made clear the needs for a broader range of strategies in order to provide more effective intervention for our increasingly culturally diverse society. Counseling psychologists in the twenty-first century will need to integrate with traditional fundamentals of counseling, the self-understanding, knowledge, and skills that form the foundation of competent multicultural counseling. Self-understanding for multicultural competence begins with an appreciation of the ongoing controversies we described regarding the meanings of the terms multicultural, cultural diversity, race, ethnicity, and minority. We then explored how self-understanding is aided by awareness of the concepts of Anglo racial identity and how the normal development of developmental and social psychological processes such as coping defenses and consensus effects all impede multicultural sensitivity.

We explained how knowledge of client cultures is more than memorizing a few facts about diverse cultures; understanding sources of within-group differences related to racial identity, acculturation, worldviews, and client beliefs about counseling are critical components of counselors making appropriate diagnoses and interventions with culturally diverse clientele.

Self-understanding and knowledge of client cultures serve as the basic foundation for developing multicultural counseling skills. Identifying and assessing the components of competent multicultural counseling skills have been the focus of considerable debate and research during the past decade. We cited many of the key principles, guidelines, and training models that have been put forth as well as the preliminary developments of assessment techniques for determining when a counseling psychologist has achieved multicultural competence. With all of the profession having an increased awareness of these issues, predoctoral, intern, and continuing education programs are all giving increased attention to helping counseling psychologists expand their multicultural effectiveness.

Beyond the achievement of multicultural competence for each counseling psychologist is the pressing need for the development of more effective research and intervention strategies for working with culturally diverse clients. In this chapter we described the knowledge being accumulated from research on areas such as (1) ethnic similarity of counselors and clients, (2) counselor knowledge of ethnic cultures, (3) modifications of conventional forms of treatment, and (4) interactions of counselor and client culture statuses. Continuation and advancement of such research will require not only multicultural competence but also the utilization of all of the very best attributes of the counseling psychologist as a scientist–practitioner.

REFERENCES

Arredondo, P., Toporek, R., Brown, S. P., Jones, J., Locke, D. C., Sanchez, J., & Stadler, H. (1996). Operationalization of the multicultural counseling competencies. *Journal of Multicultural Counseling and Development, 24,* 42–78.

Atkinson, D. R. (1994). Multicultural training: A call for standards. *The Counseling Psychologist, 22,* 300–307.

Atkinson, D. R., & Hackett, G. (Eds.). (1988). *Counseling non-ethnic American minorities.* Springfield, IL: Charles C. Thomas.

Atkinson, D. R., & Lowe, S. M. (1995). The role of ethnicity, cultural knowledge, and conventional techniques in counseling and psychotherapy. In J. G. Ponterotto, J. M. Casas, L. A. Suzuki, and C. M. Alexander (Eds.), *Handbook of multicultural counseling* (pp. 387–414). Thousand Oaks, CA: Sage Publications.

Atkinson, D. R., & Thompson, C. E. (1992). Racial, ethnic, and cultural variables in counseling. In S. D. Brown and R. W. Lent (Eds.), *Handbook of counseling psychology* (2nd ed., pp. 349–382). New York: John Wiley & Sons.

Atkinson, D. R., Thompson, C. E., & Grant, S. K. (1993). A three-dimensional model for counseling racial/ethnic minorities. *The Counseling Psychologist, 21,* 257–277.

Betz, N. E. (1989). Implications of the null environment for women's career development and for counseling psychology. *The Counseling Psychologist, 17,* 136–144.

Brown, M. T., & Landrum-Brown, J. (1995). Counselor supervision: Cross-cultural perspectives. In J. G. Ponterotto, J. M. Casas, L. A. Suzuki, and C. M. Alexander (Eds.), *Handbook of multicultural counseling* (pp. 263–286). Thousand Oaks, CA: Sage Publications.

Carter, R. T., & Qureshi, A. (1995). A typology of philosophical assumptions in multicultural counseling and training. In J. G. Ponterotto, J. M. Casas, L. A. Suzuki, and C. M. Alexander (Eds.), *Handbook of multicultural counseling* (pp. 239–262). Thousand Oaks, CA: Sage Publications.

Casas, M. (1984). Policy, training and research in counseling psychology: The racial/ethnic minority perspective. In S. Brown and R. Lent (Eds.), *Handbook of counseling psychology* (pp. 785–831). New York: John Wiley & Sons.

Coleman, H. L. K. (1995). Strategies for coping with cultural diversity. *The Counseling Psychologist, 23,* 722–740.

Coleman, H. L. K. (1996). Portfolio assessment of multicultural counseling competency. *The Counseling Psychologist, 24,* 216–229.

Coleman, H. L. K., Wampold, B. E., & Casali, S. L. (1995). Ethnic minorities' ratings of ethnically similar and European American counselors: A meta-analysis. *Journal of Counseling Psychology, 42,* 55–64.

Constantine, M. G. (1997). Facilitating multicultural competency in counseling supervision. In D. B. Pope-Davis and H. L. K. Coleman (Eds.), *Multicultural counseling competencies* (pp. 310–324). Thousand Oaks, CA: Sage Publications.

Cook, D. A., & Helms, J. E. (1988). Relationship dimensions as predictors of visible racial/ethnic group students' perceptions of cross-racial supervision. *Journal of Counseling Psychology, 35,* 268–274.

D'Andrea, M., & Daniels, J. (1997). Multicultural counseling supervision: Central issues, theoretical considerations, and practical strategies. In D. B. Pope-Davis and H. L. K. Coleman (Eds.), *Multicultural counseling competencies* (pp. 290–309). Thousand Oaks, CA: Sage Publications.

D'Andrea, M., Daniels, J., & Heck, R. (1991). Evaluating the impact of multicultural counseling training. *Journal of Counseling and Development, 70,* 143–150.

Eisenman, R. (1995). Why psychologists should study race. *American Psychologist, 50,* 42–43.

Enns, C. Z. (1993). Twenty years of feminist counseling and therapy. *The Counseling Psychologist, 21,* 3–87.

Essandoh, P. K. (1996). Multicultural counseling as the "Fourth Force": A call to arms. *The Counseling Psychologist, 24,* 126–137.

Fassinger, R. E., & Sperber-Richie, B. (1997). Sex matters: Gender and sexual orientation in training for multicultural counseling competency. In D. B. Pope-Davis and H. L. K. Coleman (Eds.), *Multicultural counseling competencies* (pp. 83–110). Thousand Oaks, CA: Sage Publications.

Fischer, A. R., Jome, L. M., & Atkinson, D. R. (1998). Reconceptualizing multicultural counseling. *The Counseling Psychologist, 26,* 525–588.

Fitzgerald, L. F., & Nutt, R. (1986). The Division 17 principles concerning the counseling/psychotherapy of women: Rationale and implementation. *The Counseling Psychologist, 14,* 180–216.

Gaines, S. O., & Reed, E. S. (1995). Prejudice. *American Psychologist, 50,* 96–103.

Gelso, C. J., & Fassinger, R. E. (1992). Personality, development, and counseling psychology: Depth, ambivalence, and actualization. *Journal of Counseling Psychology, 39,* 275–298.

Gergen, K. J., Gulerce, A., Lock, A., & Misra, G. (1996). Psychological science in cultural context. *American Psychologist, 51,* 496–503.

Grieger, I., & Ponterotto, J. G. (1995). A framework for assessment in multicultural counseling. In J. G. Ponterotto, J. M. Casas, L. A. Suzuki, and C. M. Alexander (Eds.), *Handbook of multicultural counseling* (pp. 357–374). Thousand Oaks, CA: Sage Publications.

Guidelines for providers of psychological services to ethnic, linguistic, and culturally diverse populations. (1993). *American Psychologist, 48,* 45–48.

Hall, C. C. I. (1997). Cultural malpractice. *American Psychologist, 52,* 642–651.

Hecht, M. L., Andersen, P. A., & Ribeau, S. A. (1989). The cultural dimensions of nonverbal communication. In M. K. Asante and W. B. Gudykunst (Eds.), *Handbook of international and intracultural communication* (pp. 163–185). Newbury Park, CA: Sage Publications.

Helms, J. E. (1984). Toward a theoretical explanation of the effects of race on counseling: A black and white model. *The Counseling Psychologist, 12*(4), 153–165.

Helms, J. E. (Ed.). (1990). *Black and white racial identity: Theory, research and practice.* Westport, CT: Greenwood Press.

Helms, J. E. (1992). *A race is a nice thing to have.* Topeka, KS: Content Communications.

Helms, J. E. (1994). How multiculturalism obscures racial factors in the therapy process. *Journal of Counseling Psychology, 41,* 162–165.

Helms, J. E. (1995). An update of Helms's white and people of color racial identity models. In J. G. Ponterotto, J. M. Casas, L. A. Suzuki, and C. M. Alexander (Eds.), *Handbook of multicultural counseling* (pp. 181–198). Thousand Oaks, CA: Sage Publications.

Helms, J. E., & Talleyrand, R. M. (1997). Race is not ethnicity. *American Psychologist, 52,* 1246–1247.

Hills, H. I., & Strozier, A. L. (1992). Multicultural training in APA-approved counseling psychology programs: A survey. *Professional Psychology: Research and Practice, 23,* 43–51.

Jackson, M. L. (1995). Multicultural counseling: Historical perspectives. In J. G. Ponterotto, J. M. Casas, L. A. Suzuki, and C. M. Alexander (Eds.), *Handbook of multicultural counseling* (pp. 3–16). Thousand Oaks, CA: Sage Publications.

Kerwin, C., & Ponterotto, J. G. (1995). Biracial identity development: Theory and research. In J. G. Ponterotto, J. M. Casas, L. A. Suzuki, and C. M. Alexander (Eds.), *Handbook of multicultural counseling* (pp. 199–217). Thousand Oaks, CA: Sage Publications.

Kiselica, M. S. (1998). Preparing Anglos for the challenges and joys of multiculturalism. *The Counseling Psychologist, 26,* 5–21.

LaFromboise, T. D., Coleman, H. L. K., & Gerton, J. (1993). Psychological impact of biculturalism: Evidence and theory. *Psychological Bulletin, 114,* 395–412.

LaFromboise, T. D., Coleman, H. L. K., & Hernandez, A. (1991). Development and factor structure of the Cross-Cultural Counseling Inventory—Revised. *Professional Psychology: Research and Practice, 22,* 380–388.

Leong, F. T. L. (1996). Toward an integrative model for cross-cultural counseling and psychotherapy. *Applied & Preventive Psychology, 5,* 189–209.

Leong, F. T. L., & Santiago-Rivera, A. L. (1999). Climbing the multiculturalism summit: Challenges and pitfalls. In P. Pedersen (Ed.), *Multiculturalism as a fourth force* (pp. 61–72). Philadelphia: Brunner/Mazel.

Leong, F. T. L., Wagner, N. S., & Tata, S. P. (1995). Racial and ethnic variations in help-seeking attitudes. In J. G. Ponterotto, J. M. Casas, L. A. Suzuki, and C. M. Alexander (Eds.), *Handbook of multicultural counseling* (pp. 415–438). Thousand Oaks, CA: Sage Publications.

Mintz, L. B., Bartels, K. M., & Rideout, C. A. (1995). Training in counseling ethnic minorities and race-based availability of graduate school resources. *Professional Psychology: Research and Practice, 26,* 316–321.

Neville, H. A., Heppner, M. J., Louie, C. E., Thompson, C. E., Brooks, L., & Baker, C. E. (1996). The impact of multicultural training on white racial identity attitudes and therapy competencies. *Professional Psychology: Research and Practice, 27,* 83–89.

Ottavi, T. M., Pope-Davis, D. B., & Dings, J. G. (1994). Relationship between white racial identity attitudes and self-reported multicultural counseling competencies. *Journal of Counseling Psychology, 41,* 149–154.

Paniagua, F. A. (1998). *Assessing and treating culturally diverse clients* (2nd ed.). Thousand Oaks, CA: Sage Publications.

Pedersen, P. (Ed.). (1999). *Multiculturalism as a fourth force.* Philadelphia: Brunner/Mazel.

Pedersen, P. B., Draguns, J. G., Lonner, W. J., & Trimble, J. E. (Eds.). (1996). *Counseling across cultures* (4th ed.). Thousand Oaks, CA: Sage Publications.

Phinney, J. S. (1996). When we talk about American ethnic groups, what do we mean? *American Psychologist, 51,* 918–927.

Ponterotto, J. G. (1997). Multicultural counseling training: A competency model and national survey. In D. B. Pope-Davis and H. L. K. Coleman (Eds.), *Multicultural counseling competencies* (pp. 111–130). Thousand Oaks, CA: Sage Publications.

Ponterotto, J. G., Casas, J. M., Suzuki, L. A., & Alexander, C. M. (Eds.). (1995). *Handbook of multicultural counseling.* Thousand Oaks, CA: Sage Publications.

Ponterotto, J. G., Rieger, B. P., Barrett, A., & Sparks, R. (1994). Assessing multicultural counseling competence: A review of instrumentation. *Journal of Counseling and Development, 72,* 316–322.

Pope-Davis, D. B., & Coleman, H. L. K. (Eds.). (1997). *Multicultural counseling competencies.* Thousand Oaks, CA: Sage Publications.

Pope-Davis, D. B., & Dings, J. G. (1995). The assessment of multicultural counseling competencies. In J. G. Ponterotto, J. M. Casas, L. A. Suzuki, and C. M. Alexander (Eds.), *Handbook of multicultural counseling* (pp. 287–311). Thousand Oaks, Ca: Sage Publications.

Pope-Davis, D. B., Menefee, L. A., & Ottavi, T. M. (1993). The comparison of white racial identity attitudes among faculty and students: Implications for professional psychologists. *Professional Psychology: Research and Practice, 24,* 443–449.

Pope-Davis, D. B., Reynolds, A. L., Dings, J. G., & Nielson, D. (1995). Examining multicultural counseling competencies of graduate students in psychology. *Professional Psychology: Research and Practice, 26,* 322–329.

Principles concerning the counseling and therapy of women. (1979). *The Counseling Psychologist, 8*(1), 22.

Quintana, S. M., & Bernal, M. E. (1995). Ethnic minority training in counseling psychology. *The Counseling Psychologist, 23,* 102–121.

Reynolds, A. L. (1995). Challenges and strategies for teaching multicultural counseling courses. In J. G. Ponterotto, J. M. Casas, L. A. Suzuki, and C. M. Alexander (Eds.), *Handbook of multicultural counseling* (pp. 312–330). Thousand Oaks, CA: Sage Publications.

Ridley, C. R. (1995). *Overcoming unintentional racism in counseling and therapy.* Thousand Oaks, CA: Sage Publications.

Ridley, C. R., Li, L. C., & Hill, C. L. (1998). Multicultural assessment: Reexamination, reconceptualization, and practical application. *The Counseling Psychologist, 26,* 827–910.

Ridley, C. R., Mendoza, D. W., & Kanitz, B. E. (1994a). Multicultural training: Reexamination, operationalization, and integration. *The Counseling Psychologist, 22,* 227–289.

Ridley, C. R., Mendoza, D. W., Kanitz, B. E., Angermeier, L., & Zenk, R. (1994b). Cultural sensitivity in multicultural counseling: A perceptual schema model. *Journal of Counseling Psychology, 41,* 125–136.

Rogers, C. R. (1957). The necessary and sufficient conditions of therapeutic personality change. *Journal of Consulting Psychology, 21,* 95–103.

Rowe, W., Behrens, J. T., & Leach, M. M. (1995). Racial/ethnic identity and racial consciousness: Looking back and looking forward. In J. G. Ponterotto, J. M. Casas, L. A. Suzuki, and C. M. Alexander (Eds.), *Handbook of multicultural counseling* (pp. 218–236). Thousand Oaks, CA: Sage Publications.

Rushton, J. P. (1995). Construct validity, censorship, and the genetics of race. *American Psychologist, 50,* 40–41.

Sodowsky, G. R., Taffe, R. C., Gutkin, T. B., & Wise, S. L. (1994). Development of the Multicultural Counseling Inventory: A self-report measure of multicultural competencies. *Journal of Counseling Psychology, 41,* 137–148.

Speight, S. L., Thomas, A. J., Kennel, R. G., & Anderson, M. E. (1995). Operationalizing multicultural training in doctoral programs and internships. *Professional Psychology: Research and Practice, 26,* 401–406.

Sue, D. W., Bernier, J. E., Durran, A., Feinberg, L., Pedersen, P., Smith, E. J., & Vasquez-Nuttall, E. (1982). Position paper: Cross-cultural counseling competencies. *The Counseling Psychologist, 10*(2), 45–52.

Sue, D. W., & Sue, D. (1999). *Counseling the culturally different: Theory and practice* (3rd ed.). New York: John Wiley & Sons.

Sue, S. (1998). In search of cultural competence in psychotherapy and counseling. *American Psychologist, 53,* 440–448.

Sue, S., & Zane, N. (1987). The role of culture and cultural techniques in psychotherapy: A critique and reformulation. *American Psychologist, 42,* 37–45.

Thompson, C. E., Worthington, R., & Atkinson, D. R. (1994). Counselor content orientation, counselor race, and black women's cultural mistrust and self-disclosures. *Journal of Counseling Psychology, 41,* 155–161.

Trevino, J. G. (1996). Worldview and change in cross-cultural counseling. *The Counseling Psychologist, 24,* 198–215.

Vera, E. M., Speight, S. L., Mildner, C., & Carlson, H. (1999). Clients' perceptions and evaluations of similarities to and differences from their counselors. *Journal of Counseling Psychology, 46,* 277–283.

Wirth, L. (1945). The problem of minority groups. In R. Linton (Ed.), *The science of man in the world crisis* (pp. 346–369). New York: Columbia University Press.

Wrenn, C. G. (1962). The culturally encapsulated counselor. *Harvard Educational Review, 32,* 444–449.

Yee, A. H., Fairchild, H. H., Weizmann, F., & Wyatt, G. E. (1993). Addressing psychology's problems with race. *American Psychologist, 48,* 1132–1140.

C H A P T E R 7

ON BECOMING A COUNSELING PSYCHOLOGIST: PROFESSIONAL DEVELOPMENT IN GRADUATE SCHOOL AND BEYOND

For Aspiring Counseling Psychologists

Selecting a Graduate Program

Types of Doctoral Degrees

Graduate School As Professional Development

Six Challenging Perspectives

Graduate School Years: Professional Developmental Opportunities

Elective Courses

Professional Readings

Professional Conventions

This chapter is quite different from the first six chapters, all of which provided an introduction to the foundational concepts and issues in the profession of counseling psychology. This chapter is intended to assist readers who are at least contemplating, if not already on their way to, becoming counseling psychologists. It is designed to be advisory as well as informative. Our selection of perspectives and topics presented is, for the most part, derived from more than 30 years of personal observations and discussions about which factors facilitate the career development of young counseling psychologists. We offer many suggestions that we hope will not only facilitate the career development of each reader, but also provide readers with an increased sense of self-efficacy as a result of becoming acquainted with the "normality" of the sometimes trying experiences of graduate education, choosing internships, and postdegree career options, and becoming a fully credentialed counseling psychologist. The material in Chapter 4, describing the many new developments in the profession of psychology related to the industrialization of health care, is also an important context that has influenced the information and recommendations we provide; readers are urged to read that chapter if they have not already done so, in order to more fully understand the implications of our suggestions.

Chapter 7 covers an extensive range of career development. The headings of the various sections, ranging from "For Aspiring Counseling Psychologists" to "Establishing a Career," are largely self-explanatory and can guide each reader's choice of where to begin reading in this chapter.

FOR ASPIRING COUNSELING PSYCHOLOGISTS

Selecting a Graduate Program

This section provides information and advice for readers who are not yet in graduate programs in counseling psychology yet have liked what they learned about the profession and have decided to learn more about the various kinds and levels of graduate training programs. The first difficult decision to make is whether to consider master's degree programs, typically requiring 2 years of full-time study (or several more years of part-time study); or doctoral degree programs, typically requiring 5–6 years of full-time study, including the internship. (Only a few doctoral programs allow much part-time study; part-time doctoral degrees often require 10 or more years.) As we elaborated in Chapter 4, psychology has, since the 1940s, viewed the doctoral degree as the only degree appropriate for fully independent practice. Completion of only a master's degree in psychology will impose significant limits to career opportunities in psychology. On the other hand, as also noted in Chapter 4, there are more practice opportunities for one with a master's degree in counseling, as compared to a master's degree in psychology. Readers interested primarily in a practitioner's master's degree in counseling should consider the variety of counseling programs such as mental health counseling, marriage and family counseling, rehabilitation counseling, and community counseling. Hollis and Wantz (1993) list over 400 such programs.

For those considering pursuing the doctoral degree in counseling psychology, there may be a number of reasons to complete a master's degree. First, the shorter time period required allows a more reasonable test of whether one is really interested in and likes making the kinds of academic and professional commitments needed for the several years it takes to become a counseling psychologist. Some students decide that the opportunities available as a professional counselor at the master's degree level are sufficient, especially since the doctoral degree would require another 3 (minimally) and possibly 4–5 years of study and internships.

Second, there are times when students interested in doctoral degree programs do not have the academic credentials needed to gain acceptance directly into psychology doctoral programs (often a 3.5 grade point average in extensive psychology coursework and Graduate Record Exam scores of 1100 or more), yet do have the 3.0 grade point average in general undergraduate coursework typically needed for entering a master's degree program. The choice to pursue a master's degree as a way to improve ones credentials for getting accepted into a doctoral program typically adds a year or two to the time needed to eventually earn a doctoral degree; however, this option does have the distinct advantage of increasing chances for entry into a doctoral program. There are, of course, no guarantees; however, each year a number of master's graduates are able to achieve their goal of going on to doctoral studies when initially they were ineligible for such programs.

For those considering doctoral programs in psychology, there are several major resource books that are important to consult. The first and most basic is *Graduate*

Study in Psychology, which is updated annually by the American Psychological Association (APA). This book lists all programs that offer degrees of all types of psychology in regionally accredited universities. Doctoral-level counseling, clinical, and school programs accredited by the APA are clearly indicated. Each program is briefly described in terms of the kinds of degrees it offers, the required grade point averages, and various kinds of exams required for admission to the program (e.g., Graduate Record Examination); the number of applicants versus the number accepted; amount of financial support available, and so forth. In short, the book provides a great deal of statistical information about almost every program in psychology.

A second major resource includes four "how-to" books on the process of applying to graduate school: *Getting In: A Step-by-Step Plan for Gaining Admission to Graduate School in Psychology* (APA, 1997), *Insider's Guide to Graduate Programs in Clinical and Counseling Psychology* (Sayette, Mayne, & Norcross, 1998), *The Complete Guide to Graduate School Admission* (Keith-Spiegel, 1990) and *Preparing for Graduate Study in Psychology: Not for Seniors Only* (Fretz & Stang, 1980). These books describe not only timelines and procedures for applications but also how to prepare oneself both academically and experientially to become a competitive applicant for doctoral-level programs. For example, they describe how the kinds of courses one takes as an undergraduate may be even more important than simply obtaining high grades. Other sections describe the steps that may be taken to increase the possibilities for attending graduate programs in psychology for those who lack outstanding grades or high Graduate Record Exam scores.

It is important for applicants to counseling psychology programs to understand that these programs vary greatly in how many credit hours and what specific psychology courses must be taken before becoming an applicant. Even though typical guidelines for many graduate psychology programs suggest that applicants have the equivalent of an undergraduate major in psychology, many programs—especially in counseling psychology—will consider applicants from very diverse undergraduate backgrounds, particularly if they have completed courses in statistics and research design, either as part of their own majors or as electives before or after completing their bachelor's degree.

Prospective racial and ethnic minority student applicants to counseling psychology programs can find useful suggestions and assistance in several specialized resource materials. Ponterotto, Burkard, Yoshida et al. (1995) provide some very helpful results from a qualitative study of what prospective minority students look for in application packets. Programs that have paid attention to this study will clearly highlight the opportunities for graduate students to study multicultural theory and practice as well as provide specific information on topics such as financial aid and the ethnic demography of the faculty, student body, and community in which the program is located.

Types of Doctoral Degrees

For students who are now in or expecting to be in a master's degree program and will subsequently be considering various doctoral degree programs, it is important to become aware of some actual differences and, more important, some perceptions about differences in types of doctoral degrees in terms of the opportunities they provide for both short- and long-range professional developmental goals. Doctoral programs in counseling psychology most frequently offer the Ph.D. (Doctor of Philosophy) degree; a few offer an Ed.D. (Doctor of Education) degree; some programs offer a choice of either degree. Because the Ph.D. degree has long been the primary recognized research degree from universities, it is not surprising that counseling psychology, with a scientist–practitioner emphasis, has most often offered the Ph.D. degree. However, since many APA-approved counseling psychology programs have long been housed in colleges and schools of education, some of those programs offer primarily the Ed.D. degree. In earlier times, that degree choice may have indicated less stringent research training and dissertation requirements than in other parts of a university, but that is rarely true in today's colleges of education.

The Psy.D. (Doctor of Psychology) degree is less well known in counseling psychology; these programs more typically offer specializations in clinical psychology. These more practice-oriented degree programs are often very attractive to students who are less interested in research and more interested in a primary focus on practice skills. Because of fewer research requirements, students in Psy.D. degree programs typically take about 5 years to complete their degrees compared to approximately 6 years for those in Ph.D. degree programs (Gaddy, Charlot-Swilley, Nelson, & Reich, 1995). The curriculum of Psy.D. programs regarding education for service delivery and attention to social issues is well described by Peterson, Peterson, Abrams, and Stricker (1997). With less attention to participation in research as part of Psy.D. programs, graduates from these programs are less likely to hold positions in psychology departments or medical schools that award appointments and promotions on the basis of research productivity. On the other hand, the extensive practicum training provided in Psy.D. programs makes graduates attractive to service settings that want to immediately involve new psychologists in extensive practice.

Graduate School as Professional Development

Ideally, graduate school in counseling psychology is a time of significant professional and personal growth as well as for attainment of knowledge. We have noted throughout this book the emphasis of counseling psychology on person–environment interactions. In the next two sections of this chapter we look at the interactions of graduate students (persons) and graduate schools (environments) that are essential to attaining the ideal. Graduate school environments, like most environments, tend to elicit certain feelings and behaviors. Many of these feelings and behaviors help students achieve their goals. However, others may also frequently be elicited that limit the range of goals and/or make attainment of goals more difficult and frustrating than necessary. The next section identifies six perspectives that greatly facilitate satisfaction and productivity during the graduate school years in terms of both professional and personal development. Unfortunately, many of these perspectives are poorly cultivated in the graduate school environment. In fact, there are a variety of factors in our educational system that press toward the antithesis of these perspectives. Understanding both the needs of persons developing as counseling psychologists and the environmental presses of graduate school is therefore an essential part of the next section.

Six Challenging Perspectives

Changing the Means-to-an-End Attitude
Into Professional Development

We find many graduate students enter graduate school with what we call a means-to-an-end perspective, one that served them well in high school and college. In high school, one tries to do well to have the opportunity to go to a good college; in college, one tries to do well to get into graduate school; then one focuses on surviving graduate school in order to earn the doctoral degree. Then life begins! We would like to interrupt this means-to-an-end course of study. *The end is here! You are now part of counseling psychology.* (We shift here to the second-person "you" form for the remainder of the chapter, feeling the need for a more personal frame of reference for this largely advisory material.)

We recommend your looking at graduate school as the beginning of your professional development. Such a change will require you to adopt an activist position as you encounter a variety of challenges. Essentially, you must ask how you can get the most out of each experience instead of doing just enough to get by or "over the hurdle." Taking a professional development view rather than a means-to-an-end perspective is best accomplished by understanding the 5 other challenging perspectives in this section: (1) changing self-preservation into self-actualization, (2) balancing dependence and independence, (3) finding a mentor, (4) actively coping with disappointments, and (5) finding personal development in professional development. For these five perspectives we examine some typical problem areas and frustrations you may encounter as a graduate student, then suggest ways of mastering the challenge of growing professionally and personally.

Changing Self-Preservation Into Self-Actualization

For students just beginning graduate study, turning self-preservation into self-actualization may be the most salient challenge. Graduate study in counseling psychology may bring numerous threats to one's sense of self-efficacy. We define *self-efficacy* as the "expectation that one can master the problems that one faces in a given situation." Self-efficacy has become not only a central concept in the social learning perspective in personality development and in cognitive–behavioral therapy (see Bandura, 1977), but also in understanding career development in general (Lent, Brown, & Hackett, 1994) and, even more specifically, predicting development of interest in research (Bishop & Bieschke, 1998).

The quantity and quality of the requirements of graduate courses will probably exceed those you had in undergraduate courses. Moreover, other students in the class are usually as academically talented as you (or perhaps seemingly more so). Seeing "first clients," even if only role-playing, may leave you tongue-tied. The thought of completing a dissertation ("Did you hear her dissertation was 210-pages long?") may simply be beyond your hopes of anything you could do. In the absence of some of the psychological supports we talk about later in this chapter, any student facing all these threats might well consider a different career.

The major concern we need to address about these threats to self-efficacy is the possibility that they will lead to self-doubts and avoidant behaviors—the latter in the service of a felt need for self-preservation. We are not concerned that you experience some self-doubts; you will probably not be stretched enough to reach your full potential without them. We want to "certify" that it is all right to have such doubts. How you react to them is the critical factor to be discussed here. All too often, the way any of us cope is to minimize or avoid contact with the difficult situation. At the extreme, such avoidance may mean withdrawal from graduate school and termination of a long-planned career objective. At a lesser extreme, it results in students minimizing their work in the threatening area and considering the requirement as simply a hurdle to get over. "Get by with as little as possible and get out as soon as possible" is the creed of the self-preservation specialist.

Such a strategy, however, may lead to many unfortunate disappointments for both you and your program faculty. If course demands are the threat and one responds by avoiding much material related to that course, one is engaging in a self-defeating behavior that leads to the self-fulfilling prophecy of not doing well. Relatedly, graduate students sometimes deal with the threat of research by avoiding any research activities until absolutely compelled to confront them—until they must start their dissertation.

What should you do when confronted by threats to self-efficacy? First, as we have already said, simply recognize what is happening to you. Initial feelings of acute anxiety, dread, or the need to get away from it all may simply be the result of these challenges—they are not necessarily indicating more serious psychological problems and/or unsuitability for the profession of counseling psychology. Second, at the risk of oversimplifying, we urge you to think of reframing threats to self-efficacy as a problem-solving task. The literature on personal problem-solving and counseling (Heppner & Krauskopf, 1987) describes many of the strategies for appraisal of problems, goal-setting, and problem-solving actions. There are many steps you can take on your own; also, as we discuss later, if your doubts seem overwhelming, they may be a good catalyst for considering the benefits of personal counseling for yourself. In response to demands from academic courses, you may want to consider new methods of reading, studying, or time management. For threats from initial counseling experiences, you may want to consult additional skill-building workbooks (e.g., Egan, 1994), study casebook materials, observe peers counsel, and so forth. For research, you might seek out a research team project where you would have much smaller and more defined activities than personally planning and conducting a full study.

In summary, we simply suggest that, after experiencing threats to self-efficacy, you must ask yourself what you need to do to make this an area in which you grow and develop; that is, actualize your potential. Easier said than done, we agree. (One advisee said, "I'd like to self-actualize, but I have this horrible exam next week.") If you find yourself at any time in the future looking at your own avoidant tendencies generated by self-doubts, say, "Stop! I need to look at what I can *do* rather than what I can *avoid*." If you do this, we will have accomplished our goal for this brief section of the chapter.

We do recognize that striving for self-actualization in the face of the many demands of graduate work will test your ability to set limits. There are indeed only 24 hours in a day and we all need sleep. If you are being challenged in many areas simultaneously, it may be important to sort out your priorities. Which challenges will you work on at this time versus some future time? If you entered graduate school directly from undergraduate school, you may still be working on the assumption that you will be able to reach a reasonable level of mastery on most of the tasks and demands that come with each semester. Part of the process of becoming a professional, and dealing with often vague and extensive tasks, is learning to live with the feeling that one is never truly completely "on top" and "caught up." Feelings of completeness and mastery that sometimes came at the end of semesters may be ones you have to file in long-term memory. Being a professional is not defined in terms of number of tasks for a given semester. Part of self-management as a professional is deciding throughout your entire career which tasks can be accomplished in the near future and which will have to wait for coming months or even later. The bottom line for this kind of setting of limits is to remember that you are *deferring* rather than *avoiding* work that you cannot manage at the present time.

Our final point related to changing self-preservation into self-actualization concerns the role of competition in our society, sometimes most blatantly evident in our system of higher education (e.g., curving exam scores). Such procedures obviously foster individual competitiveness, meaning that students may almost studiously avoid any collaborative work and mutual assistance. Much has been written about how such procedures are inimical to higher-level thinking and creativity. Because students in graduate programs in counseling psychology are already a very select group, there is little if any need for students to feel in competition with each other. We genuinely believe that a well-functioning graduate program will include some aspects in which students work together, for example, studying in groups for the most demanding courses, assisting each other in research projects, providing constructive peer supervision in counseling practica.

Balancing Dependence and Independence

Balancing dependence and independence and the next two perspectives—finding a mentor and actively coping with disappointments—are, in our view, inextricably bound together. Indeed, they also are, in a sense, integral to the challenge just discussed regarding self-actualization. However, we believe that there are some points that are best made by considering the perspectives separately. Both graduate and undergraduate studies exert some strong environmental press toward dependence; that is, they elicit dependent behaviors from students. Relatively clear requirements are laid out; students then perceive hurdles they must get over to obtain the coveted degree. Moreover, the threats to self-efficacy reviewed in the preceding paragraphs may also stimulate dependence on available experts (e.g., faculty and supervisors) to tell you explicitly and specifically what to do. You may also find yourself wanting more specific feedback from your faculty and supervisors: Are you adequately following the rules? Trying to do things differently, even if something different seems better to you, may seem to risk abandonment by your advisor.

One related aspect of dependence: If you have returned to graduate school after working relatively independently in another career, the structure and hurdles of graduate school, as well as the traditional roles of faculty power over students, may make you feel like you are being treated like a child. Your sense of lost independence will anger you just as much as if you were to visit your parents who tell you what time to go to bed. In our view, the push toward dependency found in many graduate programs can stimulate both passivity and rage.

On the other hand, it is also true that much effective learning can take place by depending on available program structures and resources. The challenge is to be sure that you do not limit your professional development to a passive dependence on what is routinely given to you. To the extent that you enjoy the comfort of this structure, you will probably take less initiative to find and follow other options that will enrich your graduate study. Just as living at home during your undergraduate years may limit the development of your autonomous independent living (Mendelson, 1987), being dependent on the structure of your graduate program for all your professional development will similarly limit the range of your professional development. Thus the challenge is *balancing* dependence and independence. What steps do you need to take to ensure some independent action for your professional development?

Just as with the threats to self-efficacy, the antidote begins with recognition that the push toward dependency in graduate school must be met by some counteraction on your part. First, you must ask what you *want* from your graduate program, as compared to asking "What will my graduate program provide for me?" We advise students to continually think about both long-term (e.g., 5-year) goals as well as short-term (e.g., coming year) goals. What specific kinds of practice and research experiences would you like to have during the coming year? What roles would you like to be prepared to fill in 5 years? Do you have any styles of personal interaction that you want to try to modify in the near future?

Relatedly, what arrangements have you made to have some balance, so that graduate school does not fill your entire life? The demands of graduate school can be totally absorbing. Professors are skilled in making demands on both themselves and students that will fill all available waking hours. To have any kind of avocational or recreational interests, the somewhat clichéd saying is all too appropriate: One doesn't *find* time, one *makes* time.

Finding a Mentor

Ever since the 1970s, the concept of mentoring as a significant contributor to career development in all professions has been increasingly explored (Levinson, 1980). While its definition has varied widely, the most useful definition for our purposes has been presented by Bova and Phillips (1982).

> Mentors are those who practice most of the following principles: 1. Try to understand, shape, and encourage the dreams of the protégés, 2. Often give their

blessing on the dreams and goals of their protégés, 3. Provide opportunities for their protégés to observe and participate in their work by inviting their protégés to work with them, 4. Teach protégés the politics of "getting ahead" in the organization. A mentor is usually a person of high organizational or specific career status who by mutual consent takes an active interest in the career development of another person" (p. 7).

Bogat and Redner (1985) were one of the first to call attention to the role of the mentor in graduate school as it subsequently affects one's professional development in psychology. Ellis (1992) states:

> I believe that quality graduate programs have some sort of a faculty mentor system, in which students can obtain advice, counseling, and helpful direction in their training. This must be a relationship of trust, in which ideas can be freely shared and confidences held (p. 575).

The values and characteristics of effective mentors have been explored by counseling psychologists most specifically for women (Gilbert & Rossman, 1992) and ethnic minorities (Atkinson, Neville, & Casas, 1991).

To the extent that students have a means-to-an-end perspective, they may not view faculty as people with whom they will continue to have relationships in subsequent years and therefore do not look for mentors among the faculty. Moreover, faculty and student roles in courses might sometimes seem almost adversarial—faculty seem to hold all the power and may be making course and/or program demands that students find neither valuable nor interesting—obviously not the conditions to promote mentoring. A further irony is that graduate students often feel they can relate most closely to younger junior faculty; however, the research on mentors suggests that those identified as valuable mentors have been among the more senior faculty (Bogat & Redner, 1985).

Given that the climate is often not conducive to mentor–protégé relationships, you may need to think carefully about how to initiate finding a mentor among the faculty and supervisors in your graduate program. This statement reveals one of our assumptions; that is, that career development of counseling psychologists is indeed facilitated by having a mentor. While we clearly know of many outstanding counseling psychologists who have developed rewarding and significant careers without having mentors, it is our own view that progress in the early stages of one's career—from the internship through first positions—is greatly accelerated by their assistance. We urge you to go back and reread the definition provided by Bova and Phillips (1982) and begin thinking about your current or possible future advisors as suitable to this kind of role. In short, we urge you to think about advisors as more than a signature on your course requests at the beginning of each semester!

Actively Coping With Disappointments
No matter how carefully you have researched your choice of programs, you are likely to find, at some point, a course or professor, a practicum or requirement that does not meet your own view of what you expected from graduate school.

Any system imposes limitations on you. The challenge is to learn how to work creatively within that system to obtain your key goals without sacrificing your integrity by "selling out." We often hear both students in college and professionals in a human services system argue that the "system" won't allow them to be themselves, that they feel stifled, and that they could be creative and productive "if it weren't for . . . so much reading and so many papers to write, leaving me with no time to be concerned with what I am learning . . . the silly requirements and the grading game . . . the unrealistic pressures placed on me by the professors" (Corey & Corey, 1989, p. 19).

Again, a means-to-an-end perspective leads to a passive accommodation to such disappointments. We encourage you to think about a more activist self-management response. First explore any of your disappointments with your fellow students both at your own beginning level and those at more advanced levels in the program. In this way you may (a) gain some perspective on whether the concern is widely shared or one unique to you, and (b) discover ways other students have actively dealt with that disappointment. Then, if your concern is widely shared, those of you who share it may want to bring it to the attention of the faculty or program director through student representatives, grievance procedures, or other mechanisms. In a sense, such procedures are a way of learning to cope with some inevitable disappointments in one's professional career.

When the problem is one that is not shared by others, the courses of action may seem less evident. Just as we discussed in the earlier section on changing self-preservation into self-actualization, the primary need is to reframe the concern as a problem to be solved. What, in more behavioral concrete terms, is the problem? What kinds of possible solutions can you envision? What kinds of alternatives are available? What are the costs and benefits of some of the various solutions in terms of how much they involve changes in you and changes from others? In short, the challenge is for you to be sensitive to any of your own complaining reactions to disappointments—usually a counterproductive activity for both your present mental health and your future professional development. Instead, consider how to take an activist role in reaching alternative solutions through changing something about "the system" and/or yourself—the focus of the final perspective we discuss.

Finding Personal Development in Professional Development

Graduate study in counseling psychology is qualitatively different from that in, for example, history, physics, or music. Becoming an effective counselor happens only by learning a great deal about yourself. It is not simply a matter of applying a set of techniques. *You* are the major tool—one that must be highly adaptable to be effective with a wide range of clients and interventions. To become that adaptable, many of your values, assumptions, and personal styles will have to be examined. As a counselor you might experience value conflicts with clients, for example, in matters of religion, abortion, gender roles, perceived responsibilities for family members, and so forth. Clients may be part of a culture that has a very different value system than you, leading them to close out options that you consider viable and effective choices for them. Even less obvious to most counselors are the assumptions we all make about various cultures. As we explored in Chapter 6 counselors make many assumptions and attributions about nonverbal behavior, lack of assertiveness, levels of self-disclosure, and observing promptness for appointments that may make it particularly difficult to establish a working alliance with clients from various cultural backgrounds. These assumptions and attributions may be the primary signal for areas of knowledge, skills, and attitudes that you need to make part of your professional developmental program.

Understanding how your own personality and style of interacting affects clients is also a critical part of your learning. Relatedly, some areas of your own personal struggle may be the source of significant countertransference issues (see Chapter 8) that block progress in a counseling relationship. All of these areas can often be addressed by personal counseling for yourself, a topic that has long been debated as to whether or not it should be a required part of training in counseling psychology.

You may be aware that psychoanalysis has, from its beginning, essentially required that trainees complete psychoanalysis before being fully certified as psychoanalytic practitioners. Psychologists of other theoretical orientations have been much less explicit and more varied in their opinions about the value of personal counseling as part of the training of therapists. Only a few programs take official positions in their written materials regarding whether students should consider personal counseling. A few programs regularly provide students with lists of recommended psychotherapists to consult for personal counseling.

Despite this relative lack of explicit discussion of the value of personal counseling as part of the training of counseling psychologists, Kestenbaum (1986) found two-thirds of his sample of 147 graduates from five different APA-approved counseling psychology programs had sought some personal counseling during their training. The majority of these students entered psychotherapy in order to seek help with relationship issues with family, friends, or significant others. Few of them indicated that the stresses of graduate training were the primary reason for seeking counseling, but rather indicated that their graduate training did give them a new perspective about the value of seeking professional help for their personal problems. Approximately 60% of the students who sought personal counseling during graduate training had also been in therapy before entering graduate school, a trend that apparently continues after receiving the doctorate as well. Guy, Stark, and Poelstra (1988) found that those who seek personal therapy after entering professional practice are more likely to be those who sought counseling during graduate school. Holzman, Searight, and Hughes (1996) and Kestenbaum (1986) find that the overwhelming majority of students have very favorable responses to participating in therapy while in graduate school. They felt that their counseling skills had been helped primarily through their being able to make more effective use of their feelings in their own counseling. They were able to more quickly develop an empathy with clients' difficulties. On the other hand, Kestenbaum also finds that 21% of the students feel that their counseling experience created a number of multiple role complexities for them that subsequently affected their own work with clients. More specifically, when the counselors felt that their therapy was at an impasse, they found themselves having more difficulties working with their own clients.

TABLE 7.1.   **Challenges for Graduate Students: Getting the Most From One's Training Experience.**

Challenge	How to Meet the Challenge
Changing the Means-to-an-End Attitude into Professional Development	View graduate school as the beginning of one's professional development, rather than a means to an end
Changing Self-Preservation to Self Actualization	View threats to self-efficacy as opportunities for growth, rather than reasons for avoidance
Balancing Dependence and Independence	Recognize the environmental "push" for dependency, and counteract it
Finding a Mentor	Actively seek relationships with those who can assist in one's professional growth
Actively Coping with Disappointments	Explore areas of difficulty with fellow students; take an activist role in reaching alternative solutions to problems.
Finding Personal Development in Professional Development	Become aware of how one's own personality, style of interacting, and cultural assumptions impact one's professional development and functioning.

For those who are experiencing personal distress during the graduate school years, counseling offers a way not only of dealing with that stress but also improves one's sense of skills and techniques for relating to clients. Clearly, from a professional developmental point of view, engaging in personal counseling while in graduate school may be a highly valuable option to consider.

We have now described six perspectives that we believe will help you become an effective manager of your own professional development. We turn now to some special opportunities for you to consider in planning your professional development during graduate school years.

GRADUATE SCHOOL YEARS: PROFESSIONAL DEVELOPMENTAL OPPORTUNITIES

We describe six opportunities we believe merit some special consideration in your plans for the graduate school years. These opportunities are often not made explicit in formal coursework, yet are almost always available as part of the elective aspects of counseling psychology programs.

Elective Courses

Your graduate program probably offers a number of elective courses. Undergraduates often consider electives primarily in terms of immediate interests and the demands they make on one's time—they try to find "an easy course." We encourage you to think about electives in graduate school not only in terms of any immediate interests, but also in terms of what those courses can contribute to your professional development, especially by expanding your future internship and career options.

Several surveys have documented that assessment training in counseling psychology is sometimes viewed as inadequate for the broad variety of roles in which counseling psychologists sometimes find themselves (discussed in Chapter 13). Hospital-based internships and positions expect applicants to possess a considerable amount of experience in using a variety of assessment batteries. The applications for some of these positions ask how many specific batteries of each type you have given and may in fact ask you to submit a report you have prepared from using a variety of assessment techniques with one of your clients. As noted also in Chapter 4, focused use of assessment can be a cost-effective part of case management strategies in managed care. In deciding on your electives, you will want to examine the extensiveness of assessment training in your program and determine if you should supplement it with some electives in order to be prepared for the kinds of internships and career placements you hope to obtain.

Also noted in Chapter 4 were needs for training in case management, including the diagnostic, treatment, and maintenance stages. Hopefully, this kind of training will be included as part of your practicum experience, as well as training focused on brief therapy. If your program does not incorporate such training in its required courses, you may want to seek pertinent electives.

Many counseling psychology programs have at least elective, if not required, courses in both supervision and consultation. As noted in both chapters 4 and 19, these areas are highly valued in industrialized health care settings as well as in counseling centers. Both are therefore highly commendable electives to choose.

A final area to consider is multicultural counseling. If your program is not already incorporating this area in its required coursework, electives in both the theory and practice of multicultural counseling greatly enhance your career opportunities since, as discussed in both Chapter 4 and Chapter 6, the clientele of psychologists in coming years will be increasingly multicultural. As just one example of the pragmatic utility of such skills, provider panels of health care companies that are supposedly closed are often interested in adding providers who have training and experience in working with clients from a different cultural background.

Your specific professional goals, changing times, and strengths of your program may all lead to other suggestions more pertinent than these. The fundamental point is to include consideration of your long-range professional goals when choosing electives.

Professional Readings

You may feel almost overwhelmed with the amount of reading already required in your graduate courses and cannot imagine taking on any more reading. Yet, if you are to become an effective manager of your own professional development, the time to start some elective professional reading is right now. Courses, by design, have limited breadth; moreover, professors or instructors teaching these courses do not know everything (at least the ones we know!). As a way to stay abreast of current developments in psychology in general, we highly recommend a regular perusal of the *APA Monitor,* the monthly newspaper of the American Psychological Association; and the *American Psychologist,* the primary journal of the association. The articles in the journal cover the entire gamut of psychology, and you may wish to read only an occasional article; however, the "Comments" section is one of the quickest ways to become acquainted with some of the most controversial issues in professional practice and scientific research in contemporary psychology.

For counseling psychology specifically, we recommend a similar perusal of the tables of contents of each issue of the *Journal of Counseling Psychology,* the primary empirical research journal of the field; *The Counseling Psychologist,* the primary conceptual journal of the field; and *Professional Psychology: Research and Practice,* the major journal about professional practice issues. Granted, few if any of us read any of the journals from cover to cover, yet by taking time to read the abstracts of the articles in these journals, we get a feel for the current issues and topics of greatest concern, and can take note of articles that we do specifically want to read or consult when time permits.

We also urge you to think about some elective reading in your own area of special interest. That may be a topic such as women's issues, multicultural counseling, or service delivery techniques such as behavior modification or career counseling. Almost every different population of clients, treatment technique, theoretical orientation, and/or scientific research problem has a specialized journal that is probably worth consulting with some frequency, again if only to review the table of contents, abstracts, and identify articles of specific interest. A handy way to keep up to date on recent books in your specialized area of interest is to order them directly from a publisher if you notice that several are published by the same house. The publisher will put your name on a mailing list; you will then receive biyearly if not quarterly catalogues listing many current publications in your particular area of interest.

As we close this section, we recognize that we have devoted all of our space telling you what to read, not when to read it. As we noted in one of the earlier sections of this chapter, a continual task of professional life is learning how to make time for what we think is valuable; if you wait to find time to read, your accumulation of newsletters and books will soon be as high as the Empire State Building.

Another value of regularly reading these journals is that you will soon realize that some of your own work in classes and research may be of the same caliber as that being published. Thus, you can begin to visualize yourself as a contributor to journals, not merely a reader of them. With some editorial suggestions from an advisor or faculty member, many research projects or conceptual papers of graduate students may become suitable for publication in these journals.

All of the journals mentioned, and many other specialized ones, are available at reduced rates through student memberships in various professional organizations. In the past decade, the APA and many of its more than 50 divisions have developed student memberships; for a fraction of the cost of professional membership, students can receive special newsletters, news of the division's current activities, and reduced rates on the journals. The address for the APA is found in Chapter 5; the address of the Student Affiliate Group of the Division of Counseling Psychology appears on the inside cover of each issue of *The Counseling Psychologist*. Many counseling psychology students are also interested in the American Counseling Association and its 17 divisions, for example, American Mental Health Counselors Association, National Career Development Association, and Association for Multicultural Counseling and Development. Information on student membership and journals is available from American Counseling Association, Box BA477, Baltimore, MD 21203-0477 or at their website www.counseling.org.

Professional Conventions

We could not have written wisely about professional conventions ourselves until we had been in the profession many years and slowly began to realize the many unexpected ways in which these conventions can affect graduate students' professional development. If you were to stop reading at this point and rush off to a professional convention, you might well be overwhelmingly disappointed. Regional and national psychology conventions are large and complex affairs, often with thousands of participants and many paper sessions and symposia scheduled for almost every hour. Simply attending some of these sessions and then returning to your home or hotel room is *not* how a convention contributes to your professional development.

The greatest benefits of professional conventions occur for graduate students, as we have observed them, from their presenting a paper or participating in a symposium at a convention. How can you have such an opportunity? You might expect conventions to be primarily for well-established professionals with active research programs. On the contrary, it is much easier to present a paper at a professional convention than to have a paper published. Whereas many professional journals are able to accept fewer than half or even a quarter of the papers submitted for publication, most conventions accept for presentation half or more of all the papers that are submitted. Most master's thesis research projects completed in counseling psychology programs have a good chance of acceptance for presentation at a regional or national convention poster session. Poster sessions refer to times when a large number of papers are posted on bulletin boards with accompanying illustrative tables. The authors stand by for the selected time period so that interested persons can come and discuss the papers with their authors. In contrast to poster sessions, symposia are often made up of several brief research presentations from various research team members followed by comments from a few knowledgeable discussants. Having the opportunity to present at a symposium is most often related to being part of a research team or having a mentor. At every convention, there are symposia that include several graduate students from the same program or from different universities but working on similar projects known to the symposium organizer—typically, an established researcher from a practice setting or from a faculty.

We have gradually become aware of the immense benefits of such participation by graduate students. Those who do take part in such presentations, although initially very frightened about the prospects, typically come away with a greatly increased sense of self-efficacy and feeling connected to the field of counseling psychology. Suddenly they have found a number of people (in addition to their advisor) quite interested in the details of their work and have indeed found themselves to be the expert in that particular area. That submitting a relatively brief abstract of one's ongoing work to a convention takes such a small amount of effort yet can lead to such gratifying experiences is obviously a very cost-effective investment for professional development.

It is also important to note that presenting at a convention is something that is listed on your résumé. Such a listing strongly marks your professional commitment. Most employers in both practitioner and academic settings want to be sure that they are considering someone not only competently skilled in psychological services but also involved in broader professional aspects. Such involvement is not only a promise of remaining a vitalized professional but also brings credit to an agency when staff participate in national conventions. Studies of the reputations of agencies and academic programs sometimes include tallies of the places of employment of convention presenters (Skovholt, Stone, & Hill, 1984).

There are other aspects of convention participation that are also very important for professional development. All conventions run a number of social hours; that is, occasions when the participants meet very informally. These times are especially significant for the networking experience of graduate students. This is a time to meet many other counseling psychologists of widely varying levels of experience but all with strong commitments to professional development. You can meet the most well-known practitioners and researchers as well as those who, like yourself, may just be beginning a career. Making such contacts may well lead to further correspondence that will help you with your own research and career opportunities. Osberg and Rallin (1989) provide further elaborations on how attending conventions is a primary networking technique for young professionals. Most important, those social activities can greatly enhance your sense of being part of a profession—establishing your personal professional identity as a counseling psychologist.

You can most easily learn about opportunities for presenting at conventions by being a student member of the various professional organizations described in the previous section. Additionally, your advisor and/or mentor may be able to tell you about other regional and state conventions where you may have opportunities to present conceptual or research papers you complete as part of your graduate study.

"Externships"

This section describes some of the potential benefits of participating in "externships." The word *externship* is one that has come into use since the 1970s. Up until that time, the word *internship* was used much more broadly than it is today and applied to almost any experience outside of formal practica in one's doctoral program. Internships were made up of a variety of part-time or full-time experiences spread over a number of years. Many other disciplines, in both the mental health and nonmental health fields, may use the word *internship* in this broader way and use it to refer to any field experience, even during the undergraduate years. However, as a part of the more standardized regulations for the content and training of programs developed in the 1970s, the psychology internship became defined as a 1-year full-time or a 2-year half-time experience completed only after all doctoral practicum requirements had been met.

The word *externship* then emerged to refer to practical experiences in agencies outside of program practica but prior to the internship year. Externship experiences may range from relatively formal training programs involving the student in 20 hours a week of training and service to more informally arranged training experiences for as little as a half-day a week for 1 semester. There is no official definition of *externship*; there may be significant variations from program to program in how this word is used if it is used at all.

Externships have several very specific values for subsequent internship and career opportunities for many graduate students. First, most internship programs are looking for persons who have had at least some prior significant experience in that particular kind of setting. Hospitals may be reluctant to consider an applicant who, despite a strong transcript and outstanding supervisor recommendations, has never worked in a hospital setting. Similarly, a university counseling center may be slightly reluctant to consider an intern whose total experience in practica and employment has been in inpatient psychiatric facilities. Thus, if you are planning to apply for internships or for career positions that are in settings that differ from where you completed your practica and any employment, you may well want to consider an externship of at least 1 semester or more in whatever setting to which you plan to apply.

Second, students in traditional scientist–practitioner programs may often have fairly intensive but not very extensive practicum experience in terms of number of hours of practical experience. On the other hand, graduate students in Psy.D. doctoral programs and other more practice-oriented programs may be assigned to work 20 hours a week in an agency throughout their doctoral training and therefore have literally thousands of hours of accumulated experience prior to the internship. Consequently, graduate students who have not held employment as a mental health professional (for example, after the master's degree but before entering the doctoral program) may want to consider an externship as a way of increasing the number of hours of experience. VA hospitals sometimes provide intensive summer externships of 500 hours; a variety of counseling centers and community mental health agencies provide 20-hour-a-week externships for students who are in their final years of training before going on internship.

A third value of externships is similar to one noted in the section on elective courses—students in counseling psychology may want to increase their amount of assessment experience especially if they are considering internships and careers in hospital settings. Externships specifically focused on assessment may sometimes be arranged in various hospitals and agencies.

In summary, externship choices may be a way of preparing yourself for specific internships or careers; alternatively, an externship may be chosen simply because you want the breadth of exposure available at the externship level but do not intend to pursue further such experiences at the intern or career level. There are no formal directories of externships and, in fact, information about them is often difficult to obtain. Your best sources are typically your advisor, program director, and advanced-level graduate students who have taken advantage of these opportunities.

Internships

"Managing the internship application experience: advice from an exhausted but content survivor . . . Having gone through it, I now believe preparation should begin in the first year of graduate school" (Jacob, 1987, p. 146). There have been over 200 articles published regarding psychology internships, the majority in the past decade. Many focus on advice for applicants, for example, "Preparing for Internship: Tips for the Prospective Applicant" (Mellott, Arden, & Cho, 1997); "Competitive Internship Candidates" (Gloria, Castillo, Choi-Pearson, & Rangel (1997); "A Decision-Making Technique for Choosing a Psychology Internship" (Stewart & Stewart, 1996); "A Guide to Obtaining a Psychology Internship" (Megargee, 1997); whereas others focus on what we know about internships and their contribution to professional development (Stedman, 1997).

Choosing from well over 300 recognized internship sites may seem a daunting process; moreover, since internship application, like entry into graduate school, is a competitive process, students have considerable anxiety about the process. The combination of these two features no doubt accounts for the plethora of articles on this topic. Unfortunately, most of the literature is focused on the application process and managing potential difficulties in the transition to the internship rather than looking at the longer term professional development aspects regarding the choice of internships. Our primary focus will therefore be on those aspects and we will leave to you, the reader, the task of consulting the literature for the many useful pieces of advice regarding the application process itself.

Each internship provides a somewhat different set of intensive training experiences. The primary question for you, when considering the choice of internships, is which kinds of experiences you would want to have to enhance and complement your current doctoral training. Students readily think about some of the choices regarding settings, such as hospitals, counseling centers, and community mental health centers, but are less likely to think about what the internship will offer them in terms of experience with other theoretical orientations, such as behavioral, psychodynamic, and opportunities with various client populations, whether by diagnostic category (e.g., eating disorders, career dissatisfaction, and posttraumatic stress syndrome) or demographic characteristics (e.g., gender, age, and ethnicity). An internship experience in a managed care organization might also provide valuable experience for the current more industrialized health care market (described in Chapter 4). However, as this is written, there are very few such opportunities at the predoctoral internship level since most managed care organizations require all providers to be licensed. It is hoped that eventually appropriate supervisory arrangements can be made so that both externship and internship opportunities will be available in managed care organizations. Brickey (1998) provides a fine example of the possibilities in, and advantages of, an internship in what he calls a "market-driven psychology practice."

Your choice of an internship has both direct and indirect career implications. The direct implications come from the more obvious connection between your gaining experience with a particular kind of setting or service to your marketability for that kind of career for your first job. Obviously, persons with internships completed in hospital settings will be in a stronger position when applying for psychology positions in hospitals; similarly, someone completing an internship in a university counseling center will be more competitive for a career position in a counseling center than a candidate who has completed only one practicum in a counseling center.

The more indirect career implications from choice of internship relate to the concept of networking. Typically, the persons with whom you work in your internship setting most likely know other professionals in that kind of setting and will therefore be able to tell you more about job opportunities in that setting than any other. Thus your informal network for potential jobs will be shaped in part by your choice of internship setting.

There are also some important aspects to consider about internships and their effect on your qualifications for licensure, other professional credentials, and employment. There are several hundred internships listed in the directory of the Association of Psychology Internship Centers (APIC), issued each fall, providing brief descriptions of the kinds of training available in each internship, the prerequisite qualifications for candidates, and application procedures. APIC also has developed guidelines for internship offers and acceptances and monitors compliance with these guidelines to provide assurance of compliance by both agencies and intern applicants. Constantine and Keilin (1996) provide an overview of the kinds of problems applicants experience and how their concerns may be addressed.

For licensing and other credentials as professional psychologists, internships that are APA-approved are typically fully accepted, without further question or documentation, as meeting requirements for internship-level training. Other internships listed in the APIC directory are usually acceptable, after providing some documentation from the agency, to many licensing boards and some employers (the VA and some states require that the internship be completed in an APA-approved program).

It is possible to complete a specially arranged internship in an agency that does not officially list its program in the APIC directory to gain some specialized experience (e.g., working with AIDS patients in a hospital without an internship program). While a graduate from an APA-approved doctoral training program is permitted to complete an internship that is not APA-approved but does provide appropriate supervised experience and training, the lack of formal recognition as an internship has significant licensing and career implications. Some students who know that the state in which they want to practice will admit them for licensure without having a formally recognized internship sometimes choose this route. However, we feel that this is such a high-risk choice, in case there is ever a decision to change one's employer or the state in which one practices, that we require the occasional student who chooses this route to sign a statement indicating that he or she realizes the potential limits of such an internship choice to one's licensing eligibility and career opportunities.

It is preferable that you give primary attention to the above considerations in your choice of internships before looking at the other factors that seem so tempting to graduate students—location, cost of living, distance from significant others. While all of these personal factors may be very useful secondary considerations, when used as primary considerations, they may lead to choices of internships that, in the short range, are gratifying but result in significant missed opportunities in terms of long-range career development. You might best serve your long-term career development when you are able to adopt the attitude "I can live any place for just one year."

In the process of choosing an internship, there is one special factor for counseling psychology graduate students to consider: A fairly large number of the internships listed in the APIC directory indicate that they limit their applicants to those who graduate from clinical psychology programs. While this qualification does almost always indicate that these internships want their applicants to have fairly extensive assessment training and considerable experience with clients with significant degrees of psychopathology, each year there are a number of counseling psychology students whose training includes such factors and who make the case for their appropriate suitability to be an applicant to the internship. In short, if there is an internship listed as open only to clinical psychology students that you very much want to consider and you believe you have the kinds of training described in the eligibility requirements, we encourage you to submit an application. In many cases, the staff is simply unaware of differences between counseling psychology and more generic counseling and has made some misattributions about limits to the nature of an applicant's training.

In summary, the choice of internship is a major component in long-range professional development and provides an opportunity for both depth and breadth that will complement training experiences gained in your program and any previous employment experiences as you make the transition to your first career.

At this point in your reading, it would be especially valuable for you to review the material in Chapter 4 on the emergence of accredited postdoctoral residencies. These residencies could either complement or supplement your internship experience. Residencies can be a further significant enhancement to your early career opportunities and rapid professional development.

The Dissertation

The final section of considerations for program development during graduate school applies to one of the final requirements for obtaining a doctoral degree—the dissertation. The primary purpose of this section is to help you plan your dissertation in the context of your professional development. This purpose may be challenging to fulfill.

The history of students' views toward and work on dissertations is replete with means-to-an-end perspectives. Ironically, in such a view the dissertation then gains more importance in the life of the student than it ever should. Whatever ambivalence about your program is still keeping you only partially engaged in the program and whatever threats to self-esteem have been leading you toward avoidance may all become fixated on this final hurdle. Thus, it is not surprising that Garcia, Malott, and Brethower (1988) report that nearly a quarter of those students who drop out of graduate school do so after they have completed all the course work save the dissertation.

You may rightfully say the preceding paragraph sounds like blaming the victim, as the failure to complete the dissertation is explained in terms of the students' perspectives or neuroses. Ever since the 1960s, there has been an increasing amount of literature indicating that part of this failure to complete theses is also related to a lack of supervision and effective incentives (see Garcia et al., 1988). More recently, other environmental aspects have been suggested by the work of Mallinckrodt, Gelso, and Royalty (1990), who find that Holland personality types (see Chapter 14) were not only significantly related to research interests in counseling psychology but also to delays in the completion of research requirements. "Investigative and investigative–artistic students have the highest interest in research. Enterprising interests were related to lower levels of research interest and a delay in completing training" (p. 26). Thus, both individual and environmental factors can work against the dissertation being a positive professional developmental experience.

We first attempt to address the environmental factors. One of the logical interventions that is increasingly promoted is the development of structured courses or supervisory systems that provide for a higher level of supervision of the dissertation. In one such program that has been formally evaluated, Garcia and colleagues (1988) find that students who participated in a system including weekly meetings, task specification, feedback, and incentives, completed significantly more tasks than those in a control group. Interestingly, though, there was no judged difference in the quality of the projects that were completed in either of the two groups.

If you encounter significant problems in making progress on the dissertation, you may indeed want to look into more structured opportunities for supervision and support available in your own university. If there is no structured program in your area, you may be able to find similar kinds of help from a writing center that is part of campus services. Although such centers are geared primarily for undergraduates, the writing counselors often look forward to working with the higher-level challenges that graduate students provide in contrast to those of beginning freshmen, who may still be struggling with writing coherent paragraphs.

In picking your dissertation advisor, you may want to be sure that you select an advisor not only for expertise in a topical area but also one who fits with your own style of functioning, who can assist you with relatively undefined tasks like deciding on a topic for a dissertation and then executing it. Although there may seldom be more than one faculty member with expertise in your area of interest, whenever there can be congruence between your style and the advisor's, your progress will be facilitated. If you have difficulty choosing an advisor who seems to naturally fit your style, it is not unreasonable to explore the possibility of asking your advisor to work with you in a way that might differ from his or her usual style.

There are two other bits of useful advice that come from the Mallinckrodt and colleagues (1990) study of supportive environments for research. They note that positive change in research interests is related to a program's conveying

> . . . to students that all experiments are flawed and that a particular study need not make a great contribution to knowledge to be worth doing and . . . "wedding science to practice"—that is, teaching students to use their clinical experience as a source of research ideas (p. 30).

From the professional developmental perspective, one can also look at the dissertation in its environmental context as one of the transitions, along with the internship, between your graduate school years and the beginnings of your establishment in a career as a counseling psychologist. Your choice of topic for the dissertation could well be the beginning of a program of research that you plan to continue in either a service setting or academic position. Your dissertation topic may also be one with special implications for your subsequent practice, for example, conducting research with abused spouses attending a community clinic, or with "plateaued" employees served by an employee assistance plan. In short, rather than simply looking for a dissertation topic that is feasible, you should think about the topics that will have practical use for you as well. Obviously, this is a major way to provide yourself with both intrinsic and extrinsic incentives for working on the dissertation. Topics that are supposedly feasible but are unrewarding sometimes make for the least feasible dissertations!

PROFESSIONAL DEVELOPMENT IN INITIAL POSTDOCTORAL CHOICES

The moment for which you have worked so hard finally comes. You receive the doctoral degree in psychology. The first postdoctoral requirement is that you celebrate appropriately—whatever that is for you.

In this section, we explore the professional developmental issues and implications in three areas of planning for your initial postdoctoral year. The first set of issues concerns the type of position you will enter. Despite counseling psychology's long major involvement in the study of career development, ironically, there is little formal consideration given in counseling psychology programs to either the short- or long-range implications of the type of first position one chooses. As a graduate of a counseling psychology program, you will have a diverse range of opportunities from, for example, hospital staff psychologist, to assistant professor of psychology, to supervised independent practitioner, to full-time research psychologist, to a formal postdoctoral training or research fellowship. Are there differential career implications for choosing one of these paths over another? Speaking more pragmatically, how easy is it to change from one type of position to another after a year or two? Are some career paths more satisfying than others, especially for long-range goals? Do different career choices affect how difficult it will be to maintain a sense of being part of a profession; that is, not feeling isolated?

The second set of issues is related to the rapidly changing social patterns regarding men's and women's careers and child rearing. We see an increasing number of new professionals who begin their families and careers almost at the same time. (One graduate purchased her first home, defended her dissertation, and gave birth to her first child all in the same month.) Simply managing the issues involved in two professionals sharing a life together entails numerous career implications even when both have positions they like—a tall order in itself. The addition of children exponentially increases multiple-role demands and implications. In this area there is a burgeoning literature to which we can only allude as we describe what we believe are the most salient considerations of multiple roles for postdoctoral career planning.

The third set of issues relates to managing the transition to your first job. In this area there is a reasonable amount of literature on actually searching for positions as a psychologist and some very relevant articles about this transition from graduate school to professional roles. We highlight some of these articles' recommendations as well as add some of our own.

Career Choices and Their Implications

If you are certain about which type of position you intend to enter and do not plan a change in later years, then this section will be relatively unimportant for you. If you are, however, like most counseling psychology students about to graduate, you suddenly realize that you are faced with making choices among what seem to be very different career paths. In fact, these choices *can* lead to very different career paths and lifestyles—workload, flexibility, security, income, and satisfaction. Notice that we emphasize the word *can*. We like to think of the choice of an initial career position like the choice of major for undergraduates who have some idea of interests and even a general career goal but are not sure which major to choose to get there. Just as there are several majors that can lead to any one career goal, there are several initial postdoctoral position choices that can lead to any given professional objective.

In keeping with the majors analogy, however, it is also clear that some majors lead more directly to a career goal; for example, a zoology major may provide much more extensive preparation for a career in medicine than would a political science major; to become a civil engineer one will have to take a rather extensive set of specific courses essentially equivalent to the major even if one does not major in civil engineering. In this section, we identify factors that facilitate changes in types of counseling psychology careers.

There is little pertinent published information about how to decide among specific career choices within counseling psychology. For many decades, a majority of counseling psychologists worked in campus settings either as staff psychologists in counseling centers or as professors; therefore, few options were considered by most counseling psychologists. Most older studies of new counseling psychologists adapting to their first careers are in one of these settings (e.g., Ponterotto & Furlong, 1986; Simono & Wachowiak, 1983). The experiences of new professional counseling psychologists in a much broader array of settings were nicely explored in *The Counseling Psychologist,* volume 20, number 1 (January 1992). Both very new professionals, and those with 7–10 years of experience, describe their experiences in settings ranging from private practice to general medical hospital settings as well as in traditional counseling centers and academic positions. Among the important commonalities between the older and newer studies of career development of counseling psychologists are that (1) one's first extended career position is often, but not necessarily related to the first postdoctoral position; and (2) satisfaction with the position is not related to whether one entered it early or late in one's career history.

As discussed in Chapter 4, the concept "career" in the twenty-first century will entail many more employers and positions than those in the past century. Flexibility has always been important both for perceiving the potential and achieving the reality of career moves when desired.

There are a few noteworthy points about flexibility. First, moving to any type of position is greatly facilitated by having had some prior type of work experience in a particular setting. At any point in one's career, it would be difficult to obtain employment as a hospital psychologist or a counseling center psychologist without ever having had formal training experience or work experience in one of those settings, either as part of predoctoral or postdoctoral training and experience. This on-site experience requirement is slightly less important for independent practice and community mental health centers where the most important question is whether or not you have the skills to work with the kinds of client populations to be served.

Perhaps the greatest limits regarding flexibility concern academic positions in highly rated universities. Such positions are always related to evidence of one's scholarly work as reflected in publications. The newer the counseling psychologist, the fewer the publications necessary. In fact, Ponterotto and Furlong (1986) were able to show that the more one had specialized training in what were then priority areas such as group counseling and multicultural counseling, the less critical was an extensive publication record. However, the more time that elapses since the doctoral degree, no matter what type of position one holds, the more publications that are expected of one who wishes to enter academia. Consequently, should you choose to move into a service position for the first years of your career and then plan to move to academia, unless you are able to publish articles while you are in that service position, you would be unlikely to be able to make the move into such an academic position in a counseling psychology program in a major research university. In one sense, it is usually easiest to enter an academic career directly from graduate school. If you found yourself not suited for an academic career, it would be easier to move into a service position, assuming you had a reasonable range of service experience through practica and predoctoral internship, than it would be to move from a service position to an academic one.

Finally, there are the longer-range considerations of advancement and salary related to type of position. While beginning positions in diverse settings may have quite similar salaries and all have some room for advancement in the first few years, the picture rapidly changes. Opportunities for advancement and increases in salary seem most limited in institutional settings such as counseling centers and community mental health centers. The salary scales may be relatively compressed and the only way to advance may be to move into an administrative position, of which there may be relatively few. While such factors may be comparatively unimportant for initial choices, they may have significance for your longer-range career goals. In academia, the speed with which one gets promoted and has salary increases is directly related to scholarly publications. Thus, it would be possible to find two counseling psychologists both 15 years after their Ph.D., with one being a modestly paid associate professor earning less than a counseling center psychologist and the other a full professor earning more than all but the most successful independent practitioners.

In managed care settings, initial salaries or fee scales may seem quite attractive and will indeed often exceed the initial salaries of counseling centers or community mental health clinics. On the other hand, unless one moves into administrative roles within these settings, there is essentially no career ladder. Your salary after 15 years of experience could be no greater than your initial one. If, on the other hand, you are able to build an independent practice, the opportunities for advancement and income are almost totally a function of your own initiative and time invested. Note that one does not have a salary when in independent practice; one can speak only of net income after paying office expenses. While the average income of practitioners is generally only slightly more than the average salary of those in service positions in hospitals, clinics, and counseling centers, the range and standard deviation of income in independent practice is immense. Some persons prefer to see relatively few clients simply to generate a modest income and have considerable time for other activities; others find fulfillment in investing a great deal of time and energy into a very extensive counseling practice, spending many hours each week in direct service as well as supervising others, perhaps even organizing and managing a group practice for which one receives part of the fees of each participating practitioner. In the latter case, the income level would easily double or triple the salary of the typical psychologist working in a hospital or clinic setting. Also in contrast to other settings, in independent practice there is no built-in career ladder. The day-to-day responsibilities of the professional practitioner with 25 years of experience are essentially the same as the new professional practitioner. Consequently, professional development opportunities become all the more critical for maintaining a sense of being part of a dynamic profession.

Once having decided on the type of position to seek, you can find a wide range of published advice. Most articles have been written regarding finding and interviewing for academic positions (Brems, Lampman, & Johnson, 1995; Gore, Murdock & Haley, 1998; Rheingold, 1994). Plante (1998) provides one of the more recent helpful articles for finding employment in the marketplace created by industrialized health care. The major difference between academic positions and service positions is how one finds out about them. As Ponterotto and Furlong (1986) have made clear, personal contact networks are a major factor in candidates obtaining academic positions. (Personal contacts are defined as an affirmative answer to the question "Did your graduate advisor, or any of the individuals who wrote letters of recommendation on your behalf, personally know any of the faculty in the program that hired you?") For more service-oriented positions, especially outside one's own geographic area, the most extensive information can be found in the classified-ad section of the monthly APA newspaper, the *Monitor*. Many counseling center positions are also listed in the *Chronicle of Higher Education*, a weekly newspaper that is available in most colleges and universities.

In summary, we have described the possibilities for considerable flexibility in terms of movement from one type of position or another *given the appropriate experiential background and accomplishments*. Thus, when considering first postdoctoral positions, you need to look at what other types of positions you might want to consider later in your career and determine whether or not you should be obtaining any particular kind of experience from your initial career position.

Multiple Role Considerations

As recently as a decade ago, this section might have been addressed only to women. Now we are also seeing a significant number of men who allow many of their career decisions to be affected by their roles and responsibilities as partners and parents.

In this section, we use the term *multiple roles* to refer to roles you might fill outside of specific career-related ones but which have an impact on career-related choices and behavior, thus affecting professional development. Counseling psychologists have been among the primary researchers on the issues that multiple roles present for psychological adjustment as well as for career adjustment. As O'Neil, Fishman, and Kinsella-Shaw (1987) indicate, career decisions for dual-career couples may entail a whole range of gender–role and marriage–family dilemmas. Gilbert and Rachlin (1987) point out that in "dual-career families" (that is, where both partners have careers in which they wish to advance) there are many sources of conflict that arise in relation to "allocation of family work; feelings of confidence, entitlement and power; decisions concerning career placement and advancement; and the integration of career and family priorities" (p. 33). As Petrie and Wohlgemuth (1994) spell out, there continue to be concerns that both new *and* established professionals need to address in their career planning regarding both dual-careers and parenthood.

We noted early in this chapter that part of the role of being a professional is the realization that you have to set your own priorities and limits. When you have a significant relationship with another professional person, then setting those priorities and limits is exponentially more complex, especially to the extent that there may be some significant differences in the values of partners, ranging from importance of a career to importance of a clean bathroom. Ideally, both parties of a professional couple can find positions that are satisfying and fulfilling in the same location. In large metropolitan areas, this is often possible, especially if one partner is patient—one partner finds a desirable full-time position, the other partner may have to temporarily consider a less-than first-choice position. In more rural areas, it may be extremely difficult to find two positions that are both highly desirable. Moreover, jobs and expectations change so that over time one partner usually becomes more satisfied than the other. It is our observation that most couples deal with these satisfaction differentials in one of two ways. In one strategy, one partner stays in a satisfying career while the other takes his or her turn in a less satisfying one with the understanding that at some later point in time, priority will be given to his or her being in a satisfying career. Alternatively, and sometimes as part of the first strategy, the less satisfied partner moves from job to job in an attempt to find a more satisfying one. There are any number of other less often used strategies, all of which rely for their effectiveness on explicit understandings of both members of the couple as to what is equitable and, if equity is not being experienced now, when there will be the opportunity to work toward a more equitable situation. (Dual career issues are lifelong—the quality of a marriage and well-being in retirement are directly related to the very kinds of factors that Gilbert and Rachlin [1987] noted above for dual-career marriages.)

Changing times have also meant a greater number of women and men receiving doctoral degrees in counseling psychology and also maintaining active roles as a parent. One quickly learns that effective parenting is a very time- and energy-demanding task. Managing the stress of adding the parenting role to other professional and life roles can be greatly facilitated by understanding two factors that are directly related to career planning. The more flexibility that one has in terms of time periods (flex-time) when the job can be done, the less stress there will be in

Six Irrational Beliefs of New Professionals.	TABLE 7.2.

1. As soon as I unpack my bags, I will be settled.
2. My new associates will welcome me enthusiastically and accept me as one of them.
3. I will never be an apprentice again.
4. I will easily perform the varied demands of my job.
5. I must perform perfectly, lest someone discover that I am a fraud.
6. Because I worked so hard to get here, I will love my job.

from Olson et al., 1986, pp. 416–418.

managing child-care responsibilities. Second, contrary to the expectations of yet-to-be parents, child-care responsibilities are not limited to the first few years. While the nature of the responsibilities change radically over the years, demands on time and energy will exist at least until children are of college age (and may not slow down much even then). At every age there are unexpected emotions that both fathers and mothers feel in relation to their children that will affect how much time and energy they will want to put into their work. The work of Lee (1984) on the counseling concerns of women who are first-time mothers, after having established careers, is just one example of an article that could be written for the mothers or fathers of children or adolescents of almost any age.

In summary, we believe that the career choices for a counseling psychologist who is a parent and/or partner of another career person need to include not only specific position responsibilities but also a careful and explicit exploration of how time, energy, and location demands of each position would affect responsibilities outside of work and quality time in these relationships.

The Transition: From Graduate School to First Position

"Graduate programs in psychology typically do not provide their students with anticipatory socialization concerning entry into a professional setting, the role demands of professional life, and the personal adjustments needed for professional development" (Olson, Downing, Heppner, & Pinkney, 1986, p. 415). No matter what your career choice, your preparation for this critical transition should begin with a reading of the Olson et al. article. Their analysis remains as accurate today as it was in the 1980s. We list above their six myths or what might alternatively be called "Six Irrational Beliefs of New Professionals" in Table 7.2. In the article the authors describe the realities that render these statements myths and suggest what new professionals need to do to cope with the realities. The authors suggest, and we concur, that being prepared to deal with these transitions is the greatest service you can do for yourself.

In addition to some of the factors that they point out in dealing with the realities behind these myths, we believe that there are other key surprises. As you read these, they will probably strike you as just common sense; however, again and again we find new professionals feeling unprepared for what, with hindsight, seems so obvious. Let us provide a few examples.

In a new setting you will have to learn the norms of that setting: What are the behaviors that are rewarded? Who interacts with whom? What are the taboos, for example, topics of discussion, behaviors, theoretical positions, research areas, political activities, that are deemed unacceptable or at least second class? How can you establish your own role and identity within that local culture? You will be expected, in most positions, to be able to handle the multiple roles of being a subordinate, a peer, and a superior (supervisor). Each of these positions has implications for how you will interact with others, ranging from how you address each other to what kinds of information, concerns, and issues you share with one another. Just as we discuss some of the avoidant behaviors that went with self-preservation in graduate school, you may experience similar avoidant tendencies in your professional position if you find some aspects of your position disappointing. Most especially, if you believe there is little that can be done about those disappointments, you will find yourself increasingly cynical, possibly withdrawing and even undermining others.

Schlossberg (1981, 1989), a counseling psychologist, writes extensively about the factors that determine how stressful a transition can be. In her 1989 book she describes practical strategies for coping with those changes. The skills of any counseling psychologist in assessing the strengths and limitations of both persons and environments are the fundamentals needed for implementing her recommended steps of taking stock of your situation, taking stock of yourself and supports, and taking stock of your strategies as a prerequisite for taking charge of your transitions so that they become part of, rather than an impediment to, your professional development.

Baron, Sekel, and Stott (1984) describe a variety of specific tasks they believe help the counseling center psychologist cope with the excitement and stress of the first year. They give very specific recommendations for (1) correcting unrealistic expectations, (2) making an accurate organizational assessment, (3) developing networks of support, (4) preventing overcommitment, (5) continuing professional growth, and (6) assessing future goals and needs.

ESTABLISHING A CAREER

After you have chosen your first position and begun managing the transitional phase described above, you will need to take a few more specific planning steps to guide you into a lifelong pattern of satisfying positions as a counseling psychologist. By this point in your "career" you will very likely feel over the worst hurdles and more in control of your own life, even if, as described in the previous section, your first position is not quite everything you hoped it would be. Two of the major planning steps you need to take in your first postdoctoral position have already been well described in Chapter 4 since both of these steps became salient professional issues for all psychologists in the closing decades of the twentieth century: credentialing and lifelong postdoctoral education. It is vitally important that you find out about licensing in the state where you have your first position just as soon as you accept a position. Because, as we have already noted, state regulations vary tremendously on what constitutes acceptable postdoctoral experience, you should determine just what you need to do to begin accumulating appropriately documented supervised experience. You will not be able to take the licensing exam until you have satisfied the state's postdoctoral supervised experience requirements. If you have been accumulating your own electronic file of all your coursework and supervised practicum, extern and intern assessment and intervention training and experience, you will be well on your way to having all the information you need to complete your applications for licensure and, after obtaining a license, for applying for credentials such as listing in the National Register of Health Service Providers in Psychology, and board certified status from the American Board of Professional Psychology.

Maintaining your credentials as a psychologist, as well as increasing your flexibility to consider an ever broader array of career opportunities, will require that you systematically plan for some continued education. Again, in Chapter 4 we have outlined the changes that are taking place that should make these activities more easily obtained and more intrinsically worthwhile. Just as we advised making judicious choices of electives in graduate school to maximize your learning about career opportunities, you now need to think about how your choices of continuing education activities can contribute most to your career options.

If your first position is in a group practice of psychologists or a multidisciplinary practice, you may well find yourself a bit overwhelmed by how much you do *not* know about the "nitty gritty" day-to-day duties you will have in addition to delivering the services you have been so well prepared to provide (Stone, Dew, & Sackett, 1998). Training programs in psychology have long held negative, or at least ambivalent attitudes about including in their curriculum anything about the "business of doing psychology." Until recent years, it was often difficult for new professionals to obtain good advice on how to cope with some of the business aspects. Fortunately, in the past few years, the American Psychological Association has been developing its "toolbox series" for practitioners. Depending on your particular situation, you can choose from among books with titles such as "Marketing Your Practice," "Organizing Your Practice Through Automation," "Models for Multidisciplinary Arrangements," "Practicing Outside of Third-Party Reimbursement" and so forth.

While a very large majority of psychologists consistently report satisfaction with their positions and careers, most everyone has times when a current position or status leaves much to be desired. Two counseling psychologists, Skovholt and Ronnestad (1992), prepared a fascinating report from their study of stages and themes in therapist and counselor development. In their book, *The Evolving Professional Self,* they identify three tracks of "development": developmental, moratorium, and stagnation. While we will not here go into their detailed analyses of what leads into and out of each stage, we do particularly like the process they identified as continuous professional reflection, which "consists of three essential aspects: ongoing professional and personal experiences, a searching process with others within an open and supportive environment, and active reflection about one's experiences" (p. 141). These aspects, when regularly and actively engaged in should prevent most career crises; when life's vicissitudes within and/or outside of your position create distress, the same three aspects form the major intervention needed to energize one who has moved into a moratorium or stagnation stage.

We close this chapter on professional development with what we believe to be the most cost effective use of time and energy of counseling psychologists who wish to be actively engaged in continuous professional reflection. The Division of Counseling Psychology (Division 17) of APA provides the most extensive networks for counseling psychologists to maintain active colleagueship. Even during graduate student years, you can become a member of the Student Affiliate Group (SAG) of the division and learn about special opportunities for participating in regional and national conventions and publications. In the mid-1990s the division underwent a reorganization to provide for sections and special interest groups (SIGs) so that there would be even greater opportunities for small groups of colleagues to share materials and concerns through their newsletters and Websites, as well as meet together regularly at conventions. The various sections and SIGs have been so popular with counseling psychologists, at all levels of experience, that the division has had to substantially increase scheduled meeting times at the APA convention in order to accommodate these very active groups. They hold many small group roundtable discussions that provide opportunities for students to have dialogues and interactions with both new and long-established counseling psychologists in a very supportive environment—an essential complement to the more than 40 hours of papers and symposia offered by counseling psychologists in the large meeting rooms of the APA convention. The diversity of interests represented is apparent in the titles of some of the current sections and SIGs: *Sections*—Ethnic and Racial Diversity; Independent Practice; Health Psychology; Lesbian, Gay, Bisexual Awareness; Vocational, Women; *SIGS*—Adult Development & Aging, Children & Adolescents, College Counseling Centers, Couples and Families, Group Counseling, Hypnosis in Counseling, International Affairs, Masculinity and Men's Studies, Prevention and Public Interest, Supervision and Training, Teaching and Research in Qualitative Methods, and Disability Issues.

We believe we have provided you, the reader, with both the knowledge and the strategies you need to become part of what we have found to be a profession that provides for a rare combination of extraordinary levels of fulfillment and meaningfulness in our work and an ever-expanding network of long-lasting, deeply caring interpersonal relationships for us and our families.

SUMMARY

The primary purpose of this chapter is to help the reader to develop a perspective on graduate education that marks it as the beginning of lifelong professional development. Different types of programs and graduate degrees in counseling psychology must first be considered by those who have not yet begun graduate school. Then six challenging perspectives help to explore the ramifications of a professional development view of graduate school: (1) changing the means-to-an-end attitude into professional development, (2) changing self-preservation into self-actualization, (3) balancing dependence and independence, (4) finding a mentor, (5) actively coping with disappointments, and (6) finding personal development in professional development.

First, because graduate school has a number of environmental pressures that do not serve students well in terms of managing their own career development, an alternative to a means-to-an-end perspective is realized by looking at graduate school as the first phase of *being* a counseling psychologist rather than how to *become* a counseling psychologist. Next, one must take an active role in response to perceived threats to self-efficacy, environmental pressures toward dependency, and the inevitable disappointments in any program. Of great value to the graduate student is mentoring. One must recognize the challenges to values and assumptions that come with graduate training and how personal counseling may be a significant asset in coping with such challenges as well as in learning effective counseling skills.

The next section reviewed a variety of opportunities for professional development and enrichment available in most counseling psychology programs. These opportunities are often not made explicit and therefore are overlooked. Opportunities for professional development can be obtained through elective courses, professional readings, professional conventions, externships, internships, and the dissertation. The closing parts of the chapter focused on the initial postdoctoral years and establishing a career as a counseling psychologist. Special considerations, options, and resources can be identified for considering types of career choices, the implications of multiple roles in making career choices, and then managing the transition to a full-time career. In this section, attention was given to issues in and advice for obtaining licensing as a psychologist, obtaining other valuable professional credentials, what experiences you can expect as you establish your career in practice or academic settings, planning and choosing continuing education strategies that will lead to the most satisfying career developments. The chapter concluded with a description of relatively new developments in the Division of Counseling Psychology that provide counseling psychology students and new professionals many more opportunities to become actively involved with the vigor and vitality of all members of the profession.

REFERENCES

American Psychological Association. (1997). *Getting in: A step-by-step plan for gaining admission to graduate school in psychology.* Washington, DC: Author.

Atkinson, D. R., Neville, H., & Casas, A. (1991). The mentorship of ethnic minorities in professional psychology. *Professional Psychology: Research and Practice, 22,* 336–338.

Bandura, A. (1977). Self-efficacy: Toward a unifying theory of behavioral change. *Psychological Review, 84,* 191–215.

Baron, A. Jr., Sekel, A. C., & Stott, F. W. (1984). Early career issues for counseling center psychologists: The first six years. *The Counseling Psychologist, 12*(1), 121–125.

Bishop, R. M., & Bieschke, K. J. (1998). Applying social cognitive theory to interest in research among counseling psychology doctoral students: A path analysis. *Journal of Counseling Psychology, 45,* 182–188.

Bogat, G. A., & Redner, R. L. (1985). How mentoring affects the professional development of women in psychology. *Professional Psychology: Research and Practice, 16,* 851–859.

Bova, B. M., & Phillips, R. R. (1982, November). *The mentoring relationship as an educational experience.* Paper presented at the National Conference of the Adult Education Association of the United States of America, San Antonio, TX. (Eric Document Reproduction Service, No. ED224 944)

Brems, C., Lampman, C., & Johnson, M. E. (1995). Preparation of applications for academic positions in psychology. *American Psychologist, 50,* 533–537.

Brickey, M. (1998). Integrating an internship into a market-driven psychology practice. *Professional Psychology: Research and Practice, 29,* 390–393.

Constantine, M. G., & Keilin, W. G. (1996). Association of Psychology Postdoctoral and Internship Centers' guidelines and the internship selection process: A survey of applicants and academic and internship training directors. *Professional Psychology: Research and Practice, 27,* 308–314.

Corey, M. S., & Corey, G. (1989). *Becoming a helper.* Belmont, CA: Wadsworth.

Egan, G. (1994). *The skilled helper.* Monterey, CA: Brooks/Cole.

Ellis, H. D. (1992). Graduate education in psychology: Past, present, and future. *American Psychologist, 47,* 570–576.

Fretz, B. R., & Stang, D. J. (1980). *Preparing for graduate study in psychology: Not for seniors only.* Washington, DC: American Psychological Association.

Gaddy, C. D., Charlot-Swilley, D. C., Nelson, P. D., & Reich, J. N. (1995). Selected outcomes of accredited programs. *Professional Psychology: Research and Practice, 26,* 507–513.

Garcia, M. E., Malott, R. W., & Brethower, D. (1988). A system of thesis and dissertation supervision: Helping graduate students succeed. *Teaching of Psychology, 15,* 186–191.

Gilbert, L. A., & Rachlin, V. (1987). Mental health and psychological functioning of dual-career families. *The Counseling Psychologist, 15,* 7–49.

Gilbert, L. A., & Rossman, K. M. (1992). Gender and the mentoring process for women: Implications for professional development. *Professional Psychology: Research and Practice, 23,* 233–238.

Gloria, A. M., Castillo, L. G., Choi-Pearson, C. P., & Rangel, D. K. (1997). Competitive internship candidates. *The Counseling Psychologist, 25,* 453–472.

Gore, P. A., Murdock, N. L., & Haley, S. J. (1998). Entering the ivory tower: Characteristics of successful counseling psychology faculty applicants. *The Counseling Psychologist, 26,* 640–657.

Guy, J. D., Stark, M. J., & Poelstra, P. L. (1988). Personal therapy for psychotherapists before and after entering professional practice. *Professional Psychology: Research and Practice, 19,* 474–476.

Hollis, J. W., & Wantz, R. A. (1993). *Counselor preparation.* Bristol, PA: Accelerated Development.

Holzman, L. A., Searight, H. R., & Hughes, H. M. (1996). Clinical psychology graduate students and personal psychotherapy: Results of an exploratory survey. *Professional Psychology: Research and Practice, 27,* 98–101.

Heppner, P., & Krauskopf, C. J. (1987). An information-process approach to personal problem solving. *The Counseling Psychologist, 15,* 371–447.

Jacob, N. C. (1987). Managing the internship application experience: Advice from an exhausted but contented survivor. *The Counseling Psychologist, 15,* 146–155.

Keith-Spiegel, P. (1990). *The complete guide to graduate school admission.* Hillsdale, NJ: Lawrence Erlbaum.

Kestenbaum, J. D. (1986). Perceived impact of personal counseling by counseling psychology graduate students. *Dissertation Abstracts International, 48/01B,* 266. (University Microfilms No. AAC8709088)

Lee, R. E. (1984). When mid-career mothers first return to work: Counseling concerns. *Journal of Counseling and Development, 63,* 39.

Lent, R. W., Brown, S. D., & Hackett, G. (1994). Toward a unifying social cognitive theory of career and academic interest, choice, and performance. *Journal of Vocational Behavior, 45,* 79–122.

Levinson, D. J. (1980). The mentoring relationship. In M. Morgan (Ed.), *Managing career development* (pp. 117–119). New York: Van Nostrand.

Lopez, S. J., & Edwardson, T. L. (1996). Quantifying practicum experience. *Professional Psychology: Research and Practice, 27,* 514–517.

Mallinckrodt, B., Gelso, C. J., & Royalty, G. M. (1990). Impact of the research training environment and counseling psychology students' Holland personality type on interest in research. *Professional Psychology: Research and Practice, 21,* 26–32.

Megargee, E. I. (1997). *A guide to obtaining a psychology internship* (3rd ed.). Muncie, IN: Accelerated Development.

Mellott, R. N., Arden, I. A., & Cho, M. E. (1997). Preparing for internship: Tips for the prospective applicant. *Professional Psychology: Research and Practice, 28,* 190–196.

Mendelson, C. (1987). Adjustment to college: The role of perception of childhood interactions with parents, autonomy, and social support. *Dissertation Abstracts International, 48/01B,* 3406. (University Microfilms No. AAC8725534)

Olson, S. K., Downing, N. E., Heppner, P. P., & Pinkney, J. (1986). Is there life after graduate school? Coping with the transitions to postdoctoral employment. *Professional Psychology: Research and Practice, 17,* 415–419.

O'Neil, J. M., Fishman, D. M., & Kinsella-Shaw, M. (1987). Dual-career couples' career transitions and normative dilemmas. *The Counseling Psychologist, 15,* 50–96.

Osberg, T. M., & Rallin, N. L. (1989). Networking as a tool for career advancement among academic psychologists. *Teaching of Psychology, 16,* 26–28.

Peterson, R. L., Peterson, D. R., Abrams, J. C., & Stricker, G. (1997). The National Council of Schools and Programs of Professional Psychology educational model. *Professional Psychology: Research and Practice, 28,* 373–386.

Petrie, T. A., & Wohlgemuth, E. A. (1994). In hopes of promoting cohesion among academics: New and established. *The Counseling Psychologist, 22,* 466–473.

Plante, T. G. (1998). How to find a first job in professional psychology: Ten principles for finding employment for psychology interns and postdoctoral fellows. *Professional Psychology: Research and Practice, 29,* 508–511.

Ponterotto, J. G., Burkard, A., Yoshida, R. K., Cancelli, A. A., Mendez, G., Wasilewski, L., & Sussman, L. (1995). Prospective minority students' perceptions of application packets for professional psychology programs: A qualitative study. *Professional Psychology: Research and Practice, 26,* 196–204.

Ponterotto, J. G., & Furlong, M. I. (1986). A profile of recently employed academicians in APA-approved and nonapproved counseling psychology programs. *Professional Psychology: Research and Practice, 17,* 65–68.

Rheingold, H. L. (1994). *The psychologist's guide to an academic career.* Washington, DC: American Psychological Association.

Sayette, M. A., Mayne, T. J. & Norcross, J. C. (1998). *Insider's guide to graduate programs in clinical and counseling psychology.* New York: Guilford.

Schlossberg, N. K. (1981). A model for analyzing human adaptation to transition. *The Counseling Psychologist, 9*(2), 2–18.

Schlossberg, N. K. (1989). *Overwhelmed: Coping with life's ups and downs.* Lexington, MA: Lexington Books.

Simono, R. B., & Wachowiak, D. (1983). Career patterns in counseling centers: Counseling psychologists review their past, present, and future. *Professional Psychology: Research and Practice, 14,* 142–148.

Skovholt, T. M., & Ronnestad, M. H. (1992). *The evolving professional self.* New York: John Wiley & Sons.

Skovholt, T. M., Stone, G. L., & Hill, C. E. (1984). Institutional affiliations of contributors to scholarly and professional activities in counseling psychology: 1980–1983. *Journal of Counseling Psychology, 31,* 394–397.

Stedman, J. M. (1997). What we know about predoctoral internship training: A review. *Professional Psychology: Research and Practice, 28,* 475–485.

Stewart, A. E., & Stewart, E. A. (1996). A decision-making technique for choosing a psychology internship. *Professional Psychology: Research and Practice, 27,* 521–526.

Stone, C., Dew, E., & Sackett, S. (1998, August). *Work experiences and career and job satisfaction of new counseling psychologists.* Paper presented at the American Psychological Association Convention, San Francisco, CA.

C H A P T E R 8

THE THERAPEUTIC RELATIONSHIP

Summary

References

When the beginning student first thinks about what personal counseling or psychotherapy is all about, he or she probably focuses on what psychologists view as technical factors. That is, the student thinks of therapy in terms of the application of psychological techniques and procedures, and also focuses on the idea that these techniques and procedures are applied by an expert. This expert is quite knowing, and has at least a lot of the answers to the client's problems.

The *application of techniques by an expert,* in reality, is only part of what counseling or therapy is. The "other part" of therapy, often the most important part, is what we shall be concerned about in this chapter: *the relationship that develops between the client and counselor.* We shall examine the place of the counselor–client relationship in counseling; just what is meant by a relationship; the components of the therapeutic relationship; the factors that allow for a good relationship; and what are called "facilitative conditions" that, when present to a high degree, appear to promote constructive change in clients.

THE IMPORTANCE OF THE THERAPEUTIC RELATIONSHIP

> Human beings are social animals. They live through a series of interrelationships, forming and being formed by interactions with other people. Much of what people come to feel and be is directly and indirectly related to the quality of the associations they have had with others. Much has been written about the quality of these formative relationships. If relationships help to form troubled lives (in the natural environment), then new relationships are needed to help change troubled lives. . . . the relationship that develops between patient and psychotherapist can be especially powerful in stimulating personality change. Despite the long history of successful and unsuccessful relationships the patient has had, the relationship that develops with the therapist, *quite apart from the techniques the therapist uses* [italics added], can facilitate the patient's growth (Lambert, 1983, p. 1).

The above quote is the beginning paragraph of a book devoted entirely to the counselor–client relationship, its causes and effects, in a variety of approaches to counseling and therapy. Based on years of both empirical research and counseling experience, nearly all professionals who practice counseling, as well as those who study it, would agree with Lambert's above statement that the counselor–client relationship is very important. Furthermore, many if not most therapists believe that the relationship is the bottom line—the key factor in successful counseling. In their extensive review, Highlen and Hill (1984) state this position clearly:

Certainly everything else that transpires is inextricably embedded in the matrix of this relationship. . . . In order for the counselor to become a potent source of influence in client change, a bond between the participants must be developed. If this solid base is not established, clients will not risk themselves to engage in the "pain of change" (pp. 360–361).

Although virtually all practicing counselors would view the relationship as important, there are wide differences of opinion as to just how important it is to successful counseling. Some, such as Hycner and Jacobs (1995), see the counselor–client relationship as the sine qua non of effective intervention. Others go even further. They suggest that not only is the relationship the most important factor in change, but that certain relationship conditions are all that is needed for successful therapy. These conditions are both *necessary* and *sufficient* for constructive behavior and personality change in a wide range of interventions (see Patterson, 1984).

On the other side of the ledger, there is probably only a handful of therapists, mostly those who align themselves with a radical behaviorism (see Chapter 11), who view the relationship as unimportant. Still, on this same end of the continuum, but a step closer to the middle, some view the counselor–client relationship as important, but running a rather weak second to technical factors, for example, counselor techniques in terms of what promotes client change. At about the midpoint on this continuum of importance is probably the therapist who views the relationship as very important and who sees a good relationship between therapist and client as a necessary factor for positive change, but not a sufficient factor. Other factors, such as counselor techniques, client characteristics, and so forth, are also important.

As will be discussed later in greater detail, conceptions of the role and importance of the therapeutic relationship seem to follow closely one's theoretical orientation. In terms of the *way* in which the relationship affects clients and client change, Prochaska & Norcross (1999) suggests that the counselor–client relationship can be seen as (a) one of the *preconditions* for therapy to proceed (as in rational–emotive or perhaps behavior therapy); (b) an *essential process* that itself produces change (as in certain humanistic approaches); or (c) a primary *source of content* to be talked about and processed in therapy (as in most of the psychodynamically oriented approaches). In terms of *importance,* in the humanistically oriented approaches such as person-centered therapy, existential therapy, and gestalt therapy, the relationship is highly central to client change. This is also the case in most of the psychodynamically oriented therapies (e.g., Freudian analysis, neoanalytic approaches, Adlerian therapy). Thus, although the humanistic and psychodynamic therapies work within the counselor–client relationship in different ways, they both view it as deeply important.

In the learning-based approaches (behavior therapy, cognitive therapy, rational-emotive therapy, etc.), on the other hand, views of importance appear to range from those few who contend the relationship to be unimportant to those who see it as moderately important. Some learning-oriented therapists do indeed view the relationship as more central to change than we have implied, but the general tendency is for learning-oriented therapists to view relationship factors as second in importance to counselor techniques. There have, however, been recent changes among learning-oriented counselors regarding conceptions of the therapeutic relationship, and these changes will be examined in Chapter 11.

THE THERAPEUTIC RELATIONSHIP DEFINED

Despite the fact that the relationship has been a key construct in theory, practice, and research for many years, little effort has gone into defining just what a therapeutic relationship is, and how relationship factors may be differentiated from non-relationship factors. The inattention to definition is most surprising on the part of theories placing the relationship at the center of change. For example, in relationship-oriented therapies such as client-centered therapy (now called person-centered therapy; see Chapter 12), no more effort seems to have been put into matters of definition than in other approaches in which the relationship is not so crucial. These relationship approaches most often discuss so-called relationship conditions that are necessary and/or sufficient for positive change to take place. The conditions represent qualities and/or behaviors in the therapist, and the client's role essentially is to perceive or take in the conditions. For example, from the time of Rogers's (1957) famous statement about the necessary and sufficient conditions for positive change in therapy, virtually all client-centered therapists have viewed empathic understanding on the part of the counselor as one of these conditions. Thus, if constructive change is to take place, the counselor must empathically understand the client (as defined later in the chapter), and the client is to perceive the counselor's empathy.

Although therapist-offered conditions may be quite important, perhaps even necessary, they do not help us much in attempting to define what a relationship is and is not. Along with being conditions that contribute to a relationship rather than necessary elements of a relationship, they are one-sided. Therapist-offered conditions minimize the role of the client in the relationship and do not incorporate the reciprocal interaction and influence that must be part of a dyadic relationship.

A definition that does capture the reciprocal nature of relationships has been offered by Gelso and Carter (1985, 1994) and Gelso and Hayes (1998). This definition is simple and general: The relationship *is the feelings and attitudes that counseling participants have toward one another, and the manner in which these are expressed.* In this definition, the techniques used by the counselor that come from his or her theory may be influenced by and influence the relationship, but these techniques do not define the relationship. For example, the interpretations offered by the psychoanalytic therapist are techniques, and they are prescribed by that therapist's theory of counseling (i.e., psychoanalytic theory of therapy). Likewise, when the behavior therapist uses conditioning techniques, we could not say that is the relationship. This therapist is following the dictates of his or her theory of counseling.

Thus, the counseling interaction consists of two elements. The first is the relationship, as defined above. The second is the technical side, consisting of the techniques used by the counselor and the theoretically dictated roles that the counselor and client engage in; for example, in client-centered therapy, the client expresses his or her feelings in the moment, as she or he experiences them, and the counselor seeks to empathically understand the client.

The differentiation between relationship and technical factors in therapy can be useful in helping us understand this highly complex enterprise. Yet, more often than is probably recognized, relationship factors color and give shape to how technical factors are actualized in counseling (Gelso & Carter, 1985, 1994; Gelso & Hayes, 1998). Thus often subtle feelings and attitudes the counseling participants hold toward one another will strongly influence just how they enact their theoretically prescribed roles. On the counselor's side, for example, if the counselor is psychoanalytically oriented and thus places a premium on the technique called *interpretation,* how and what that counselor feels toward the client will influence the nature, depth, frequency, length, and content of the interpretations that are offered. Even when the counselor is astute in his or her ability to understand his or her own feelings and not let them interfere with the work, then these feelings must color the interpretations.

Not only does the relationship influence how the counseling participants enact their theoretically prescribed roles, these roles also affect the relationship. For example, whether the counselor primarily reflects feelings, interprets, gives advice, or engages in conditioning exercises will each affect the relationship differently. Also, it goes without saying that the *manner* in which these roles are enacted both is affected by the emerging relationship and influences and alters that relationship.

In sum, then, although relationship and technical factors can be thought of as two elements of any therapeutic encounter, the two are highly interdependent. Each affects the other to a marked degree. In terms of the relationship, it often emerges silently, as the participants' feelings and attitudes toward one another develop. The therapist and client each do what they are supposed to do, according to the counselor's theory and the client's needs and compatibility with that theory. Ordinarily, the relationship comes to the fore either when something goes awry (e.g., when negative feelings arise) or when something special happens (e.g., the client feels especially moved by a feeling expressed by the counselor).

In attempting to capture the complexity of the relationship, we conclude this section with a quote from a psychologist who has devoted his career to studying the meanings of therapeutic relationships. In commenting on Gelso and Carter's (1985) definition, Barrett-Lennard (1985) provides a discussion that highlights the richness, fluidity, and indeed the elusiveness of the therapist–client relationship.

> One may think of a (dyadic) relationship as being centered on the qualities and contents of experiencing of the two participant individuals with, and toward, one another. This covers a lot of territory but it does not fully encompass the ways in which the participants communicate with each other, the messages that are passed back and forth, the moment-by-moment or generalized image that A has of B's awareness of A, or of B's feeling toward A, and likewise in respect to B's image of A's interperceptions. Neither of these levels fully encompasses "a relationship" as an emergent entity that develops a life and character of its own, existing in intimate *inter*dependence with the single-person components, a "we" in the consciousness of member persons and a distinctive "you" or "they," or the like, as seen from the outside. Any of these levels of relationship can be viewed in terms of what is present or typical at a given time in the life of the relationship, or from a developmental standpoint; and interest may center on the interior process of the relationship, or on the ways the relationship system maintains itself or is altered under the influence of external forces (Barrett-Lennard, 1985, p. 282).

COMPONENTS OF THERAPEUTIC RELATIONSHIPS

As was the case with defining the relationship, ironically few psychologists have devoted attention to the parts or components into which the relationship might be divided. Perhaps that was so because those who were most concerned with the relationship were, for many years, devoting themselves to the study of the counselor-offered relationship conditions (e.g., empathy, unconditional positive regard, and congruence, as discussed in the latter part of this chapter). Although research on these conditions has been quite fruitful, uncovering many interesting findings, it may have interfered with further theorizing about the relationship.

In any event, from the time of Sigmund Freud's early writing (Freud, 1912/1959), at least some psychoanalysts have occupied themselves with theorizing about different dimensions of therapeutic relationships. Although in psychoanalysis the transference element of the relationship has always garnered the greatest interest, from Freud on, a number of analysts have proposed that there is more of interest to analysis than the transference relationship. Freud himself believed that there were two significant components to analytic relationships. The first was the transference proper, or the neurotic transference. This component needed to be analyzed and worked through. Juxtaposed with this neurotic transference, however, were what Freud called the "friendly" and "affectionate" feelings of the analysand toward the analyst. Even though these feelings were also part of the transference (i.e., were distortions of the analyst), Freud felt them to be essential to successful analysis. They should not be interpreted to the analysand as transference.

Other psychoanalysts over the years developed formulations about components of the relationship that went beyond or at least were different from the neurotic transference; but it remained for Ralph Greenson (1967) to theorize that analytic relationships could be divided into three parts: the working alliance, the transference proper, and the real relationship. Greenson's writing has had an important impact within psychoanalysis. Gelso and Carter (1985) extended Greenson's propositions to essentially all theoretical approaches (not only psychoanalysis). In a pantheoretical statement, they propose that *"all therapeutic relationships consist of these three components [working alliance, transference, real relationship], although the salience and importance of each part during counseling or therapy will vary according to the theoretical perspective of the therapist and the particulars of a given therapy"* (p. 161).

In the remainder of this section we shall examine these three components of therapeutic relationships. In our discussion, we draw heavily on the initial conceptions of Gelso and Carter (1985) and more recent revisions (Gelso & Carter, 1994; Gelso & Hayes, 1998). Before beginning our discussion, it should be underscored that, although we discuss the three components as separate constructs, they are in fact quite interrelated in counseling practice. The way in which they operate together will be explored at the end of this discussion. It should be kept in mind that the three components are seen by Gelso and collaborators, and by the present authors, as being applicable to all relationships. They are in no way restricted to psychoanalysis.

Components of the Counseling Relationship.   **TABLE 8.1.**

Component	Summary Definition
Working Alliance	Joining of client's reasonable/observing side with counselor's working side.
Transference Configuration	
Client transference	Client experience of therapist involving feelings and perceptions belonging rightfully to early significant relationships.
Therapist Countertransference	Therapist transference to client's material.
Real Relationship	Genuine and realistic part of counselor–client relationship.

The Working Alliance

In recent times, the working alliance (also called the helping alliance, the working relationship, and the therapeutic alliance) has been empirically investigated more than perhaps any other construct pertaining to the counselor–client relationship. A number of measures have been developed to study the alliance (see Horvath & Greenberg, 1994), and it has been clearly documented that this alliance is a key part of the therapy relationship (Gelso & Hayes, 1998; Horvath & Greenberg, 1994).

What is the working alliance? What are its ingredients? What counselor and client characteristics and behaviors facilitate or inhibit its development? Following Gelso and Carter's (1985) thinking, we may consider the working alliance as *the alignment or joining together of the client's reasonable and observing side (the reasonable/observing ego in psychoanalytic terms) with the counselor's working or "therapizing" side (the counselor's observing ego applied to the counseling) for the purpose of facilitating the work of counseling.* This definition is based on the notion that two rather disparate qualities exist in human personality. The first is that which permits us to "stand back" and reasonably observe phenomena, including ourselves, and our own functioning, motives, and feelings. This is the side that could be seen as the reasonable/observing ego. The second quality allows us to experience and feel unreflectively and may be viewed as the experiencing side of the ego or the experiencing ego.

In therapies that may be considered expressive or insight-oriented treatments (e.g., psychodynamic and humanistic therapies), and perhaps in the behavioral and cognitive therapies as well, the client needs to be able to oscillate between the experiencing and observing sides of his or her personality. Thus, the client needs to be able to feel and experience, and then look and reflect upon those feelings and experiences.

Once again, in the working alliance the counselor and client's reasonable sides join together so that each can carry out their roles in the work successfully. Both counselor and client share a reasonable belief that this experience will be worthwhile for the client, and because of this, both are committed to their collaboration in the work.

What makes the working alliance so important? Not only does it reflect the participants' commitment to the work, and an intent to collaborate, it is also what allows the client to continue in the work during difficult times. For example, if and when the client's defenses and negative transference reactions push him or her in the direction of discontinuing counseling, it is the working alliance that most potently aids the client to stand back from these feelings and recognize them as defensively based. Thus, although the alliance is always important during the counseling experience, it is especially important during difficult times between the counselor and client.

Probably the most seminal theoretical statement about the working alliance as it operates across diverse forms of psychotherapy has been offered by Edward Bordin (1979). Bordin proposes that the alliance consists of three parts: agreement between counselor and client on the goals of counseling, agreement about the tasks of the work, and the emotional bond that forms between the participants. Agreement on goals implies that the participants share the goals of the work, regardless of whether this agreement is explicitly stated or indeed whether the goals themselves are explicitly stated. Agreement on tasks implies that therapist and client also share a common view of how those goals may best be attained. It is important here to understand that Bordin is not talking about tasks as structured work tasks. Rather, he is referring to any of the in-therapy or extra-therapy role behaviors expected of the participants. For example, in most forms of therapy an expected client task is for that client to talk about himself or herself and to express feelings. In analysis, the in-therapy task is for the analysand to free-associate, whereas in more structural treatments, a frequent task is for the client to carry out homework assignments. In any event, if the alliance is to be strong, client and counselor need to reach sound agreements on the value of the main tasks of a given therapy. Last but not least, there needs to be an attachment between counselor and client if the alliance is to be strong.

In our way of thinking about a working alliance, agreement on tasks and goals and bonding contribute to the strength of the alliance. In turn, the strength of the alliance facilitates agreement on tasks and goals as well as on emotional attachment. Thus there is a reciprocal causal relationship between alliance and the three dimensions discussed by Bordin (1979). Implicit in this reciprocal relationship is the fact that the working alliance exists on a continuum, ranging from weak or nonexistent to very strong. Relatedly, bonding and agreement on tasks and goals also exist on continua, varying in the same way as does the working alliance.

As should be clear by now, the working alliance is interactive in that both the counselor and the client contribute to it. Regarding the counselor's contribution, we would expect a number of qualities and behaviors to be important. The counselor's professional concern, compassion, and willingness to persist in the work seem highly pertinent. Also, the well-known "facilitative conditions" of empathic understanding, unconditional positive regard, and congruence (to be discussed in detail later in this chapter) would appear to be vital to a strong alliance. Just as is the case with the client, if the alliance is to be strong, the counselor must make use of his or her reasonable or observing side so that the feelings he or she experiences toward the client may be used appropriately. Counselors experience a range of emotional reactions to clients, and it is imperative that we use our reasonable/observing capacities to understand these reactions. Then, as a bottom line, we must try to use our emotional reactions in the service of the client, to the client's benefit, and not in antitherapeutic ways.

In terms of the client's contribution to the working alliance, probably the most essential feature is a capacity to trust. Without this, there can be no healthy bonding, no positive attachment. As uncovered in a study by Gaston, Marmar, Thompson, and Gallagher (1988), client defensiveness or resistance tends to affect the alliance negatively, at least in brief therapy (analytic, behavioral, and cognitive) with depressed elderly patients. Perhaps most basically, though, the client must have a strong enough, reasonable, observing side, or ego, to allow him or her to stand back and observe what is transpiring in him or her and in the work.

Gelso and Carter (1994) and Gelso and Hayes (1998) present a series of theoretical propositions about how the alliance operates in, and affects the process and outcome of, therapy. These propositions are aimed at facilitating both counseling practice and research. Gelso and Hayes's (1998) work, along with Horvath and Greenberg's (1994) book-length treatment of the working alliance, should be consulted by the reader who is interested in studying this construct further. In terms of research support, probably the clearest finding at this early stage of empirical investigation is that *the strength of alliance, as measured within the first few sessions of counseling or therapy, is related to a wide variety of measures of outcome. The stronger the alliance in the first few sessions, the more positive are the results of counseling.* This finding appears quite robust, as it holds up for both brief and longer-term therapy, for counseling from a range of theoretical perspectives (analytic, behavioral, cognitive, humanistic, gestalt, etc.), and with several different types of alliance measures (Bordin, 1994; Gelso & Hayes, 1998; Horvath & Symonds, 1991).

In sum, the findings do appear to support the proposition that it is quite important to establish a sound working alliance very early in counseling. This formation of an early alliance is especially important in briefer counseling, in which the counselor does not have the luxury of time to devote to the gradual cultivation of an alliance. Based on the authors' counseling experiences, we would go even further and suggest that the greatest attention needs to be given to promoting this aspect of the total relationship because without an alliance, it is hard to imagine the work of therapy being done with much ultimate effectiveness.

According to Gelso and Hayes (1998), two concepts are fundamental to any conception of the working alliance: *collaboration* and *attachment* (or bonding). Regarding collaboration, counselor and client must invest in the work jointly. If this sense of collaborativeness is not strong at the beginning of counseling, it is necessary that it develop as the work unfolds. Regarding attachment, it is essential that counselor and client form a bond with each other for the purpose of the work. These two elements—collaboration and attachment—are common across all of the measures of working alliance that have been developed in recent times (Horvath, Gaston, & Luborsky, 1993).

Just what constitutes a sound or sufficiently strong working alliance may depend on a host of factors. For example, interventions that are more emotionally demanding on the client may require a stronger alliance than less demanding treatments. Also, the alliance may need to be especially strong during certain critical points in the therapy, for example, when negative transference or certain resistances threaten the work or when the client feels particularly vulnerable. Finally, certain aspects of the alliance may need to be stronger at certain times in the work. An example of the latter may be that early in the work the agreement on tasks may be essential, whereas later in the counseling the bonding aspect may be more important.

In summary, although the concept of a working alliance has existed in counseling literature for many decades, it is only in recent times (beginning in the 1970s and 1980s) that theory and research have addressed how the alliance operates in different approaches to therapy, and how it affects the counseling process and outcomes. Research suggests that the working alliance is one of the key elements of therapy, perhaps the very foundation of the therapy relationship (Gelso & Hayes, 1998; Horvath & Greenberg, 1994). In the years ahead, research is likely to address how client, therapist, and treatment factors combine to help form and preserve effective working alliances.

The Transference Configuration

The second component of the therapeutic relationship that will be discussed has historically been embedded in psychoanalytic theory. Indeed, many consider the discovery of transference to be Freud's most significant achievement, and modern psychoanalysis is defined by many as the systematic analysis of the transferences (see Chapter 10).

Despite its centrality in psychoanalytic theory, one may consider transference (and countertransference) to be a part of all therapeutic encounters, and to be a component of all therapeutic relationships. In fact, as Freud (1912/1959) clearly formulated, transference can be seen as occurring in all human relationships. It is a natural human tendency that becomes magnified and intensified in therapeutic relationships because of the nature of such relationships. That is, because therapeutic interactions focus on help giving, with one person seeking to provide conditions for psychological growth in another, the tendency to experience and manifest transference reactions becomes heightened.

Just what is transference? In the classical Freudian view, transference is seen as the reliving of Oedipal issues in the therapy relationship. The therapist is reacted to as if he or she were any or all of the participants in the client's early Oedipal situation, most often the client's mother and/or father. Because of the exclusive focus on the Oedipal context, this definition is quite narrow and restrictive, and of course requires that the therapist share the psychoanalytic view of the critical importance of the Oedipus complex in human development.

When we view transference as an element of all therapeutic relationships, a broader conception of this construct is in order. Such a conception, in keeping with more current thought, has been offered by Gelso and Hayes (1998, p. 51). Transference is defined as *the client's experience of the therapist that is shaped by the client's own psychological structures and past and involves displacement onto the therapist of feelings, attitudes, and behaviors belonging rightfully in earlier significant relationships*. To the extent that the client's reactions to the counselor are transference-based, the client is responding to the counselor *as if* the counselor represented aspects of the transference source, for example, mother, father, sibling. It is important to understand that the client does not really think or believe that the therapist *is* mother, father, or sibling when transference reactions are occurring. Rather, the client transfers significant aspects of the parents' reactions toward him or her from earlier times onto the therapist, such that the therapist is erroneously assumed to be exhibiting those reactions (motives, attitudes, feelings, etc.).

In transference situations such as those discussed above, the client may react to the therapist as if the therapist does not like him or her, is being critical, will abandon him or her, is not trustworthy, is perfect, is wonderful, and so on. In other words, an almost infinite array of affects, characteristics, motives, and behaviors may be attributed to the counselor erroneously. Inspection of these client perceptions, sometimes over long periods of time, usually reveals them to be displacements from earlier significant relationships. Examples of transference reactions from cases actually worked with by one of the authors are given below.

- *Case 1:* Over many sessions, this client felt sure that the therapist could give her solutions to her life problems, which in fact were profound. She felt that the therapist really knew the solutions but was withholding them. He was not giving her her fair share—what she deserved to have. Because of this she experienced a chronic sense of deep anger toward the therapist. During one session in which she angrily criticized and pleaded with the therapist to "tell her," he pointed out the bitterness in her request and how her feelings must echo feelings from long ago. She responded by tearfully expressing how she never got her share from her parents, how she was never taken care of. This interaction was a critical step in the work toward her coming to understand her transference and work through the conflicts underlying them.
- Case 2: Despite the fact that the client experienced the therapist's empathy and concern in an ongoing way, during periods of the work he responded to the therapist as a critical, demanding, and deeply attacking figure. The sound working alliance and the client's strong observing ego helped him stand back from these feelings and come to grips with where they were coming from. A good bit of the work centered on the client's conflicts with a highly critical, demanding father, and the effects of this relationship on his self-concept and relationships with others.
- Case 3: During the early weeks of a long counseling experience, this client, among other things, could never break silences by offering new material. Her mind would go blank. She feared and fully expected that the therapist would feel critical of her initiating new topics and of any material she might initiate, despite the reality of the treatment situation; that is, her initiation was welcomed. A significant proportion of the counseling focused on this client's injurious relationship with her mother, a deeply narcissistic woman who had few boundaries, and whose needs this client had to constantly attend to. In close relationships, this client consistently carried with her a sense that the only way she could be cared about was if she, in effect, denied any of her needs and attended to the other's. She became a stranger to her own needs, and much of the counseling aimed at helping her learn about what she wanted and needed, and psychically disengage from the often unconscious entanglement with her mother.

Just as in all counseling relationships, in these three cases there were many transference elements. We have presented what may be seen as single strands of these transferences so as to clarify how transference reactions may occur in counseling. As a way of further clarifying this complex concept, the following rules of thumb about transference may be useful.

1. *Transference is always an error.* By definition, the perceptions the client has of the counselor, when transference-based are, to an important extent, erroneous. They represent displacements that were appropriate (not an error) to other relationships, from another time and place. It needs to be stated here that by no means are all perceptions the client has of the counselor erroneous, neither are all emotional reactions clients have toward their counselors based on misperceptions. It is important for the counselor to understand which reactions are realistic and which are based on transference.

   Although we think of transference in terms of errors in perception and displacement, it should be noted that there is at least an element of reality in all transference reactions. Often something in the therapeutic relationship serves as a trigger for transference (e.g., something the therapist says or does, verbally or nonverbally). Fundamentally, though, the client is experiencing the therapist and the relationship in a way that does not befit the therapist and his or her behavior, but instead echoes relationships and issues from the client's earlier life.

2. *Transference may be positive or negative.* The misperceptions that are part of transference reactions are just as likely to be positive as negative. Thus, the client may project positive attitudes onto the counselor, based on needs tied to past conflictual relationships, for example, because of the client's deprivations with a parent, she or he may need to see the counselor as more loving or powerful than is realistically the case. Because counselors' feelings are most often positive, and because the counseling role is a positive one, positive transferences are often more difficult to appreciate *as transferences* than are negative transferences.

3. *The emergence of transference in the counseling is facilitated by the therapist's neutrality and ambiguity.* The concept of neutrality is one of the most misunderstood in all of the psychotherapy and counseling literature. By *neutrality* we do not mean bland indifference or lack of caring. Instead, we refer to the therapist's not taking sides and not imposing his or her values and beliefs on the client. *Ambiguity* is a similar but not identical concept. It refers to the tendency not to present a clear picture of one's feelings, life, and attitudes; and counselors as well as theoretical approaches to counseling vary widely in the extent to which they endorse the concept of ambiguity.

   In any event, it is generally agreed that counselor ambiguity and neutrality create an environment in which transference is more likely to develop and emerge fully. This is not to say that transference does not occur in active therapies, where the therapist is very open about his or her values and may take sides. It occurs there, too; but ambiguity and neutrality allow it to develop and come into the open more fully and in a way that many counselors believe to be less "contaminated" (by the reality of the counselor). It must be added that the extent to which transference *should* be encouraged to develop and emerge is not nearly agreed on by counselors. As shall be seen in chapters 10, 11, and 12, theories vary widely on this point.

4. *Transference is not conscious.* Although the client's feelings toward the counselor may be fully conscious, the fact that they are displacements from other, earlier relationships is not. Some approaches to counseling (especially those psy-

chodynamically based) seek to make them conscious, with the aim of resolving or correcting transference distortions.

5. *Transferences are most likely to occur in areas of greatest unresolved conflict with significant others earlier in one's life.* The final rule of thumb implies that humans are more likely to misperceive the present based on the past (i.e., erroneously project the past into the present) in areas in which there were significant unresolved conflicts in past important relationships. Thus, for example, if a central area of unresolved conflict in one's childhood had to do with dependency, issues around dependency are likely to be evidenced in the transference relationship with the therapist.

It should be reiterated that what we have presented above are rules of thumb about the operation of transference in counseling and therapy. Some of these are a basic part of the definition of *transference* (e.g., it is an error, it is not conscious); others have never been tested in a rigorous scientific manner. The concept of transference (and countertransference, as will be discussed next) is one of the most complex in psychology today, and it has been extremely difficult to develop methods of studying it scientifically. That is because theoretical propositions that incorporate unconscious processes are not easily tested with traditional scientific methods. In recent years, though, empirical research has begun to develop. A number of methods of studying transference have emerged, including both quantitative and qualitative methods. Some of these methods make use of therapists' judgments (e.g., Gelso, Hill, Mohr, Rochlen, & Zack, 1999; Gelso, Kivlighan, Wine et al., 1997; Patton, Kivlighan, & Multon, 1997), whereas others use judgments made by raters based on audio- or videotapes of sessions (see Luborsky and Barber's [1994] review). We expect research on transference to increase in the years ahead, both in the area of psychoanalytic treatment and nonanalytic counseling.

How does transference operate in different forms of therapy? How is it handled and how should it be dealt with by the counselor? We refer the reader to subsequent chapters of this book (chapters 10, 11, and 12) and to Gelso and Hayes (1998) for detailed discussion of these complex questions. For now, suffice it to say that although we propose that transference is a component of the therapy relationship in all forms of counseling, some approaches more than others provide conditions allowing the transference to develop more fully, and then work with these reactions with the aim of helping the client gain insight into them. Generally, the psychoanalytically based approaches do this. Other approaches pay less attention to transference.

In general, transference will develop and become manifest to a greater extent in therapies that view it as central and aim to work with transference reactions. At the same time, there is evidence that it does occur even in therapies in which it is viewed as unimportant (see studies by Rhoads and Feather [1972], and Ryan and Gizynski [1971] regarding the operation of transference in behavior therapy). Counselors of all theoretical persuasions should be trained to at least recognize signs of transference and to deal with transference issues when they are interfering with progress. As Gelso and Hayes (1998) discuss, therapists can do this and still remain faithful to the theoretical approaches they are practicing. For example, the behavior therapist can help the client understand transference difficulties that are negatively affecting the counseling, without violating any principles of behavior therapy.

Countertransference: The Counselor's Transference

Given that the client–counselor relationship is a two-way street, involving contributions from both participants, it is important to look at the counselor's contributions to the transference configuration. As implied earlier, the counselor can behave in ways that evoke certain transference reactions and, by so doing, the counselor will contribute to the client's transference. But it is important to note that the counselor also contributes his or her own transference reactions, and these are called *countertransference.*

Just as we propose that client transference occurs in all therapy, so too is countertransference seen as universal. No matter how emotionally mature the counselor, and how effectively he or she has overcome inevitable conflicts, the counselor is a human being, and as such will have areas of unresolved conflict. These sore spots contain the issues that are likely to develop into countertransference reactions. This occurs when material presented by the client touches areas of unresolved conflict in the counselor. The universal nature of countertransference has been recently documented empirically (Hayes, McCracken, McClanahan, Hill et al., 1998).

The above discussion may seem to imply that there is some agreed-upon definition of *countertransference.* Actually, this construct has been one of the most confused and confusing ones in the history of psychology (and of psychoanalysis). A wide array of definitions can be found in the literature. These range from the broadest, called the *totalistic* definition, to the narrowest, called the *classical* definition. The totalistic definition of countertransference views this phenomenon as including virtually all of the counselor's emotional reactions to the client. Thus, realistic reactions, not based on particular conflicts within the counselor, will be seen as countertransference, just as will conflict-based reactions.

The classical definition of *countertransference* is the "counselor's transference to the client's transference." This is very narrow in that only client transference reactions, and not reactions that are nontransferential, can be the trigger for countertransference. An intermediate definition may be the most useful one. *Countertransference* can thus be defined as *the counselor's transference to the client's material—to the transference and nontransference communications presented by the client.* As Langs (1974) suggests, countertransference may be seen as

> . . . one aspect of those responses to the patient which, while prompted by some event within the therapy or the therapist's real life, are primarily based on his past significant relationships; basically they gratify his needs rather than the patient's therapeutic endeavors (p. 298).

Is countertransference therapeutic or antitherapeutic? Does it hinder or help progress in counseling? The answers to these questions depend on whether countertransference is considered an overt behavior or an internal experience in the counselor. Earlier writing, usually in psychoanalysis, appeared to focus on external behavior, what the analyst *did* with the client based on internal conflicts in the work.

When viewed as an external behavior, countertransference is something to be controlled and ideally to be worked through because it is important that therapists not act out their own conflicts with and on their clients. Such acting out may take numerous forms. For example, the counselor who, because of his or her unresolved issues, becomes inappropriately angry, submissive, or unresponsive and may be viewed as acting out the countertransference.

In recent times, countertransference has more often been viewed as an internal experience in the counselor (Gelso & Hayes, 1998). When seen as an internal experience (rather than as a behavior that is acted out with the client), countertransference can be extremely helpful to counseling—*if* it is understood and effectively managed by the counselor (see empirical studies by Hayes, Riker, and Ingram [1997] and Latts and Gelso [1995]). For example, if the counselor uses his or her internal countertransference-based experiences to better understand the impact of the client on him or her and on others, this can greatly benefit the work. This in fact requires that the counselor be willing to focus on his or her feelings toward the client when these are experienced as conflictual. It also requires that the counselor is willing and able to try to understand where these feelings come from in his or her own life, a task that can be anxiety-provoking but extremely important.

In summary, like transference, countertransference is seen as a component of all therapy relationships. The countertransference experience can be for better or worse, depending on the counselor's willingness to inspect his or her own experience, and the roots of his or her conflict-based reactions to clients. Also, as is the case with transference, whereas countertransference had been ignored by researchers for many years, empirical work is currently on the increase (e.g., Hayes et al., 1997, 1998; Latts & Gelso, 1995; Lecours, Bouchard, & Normandin, 1995). Particularly important will be research that seeks to understand how therapists can effectively manage and make use of their countertransference reactions (Gelso & Hayes, 1998; Hayes et al., 1998).

The Real Relationship

Coexisting in an interrelated way with the working alliance and transference components of the counseling relationship is a third component. Following the lead of psychoanalyst Ralph Greenson (1967), this component has been labeled the "real relationship" (Gelso & Carter, 1985, 1994; Gelso & Hayes, 1998). Although we will use *real relationship,* this term can be confusing, implying as it does that relationships vary in how "real" they are. All relationships are of course real in the sense that they actually exist; and it is probably safe to say that none exists any more than others.

The construct of "real relationship" is conceptualized as having two main defining features: genuineness and realistic perceptions. Counseling relationships would rate high on the real relationship component if both participants were highly genuine and perceived each other in a realistic (undistorted) way. Conversely, lack of genuineness and realistic perceptions would make for a low rating on this component.

The concept of "genuineness" has been central in counseling and therapy for many years, especially in the humanistic therapies (e.g., person-centered, gestalt).

When genuineness is discussed in the counseling literature, what is usually being referred to is the *therapist's* genuineness; and, especially in the humanistic approaches, therapist genuineness is seen as an important facilitative factor.

What is meant by *genuineness?* We define it as the ability and willingness to be what one truly is in the relationship, to be honest, open, and authentic. As noted above, the counseling literature has tended to focus on therapist genuineness, and in this sense has neglected the fact that the relationship goes two ways. In order for the relationship to be high in genuineness, both parties must be open, honest, and authentic, or at least they must work to express these qualities with each other. As Greenberg (1985) puts it, in a genuine relationship, the two participants in the counseling situation are "stubbornly attempting to dispense with appearances and reveal themselves as they truly are in the moment" (p. 254). Along a similar vein, a relationship that is highly genuine would tend to be what is often described as an *I–thou relationship.* To follow Greenberg's (1985) thinking further, the genuine involvement in an I–thou relationship is seen as "the attempt for people to break down barriers between inside and outside, between image and experience, and to communicate intimately their moment-to-moment inner experience" (p. 254).

Because the counselor and client's roles differ in the relationship, however, their expression of genuineness is quite different. From the client's side, he or she is expected to try to express feelings, thoughts, and inner experience essentially at all times, although it is of course not expected that the client will always be successful at accurately expressing these inner qualities. In this sense, though, the client is expected to be genuine, or struggle to be so, throughout the work.

The counselor's contribution to a genuine relationship is more complicated than the client's role. No approach to counseling and therapy would advise the counselor to say whatever is on his or her mind, and express or act out his or her feelings unreflectively. Relatedly, Greenberg (1985) points out that: "The relationship is therefore not a strictly mutual I–thou relationship in which the counselor is equally acknowledged and confirmed by the client in an ongoing fashion" (p. 255). Greenberg refers to philosopher Martin Buber's (1958) famous book on the I–thou relationship, and cites Buber's term, "one-sided inclusion," as fitting counseling relationships because of the differing roles. Thus, one can have an I–thou relationship in counseling, but it differs from the ordinary I–thou relationship. The counselor puts many of his or her needs aside and is in the service of the client's needs and growth during the time of the work. Returning to the issue of genuineness, the extent and ways in which the counselor should be open, honest, and authentic must depend on what is best for a given client at a given point in the work. In this sense, the counselor must practice a kind of "controlled spontaneity"—expressing what he or she feels, what is on his or her mind, after reflecting on what is best for the client and deciding that expression of this feeling would be appropriate.

In summary, the counselor spends much of the time in counseling paying attention to the client and his or her expressions and commenting on these. The counselor thinks about what is going on in the work, in the client, in himself or herself, and in the relationship. At certain points the counselor may express his or her emotions and feelings toward and about the client. It must be emphasized, however, that our comments do not imply that the counselor ought to be *disingenuous* or dishonest at any point. Although whether and how particular feelings ought to be directly expressed is open to debate, we would contend that there is no place in counseling for counselor dishonesty or disingenuousness.

The second aspect of the real relationship is *realistic perceptions*. Here the participants perceive each other in a realistic and accurate way, undistorted by transference experiences or other defenses. From the first moment of contact, at least some of the therapeutic relationship contains such realistic perceptions on the part of *both* client and counselor. We emphasize the word *both* here because some theoretical approaches (particularly those psychoanalytically based) appear to imply that, whereas the therapist's perceptions may be mostly realistic from the beginning of the work, all or nearly all of the client's perceptions are transference-based. On the contrary, not only does the client perceive or "subceive" aspects of the counselor realistically, but this realistic or accurate picture builds and increases throughout the work. Relatedly, as transference distortions are worked through (whether or not they are interpreted to the client as such), realistic perceptions take their place, at least in part.

Even counselors who practice the "blank screen" notion of counseling (discussed in Chapter 10), in the sense of being highly ambiguous about themselves and their personal opinions, communicate their personhood in numerous ways—from their office decor to their attire and general appearance to their sense of humor to the questions they ask, and so forth. And even clients with very strong transference proclivities and tendencies to distort will be able to perceive the counselor realistically to an extent.

How important is it for the relationship to be on the positive side (characterized by highly genuine and realistic perceptions on the part of both participants) of a real relationship continuum? All forms of therapy would probably advocate that the therapist perceive the client realistically (e.g., undistorted by countertransference reactions and other personal needs). Virtually all would want the client to perceive the counselor accurately or, more important, to be moving in the direction of accurate perception. Similarly, client genuineness would be seen as a plus in virtually all approaches. The most controversial element, though, is counselor genuineness. The when, how, and to what extent of counselor genuineness varies significantly across therapies, as shall be discussed in greater detail later in the book. At the same time, no theory suggests that the counselor wear a professional facade that misrepresents who he or she is as a person.

What does research tell us about the real relationship in counseling? Of the components we have discussed, the real relationship has received by far the least research attention. The few studies that have been done (Eugster & Wampold, 1996; Gelso et al., 1999; Knox, Hess, Petersen, & Hill, 1997) point to the importance of a positive real relationship in counseling. These studies, however, have barely scratched the surface, and much work is needed on this construct. At the same time, there is a great deal of research on one of the elements of the real relationship: therapist genuineness. This shall be discussed in the next section on therapist facilitativeness.

A Perspective on Relationship Components

We noted in the beginning of this section that the three components of the therapeutic relationship are interrelated in practice. We shall conclude this section by discussing how they are interrelated and how they might be expected to operate together in counseling.

Early in counseling, the working alliance is especially important. The reasonable sides of the counselor and client will need to join together, to bond, so that the value of working together can be appreciated, and emotional threats to the emerging relationship can be looked at without destroying what has begun to build. The counselor and client must also come to agree—implicitly or explicitly—on the goals and tasks of counseling, as discussed earlier. Utmost attention needs to be given to the cultivation of this alliance early in counseling. Initial positive transference and a positive real relationship aid considerably in alliance development. Even though transference reactions are displacements from earlier relationships (i.e., errors, as described earlier), if they are positive, they can help create warm friendly feelings that serve to solidify the working bond between counseling participants. In a like manner, if each participant feels positively toward the other, who is seen realistically and who has genuinely expressed himself or herself, the working alliance will be strengthened. In this way, genuine and realistic caring, which itself creates and is part of a personal, emotional bond, also furthers the working bond of the alliance.

In turn, when the working alliance is sound, the client is able to experience negative feelings toward the counselor in the transference relationship without these feelings injuring the work. In fact, the strength of the alliance allows one to work through the negative transferences and thus further strengthen the total relationship. On the other hand, when negative transference develops early in the work and before a strong working alliance has had a chance to develop, it is important, perhaps essential, that these feelings be explored and their transference roots uncovered. Without this, the alliance may be irreparably damaged by the negative transference, and the relationship may end or stagnate. (See Horwitz's [1974] examination of such phenomena based on a 20-year process outcome study done at the Menninger Clinic.) When such negative transference is explored and understood, the result is better and more successful counseling (Gelso, Hill, & Kivlighan, 1991; Gelso et al., 1997). We should note here, though, that negative transference is not always present to a significant degree and is not always an important part of treatment (Gelso et al., 1997; Patton et al., 1997).

As counselor and client continue to work together and their alliance strengthens, we would expect the real relationship to strengthen. The client is able to be increasingly genuine and to perceive the counselor more realistically. The working alliance facilitates this and is thus a factor in the strengthening of the real relationship, just as the real relationship affects the working alliance.

What is the developmental course of the three components during counseling? As indicated earlier, the working alliance is most salient early in the relationship. After the early phase, when it becomes established to a satisfactory degree, the alliance tends to fade into the background, only coming to the fore when needed, for example, when the relationship is threatened by negative feelings that may result from transference. There is also emerging evidence indicating that in successful counseling the working alliance declines in strength for a period. That is, after being initially strong, the alliance will weaken as the counselor begins to focus on the client's resistances or basic emotional issues. Subsequently, the alliance will again strengthen.

This high–low–high pattern does not appear to occur in less-successful counseling (see Gelso and Hayes [1998], Chapter 2, for a review of research on this pattern).

The real relationship, on the other hand, may well build throughout the relationship, becoming most salient in the later phases of the work, when the participants come to know each other most deeply, have become increasingly genuine, and perceive each other most realistically. Transference continues throughout counseling, but is increasingly understood by the client (Gelso et al., 1997; Graff & Luborsky, 1977; Patton et al., 1997), at least in therapies that focus on these transference reactions. In therapies that do not, we would expect the transferences to become less salient as other phenomena are attended to—unless these transferences are injurious to the work. In such cases, they need to be dealt with and resolved, or the effects can be irreparably damaging.

In summary, each component of the counseling relationship develops in its own way, although each is also interdependent. Additional theory and research are needed to further our understanding of the course of development of the various components in both successful and unsuccessful counseling.

FACILITATIVE CONDITIONS AND THE COUNSELING RELATIONSHIP

At several points in this chapter reference has been made to therapist-offered conditions, necessary and sufficient conditions, and relationship conditions. All of these references pertain to a set of conditions initially formulated over 40 years ago by Rogers (1957), the founder of client-centered therapy, which is now known as *person-centered therapy* (see Chapter 12). Rogers's original theoretical statement was one of the most influential in the history of counseling psychology. It has generated a great deal of research and had a profound effect on counseling practice. In this section of Chapter 8 we explore the major conditions proposed by Rogers in some detail, as these conditions are crucial to the counselor–client relationship as defined earlier.

As a preface to his famous statement, Rogers asked, "Is it possible to state, in terms which are clearly definable and measurable, the psychological conditions that are *both necessary and sufficient* [italics added] to bring about constructive personality change" (1957, p. 95)? Rogers answered his question by stating the six conditions presented in Table 8.2.

According to these conditions, the client needs to be in contact with the counselor and needs to be in a state (i.e., incongruence, anxiety, vulnerability) that makes him or her receptive to help. The client also must perceive or take in what the counselor has to offer. Despite the importance of these client contributions, though, the features of Rogers's statement that have been given the greatest attention over the years are items 3, 4, and 5 in Table 8.2, the three therapist-offered conditions. As implied in Rogers's own work, as well as the research of many others, the three therapist-offered conditions, or the relationship conditions, constitute the bulk of his theoretical statement.

Before discussing each of the three conditions, we will clarify our use of the term *facilitative conditions*. Much of the research evidence suggests that the

TABLE 8.2.   **Rogers's Necessary and Sufficient Conditions for Constructive Change in Counseling.**

1. Two persons are in psychological contact.
2. The first, whom we shall term the client, is in a state of incongruence, being vulnerable or anxious.
3. The second person, whom we shall term the therapist, is congruent or integrated in the relationship.
4. The therapist experiences unconditional positive regard for the client.
5. The therapist experiences an empathic understanding of the client's internal frame of reference and endeavors to communicate this experience to the client.
6. The communication to the client of the therapist's empathic understanding and unconditional positive regard is to a minimal degree achieved.

   No other conditions are necessary. If these six conditions exist, and continue over a period of time, this is sufficient. The process of constructive personality change will follow. (italics added)

Source: C. R. Rogers. (1957). The necessary and sufficient conditions of therapeutic personality change. *Journal of Consulting Psychology, 21,* p. 96.

therapist-offered conditions are not sufficient (see reviews by Beutler, Machado, and Neufeldt [1994]; Orlinsky, Grawe, and Parks [1994]; and comments by Bohart and Greenberg [1997, pp. 18–19]) for positive counseling outcomes in many or most cases. In other words, more is needed than just these three conditions (or even the six conditions originally specified by Rogers). Also, evidence suggests that these conditions are best not viewed as necessary, as it is conceivable that at least some clients in some kinds of counseling treatment change positively when these therapist-offered conditions are present only to a minimal degree. Yet, as will be elaborated later in the chapter, it appears that these conditions do in most cases facilitate positive change and are important for change. Thus, the conditions discussed below are labeled facilitative conditions, although they are viewed as unnecessary in some cases and certainly not sufficient in most.

Empathic Understanding

Of the three facilitative conditions, that which has the greatest appeal theoretically and clinically, and which has received the greatest amount of empirical support in terms of being associated with positive counseling outcomes (Orlinsky et al., 1994), is empathic understanding. Indeed, it is hard to envision effective counseling if the counselor is not able to empathize with the client and his or her issues. Therapists from virtually every theoretical orientation have noted the importance of empathy. (See, for example Eagle and Wolitzky's [1997] in-depth discussion of the importance of empathy in psychoanalysis, and Linehan's [1997] discussion of its role in cognitive-behavior therapy.)

In describing his view of empathy, Rogers (1957) tells us:

> To sense the client's private world as if it were your own, but without ever losing the "as if" quality—this is empathy, and this seems essential to therapy. To sense

the client's anger, fear, or confusion as if it were your own, yet without your own anger, fear, or confusion getting bound up in it, is the condition we are attempting to describe. When the client's world is this clear to the therapist, and he moves about in it freely, then he can communicate his understanding of what is clearly known to the client and can also voice meanings in the client's experience of which the client is scarcely aware (p. 98).

Shortly after Rogers's seminal statement, G. T. Barrett-Lennard (1962), who had studied with Rogers, published an inventory that sought to measure empathic understanding and the other therapist-offered conditions from the vantage point of the client receiving counseling. Over the years, Barrett-Lennard has done careful and important research on the Relationship Inventory (RI) and revised it several times (see Barrett-Lennard, 1986). Because of that, the RI continues to be the most effective method of measuring the facilitative conditions in a manner that is true to Rogers's theory. Some items from the RI will help clarify the meaning of empathy. Pluses indicate high, and minuses low, empathy.

> (+) He appreciates exactly how the things I experience feel to me
> (-) He may understand my words but doesn't see the way I feel
> (+) He usually understands the whole of what I mean
> (-) Sometimes he thinks *I* feel a certain way, because that's the way he feels
> (+) He realizes what I mean even when I have difficulty saying it

In his initial definition and many of his subsequent writings (e.g., Rogers, 1975), Rogers stressed that empathy and the other conditions were *attitudes and subjective experiences with the therapist.* Yet, as Hackney (1978) notes, over the years a shift occurred in how empathy was viewed. More and more it came to be seen as a communication *skill* and less and less as a subjective experience that could be expressed by the therapist in a variety of ways. Increasing stress was placed on the idea that empathy was observable, measurable, and readily trainable—that is, often requiring only a few hours of training (see Carkhuff, 1969; Truax & Carkhuff, 1967). What Rogers and many others (see Bozarth, 1984, 1997) had seen as "a way of being" was reduced and narrowed to a trainable skill.

As part of this development, it appeared that empathy became almost equated with the counseling technique called *reflection of feeling* in which the counselor paraphrases or reflects back to the client the feelings involved in what the client has just communicated (see Chapter 6). Bozarth (1997) points out that many in the counseling field came to believe that reflection of feeling *is* empathy and empathy *is* reflection of feeling.

Although the technique of reflection may aid the counselor in expressing his or her empathy, equating the two oversimplifies and excessively narrows the concept of empathy. In his thoughtful clarification of why empathy and reflection must be differentiated, Bozarth (1984) presents the following multiple-choice item, asking his reader to indicate which statement is the most empathic: (1) I'm having strong sexual feelings toward you; (2) When I took my Volkswagen engine out, the car rolled down the hill, hit the rabbit pen, etc., etc.; (3) You feel as though you have lost contact with the physical world. The third response is a standard reflection of feeling, but Bozarth presents compelling case data to show how alternatives 1 and 2 were highly empathic. For example, in alternative 2, the client experienced an intense and painful communication block in one session. She began the next session by asking the therapist, "What have you been doing?" He responded by telling her a nearly session-long story about his car. She later expressed appreciation that the therapist did not try to force her to reconfront her struggle; she needed a respite from it. She also described how the session helped her identify the core of her difficulties.

The above shows how nonreflective responses can be empathic. On the other side of the ledger, reflections, even accurate ones, may signify a lack of empathy. One of the authors vividly recalls an instance when a colleague accurately reflected another colleague's underlying feelings during a meeting, resulting in the recipient tearfully and, to her, shamefully breaking down. This colleague, at that time, neither needed nor wanted someone to illuminate her underlying feelings, and doing so was a deeply unempathic act, although it entailed an accurate reflection of feeling.

There are many ways in which one can become empathic. As Hackney (1978) recommends, the counselor needs to "experience the feeling, first, comprehend it as best you can, then react to it" (p. 37). Modes of being empathic can and should be based on who the therapist is as a person, who the client is as a person, the therapist–client interactions, and probably some other factors. In essence, according to Bozarth (1984, 1997) what is needed is *idiosyncratic empathy* in which the empathy that is subjectively experienced is expressed in a way that fits the counseling participants and their relationship. Numerous responses (silence, reflection of feeling, interpretation, storytelling, etc.) may express empathy.

Before leaving our discussion of empathic understanding, we should note two important developments in research and theory on this construct. The first development is that empathy is increasingly being viewed as a multistage process (Barrett-Lennard, 1981, 1986; Bohart & Greenberg, 1997; Gladstein, 1983). Gladstein points out that several conceptualizations of empathy seem to include some common stages. First, empathy is experienced emotionally, through a process of identification with the client. This is not complete identification. Rather, it is a process in which the counselor to some extent experiences what the client feels and yet maintains the necessary separateness. Second, there is cognitive activity, in which the counselor consciously sifts through the client's expressions and considers their meanings to the client. Third, in Rogers's (1975) and Barrett-Lennard's (1986) conceptualizations, there is a communication of that empathy to the client; and, as discussed above, this communication may take many forms. Finally, there exists the client's "sense and perception of the degree to which the therapist is attuned and actually 'with' him, or her, in immediate personal understanding" (Barrett-Lennard, 1986, p. 446). As further noted by Barrett-Lennard, it is useful to conceptualize the stages of empathy as recycling throughout the counseling encounter.

The second development in research and theory on empathic understanding has been the growing awareness over the years that there are different kinds of empathy (Bohart & Greenberg, 1997; Duan & Hill, 1996; Gladstein, 1983). For example, empathy may be divided into overlapping types, with each having significantly different implications for counseling. The first may be called *cognitive empathy* (or intellectual empathy, as in Duan and Hill [1996]). Cognitive empathy involves the counselor's "taking in" the client's perspective and comprehending what the client feels. *Affective empathy* (or empathic emotions, as in Duan and Hill [1996]), on the other hand, entails the counselor's emotional identification with the client and actually *feeling* at least some of what the client feels.

Gladstein (1983) presents a thoughtful discussion of how each of these types of empathy may or may not be helpful, depending on what the goals of counseling are, which stage the counseling is in, and what the client's preferences are in the relationship. The key point is that certain kinds of empathy may be helpful or not helpful, and that simple statements about how empathy helps are not sufficient.

Finally, awareness that empathy is a multistage process and that there may be different types of empathy may help resolve one of the most confusing and disturbing findings in the empathy literature. A number of studies have noted that different measures of empathy are at best modestly related to one another. Although puzzling at first glance, this finding makes sense because the various measures are tapping different aspects and stages of empathy. Thus one would not expect them to be highly interrelated (see Barrett-Lennard, 1981; Duan & Hill, 1996; Gladstein, 1983).

Unconditional Positive Regard

Of the three facilitative conditions, unconditional positive regard is the most controversial and perhaps also the most complex. At various points in the history of this construct, it has been viewed as synonymous with any and all of the following: warmth, nonpossessive warmth, acceptance, unconditional acceptance, respect, regard, and caring.

In Rogers's (1957) original theoretical statement, he discussed unconditional positive regard in this way:

> To the extent that the therapist finds himself experiencing a warm acceptance of each aspect of the client's experience as being a part of that client, he is experiencing unconditional positive regard. . . . It means that there are no *conditions* of acceptance, no feeling of "I like you only *if* you are thus and so." It means a prizing of the person. . . . It is at the opposite pole from a selective evaluating attitude—"You are bad in these ways, good in those." It involves as much feeling of acceptance for the client's expression of negative, "bad," painful, fearful, defensive, abnormal feelings as for his expression of "good," positive, mature, confident, social feelings, as much acceptance of ways in which he is inconsistent as of ways in which he is consistent. It means a caring for the client, but not in a possessive way or in such a way as simply to satisfy the therapist's own needs. It means a caring for the client as a *separate* person, with permission to have his own feelings, his own experiences (p. 98).

As can be seen from Rogers's original definition, virtually all of the terms that have been used interchangeably with unconditional positive regard are included in his formulation. As Lietaer (1984) points out, some of the controversy and ambivalence surrounding the concept of unconditional positive regard is due to the fact that Rogers did not elaborate much further or at least did not examine some of the problems with the concept.

The controversy surrounding the concept of unconditional positive regard most basically relates to the notion that the therapist can be unconditional in his or her reactions to clients. Critics maintain that it is unrealistic to expect a therapist to experience any feelings toward a client without conditions. In this way, the concept of unconditionality runs into conflicts with the third facilitative condition, genuineness, or congruence. Except in extremely rare circumstances, critics argue, one cannot be unconditionally positive in one's regard for the client and genuine or congruent—simply because unconditionality is not possible.

Responses to these criticisms have been twofold. First, the extent to which a therapist experiences unconditional positive regard can be viewed as a matter of degree. Rogers himself made this point in his "necessary and sufficient conditions" paper (Rogers, 1957). As Berenson and Carkhuff (1967) note, completely unconditional positive regard exists only in theory, and from a clinical and experiential viewpoint the most accurate statement is that the effective counselor experiences unconditional positive regard during many moments of his or her contact with the client. At times, the therapist experiences only a conditional regard, and perhaps at times the regard is negative.

The second response to the criticisms of the concept of unconditional positive regard entails an important distinction. Lietaer (1984) argues persuasively that in considering the concept of unconditionality, one must distinguish the client's inner experience from his or her external behavior. *Unconditionality* refers to acceptance of the client's experience (feelings, fantasies, thoughts, desires). Lietaer states: "My client ought to experience the freedom to feel *anything* with me; he should sense that I am open to his experience and will not judge it" (p. 46; italics added). Further, as Bozarth (1997) notes, if the counselor truly climbs into the client's world empathically, that counselor will indeed fully accept the person. Lietaer, however, notes that his receptiveness to the inner experiential world of the client does not mean that all behavior is equally welcome: "Both within and without the therapeutic relationship there can be specific behaviors of which I disapprove, would like to change, or simply cannot accept" (Lietaer, p. 48). At the same time, it is important that the counselor attempt to look beyond the behavior of which he or she disapproves. The counselor should try to understand the behavior from the perspective of everything the client has experienced in his or her life. Lietaer adds: "Without approving of it, I accept his behavior as something that is there 'for the time being' and go with him into the personal problems that lie behind it" (p. 47). In being unconditional, though, Lietaer underscores that, whatever the counselor's reactions to the client's behavior, the counselor must "*keep on valuing the deeper core of the person, what she basically is and can become*" (p. 47).

Given the complexity of the concept of unconditional positive regard, it is not surprising that studies have shown it to be multidimensional. That is, the concept appears to be composed of several relatively independent dimensions (see Barrett-Lennard, 1986; Gurman, 1977; Lietaer, 1984). In terms of the dimensions that are important across different forms of therapy, the two that Barrett-Lennard (1986) formulates seem most pertinent: *level of regard* and *unconditionality of regard*. He defines level of regard as "the overall level or tendency of one person's affective response to another" (p. 440). Positive regard entails warmth, liking, caring, "being drawn toward," and valuing the client in a nonpossessive way. Examples of positive items (the first three below) and negative items (the last three) from Barrett-Lennard's aforementioned Relationship Inventory are:

> She respects me as a person.
> I feel appreciated by her.
> She cares for me.
> I feel that she disapproves of me.
> She feels that I am dull and uninteresting.
> At times she feels contempt for me.

Whereas level of regard pertains to the degree of positive or negative feelings toward the client, unconditionality of regard refers to the degree of constancy in accepting the client, or, as Lietaer states, the extent to which the client is accepted without *ifs*. Unconditionality of acceptance implies that the therapist's basic attitude toward the client does not fluctuate according to the client's emotions or behavior. Positively (first two) and negatively (last two) worded conditionality items from Barrett-Lennard's Relationship Inventory suggest how this construct may be operationalized:

> How much he likes or dislikes me is not altered by anything that I tell him
>   about myself.
> Whether the ideas and feelings I express are "good" or "bad" seems to make
>   no difference to his feelings toward me.
> Sometimes I am more worthwhile in his eyes than I am at other times.
> Depending on my behavior, he has a better opinion of me sometimes than he
>   has at others.

Congruence

Congruence, or genuineness, as it is often termed, has been considered a foundation variable since Rogers's initial statement. This means that, as Barrett-Lennard (1986) notes, empathy, positive regard, and unconditionality cannot have their desired effects if the therapist is not congruent or genuine. In fact, theoreticians such as Barrett-Lennard question whether one can really be empathic or unconditionally positively regarding in the absence of congruence. In this sense, congruence sets an upper limit on the degree to which the other conditions can exist and have their expected effects. (Stating these terms in an either/or fashion helps to clarify how the concepts operate interactively. In fact, each is better seen as existing on a continuum, with the *extent* of congruence influencing the *extent* to which one can be empathic and regarding.)

What do we mean by the words *congruence*, or *genuineness?* The concept of genuineness was discussed earlier in this chapter as part of the "real relationship" in counseling. We shall now examine this condition further. Rogers (1957) believed that congruence meant the following:

> . . . within the relationship he [the counselor] is freely and deeply himself, with
> his actual experience accurately represented by his awareness of himself. It is the
> opposite of presenting a facade, either knowingly or unknowingly. . . . It should

be clear that this [being congruent] includes being himself even in ways which are not regarded as ideal for psychotherapy (p. 98).

Then, regarding whether the counselor must be congruent at all times, Rogers tells us:

It is not necessary (nor is it possible) that the therapist be a paragon who exhibits this degree of integration, of wholeness, in every aspect of his life. It is sufficient that he is accurately himself in this hour of this relationship, that in this basic sense he is what he actually is, in this moment of time (p. 98).

When one studies Rogers's observations, a number of questions about congruence arise. Why does Rogers refer to congruence as implying integration or wholeness? Is the congruence between one's underlying experience and awareness of that experience, between that underlying experience and one's overt communication with the client? between awareness and communication? or among all of these levels? How does congruence relate to therapist spontaneity and to acting out of one's impulses in counseling? In an effort to be congruent, to what extent should the therapist focus on expressing his or her own feelings to the client?

These complex questions have been addressed over the years by Rogers and other theoreticians who have studied the facilitative conditions. As we shall see, the answers must be interrelated. For example, in response to why Rogers seems to equate congruence with integration and wholeness, from its inception, the concept of congruence has implied a consistency among the different levels of experience. One's underlying experience, awareness, and communication are all consistent. In this sense, the person is integrated. Clearly, when theorists who write about the facilitative conditions discuss wholeness and integration, they do not mean that the therapist has all positive feelings, or has no problems of his or her own. In Rogers's first statement above he makes that clear. The counselor may have negative feelings in the relationship, and be whole, integrated, and congruent if he or she is able to be nondefensively aware of these feelings and share them when appropriate. But, again, integration and wholeness refer to a consistency among the various levels of experiencing and communication.

The concept of *experience* or *experiencing* as it relates to counselor congruence is complicated and requires further clarification. Barrett-Lennard (1986) notes that experience

. . . includes all of the ways in which the person is aroused and active at a given moment which *could*, in the nature of the human organism, register and be integrated in conscious awareness. Implied is the notion that persons may be more or less "open to experience" at a given time, as a function both of situational and personality determinants (p. 444).

If the counselor is not open to his or her experience, then what is experienced at an underlying level will not be in awareness. In effect, the counselor is not conscious or aware of this experience, and to that extent there is incongruence between experience and awareness. This state will also create incongruence between experience and overt communication with the client because experience tends to be expressed indirectly to the client—verbally and nonverbally—and this may contradict what the therapist communicates overtly.

We noted in our earlier discussion of the real relationship in counseling that the concept of counselor genuineness is controversial. Although no theoretical approach advocates therapist phoniness or disingenuousness, approaches differ in the extent to which they advocate the counselor's sharing his or her feelings about the client, the counseling, and the relationship directly with the client. In general, psychoanalytic approaches promote *less* direct sharing of counselor feelings, and humanistic approaches promote *greater* sharing. Virtually no legitimate approach, though, would advocate the counselor's acting out his or her impulses with the client, discussing his or her personal problems with the client except in some unusual circumstances, or telling the client whatever is on the counselor's mind. In terms of direct communication of negative feelings about the client or the relationship, the humanistic perspective would generally support such expressions and in fact view them as extremely important, especially if the counselor's experienced feelings were interfering with his or her counseling effectively and experiencing empathy and regard.

Finally, as for the other facilitative conditions, items from Barrett-Lennard's Relationship Inventory provide operational examples of the concept of congruence. The first two items are positively stated for congruence and the last two are negatively stated:

> I feel that she is real and genuine with me.
> I feel that what she says nearly always expresses exactly what she is feeling
>   and thinking as she says it.
> At times I sense that she is not aware of what she is really feeling with me.
> I believe that she has feelings she does not tell me about that are causing
>   difficulty in our relationship.

A Perspective on Facilitative Conditions

As noted at the beginning of this discussion of the facilitative conditions, research over the years strongly supports the contention that these conditions are generally not sufficient and probably not even necessary in some cases. Yet the research also just as clearly suggests that the conditions are indeed facilitative. They are facilitative of a constructive positive counseling process and of a range of desirable outcomes.

Actually, the history of research on these conditions is not as stable, and the results not as consistent, as the statement above might lead one to believe. Shortly after Rogers's statement about the "necessary and sufficient conditions," research studies rather quickly accumulated attesting to the positive effects of the conditions. It appeared that some bottom-line conditions had been discovered and that these conditions seemed among the most powerful ever studied in counseling and psychotherapy (see Truax & Carkhuff, 1967; Truax & Mitchell, 1971). Beginning around the early 1970s, though, more negative results began to emerge. This occurred when investigators who were perhaps more skeptical of Rogers's theory sought to test it rigorously and in a context that differed from Rogers's client-centered therapy (the theoretical position from which the conditions originated). Because of these negative results and the many concerns voiced about the methodology of the earlier research, disappointment set in about the facilitative conditions (see, for example, Parloff, Waskow, & Wolfe, 1978).

Reviews conducted since those early ones present a more balanced picture. First, the conditions do have a positive effect on a range of indicators of the outcomes of counseling, although that effect does not seem as powerful and far-reaching as the research of the 1960s and early 1970s suggested. Second, the extensive recent reviews (i.e., Bohart & Greenberg, 1997; Orlinsky et al., 1994) as well as a notable earlier one (Gurman, 1977) clearly indicate that the facilitative conditions are much more strongly related to a range of counseling outcomes when these conditions are *based on the client's perception rather than on the ratings made by outside judges (who, for example, base ratings on taped segments of sessions)*. In other words, when the client rates his or her therapist in terms of the facilitative conditions (on, for example, Barrett-Lennard's Relationship Inventory), these ratings will be far more related to how the counseling turns out (e.g., effective, ineffective) than will ratings of the facilitative conditions as viewed by outside raters. Although some observers believe this indicates that the facilitative conditions are not that important, in our view this finding is entirely consistent with Rogers's initial theory. Rogers's focus was on the client's perception of the relationship as the most important indicator of the effects of the conditions, not on "objective" ratings made by nonparticipants in the relationship. We should note that this relationship of clients' ratings of their therapists' facilitativeness and how counseling turns out is also consistent with Elliott, Clark, and Kemeny's (1991) finding that clients feel that being understood is the most important variable in therapy.

A third noteworthy feature of research reviews on the facilitative conditions is that the effects do not seem equivalent for the different conditions (Orlinsky & Howard, 1986; Orlinsky et al., 1994). For example, empathic understanding seems to have a more consistent positive effect across studies than does congruence, although congruence does seem important also, especially (again) from the client's perspective. In terms of important directions for future research on the facilitative conditions, we refer the reader to these excellent reviews as well as discussions by Watson (1984) and Duan and Hill (1996).

RELATIONSHIP COMPONENTS, FACILITATIVE CONDITIONS, AND THE THERAPEUTIC PROCESS

Do the facilitative conditions, as discussed above, and the relationship components, as explored earlier in this chapter, interrelate during counseling? If so, how would this occur? All that can be offered is theoretical speculation. Research is needed to help inform this speculation.

Gelso and Carter (1985) suggest that the facilitative conditions are probably central in the development of the working alliance. Thus, the working alliance will be more positive and stronger to the extent that the therapist is empathic, unconditionally and positively regarding, and congruent.

Gelso and Carter also speculate that the facilitative conditions may have their effect *through* the alliance they foster. We would go a step beyond this and suggest that the therapist-offered facilitative conditions have their effect on the client through their effects on the transference and real relationship, as well as on the working alliance. For example, the therapist who is high on empathy, unconditionality, positive regard, and congruence will probably foster positive transference. At least as important, though, is that the counselor who is facilitative, and experienced as such by the client, will create the kind of safe climate that allows the client to explore negative transference reactions when they occur. If one feels deeply understood, cared about, and accepted personally with few if any conditions by a therapist who is experienced as genuine, the exploration and expression of negative feelings when they boil up are more possible. Of course, given a sound alliance (which is also affected by therapist facilitativeness), the client is better able to stand back, observe, and ultimately understand these feelings for what they are; that is, transference.

The counselor's facilitativeness both affects and *is a part of* the real relationship. It will be recalled that genuineness is one of the defining features of the real relationship, and of course counselor genuineness is one of the facilitative conditions. In this sense, facilitativeness is part of the real relationship. Also, the facilitative therapist will promote realistic and genuinely positive feelings on the part of the client toward that therapist. We would then expect a reciprocal effect. To the extent that the client experiences and expresses positive feelings toward the therapist, in the context of the real relationship, the therapist will do likewise.

The above discussion would appear to imply that therapist facilitativeness is a basic causal factor, having desirable effects on the counseling outcomes and a favorable impact on the relationship components. Yet clinically we know that some clients are easier to be facilitative with than others. Thus the client affects how facilitative the therapist can and will be. An important research direction is the study of both the client factors, and relationship factors that promote or retard therapist facilitativeness. The reader is referred to Gelso and Hayes (1998) for an extensive discussion of how therapist facilitativeness is related to each of the components of the therapeutic relationship.

SUMMARY

The relationship in counseling and therapy is defined as the feelings and attitudes that counseling participants have toward one another and the manner in which these are expressed. A distinction was made between relationship factors and technical factors in counseling, although it was suggested that the relationship that develops between counselor and client will influence how technical factors are enacted in the work.

The way in which the relationship affects the counseling process is seen differently in the various theoretical approaches to counseling. Most counselors and therapists, however, view the relationship as a very important part of counseling, and research supports this view.

The therapeutic relationship consists of three components: the working alliance, the transference configuration, and the real relationship. The *working alliance* is defined as the alignment of the client's reasonable and observing side with the counselor's working, or therapizing, side for the purpose of facilitating the work of counseling. The construct of the working alliance is one of the most promising in all of counseling psychology in terms of its effect on the counseling process and its outcome.

Client transference is defined as the client's experience of the therapist that is shaped by the client's psychological structures and past, and involves displacement onto the therapist of feelings, attitudes, and behaviors belonging rightfully in earlier significant relationships. Five rules of thumb were offered to clarify the concept of transference: (1) transference is always an error; (2) transference may be positive or negative; (3) the emergence of transference is eased by therapist neutrality and ambiguity; (4) transference is not conscious; and (5) transferences are most likely to occur in areas of greatest unresolved conflict from earlier in life. Client transference occurs in all therapies. Counselor transference, too, is a given. *Countertransference* is a potential aid to the therapist in understanding the client and the counseling process, *if* the therapist is willing to focus his or her attention on conflictual feelings that may be experienced toward the client.

The *real relationship* consists of the realistic and genuine perceptions the participants have of one another. The real relationship, expectations of the counselor and the client regarding it, and the differing roles of the participants all interact during the course of counseling.

One of the most influential theoretical statements in the history of counseling psychology was Carl Rogers's formulation of the necessary and sufficient conditions for effective therapy. These conditions were presumed to be part of the counselor–client relationship which, in turn, was seen as the most important ingredient of effective counseling. Of the conditions Rogers theorized about, the three that have been most focused on in theory, research, and practice are the therapist-offered conditions of *empathic understanding, unconditional positive regard* (including both unconditionality and positive regard), and *congruence*. The research evidence strongly suggests that these conditions are indeed facilitative, although they are generally not sufficient, and at times probably not necessary. The conditions are especially important in their relationship to counseling outcomes when measured from the vantage point of the client.

More research is needed on the manner in which the facilitative conditions and the relationship components interact in counseling.

REFERENCES

Barrett-Lennard, G. T. (1962). Dimensions of therapist response as causal factors in therapeutic personality change. *Psychological Monographs, 76* (43, Whole No. 562).

Barrett-Lennard, G. T. (1981). The empathy cycle: The refinement of a nuclear concept. *Journal of Counseling Psychology, 28,* 91–100.

Barrett-Lennard, G. T. (1985). The helping relationship: Crisis and advance in theory and research. *The Counseling Psychologist, 13,* 279–294.

Barrett-Lennard, G. T. (1986). The Relationship Inventory now: Issues and advances in theory, method, and uses. In L. Greenberg and W. Pinsoff (Eds.), *The psychotherapeutic process.* New York: Guilford Press.

Berenson, B. G., & Carkhuff, R. R. (Eds.). (1967). *Sources of gain in counseling and psychotherapy.* New York: Holt, Rinehart & Winston.

Beutler, L. E., Machado, P. P., & Neufeldt, S. A. (1994). Therapist variables. In A. E. Bergin and S. L. Garfield (Eds.), *Handbook of psychotherapy and behavior change* (4th ed., pp. 229–269). New York: John Wiley & Sons.

Bohart, A. C., & Greenberg, L. S. (1997). Empathy and psychotherapy: An introduction and overview. In A. C. Bohart and L. S. Greenberg (Eds.), *Empathy reconsidered: New directions in psychotherapy* (pp. 3–31). Washington, DC: American Psychological Association.

Bordin, E. S. (1979). The generalizability of the psychoanalytic concept of the working alliance. *Psychotherapy: Theory, Research and Practice, 16,* 252–260.

Bordin, E. S. (1994). Theory and research on the therapeutic working alliance: New directions. In A. Horvath and L. Greenberg (Eds.), *The working alliance: Theory, research, and practice* (pp. 13–37). New York: John Wiley & Sons.

Bozarth, J. D. (1984). Beyond reflection: Emergent modes of empathy. In R. Levant and J. Shlien (Eds.), *Client-centered therapy and the person-centered approach.* New York: Praeger.

Bozarth, J. D. (1997). Empathy from the framework of client-centered theory and the Rogerian hypotheses. In A. Bohart and L. Greenberg (Eds.), *Empathy reconsidered: New directions in psychotherapy* (pp. 81–102). Washington, DC: American Psychological Association.

Buber, M. (1958). *Between I and thou.* New York: Scribner.

Carkhuff, R. R. (1969). *Helping and human relations* (Vols. 1 and 2). New York: Holt, Rinehart & Winston.

Deffenbacher, J. L. (1985). A cognitive-behavioral response and a modest proposal. *The Counseling Psychologist, 13* 261–269.

Duan, C., & Hill, C. E. (1996). The current state of empathy research. *Journal of Counseling Psychology, 43,* 261–274.

Eagle, M. N., & Wolitzky, D. L. (1997). Empathy: A psychoanalytic perspective. In A. Bozart and L. Greenberg (Eds.), *Empathy reconsidered: New directions in psychotherapy* (pp. 217–244). Washington, DC: American Psychological Association.

Elliott, R., Clark, C., & Kemeny, V. (June 1991). *Analyzing clients' post-session accounts of significant therapy events.* Paper presented at annual meeting of the Society for Psychotherapy Research, Lyon, France.

Eugster, S. L., & Wampold, B. E. (1996). Systematic effects of participant role on evaluation of the psychotherapy session. *Journal of Consulting and Clinical Psychology, 64,* 1020–1028.

Freud, S. (1959). The dynamics of transference. In E. Jones (Ed.) and J. Riviere (Trans.), *Collected papers* (Vol. 2). New York: Basic Books. (Original work published in 1912)

Gaston, L., Marmar, C. R., Thompson, L. W., & Gallagher, D. (1988). Relation of patient pretreatment characteristics to the therapeutic alliance in diverse psychotherapies. *Journal of Consulting and Clinical Psychology, 56,* 483–489.

Gelso, C. J., & Carter, J. A. (1985). The relationship in counseling and psychotherapy: Components, consequences, and theoretical antecedents. *The Counseling Psychologist, 13,* 155–243.

Gelso, C. J., & Carter, J. A. (1994). Components of the psychotherapy relationship: Their interaction and unfolding during treatment. *Journal of Counseling Psychology, 41,* 296–306.

Gelso, C. J., & Hayes, J. A. (1998). *The psychotherapy relationship: Theory, research, and practice.* New York: John Wiley & Sons.

Gelso, C. J., Hill, C. E., & Kivlighan, D. M. (1991). Transference, insight, and the counselor's intentions during a counseling hour. *Journal of Counseling and Development, 69,* 428–433.

Gelso, C. J., Hill, C. E., Mohr, J., Rochlen, A., & Zack, J. (1999). Describing the face of transference: Dynamic therapists recollections about transference in cases of successful long-term psychotherapy. *Journal of Counseling Psychology, 46,* 257–267.

Gelso, C. J., Kivlighan, D. M., Wine, B., Jones, A., & Friedman, S. C. (1997). Transference, insight, and the course of time-limited therapy. *Journal of Counseling Psychology, 44,* 209–217.

Gladstein, G. A. (1983). Understanding empathy: Integrating counseling, developmental, and social psychology perspectives. *Journal of Counseling Psychology, 30,* 467–482.

Graff, H., & Luborsky, L. (1977). Long-term trends in transference and resistance: A report on quantitative–analytic methods applied to four psychoanalyses. *Journal of the American Psychoanalytic Association, 25,* 471–490.

Greenberg, L. (1985). An integrative approach to the relationship in counseling and psychotherapy. *The Counseling Psychologist, 13,* 251–260.

Greenson, R. R. (1967). *The technique and practice of psychoanalysis* (Vol. 1). New York: International Universities Press.

Gurman, A. S. (1977). The patient's perception of the therapeutic relationship. In A. Gurman and A. Razin (Eds.), *Effective psychotherapy: A handbook of research.* New York: Pergamon Press.

Hackney, H. (1978). The evolution of empathy. *Personnel and Guidance Journal, 57,* 35–38.

Hayes, J. A., McCracken, J. E., McClanahan, M. K., Hill, C. E., Harp, J. S., & Carozzoni, P. (1998). Therapist perspectives on countertransference: Qualitative data in search of the theory. *Journal of Counseling Psychology, 45,* 468–472.

Hayes, J. A., Riker, J. R., & Ingram, K. M. (1997). Countertransference behavior and management in brief counseling: A field study. *Psychotherapy Research, 7,* 145–153.

Highlen, P. S., & Hill, C. E. (1984). Factors affecting client change in individual counseling: Current status and theoretical speculations. In S. Brown and R. Lent (Eds.), *The handbook of counseling psychology* (pp. 334–396). New York: John Wiley & Sons.

Horvath, A. O., Gaston, L., & Luborsky, L. L. (1993). The therapeutic alliance and its measures. In N. E. Miller, L. Luborsky, J. P. Barber, and J. P. Docherty (Eds.), *Psychoanalytic treatment research: A handbook for clinical practice* (pp. 247–273). New York: Basic Books.

Horvath, A. O., & Greenberg, L. (1994). *The working alliance: Theory, research, and practice.* New York: John Wiley & Sons.

Horvath, A. O., & Symonds, B. D. (1991). Relation between working alliance and outcome in psychotherapy: A meta-analysis. *Journal of Counseling Psychology, 38,* 133–149.

Horwitz, L. (1974). *Clinical prediction in psychotherapy.* New York: Jason Aronson.

Hycner, R., & Jacobs, L. (1995). *The healing relationship in gestalt therapy.* New York: Gestalt Journal Press.

Knox, S., Hess, S. A., Peterson, D. A., & Hill, C. E. (1997). A qualitative analysis of client perceptions of the effects of helpful therapist self-disclosure in long-term therapy. *Journal of Counseling Psychology, 44,* 274–283.

Lambert, M. J. (Ed.). (1983). *A guide to psychotherapy and patient relationships.* Homewood, IL: Dow Jones–Irwin.

Langs, R. J. (1974). *The technique of psychoanalytic psychotherapy* (Vol. 2). New York: Jason Aronson.

Latts, M. G., & Gelso, C. J. (1995). Countertransference behavior and management with survivors of sexual assault. *Psychotherapy, 32,* 405–415.

Lecours, S., Bouchard, M., & Normandin, L. (1995). Countertransference as the therapist's mental activity: Experience and gender differences among psychoanalytically oriented psychologists. *Psychoanalytic Psychology: 12,* 259–280.

Lietaer, G. (1984). Unconditional positive regard: A controversial basic attitude in client-centered therapy. In R. Levant and J. Shlien (Eds.), *Client-centered therapy and the person-centered approach*. New York: Praeger.

Linehan, M. M. (1997). Validation and psychotherapy. In A. Bohart and L. Greenberg (Eds.), *Empathy reconsidered: New directions in psychotherapy* (pp. 353–392). Washington, DC: American Psychological Association.

Luborsky, L. & Barber, J. P. (1994). Perspectives on seven transference-related measures applied to the interview with Ms. Smithfield. *Psychotherapy Research, 3/4*, 172–183.

Orlinsky, D. E., Grawe, K., & Parks, B. K. (1994). Process and outcome in psychotherapy—noch einmal. In A. E. Bergin and S. L. Garfield (Eds.), *Handbook of psychotherapy and behavior change* (4th ed., pp. 270–376). New York: John Wiley & Sons.

Orlinsky, D. E., & Howard, K. I. (1986). Process and outcome in psychotherapy. In S. Garfield & A. Bergin (Eds.), *Handbook of psychotherapy and behavior change* (pp. 311–381) (3rd ed.). New York: John Wiley & Sons.

Parloff, M., Waskow, I., & Wolfe, B. (1978). Research on therapist variables in relation to process and outcome. In S. Garfield and A. Bergin (Eds.), *Handbook of psychotherapy and behavior change* (pp. 233–282) (2nd ed.). New York: John Wiley & Sons.

Patterson, C. H. (1984). Empathy, warmth, and genuineness in psychotherapy: A review of reviews. *Psychotherapy: Theory, Research and Practice, 21*, 431–439.

Patton, M. J., Kivlighan, D. M., & Multon, K. D. (1997). The Missouri psychoanalytic counseling research project: Relation of changes in process and outcome. *Journal of Counseling Psychology, 44*, 189–208.

Prochaska, J. O. & Norcross, J. P. (1999) *Systems of psychotherapy: A transtheoretical analysis.* (4th ed.) Pacific Grove, CA: Brooks-Cole Publishing Company.

Rhoads, J. M., & Feather, B. F. (1972). Transference and resistance observed in behavior therapy. *British Journal of Medical Psychology, 45*, 99–103.

Rogers, C. R. (1957). The necessary and sufficient conditions of therapeutic personality change. *Journal of Consulting Psychology, 21*, 95–103.

Rogers, C. R. (1975). Empathy: An unappreciated way of being. *The Counseling Psychologist, 5*, 2–10.

Ryan, V. L., & Gizynski, M. N. (1971). Behavior therapy in retrospect: Patients' feelings about their behavior therapies. *Journal of Consulting and Clinical Psychology, 37*, 1–9.

Truax, C. B., & Carkhuff, R. R. (1967). *Toward effective counseling and psychotherapy.* Chicago, IL: Aldine.

Truax, C. B., & Mitchell, K. M. (1971). Research on certain therapist interpersonal skills in relation to process and outcome. In A. Bergin and S. Garfield (Eds.), *Handbook of psychotherapy and behavior change* (pp. 299–344). New York: John Wiley & Sons.

Watson, N. (1984). The empirical status of Rogers' hypotheses of the necessary and sufficient conditions for effective psychotherapy. In R. Levant and J. Shlien (Eds.), *Client-centered therapy and the person-centered approach*. New York: Praeger.

C H A P T E R 9

THE COUNSELOR'S RESPONSE TO THE CLIENT: TACTICS AND TECHNIQUES OF COUNSELING

Levels of Counseling Technique

Nonverbal Behavior

Verbal Behavior: The Response Modes Approach

Covert Behavior

Interpersonal Manner: The Counselor and Interpersonal Influence

Summary

References

In Chapter 5 we examined the counselor–client relationship as one of the two vital elements of counseling. Within the context of this ever-developing relationship exists the second key element: the techniques used by the counselor in his or her work with the client. Such techniques consist of the actual verbal and nonverbal responses made by the counselor to the client. The word *tactics* is often used interchangeably with *techniques,* and in this chapter we use the latter as a shorthand term for both.

In this chapter, we describe the range of techniques used in counseling. In so doing, we are not seeking to provide the student with a cookbook on how to counsel. Rather, the aim is to give an overall picture of the kinds of responses counselors make to clients in an effort to promote positive change. We first present an overall classification of the levels of counseling technique and then discuss the differing types of techniques or responses within each level.

Just what is meant by the word *technique* in counseling? In fact, there are a range of definitions in the literature, and these vary from the most general to the very specific. An example of the most general definition is provided by Highlen and Hill (1984), who conceptualize technique as "anything the counselor performs within the session" (p. 366). A more specific and probably typical definition is that offered by Harper and Bruce-Sanford (1989). These authors define *technique* as: "A defined tool or method that is employed by the counselor in order to facilitate effective counseling or positive behavior change in the client" (p. 42).

Implied in the more specific definitions such as Harper and Bruce-Sanford's is the idea that techniques are deliberate. That is, they are verbal and nonverbal responses made by the counselor with the conscious intent of fostering certain behavioral or internal reactions in the client. Also, techniques are ordinarily connected to theory. For example, client-centered counselors (Chapter 12) use techniques that differ from behavioral counselors (Chapter 11). And psychoanalytic theory (Chapter 10) supports techniques that differ even further from those advocated by client-centered and behavioral approaches. Thus, each theory has both its own vision of the counselor–client relationship (discussed in the previous chapter), and the techniques to be used in counseling.

It is useful to think of technique in both the more general and more specific senses, as the following discussion will make apparent. Before proceeding, however, a caution is in order about the idea and use of techniques in counseling (i.e., especially with reference to the more specific usage of the word *technique*). Over the years, many counselors and theoreticians have been concerned that the field could become too "technique-oriented" and focus on the simplistic use of a set of techniques without deeper understanding. There has also been much concern that basic counselor attitudes (e.g., empathy, regard, congruence) could easily be neglected if the counselor focuses too much on techniques.

The view advocated in this book is that techniques (again, using the more specific definition) are extremely important in counseling, but that they must be used in a context. As Brammer, Abrego, and Shostrom (1993) remind us, the value of techniques is very limited unless the counselor has a good understanding of the therapeutic goals for which he or she is striving, of the basic attitudes that are central to counseling (such as those discussed in Chapter 8), and of the theoretical assumptions to which the techniques are tied. In essence, the use of techniques without a broader understanding of counseling will be ineffectual in the long run. Brammer and colleagues (1993) bring this point home when they note that: "One characteristic of a charlatan is blind adherence to pat techniques applied indiscriminately to all clients" (p. 111).

LEVELS OF COUNSELING TECHNIQUE

As a way of systematizing the numerous variables that may be considered under the heading of "counselor techniques," we have developed the classification scheme presented in Table 9.1. This is a modification of the earlier scheme by Highlen and Hill (1984). It is based on the most general definition of *technique*; that is, "anything the counselor performs within the session."

This classification scheme is organized into five levels or categories. The first categories contain the most specific and observable levels of counselor technique. Techniques at these levels are not necessarily derived from particular theories of counseling, for example, open questions, which come under the heading "Verbal Behavior" and used in all theories. The latter categories tend to contain more abstract and general variables that must be inferred from behavior, but are not directly observable. These variables are often derived from particular theories of counseling. For example, the "empty chair technique" derives from gestalt therapy.

In the remainder of this chapter, counselor techniques under four of the five levels will be discussed. Level 4, General Strategies, will be examined in the next three theory chapters.

Nonverbal Behavior

Imagine yourself in counseling with a psychologist whose actual words to you seem to convey caring, interest, and respect as you relate some emotionally painful experiences. At the same time, this counselor looks out the window rather than at you most of the time, speaks in a flat and emotionless tone of voice, sits with arms folded while leaning back in an easy chair, and when sitting up frequently taps his or her foot. Despite the counselor's positive words, you would not have to be a psychologist yourself to feel that something was wrong here, and to feel hurt by the psychologist's nonverbal responses. You probably would not stay around for counseling very long unless this changed. (We *hope* not!)

As far-fetched as this example may seem to you, both authors have observed counselors whose nonverbal behavior was vastly inconsistent with their verbal behavior. (Our observations have been largely of students just learning to be counselors, but unfortunately such inconsistencies also occur occasionally among experienced counselors.) Effective counselors, on the other hand, are aware that they are *always* communicating with clients through a wide range of nonverbal mechanisms, realizing that they as well as their clients cannot *not* communicate messages and cues nonverbally. These counselors pay attention to their own and their clients' nonverbal behavior and are able to read such behavior effectively. At the same time, effective counselors are not overly preoccupied with their bodies as a source of nonverbal communication. It does appear, however, that the most effective counselors are able to use their bodies as instruments of communication with clients without this interfering with the naturalness of their counseling.

Classification of Counselor Nonverbal Behavior.   **TABLE 9.1.**

Level and Category	Definition	Example
Level 1 Nonverbal Behavior	Behavior not expressed through formal language	Facial expression, eye movements, body language, nonlanguage sounds, touch, silence
Level 2 Verbal Behavior	Classes of verbal responses counselors make with clients	Minimal encourager, approval, information, direct guidance, questions, paraphrase, interpretation, confrontation, disclosure
Level 3 Covert Behavior	Intentions behind counselor's overt responses to client	Counselor's internal plans and strategies for counseling
Level 4 General Strategies	Broader procedures usually tied to theory	Empty chair technique, systematic desensitization
Level 5 Interpersonal Manner	General ways counselor comes across to client	Impression of expertness, attractiveness, and trustworthiness

Categories of Nonverbal Behavior

As discussed by Hill and O'Brien (1999), nonverbal behavior can be divided into several categories: paralanguage, facial expression, kinesics, eye contact, and proxemics. When such behavior pertains to the counselor's reactions, it is often referred to as *attending behavior* (how the counselor physically orients himself or herself to the client). We should note that nearly all the research on nonverbal communication in counseling was done in the 1970s and 1980s, with very little being done later (Hill & Williams, 2000). This is an area of investigation that is in need of reinvigoration.

Paralanguage pertains to *how* things are said rather than *what* is said. Paralinguistic cues qualify how a word or verbal message is sent or received. For example, the flat and emotionless voice tone used by the counselor described at the beginning of this section was a paralinguistic cue, qualifying as it did the counselor's verbal expression of interest, caring, and respect; making that expression, in effect, less believable to the client. In addition to voice tone, paralanguage includes spacing of words, emphasis, inflection (loudness and pitch), pauses, various nonlanguage sounds (e.g., moans, yells), and nonwords ("uh," "ah"). Examples of paralinguistic cues often seen and heard during counseling are laughter, yawning, speaking in a low voice, pausing between words, silence, raising of voice, stuttering or constant restatement, using a high-pitched voice, deep sighing, deliberate coughing, swallowing unnaturally, heavy breathing, and responding with "uh-huh," "uh," and "um." (See Harper and Bruce-Sanford [1989] for examples of what each of these cues might mean in counseling in our culture and Table 9.2.)

Facial expression is another area of nonverbal behavior. Based on their extensive review of the research literature, Harper, Wiens, and Matarazzo (1978) conclude that facial expression may be the most important of all nonverbal cues in counseling. The importance of the human face as a communicator is summarized by Knapp (1972):

TABLE 9.2. Categories of Nonverbal Behaviors in Counseling.

Category	Definition
Paralanguage	*How* things are said rather than what is said.
Facial expression	Facial movements that communicate meaning and intent.
Kinesics	Body movements other than facial expression and eye movements. "Touch" is a form of kinesics.
Eye contact	Extent to which participants look at each other and how they look at each other.
Proxemics	How space is structured and used, for example, seating distance between counselor and client.

> The face is rich in communicative potential. It is the primary site for communicating emotional states; it reflects interpersonal attitudes, it provides nonverbal feedback on the comments of others; and some say that, next to human speech, it is the primary source of giving information. For these reasons and because of its visibility, we pay a great deal of attention to what we see in the faces of others (pp. 68–69).

The importance of facial expressions to clients is demonstrated effectively in a study by Lee, Uhlemann, and Haase (1985). Counseling interviews of 20 minutes' duration were conducted by graduate students training to be counselors. The clients were undergraduate students who volunteered to discuss personal concerns in a study of counseling techniques. Among other things, the researchers were interested in whether these clients' judgments of their counselors' nonverbal behavior correlated with the clients' perceptions of how expert, attractive, and trustworthy the counselors were. In fact, of the eight nonverbal categories studied, counselor facial expression (indicative of warmth and concern) and timely smiling were the best predictors of clients' perceptions that their counselors were expert, attractive, and trustworthy.

Kinesics pertains to body movements other than facial expression and eye movements. In the example used to begin our discussion of nonverbal behavior, the counselor's leaning back, arm folding, and foot tapping were body movements that fit this category. Ekman and Friesen (1969) categorize body movements into four types. *Emblems* are movements that can clearly substitute for words, for example, waving goodbye. *Illustrators* are movements that occur at the same time as speech and serve to clarify visually what is being said, for example, dropping one's head in cupped hands to indicate sadness. *Regulators* monitor the flow of verbal interaction, for example, head nods, shifts in posture. Finally, *adaptors* are body movements without conscious communicative purpose, although they are often indicators of inner thoughts and feelings, for example, head scratching, foot tapping, biting one's lips.

The study of kinesics in counseling has a fairly long history. For example, approximately 35 years ago Fretz (1966) found that counselors' forward body lean and direct body orientation were related to positive evaluations of counseling by clients. In an important study by Maurer and Tindall (1983), it was found that when experienced counselors deliberately used the same arm and leg positions during career counseling as did their high school student clients, these clients gave higher empathy ratings to the counselors than when counselors used different arm and leg positions (despite the fact that counselors in the two conditions were matched on empathy). Thus, how the counselor uses his or her body in counseling communicates something to the client, whether or not the client is aware that she or he is so affected. Also, the counselor's, as well as client's, feelings are often evidenced through body movements, even when they are not conscious or evidenced in the words used (as in the use of adaptors described above).

An area of nonverbal behavior that is often classified under kinesics is that of *touch* in counseling. This may well be the most controversial of the nonverbal topics. Some therapists (e.g., Langs, 1973; Wolberg, 1967) maintain that touch should never occur in counseling or therapy, with the possible exception of handshakes, for example, upon meeting, after initial sessions, before or after vacations, at termination. Similarly, most counselors have a conservative bias about touching clients, believing that this nonverbal behavior should be engaged in with great caution. The concern about physical contact is that it may overstimulate clients' dependency, arouse sexual impulses or fears of the counselor's sexual motivations, and move the counseling away from being a "talking cure" and toward physical acting-out. Within this conservative bias, some counselors do believe that certain kinds of physical contact with clients are appropriate and even helpful in certain, specific situations. For example, in moments of crisis or great emotional pain, touching the client's hand can helpfully communicate concern and provide comfort (Hunter & Struve, 1998).

Just as opinion about touch is controversial, the research findings have been mixed. As Suiter and Goodyear (1985) summarize, some studies have shown certain kinds of touch (e.g., of the client's hand, arm, shoulder) to have positive short-term effects, whereas other studies have demonstrated no effect. On the other hand, when counselors and clients watched videotapes of therapy, Suiter and Goodyear found that the counselor's semi-embrace of the client on tape resulted in lower evaluations of that counselor's trustworthiness. Apparently, this degree of physical contact symbolized greater intimacy than both counselors and clients felt appropriate.

Eye contact is also a category of nonverbal behavior. The extent to which interactants look at each other and how they look at each other during their interaction are clearly important communicators in relationships in general and counseling in particular. Most counseling studies of nonverbal behavior use counselor-to-client eye contact as one of the key nonverbal counselor behaviors. For example, Tyson and Wall (1983), in arranging an experiment on what they viewed as responsive and nonresponsive nonverbal behavior, considered counselor eye contact 80% of the time as responsive and 20% of the time as nonresponsive. Regarding the importance of this nonverbal category, Lee et al. (1985) found counselor eye contact to be related to clients' ratings of counselors' expertness, attractiveness, and trustworthiness as counselors.

One aspect of eye contact in counseling that cannot be ignored is its relation to racial and cultural factors. As just one of many examples, Hill and O'Brien (1999) note that Anglo middle-class North Americans tend to maintain eye contact while listening but look away when speaking. Conversely, African Americans tend to maintain eye contact when speaking but look away when listening. Brammer and MacDonald (1996) note that sustained eye contact is considered a sign of disrespect by some Native American groups. As Sue and Sue (1977) discuss, some cultural groups may avoid eye contact as a sign of respect and deference. As always, racial and cultural factors need to be incorporated by the counselor to be maximally effective.

Proxemics refers to the area of nonverbal behavior dealing with the structure and use of space in human interaction. Perhaps the most important scientific work on this topic has been done by Hall (1963, 1968), who notes four distance zones among middle-class Americans: intimate (0–18 inches), personal (1.5–4 feet), social (4–12 feet), and public (12 feet or more). If cultural factors affect eye contact, they seem even more influential in personal space. Hall (1963), for example, discusses the major differences between Americans and Arabs in how much space they prefer between interactants. In counseling, at least where the participants are Anglo, middle-class Americans, Lecomte, Bernstein, and Dumont (1981) find that intermediate distances between counselor and client (approximately 50 inches) results in the most effective communication from both parties.

The Deliberate Use of Nonverbals in Counseling

As already noted, the effective counselor knows that nonverbal communication is always occurring between himself or herself and the client. Also, this counselor is able to use his or her body as an instrument of communication; that is, as an intentional means of communication. Are there any suggestions that may be offered to the beginning counselor regarding how specific nonverbals may be used? Authors who discuss beginning counseling skills, often called *microskills* because of their specific nature, usually outline certain nonverbals. For example, in one of the most prominent skills-oriented texts in counseling, Egan (1998) uses the acronym SOLER as a device for teaching various nonverbal behaviors as a starting point for beginning counselors. It should be emphasized that Egan is appropriately tentative and flexible about them. Not only does he stress the need for flexibility in application but he emphasizes that his guidelines relate mostly to North American culture. The five prescriptions in Egan's SOLER are the following.

S: Face the client squarely; that is, adopt a posture that indicates involvement. Egan notes that facing someone squarely is considered a posture of involvement, and communicates the message, "I'm available to you; I choose to be with you." Egan also notes that the word *squarely* need not be taken literally. What is important, he underscores, is that the bodily orientation you adopt conveys a message of involvement.

O: Adopt an open posture.   Crossed arms and legs may communicate defensiveness and lessened involvement, whereas an open posture can be a sign that you are open to what the client is able to share. Again, the word *open* need not be taken literally, as Egan notes that if your legs are crossed, that does not necessarily mean that you are uninvolved. The important thing is that the counselor ask himself or herself, "To what degree does my posture communicate openness and availability to the client?"

L: Remember that it is possible at times to *lean* toward the client.   Leaning toward the other person often communicates that "I'm with you and interested in what you have to say right now"; whereas leaning back or slouching may communicate "I'm not that interested" or even boredom. Egan also notes, though, that leaning too far forward or doing so too soon may be anxiety-provoking to the client. It may be experienced as a demand for too much closeness, too soon. Perhaps the most effective helpers are not rigid but are able to move backward and forward naturally and flexibly, according to what is happening in the counseling.

E: Maintain good *eye* contact.   Fairly steady eye contact is natural in personal discussions and tends to communicate attention and interest, although the racial and cultural modifiers of this rule of thumb, as noted above, must be kept in mind. At the same time, one can maintain such steady and intense eye contact, that the client feels he or she is being "analyzed." Generally, though, a high degree of eye contact (that is neither staring nor too intense for the client) communicates the appropriate interest. Egan notes that although there is no problem with occasionally looking away, if you catch yourself doing so frequently, this may be a clue about your reluctance to get involved.

R: Try to be relatively *relaxed* while engaging in these behaviors.   To Egan, this means two things: not fidgeting nervously or engaging in distracting facial expressions and becoming comfortable with using your body as a vehicle of involvement and expression. When you feel comfortable engaging in these behaviors, Egan suggests that they will then help you focus attention on the client and punctuate your verbal dialogue through the use of nonverbals.

Although microskills such as the above were offered as clear prescriptions by counseling authorities in the past, more recent thinking, aided by research, has helped us become aware that suggestions such as SOLER may only be used as rough and very tentative guidelines. Egan (1998) makes this clear, as we have noted; authors such as Hill and O'Brien (1999) emphasize this point even more strongly. They believe that each counselor–client dyad may establish its own set of rules for nonverbal behavior and that each dyad needs to be studied individually rather than trying to establish a universal set of nonverbal qualities applicable to all. In considering the various viewpoints, we suggest that some general principles or guidelines may be established for the use of nonverbals in counseling, but there will be great variability from case to case. The counselor must always be mindful of individual differences in clients' needs and behavior, including nonverbal behavior. To further complicate matters (which matches the great complexity of the real world of counseling), certain verbal or nonverbal behaviors may be used unconsciously by the counselor to compensate for other nonverbals. Highlen and Hill (1984) use the example of good eye contact compensating for a backward lean. As another example, Hermansson, Webster, and McFarland (1988) found that when the counselors they studied were instructed to lean backward or forward, their verbal behavior compensates for their nonverbals; for example, they were the most empathic when experimentally required to lean backward!

Verbal Behavior: The Response Modes Approach

Much of what goes on between counselor and client is at a verbal level. Over the years, there has been a great deal of research attention given to counselor verbal behavior, and a number of approaches to understanding and classifying the counselor's verbal behavior have been developed.

A most useful approach to understanding counselor verbal behavior is called the *response modes* approach. Here, the focus is on the grammatical structure of the counselor's verbal response, rather than on the content. Thus, for example, we classify counselor responses into categories or types, such as reflection, advice, question, and interpretation; and we look at how these types relate to a wide range of other variables in counseling. Of the different approaches, the response modes approach has been the most extensively studied over the years. For the most part, when one observes a counseling session, the observer can readily and reliably (with a little training) classify virtually all of the counselor's responses by using a response modes approach. Because of this, and because counselors must typically learn the different response modes as part of their training, we shall focus the remainder of this section on these responses. Note that such response modes are what we ordinarily mean when we talk about techniques; that is, when using the more specific definition of *technique,* as discussed earlier.

Hill and Williams (2000) note that there are over 30 different measures of, or systems for, classifying counselor response modes. Although there are naturally variations among the systems, there are probably more similarities than differences. They all appear to include the following six techniques or counselor response modes in their classifications: question, information, advice, reflection, interpretation, self-disclosure (Elliott, Hill, Stiles et al., 1987). Using a slight modification of the classification system developed by Hill (1985, 1986), and revised by Hill and O'Brien (1999), let us now look at each counselor response. Note that there are 11 different response modes in this system, and they are divided into four general categories: minimal responses, directives, information seeking, and complex counselor responses.

Minimal Responses

In Hill's (1985, 1986) system of categorization the first two response modes are called *minimal encouragers* and *silence*. These response modes are not truly "verbal" in the strict sense; they fit the paralinguistic category discussed above. We shall also briefly discuss them here because of their frequency in a typical counseling interview.

The minimal encourager is a very short phrase that may show simple acknowledgment, agreement, or understanding. It usually reflects acceptance of the client, and encourages the client to continue talking. The minimal encourager tends to be neutral in that it does not imply approval or disapproval (see below), even though it usually seeks to show acceptance.

Examples of minimal encouragers are "Go on," "I see," and "Okay." The most commonly used minimal encourager is the response "Mm-hm." In the development of client-centered therapy (see Chapter 9), "mm-hm" was seen as an indication of simple acceptance of the client, and this usage has continued today. Benjamin (1987) tells us that this response generally indicates permissiveness on the therapist's part, suggesting to the client, "Go on, I'm with you"; "I'm listening and following you." Despite the intended acceptance, phrases like "mm-hm" can at times be used too frequently, so that the flow of the session is impeded by the seemingly constant use of "encouragers."

It is probably safe to say that beginning counselors undervalue silence. It makes them anxious, as they feel they must be *saying* something. In fact, silence may be filled with meaning. Silence may facilitate counselor and client getting closer, emotionally touching; or it may indicate that something is awry in the working alliance. Generally we like to differentiate "pregnant silences" from "empty silences." In a pregnant silence, the client is doing his or her "work," for example, thinking or feeling about what is transpiring. In an empty silence, little positive is going on and the client typically shows signs of anxiety, such as fidgeting. Our general rule of thumb is that pregnant silences should not be interrupted by the counselor, whereas empty silences should. Also, Benjamin (1987) notes that unless the counselor is very sure of what he or she is doing, extensive silences should be avoided. A minute of meaningful silence is a long time!

Directives

The category of *directives* involves directing the client to do something. In using directives, the counselor may try to get the client to continue what he or she is already doing (the response mode of approval) or provide information or guidance regarding what the client should do.

When the therapist uses the response mode of *approval,* he or she may be offering support, explicit approval of some aspect of the client or the client's behavior, reassurance, and/or reinforcement. Sympathy also fits this category, although counseling educators and theorists generally agree that offering sympathy is not a desirable counseling response, except under unusual circumstances. Responses within the response mode of approval may be very short, for example, "Very good," or they may be much longer. Examples of specific responses that fit this category are: "It'll get better"; "Don't worry about it"; "I think you did the right thing"; "Everyone feels that way from time to time"; "Right, you're right"; "That's really tough to handle"; "It'll be hard"; "I'm concerned about you."

As Benjamin (1987) notes, when we offer reassurance, we are saying, in effect, that the client needs an external influence to keep him or her going or to get started, and this we shall provide. Benjamin uses the following examples that range from mild to heavy reassurance (*Note:* CL = client; CO = counselor).

CL: I can't face him.
CO: You haven't tried; it may not be as hard as you think.
CO: I'm not so sure; I rather suspect you can.
CO: Can't you; that's one man's opinion and this man thinks otherwise.
CO: Of course you can. I really can't be there but I'll be there in spirit.
CO: It's hard, I know; but you can and you must.

There is evidence in the therapy literature that it is helpful to show approval of and support for the client as a person and in a general way (see Hill, 1989, 1990), but counseling can also be too supportive. One can be so supportive that the client's own strengths are not marshalled. Also, as with all techniques, it is crucial that we differentiate effective from ineffective use. Well-timed support or reassurance can indeed move the client forward, whereas certain kinds of reassurance offered in certain ways may be experienced as hollow and impede client growth. For example, implying that "everything will be okay" is often experienced as a lack of empathy, and such reassurances may interfere with the client's working through affects that need to be lived and experienced (see Hill & O'Brien, 1999).

The second response mode under directives is called *providing information*. Counselor responses that fall into this category supply information to the client in the form of facts, data, opinion, or resources. The information that is given may be related to the counseling process, the counselor's behavior, or counseling arrangements such as meeting time and place, fee, and so forth. Examples of providing information are as follows.

CL: So what do you make of these interest test results. What do you think are my best interests?
CO: It looks like your strongest interests are in wildlife management, although there is also a second group of interests that seem to involve sales.
CL: The time went by so fast. Now that I've talked to you, I'm really glad I came. How often do we meet?
CO: We meet weekly, for up to 12 sessions, which is the session limit at the center. (In addition to providing this information, an effective response here would acknowledge the client's positive feelings and perhaps also express enthusiasm.)

The provision of information in counseling can be quite important. Certainly we do not support the caricature of the "nondirective" counselor who takes his or her nondirectiveness so seriously that he or she never provides information:

CL: (passing a counselor in the hallway) Could you tell me where the men's room is?
CO: You are wondering and unsure of where the men's room is.

At the same time, the counselor can become too involved in being an expert information giver, forgetting the fact that simple information rarely has an impact on underlying feelings and attitudes. The counselor also needs to be sensitive to the possibility that the client seeks information as a way of avoiding self-exploration and possibly painful feelings.

The third response mode under directives is *direct guidance*. This involves directions, suggestions, or advice offered by the counselor. Whereas the mode of providing information involves giving facts and data, direct guidance requests or suggests that the client *do* something. One can think of direct guidance as being of two kinds: that which offers advice or directions within the session, and that which does so outside the session. Examples of direct guidance within the session are:

> CO: Relax right now and take a deep breath.
> CO: I would like you to tell me whatever crosses your mind when you think about your mother. Try not to edit and don't worry about how irrational or silly you may feel it sounds.

Examples of direct guidance regarding behavior outside the session are:

> CO: I really think it would be a good idea to talk this over with Jim.
> CO: I think you should talk with your math professor about why you had problems with the exam last week.
> CO: As homework, I would like you to keep a record of how many times you feel anxious during each day, and of what was occurring at those moments.

The use of direct guidance, especially in the form of advice to the client regarding behavior outside the counselor's office, has always been a controversial issue. Many counselors do not believe advice should be given, except in extraordinary circumstances, whereas in the therapies that are more "directive," advice is viewed as a desirable element of the process. In our view, all therapists need to sort out for themselves whether they have the right, as Benjamin (1987) puts it, "on moral, professional, or simply human grounds to give advice. If I conclude that I do not, I should say so openly and clearly" (pp. 234–235). We also agree with Benjamin that the first step in responding to a request for advice should be to explore what the client thinks about the situation being discussed and what alternatives have been considered— and what the client's hopes and fears are regarding the conflict situation:

> CO: I realize that you are terribly concerned about this. Perhaps if you can tell me the various alternatives you have considered and how you feel about them, we may be able to arrive at something that makes sense to you (from Benjamin, 1987, p. 234).

Often such an exploration eliminates the need for advice from the counselor. The client is able to follow his or her own dictates.

Information Seeking

Counselor responses used to elicit information of some sort from the client are classified as *information seeking*. Generally, there are two counselor response modes here: *closed questions* and *open questions*.

Closed questions are used by the counselor to gather data and typically request a one- or two-word answer, a "yes" or "no" or a confirmation. Examples are:

CL: I just don't think I am studying enough in geometry. The problem is more the time I'm putting in than my study skills.
CO: How many hours a night do you study for geometry on the average?
CL: Jane and I finally got away for a weekend without the kids.
CO: Did you have a good time?
CL: My boyfriend thinks I ought to lose 10 pounds.
CO: What do you weigh?

Open questions, rather than delimiting the client's response, seek client exploration or clarification. Usually one is not looking for a specific and short answer when asking an open question. Using the same client statements as given above, examples of open questions might be:

CL: I just don't think I am studying enough in geometry. The problem is more the time I'm putting in than my study skills.
CO: What do you think gets in the way of your studying more?
CL: Jane and I finally got away for a weekend without the kids.
CO: What was the experience like for you?
CL: My boyfriend thinks I ought to lose 10 pounds.
CO: What are your feelings about losing the weight?

As you can see from these responses, the counselor, when using open questions, is seeking to facilitate exploration by the client. This exploration may pertain to the client's feelings, thoughts, behavior, personality dynamics, and/or expectations about counseling.

Although both open and closed questions have their place among counseling techniques, and may be helpful at times, many of those who write about technique believe questions are much overused in counseling. Benjamin (1987) presents this view emphatically when he states:

Yes, I have many reservations about the use of questions in the interview. I feel certain that we ask too many questions, often meaningless ones. We ask questions that confuse the client, that interrupt him. We ask questions that the client cannot possibly answer. We even ask questions that we don't want the answers to, and consequently, we do not hear the answers when they are forthcoming (p. 134).

At the same time, Benjamin goes on to discuss how open questions are superior to closed questions, a view shared by many researchers and trainers (e.g., Egan, 1998; Hill & O'Brien, 1999). Benjamin (1987), in expressing this general viewpoint, tells us: "The open question may widen and deepen the contact; the closed question may circumscribe it. In short, the former may open wide the door to good rapport; the latter usually keeps it shut" (p. 136). It appears that open questions are in fact used frequently in counseling, ranging from about 8 to 13% of all counselor responses (Hill & O'Brien, 1999).

The research on therapist techniques tends to support this perspective on questions. In Hill's (1989) intensive study of eight psychotherapy cases in which highly experienced therapists conducted the therapy, clients typically gave low helpfulness ratings to closed questions. This technique created a feeling in the clients of being interviewed rather than being invited to become emotionally involved in a therapeutic relationship.

Open questions, on the other hand, have been found to be useful in encouraging clients to talk longer and more deeply about their feelings and problems (Hill & O'Brien, 1999). Yet among Hill's (1989) eight cases, while some clients apparently liked the challenge involved in open questions, others experienced them as too threatening. It appears that the effectiveness of open questions depends on many factors—for example, how well timed the questions are, whether the client is ready for them, the issues with which the client is dealing, and of course the specific nature of the questions being asked.

Complex Counselor Responses

In Hill's (1985) classification system, called the *Counselor Verbal Response Modes Category System,* the four *complex* counselor response modes or techniques include paraphrase, interpretation, confrontation, and self-disclosure. These four response modes are complex in that they are more abstract than the other modes, and each of them may be divided into two or more subtypes. Also, their effectiveness depends greatly on complex and often subtle issues of timing, precise phrasing, and sensitivity to the client's dynamics and feeling states at the moment as well as more generally. Because of these considerations, the four complex techniques are more difficult to learn, and certainly more difficult to master, by counselors. Let us examine each of these techniques.

Paraphrase.   The technique of paraphrase may be divided into four kinds of responses that have much in common with each other: restatements, reflections, nonverbal referents, and summaries. All four basically paraphrase, mirror, or summarize what the client has communicated to the counselor, either at the verbal or nonverbal level. The counselor does not add his or her perspective to the communication but rather gives back to the client what the counselor hears the client expressing.

When the counselor verbalizes a *restatement,* she or he essentially restates or rephrases what the client has said, usually using similar but fewer words. In a good restatement, the counselor's expression is clearer and more concrete than the client's, and this fosters the client's examination of what he or she is expressing.

> CL: I just don't know if I have produced enough to be promoted to the next level at the university; and if I'm not, I'll have to begin looking around for what I can find; for another job.
> CO: You're not sure if you'll make the cut and may need to find a new job.
> CL: It has just seemed like one thing after another this year. There was my wife's illness, and then Heather's accident was almost more than I could take. Now my 8-year-old son has to have this operation. I just wonder if it will ever end.
> CO: It just seems like the problems never stop and you're wondering if they ever will.

In contrast to a restatement, a *reflection* rephrases the client's expression with explicit attention to the feelings involved in that statement. These feelings may have been stated by the client or they may be implicit. In the latter case, the feelings are inferred by the counselor from the client's nonverbal behavior or from his or her total communication. To reflect feelings that are unstated, the counselor must listen empathically, and often a deeply empathic kind of listening is required. When reflecting, the therapist does not add his or her own viewpoint, as would be so with interpretation, a technique we will soon examine. Instead, the reflecting counselor brings to the surface those feelings underneath the client's words. The counselor in this sense is a mirror to the deeper feelings the client may be struggling to explore. The exchange below exemplifies this sort of reflection.

> CL: It's hard to talk about this stuff or even to think about it. I mean, I've been complaining about not having a relationship for a long time, and now that there's a possibility, what do I do?
> CO: It's upsetting to see how fearful and avoiding you are of just what you thought you wanted.
> CL: That's for sure. I just don't know if John is the person for me. He seems too nice, and yet he has everything I *should* want. I just don't know.
> CO: You're feeling confused about whether you want John or should want John.
> CL: Yes, but as I think about it, that's the way I've always been. When someone cares about me and is good to me, I move away; when someone doesn't want me, I want them. What a mess this is. Will I ever improve?
> CO: You feel discouraged, wondering if you will ever connect when the other person cares.

The *nonverbal referent* is similar to reflection and restatement but points to the client's nonverbal behavior as an indication of his or her feelings. *Nonverbals* here may refer to body posture, facial expression, tone of voice, gestures, and so forth.

> CL: I don't know what's wrong. I should be happy with Sally's attention but I'm not.
> CO: Your face has a sad expression as you talk about this.
> CL: But, darn it, I do care about John, despite his craziness and social discomfort.
> CO: Your voice was very soft as you said that.
> CL: I feel happy in this relationship for the first time ever.
> CO: Your voice sounds alive when you say that.

The final kind of paraphrase is called a *summary*, which verbalizes the major themes in what the client has expressed. The summary may cover a part of a session, the entire session, or the treatment as a whole.

> CO: It looks like the basic issue you've been struggling with today is your fear of relationships and how you avoid involvements that are good for you.
> CO: In sum, you've spent several weeks sorting through what you want and have come to realize engineering isn't it. You are now focusing on management and feel really good about that.

As a general technique, the four types of paraphrase have a long history in counseling and therapy. Beginning in the 1940s, paraphrase became a prominent verbal technique, when what was called *nondirective therapy* (later client-centered, then person-centered therapy) became popular. But even therapists who are not client-centered or nondirective with their clients use paraphrases. Hill (1989), for example, finds paraphrase to be one of the most frequently used techniques among the eight experienced therapists in her study, none of whom were client-centered in their theoretical orientation.

Each of the four types of paraphrases may be of significant help to clients. They show the client that the therapist is listening and enable the client to continue exploration and often communicate the counselor's empathic understanding to the client. Paraphrases also let therapists check out their understanding of what clients are saying. On the other hand, as with all techniques, paraphrase can be misused. Continual use of restatement can be an irritant to the client, especially if the counselor approaches exact restatement of the client's verbalizations. Egan (1998) refers to merely repeating what the client has said as "parroting," and views this as a parody of empathy. He states that "mere repetition carries no sense of real understanding of, no sense of being with, the client. Since real understanding is in some way 'processed' by you, since it passes through you, it should convey some part of yourself" (pp. 96–97).

We agree with Egan that the effective counselor is always looking for the core of what is being expressed—that he or she becomes highly expert at finding that core and communicating it to the client. This kind of response is more likely to be *reflection* than *restatement*. And, in fact, in Hill's (1989) intensive analysis, reflection was experienced by clients as the most helpful of the paraphrase techniques. It made clients feel accepted and facilitated their getting in touch with their feelings.

Interpretation.   Of the complex counselor responses, interpretation is probably the most complex. It requires greater skillfulness, in our view, and may have the greatest potential for both moving the client forward and interfering with progress. Whereas paraphrase techniques stay with the client, and give back to him or her what the therapist hears in that client's expression, *interpretations go beyond what the client has stated or recognized.* An interpretation usually offers new meaning and points to the causes underlying the client's actions and feelings. Here the therapist's frame of reference emerges as he or she reframes the client's material in terms of the therapist's view of what is happening. This seeks to help the client see things from a new perspective and in a new way.

The complex nature of interpretation is underscored by the fact that this response encompasses several different types. In Hill's (1985, 1986) category system, for example, five types are described.

A common type of interpretation *establishes connections between seemingly isolated statements, problems, or events.* For example, to a client who has been discussing his fear of giving speeches, his low self-esteem, and his problems with relationships, the counselor may eventually point out how all three problems are interconnected and, further, how this client's excessive standards and expectations of himself appear to underlie each problem.

A second type of interpretation *points out themes or patterns in the client's behavior or feelings.* An example of this type might occur in response to the client who continues to become disenchanted with jobs after having high hopes initially. The counselor might note, "Each time it seems that you feel very excited about the possibilities of a job, and then when you see the inevitable problems, you turn away." The counselor might follow this interpretation with an open question about what the meaning of this pattern might be, or the counselor can provide a further interpretation, assuming of course that the client has provided enough material, for example, "Based on what we have been talking about, I suspect that your turning away is a way of dealing with your fear of failing." This follow-up statement demonstrates how the skilled therapist can connect two or more different types of interpretations within the same response.

The last interpretation above pointed to the client's underlying defense ("turning away") against anxiety (fear of failure). This type of interpretation falls within the third type discussed by Hill (1985); that is, *interpretation of defenses, resistance, or transference.* Interpretation of transference is probably the central technique in psychoanalytic treatment. Here the therapist points out how the client's perceptions of the therapist's feelings, behavior, or attitudes are distortions based on past relationships, usually with father or mother. (See the discussions of transference in chapters 5 and 7.) In an effort to help the client gain insight, the counselor shows the client how she or he is reacting to and perceiving this counselor as if she or he were a significant person in the client's childhood. For example:

> CL: I just can't seem to talk to you comfortably about my gayness. It's as if you are sitting there and quietly judging me, thinking I'm an unmasculine shit. Even though you seem accepting of me, I can't trust that, and have this fear that you are critical of me as a person. I half expect you to start yelling at me, to really explode.
> CO: As I listen to you I'm struck with how you are seeing me as so similar to the way your father was. It's as if you're putting father into me.

The fourth type of interpretation *relates present events, experiences, or feelings to the past.* When making this type of interpretation, the therapist aims to help the client see how present problems and conflicts are tied to the past—are causally linked to that past. We say to the client, in effect, "You are misperceiving the present or behaving in ways that hurt you or others in the present because of these issues or experiences in your past." For example:

> CL: I don't know—I just seem to avoid men who are good for me, and get hooked up with these bastards who abuse me. And I turn into such a nag. Nag, nag, nag—I nag so much that I'll turn them into bastards even if they aren't to begin with. I just don't know why I do these things.
> CO: It seems like you consistently get into, and create, situations that are just like your mother and father's relationship when you were a child.

The fifth and final type of interpretation in Hill's (1985) system entails *giving a new framework to feelings, behaviors, or problems.* Counselors use this technique to provide clients with a fresh, new way of looking at some aspect of themselves and their lives. Hill exemplifies this process as follows:

> **CL:** He just never does anything around the house, and he goes out drinking with the guys all the time. I get stuck taking care of the kids and doing everything around the house.
> **CO:** He seems to be saving you from any decision about what you are going to do with your life and your career.

We began the discussion of interpretation by noting how complex this technique is and how, more than most techniques, it can be for better or worse—it can help or harm the client. Probably more than any technique, the issues of *depth* and *timing* are absolutely crucial in determining whether an interpretation has its desired effect. Throughout psychoanalytic theory on technique, for example, one finds a great sensitivity to the use of interpretations that are only slightly ahead of the client's level of insight, enabling the client to take a short step forward in understanding. In this sense, the "good interpretation" is never a depth interpretation, or at least it is never so deep that it does not make contact with the client's awareness. In terms of timing, an effective interpretation must be made when the client can absorb it—can take it in, so to speak. No matter how accurate or well stated an interpretation may be, if it is ill timed, the client's response will not be what the therapist is hoping for—one of insight and awareness. Recent reviews of research (Hill & O'Brien, 1999; Hill & Williams, 2000) do in fact clearly support the importance of interpretations being well timed and of moderate depth.

Another factor in whether interpretations are helpful relates to the characteristics of the client. In an important article on research on interpretation, for example, Spiegel and Hill (1989) suggest that clients with higher levels of self-esteem, psychological-mindedness, and cognitive complexity are the most receptive to interpretive approaches to counseling. Such individuals seem to like and profit from the therapist's explanations, even though they may not always agree with them (Hill, 1989). The other side of this coin is that counselors need to be aware of the kinds of persons who do not profit from such approaches and to use interpretations guardedly if at all with such clients.

Research on the helpfulness of interpretation is more positive than for any other technique. In fact, interpretation, along with approval, are the only techniques consistently found to be helpful (Hill, 1989, 1990; Hill & Williams, 2000). It can be concluded from this that therapists, on the whole, are well aware of the complexity and potential power (for better or worse) of interpretation, and they tend to use it with appropriate caution and skill.

Confrontation.   The next technique to be discussed is controversial because for many therapists and clients it conjures up the image of attacking and being attacked. In fact, *confrontation* may be gentle as well as aggressive and, although some confrontations may be explicitly hostile, we believe the most effective ones are embedded in a caring relationship and are neither hostile nor attacking.

Confrontation may be seen as any therapist response that challenges the client's behavior. The challenge most often focuses on discrepancies or contradictions in the client's behavior, thoughts, or feelings. Challenges may also focus on distortions, evasions, games, tricks, excuse making, and smoke screens in which clients involve themselves, and which ultimately keep them from solving their problems.

The kind of confrontation that focuses on discrepancies or contradictions usually has two parts. In the first part, the therapist states or refers to some aspect of the client's behavior; in the second part, which often begins with a *but,* the discrepancy is presented. Note that, unlike interpretations, confrontations do not state the cause of the discrepancy.

An example of confronting a discrepancy between the client's words and behavior (or between verbal and nonverbal behavior) might be:

> CL: I've been looking forward to coming to this session today because I get so much out of our work together.
> CO: You say this but you were 15 minutes late and have been sitting silently with your arms folded. (The counselor might follow up this confrontation with an open question, e.g., "What do you make of this difference between what you've expressed and your behavior?")

A slight modification of a case noted by Egan (1986) provides a good example of confronting distortions. Eric, a young gay male, blames his problems on an older brother who seduced him during his early years of high school:

> CO: Eric, every time we begin to talk about your sexual behavior, you bring up your brother.
> CL: That's where it all began!
> CO: Your brother's not around any more. . . . Tell me what Eric wants. But tell me as it is.
> CL: I want people to leave me alone.
> CO: I don't believe it because I don't think you believe it. . . . Be honest with yourself.
> CL: I want some one person to care about me. But that's deep down inside me. . . . What I seem to want up front is to punish people and make them punish me.

As discussed with respect to interpretation, confrontation can be for better or worse. Research studies clearly point to the fact that confrontation can stir up client defen- siveness and make clients feel misunderstood (Hill & Williams, 2000). Perhaps because of such negative reactions, confrontations tend to be used infrequently, accounting for approximately 1%–5% of all therapist statements (Hill & Williams, 2000). Yet there is also evidence that confrontations can lead to arousal and make clients more receptive to change. Further, client's differ in how they respond to confrontations. For example, in one major study (Hill, 1989), some clients responded well, whereas others experienced confrontations as too upsetting, even when presented very gently. Some clients found confrontations uncomfortable, but profited from them nonetheless.

As we reflect on the above research, as well as our own counseling experiences, we conclude that a key part of being sensitively empathic and skillful as a therapist is knowing when and how to confront clients, as well as sensing which clients may be helpfully confronted. In general, confrontations work best in the context of a trusting relationship wherein the client feels understood and cared about. We also find Egan's (1986, pp. 227–228) guidelines useful in thinking about the do's and don'ts of effective confrontation.

1. *Avoid labeling.* Derogatory labels, in particular, make clients feel put down and increase resistance to feedback. Words such as *dumb, selfish, arrogant, manipulator, lazy,* and so forth, should be avoided, both because they are not effective and convey a lack of respect for the other person.

2. *Describe the situation and the relevant behaviors.* Rather than labeling, describe the context and self-limiting behaviors as specifically and accurately as possible. Even when you do this, don't dump everything on the client at once. You are not trying to build a case for a trial!

3. *Describe the impact or consequence of the behavior.* Point out how relevant parties (e.g., the counselor, client, significant others) are affected by the behavior in terms of both emotions and behavior. Note, though, that this should not be done with all confrontations; do this selectively.

4. *Help clients identify what they need to do to manage the problem.* Showing clients alternatives, or, even better, helping them explore alternatives, can be valuable when you challenge some aspect of their behavior.

Self-disclosure.   The final technique to be discussed is controversial. The merits and liabilities of self-disclosure have been debated for many years in the counseling and therapy literature. Generally, humanistic counselors (see Chapter 12) believe therapist self-disclosure can be a very helpful way of facilitating a genuine I–thou relationship between counselor and client. When counselors self-disclose, they take themselves off the therapist pedestal and show themselves to be human beings, just like clients. To the humanist, this is a notably positive development. At the other end of the continuum are the traditional psychoanalytic therapists (see Chapter 10). To the traditional analytic therapist, disclosure contaminates the emerging transference and, more important, may foster clients' consciously or unconsciously imitating the therapist, rather than seeking to understand themselves.

Generally, self-disclosure may be divided into *involving statements* and *disclosing statements* (McCarthy & Betz, 1978). In the involving disclosure, the counselor communicates to the client his or her feelings or perceptions, usually (but not always) in the moment, and about the client and/or relationship. Examples of such statements might be: "Sometimes, like right now, it's real hard to know how to respond to you in a way that would feel helpful," or "I feel sad as I listen to your continual attacks on yourself," or "I feel like we have had a good relationship, and although I know we must end now, it's a loss for me as well." Disclosing statements reveal something about the counselor or his or her life that does not directly relate to the client or the relationship. These disclosures may be facts about the therapist; similarities between the therapist and client, including how they feel; or therapeutic strategies used by the therapist. Examples of disclosing statements in these different categories might be: "If someone responded to me that way, I, too, would have a lot of feelings—anger, helplessness, and so on" (disclosure of similarities in feelings); "I understand because I have two teenagers also" (disclosure of similarities); "One of the things that has worked well in my practice and my life has been to listen carefully and not interrupt" (disclosure of strategy); "I got my degree in counseling psychology from Ohio State in 1980 and have been practicing for 20 years" (disclosure of facts).

In addition to the division between involving and disclosing types of self-disclosure, we can make a further distinction: Self-disclosures may be either *positive* or *negative*. Positive disclosures are reassuring in that they support, reinforce, or legitimize the client's perspective, for example: "I, too, feel very good about our work and our relationship" (Hill, Mahalik, & Thompson, 1989). The negative disclosure, on the other hand, tends to be challenging in that it confronts the client's perspective, way of thinking, or behavior, for example: "You say it's okay, but if someone responded to me in that way, I'd feel pretty upset" (see Hill et al., 1989).

Although the research is mixed, the evidence generally seems to favor the merits of involving over disclosing statements, and positive over negative disclosures. At the same time, if offered skillfully, each kind of disclosure may have a positive impact. For example, it has been found that in both brief counseling (Hill, 1989) and long-term therapy (Knox, Hess, Peterson, & Hill, 1997), therapist self-disclosure is rated positively by clients and results in increased self-exploration and insight. Such findings about the desirable effects of self-disclosure are typical (Hill & Williams, 2000). At the same time, it is important to note that counselor self-disclosure is infrequently used, accounting for only 1%–4% of all counselor responses (Hill & O'Brien, 1999). Thus, judicious and cautious use of counselor self-disclosure can be, and usually is, facilitative. Frequent self-disclosures, on the other hand, may serve the counselor's needs more than the client's.

To aid the reader in integrating the material we have presented in this section, a summary is provided in Table 9.3. For each response mode, we present a brief definition and an example.

The Frequency, Patterning, and Intent of Verbal Techniques

Because research has found a particular response mode or technique to be effective does not mean that the more it is used the better will be the counseling. Conversely, because some techniques have been shown to be minimally effective does not imply that they should not be used at all.

As an example of the effective techniques, much research has demonstrated the technique of interpretation to be a helpful mode. Yet, for an interpretation to be effective, it is important that the counselor patiently await the right moment to offer one. Many counselors do not at all make interpretations during about the first half of a therapy session. Rather, they wait for material to accumulate and then fit one or more interpretations into the latter part of the session. Often several sessions may go by before an interpretation is offered even by the analytic counselor, who values this technique above all others. This same point may be made for self-disclosure.

Counselor Techniques in Terms of Response Modes.   TABLE 9.3.

Response Mode	Definition	Example
Minimal Responses		
Minimal encourager	Short phrase or sound that indicates acceptance	"um-hm," "I see"
Silence	Absence of verbalization	—
Directives		
Approval	Agreement with/support of client	"That was a really effective response"
Provide information	Provision of facts, opinions, data, resources	"Dr. Gelsomini in Zoology would be a good source of info"
Direct guidance	Offering directions, suggestions, or advice	"I think it might be helpful to share your feelings with Ralph"
Information Seeking		
Closed question	Questions requiring one- to two-word answer	"Are you sad?"
Open question	Questions fostering exploration	"How do you feel?"
Complex Counselor Responses		
Paraphrase	Summary of what client has communicated. Several kinds.	"You feel hurt by your friend's response"
Interpretation	Statement of connections, hidden causes, underlying themes in client's material	"You seem to react to Jane as your father reacted to you"
Confrontation	Response that challenges client	"You say you want friends, but you avoid returning phone calls and other approaches"
Self-disclosure	Revelation to client of facts about or feelings of therapist	"I feel happy about how you have grown"

This may be the least frequently used technique, as well as a consistently helpful one in clients' eyes. It must be reiterated that frequent use of self-disclosures likely interferes with therapeutic movement.

On the other side of the ledger, a technique like the closed question is minimally effective, and clients most often evaluate it in a neutral fashion. Yet there are times in treatment when it is important to ask closed questions, for example, when the counselor needs to gather information about a client.

The *patterning* of techniques may well be as important or even more important than the particular techniques used. Thus how the therapist combines techniques in a given treatment may be highly influential. For example, Hill (1989) uncovered some fascinating evidence that interpretations are most often used in the context of approval, are preceded by questions and followed by suggestions. Could it be that the interpretations were helpful because of the context in which they were embedded? This seems to make sense especially given their emotionally challenging or disruptive nature. When using both confrontations and interpretations, it may be particularly important to do so within a context of supportive techniques.

The final point in this section is in fact prefatory to the next: What the therapist is aiming for or intending with a given response may be more important than the technique or response itself in terms of the effect on a client. This brings us to the issue of *therapist intentions,* a topic of considerable interest in counseling psychology.

Covert Behavior

It will be recalled that the most general definition of *technique* was "anything the counselor performs within the session" (Highlen & Hill, 1984, p. 366). When viewed in this general way, counselors' *internal* responses to clients and to the counseling situation may be seen as at least a part of their technique. This internal or *covert* level is the third level of counseling technique (the first and second being nonverbal behavior and verbal behavior).

The internal responses of the counselor to the client and the counseling situation are extremely important because they significantly influence the counselor's treatment of the client, verbally and nonverbally. Thus, what the counselor thinks, feels, hypothesizes, and plans has a major impact on the counseling process. As surprising as it may seem, there has not been a great deal of empirical study of the covert behavior of the counselor. A fruitful line of research, however, has developed on a covert variable called counseling *intentions*. This work, like the response modes approach just discussed, has been spearheaded by Hill and colleagues (Hill 1985, 1986; Hill & O'Brien, 1999). Let us look at these intentions as an example of covert or internal counselor processes that influence counseling.

Intentions may be defined as "a therapist's rationale for selecting specific behavior, response mode, technique, or intervention with a client at any moment within the session" (Hill & O'Grady, 1985, p. 3). Thus, an intention is the *cognitive* component that mediates the specific responses counselors make to their clients. As such, intentions get us closer to what therapists think about what they are doing. They give us a glimpse of the *why* behind counselors' overt behavior; that is, the goals counselors have when they respond to clients.

To determine what therapists intend when they respond to clients, Hill and colleagues conducted a series of studies. Generally, they had therapists listen to tapes of their sessions with clients and note what their intentions were behind each response. Based on studies using this method, Hill and O'Grady (1985) devised a list of 19 such intentions. Although some of these overlap and may be clustered to shorten the list, it is useful to look at all 19 as a general guide. These are outlined in Table 9.4.

A number of valuable findings have emerged regarding counselor intentions (Fuller & Hill, 1985; Hill, Helms, Tichenor et al., 1988; Hill & O'Grady, 1985; Hill, O'Grady, Balenger et al., 1994; Stiles, Startup, Hardy et al., 1996). It does seem clear that intentions are linked to the counselor's actual verbal responses. For example, when counselors intend to stimulate insight, they are most likely to use the response mode of interpretation, and least likely to use the mode of approval; when counselors seek to facilitate exploration of feelings, they are most likely to use open questions and reflections, and least likely to give information.

List of Intentions.

1. **Set limits:** To structure, make arrangements, establish goals and
   methods to attain goals, correct expectations about treatment,
   relationship (e.g., time, fees, cancellation policies, homework).

2. **Get information:** To find out specific facts about history, client functi...

3. **Give information:** To educate, give facts, correct misperceptions or mis...
   for therapist's behavior or procedures.

4. **Support:** To provide a warm, supportive, empathic environment; increase tru...
   build relationship; help client feel accepted, understood, comfortable, reassured,
   help establish a person-to-person relationship.

5. **Focus:** To help client get back on the track, change subject, channel or structure the d...
   he or she is unable to begin or has been diffuse or rambling.

6. **Clarify:** To provide or solicit more elaboration, emphasis, or specification when client or th...
   has been vague, incomplete, confusing, contradictory, or inaudible.

7. **Hope:** To convey the expectation that change is possible and likely to occur, convey that the ther...
   pist will be able to help the client, restore morale, build up the client's confidence to make changes.

8. **Cathart:** To promote relief from tension or unhappy feelings, allow the client a chance to let go or
   talk through feelings and problems.

9. **Cognitions:** To identify maladaptive, illogical, or irrational thoughts or attitudes (e.g., "I must be
   perfect").

10. **Behaviors:** To identify and give feedback about the client's inappropriate or maladaptive behaviors
    and/or their consequences, do a behavioral analysis, point out games.

11. **Self-control:** To encourage client to own or gain a sense of mastery or control over his or her own
    thoughts, feelings, behaviors, or impulses; help client become more appropriately internal rather
    than inappropriately external in taking responsibility for his or her role.

12. **Feelings:** To identify, intensify, and/or enable acceptance of feelings; encourage or provoke the client
    to become aware of or deepen underlying or hidden feelings or affect or experience feelings at a
    deeper level.

13. **Insight:** To encourage understanding of the underlying reasons, dynamics, assumptions, or uncon-
    scious motivations for cognitions, behaviors, attitudes, or feelings. May include an understanding
    of client's reactions to others' behaviors.

14. **Change:** To build and develop new and more adaptive skills, behaviors, or cognitions in dealing
    with self and others. May be to instill new, more adaptive assumptive models, frameworks, expla-
    nations, or conceptualizations. May be to give an assessment or option about client functioning
    that will help client see self in new way.

15. **Reinforce change:** To give positive reinforcement or feedback about behavioral, cognitive, or affec-
    tive attempts at change to enhance the probability that the change will be continued or maintained;
    encourage risk taking and new ways of behaving.

16. **Resistance:** To overcome obstacles to change or progress. May discuss failure to adhere to thera-
    peutic procedures, either in past or to prevent possibility of such failure in future.

17. **Challenge:** To jolt the client out of a present state; shake up current beliefs or feelings; test validity,
    adequacy, reality, or appropriateness of beliefs, thoughts, feelings, or behaviors; help client ques-
    tion the necessity of maintaining old patterns.

18. **Relationship:** To resolve problems as they arise in the relationship in order to build or maintain a
    smooth working alliance; heal ruptures in the alliance; deal with dependency issues appropriate to
    stage in treatment; uncover and resolve distortions in client's thinking about the relationship that
    are based on past experiences rather than current reality.

19. **Therapist needs:** To protect, relieve, or defend the therapist; alleviate anxiety. May try unduly to
    persuade, argue, or feel good or superior at the expense of the client.

Source: Reprinted from Hill and O'Grady (1985).

elor intentions also seem clearly linked to theoretical orientation. For ex-
ounselors who are psychoanalytic in their orientation more often have in-
ns to promote insight and feeling exploration. Behaviorally oriented coun-
s, on the other hand, are more likely, in their responses to clients, to intend to
omote change, reinforce change, and set limits.

Another interesting finding about intentions is that different ones are used at various points within a given session. In the beginning of a counseling session, the most frequent counselor intentions are to clarify and get information; but as the session develops, the intentions of catharsis, insight, and change become more prominent. This progression during a session makes sense clinically. Counselors begin sessions intending to sort out information and clarify what the client is expressing. Then, as things get clearer with the unfolding of the session, the counselor moves closer, seeking to deepen the client's understanding and emotional experience and to promote change. This progression of intentions has been found to occur, with some variations, across an entire counseling experience as well as within a given hour (see Hill & O'Grady, 1985).

How Intentions Operate in Counseling

How are intentions played out in a counseling experience? Each client brings to counseling his or her own set of problems and issues, as well as a unique personality. Using the lenses that are inevitably colored by his or her personality and theoretical orientation, the counselor takes in and processes the material offered by the client. This is usually a tremendous amount of material, and the counselor processes it in an incredibly quick and sophisticated manner—the parallel to a computer is inescapable. Based on their experience and theoretical orientations, counselors organize this client material or data according to goals they wish to accomplish at given points in a session. These goals (intentions) may be conscious in the therapist, or they may not be in awareness. Nevertheless, the intentions guide the counselor's choice of interventions. (For elaboration, see Hill & O'Brien [1999] and Hill & O'Grady [1985].)

A given intention can be implemented through a range of responses, both verbal and nonverbal. Hill and O'Grady (1985) use the example of a counselor intending to intensify client feelings. The counselor may do any of the following: lean forward, touch, reflect feelings, be silent, confront, self-disclose, respond with particular warmth, and so on. As noted above, however, therapists will refrain from making responses for a given intention as well; for example, if they want to intensify feelings, they typically will not give information. The counselor's choice of the intervention(s) used to implement a given intention depends on many factors—comfort with various techniques, theoretical orientation, and understanding of the client's dynamics and response patterns.

In any event, following the intervention, the client will then make a response based on his or her immediate integration of the intervention. In turn, the client's response helps shape the counselor's subsequent intention (and intervention). Thus, for example, if the counselor feels the client's responses suggest a weak working alliance, the counselor is likely to intend to assess, support, and explore feelings (Kivlighan,

1990). When the therapist senses a high degree of transference in the client's response, the therapist will likely intend to foster insight, feeling exploration, and resolution of problems in the therapeutic relationship (Gelso, Hill, & Kivlighan, 1991).

This reciprocal process continues throughout the counseling encounter. Each participant, counselor as well as client, adjusts his or her responses to the immediate response of the other, combined with all that preceded. The counselor's intentions are thus continually shaped by the client, and these intentions, in turn, continually affect both the counselor's intervention and the client.

Interpersonal Manner: The Counselor and Interpersonal Influence

The final level of technique to be examined in this chapter is called "interpersonal manner." This is the most abstract and global of the technical levels discussed so far and does not refer to specific behaviors and techniques. Rather, interpersonal manner refers to constellations of verbal and nonverbal behaviors that sum up the personal style of a counselor. At the most general level, manner entails how the counselor comes across to the client, and is defined by the impressions that the counselor creates in his or her clients.

Highlen and Hill (1984) point out that the variables of interpersonal manner (attitudes, involvement, communication patterns) compose the gestalt of overt behavior. These variables are numerous, including those of empathy, positive regard, and congruence. Thus, issues of technique (as examined in this chapter) come to overlap with the issues of counselor–client relationship (as discussed in Chapter 8).

In this final section we shall focus on a set of variables that have been studied extensively in counseling psychology for more than three decades and that are often referred to as the counselor's *social influence*. The major initial theoretical statement about social influence in counseling was offered by Stanley Strong (1968, 1970), and much of the development of this line of thought is a testimony to Strong's theoretical work and empirical research.

In drawing from research and theory in social psychology, Strong proposed that counseling was a process of social influence in which the counselor sought to influence the client toward attitude and behavior change. He theorized that counselors' attempts to induce change in clients created a state of cognitive dissonance. Clients, as do all humans, would then seek to reduce dissonance, and they could do this in any of several ways: they could either (a) change in the direction advanced by the counselor; or (b) not do so, for example, by discrediting the counselor or issue. Strong hypothesized that positive client change would be most likely to the extent that clients perceive their counselors as being high in the qualities of *expertness, attractiveness,* and *trustworthiness* (EAT).

In line with the above propositions, Strong formulated counseling to be a two-stage process. In the first stage, the counselor does what is necessary to enhance the client's perceptions of the counselor's EAT. Then, in the second stage, the counselor influences client change. The specifics of this attempt to influence are not spelled out. Apparently, any of a range of specific procedures may be used, as advocated by the different theoretical approaches to counseling (see the next three chapters).

The key constructs in social influence theory are EAT. According to Strong (1968), expertness is the degree to which the counselor is seen as a source of valid assertions. Perceptions of E may be affected by "(a) objective evidence of specialized training such as diplomas, certificates, and titles; (b) behavioral evidence . . . such as rational and knowledgeable arguments and confidence in presentation; and (c) reputation as an expert" (p. 216). Counselor attractiveness is based on "perceived similarity to, compatibility with, and liking for" the counselor (Strong, 1968, p. 216). Strong feels that the facilitative conditions discussed in Chapter 5 critically influence clients' perceptions of counselor attractiveness. Counselor self-disclosure is also seen as central. Finally, counselor trustworthiness, according to Strong, is based on "(a) reputation for honesty; (b) social role, such as physician; (c) sincerity and openness; and (d) lack of motivation for personal gain" (p. 217).

Because of the cogency, clarity, and testability of Strong's theoretical statements (Strong, 1968; Strong & Matross, 1973), dozens of studies have been done over the past three decades on counselor social influence. Because client-perceived EAT, often referred to as "source characteristics," are so central to the theory, much of the research has examined what factors may be included under these three variables and how to enhance clients' perceptions of them. Among other things, the research has generally supported Strong's original statements about which factors affect perceptions of this well-known triad. Interestingly, this research has also pointed to the great importance of the counselor's *nonverbal behavior* in the client's perceptions of EAT. Generally, the nonverbals in the acronym SOLER appear to affect such client perceptions.

How important is EAT for Strong's stage 2, the actual attempt to influence change? The results generally support the importance of client-perceived EAT in counseling outcome (Heppner & Claiborn, 1989), but this is still an open question. Despite the great amount of research devoted to it over many years, counselors have always questioned the usefulness of social influence theory. It has never been clear, for example, just how the theory, or other theories derived from social psychology, may be applied to practice (e.g., Frazier, Gonzales, & Rudman, 1995). At first glance, it may appear that the theory dictates that the counselor do whatever is necessary to make himself or herself appear expert, attractive, and trustworthy—that nothing else is needed, as change will follow automatically from the client's perceptions of these source characteristics. If one follows this approach, what results is a caricature of counseling, with a focus on superficial appearances rather than the deeper, more central qualities that make for good counseling.

Social influence theory and its application is in effect a very general, pantheoretical set of principles about behavior change. This theory, in our view, should *not* be applied in any direct, straightforward fashion. Knowing about EAT and integrating such knowledge into one's general theory of counseling may help the counselor understand the process and at times offer some hints about application. But the focus of counseling should be on understanding the client (and one's own reactions to the client and situation), developing the relationship, and applying one's substantive (e.g., psychoanalytic, behavioral) theory of counseling to the situation. The use of techniques, as discussed in this chapter, is best seen as occurring within this context. Furthermore, within this context, it is rare that the practitioner should seek to *appear* expert, trustworthy, and attractive. Rather, she or he should seek to *be* truly expert in his or her practice, genuinely trustworthy, and perhaps an attractive human being in the most general sense.

SUMMARY

There is a range of definitions of the word *techniques*, from the most general (anything the counselor performs with the client) to the more specific (a tool or method employed by the counselor to facilitate effective counseling). Using the most general definition, four levels of technique are discussed in this chapter: (1) nonverbal behavior, (2) verbal behavior, (3) covert behavior, and (4) interpersonal manner.

The general domain of nonverbal behavior comprises *paralinguistics, facial expression, kinesics, visual behavior,* and *proxemics*. The effective counselor is aware that he or she is always communicating with clients nonverbally and that the client, too, is doing so. With experience the counselor learns to use nonverbals to enhance counseling. The acronym *SOLER* is a way of summarizing how the counselor might deliberately use nonverbal behavior to enhance counseling.

In the *response modes approach*, the focus is on the grammatical structure of the counselor's verbal response, rather than the content. Response modes are what is ordinarily meant by the word *technique* when used in the more specific sense. Hill's (1985) Verbal Response Category System serves to classify response modes, 11 of which can be distinguished: *minimal encouragers, silence, approval, providing information, direct guidance, open and closed questions, paraphrase, interpretation, confrontation,* and *self-disclosure*. It is important that techniques such as response modes be used in the context of an understanding of counseling goals and a stable counselor–client relationship. The theoretical basis for applying techniques must also be understood.

Covert behavior can be discussed in terms of the *intentions* behind the counselor's response to the client. The study of counselor intentions has furthered our understanding of counseling processes and outcomes.

The last level of technique discussed in this chapter is *interpersonal manner*, or the general way in which the counselor "comes across" to the client. The counselor's *expertness, attractiveness,* and *trustworthiness* (EAT), as perceived by the client, are an example of this interpersonal manner. Strong's (1968) theory of social influence in counseling, which incorporates EAT as central ingredients, posits that client's attitudes and behavior will change during counseling to the extent that clients perceive their counseling as high on the EAT variables. Although the direct applicability of social influence theory to counseling is limited, it has been a useful guide to understanding the change process in counseling.

REFERENCES

Benjamin, A. (1987). *The helping interview.* Boston: Houghton Mifflin.

Brammer, L. M., Abrego, P. J., & Shostrom, E. L. (1993). *Therapeutic counseling and psychotherapy* (6th ed.). Englewood Cliffs, NJ: Prentice-Hall.

Brammer, L. M., & MacDonald, G. (1996). *The helping relationship: Process and skills* (6th ed.). Boston: Allyn & Bacon.

Egan, G. (1986). *The skilled helper* (3rd ed.). Monterey, CA: Brooks/Cole.

Egan, G. (1998). *The skilled helper: A problem-management approach to helping* (6th ed.). Pacific Grove, CA: Brooks/Cole.

Ekman, P., & Friesen, W. V. (1969). The repertoire of non-verbal behavior. *Semiotica, 1,* 49–98.

Elliott, R., Barker, C. B., Caskey, N., & Pistrang, N. (1982). Differential helpfulness of counselor verbal response modes. *Journal of Counseling Psychology, 29,* 354–361.

Elliott, R., Hill, C. E., Stiles, W. B., Friedlander, M. L., Mahrer, A. R., & Margison, F. R. (1987). Primary response modes: A comparison of six rating systems. *Journal of Consulting and Clinical Psychology, 55,* 218–223.

Frazier, P. A., Gonzales, M. H., & Rudman, L. A. (1995). Evaluating the effectiveness of applying social psychological theory to counseling. *The Counseling Psychologist, 23,* 691–696.

Fretz, B. R. (1966). Postural movements in a counseling dyad. *Journal of Counseling Psychology, 13,* 335–343.

Fuller, F., & Hill, C. E. (1985). Counselor and helpee perceptions of counselor intentions in relation to outcome in a single counseling session. *Journal of Counseling Psychology, 32,* 329–338.

Gelso, C. J., Hill, C. E., & Kivlighan, D. M. (1991). Transference, insight, and counselor intentions during a counseling hour. *Journal of Counseling and Development, 69,* 428–433.

Hall, E. T. (1963). A system for the notation of proxemic behavior. *American Anthropologist, 65,* 1003–1026.

Hall, E. T. (1968). Proxemics. *Current Anthropology, 9,* 83–108.

Harper, F. D., & Bruce-Sanford, G. C. (1989). *Counseling techniques: An outline and overview.* Alexandria, VA: Douglass Publishers.

Harper, R. G., Wiens, A. N., & Matarazzo, J. D. (1978). *Nonverbal communication: The state of the art.* New York: John Wiley & Sons.

Heppner, P. P., & Claiborn, C. D. (1989). Social influence research in counseling: A review and critique. *Journal of Counseling Psychology* [Monograph], *36,* 365–387.

Hermansson, G. L., Webster, A. C., & McFarland, K. (1988). Counselor deliberate postural lean and communication of facilitative conditions. *Journal of Counseling Psychology, 35,* 149–153.

Highlen, P. S., & Hill, C. E. (1984). Factors affecting client change in individual counseling: Current status and theoretical speculations. In S. Brown and R. Lent (Eds.), *Handbook of counseling psychology* (pp. 334–396). New York: John Wiley & Sons.

Hill, C. E. (1985). *Manual for the Hill counselor verbal response modes category system* (rev. ed.). Unpublished manuscript, University of Maryland.

Hill, C. E. (1986). An overview of the Hill counselor and client verbal response modes category systems. In L. Greenberg and W. Pinsoff (Eds.), *The psychotherapeutic process: A research handbook* (pp. 131–160). New York: Guilford.

Hill, C. E. (1989). *Therapist techniques and client outcome: Eight cases of brief psychotherapy.* Newbury Park, CA: Sage Publications.

Hill, C. E. (1990). Review of exploratory in-session process research. *Journal of Consulting and Clinical Psychology, 58,* 288–294.

Hill, C. E., Helms, J. E., Tichenor, V., Spiegel, S. B., O'Grady, K. E., & Perry, E. (1988). The effects of therapist response modes in brief psychotherapy. *Journal of Counseling Psychology, 35,* 222–233.

Hill, C. E., Mahalik, J., & Thompson, B. J. (1989). Self-disclosure. *Psychotherapy, 26,* 290–295.

Hill, C. E., & O'Brien, K. M. (1999). *Helping skills: Facilitating exploration, insight, and action.* Washington, DC: American Psychological Association.

Hill, C. E., & O'Grady, K. E. (1985). List of therapist intentions illustrated in a case study and with therapists of varying theoretical orientations. *Journal of Counseling Psychology, 32,* 3–22.

Hill, C. E., O'Grady, K., Balenger, V., Busse, W., Falk, D., Hill, M., Rios, P., & Taffe, R. (1994). Methodological examination of videotape-assisted review in brief therapy: Helpfulness ratings, therapist intentions, client reactions, mood, and session evaluation. *Journal of Counseling Psychology, 41,* 236–247.

Hill, C. E., & Williams, E. N. (2000). The process of individual therapy. In S. Brown and R. Lent (Eds.), *Handbook of counseling psychology* (3rd ed. pp. 670–710). New York: John Wiley & Sons.

Hunter, M., & Struve, J. (1998). *The ethical use of touch in psychotherapy.* Thousand Oaks, CA: Sage Publications.

Kivlighan, D. M. (1990). Relation between counselors' use of intentions and clients' perceptions of the working alliance. *Journal of Counseling Psychology, 37,* 27–32.

Knapp, M. L. (1972). The field of nonverbal communication: An overview. In C. Stewart and B. Kendall (Eds.), *On speech communication: An anthology of contemporary writings and messages.* New York: Holt, Rinehart and Winston.

Knox, S., Hess, S., Peterson, D., & Hill, C. (1997). A qualitative analysis of client perceptions of the effects of helpful therapist self-disclosure in long-term therapy. *Journal of Counseling Psychology, 44,* 274–283.

Langs, R. J. (1973). *The technique of psychoanalytic psychotherapy* (Vol. 1). New York: Jason Aronson.

Lecomte, C., Bernstein, B. L., & Dumont, F. (1981). Counseling interaction as a function of spatial–environmental conditions. *Journal of Counseling Psychology, 28,* 536–539.

Lee, D. Y., Uhlemann, M. R., & Haase, R. F. (1985). Counselor verbal and nonverbal responses and perceived expertness, trustworthiness, and attractiveness. *Journal of Counseling Psychology, 32,* 181–187.

Maurer, R. E., & Tindall, J. H. (1983). Effect of postural congruence on client's perception of counselor empathy. *Journal of Counseling Psychology, 30,* 158–163.

McCarthy, P. R., & Betz, N. E. (1978). Differential effects of self-disclosing versus self-involving counselor statements. *Journal of Counseling Psychology, 25,* 251–256.

Spiegel, S. B., & Hill, C. E. (1989). Guidelines for research on therapist interpretation: Toward greater methodological rigor and relevance to practice. *Journal of Counseling Psychology, 36,* 121–129.

Stiles, W., Startup, M., Hardy, G., Barkham, M., Rees, A., Shapiro, D., & Reynolds, S. (1996). Therapist session intentions in cognitive–behavioral and psychodynamic–interpersonal psychotherapy. *Journal of Counseling Psychology, 43,* 402–414.

Strong, S. R. (1968). Counseling: An interpersonal influence process. *Journal of Counseling Psychology, 15,* 215–224.

Strong, S. R. (1970). Causal attribution in counseling and psychotherapy. *Journal of Counseling Psychology, 17,* 388–399.

Strong, S. R., & Matross, R. P. (1973). Change processes in counseling and psychotherapy. *Journal of Counseling Psychology, 20,* 25–37.

Sue, D. W., & Sue, D. (1977). Barriers to effective cross-cultural counseling. *Journal of Counseling Psychology, 24,* 420–429.

Suiter, R. L., & Goodyear, R. K. (1985). Male and female counselor and client perceptions of four levels of counselor touch. *Journal of Counseling Psychology, 32,* 645–648.

Tyson, J. A., & Wall, S. M. (1983). Effect of inconsistency between counselor verbal and nonverbal behavior on perceptions of counselor attributes. *Journal of Counseling Psychology, 30,* 433–437.

Wolberg, L. R. (1967). *The technique of psychotherapy* (2nd ed.). New York: Grune & Stratton.

THE PSYCHOANALYTIC APPROACH

The Centrality of the Unconscious

The Role of Defenses

Repetition and Transference

The Role of the Client–Therapist Relationship

Interpretation and Other Techniques

The Ideal of Insight

Time-Limited Psychotherapy (TLP): An Approach for Counseling Psychologists

James Mann's Time-Limited Psychotherapy

The Psychoanalytic Approach in Perspective

From Strange Bedfellows to Compatible Partners

Science, Research, and Psychoanalysis

Summary

References

There are virtually dozens of theories of counseling and psychotherapy today, and indeed each practitioner may be seen as developing his or her own unique theory. At the same time, it is possible to combine the most prominent theories into three main clusters. In this chapter and the following two, we shall examine the three theory clusters that have been dominant in counseling psychology and in the counseling and therapy that is practiced by counseling psychologists. These clusters may be labeled *psychoanalytic* (including Freudian approaches, their derivatives, and departures), *learning* (including the behavioral, cognitive, and cognitive–behavioral approaches), and *humanistic* (including experiential and existential).

Many excellent presentations of theories of counseling are available. Our goal in the following three chapters is not to duplicate these. Rather, we aim to delineate the major ingredients of each of the three theory clusters, exemplify treatment approaches and procedures within each, and clarify the place of each perspective in counseling psychology. Key references will enable the student to pursue each individual theory in greater depth.

Will the real psychoanalytic practitioner please stand up? If this question was asked of a large group of therapists, those who stood would probably represent a dizzying array of viewpoints about personality development, health and psychopathology, and psychological interventions. It is not surprising that the beginning student often feels overwhelmed by the enormous diversity of views and approaches within the general psychoanalytic perspective. This diversity, along with the awesome complexity inherent in psychoanalytic theories, makes it difficult for the beginner to decipher just what is and is not psychoanalytic. With experience, practice, and much reading, things do become clearer, although the seasoned practitioner and scholar does not have an easy time with this question either.

One of the principal goals of this chapter is to provide the reader with a framework for understanding common ingredients of the multifold approaches found under the psychoanalytic umbrella. We will also explain how psychoanalysis fits with counseling psychology.

We begin by taking a glimpse at the life and personality of the originator of psychoanalysis, Sigmund Freud. Subsequently, we (1) examine some distinctions that have too often remained unclarified and are frequent sources of confusion for the beginning student of psychoanalysis; (2) clarify the main theory clusters within psychoanalysis; (3) discuss ingredients that are common to all psychoanalytic approaches; (4) present a theoretical approach to psychoanalytic therapy that seems well suited to counseling psychology; and (5) conclude with a discussion of the relationship of psychoanalysis to counseling psychology—the ways in which these two endeavors have not meshed, and how their "fit" has become much better in recent years. Research issues and findings related to psychoanalytic interventions are also presented in the final section of the chapter.

It should be noted that the material in this chapter assumes the reader has a beginning understanding of basic psychoanalytic concepts such as Freud's psychosexual stages (e.g., oral, anal, phallic stages, and the Oedipus complex), structures of the psyche (id, ego, super ego), defense mechanisms, and levels of consciousness (unconscious, preconscious, conscious). Excellent discussions of these concepts are provided by Prochaska and Norcross (1999) and Sharf (1996). The advanced student can consult Brenner's (1973) classic work.

THE FIRST FREUDIAN AND THE BEGINNINGS OF PSYCHOANALYSIS

All fields of psychology in which counseling interventions are involved must be indebted to psychoanalysis and especially to Sigmund Freud for the beginning development of therapeutic treatment. It was Freud, after all, who discovered and developed the "talking cure," the treatment upon which the entire field of verbal counseling has been built. Because of the profound impact of Freud and his early work on all approaches to psychological intervention, it is worth examining his life and the early psychoanalytic movement in some depth.

Sigmund Freud was born in 1856 in Freiberg, Moravia (formerly Austria). His father, Jakob, was a wool merchant in Vienna, where Freud lived from the age of 4. Jakob was married twice; Sigmund was the first child of Jakob's second marriage to Amalie, a 20-year-old woman who was also 20 years Jakob's junior. Jakob and Amalie bore seven other children, so Sigmund was the eldest child of a large family. Freud's childhood seems to have been a relatively happy one. Jakob was a liberal-minded Jew with progressive views. He was apparently a loving father with a good sense of humor, although he seemed to represent discipline and authority to Sigmund. Freud's relationship with his father seemed somewhat distant. Freud's mother is described as having a lively personality, and gave Sigmund considerable affection and attention. She was proud of her first-born, and Sigmund remained fond of her until her death at age 95.

A deep scholarly orientation pervaded Freud's life from very early on. His great intellectual capacity was recognized early by his family, and it was established that he would be a scholar. His destiny was incontestable: Freud's study–bedroom was the only one in his house equipped with an oil lamp—the other members' rooms had candles. Freud was a precocious reader, who studied a great deal. He began to enjoy Shakespeare at the age of 8 and, as a teenager, ate his evening meals in his room so he would lose no time from his studies. Freud's passion for learning and understanding never faded. In fact, although Freud was steeped in psychoanalytic practice throughout most of his adult life, his most passionate interests revolved around understanding what makes people tick—the workings of the human psyche—rather than in providing psychological help.

Freud received his M.D. from the University of Vienna in 1881, after which he took a position at the city's well-known general hospital. There he engaged in general medical services, and also spent five months studying brain anatomy and neuropathology under Theodore Meynert at a nearby psychiatric clinic. His practice flourished, and he wrote books on aphasia and infantile cerebral paralysis. It looked as though the young Freud was destined for a smooth and lucrative career. Things were not to be easy, though, for Freud's restless and creative genius goaded him to new and deeper understandings of the human psyche—understandings that were to be the source of much professional ferment and emotional pain in his life. In his practice, he began to see patients with hysterical disorders and in 1886 presented his first paper on hysteria. It was badly received by his medical colleagues. This was probably the first in what became a long series of rejections for one of the great minds of history.

While a medical student, Freud met Joseph Breuer, a prominent general practitioner 14 years his senior. They became friends, and their friendship continued over the years. Breuer discussed with Freud a case he treated from 1880 to 1882, the now-famous case of Anna O, in which a variety of symptoms, including conversion reactions, were cured by means of hypnosis and the free discharge of emotions, called *catharsis*. Freud was fascinated by this case and by what he felt to be a remarkable discovery. Following his return in 1889 from the Nancy School, where he studied hypnotic suggestion with Bernheim and Liebault, Freud further tested the new method of catharsis, or abreaction, along with hypnosis.

Breuer and Freud eventually published the case of Anna O in *Studies in Hysteria* (1895), but the book did not receive the acceptance they had hoped for. The medical profession of that time explained all symptoms on the basis of some organic lesion; if a physical problem could not be found, it was assumed that something in the brain was the culprit. As Freud continued to develop his views about the sexual basis of the neuroses, things heated up further. When Freud theorized that hysterical and other symptoms were, at their core, the results of sexual repression, Breuer withdrew from the work. Freud essentially worked alone, and was the object of professional ridicule by fellow physicians. He was seen as a crackpot, and his private practice nearly dried up. For example, in early 1900 Freud reported that he had had no new cases for months, and his financial outlook was again bleak. Having a wife, six children, and a mother to support (Freud's father had died) surely added stress.

The final years of the nineteenth century were crucial for Freud and psychoanalysis. During this period, Freud worked essentially alone. He began his self-analysis as a way of understanding the psyche and resolving some personal neuroses, and further developed his theories about sex, producing one of his most important works, *The Interpretation of Dreams* (1900). He soon was to discontinue the use of hypnosis. Too many patients could not be hypnotized, and too many of the "cures" were short-lived. Instead, Freud began to use a procedure he called *free association* to get his patients to remember repressed experiences and feelings from their past, and thus began the revolutionary new method, psychoanalysis.

Freud's work began to receive positive recognition in the early 1900s. Although he continued to work largely alone, during this time Freud met a number of men who were to form the inner sanctum of psychoanalysis. For example, in 1902 he initiated weekly discussions in his home with a small group of budding analysts—the famed Vienna Psychoanalytic Society. Given the great struggles and isolation that Freud endured during his initial years of developing psychoanalysis, as well as some aspects of his character structure, it was perhaps inevitable that psychoanalysis would become a system revolving around the beliefs of one man.

As the first decade of the twentieth century was drawing to a close, Freud's views were becoming increasingly influential. A major marker of the great recognition he and psychoanalysis were beginning to receive was the invitation from G. Stanley Hall for Freud to give a series of lectures in the United States, commemorating the twentieth anniversary of Clark University. Freud's lectures had a great impact on that august body, including the famous William James, who became a supporter of psychoanalysis.

Interestingly, although Freud's genius is now almost universally recognized, he often complained of not having been born with a better brain. He believed that his main virtue was his courage, an assertion that could hardly be denied. He also once stated that his next best attribute was his self-criticalness, and this seems equally inarguable. These qualities—courage and self-criticalness—constantly pushed Freud to further his and our understanding of the deepest aspects of the human psyche in the face of professional rejection and even humiliation. His self-criticalness also must have been part of his continual analysis, reanalysis, and modification of his own views.

Freud often changed his views, and did so even when giving up a cherished theory was painful to him. Yet he had difficulty with others deviating from his position, especially if they used the word *psychoanalysis* as a label for their theorizing. Psychoanalysis was Freud's creation, and he alone could decide what rightfully belonged in its province. Once Freud was convinced that a theory was valid, he maintained it with complete conviction. He could not admit contradiction. As Ellenberger (1970) noted, his opponents viewed this as intolerance, whereas Freud's followers saw this trait as a passion for truth.

Whatever the case may be, Freud inarguably was deeply passionate about his intellectual pursuits, and had an enormous capacity for work. A look at his daily schedule gives a picture of how totally devoted he was to it. On a typical day, Freud saw his first patient at 8 A.M., and continued his clinical practice until 1 P.M., with a 5-minute break between sessions. At 1 P.M. he ate lunch and took a walk with his family. He then saw more patients from 3 until 9 or 10 P.M., followed by dinner and another walk with his wife. He then returned to his study and wrote from 11 until 1 or 2 A.M. This amounted to about an 18-hour workday. In commenting on this, Prochaska and Norcross (1999) note the irony that a man whose professional life was so devoted to understanding sex appeared to have left so little time in his life for his own sexuality.

Freud was a man of compassion, who cared deeply about his patients and people in general. His courage and passion for knowledge, though, truly stand out. These qualities were evidenced clearly in how he dealt with his terribly painful cancer of the jaw and palate. In 1923 he was operated on for this cancer, the first of 33 such operations. For 16 years Freud suffered agonizing pain. His speech, hearing, and eating were seriously affected. Despite the worsening cancer, Freud worked on, usually without medication (which he felt clouded his thinking), until his death in 1939. Some of his most profound works were produced during these years, including *An Outline of Psychoanalysis* (1940), his final statement about revised psychoanalytic theory.

For in-depth reading on Freud's life and the background of the psychoanalytic movement, the reader is referred to the three-volume biography by one of Freud's most trusted colleagues, Ernest Jones (1953, 1955, 1957).

PSYCHOANALYTIC INTERVENTIONS: SOME KEY DISTINCTIONS

To understand modern psychoanalytic thought, it is helpful to make some key distinctions that are often ignored in the psychoanalytic literature. Three such distinctions are discussed below.

Theories of the Person Versus Theories of the Treatment Process

Psychoanalysis is a diverse and complex set of assumptions, theories, and laws about how human beings develop as they do. There are psychoanalytic personality and development theories, and psychoanalytic theories of health and psychopathology. We call these viewpoints about human personality development, health, and psychopathology *theories of the person*. Later in this section, we shall present four theories of the person that are prominent in psychoanalysis.

In addition to developing theories of the person, psychoanalysis formulates theories of the treatment process. Such theories examine, for example, what goes on during analysis or therapy between the therapist and client and how the client's issues are expected to unfold within the hour and during the course of treatment. Psychoanalytic theories of treatment specify the techniques that the analyst or therapist is to use with the client and, more generally, how the therapist is to behave during the sessions.

Most psychoanalytic practitioners would agree that the therapist should strive for a deep understanding of both psychoanalytic theories of the person and psychoanalytic theories of intervention. At the same time, it is important to keep in mind that these two theories are by no means the same. One can conceptualize the individual client in psychoanalytic terms (using any psychoanalytic theory) but provide treatment that is decidedly nonanalytic. On the other hand, if the therapist conceptualizes the treatment process in analytic terms (e.g., focus on interpretation and insight, transference and countertransference), she or he has probably also relied on psychoanalytic formulations of the person.

The central point here is that when we talk about psychoanalysis, we need to be clear on whether we refer to formulations about the person (his or her personality, development, degree of health, and degree or kind of psychopathology) or about the treatment being offered.

Psychoanalytic Theory Versus Psychodynamic Theory

Although the words *psychoanalytic* and *psychodynamic* are often used interchangeably, it is useful to differentiate them. The word *psychodynamic* is the broader of the two. This word has different meanings to different people, but even differing definitions share the assumption that underlying processes (feelings, ideas, impulses, drives, etc.) influence much of overt behavior; that these underlying processes are often not at the conscious level; and that humans frequently use defense mechanisms to keep anxiety-provoking feelings, ideas, and impulses out of conscious awareness. Theories that are psychodynamic in nature may or may not be psychoanalytic (Robbins, 1989). For example, gestalt therapy is an explicitly psychodynamic theory, but just as clearly it is not psychoanalytic.

What then makes a theory *psychoanalytic?* In addition to incorporating unconscious processes and defense mechanisms (as do psychodynamic theories), virtually all modern psychoanalytic theories also (a) are developmental in that they posit a sequence to learning and development often in the form of stages that may be psychosexual (e.g., Freud, 1923/1961), psychosocial (e.g., Erikson, 1950), or relational (e.g., Mahler, Bergman, & Pine, 1975); (b) attend to the interplay of instinctual, social, interpersonal, and biological determinants (although theories vary in their emphasis on these four classes); and (c) subscribe to the primacy of mental functions

TABLE 10.1.   Levels of Psychoanalytic Interventions.

Treatment	Session Frequency (Per Week)	Duration	Major Techniques	Practitioner*
Psychoanalysis Proper	3–5	3–7 years	Interpretation Free association	Psychoanalyst
Psychoanalytically Oriented Therapy	1–2	a few months to years	Interpretation & others	Mental health professional
Supportive–Analytic Counseling	1	a few sessions to years	Support, suggestions, reinforcement	Mental health professional
Analytically Informed Counseling	1–3	varied	Technically eclectic	Mental health professional

Note: *Mental health professionals may be psychoanalysts, or nonpsychoanalyst psychologists, psychiatrists, social workers, or counselors.

or structures, which are constitutionally determined or learned early in life. Once these structures (e.g., the ego) are in place, they have a great impact on the person's life, including what environments and relationships are consciously or unconsciously sought out (Gelso & Hayes, 1998; Robbins, 1989). These ingredients are discussed further in the section, "Common Elements Among Psychoanalytic Approaches."

The distinction between psychodynamic and psychoanalytic theories largely pertains to theories of the person. When referring to theories of the treatment process, the distinction is much less clear and not especially useful. This is especially so when we move beyond "psychoanalysis proper," as discussed in the next section.

Levels of Psychoanalytic Intervention

When examining psychoanalytic interventions (the word *psychodynamic* also fits here), it is useful to differentiate among four levels of treatment: psychoanalysis proper, analytically oriented therapy, supportive–analytic therapy, and analytically informed therapy. These four levels are summarized in Table 10.1. Below we describe each level in greater detail.

Psychoanalysis Proper

Psychoanalysis is the most intensive and depth-oriented form of therapeutic intervention. Sessions occur usually 3–5 times a week, and analysis is virtually always long-term. Length of treatment is typically from 3–7 years. Analysis is carried out by a certified psychoanalyst, who ordinarily has received an M.D. degree with a specialization in psychiatry or a Ph.D. degree in psychology. After receiving the M.D. or Ph.D., the psychoanalyst receives several years of additional training in

✓ or the many psychoanalytic training institutes. For several ___ese training institutes only admitted practitioners with M.D. degrees, but during the 1980s (Slavin, 1989), training in psychoanalysis became widely available to psychologists.

Psychoanalysis proper is ordinarily carried out with the analyst sitting behind the analysand, while the analysand in turn reclines on a couch. The analysand's main task is to *free-associate;* that is, to say whatever comes to his or her mind without editing or trying to formulate intellectually the meaning of his or her associations. Another task of the analysand is to report dreams to the analyst. From the time of Freud's seminal work on the meaning of dreams (Freud, 1900/1938), dreams and their interpretation have held a special place in psychoanalysis. Analysts believe that dreams provide a powerful way of accessing the analysand's subconscious. On reporting dreams during the analysis, the analysand is asked to free-associate to parts of the dream. The analyst subsequently offers interpretations as to the meanings of these dreams in terms of the analysand's dynamic issues.

The analyst's task throughout the analysis is to be noninterfering, to offer what Freud called "even-hovering attention," and to make interpretations as the emerging material from the analysand makes sense to him or her. These interpretations should be close to the analysand's level of awareness and experience; if they become too removed from what the analysand is feeling, the treatment can become a sterile intellectual exercise.

Three interrelated features of the analyst's interactions with the analysand deserve special note because they are fundamental to psychoanalysis. First, throughout the work the analyst seeks to maintain what is called the *analytic attitude.* This attitude is one in which the analyst's most basic mission is to engage the analysand in an exploration—an investigation—of the analysand's internal world. Virtually all of the work is aimed at fostering this in-depth exploration and the resulting insights.

The second feature of the analyst's interaction with the analysand is the analyst's stance toward gratifying the analysand's wishes or demands to be loved and taken care of in the analysis. Given that all therapeutic interactions involve a strong press toward giving and receiving help, it is inevitable that the analysand experiences these wishes or demands. Yet the analyst follows Freud's *rule of abstinence* and in so doing avoids direct expressions of affection and advice. There are two good reasons for this. First, directly gratifying affectional and dependency needs runs the risk of fueling these needs and thus increases the likelihood that the analysand will become too attached to the treatment rather than to the goal of resolving his or her problems. Second, when such needs are gratified in the analysis itself, it is less likely that the underlying issues will become conscious. Thus gratification works against the analyst's mission of fostering insight.

The third element of the analyst's interaction that deserves special note is highly related to the first two. This element involves the analyst's stance of *neutrality* and *ambiguity.* This stance is often misunderstood by the beginning student, who interprets it as a kind of coldness, aloofness, or impersonality. This is far from the case in good analytic work. The analyst is deeply involved in the analysand's inner experience, and the analyst certainly cares about the analysand (see Greenson, 1967; Langs, 1976). Neutrality, however, implies that the analyst does not take sides in

the analysand's struggles. Although the analyst is o.
healthy ego, he or she does not, for example, agree or disa
feelings toward significant others in his or her life and genera.
sition on what the analysand should do in his or her life. Again, t.
to help the analysand understand himself or herself as deeply as poss.
position on what the analysand should do or who is right or wron.
analysand's struggles interferes with the analyst's main task.

The concept of ambiguity, similarly, implies that analysts should refrain fro.
displaying too much of their own issues, lives, viewpoints, and so forth. Such restraint provides an atmosphere in which the analysand's issues may unfold without
these being confounded by the analyst's. The analyst's ambiguity also permits the
analysand to project feelings and thoughts onto him or her, and in this way the all-
important transferences are allowed to develop more purely than would be the case
if the analyst's person intruded on the work.

During the course of analysis, as the analysand continues to free-associate and
the analyst carries out the tasks discussed above, the analysand naturally regresses
in his or her associations. That is, the analysand's associations and memories continually move backward in time (although not in a straight line). As this happens,
the analysand gets more and more into the childhood conflicts and issues that form
the fabric from which the present problems derive. Also, as this occurs, transference
reactions (discussed in Chapter 8) continue to develop and build.

If there is a pivotal point around which psychoanalysis revolves, it is this unfolding transference. Indeed, many analysts (e.g., Gill, 1994; Kernberg, 1975) define psychoanalysis itself as *the systematic analysis of the transferences*. As these
transferences develop, they become increasingly intense, until what is called a *transference neurosis* emerges. During this transference neurosis, it is as if great amounts
of energy are invested in the analyst, and the core of the analysand's neurosis gets
funneled into and fuels the analysis. At this stage the analyst becomes very central
to the analysand.

It must be remembered that transferences are by definition distortions of the
analyst. As defined in Chapter 8, *transference* is a repetition of past conflicts with
significant others, displacing feelings, behaviors, and attitudes belonging rightfully
in those earlier relationships onto the analyst or therapist. In psychoanalysis, the
key to helping the analysand resolve neurotic conflicts resides in providing insight
into the distortions involved in the transferences. As the transference intensifies, the
analyst maintains his or her ambiguity and neutrality, and this permits the continuing unfolding of these projections. The cure in analysis occurs as the transferences
are repeatedly interpreted, worked through, and resolved. The analyst's timing in
offering interpretations is crucial.

As the transferences are worked through, the analysand develops deep insight
into how his or her early conflicts cause him or her to distort and misperceive the
self and others. The analysand's defenses become reduced so that he or she can lead
a better life. Again, the aim of analysis is this depth insight, most centrally of the
analysand's hidden needs and issues, as manifested in the transferences. There is an
assumption that the amount and type of transference that develops in analysis reflect in a deep and significant way the analysand's inter- and intrapersonal conflicts

outside of the analytic setting. Thus working through the transferences in analysis deeply and positively affects the analysand's relations with others as well as with the self. It results in deep-seated changes in personality structure.

Psychoanalytically Oriented Therapy

Much of what is called psychoanalysis in beginning texts is really psychotherapy with an analytic orientation, rather than analysis proper, as described above. In psychoanalytic therapy the client and therapist usually sit face-to-face. Sessions are usually once or twice a week, and the duration of the work may be anywhere from a few months to several years. Although practitioners of psychoanalytic therapy may be certified psychoanalysts, they may also be psychologists, psychiatrists, and psychiatric social workers who are not analysts but who have training in psychoanalytic treatment.

Differences between analysis proper and analytic therapy are generally differences of degree rather than kind, and many believe these two treatments represent the same underlying processes (Fosshage, 1997). Because of the less frequent meetings, analytic therapy is not considered as intensive a treatment as analysis. Although transference reactions are central in this therapy, the therapist does not seek to cultivate the transference neurosis. Relatedly, free association may be used at times during analytic therapy, but it is not the modus operandi as in analysis. The focus tends to be on the problems the client is experiencing in his or her life and what is going on inside—the intrapsychic factors—that have made the client come to grief. Just as there is somewhat less focus on transference in this therapy, there is greater emphasis on helping the client cope with and solve real-life problems (as opposed to purely intrapsychic issues).

The therapist's stance in analytic therapy is very similar to the analyst's stance, and again the differences are matters of degree. Interpretation is still the major technique, but deviations from this interpretive stance are more frequent in therapy. The analytic therapist still subscribes to the analytic attitude, follows Freud's rule of abstinence, and maintains neutrality and ambiguity. But the therapist is more willing to depart from these positions, to be involved in a give-and-take interaction with the client, and to guide the session more actively. The goals of psychoanalytic therapy are similar to those of analysis, although psychoanalysts make the arguable point that the changes occurring in this treatment are not as pervasive and deep as in analysis.

Supportive–Analytic Counseling

Supportive–analytic counseling typically occurs in once-a-week sessions and takes place in a face-to-face context. This form of analytic intervention may last anywhere from a few sessions to several years. Long-term supportive–analytic therapy is most often indicated for clients who have severe emotional problems but for whom the more insight-oriented therapies are either not clinically dictated or are not possible because of situational constraints—for example, the client cannot afford more than once-a-week therapy, or the client needs supportive work. Briefer supportive–analytic counseling occurs when the client seeks help through a crisis and/or when the client or the situation does not allow for long-term insight-oriented work. The supportive–analytic therapist may be a psychoanalyst, psychologist, psychiatrist, or social worker.

Supportive–analytic therapy differs from analysis proper and analytic therapy in that the therapist is clearly more supportive in this approach and strives less for depth insight. In treating the client, the therapist has made the decision that he or she needs support and will not respond well to an insight-oriented approach. As part of the supportive stance, the therapist may provide appropriate suggestions, reassurance, and reinforcement to facilitate the client's positive steps in resolving life problems and to boost self-esteem. The therapist may at times take an educational posture, providing information and even teaching when necessary.

Analytically Informed Therapy or Counseling

Analytically informed counseling is actually not on the same continuum as the three interventions discussed above, but is included here because, in our opinion, it is the psychoanalytically related intervention that is most often used by counseling psychologists and other nonpsychoanalyst psychologists. In this treatment, psychoanalytic theories of the person are used to inform the work—to gain an understanding of the client and his or her dynamics as well as of how these dynamics are expected to play out in counseling or therapy. But the techniques and procedures used by the counselor are many and varied. In essence, the therapist uses an analytic theory of the person but does not necessarily use an analytic approach to the treatment. Rather, the therapist is technically eclectic in the sense that she or he uses whichever techniques and procedures seem to best fit the client.

An example of analytically informed therapy might be that of a therapist working in a university counseling center who conceptualizes student–clients in terms of dynamics and defenses and even formulates these defenses as id–ego conflicts, just as a classical psychoanalytic theorist would. This therapist, however, uses a range of techniques that take into account the fact that treatment at the center is brief and time-limited, having, for example, a 12-session duration limit. With a given student–client, for example, the therapist might use primarily gestalt therapy techniques (see Chapter 12) along with verbal reinforcement of behavior changes in the desired direction (see Chapter 11). Reflective techniques (Chapter 12) are also used to help the client explore feelings. All these techniques together might help shorten the treatment time from that if strictly analytic techniques, procedures, and attitudes were used; for example, analysis of transference, interpretation, analytic attitude, abstinence. The therapist also has greater latitude in terms of technique than is the case with supportive–analytic therapy and, unlike that treatment, this analytically informed counseling may or may not be supportive.

As the reader would suspect, analytically informed therapy may be practiced by counselors from several disciplines. It may occur once, twice, or even three times a week, and the duration of treatment depends more on the treatment setting than anything inherent in the treatment itself. In fact, techniques of treatment are often selected to fit the setting. For example, different techniques might be used in a university mental health clinic specializing in brief therapy than in a private clinic specializing in longer-term treatment.

A Perspective on Levels of Psychoanalytic Intervention

The main factor that differentiates psychoanalytically oriented practitioners is their theory of the person. Thus, for example, a psychoanalytic–self psychologist following the theories of Heinz Kohut (1971, 1977, 1984) would attend to somewhat different aspects of the personality than would an analytic practitioner using orthodox Freudian drive theory. These practitioners would attend to different issues because the theories they espouse make different, often divergent, statements about how personality develops, how intrapsychic problems occur, and the forces or factors that serve to foster health and psychopathology. At the same time, however, and with some notable exceptions, the levels of analytic intervention discussed above cut across the differing psychoanalytic theories of the person. Thus our discussion of psychoanalysis proper applies largely without regard to the analyst's perspective: Freudian drive theory, ego psychology, object relations theory, or psychoanalytic–self psychology. These different theoretical perspectives guide the practitioner's understanding of the person, and suggest content for the therapist to focus on; but the different theories generally say little about the process of treatment or how the therapist should work with the client. Below we explore each of the four main theory clusters that dominate psychoanalytic thought.

THE FOUR PSYCHOLOGIES OF PSYCHOANALYSIS

A common misconception is that psychoanalysis as a theory of the person and the treatment process is restricted to Freud's basic theories. Departures from Freudian conceptions are seen as something other than psychoanalysis, often given the ill-defined term, *psychodynamic*. In fact, many theories have developed within psychoanalysis, some being significant departures from Freudian ideas. During the past few decades in particular, major changes have occurred, changes that to many appear revolutionary in nature (Mitchell, 1993). As a way of organizing this growing diversity, several authors (e.g., Gelso & Hayes, 1998; Mishne, 1993; Pine, 1990) have divided the psychoanalytic pie into four theory clusters or what are referred to as "psychologies." The first two of these (in terms of their historical emergence) are Freud's *drive psychology* and *ego psychology*. These clusters are often referred to as classical psychoanalytic theory. The next two, *object relations theory* and *psychoanalytic self* psychology, have emerged into prominence in recent times, and may now be seen as ruling the theoretical roost in psychoanalysis (Gelso, 1995). Although there is significant overlap among the four psychologies of psychoanalysis, there are also substantial differences in their visions of human development, functioning, and therapy. Because of these differences, it is important for the student to understand the major features of the four psychologies. The four major theory clusters within psychoanalysis are summarized in Table 10.2. The key concepts for each cluster given on the right side of the table pertain to theories of the person rather than to treatment. This is because the key concepts about treatment are highly overlapping across the four clusters.

TABLE 10.2.   Summary of the Four Psychologies of Psychoanalysis.

Theory	Originator(s)	Key Concepts
Drive psychology	Sigmund Freud	Basic drives (sex and aggression) Psychosexual stages Unconscious processes
Ego psychology	Heinz Hartmann Anna Freud	Adaptation Ego defenses Ego strength and weakness
Object relations	Ronald Fairbairn Melanie Klein H. S. Sullivan	Human relatedness and relationships Internal representations
Self psychology	Heinz Kohut	Healthy and pathological narcissism Lines of development (grandiose self and omnipotent object) Empathy

Freud's Drive Psychology

In Freud's writing, *drive* and *instinct* are the same. They are part of our biology and a source of energy that produces psychic excitation. This excitation (or tension) stirs the individual toward action. The person does not of course feel a drive, but rather drives are experienced as urges, which themselves lead to wishes and fantasies. The key point is that the urges, wishes, and fantasies experienced by human beings are rooted in our biology in the form of basic drives. The specific urges that are experienced vary with the psychosexual stages the growing child is in, for example, oral, anal, phallic, latency, genital. Early experiences, especially with parents, are deeply important in Freud's drive psychology, but these experiences always occur in the context of basic drives, and affect the individual through the basic drives.

Freud's drive psychology posits two basic drives: sexuality and aggression. Not only does drive psychology seek to understand these two general drives, it also focuses on the urges that spring from them, on the conflicts such urges create, and on the defenses that humans use to keep potentially dangerous urges out of awareness. Many urges stir anxiety, guilt, or shame, and the individual responds by subconsciously repressing such urges through the use of defense mechanisms (e.g., repression, sublimation, projection, denial). Dangerous and conflictual urges thus become hidden, channeled, and transformed. As a result, the individual's actual behavior may appear very different from the underlying urges that the behavior expresses. For example, the client who seems perpetually "nice" may be unconsciously expressing his or her anxiety-provoking yearning to be loved, or perhaps his or her frightening aggressive urges. Or the excessively moralistic person may be defending against threatening sexual feelings. Innumerable examples may be generated of how outward behavior differs vastly from underlying urges, and the student is encouraged to reflect on such examples.

In the above summary of drive psychology, we can see basic Freudian concepts of sexual and aggressive instincts; psychosexual stages (e.g., oral, anal, phallic); and levels of consciousness (e.g., conscious, unconscious). Drive psychology is often referred to as an *id* psychology in the sense that the drives or instincts are seen as residing in the id (rather than in other agencies of the mind, such as ego or superego).

Regarding treatment, much of what we have described under "psychoanalysis proper" fits well with drive psychology. Perhaps the key feature of psychoanalytic treatment from a drive perspective is the attempt to understand the client's urges and wishes, and the defenses and conflicts surrounding them. Concepts such as therapist neutrality, ambiguity, and abstinence, as described under "psychoanalysis proper," are deeply rooted in drive psychology. So is the concept of transference as being almost purely the client's projection onto a neutral, ambiguous analyst. The unique person of the analyst matters little, as the analysand would transfer the same material unto any well-functioning analyst. The analyst's role is then to help the analysand understand these transference projections and resolve the conflicts underlying them.

Ego Psychology

Although Freud's early theorizing represented an id psychology, he eventually grew much more concerned with the role of ego (Freud 1923/1953). This concern became apparent when he created his famous structural model, where ego was given a key role, as it was in all of Freud's later theorizing. At the same time, in Freud's thinking, the ego grew out of and derived its energy from the id; and the ego's role was to erect defenses against the urges emanating from the id when those urges threatened the individual. The id was still the fundamental agency of the mind.

It remained for key figures such as Anna Freud (the daughter of Sigmund) and, in particular, Heinz Hartmann to craft an ego psychology in which the ego played a more fundamental role in psychic life (A. Freud, 1936/1966; Hartmann, 1939/1958). Hartmann, for example, viewed ego as the agency within the individual that enabled adaptation to the world outside the individual. Whereas drive psychology focuses on the taming, socialization, and gratification of drives, ego psychology "emphasizes the development of defenses with respect to the internal world, adaptation with respect to the external world, and reality testing with respect to both" (Pine, 1990, p. 50). Thus, to the ego analytic therapist, the ego does much more than erect defenses against threatening inner urges or against the dictates of a harsh superego. It is also the part of the mind that helps us adapt to our outer world, including the world of relationships and, through the process of perception, it helps us perceive relationships and other aspects of life realistically (referred to as reality testing).

Just as a strong healthy ego is part of emotionally healthy development, a weak or defective ego is seen as forming the seeds from which psychopathology grows. The ego's strength is determined by both constitutional factors and early family relationships. Once ego defects occur in early life, they have major implications for subsequent development. Such defects may result in the individual having weaknesses in reality testing, difficulties in regulating feelings, and a lack of firm boundaries between the self and others. Also, a weak ego is part of why people cannot control impulses effectively, why they have difficulty handling strong feelings, and why they may have panic reactions in certain situations (Mishne, 1993). Because early ego development is so crucial, psychoanalytic ego psychologists focus much of their theory on very early life, for example, prior to the oedipal period at age 4–6.

Psychoanalytic treatment from an ego psychology perspective is similar to therapy from a drive perspective. The concepts we have noted under "psychoanalysis proper" would apply readily to psychoanalysis within an ego analytic framework. The most distinctive feature of ego analytically oriented treatment is its content: A greater focus on the client's conscious experience and adaptation to the world outside, on reality testing in the world, and on the effectiveness of his or her defense mechanisms. Also, in psychoanalytically oriented therapy (as opposed to psychoanalysis proper), the therapist is likely to be more active and engage in more give-and-take as part of the focus on the client's adaptation to the outer world. When the client has a weak ego, the ego analytic therapist is more likely to take a supportive, reality-oriented, guiding approach to treatment.

Object Relations Theory

Object relations theory developed out of a belief by many that something fundamental was missing from drive and ego psychology: A central emphasis on human relationships and the human need for relatedness. There are several different theories that fall under the object relations umbrella, for example, those referred to as the relational perspective, attachment theory, and interpersonal theory (Greenberg & Mitchell, 1983; Mishne, 1993; Osofsky, 1995; Silverman, 1998). Although viewpoints within the general object relations camp often seem to clash, the tie that binds them all, and differentiates object relations theory from the other psychoanalytic theories, is the proposition that people are fundamentally object- or relationship-seeking rather than drive- or pleasure-seeking. (Note: the word *object* in psychoanalysis is generally used as a substitute for the word *person*.) In this sense, all object relations theories posit an inherent tendency toward relatedness and relationships. This need is hard-wired into us as a basic part of human nature (Eagle, 1984).

Although object relations theories are deeply concerned with human attachments and relationships, that is not their sole concern. Also crucial is the concept of *internal representations*. These representations are usually formed early in life, and are of significant others (e.g., parents, siblings). Representations are far from exact replicas. They are based on how the other is experienced by the person, which is itself determined by many factors. Pine (1990) captures the essential role of such representations.

> [T]he individual is seen in terms of an internal drama, derived from early childhood, that is carried around within memory (conscious or unconscious) and in which the individual enacts one or more or all of the roles. . . . These internal images, loosely based on childhood experiences, also put their stamp on new experience, so that these in turn are assimilated to the old dramas rather than being experienced fully in their contemporary form. These internal dramas are understood to be formed out of experiences with the primary objects of childhood, but are not seen as veridical representations of those relationships. The object relation *as experienced* by the child is what is laid down in memory and repeated, and this experience is a function of the affect and wishes active in the child at

the moment of the experience . . . the same quietly pensive and inactive mother will be experienced as a depriver by the hungry child, but perhaps as comfortingly in tune by the child who is contentedly playing alone. Significant for the clinical relevance of the object relations psychology is the tendency to repeat these old dramas, a repetition propelled by the efforts after attachment or after mastery or both (pp. 34–35).

The psychologically healthier person has greater ability to take current relations for what they are, rather than experiencing and perceiving the present to a great extent as a repetition of internal representations. Also, for the healthier person, the representations are more positive, nurturant, and supportive. Regarding the internal drama referred to by Pine (1990), stated simply, some dramas are healthier (more positive) than others (Gelso & Hayes, 1998).

What is psychoanalytic treatment like from an object relations perspective? How might such treatment differ from therapy derived from the other psychoanalytic clusters? As we have noted, the single most distinctive feature of object relations oriented treatment is the central focus on relationships in the client's life and on the client–therapist relationship. Although drive psychology is more oriented toward relationships than it is often given credit for (see Frank, 1998), to the object relations therapist, interpersonal relationships, internal representations of earlier relationships, and the therapeutic relationship are the pivotal points around which everything else revolves. Since the client is inherently object- and relationship-seeking, even when defending against this basic need, the therapist becomes a key person to be related to; and the person of the therapist matters a great deal. Everything the therapist does contributes to the relationship (including the transference), and in fact, the therapist along with the client shape that relationship. Even the therapist's neutrality contributes. In other words, the person of the therapist is seen as more important in object relations therapies than other analytic approaches.

Gelso and Hayes (1998) note that to current object relations theorists, the client–therapist relationship is seen as having curative elements in itself. The good therapeutic relationship allows the client to "rework internal object representations so that the images carried with the person are more constructive and more responsive to realities of current relationships, rather than distortions of them" (p. 176). Although transference and countertransference are quite central, there is also a deep person-to-person relationship that coexists with transference that helps heal the client's emotional wounds.

Psychoanalytic Self Psychology

This fourth and most recent psychology of psychoanalysis has developed out of the writings of Heinz Kohut (1971, 1977, 1984). As the term implies, *psychoanalytic self psychology* is concerned with development of the self; the word *narcissism* is often used liberally as a synonym for self. Rather than reflecting psychopathology as in other theories, narcissism is seen as a fundamental characteristic of all persons, a characteristic that may develop in healthy or unhealthy ways, depending on how the growing child is responded to by parents and other significant persons in his or her life.

In Kohut's original work (Kohut 1971), he posited two lines of self or narcissistic development: That of the grandiose self and that of the omnipotent object. The first of these pertains to the young child's sense of greatness and need to show off his or her accomplishments. The proper mirroring of these needs by parents (e.g., genuinely appreciating the child's accomplishments) results in healthy maturation of the grandiose exhibitionistic self.

The second line of self development (the omnipotent object) reflects the child's need for all-powerful parent figures. This connection between the self and the all-powerful self–object provides the child with strength and protection. As the child gradually sees that the parent is imperfect, the child is able to internalize the strength that the parents had provided. Problems of the self occur if parents fail to provide sufficient empathic mirroring and all-powerful self–object experiences. As examples of self or narcissistic problems, the child may grow to feel empty inside, constantly crave attention, continually seek all-powerful figures to align and merge with, lack sustained emotional energy, or be unable to love others as others (rather than as extensions of the self).

Analytic therapy from a self psychology perspective follows from the developmental issues noted above. Growth occurs importantly through the client's connection with an empathic therapist who mirrors the client's needs, and who allows himself or herself to be idealized by the client. The client's experience of the therapist as a good mirror and an all-powerful parent figure are referred to, respectively, as mirror transferences and idealizing transferences. Through understanding and interpretation, the therapist helps the client work through these transferences and the profound self issues they reflect.

In comparison to therapies conducted from the perspective of the other three psychologies, the self psychologist is more likely to focus on empathically understanding the client or analysand. Empathy aids therapy because it allows the therapist to deeply understand the client's inner world and thus form more effective interpretations. It is also seen by self psychologists as curative in itself through its direct effects on the client (e.g., Wolf, 1991).

Psychoanalytic self psychologists are deeply concerned with being responsive to the client, and seek to develop—more than the other analytic approaches—a climate of "interested and attuned responsiveness" (Doctors, 1996; MacIsaac, 1996; Wolf, 1991). The therapist aims to provide as much empathy, support, and guidance as is necessary to facilitate the process of "uncovering, illuminating, and transforming" the client's needs (Linden, 1994).

COMMON ELEMENTS AMONG PSYCHOANALYTIC APPROACHES

Now that we have reviewed the four basic theory clusters within psychoanalysis, we may ask the question, "What elements are common among all psychoanalytic theories?" We briefly referred to such common elements when differentiating the words *psychoanalysis* and *psychodynamics*. Now we shall elaborate the eight ingredients that are characteristic of all psychoanalytic theories of the person and the treatment process.

Psychic Determinism

Generally speaking, scientific theories in psychology are deterministic, which implies that behavior is caused or determined and may thus be explained in terms of those causes or determinants. Psychoanalytic theories are no different from other scientific theories in this sense. Where psychoanalytic theories do tend to differ, however, is in their emphasis on *intrapsychic* factors as determinants. Such an approach may be most readily contrasted to behavioristic theories (Chapter 11), which are also deterministic but which do not look inside the person's mind or psyche for causes. For the behaviorist, causes are to be found outside the person, in terms of the outside reinforcers and punishers of behavior. In psychoanalytic theories, in contrast, a variety of factors (biological, social, familial) are seen as shaping the person's intrapsychic world early in life. Once this intrapsychic world or psyche is formed, it becomes a crucial determinant of behavior. The psyche contains the basic structures in the form of id, ego, superego; basic drives, wishes, beliefs, conflicts, and needs; and differing levels of consciousness.

One derivative of the principle of psychic determinism that has great implications for psychoanalytic treatments is that because virtually all of the client's behaviors are caused by the interplay of these intrapsychic forces, all behavior in treatment is seen as meaningful. Everything the client does and says has purpose, meaning, and relevance to the therapist's understanding of and working with that client, and psychoanalytic practitioners place a premium on understanding their clients in terms of these intrapsychic determinants.

The Genetic–Developmental Hypothesis

A fundamental assumption of all psychoanalytic theories is that the past crucially determines the present and that in order to understand the present inter- and intrapersonal functioning of the client as fully as possible, we need to examine the person's past. What is meant by the past is usually the person's childhood years, and the more classical analytic theories tend to focus on the earliest years as the key in personality development. For example, in analytic theories such as orthodox Freudian, object relations, and self psychological theories, the first 6–7 years of life are seen as crucial to the development of one's basic personality.

The genetic–developmental hypothesis not only implies that the client's childhood is crucial in personality formation and in health/psychopathology, this model also incorporates the idea of developmental stages. Thus Robbins (1989) notes that all contemporary psychoanalytic theories subscribe to stages of development. Just what defines these stages, however, may differ across the various analytic theories. Freudian theory, for example, posits what are called *psychosexual* stages—oral, anal, phallic, latency, and so forth. For a clear discussion of these stages, with implications for counseling interventions, the reader is referred to Patton and Meara's (1992) work. Erikson's theory, on the other hand, conceptualizes personality development in terms of a series of *psychosocial* stages (see Erikson, 1950, 1968).

The psychoanalytic implications of stage theory become clearer when we consider two additional concepts: *fixation* and *regression*. Using the earlier years as an example, as children pass through the various stages of development, whether psychosexual or psychosocial stages, their healthy development is facilitated by parents who gratify their psychological needs to an optimum extent. Too much gratification or, as is more often the case, too much deprivation of needs that become most pressing during given stages will result in fixation or regression, or both. Part of the child's psyche becomes stuck (fixated) at the stage in which he or she experienced too much frustration, or the psyche regresses back to an earlier stage at which there was neither too much nor too little frustration. Once fixation or regression occurs during development, the remnants of this tend to show themselves in one's personality throughout development. The seeds of the neuroses and other psychological difficulties are to be found in the person's childhood experiences of frustration or overgratification of needs and in the resulting tendency to become fixated or to regress. (See Fenichel's [1945] psychoanalytic classic for a full discussion of fixation and regression.)

What are the implications of the genetic–developmental hypothesis for intervention? Just as the past determines the present, and just as the seeds of human emotional problems are contained in childhood, so the most powerful and far-reaching treatments facilitate the in-depth exploration of childhood issues. Even more, the most powerful treatments, from the analytic perspective, aid the client in emotional reliving and working through of the early experiences that form the core of his or her neurosis. (Note that we are not talking about a sterile, intellectual inspection of the past, but rather an emotional reliving of it in the present.) It is not that all psychoanalytically based treatments do, in fact, require this exploration and reliving. Many do not, especially for practical reasons, for example, time constraints. And analytic practitioners generally would agree that effective treatment can be carried out in the absence of an in-depth examination of the past. Yet psychoanalytic theories believe that such examination makes for the most effective intervention.

The Centrality of the Unconscious

In essentially all psychoanalytic theories of the person, primacy is placed on forces outside of the person's conscious awareness that motivate behavior. In Freud's earlier theorizing, the conscious mind had only a relatively minor role in determining behavior. As we have noted, early Freudian psychology was an id psychology. With the development of ego psychology by Freud and others (e.g., Anna Freud, Heinz Hartmann), significantly more attention was given to conscious experience, since much of the ego involved the conscious mind. In contemporary psychoanalytic thought, consciousness continues to play a more important role than in early Freudian theory.

Be that as it may, unconscious factors are still seen as extremely important in personality development within all analytic theories, and the most effective interventions work, at least to an extent, to make the unconscious conscious. Underlying and unconscious beliefs, wishes, and needs are seen as being implicated in most or all pathological symptoms and behaviors. And from an analytic perspective, the most effective treatments must go beyond work on those symptoms or overt and maladaptive behavior. Interventions need to work with and through the unconscious, core conflicts underlying the symptoms. This value on making the unconscious conscious can be seen in Freud's famous dictum regarding the goals of analytic treatment: "where there was id there shall be ego."

Most analytic practitioners, it should be stressed, would agree that treatment may still be effective without making the unconscious conscious or resolving core unconscious conflicts. Indeed, research conducted at the Menninger Clinic on several types of psychoanalytic interventions clearly supports the view that durable change can occur in the absence of such resolutions (Wallerstein, 1989). The general view, though, is that (a) unconscious processes are tremendously important in personality development, and (b) the most effective treatments help clients, at least to some extent, become conscious of previously unconscious conflicts, beliefs, and so forth.

The Role of Defenses

The concept of defense is a key one in contemporary psychoanalytic theories. As discussed by Brenner (1973) and further clarified in Patton and Meara (1992), a defense is any operation of the mind that aims to ward off anxiety or depression. Defenses are usually thought about in terms of the now well-known defense mechanisms, for example, repression, denial, rationalization, intellectualization, isolation, projection, displacement, and reaction formation. In essence, one may experience wishes, impulses, thoughts, beliefs, or affects that are seen as bad or potentially harmful to oneself. For example, they threaten loss of love from parental figures; abandonment; or punishment, either from one's conscience or external figures. These wishes (for example) are prevented from becoming conscious, and thus from causing anxiety or depression, by the use of defenses. The wishes are usually seen as coming from the id, and it is the ego that erects defenses against them to protect the individual from internal punishment (from the superego) or external harm.

Although defense mechanisms are often seen as operations of the ego, one can view them more broadly as any intrapsychic operations that reduce anxiety or other painful states. Thus, personality traits, attitudes, and perceptions could serve as defenses. For example, the character trait of extreme orderliness may serve as a defense against anxiety caused by the individual's impulses or wishes to be messy and out of control. Why such wishes would cause anxiety in the first place may be explained in terms of the specifics of the individual's interactions with parents, often during the anal stage, the psychosexual stages during which issues of control are primary.

Regarding treatment, psychoanalytic interventions seek to affect defenses. The aim may be to reduce or eliminate defenses or to help the client institute healthier defenses. Through working with and on the client's defenses, the treatment helps previously unconscious or subconscious reactions to become conscious and thus to be under the client's rational control. Working through defenses also frees up energy that had been expended unconsciously in maintaining these defenses so that it may be used for healthier purposes. In effective therapy, the therapist is highly sensitive to the issue of the client's need for his or her defenses. Therapeutic interventions are paced such that defenses are worked on and through as the client is emotionally ready to give them up.

Repetition and Transference

From the time of Freud's early theorizing, psychoanalytic theorists have noted how the individual's past unresolved problems get repeated and lived out in present life and, in turn, how the individual's emotional problems in the present are tied to unresolved conflicts in the past. Freud's in-depth analysis of the compulsion to repeat, the *repetition compulsion,* was his attempt to struggle with and understand why the conflictual past is so often repeated in the present and why in fact people distort the present so that it becomes consistent with the past (see Gelso and Carter's [1985] discussion [pp. 169–173]). This concept of repetition has become a deep and inherent part of contemporary as well as earlier psychoanalytic theory, and the repetition of unresolved conflicts tends to be viewed as a universal aspect of the human experience.

Examples of the kind of repetition we are referring to abound in clinical practice and in everyday life. The client who has experienced too much or too early loss (emotional or physical) in his or her early years with parents tends to carry a fear of being abandoned by others. He or she responds to friends and lovers as if they were similar to his or her parents, clings to them for fear of being again abandoned and thus pushes others away. The client who constantly oscillates between defiance and excessive obedience with authority figures (bosses) at work is repeating in the present the early and unresolved issues with a dominant father, toward whom the person felt fearful when defiant and angry when obedient. The client who needs to attract and conquer women but loses interest after doing so is acting out the unresolved conflict originating in his relationship with mother and father much earlier in his life.

Psychoanalytically based interventions seek to help the client understand repetitions such as those above, and through this understanding the client is able to perceive the present more accurately or at least to better control the repetitions. It should be noted that analytic treatment would not seek to help the client understand and work through all such repetitions. Rather, the therapist or analyst will tend to focus on certain core issues and the repetitions stemming from them. Usually, the focus would be on the issue or issues that were causing the greatest suffering in the client's life.

A key point regarding analytic treatment and repetition is that the unresolved issues going back to earlier times in the client's life tend to get played out in the treatment hour itself, especially through the transferences that are developed toward the therapist/analyst. This fact gives the therapist a powerful tool for dealing with neurotic repetitions. That is, as sufficient material unfolds to allow for convincing interpretations, the therapist is able to point out to the client how he or she is distorting in the present real-life situation of the therapy, and how these distortions (i.e., transferences) represent repetitions. Therapist and client can thus work together to seek understanding of the client's issues underlying the distortions.

Common Elements of All Psychoanalytic Theories.   **TABLE 10.3.**

Concept	Basic Proposition
Psychic determinism	Human reactions are caused by intrapsychic factors.
Genetic–developmental hypothesis	Early childhood crucially determines personality, psychological health, and psychopathology. Development occurs in stages (psychosexual or psychosocial).
Unconscious processes	Unconscious processes are crucial determinants of human behavior.
Defense mechanisms	Threatening internal impulses are repressed by unconscious defense mechanisms.
Repetition and transference	Humans tend to repeat in the present unresolved issues from the past. Insight into transference, a form of repetition, can greatly benefit the client.
Therapy relationship	The client–therapist relationship is of central importance, especially the working alliance and transference components of the relationship.
Treatment techniques	Interpretation is the key technique of insight-oriented therapy.
Client insight	Insight is the key internal mechanism that instigates and represents change in behavior.

The Role of the Client–Therapist Relationship

In an early large-scale investigation of psychotherapy (Sloane et al., 1975), the researchers noted that for the psychoanalytic therapists they studied, the client–therapist relationship and psychoanalytic treatment were almost synonymous. The client–therapist relationship is extremely central to the process and outcome of treatment in virtually all contemporary psychoanalytic interventions (Gelso & Hayes, 1998).

In trying to understand the particular ways in which the relationship is central, it is useful to think back to Chapter 8, where components of the therapeutic relationship were discussed: the working alliance, the transference configuration, and the real relationship. Although all contemporary psychoanalytic approaches to treatment would agree that a sound working alliance is essential if analytic work is to be effective, the real hallmark of psychoanalytic interventions is attention to the transference relationship, including therapist countertransference. For what we have labeled "psychoanalysis proper," cultivation, interpretation, and working through of the transferences are the heart of treatment. For analytic interventions other than analysis proper, transference is still central in terms of its unfolding and interpretation in the work and/or its use as a vehicle to aid the therapist in understanding the client's dynamics. The real relationship, on the other hand, has not been an important part of psychoanalytic thinking, although because of conceptualizations such as

Greenson's (1967), greater emphasis on the real relationship has appeared in recent years (Gelso & Hayes, 1998).

Interpretation and Other Techniques

In the sense of verbal response modes as discussed in Chapter 9, the single technique that distinguishes psychoanalytic treatments from other therapies is *interpretation*. In his classic treatise on psychoanalysis, Greenson (1967) notes that interpretation is the ultimate and decisive instrument. Other techniques are seen as deviations from this baseline and are to be used only in exceptional circumstances. For example, when conducting psychoanalysis the analyst may on rare occasions offer direct guidance, but for him or her to do so, there would need to be a clear and pressing need, for example, an indication that the analysand will do something that would have long-term and very negative consequences.

The aim of interpretations is to provide insight; that is, to help make conscious what was heretofore unconscious. The analyst allows the analysand's material to unfold during the hour or a series of hours and, when the time is right, offers an interpretation. Such interpretations seek to illuminate the hidden connections between aspects of the analysand's communications and/or uncover hidden causes. In fact, as Greenson (1967) clarifies, rather than making a single interpretation, the analyst usually offers a series of partial interpretations over a period of sessions, each aimed at shedding light on particular dynamics. Great emphasis is placed on offering interpretations that are well timed, constitute an effective dosage, and are tactfully presented. Timing is perhaps the most complex of these issues. Interpretations are well timed if the client is ready to hear and work with them, and for this to be the case, sufficient material pertinent to that interpretation needs to have already come to light. Only then will there be enough emotional evidence to make the interpretation convincing to the client.

In psychoanalytic treatments other than psychoanalysis proper, interpretation is still a key technique, although greater latitude is permitted to the therapist. As we move from analysis proper to analytically oriented therapy to supportive–analytic therapy, there is an increasing flexibility in technique. More active techniques, even those in the category of directives (see Chapter 9), may of course be used very carefully and with a well-thought-out rationale. (These comments would not apply so clearly to what we have termed "analytically informed" therapy because this form of therapy is eclectic regarding techniques.) An especially helpful discussion of the interpretive process within the context of psychological counseling is presented by Patton and Meara (1992). We should note that, although interpretation continues to be seen as the most powerful and appropriate technique in psychoanalysis, there has been a trend in recent years toward permitting a broader range of techniques and seeing other techniques as useful (Fosshage, 1997; Holinger, 1999).

The Ideal of Insight

Baker (1985) states that, broadly speaking, all forms of psychoanalytic treatment tend to share five basic psychotherapeutic goals: (1) a reduction in the intensity of irrational impulses and a corresponding increase in the mature management of instinctual striving; (2) an enhancement of the repertoire, maturity, effectiveness, and flexibility of defenses used by the individual; (3) the development and support of values, attitudes, and expectations based on an accurate assessment of reality and that facilitate effective adaption; (4) the development of capacity for mature intimacy and productive self-expression; and (5) lessening of punitiveness of superego and perfectionism rooted in the demands and prohibitions of the conscience.

What is the mechanism or vehicle for the attainment of these goals? The central internal mechanism in psychoanalysis is called *insight* (Gelso & Hayes, 1998). Thus, it is through insight, attained during the treatment hour and beyond, that the client is enabled to move forward and attain the healthy goals noted by Baker. Such insight fosters healthy goal attainment through essentially two means. First and foremost, through the self-awareness that comes with insight, the client experiences increased conscious control (Baker, 1985). When needs, impulses, and strivings are brought under conscious control, the client is better able to make logical choices and is less driven by self-destructive and nonproductive patterns of behavior. The second means through which insight facilitates attainment of healthy goals is called "objectification of the self." In essence, through insight, the client is better able to stand back and observe himself or herself and thus gain a clearer and more accurate perspective.

What precisely do we mean by *insight?* Patton and Meara (1992) define *insight* as client and therapist production and understanding of factors within the client that contribute to his or her emotional difficulties. Within the treatment itself, client insight may pertain to any of a number of arenas: how present conflicts are related to past issues; the defenses being employed; the feelings and needs being covered; how one's conflicts are being played out in current life; how these conflicts are being acted out in the transference relationship with the therapist, and so forth.

In psychoanalytic writing, two kinds of insight are often differentiated. *Intellectual insight* reflects an understanding of cause–effect relationships in one's life but lacks depth because it does not connect this understanding to one's feelings. It is more like observing the self from a distance, without the feelings that go along with what is being observed. *Emotional insight,* on the other hand, connects affect to intellect—the client is emotionally connected to his or her understanding. As the client comes to understand his or her issues, strong feelings are likely to surface. The simultaneous experience of self-understanding with these feelings is insight in the most powerful and curative sense, emotional insight.

We must note that not all treatments of a psychoanalytic nature strive for depth insight. The shorter more focused treatments (e.g., less than 6 months), while often insight-oriented, tend to promote more limited insight into one or a few central problem areas. In addition, even long-term work of an analytic nature may not strive for depth insight when the therapist believes that support is the client's crucial need. This may be especially the case with the more troubled client whose fragile ego and/or degree of dysfunction dictates supportive strategies. Nonetheless, in contemporary psychoanalytic approaches of all types, insight tends to be seen as the most powerful vehicle for deep and durable change in the client, and it is to be sought whenever the clinical situation allows.

TIME-LIMITED PSYCHOTHERAPY (TLP): AN APPROACH FOR COUNSELING PSYCHOLOGISTS

Of the many different psychoanalytic approaches to treatment, the ones that seem most relevant to the counseling psychologist are those that shorten the usually very long-term nature of psychoanalytic treatment. Such approaches gained popularity over the decades of the 1980s and 1990s for many reasons (see Chapter 4; Johnson & Gelso, 1980; Messer & Warren, 1995). There is now a wide range of brief psychoanalytic and psychodynamic therapies (see comprehensive reviews by Crits-Christoph and Barber [1991] and Messer and Warren [1995]). All of these approaches share some common assumptions about brief analytic interventions: (a) clients who have long-standing psychological problems could be treated with dynamically based therapy in a much shorter time than had been previously thought; (b) basic principles of psychoanalytic/psychodynamic treatment could be applied to time-limited treatments; and (c) time-abbreviated therapies could effect lasting changes in the client's basic personality.

In this section, we shall discuss one approach that seems well suited to the work of counseling psychologists: James Mann's Time-Limited Psychotherapy, or TLP (Mann, 1973, 1991; Messer & Warren, 1995). This psychoanalytic approach is compatible with counseling psychology's emphasis on clients' strengths, is suited to work with intact personalities, and places a premium on brevity. TLP uses a 12-session limit, which is established at the beginning or in the early phase of the work. This time limitation fits well with the growing emphasis in professional psychology in general on abbreviating treatments.

In focusing on TLP, we do not mean to imply that it is the only brief dynamic approach suited to the work of the analytically oriented counseling psychologist. Our aim in presenting Mann's approach in some detail is to provide an example of how psychoanalytic principles are applied systematically to a brief therapy. Other brief analytic/dynamic therapies, however, also have relevance to counseling psychology. Strupp and Binder's time-limited dynamic therapy, for example, has some features very similar to Mann's, and may be the treatment of choice when more extended time-limited work (25–30 sessions) is preferred (Binder & Strupp, 1991; Strupp & Binder, 1984). The counseling psychology student (or agency) interested in time-limited analytic treatment may well study both approaches in tandem in developing his or her own time-limited strategies.

James Mann's Time-Limited Psychotherapy

James Mann, a Boston psychoanalyst, developed an approach to time-limited therapy that more than any other seeks to capitalize on universal human conflicts about time on the one hand, and separation and loss on the other. His time-limited psychotherapy (TLP) has an explicit 12-session duration, and a beginning, middle, and ending phase. TLP is an approach that can be used within the framework of each of the four theoretical clusters that we have described. In fact, although Mann does not explicitly say so, careful reading of his theory suggests that in TLP all four psychologies (drive theory, ego psychology, object relations theory, and self psychology) come into play, depending on the needs and issues of individual clients. In this sense, TLP may be seen as an integrative analytic approach (Messer & Warren, 1995).

Personality, Dynamics, and Dysfunction

According to Mann, the recurring life crisis of separation–individuation is the basis upon which his TLP rests. This crisis is rooted in the separation–individuation phase, which occurs from around the third month through the third year of life. During this phase, individuals must psychologically separate from their primary caretakers, usually the mother, if they are to develop their own selves and individuality. Yet there always is a conflict about such separation, for it entails giving up the wonderful gratification and omnipotence tied to the mother–infant bond. Giving up such things is always a loss, and this is perhaps the original loss in a long series of losses that the individual inevitably faces throughout life. A key loss that stems from separation and individuation is that of a sense of infinite time. As the person grows, she or he must face the fact that time is finite, that life itself must end.

If the issues around separation from mother during the separation–individuation phase are not handled effectively by the parents, the individual is left with a special vulnerability to issues of separation and loss. Since parenting around this issue, as with all issues, is imperfect, however, all of us have some conflicts about separation. These conflicts are fueled throughout life by the losses most people typically experience, even as they gain new things, for example, the losses incurred at weaning, the Oedipal stage, puberty, college or work, marriage, birth of children, menopause, and old age. In addition to the typical losses involved in such life events and stages, Mann points out, there are countless experiences throughout life that revive repeatedly the sense of loss and anxiety related to the separation–individuation phase. Loss of money, of power, of a relationship, of self-esteem, and of a job—these are obvious examples, but there are many other subtle losses that form a constant accompaniment to life.

If the recurring life crisis of separation–individuation is the foundation of TLP, resolution of issues around the self is the primary goal. Thus, Mann (1991) repeatedly refers of diminishing negative self-image, enhancing sense of self, and improving self-concept as the basic goals of TLP. Strengthening the ego, enhancing positive internal representations, fostering adaptation are also noted, but issues around the self seem most fundamental to TLP.

Treatment Agreement and the Central Issue

TLP begins with 1–3 consultation interviews, during which the therapist seeks to understand the client's *central issue,* and the guidelines for treatment are clearly established. Once the therapist has decided that 12-session TLP is suitable, this limit is presented very explicitly during the initial phase. The 12 sessions, typically held weekly, begin at this point.

When Mann presents this time-duration guideline to his clients, he goes so far as to mark the ending date of his calendar in the presence of the client, driving home the point that the treatment relationship is limited in time. This limitation sets into motion a series of dynamic events (described in the next section) that is the key feature of TLP. Clients will at times ask the therapist if he or she believes that 12 sessions will be enough, given that the issues may be long-standing. The response is always a clear and unequivocal "yes," as the therapist's confidence in the treatment is essential.

A crucial event in TLP is the therapist's statement of the client's central issue. Here the therapist makes use of his or her psychoanalytic understanding to detect an underlying dynamic theme or pattern in the client's life that has roots in the past, exists in the present, and is expected by the client to be an issue in the foreseeable future. Because of its continuity in the client's life, Mann refers to the central issue as reflecting the client's *present and chronically endured pain.* In order to detect this theme or pattern, the therapist must make use of his or her empathic ability. As the client relates many painful incidents, the therapist asks himself or herself, "How must this person have felt about himself or herself as he or she was experiencing, living, and enduring the particular incident" (Mann, 1991, p. 25)? This question is silently repeated many times as the therapist tries to frame the client's central issue.

The central issue is almost never the same as the client's explicit reason for seeking help. Clients seek therapy for anxiety, depression, interpersonal problems, addictions, and other symptoms. The central issue, however, reflects deep underlying self issues that have plagued the client's existence from very early in his or her life. Further, the central issue must be framed for the client in feeling terms, never in technical jargon. Witness the following examples given by Mann (1991, pp. 32–33):

> To a 36-year-old member of a minority [group] who found himself in a conflictual situation in his field of work and became physically sick followed by depression: "You are a man of ability in your particular field and have done very well in it. Yet you feel and have always felt that there is something about you that makes you feel that you are unwanted, even irrelevant."

> To a 42-year-old woman who suffered an acute disorganizing experience, which led her to consider divorce: "You have tried hard all your life to be and to do acceptable things. What hurts you now and always has is the feeling that you are stupid and a phony."

> To a 22-year-old man, a graduate student struggling with the question of staying in or leaving school: "You are a man of high intelligence and you know it. You also know that you can succeed in the work you have begun. However, what bugs you now and always has is the feeling that you are second-rate, unacceptable."

> To a 35-year-old professional man with an acute phobia: "You are a big man (physically and in his field of work) who has achieved success and yet when you are alone you feel helpless."

Once the central issue is established, the therapist maintains his or her focus on it, being sure not to deviate into other issues or problems. To be effective, TLP must be a focused therapy. To be sure, the client's past is explored and connected to the present, but this exploration is limited to experiences directly relevant to the central issue.

Sequence of Dynamic Events

The strict time limit and the clear statement of a central issue set into motion a series of dynamic events. Proscription of time runs counter to and stirs up the unconscious and infantile fantasy of timelessness and unending union with an all-giving parental figure. The time limit and statement of a central issue also give the client a sense that his or her problems are understandable and can be resolved. The client experiences *at once* a sense of optimistic urgency, pessimism, and disappointment.

TLP consists of three stages, each lasting roughly 3–4 sessions. In the first, negative feelings about termination and endings are repressed, as is indeed the termination date itself. The limitation of time, the selection of a central focus that is both consciously meaningful and connected to significant unconscious issues, and the therapist's confidence that something can be done in a short time all come together to mobilize the client's optimism. An intensely positive transference develops in this initial stage. As a result of these positive affects, Mann asserts that one regularly sees rapid symptomatic improvement during the first stage. The client feels better and seems to be getting better. Important aspects of the current problem, how the client has coped with it, and its roots in the past are all explored. The client bares his or her soul. There is a great temptation on the part of the therapist to explore peripheral issues, but he or she must refrain from doing so. Instead, the therapist maintains the focus and actively seeks to understand and support the client in his or her exploration.

As the work continues into the second stage, the client's enthusiasm begins to wane. The client says, in effect, "There is so much to be done, and so little time." This is a clear signal to the therapist that the honeymoon is over. Negative transference takes the place of the previous positive transference. Mann notes that the characteristic feature of any middle point is that

> one more step, however small, signifies the point of no return . . . the client must go on to a conclusion that he does not wish to confront. The confrontation that he needs to avoid and that he will actively seek to avoid is the same one he suffered earlier in his life; namely, *separation without resolution from the meaningful, ambivalently experienced person* (1973, p. 34).

As these feelings and defenses emerge, the therapist's stance, while still supportive of the client's simultaneous growth strivings, becomes more interpretive. The therapist begins to interpret how feelings about the therapist and about ending are tied to earlier feelings about separation and about transference sources, usually parents. All of this is done within the context of the central issue.

Emerging feelings about separation and endings signal entrance into the third and final stage. According to Mann, the last three or four sessions must deal insistently with the client's reaction to termination. This does not mean that the total focus of the sessions is on ending but rather that issues about ending are a central theme during the last stage. The therapist is tempted here to evade such termination work, since she or he, too, has conflicts around separation. Yet such work must not be avoided. Attention to termination and helping the client see how feelings about separation relate to the central problem and stem from unresolved issues in the past, are deeply growth-enhancing. They not only help the client grow in terms of the central focus but also help him or her work through separation issues as manifested in one or more of the four conflict situations (independence–dependence, activity–passivity, self-esteem, unresolved grief).

The Therapist and the Client in TLP

The therapist is more active in TLP than in most analytic interventions, especially psychoanalysis per se. The therapist is questioning, encouraging, supportive, and educative. Regarding this last role, although the therapist should never lecture, she or he may provide information to the client when that seems useful. As the second stage is entered, the therapist becomes more interpretive. She or he seeks to clarify and interpret the client's resistances and, especially in the latter part of the treatment, works with client transferences. Unconscious feelings from the past, their invasion into the present, and their intrusion into the therapy relationship are interpreted and worked through. Of special interest are conflicts around the client's "feeling or behavioral style" as this relates to unresolved issues in the past and the present. It must be kept in mind, though, that this interpretive work occurs in a setting of warmth, empathy, encouragement, support, and optimism.

In keeping with counseling psychology's emphasis on clients' strengths, Mann notes this precondition for the successful practice of his TLP:

> [T]he conviction that, given a modicum of help, all human beings have emotional, intellectual, and adaptive assets that they are ready to channel into reasonably gratifying directions. It is imperative that we appreciate . . . what a patient can do for himself (Mann, 1973, p. 51).

For what kinds of clients might TLP be contraindicated? Are there clients who are especially well suited to this treatment? Generally, TLP is suitable for a broad range of clients. It is not so much the severity or type of client disorder that determines suitability as degree of client motivation for treatment and the ability of client and therapist to establish a central issue. Also crucial are the client's ability to become rapidly involved affectively and to disengage rapidly—an indication of capacity to tolerate loss, which is very important in time-limited therapy. On the negative side, Mann notes that many clients with strong dependent longings or narcissistic disorders will refuse short-term treatment. He also notes some clear contraindications for TLP: schizophrenia (including all subtypes), bipolar affective disorder, schizoid personality disorders, and certain obsessional character disorders (e.g., those whose defenses severely limit their ability to experience feelings). The more severe borderline disorders are not responsive to TLP (contraindicated).

The applicability of TLP to counseling psychology is indicated in Mann's statements about the clients who are ideally suited to TLP. College students who are suffering from what Mann calls "maturational crises" and who, relatedly, have problems

From Strange Bedfellows to Compatible Partners

Historically, psychoanalysis and counseling psychology could be seen as strange bed-fellows for several reasons. For one, the focus in psychoanalysis on lengthy treatment, often lasting many years, ran counter to counseling psychology's emphasis on brevity. Whereas counselors were interested in abbreviating interventions often to a few sessions, within psychoanalysis there appeared to be an ethos suggesting that only very extended treatments were valuable. A second source of incompatibility (historically) pertains to the tendency within psychoanalysis to focus on psychopathology, or underlying lack of health, in contrast to counseling psychology's focus on individuals' assets and strengths. In this area, the two fields actually seemed to move in opposite directions: Psychoanalysis paid attention to the deficits or pathology of even relatively healthy people, whereas counseling psychology focused its energies on the strengths of even very disturbed clients. Third, over the years psychoanalysis singled out internal, or intrapsychic, factors to explain human behavior, whereas counseling psychology placed its focus at once on the person (intrapsychic), the environment (external), and the person–environment interaction as the root causes of behavior.

Things have been changing in recent times, however, so that the two fields have become more compatible. The differences noted above are still present, but are much less extreme than in the past. In the early chapters of this book we discussed changes in counseling psychology. Let us now look at some of the changes in psychoanalysis that have made it more compatible with the work of the counseling psychologist.

Perhaps most fundamental, drive psychology has diminished in popularity, and ego psychology, certain versions of object relations theory, and psychoanalytic self psychology have gained ascendency. This basic shift has resulted in several major changes in emphases. First, a greater stress has been placed on the environmental, cultural, and interpersonal factors that contribute to psychological health and maladaptive behavior. In addition, in current thinking Freud's psychosexual states (e.g., oral, anal, phallic) are often translated into psychosocial stages during which the maturing individual's experiences with significant others (rather than hidden sexual impulses) are seen as the key determinants of development. These interpersonal experiences are seen as influencing behavior throughout life, rather than only during childhood. Thus, in current analytic theories, psychological development is viewed as a lifelong process, although early childhood is still seen as highly significant in establishing a psychological blueprint for later development.

Ego analytic, self psychology, and object–relations approaches pay significant attention to psychological health and the processes of normal development. In addition, they pay much attention to positive human strivings for creativity, mastery, and the capacity for love. The ego analysts, for example, view the ego's functions as going well beyond creating defenses against anxiety. The ego also serves to help people *adapt*—to stress, to life situations, to interpersonal relations, and so forth. The emphasis is on coping and even mastery, rather than simply defense.

One of the difficulties with orthodox Freudian theory that limited its relationship with counseling psychology was its inattention to female sexual development and portrayal of women as psychologically inferior (Gelso & Fassinger, 1992). Classical analytic concepts such as penis envy seem archaic and sexist and have been unrevolving around separation–individuation fit neatly into the issues TLP aims to address. These separation–individuation issues, along with the degree of flexibility of this client group, make the termination phase of TLP a genuine growth-consolidating experience, according to Mann. The time limit in TLP addresses the client's desire and need for independence; the treatment helps such a client mature, separate from childhood in a healthy way, and grow. Beyond this group, though, Mann's comments suggest that TLP is suitable to the large majority of clients treated by counseling psychologists.

Comments on Time-Limited Psychotherapy

Although TLP is a creative approach to abbreviating lengthy treatment, some questions may be raised about its emphasis on separation–individuation. Issues of separation and loss are absolutely crucial in this approach, and yet both the beginning student and the seasoned counselor alike may well disagree as to whether such a focus is a necessity. Perhaps not all clients who are suitable for brief therapy or counseling have basic issues of separation, and it is not clear that great emphasis on such issues during the termination phase is as essential as Mann suggests. Empirical research does, however, suggest that from the client's perspective, issues of termination should be dealt with in counseling, and in fact such issues are dealt with by most counselors (Gelso & Woodhouse, 2000). The question is whether Mann overemphasizes separation and loss. The available research evidence does indicate there are not as many loss issues involved in termination as appear to be proposed by Mann (Gelso & Woodhouse, 2000).

Be that as it may, the delineation of a central issue and the maintenance of a focus on that issue are worthwhile aspects of this brief analytic intervention. The selection of an underlying issue that clarifies how the client's present pain is connected to the past and to the client's attempts to cope is clearly true to the analytic roots of TLP. It aims to go well beyond simply treating overt symptoms. The focus on the client-therapist relationship, with a particular emphasis on transference, is also true to the analytic focus, although like many brief analytic treatments and in contrast to longer-term analytic therapies, Mann also emphasizes the importance of the therapist's being active, supportive, and guiding.

THE PSYCHOANALYTIC APPROACH IN PERSPECTIVE

An important and lively strand of psychoanalytic thinking in counseling psychology throughout the years is seen in the writing of Bordin (e.g., 1968, 1980) and King (e.g., 1965). Both these theoreticians exert thoughtful and valuable effort to apply psychoanalytic concepts to the needs of counselors who, for example, work with relatively normal clients in educational settings. Yet over time the influence of psychoanalysis on counseling psychology has tended to be marginal because, for a variety of reasons discussed below, there were some deep incompatibilities between the two fields. As we shall see, however, recently things have changed substantially.

supportable scientifically. The more recent "psychologies," however, have been much less likely to conceptualize female development in such a manner and have demonstrated willingness to seriously study female sexual development. At the roots of this change has been the reformulation of the dynamics of the Oedipus complex, which they are more likely to see in psychosocial, rather than sexual, terms.

Finally, the movement during the past few decades toward abbreviating the length of analytic interventions has taken a huge step in making analytically based treatments more suited to counseling psychology, at least as practiced in places like university counseling centers and other community mental health agencies. Especially pertinent in this respect are the brief or time-limited therapies noted earlier (Crits-Christoph & Barber, 1991; Messer & Warren, 1995).

Science, Research, and Psychoanalysis

One major area of incompatibility historically between psychoanalysis and counseling psychology has been their divergent viewpoints about scientific research. Psychology (including counseling psychology) has deeply invested in its self-definition as a science (as well as a field of practice), seeing controlled empirical research as a major way in which science is to be practiced.

Psychoanalysis has also viewed itself as a science (as well as a field of practice), but from Freud on has taken a pessimistic stance toward the value of controlled empirical research. Stated in the extreme (which was all too frequently also the norm), the view has been that controlled research could not possibly help understand the great complexities of human personality and the psychoanalytic treatment situation. In fact, the only kind of research that could be revealing is that done by a psychoanalyst *during* psychoanalysis. In this view, the psychoanalyst's observations and inferences during the psychoanalytic treatment process constitute science and further, are the only kind of research that can help us understand the human psyche and the psychoanalytic treatment situation.

Unfortunately, there are enormous scientific problems with such research: the psychoanalyst's biases, which are free to invade the process; the nearly total lack of controls and control groups; extremely global observations; and so forth. Such problems, however, seemed either to be unrecognized within psychoanalysis or were seen as problems that simply had to be lived with. Moreover, undergirding this viewpoint of science was belief that truth could be revealed through the expert psychoanalyst's observations of the analysand—these serve as both a sufficient vehicle for theory construction and an adequate method for testing theory.

Historically, psychology was not without its contribution to the problem. Stated in the extreme (which was all too frequently the norm), the only road to truth and only viable form of good science in psychology, was the controlled experiment, preferably done under laboratory conditions, whereby very specific forms of overt behavior could be studied with great precision. Anything else was seen as subjective and thus unscientific.

Fortunately, things have changed in recent years to bring psychoanalysis and psychology closer together in their views of science and research. Psychoanalysts and psychoanalytic psychologists have clearly become more accepting of controlled empirical research. Such research is evident in publication outlets such as *Psychoanalytic Psychology,* published by the Division of Psychoanalysis (Division 39) of the American Psychological Association. Although it appears that psychoanalysis as research is still the most prominent approach, there is growing recognition of the need for scientific controls and, in fact, the quantity of controlled research has been growing, especially in psychoanalysis within psychology (in contrast to psychoanalysis within medicine). At the same time as these changes in psychoanalysis have occurred, views of acceptable scientific methods in psychology in general have broadened. This is most clearly seen within counseling psychology in the "alternative methodology movement" (see Chapter 3). Counseling psychologists in particular are becoming much more accepting of research that is qualitative in nature, focuses on the individual, is done in a field setting, and seeks to examine broad patterns of behavior and subjective meaning.

What has controlled research revealed about psychoanalytic interventions? In regard to psychoanalysis proper, it is extremely difficult to conduct controlled outcome research on this treatment, given its long-term nature. Thus, little research exists; the findings that do exist, however, are favorable. Psychoanalysis, from a variety of perspectives (e.g., object–relations), does appear to have positive effects on analysands on a variety of dimensions, effecting, for example, deeper personality change (Lambert & Bergin, 1994; Wallerstein, 1989).

The picture is equally positive for psychoanalytically-oriented counseling or therapy. Controlled outcome studies indicate that clients who receive such treatments improve, on the whole, in a range of ways, including when the interventions are relatively brief and/or time limited (Lambert & Bergin, 1994; Sloane et al., 1975). Undemonstrated is psychoanalytic-oriented interventions' superiority to any other theoretical approach. All major approaches appear to be effective. Yet to be clarified is which approach is most effective for which clients under what conditions.

In addition to research on the outcome of psychoanalytic interventions, during the past decade there has been a substantial increase in research on the process of such treatments. This process research examines how treatment unfolds from session to session, which factors within the client and the therapist relate to this unfolding, and which factors relate to client improvement during treatment. Although this research is too extensive to summarize here, it is worth noting that much of it has focused on aspects of the therapeutic relationship (e.g., working alliance, transference, countertransference) and analytic techniques, such as interpretation (see, for example, Gelso, Hill, Mohr, Rochlen, & Zack, 1999; Henry, Strupp, Schacht, & Gaston, 1994; Miller, Luborsky, Barber, & Doherty, 1993).

SUMMARY

The originator of psychoanalysis and all talking cures was Sigmund Freud. His great genius, courage, and thoughtfulness were evident throughout his career and are part of his legacy to psychoanalysis as a science and as an approach to psychological treatment.

In getting a grasp on psychoanalysis, it is useful to make a number of distinctions. First, psychoanalysis is both a *theory of the person and of the treatment situation*. Second, the words *psychodynamic* and *psychoanalytic* must be distinguished: The former is broader than the latter and includes approaches that are nonanalytic. Third, there are different levels of psychoanalytic treatment; namely, psychoanalysis proper, psychoanalytic psychotherapy, supportive–analytic counseling or therapy, and psychoanalytically informed therapy. Psychoanalysis proper is the most long term and intensive of these. Psychoanalytically informed therapy makes use of psychoanalytic theories of the person to understand the client but uses whichever treatment techniques best fit the client and his or her situation.

It is a common error to view the theories of Freud and his followers as the *only* psychoanalysis. Actually, at least four major clusters of theories, often referred to as "psychologies," may be placed under the broad umbrella of psychoanalysis: Freud's drive psychology, ego psychology, object relations theory, and psychoanalytic self psychology.

Eight common ingredients of psychoanalysis as theory of the person and of the treatment situation are: (1) psychic determinism, (2) the genetic–dynamic hypothesis, (3) the centrality of the unconscious, (4) the role of defenses, (5) repetition and transference, (6) the therapeutic relationship, (7) techniques in psychoanalysis, and (8) insight as the ideal outcome of psychoanalysis.

Of the many psychoanalytic treatment approaches, those most relevant to the counseling psychologist seek to abbreviate the typically long-term nature of analytic treatment. A number of short-term approaches have become popular in recent years. One example of how psychoanalytic principles have been applied to brief therapy is the time-limited psychotherapy (TLP) of James Mann. This 12-session therapy revolves around the universal issues of separation and loss. In the first session or so, the therapist delineates a central focus for the work, which is maintained throughout. This focus represents the client's present and chronically endured pain. The therapist's stance in TLP is active and supportive, although persistent emphasis is on interpretation and insight. Transference, especially around loss and separation, is actively interpreted, mainly during the last stage.

Stressing clients' strengths, TLP is particularly well suited to young clients (e.g., college students) with developmental problems. In this way, it is highly compatible with counseling psychology.

Over the years psychoanalysis and counseling psychology, once strange bedfellows, have become potentially compatible partners. Research on psychoanalytic interventions strongly supports the efficacy of such treatments, although there is no evidence that psychoanalytic treatments are more or less effective than others. Research on the process of psychoanalytic treatments has increased substantially, and has tended to focus on the main components of the therapeutic relationship and their effects, as well as on key treatment techniques.

REFERENCES

Baker, E. (1985). Psychoanalysis and psychoanalytic psychotherapy. In S. Lynn & J. Garske (Eds.). *Contemporary psychotherapy: Methods and models.* Columbus, OH: Merrill.

Binder, J. L., & Strupp, H. H. (1991). The Vanderbilt approach to time-limited dynamic psychotherapy. In P. Crits-Christoph and J. P. Barber (Eds.), *Handbook of short-term dynamic psychotherapy* (pp. 137–165). New York: Basic Books.

Bordin, E. S. (1968). *Psychological counseling.* New York: Meredith Corporation.

Bordin, E. S. (1980). A psychodynamic view of counseling psychology. *The Counseling Psychologist, 9*(1), 62–70.

Brenner, C. (1973). *An elementary textbook of psychoanalysis.* New York: International Universities Press.

Breuer, J., & Freud, S. (1955). Studies on hysteria. *The standard edition of the complete works of Sigmund Freud* (Vol. 2, pp. 1–305). London: Hogarth Press. (Original work published in 1895)

Crits-Christoph, P., & Barber, J. P. (Eds.). (1991). *Handbook of short-term dynamic psychotherapy.* New York: Basic Books.

Dasberg, H., & Shefler, G. (1989, June). *A randomized controlled outcome and follow-up study of James Mann's time limited psychotherapy in a Jerusalem community mental health center.* Paper presented at the meeting of the Society for Psychotherapy Research, Toronto.

Doctors, S. R. (1996). Notes on the contribution of the analyst's self-awareness to optimal responsiveness. In A. Goldberg (Ed.), *Basic ideas reconsidered—progress in self psychology, Volume 12* (pp. 55–66). Hillsdale, NJ: The Analytic Press.

Eagle, M. N. (1984). *Recent developments in psychoanalysis.* New York: McGraw-Hill.

Ellenberger, H. (1970). *The discovery of the unconscious.* New York: Basic Books.

Erikson, E. (1950). *Childhood and society.* New York: Norton.

Erikson, E. (1968). *Identity, youth, and crisis.* New York: Norton.

Fenichel, O. (1945). The psychoanalytic theory of neurosis. New York: Norton.

Fosshage, J. L. (1997). Psychoanalysis and psychoanalytic psychotherapy: Is there a meaningful distinction in the process? *Psychoanalytic Psychology, 14,* 409–425.

Frank, G. (1998). On the relational school of psychoanalysis: Some additional thoughts. *Psychoanalytic Psychology, 15,* 141–153.

Freud, A. (1966). The ego and the mechanisms of defense. In *The writings of Anna Freud* (Vol. 2). New York: International Universities Press. (Original work published 1936)

Freud, S. (1938). *The interpretation of dreams.* In A. A. Brill, *The basic writings of Sigmund Freud.* New York: Random House. (Original work published in 1900)

Freud, S. (1940). *An outline of psychoanalysis. International Journal of Psycho-Analysis, 21,* 27–82.

Freud, S. (1953). The ego and the id. In J. Strachey (Ed.), *Standard edition of the complete psychological works of Sigmund Freud* (Vol. 19, pp 3–66). London: Hogarth Press. (Original work published 1923)

Freud, S. (1961). The ego and the id. In J. Strachey (Ed. and Trans.), *The standard edition of the complete psychological works of Sigmund Freud* (Vol. 19, pp. 3–66). London: Hogarth Press. (Original work published in 1923)

Gelso, C. J. (1995). A theory for all seasons: The four psychologies of psychoanalysis. *Contemporary Psychology, 40,* 331–333.

Gelso, C. J., & Carter, J. A. (1985). The relationship in counseling and psychotherapy: Components, consequences, and theoretical antecedents. *The Counseling Psychologist, 13,* 155–243.

Gelso, C. J., & Fassinger, R. E. (1992). Personality, development, and counseling psychology: Depth, ambivalence, and actualization. *Journal of Counseling Psychology, 39,* 275–298.

Gelso, C. J., & Hayes, J. A. (1998). *The psychotherapy relationship: Theory, research, and practice.* New York: John Wiley & Sons.

Gelso, C. J., Hill, C. E., Mohr, J. J., Rochlen, A. B., & Zack, J. (1999). Describing the face of transference: Psychodynamic therapists' recollections about transference in cases of successful long-term therapy. *Journal of Counseling Psychology, 46,* 257–267.

Gelso, C. J., & Woodhouse, S. S. (2000). The termination of psychotherapy: What research tells us about the process of ending treatment. In G. S. Tryon (Ed.), *Counseling based on process research: Applying what we know*. Needham Heights, MA: Allyn & Bacon.

Gill, M. M. (1994). *Transitions in psychoanalysis*. Hillsdale, NJ: Analytic Press.

Greenberg, J., & Mitchell, S. A. (1983). *Object relations in psychoanalytic theory*. Cambridge, MA: Harvard University Press.

Greenson, R. R. (1967). *The technique and practice of psychoanalysis* (Vol. 1). New York: International Universities Press.

Hartmann, H. (1958). *Ego psychology and the problem of adaptation*. New York: International Universities Press. (Original work published in 1939)

Henry, W. P., Strupp, H. H., Schacht, T. E., & Gaston, L. (1994). Psychodynamic approaches. In A. E. Bergin and S. L. Garfield (Eds.), *Handbook of psychotherapy and behavior change* (4th ed., pp. 467–508). New York: John Wiley & Sons.

Holinger, P. C. (1999). Noninterpretive interventions in psychoanalysis and psychotherapy: A developmental perspective. *Psychoanalytic Psychology, 16*, 233–253.

Johnson, D. H., & Gelso, C. J. (1980). The effectiveness of time limits in counseling and psychotherapy: A critical review. *The Counseling Psychologist, 9*(1), 70–82.

Jones, E. (1953). *The life and works of Sigmund Freud* (Vol. 1). New York: Basic Books.

Jones, E. (1955). *The life and works of Sigmund Freud* (Vol. 2). New York: Basic Books.

Jones, E. (1957). *The life and works of Sigmund Freud* (Vol. 3). New York: Basic Books.

Kernberg, O. (1975). *Borderline conditions and pathological narcissism*. New York: Jason Aronson.

King, P. T. (1965). Psychoanalytic adaptations. In B. Stefflre (Ed.), *Theories of counseling*. New York: McGraw-Hill.

Kohut, H. (1971). *The analysis of the self*. New York: International Universities Press.

Kohut, H. (1977). *The restoration of the self*. New York: International Universities Press.

Kohut, H. (1984). *How does analysis cure?* Chicago, IL: University of Chicago Press.

Lambert, M. J., & Bergin, A. E. (1994). The effectiveness of psychotherapy. In A. E. Bergin and S. L. Garfield (Eds.), *Handbook of psychotherapy and behavior change* (4th ed., pp. 143–189). New York: John Wiley & Sons.

Langs, R. J. (1976). *The bipersonal field*. New York: Jason Aronson.

Linden, J. A. (1994). Gratification and provision in psychoanalysis: Should we get rid of the "rule of abstinence"? *Psychoanalytic Dialogues, 4*, 549–582.

MacIsaac, D. S. (1996). Optimal frustration: An endangered concept. In A. Goldberg (Ed.), *Basic ideas reconsidered—progress in self psychology, Volume 12* (pp. 3–16). Hillsdale, NJ: Analytic Press.

Mahler, M. S., Bergman, A., & Pine, F. (1975). *The psychological birth of the human infant*. New York: Basic Books.

Mann, J. (1973). *Time-limited psychotherapy*. Cambridge, MA: Harvard University Press.

Mann, J. (1991). Time-limited psychotherapy. In P. Crits-Christoph and J. P. Barber (Eds.), *Handbook of short-term dynamic psychotherapy* (pp. 17–44). New York: Basic Books.

Messer, S. B., & Warren, C. S. (1995). *Models of brief psychodynamic therapy*. New York: Guilford Press.

Miller, N. E., Luborsky, L., Barber, J. P., & Doherty, J. P. (Eds.). (1993). *Psychodynamic treatment research*. New York: Basic Books.

Mishne, J. M. (1993). *The evolution and application of clinical theory: Perspectives from four psychologies*. New York: Free Press.

Mitchell, S. A. (1993). *Hope and dread in psychoanalysis*. New York: Basic Books.

Osofsky, J. D. (1995). Perspectives on attachment in psychoanalysis. *Psychoanalytic Psychology, 12*, 347–362.

Patton, M. J., & Meara, N. M. (1992). *Psychoanalytic Counseling*. New York: John Wiley & Sons.

Pine, F. (1990). *Drive, ego, object, and self: A synthesis for clinical work*. New York: Basic Books.

Prochaska, J. O., & Norcross, J. C. (1999). *Systems of psychotherapy: A transtheoretical analysis* (4th ed.). Pacific Grove, CA: Brooks/Cole.

Robbins, S. B. (1989). Role of contemporary psychoanalysis in counseling psychology. *Journal of Counseling Psychology, 36*, 267–278.

Sharf, R. S. (1996). *Theories of psychotherapy and counseling: Concepts and cases*. Pacific Grove, CA: Brooks/Cole.

Silverman, D. K. (1998). The tie that binds: Affect regulation, attachment, and psychoanalysis. *Psychoanalytic Psychology, 15*, 187–212.

Slavin, J. H. (1989). Post-doctoral training for psychologists in psychoanalysis. *Psychologist Psychoanalyst, 9*, 8–11.

Sloane, R., Staples, F., Cristol, A., Yorkston, N., & Whipple, K. (1975). *Psychotherapy versus behavior therapy*. Cambridge, MA: Harvard University Press.

Strupp, H. H., & Binder, J. L. (1984). *Psychotherapy in a new key*. New York: Basic Books.

Wallerstein, R. (1989). Psychoanalysis and psychotherapy: An historical perspective. *International Journal of Psycho-Analysis, 70*, 563–591.

Wolf, E. S. (1991). Advances in self psychology: The evolution of psychoanalytic treatment. *Psychoanalytic Inquiry, 11*, 123–146.

CHAPTER 11

THE BEHAVIORAL AND
COGNITIVE APPROACHES

The Cognitive Therapy of Aaron T. Beck

The Behavioral and Cognitive Approaches in Perspective

The Efficacy of Behavioral and Cognitive Therapies

Counseling Psychology and the Behavioral and Cognitive

Approaches

Summary

References

The theory cluster discussed in this chapter is actually a combination of two over-lapping approaches to counseling: behavioral and cognitive. As will be seen, each approach relies heavily on the other in the modern practice of counseling, and the two perspectives are theoretically compatible. The cognitive and behavioral approaches, along with the currently popular combination of the two, called *cognitive–behavioral therapy,* have become a major force in the practice of counseling psychology. For example, studies of counseling psychologists (Johnson & Brems, 1991; Norcross, Sayette, Mayne, Karg, & Turkson, 1998; Watkins, Lopez, Campbell & Himmell, 1986; Zook & Walton, 1989) indicate that well over half of the large samples of faculty and practitioners who were surveyed were heavily influenced by cognitive and behavioral approaches to counseling, as either their primary or secondary theoretical orientation. Although some of these studies were done several years ago, all indications are that the cognitive and behavioral approaches are just as influential in current practice (e.g., Beidel & Turner, 1998; Norcross et al., 1998; Sundel & Sundel, 1999).

We begin this chapter by giving a brief historical review of the development of behavioral and cognitive approaches. This is followed by an examination of nine basic assumptions common to both. In reviewing these assumptions, it will become clear that, just as with the other major theory clusters, there is no single behavioral or cognitive approach that dominates the current counseling scene. Rather, the present-day practice of behavior therapy and its cognitive cousin is marked by diversity and heterogeneity, which many believe to be a sign of health and growth.

The third section of the chapter delves into specific methods and techniques of the two approaches, exploring their common ground as well as their distinctiveness. After reviewing behavioral procedures, two primarily cognitive therapies are singled out and summarized. Finally, the chapter concludes with a perspective on behavioral and cognitive therapy in today's practice of counseling psychology.

A HISTORICAL SKETCH

Of the two approaches reviewed in this chapter, the behavioral developed much earlier. Wilson (1995) notes that two historical events overshadow all others in the development of behavior therapy. The first is the rise of behaviorism—the theoretical and philosophical foundation of at least early behavioral treatments—at the beginning of this century. In the United States, this movement's leading figure was John B. Watson. Watson's viewpoints were a reaction to the then prevalent "introspectionist" theories, which proposed that to understand human behavior one must look inside. In contrast, Watson posited that such "mentalistic" approaches were unscientific and not very fruitful. Instead, psychology ought to be the study of *overt* behavior. Watson saw human behavior as fully caused by environmental factors (those outside the person), and believed that behavior could be fully understood as a result of learning. This extremist position implied that humans could learn to be anything, could learn and unlearn any and all behaviors—virtually any human could be conditioned to become a doctor, a lawyer, a criminal, and so forth.

Watson's position, popular in the earlier part of this century, has been widely rejected in recent years. The call of behaviorism has been taken up by more sophisticated versions, the primary example being B. F. Skinner's radical behaviorism. Although Skinner saw internal events, as well as one's biological makeup, as important, he promoted the view that human behavior is best understood and modified through the study of overt stimuli and behavior. Operant conditioning principles (i.e., principles of reinforcement and punishment), in the Skinnerian view, are the most powerful influences determining behavior. Skinner's views have had a deep impact on both behavior therapy and psychology in general.

The second historical event crucial to the development of behavior therapy was experimental research on the psychology of learning and the consequent discovery of principles of classical and instrumental conditioning. The most seminal event took place near the turn of the century: Russian physiologist Ivan Pavlov's experiments demonstrating classical conditioning principles, as revealed in the salivation responses of dogs. Around the same time in this country, E. L. Thorndike was developing his famous law of effect, in which he detailed how behavior was learned according to principles of reward and punishment. Similarly, in the late 1930s, Skinner elaborated the principles of instrumental learning with his work on operant conditioning.

These two interrelated events, the rise of behaviorism and the development of the experimental study of learning, however, did not quickly pave the way toward behavioral therapy. Applications of conditioning principles to clinical problems had in fact occurred early in the century. For example, in the 1920s, Mary Cover Jones demonstrated the use of conditioning in overcoming certain fears in children. Likewise, in the 1930s, O. Hobart Mowrer and E. Mowrer used conditioning procedures (which remain effective today) to treat bed-wetting problems in children. Yet such behavioral treatments did not take hold in applied psychology, for, as Wilson (1995) notes, they were seen as simplistic by practicing psychologists. In the schism that developed, behavioral treatments were seen as part of academic–experimental psychology, whereas practitioners were most often psychodynamically oriented, and concerned themselves with clients' unconscious issues and motivations.

Enter Behavior Therapy

It remained for Joseph Wolpe (1958) to present what may have been the single most important book in the development of behavior therapy, *Psychotherapy by Reciprocal Inhibition*. Until that time, counselors and therapists lacked a set of techniques that would allow them to apply conditioning principles to their work with clients. For several years Wolpe, working in his clinic in South Africa, devised and applied behavioral techniques to his work with clients. Like psychoanalysts, Wolpe theorized that all neurotic problems were caused by anxiety. But here the similarity to psychoanalysis ended. Wolpe used a combination of classical conditioning theory and Clark Hull's then-popular learning theory as the basis for his work. Anxiety was learned through conditioned autonomic reactions, and Wolpe devised several techniques to extinguish this anxiety. The most widely cited and used of these was Wolpe's systematic desensitization, which continues to be a powerful behavioral treatment today (Sundel & Sundel, 1999; Wilson, 1995). Moreover, Wolpe maintained that fully 90% of the adult neurotic patients he treated with his behavioral approaches improved markedly.

By the time Wolpe presented his ground-breaking work, another behavioral therapist, Hans J. Eysenck (1952), had already published one of the most controversial papers in the history of counseling and therapy. Eysenck reviewed existing studies on the outcomes of psychoanalytic and eclectic psychotherapy with neurotic clients and found that their improvement rates were no better than for neurotics receiving no formal therapy. About two-thirds of both groups improved significantly. Although the validity of these findings was debated for years and were decisively refuted only after many years of research (Lambert & Bergin, 1994), they had a profound effect on the professionals training to be counselors and therapists in the 1950s and 1960s. When Eysenck's findings were viewed in light of Wolpe's claim of very high cure rates in behavioral therapies (and that of other behavior therapists, including Eysenck himself in the early 1960s), the popularity of these approaches increased dramatically.

After its healthy birth in the late 1950s, and christening in 1959 by a parent figure (see Hans Eysenck's [1959] statement), behavior therapy grew quickly in the 1960s. As Rimm and Cunningham (1985) note, psychologists seeking an alternative to psychodynamic approaches found a convincing one in an amalgamation of Skinner's operant conditioning and Wolpe's classical conditioning. The 1960s began with the appearance of the first textbook in behavior therapy, Eysenck's (1960) *Behavior Therapy and the Neurosis*. In the mid-1960s, Ullmann and Krasner (1965) produced their famous *Case Studies in Behavior Modification*, which demonstrated the use of Skinnerian operant conditioning principles with a wide range of psychological problems. Within counseling psychology, the behavioral banner was carried most effectively by John D. Krumboltz and Carl E. Thoresen, and behavioral treatments developed so quickly that Krumboltz wrote about the *Revolution in Counseling* (Krumboltz, 1966).

The 1960s ended as significantly as they had begun. Albert Bandura (1969) published the tremendously influential *Principles of Behavior Modification.* Among the many important aspects of this book was the concept of *modeling,* or *imitation learning.* Bandura reasoned that classical and operant conditioning were insufficient to explain how people learn. (In trying to learn to fish or hunt, using the principles of operant conditioning, you would receive reinforcement only after appropriate responses—a highly inefficient way to learn.) People also learn by observing others, models so to speak, and *then* by being reinforced for performing whatever was modeled.

The Cognitive Revolution

As the behavior therapies mushroomed in the 1960s, another therapeutic approach was just beginning to take shape. The seeds of the cognitive approach were planted with the 1962 publication of Albert Ellis's famous *Reason and Emotion in Psychotherapy.* In it, he argued that our feelings and behavior are caused by our cognitions; that is, what we think and say to ourselves. Ellis's rational–emotive therapy gained in popularity during the 1960s, but it was not until the 1970s, when it was joined by the cognitive revolution in psychology in general, that it flourished.

Behaviorism was the ruling force within psychology in general from the time of Watson through the 1960s. In the 1970s, however, theories about how cognitive processes determined behavior not only caught on, but appeared to become the ruling force among theories of behavior. Within applied psychology, including cognitive psychology, this movement was evidenced in the increased popularity of Ellis's approach, and perhaps even more significantly in the incorporation of cognitive concepts *within* behavioral counseling approaches. Bandura (1969) was one of the original forces promoting such an integration of cognitive and behavioral theories. Behavior therapists continued to be concerned with overt behavior, but also began to pay close attention to the interaction of thoughts, beliefs, values, and other internal and cognitive mechanisms, and how these affect behavior. For example, one of the most important investigated concepts in recent years is Bandura's (1977, 1997) concept of self-efficacy (people's beliefs about what they are able to do). Self-efficacy has been found to influence a wide range of behaviors, for example, sports performance, social skills development, educational achievement, and career development (see Bandura, 1997; Lent, Brown, & Hackett, 1994).

As part of this cognitive revolution, a number of treatment theories were developed. Although some of these cognitively oriented theories were developed within and some outside the behavioral tradition, all are compatible with behavior therapy in that they make use of behavior therapy techniques and can be conceptualized in learning terms. Beck (1976), for example, developed a cognitive therapy best known for its treatment of depression but which has much wider applications. His approach is basically cognitive, but employs many behavioral methods. Meichenbaum (1977), on the other hand, developed a form of counseling that from the beginning sought to integrate cognitive and behavioral notions. These cognitive–behavioral approaches have each been updated and further developed during the 1990s (e.g.,

Beck & Weishaar, 1995; Goldfried & Davison, 1994). To be sure, at the beginning of the twenty-first century, the integration of cognitive and behavioral approaches has been remarkable. There are few, if any, pure behavior or cognitive therapists.

Whereas behavior therapy discovered "mind" (cognition) in the 1970s, according to Wilson (1995), the 1980s and 1990s witnessed growth in the interest in feelings and emotions and how these states interact with cognitions and overt behavior. Also, within behavior therapy much greater attention was given to the biological bases of behavior, including "biobehavioral" interactions (O'Leary & Wilson, 1987). Throughout the 1990s, the diversity of cognitive and behavioral approaches further expanded, so that at times it is difficult to distinguish these approaches from other theories (Wilson, 1995). There continues to be a number of distinguishing features, however, and these shall now be addressed.

BASIC APPROACHES AND ASSUMPTIONS OF BEHAVIORAL AND COGNITIVE TREATMENTS

Although counseling encompasses a wide range of cognitive and behavioral treatments, Wilson (1995) provides a useful framework in identifying three basic approaches. These three differ in the extent to which each focuses on overt behavior or cognitive processes. Before discussing the nine common assumptions of the behavioral and cognitive perspectives, we shall briefly summarize these three approaches.

The Three Basic Approaches

First, *applied behavior analysis,* or radical behaviorism, focuses exclusively on overt behavior, with cognition seen as excess baggage—unnecessary to the understanding and modification of behavior. Its leading spokesperson has been B. F. Skinner, and operant conditioning (see below) has been its main procedure.

Second, the *neobehavioristic mediational stimulus–response model* makes use of the learning theories of such eminent psychologists as Clark Hull, Neil Miller, and Kenneth Spence. Mediational models pay attention to what goes on inside the organism. Wolpe's systematic desensitization (SD, described later) is a prime example of such a model. SD seeks to extinguish anxiety (an internal response). As part of this process, the client uses imagery (another internal event) to visualize scenes that arouse anxiety. Internal processes are considered to follow the same laws of learning as do overt behaviors.

The third approach within the behavioral and cognitive perspective is the social–cognitive model. Based on the work of Albert Bandura (1977, 1986, 1997), behavior is seen as dependent upon the interaction of three systems: (a) external stimulus events, (b) external reinforcement, and (c) cognitive mediational processes.

According to the social–cognitive model, just how the environment affects behavior depends on how the person *perceives* and *interprets* these environmental events and stimuli, rather than on the environmental events themselves. These perceptions and interpretations are fundamentally cognitive. Also, reciprocity is a key concept in social–cognitive theory. For example, one's behavior itself affects how the environment (e.g., other persons) responds, and the reinforcements that are received. These environmental reinforcements, in a reciprocal fashion, have a marked effect on behavior. The experiences that we have based on our behavior partly affect what and how we think, expect, and can do; these cognitive processes, in turn, alter behavior. Thus, there is a constant interaction between behavior, cognitive processes, and the environment.

In terms of counseling, the social–cognitive model has fueled the integration of cognitive and behavioral approaches. Behavior therapy, for example, has increasingly used the methods of cognitive therapy (e.g., see discussions of Aaron Beck and Albert Ellis later in this chapter), and thus focuses on the internal cognitions that underlie human problems and conflicts. When cognitive and behavioral approaches are combined based on the social–cognitive model, the person is seen more as the fundamental agent of change, rather than as a passive recipient of stimuli, as in earlier models of behavioral treatment.

Nine Basic Assumptions

In discussing the nine basic assumptions of the behavioral and cognitive perspectives, we do not mean to imply that all these assumptions are uniformly held by all counselors. Indeed, there is so much diversity, even among the strictly behavioral approaches, that many critics have wondered if behavior therapy really exists. At the same time, there are many more differences between the cognitive–behavioral and psychoanalytic or humanistic clusters than there are within the cognitive and behavioral cluster. In discussing the nine assumptions, we shall try to make clear what differences exist *within* the behavioral and cognitive approaches as well as *between* them and the psychoanalytic and humanistic perspectives. For the reader's convenience, these nine assumptions are summarized in Table 11.1. Below we discuss these in greater detail.

Attention to Overt Behavior and Processes Close to Overt Behavior
Virtually all behavioral and cognitive therapies pay close attention to overt behavior, although the radical behaviorists (applied behavior analysts) are the only ones who focus exclusively on such overt processes. As one moves more toward the cognitive side of the continuum (with cognitive modification at the end point), the counselor's attention shifts toward more internal processes, such as cognitions. At the same time, the amount of attention given to the modification of overt behavior is high in all of these approaches, even the explicitly cognitive ones, and is greater than that for the other theory clusters, for example, psychoanalysis.

Even when behavior therapists' attention shifts away from overt behavior, they will be inclined to address processes nearer the surface (nearer overt behavior) than will, for example, psychoanalytic therapists. Thus, in Wolpe's systematic desensitization, counselors seek to work directly on conditioned anxiety (an internal state),

TABLE 11.1.   Nine Assumptions of Cognitive–Behavioral Approaches to Counseling.

1. When intervening, it is best to attend to overt behavior or at least processes close to the overt level.
2. Behavior is learned and can thus be unlearned and relearned.
3. The most effective treatment integrates cognitive and behavioral approaches.
4. Although the past is important in shaping behavior, it is most effective to focus on the present when attempting to change behavior.
5. The client's presenting problem and symptoms should be the focus of treatment.
6. Counseling proceeds most effectively when clear and specific goals have been established for the treatment.
7. The cognitive–behavioral counselor most frequently and effectively works in an active, directive, and prescriptive manner.
8. The client–counselor relationship is important in cognitive–behavioral counseling, but it is not sufficient for constructive change.
9. The cognitive–behavioral counselor is an applied behavioral scientist who stays abreast of and applies research findings to practice.

and cognitive therapists may go even further and work with the cognitions presumed to cause that anxiety. Psychoanalysts, on the other hand, tend to posit a number of forces even further removed from overt processes. A phobia may be seen by the analyst as a defensive maneuver stemming from the unconscious need to restrict anxiety to one situation rather than a range of them. This anxiety, in turn, may be conceptualized as stemming from unconscious childhood fears of punishment, tied to the wish to do away with father and the accompanying wish to win over mother. Here we have an unconscious defense (the phobia itself) caused by even more deeply unconscious fears, in turn, caused by equally deep unconscious wishes! Contrast this to Wolpe's view, in which the phobic avoidance and internal anxiety are seen as conditioned reactions to the feared object or situation.

The Belief That Behavior, Including Cognitive Behavior, Is Learned and Can Be Unlearned and Relearned

Although nearly all theories of personality and therapy now assume that human functioning is a result of the interaction of biological predispositions and environmental factors, the behavioral and cognitive approaches focus more on how humans go about learning behavioral, emotional, and cognition reactions and patterns. Despite biologically based predispositions, behavior still tends to be learned, the three basic models of learning being instrumental learning, classical conditioning, and modeling. Further, it is *not* assumed that maladaptive behavior is acquired through processes that differ from those for adaptive (healthy) behavior. Both are acquired according to the same fundamental principles of learning. Just as behavior is learned according to certain principles, it can be unlearned and relearned. The same principles may be used to explain this unlearning and relearning process. Let us look briefly at each of the three forms or models of learning and the principles they include.

Instrumental Learning.   In this form of learning, often referred to as *operant conditioning,* behavior is seen as controlled by its consequences. The consequence, *positive reinforcement,* is anything that increases the probability of a response. If a counselor, for example, responds favorably ("Great idea!") when her career-counseling client says he plans to gather more information, and if such a favorable response is followed by increased information-seeking, we would call the counselor's response a positive reinforcer. Positive reinforcement is seen as the most powerful procedure through which behavior is learned.

In like fashion, *negative reinforcement* is anything that increases the probability of a response as a result of avoiding something negative that would have occurred had the escape behavior not been emitted. An example of this would be a client whose avoidance of public speaking is strengthened by the relief that comes from avoiding such activity. A similar concept, *punishment,* refers to the aversive consequences of a response and is often followed by a decrease in that response. For example, a student whose question is ridiculed by a professor would likely reduce his or her questioning. However, the use of an aversive stimulus often has undesirable side effects, so behavior therapists usually prefer a second kind of punishment—the removal of a positive reinforcement. An often used example of this form of punishment is called *time out* (see Sundel & Sundel, 1999). Typically, the individual is taken to a place lacking the usual reinforcers (the misbehaving child is placed in a room holding no rewarding stimuli such as toys or TV).

The final concept to be mentioned under operant conditioning is *shaping,* or *approximation,* whereby a person is rewarded for successively closer approximations of the desired behavior or end state. For example, a young child utters "mmmm" in the presence of his mother and is reinforced by her pleasurable response. Then the child is similarly reinforced for uttering "ma," and then only for the gold-star response: "Ma, ma!"

Classical Conditioning.   This form of learning was discovered by Pavlov in his experiments with dogs. When a stimulus that is neutral is paired with a stimulus that has an effect—the *unconditioned stimulus* (UCS); for example, food in the presence of hungry dogs—the associated *neutral stimulus* begins to elicit the same effects as the UCS. In other words, the bell becomes a *conditioned stimulus* (CS), in that, just like the food, it elicits salivation in the dog. The dog's response to the food, or UCS, is called an *unconditioned response* (UCR); its response to the bell, once the bell becomes a CS, is called a *conditioned response* (CR). Even after the dog is conditioned, its CR will *extinguish* if the CS is presented repeatedly without at least an occasional occurrence of the UCS. (This is similar to extinction of an operant response when reinforcement does not occur.)

In both classical and operant conditioning, two additional principles are crucial to the learning process. The first is *stimulus generalization,* the process through which a person generalizes to others from a specific conditioned or reinforced stimulus. For example, the male client who has learned to trust his mother may also tend to trust other women unless there is reason not to trust. The child who has learned to stay away from fast-moving cars also stays away from other fast-moving objects. However, both accurate and inaccurate generalizations are possible. Thus, a principle called *discrimination*—the learning of proper differentiations among stimuli—must work in tandem with stimulus generalization. The client who grew up with an emotionally destructive father needs to learn not to generalize her reactions to all males, but to discriminate among males regarding their capacity for kindness versus destructiveness.

There are innumerable examples of how classical conditioning may operate in the learning and unlearning of complex behaviors, and the student is invited to suggest such examples as they may apply to the counseling situation. One point we add here is that classical conditioning is no longer seen as the simple pairing of a single US with a single CS. Rather, as Wilson (1995) notes, the correlations between entire classes of stimulus events can be learned. The examples above of generalizing from mother or father to other women or men demonstrate such global conditioning.

Modeling.   The third form of learning, modeling, is also referred to as *imitative learning* and *vicarious learning*. Much human behavior is learned by observing others (the *models*), doing what they do, and emotionally experiencing and imitating what they are seen experiencing. Much of what we learn could not at all be learned or could be learned only very inefficiently without modeling.

Of the three forms of learning, modeling is the newest to be theorized about, and some psychologists continue to believe that modeling is only a subset of classical and operant conditioning. It is true that aspects of operant and classical conditioning are part of the modeling process. For example, to an important extent, modeling occurs because the behaviors exhibited by the model are reinforced, in either the model or learner, or both. Yet modeling seems distinctive enough to warrant its separate discussion. Think about learning any complex skill (flying an airplane, driving a car, becoming an effective counselor) through only operant and classical conditioning (that is, without modeling). It is hard to imagine learning with any degree of efficiency or, in some cases, even safety. At the same time, one can readily see how the other two forms of learning may be added to modeling. In learning to be a counselor, you observe others both directly (on film, in practice sessions) and through reading. But you also receive reinforcement of appropriate counseling reactions and approximations of them. Further, you may observe others as they experience emotional responses to certain client behaviors; and, through vicarious classical conditioning, you may experience the same reactions to such behaviors when you begin counseling.

Before concluding this discussion of the three forms of learning (instrumental learning, classical conditioning, and modeling), it should be emphasized that even therapists who lean toward the cognitive side of the cognitive–behavioral continuum are also inclined to conceptualize their clients' problems, at least partly, in learning terms. Ellis (1995), for example, talks about how individuals are socially conditioned to perceive and cognize in certain ways. In like fashion, Beck and Weishaar (1995) endorse social learning theory and the importance of reinforcement in an attempt to understand how cognitive processes develop, go awry, and can be changed.

The Melding of Behavioral and Cognitive Approaches in Practice

Although the primarily cognitive approaches to counseling (such as Ellis's rational–emotive therapy and Beck's cognitive therapy) were developed outside the mainstream of behavior therapy, behavioral and cognitive approaches tend to be melded in the present-day practice of counseling psychology, as we have noted, so that practitioners usually consider themselves cognitive–behavioral counselors rather than one or the other. This melding has occurred both because (a) the cognitive theories have stated explicitly their use of behavioral techniques and their conceptualization of human behavior in learning terms, and (b) the most popular behavior therapy theories consider internal constructs (e.g., cognition) crucial to development and change.

As implied in (b) above, the behavior therapy scene has encountered dramatic changes in recent years. Applied behavior analysis, a form of radical behaviorism focusing on only overt behavior, was a dominant force in American psychology (including applied psychology) in the not-so-distant past. In the twenty-first century, however, few radical behaviorists still practice. Social–cognitive theory, as represented by the work of Albert Bandura, its leading spokesman, now prevails. Internal constructs, such as expectancies, values, thoughts, and self-efficacy, are key concepts in this approach. Overt behavior still receives much attention in social–cognitive theory, but internal cognitive concepts are now studied in addition to external behavioral concepts. Thus, the modern behavioral counselor is almost always a cognitive–behavioral counselor.

The Predominance of the Present

All cognitive and behavioral approaches place a premium on the here and now. Problems reside in the present and thus it is the present that requires attention in counseling. To be sure, virtually all agree that the past is important in shaping present cognitive and behavioral patterns. Thus, behavioral and cognitive therapists are interested in the client's learning history, and many gather careful assessment data about it. A counselor may, for example, solicit detailed information about the development of a client's social phobia because the sheer duration of this phobia over time is relevant to the methods of treatment. In the same way, the counselor examines past performance because this reveals important information about the client's assets.

Although the assessment of the client's learning or reinforcement history is seen as valuable, even crucial by some, treatment focuses on the present problem. Few, if any, behavioral–cognitive counselors seek in-depth insight into material buried in the client's past; such insight is not seen as especially helpful in resolving current problems. The past may be very interesting, but its revelations alone change nothing. Nevertheless, behavioral and cognitive counselors may indeed search for other kinds of insight—for example, insight into what clients are telling themselves, or insight into the conditions under which certain fears occur. But these kinds of insight are very different from that sought in psychoanalytic or even humanistic treatments.

The emphasis on the here and now clearly separates the cognitive–behavioral counselor from the more classical psychoanalytic therapist. On the other hand, centeredness on the present in cognitive and behavioral approaches is similar to the orientation of humanistic counselors.

Taking the Presenting Problem Seriously

A client seeks counseling because of anxiety about speaking in class. The problem has become more pressing because this client has just been admitted to a graduate program in counseling where the class sizes are very small and emphasis is placed on class discussion. The behavioral counselor would make a careful assessment of this problem—its frequency, intensity, and duration—but would likely view the speaking problem as the key intervention issue. The cognitive therapist may go a step beyond and work on the cognitive beliefs that contribute to the speech anxiety, but this counselor will also stay very close to the presenting problem.

The psychoanalytic or humanistic counselor, on the other hand, may view the speaking problem as a symptom of other issues. These issues are generally seen as unconscious (by the analytic therapist) or outside awareness (by the humanist). What needs treatment is not the symptom but the "real" cause that underlies it. The primarily behavioral counselor, however (differing somewhat from the cognitive), will treat the symptom itself. In fact, behavioral counselors have traditionally adhered to the expression: "The problem is the symptom, and the symptom is the problem."

The Importance of Specific, Clearly Defined Goals

Behavioral and cognitive counselors have a particular aversion to counseling goals that are stated in global—or what they consider "fuzzy"—terms. Thus, goals such as "self-actualization," "personality reorganization," and "resolution of core unconscious conflicts" have always been eschewed by such counselors. Even when clients seek counseling for such reasons, and express their goals in these terms, the behavioral–cognitive counselor works hard to help them be clear and specific. In fact, the counselor usually tries to *operationalize* what constitutes client improvement; that is, tries to state goals so that they are readily measurable and subject to public scrutiny.

An example of this might be seen in a female university student who seeks counseling because she vaguely senses that she does not think highly enough of herself. Careful assessment reveals that this client holds unattainable standards, and harshly criticizes herself when she fails to meet these. The counselor also observes that she tends to denigrate herself verbally. The counselor and client enunciate three goals: The client is to make fewer self-deprecating remarks, reduce her self-critical cognitions, and develop more attainable standards. Such specific problems and goals can be worked on through a variety of behavioral and cognitive interventions. They can also be readily measured.

Similarly, with a client who seeks counseling for specific problems, goals are likewise stated as far as possible in terms of specific behavioral and emotional changes. For example, a male agoraphobic client who fears both enclosed spaces and the outdoors may have counseling goals expressed in terms of increasing the frequency of his visits to a local food store, and lowering his anxiety level during such visits. The client suffering from depression might seek to smile more, make fewer self-blaming comments, engage in a greater number of positive activities, and achieve a more favorable score on an inventory of depression.

A Value on the Active, Directive, and Prescriptive Counselor Role

Behavioral and cognitive counselors work actively with their clients to develop the goals of counseling. As counseling proceeds, the counselor's stance (much more than for humanistic and psychoanalytic counselors) is active, directive, and prescriptive.

Thus, the counselor will actively guide the client during the interview; make suggestions about what the problem is and how it can best be resolved; suggest activities to be engaged in *within* the interview (e.g., role-playing, imagery, and desensitization); and prescribe client behaviors *outside* the interview. Such outside activities, called *homework,* are a hallmark of the behavioral and cognitive approaches. Much in treatment is accomplished *between* sessions, through what the client finds out about himself or herself, practices, and attempts as the result of homework assignments.

Cognitive and behavioral counselors are thus far from the stereotype of the silent analytic counselor. They do not hesitate to talk during the session. In return, the counselor expects parallel client activity. As Wilson (1995) makes clear: "Perhaps more than any other form of treatment, behavior therapy involves asking a patient to do something such as practice relaxation training, self-monitor daily caloric intake, confront anxiety-eliciting situations, and refrain from carrying out compulsive rituals" (p. 208).

The Counselor–Client Relationship as Important But Not Sufficient

When behavior therapy first hit the applied psychology scene in the late 1950s and early 1960s, it presented itself as the superscientific alternative to treatment approaches such as client-centered therapy and, especially, psychoanalysis, both of which were portrayed as something less than scientific. In the behavior therapy literature, the apparent need for rigor was expressed in the use of impersonal language, such as "experimenter and subject" for "therapist and client." Given the premium placed on scientific objectivity, the role of the client–counselor relationship was downplayed as a "soft" factor. It was not a readily observable overt behavior and did not lend itself to rigorous scientific measurement.

As behavior therapy has matured and become more open to the study and treatment of internal processes, and as notions of science and what is scientific have expanded and liberalized (see Chapter 3), the role of the counselor–client relationship has received much greater attention. Virtually all cognitive and behavioral counselors now express the belief that effective treatment is more than the application of a set of techniques, and that the counselor–client relationship is highly important to the change process. At the same time, unlike Carl Rogers and devotees of the person-centered approach, cognitive and behavior therapists do not believe that a good relationship is in itself sufficient to bring about durable change. The relationship is important, rather, inasmuch as it sets the stage for the effective use of techniques. The role of the relationship in behavior therapy as portrayed by Brady (1980) two decades ago is still fitting.

> In general, if the patient's relationship with the therapist is characterized by belief in the therapist's competence . . . and if the patient regards the therapist as an honest, trustworthy, and decent human being with good social and ethical values (in his own scheme of things), the patient is more apt to invest himself in the therapy. Equally important is the quality and tone of the relationship he has with the therapist. That is, if he feels trusting and warm toward the therapist, this generally will facilitate following the treatment regimen, will be associated with higher expectations of improvement, and other generally favorable outcomes.

The feelings of the therapist toward the patient are also important. If the therapist feels that the patient is not a desirable person or a decent human being or simply does not like the patient for whatever reasons, he may not succeed in concealing these attitudes toward the patient, and in general they will have a deleterious effect (pp. 285–286).

The relationship in behavioral therapies is important but is not an end in itself. It provides leverage for the counselor to have the client follow the treatment regimen, and it makes the therapist a more effective reinforcer. Thus the role of the relationship is very different from either psychoanalytic or humanistic interventions. (See Chapter 8 on the therapeutic relationship and chapters 10 and 12 on psychoanalytic and humanistic counseling, respectively.)

The Value of Empirical Data and Scientific Methods

There have been so many changes in behavior therapy over the years that even its definition is no longer clear. This confusion has become especially salient as behavior therapy has incorporated cognitive theory and as cognitive therapy has adopted both behavioral techniques and learning theory as basic explanatory tools. At the same time, it is possible that the only assumption or element common to all so-called behavioral and cognitive approaches is the great value placed on careful empirical study of treatment techniques. Probably more than counselors of any other theoretical persuasion, the behavioral counselor sees himself or herself as an applied behavioral scientist who gathers scientific data and uses research findings about specific treatments in his or her counseling (Goldfried & Davison, 1994; Wilson, 1995).

Given the great emphasis on specificity in behavioral counseling, it is not surprising that practitioners value careful and precise investigations of specific treatment techniques for use with particular client populations. The aim is to build an armamentarium of specific techniques of scientifically demonstrated effectiveness for use with certain client problems in particular situations. It is also not surprising that the impetus for the "empirically validated treatments" movement, as described in Chapter 3, has emanated from researchers aligned with cognitive–behavior therapy. The value on rigorous scientific study of treatment techniques is a deep and inherent part of the cognitive–behavioral approach.

METHODS AND PROCEDURES OF BEHAVIORAL AND COGNITIVE APPROACHES

In this section we summarize a variety of selected assessment and treatment procedures and methods often used by cognitive–behavioral therapists. We follow with a presentation of two primarily cognitive theories of counseling, Ellis's rational–emotive behavior therapy and Beck's cognitive therapy. This section constitutes, however, only a skeletal summary of some frequently used methods and procedures. For a fuller presentation, the reader is referred to book-length discussions by Goldfried and Davison (1994), Kazdin (1994), and Sundel and Sundel (1999). Readable and useful chapters have been presented by Glass and Arnkoff (1992), Rimm and Cunningham (1985), and Wilson (1995).

Assessment Procedures

The first task of the cognitive–behavioral counselor is to develop a sense of rapport and trust with the client. The counselor listens sensitively and empathically as the client discusses the presenting problem. The emerging relationship allows the counselor to seek information from the client that might be too upsetting to divulge in the absence of such a bond. In the initial meeting or meetings, the therapist seeks full understanding of the client's presenting problem. Using his or her theory of behavior and counseling as a guide, the counselor elicits detailed information about the client's problem—how and when it developed; its duration, frequency, intensity, and severity; and the situations in which it occurs. The client's thoughts and feelings about the problem and how the client has tried to cope with it (including past attempts at counseling) are explored. The counselor looks carefully for the environmental and cognitive influences that may be maintaining the problem and that may be expressed through the client's thoughts, feelings, or behavior.

As Wilson (1995) indicates, cognitive and behavioral counselors rarely ask "why" questions, for example, "Why do you get anxious before exams?" or "Why do you feel stressed out at work?" Such questions may be central to the assessment work of the psychoanalytic therapist, but cognitive and behavioral therapists strongly prefer *how, when, where,* and *what* questions as they seek to understand the factors maintaining the problem behavior and situation. The counselor relies heavily on the client's self-reports but does not necessarily take them at face value. Instead, the therapist looks for ways in which the client's reports seem inconsistent or otherwise inaccurate. Such inconsistencies are gently probed or silently noted for later use. As an effort to develop a picture of the problem and its context, the counselor helps the client to be as specific as possible, particularly in terms of how, when, and where the problem is manifested.

As aids in assessment, the counselor uses a variety of techniques in addition to verbal interaction. Among the most prominent are role-playing, guided imagery, self-monitoring, behavioral observation, and psychological testing. In using *role-playing,* the counselor may ask the client to role-play a particular interpersonal situation that seems to be troubling. The counselor can take the role of the person with whom the client is having difficulty or may engage in role reversal, whereby the client plays the other person while the therapist plays the client, or both of these activities. Such role-playing provides the counselor with some preliminary behavioral observations of the client and also helps the client see more clearly what motivates the interaction with the person with whom he or she has a problem.

In *guided imagery* the counselor asks the client to create a visual image of the problem situation and then verbalize this image to the counselor. This enables both counselor and client to get a step closer (more than simple verbal explanation) to what actually goes on in the problem situation and to what the client thinks and feels in that situation. *Self-monitoring* entails the client's keeping a careful daily record of events or reactions that indicate the main problem. For example, the client with anxiety problems may keep a record of situations in which she or he feels anxious, the amount of anxiety experienced, and what triggered the anxiety. As a result, both client and counselor should develop a clearer, more detailed picture of the problem and what is maintaining it.

Unlike the other techniques, *behavioral observations* are ordinarily used by people other than the client (e.g., parents, teachers, hospital personnel) and are created in the client's natural environment (school, home, hospital), where the problem is occurring. The behavioral counselor shows these people how to observe and record the client's behavior objectively. Most often, this procedure is used from an operant conditioning perspective. The observer learns to observe the client's behavior, for example, in the classroom or at home and note the reinforcers and punishers that may influence the behavior. The observers can then be taught how to modify their own behavior so as to help change the client's behavior. For example, parents often learn about reinforcement procedures and how their own behavior may reinforce the problematic behaviors of their child. The parents can then be taught how to use reinforcements to produce the desired behaviors.

Psychological tests, questionnaires, and *checklists* are used by behavioral and cognitive counselors, but only when these measure specific qualities directly relevant to the client's problem situation or behavior. General psychodiagnostic tests, such as the Minnesota Multiphasic Personality Inventory (MMPI), or the varieties of projective devices, are clearly *not* favored. Instead, checklists and questionnaires that assess, for example, fears, anxiety, depression, or assertiveness may be quite useful in obtaining a preliminary picture of the level of severity of the client's problem and determining how the degree of this severity changes across the course of treatment.

As a final note, it must be added that assessment does not cease after the presenting problem has been fully studied. The behavioral–cognitive counselor continues assessment throughout treatment. In such counseling, in fact, assessment is an integral part of the ongoing treatment.

Behavioral and Cognitive Treatment Procedures

More than counselors of any other theoretical orientation, the behavioral–cognitive counselor attempts to match specific treatment techniques to particular client problems. Techniques are selected on the basis of all aspects of the client's problem, the research literature on the effectiveness of the techniques, and the counselor's own clinical judgment about what will work best with the client. Below is a sample of behavior therapy techniques. As we present these, it is important to keep in mind that in actual treatment, various methods are usually combined and that both cognitive and behavioral procedures are frequently used with the same case.

Operant Conditioning
Operant conditioning is both a set of principles that explain how behavior is learned and a technique for modifying behavior. The use of operant conditioning techniques

Some of the Many Techniques of Cognitive–Behavior Therapy.   TABLE 11.2.

Operant conditioning	Assertiveness and social skills training,
Positive reinforcement	behavior rehearsal
Shaping	Flooding
Desensitization	Participant modeling
Systematic desensitization	Self-control procedures
In vivo desensitization	Aversive conditioning
Cognitive restructuring	

may occur in the counselor's office as well as in the environment in which the client's problems occur. Let us look at within-session operant conditioning first.

If the client feels a sense of positive connection to the counselor or at least values the counselor's expertise, he or she will be receptive to the counselor's views and reactions. The counselor in this instance can be a potent reinforcer of behavior change. The behavioral counselor decides which behaviors are to be changed and, if within-office reinforcement techniques seem to fit the situation, the counselor will apply them, usually verbally. For example, in working with a client trying to resolve some career problems and move in a more suitable career direction, the counselor may believe that it is highly important for the client to seek occupational information. If the counselor senses that the client will tend to resist such activity, he or she will verbally reinforce (e.g., "Great idea!" or "That sounds like a real step in the right direction") any hints on the client's part that such information would be helpful. Then, as the work proceeds, the counselor positively reinforces the client's expressed willingness to seek information. Positive reinforcement is thus combined with a shaping procedure. Such methods have been found to be highly effective in promoting occupational information-seeking.

In the above example, positive reinforcement is used to increase a response. What about operant conditioning procedures to extinguish a behavior? Using an out-of-session example, suppose a mother, Ms. Weary, seeks counseling because her 3-year-old child, Jimmy, has recently been having frightful, disruptive temper tantrums in which he holds his breath and throws his toys. The counselor carefully interviews Ms. Weary about the conditions under which the problem occurs and finds that they only occur in the presence of the mother, who has just begun a new job that reduces her time at home with Jimmy. The counselor decides to visit the Weary household to directly observe the situation. It becomes apparent that Ms. Weary picks up her son warmly, and verbally expresses affection, whenever he grows angry. Jimmy is thus getting reinforced for angry behavior. Further discussion reveals that Ms. Weary feels guilty about being away from home, although her new job is stimulating and a clear step forward for her vocationally. The counselor works with Ms. Weary to help her to stop reinforcing Jimmy's angry behavior and ignore it instead. Ms. Weary is to leave the room whenever the tantrums begin. The counselor also suggests that she provide Jimmy with lots of physical and verbal affection when he behaves well. The father, too, who often would get preoccupied with work issues while spending time with the child, is shown how to be more reinforcing when the child is well behaved. In a short time, Ms. Weary, who has been keeping careful records as part of the counseling, reports that Jimmy has essentially stopped his tantrums, is getting lots of loving from both parents, and seems happier generally.

Desensitization

Systematic desensitization (SD) is one of the most thoroughly studied behavioral interventions for extinguishing anxiety and other fear-based responses; it has been found effective for a wide range of anxiety-related problems (Goldfried & Davison, 1994). Growing out of studies that sought to remove conditioned fears in animals, it was adapted for use with humans by Joseph Wolpe (1958). The idea is that when anxiety is systematically paired with an incompatible state, the anxiety will disappear as a result of counterconditioning or will be inhibited, according to the principle of *reciprocal inhibition*. The response used most frequently to inhibit anxiety is relaxation, specifically deep-muscle relaxation.

SD comprises four steps (Deffenbacher & Suinn, 1988). The first is to give the client a rationale for the procedure. This should be stated in a nontechnical manner, and impart the concept that fears are learned and thus can be unlearned through desensitization. The second step is relaxation training. The client is usually taught progressive deep-muscle relaxation, a technique Wolpe adapted from Jacobson (1938). The client is also asked to remember a specific experience in which she or he felt deeply relaxed, and the counselor helps the client construct a scene around this. Third, the counselor and client work together to construct a visual hierarchy of anxiety-arousing scenes, ranging from nonanxiety-arousing to extremely upsetting, all related to the specific problem. For example, if the client is seeking counseling because of exam anxiety, the most upsetting scene may picture that student sitting in a classroom about to receive the final exam from the teacher. Visual hierarchies typically include 8–15 scenes, none of which should elicit more anxiety than those next to it. Usually the counselor tries to space scenes evenly according to their anxiety-arousing potential.

The final step in SD is desensitization proper, in which the scenes in the hierarchy are, step by step, paired with relaxation. Typically, after the client is deeply relaxed, the counselor asks him or her to visualize the least anxiety-arousing scene in the hierarchy. If the client feels any significant anxiety when visualizing this scene, he or she is to raise a finger. If this happens, the client is instructed to visualize the highly relaxing experience they initially worked on. If no anxiety is felt after two or more trials of the first scene, the counselor asks the client to visualize the next one on the hierarchy. If anxiety is experienced, the counselor drops back to the previous scene and repeats the visualization of that scene two more times. This process continues until the client is able to visualize all scenes on the hierarchy without experiencing anxiety. Termination of counseling occurs when the client is able to experience success in dealing with the actual feared situation—for example, the test-anxious client is able to take exams with relative ease; the person with a phobia is able to perform activities that he or she was phobic about earlier.

One variant of SD is *in vivo desensitization*. The procedure is the same as in SD, except that the hierarchy is presented in real life. The house-bound agoraphobic client may have a hierarchy that begins with stepping outside the house and ends with shopping at the local grocery store. The counselor usually accompanies the client in moving through the hierarchy. If the client becomes anxious, she or he is assisted in relaxation behavior. In vivo desensitization can be a powerful procedure and is recommended whenever it is viable (see Beidel & Turner, 1998; Goldfried & Davison, 1994). To be effective, however, the counselor must have full control over the implementation of the hierarchy. This is not always feasible, for example, when anxiety is tied to public speaking, social interaction, or sexual situations.

It should be noted that the progressive relaxation component of SD is often used as a treatment in itself and can be an effective procedure for coping with anxiety and stress. Another variant of SD, called *covert sensitization*, is used to extinguish undesirable behaviors such as alcoholism and certain sexual disorders, for example, exhibitionism. Here, the client is asked to imagine aversive consequences in response to the undesired acts. An alcoholic might be asked to imagine nausea at the thought of a drink, an exhibitionist to imagine being handcuffed in public by the police. A hierarchy of scenes that depict the unwanted behaviors is developed, and each scene is presented in a step-by-step fashion until the client is able to control the problem behavior.

Flooding

In certain ways, flooding is the opposite of SD. SD seeks to *minimize* anxiety by pairing small doses of it with a contradictory state (e.g., deep relaxation). Flooding *maximizes* anxiety. The agoraphobic client might be asked to imagine being away from home, in a crowded supermarket, without having first gone through a hierarchy of scenes. The anxiety here will be quite high, but it usually dissipates if the client stays with the scene long enough. Thus, through repeated exposure to high-anxiety scenes, in the absence of any actual harm, anxiety becomes extinguished.

A form of flooding that is frequently used is *in vivo flooding*, which has been found to be effective with agoraphobics. Again, using a trip to the supermarket as our example, the client might first approach the task in a graduated fashion (as in vivo desensitization). Then, once the client is able to approach the supermarket, the counselor may go with the client to the market, urging him or her to stay there regardless of the anxiety, until the anxiety subsides. The principle, again, is that anxiety will disappear if not reinforced. The client sees that he or she is not endangered, that nothing bad happens, so the anxiety eventually dissipates.

Flooding is a potentially useful method, but it is also clearly a high-stress method that inexperienced counselors should not attempt without supervision. Rimm and Cunningham (1985) point to evidence that flooding may be especially effective, for example, with agoraphobics, when combined with drug therapy. Medication, such as tricyclics or monoamine oxidase (MAO) inhibitors, is administered first, and then followed by the application of in vivo flooding.

Assertiveness and Social Skills Training

Counselors often work with clients who are inhibited in expressing their emotions and who do not stand up for themselves. Such people lack assertiveness, a skill that behavioral and cognitive counselors have worked with considerably over the years. The major strategy used within assertiveness training is called *behavior rehearsal*. Here the counselor helps the client specify situations in which he or she is unassertive. The counselor then plays the role of the person toward whom the client wants to be more assertive while the client role-plays assertiveness. The client pays attention to his or her feelings during and after the role-playing; the counselor observes specific strengths and weaknesses, positively reinforcing positive behavior and nonjudgmentally noting the negative. In addition, the therapist often models effective assertive behaviors for the client. Therapist modeling is especially effective if the client lacks knowledge about effective assertiveness; it also gets the client in touch with what it feels like to be the target of the modeled response.

Following counselor modeling, the client imitates the modeled responses, and the counselor verbally reinforces improvements (*shaping*), attending to both verbal and nonverbal client behavior. If the client is working on expressing negative emotion, it is best to have the client begin with a mild response. Doing so aims at reducing the chances that the target person will be "backed into a corner" and forced to respond defensively (Rimm & Cunningham, 1985). In case the minimal responses are not effective, assertiveness training helps the client learn how to escalate assertions. Also, it may be best for the counselor to fade out both modeling and reinforcement during treatment, since modeling does not occur in the real world and the client must learn to be *self-reinforcing*. This fading out is thought to lead the client to greater self-directed mastery and persistence in his or her natural environment (Rimm & Masters, 1979).

Participant Modeling

In discussing assertiveness training, and at other points, we have commented on the use of modeling in counseling. The term *participant modeling* (or equivalents such as *contact desensitization, demonstration plus participation*) is often used to describe a specific set of procedures that involve the counselor's modeling through demonstration, followed by the client's imitation of the modeled responses. These procedures are carried out in a graduated fashion. Participant modeling has been found to be effective for a wide range of specific fears and anxieties and is currently being used a great deal to treat social phobias (e.g., agoraphobia).

Consider the steps that might be taken with participant modeling in treating the client suffering from agoraphobia. The goal of treatment might be for the client to be able to walk comfortably to the local food market. The first step would be to teach the person relaxation techniques, with a focus on deep breathing. The next step would be for the counselor to walk out onto the client's sidewalk, in the client's full view, and then do some deep breathing. Then the counselor and client would walk together out onto the sidewalk, with the counselor offering instruction and support. Finally, the client would perform this task alone, using the skills she or he has just learned. This same procedure (counselor first, the client and counselor together, and finally client alone), is used for each step, the final step being the goal—the client's comfortably walking to the local market. At each step, the counselor should positively reinforce the client's behavior with verbal praise.

Self-Control Procedures

Self-control methods grew out of behavior therapists' desire to help clients control their own destiny rather than be passive recipients of conditioning procedures. Self-control methods emphasize the client as an active agent who can cope and exert effective control in problem situations. These methods are most appropriate in situations where natural reinforcements are long term and no short-term reinforcements are available for the desired behavior. An example is academic performance, wherein effective study behavior is usually not reinforced soon after it occurs. Rather, the student must wait until the next exam or even the end of a semester for reinforcement. Such delays make it extremely difficult to learn new desired behaviors or extinguish old, undesirable ones. Self-control methods provide short-term reinforcements until the longer-term reinforcers become available.

Clients who use self-control methods serve as their own therapists in administering their own rewards and punishments. Because of this, therapists often give such clients instruction in behavior modification, with particular emphasis on operant conditioning principles. Thus, clients are taught basic learning principles, the importance of reinforcement being contingent on given behaviors, and the idea of stimulus control.

Behavior therapists now use a range of self-control procedures (Glass & Arnkoff, 1992; Kanfer, 1977). Kanfer and colleagues devised a multistage procedure for helping clients enhance their self-control, a procedure that has been particularly effective in the treatment of obesity (Rimm & Cunningham, 1985). The first stage entails the client's carefully monitoring his or her behavior, for example, the frequency of eating (how much, how fast, how often) and the surrounding situations (when watching TV, late at night). This gives the counselor and client a baseline for the problem behavior. The second stage entails establishing goals. It is essential that these be specific, reinforceable, and short term. Thus the counselor might work with the client to specify daily caloric intake. When goals are short term, the client is able to experience more reinforcements; when goals are specific, the client has a clearer sense of what is needed.

The third step is the actual treatment in which the self-control methods are applied. Rimm and Masters (1979) detail the following procedures for the treatment of obesity: (1) removing undesirable foods from the house, particularly high-calorie foods that do not require preparation; (2) changing eating behavior, for example, returning eating utensils to the table between bites, taking short breaks during the meal; (3) stimulus narrowing—restricting eating to certain places; (4) having the client eat in situations where he or she does not typically overeat; (5) reinforcing improvements in eating behavior; and (6) encouraging competing responses, for example, taking a walk while delaying eating.

Contingency Contracting

Contingency contracting, which relies on operant conditioning principles, is a form of behavioral management in which the rewards and punishments for desired and undesired behaviors are established in advance, frequently by a *written contract* with the client (Rimm & Masters, 1979). The first step is assessment. The counselor and client work together to specify the behaviors that need to be modified. They may work toward increasing the frequency of desired behaviors that occur too seldom or decreasing undesirable behaviors undertaken too often. During assessment, counselor and client decide on who will dispense the rewards and punishments (e.g., client, parent, or teacher), and what these will be. Rewards might be money, praise, being allowed to attend movies—anything that the client enjoys. Punishments usually entail withholding the preferred rewards. During the assessment, it is helpful to get a baseline for the target behaviors. Note that such monitoring and recording of the behaviors is also useful during treatment, to get a clear picture of change. Also, seeing change is in itself reinforcing.

Treatment involves simply enforcing the contingencies. Again, this can be done by the client (a self-control method) or someone else. The reinforcers should be applied each time the target behavior is manifested. If this is not possible, "points" can be given for each performance of the target behavior. After reaching a specified amount, the points would convert into a reward or punishment. A good example of contingency contracting as a self-control procedure might be a college student who seeks help because of poor study behaviors. The counselor and client would work together to specify the desired study behaviors to be rewarded and the undesirable ones to be punished. Care would be taken to allow for rewards for effective short-term steps (shaping); for example, if the student typically studies only a half-hour per day, points or rewards could be given for studying 1 hour per day at first, with study time gradually increasing. With the counselor's guidance, the student would decide on the reinforcers. These could include self-praise, often an effective reinforcer. Note that the treatment occurs *between* sessions. During the sessions themselves, the counselor and client review progress and adjust the contract if necessary. The counselor could also provide verbal reinforcement for desired behavior.

Cognitive Restructuring

On a cognitive–behavioral spectrum, the methods and procedures discussed so far would be found on the behavioral end. Cognitive restructuring, on the other hand, is the one overarching method that would be found on the cognitive end. The assumption underlying this method is that, in one way or another, what clients say to themselves and how they say it (their self-talk or cognitions) determine or shape their problems. Thus cognitive restructuring entails helping clients change their cognitions.

Cognitive restructuring is a broad term that includes identifying and changing anxiety-causing cognitions. As detailed by Meichenbaum and Deffenbacher (1988), these cognitions may be in the form of cognitive *events,* cognitive *processes,* cognitive *structures,* or all these. Cognitive events are what people say to themselves, and the images they have, that they are aware of and can report. Cognitive processes operate at an automatic and "unconscious" level and include the *way* people process information—how they appraise events, selectively attend to and remember events, and incorporate information consistent with their beliefs. Cognitive structures are even broader, constituting the individual's assumptions and beliefs about the self and the world in relation to the self. There is clearly much overlap in these three concepts, and it may be useful to think of them as existing on a continuum ranging from specific thoughts to global assumptions. The latter have a pervasive and general effect on how people behave and feel.

A wide variety of cognitive approaches now exists (Kazdin, 1994) but as Meichenbaum and Deffenbacher (1988) note, all cognitive restructuring procedures include the following: (1) evaluating how valid and viable are the client's thoughts and beliefs; (2) assessing what clients expect, what they tend to predict about their behavior and others' responses to them; (3) exploring what might be a range of causes for clients' behavior and others' reactions; (4) training clients to make more effective attributions about these causes; and (5) altering absolutistic, catastrophic thinking styles (discussed below under rational–emotive therapy).

Two Primarily Cognitive Approaches to Counseling

Below we summarize the two most prominent cognitive approaches to therapy, Ellis's rational emotive behavior therapy and Beck's cognitive therapy. We single out these because each is a theory of therapy in and of itself, is well known, and has substantial research support. Both are cognitive–behavior therapies, relying on principles of learning and using behavioral methods in addition to focusing on cognitive change. But, at the core, the two approaches are more cognitive than behavioral because they posit that cognitions are the primary motivators of behavior and emotions, and that changing cognitions provides the most effective treatment.

In addition to the two approaches discussed below, the interested student may consult Goldfried's (1988) rational restructuring, a method that provides more structure to Ellis's rational emotive behavior therapy and a greater focus on personal coping skills. Also, Meichenbaum's stress inoculation training (see Meichenbaum & Deffenbacher, 1988) is substantially cognitive and has proven effective for many anxiety-related problems (Sandel & Sandel, 1999). In Table 11.3 we summarize the key concepts of these two therapies as well as the therapist's approach to the client. Below we describe Ellis and Beck's theories in greater detail.

The Rational Emotive Behavior Therapy of Albert Ellis

Albert Ellis began his clinical practice by conducting psychoanalytic psychotherapy but found that such treatment did not yield the degree of change that he sought, particularly given the long duration of analysis. As a consequence, he developed his own system of therapy, labeled *rational–emotive therapy*. The work that provided the basis for this treatment and for all Ellis's subsequent and prolific writing was his *Reason and Emotion in Psychotherapy* (Ellis, 1962). Recently, Ellis changed the name of his therapy from rational–emotive therapy to rational emotive *behavior* therapy (REBT) (Ellis, 1995). Although his theory continues to be fundamentally cognitive, the name change was due to that fact that Ellis has always considered behavior change an important element of treatment. He points out how behavior and

TABLE 11.3.   **Key Concepts of Ellis's Rational Emotive Behavior Therapy and Beck's Cognitive Therapy.**

Theory	Originator	Key Concepts	Therapist Approach
Rational–Emotive behavior therapy	Albert Ellis	ABC Theory Irrational beliefs catastrophizing musturbating absolutistic thinking	active–directive–persuasive
Cognitive therapy	Aaron Beck	Cognitive Distortions arbitrary inference selective abstraction overgeneralization magnification and minimization personalization	collaborative empiricism Socratic dialogue

cognitions reciprocally influence each other, and pays close attention to his client's behavior as he seeks to affect their cognitions (Ellis, 1995).

The most fundamental aspect of REBT is what Ellis calls his ABC theory. In this theory, A is the activating event, B is the client's beliefs or cognitions, and C is the client's resulting emotional reactions and behavior (the outcome). In most conceptions the activating event (A) is seen as causing the client's feelings and behavior (C). This is not so in Ellis's theory. Instead, it is point B, the client's beliefs or cognitions, that cause the resulting behavior and feelings. In other words, it is how we cognitively interpret activating events that most basically determines our resulting emotional reactions and behavior. These cognitions include what the client tells himself or herself about A and about the self in relation to A; they are so to speak internalized sentences the person utters. The cognitions of B may also be broader, representing the client's belief system. Emotional difficulties are caused when the person's cognitions are irrational and self-defeating. The job of REBT is to correct these irrational beliefs and replace them with rational and emotionally healthy beliefs.

Ellis (1995) uses as an example of irrational beliefs at point B a woman with severe emotional problems who is rejected by her lover. This troubled woman does not simply feel that it is undesirable to be rejected. Rather, she is inclined to also believe that "(a) it is *awful;* (b) she *cannot stand* it; (c) she *should not,* must not be rejected; (d) she will *never* be accepted by any desirable partner; (e) she is a *worthless* person because one lover has rejected her; and (f) she *deserves to be damned* for being so worthless" (p. 164).

In his earliest work, Ellis listed 11 basic irrational, "senseless" ideas that are common in our culture and lead to neurosis. Perhaps the two most common (Goldfried, 1988) involve approval from others and perfection. An example of the former is: "If I am not liked and approved of by others, that is terrible and I am no good." An example of the latter: "If I don't do a perfect job at everything I try, then I am no good." The common element of such beliefs is "catastrophizing" (if this or that happens or does not happen, it would be terrible and a catastrophe), "musturbating" (such and such must happen or must not happen), and "absolutistic" thinking (this or that is always so).

Where do such irrational beliefs and schemas come from, and how are they to be treated? Although human beings have vast resources for growth, they also have powerful inborn tendencies to think irrationally and harm themselves. They are born with "an exceptionally strong tendency to want, to 'need,' and to condemn (1) themselves, (2) others, and (3) the world when they do not immediately get what they supposedly 'need' " (Ellis, 1995, p. 170). These tendencies are then deeply influenced by one's family upbringing and by social conditioning; early conditioning is the most durable. The irrational beliefs, once conditioned, are maintained by the person's continual reindoctrination of himself or herself. By the time a client seeks counseling, his or her cognitive beliefs and assumptions are deeply ingrained.

Counseling is most effective if the counselor actively exposes and corrects the client's irrational, self-defeating thinking. Because irrational thinking is deeply ingrained, it requires active and powerful treatment methods to change. The more passive approaches, for example, psychoanalysis, are less effective than active and directive therapy. On the other hand, Ellis (1995), who does not mince words, tells us that irrational beliefs, such as those of the woman rejected by her lover, "can be elicited and demolished by any scientist worth his or her salt, and the rational–emotive therapist is partly that: an exposing and skeptical scientist" (p. 164). The rational–emotive therapist uses a wide range of techniques: role-playing, assertion training, operant conditioning, desensitization, humor, suggestion, support, and so forth. But above all, REBT entails active, vigorous, logical *persuasion* to help the client see and change irrational thinking and behavior.

REBT does not place value upon insight into the unconscious or childhood causes. Rather, REBT therapists help their clients develop insights into how their own beliefs and assumptions, once learned, are the root causes of their problems because clients keep reindoctrinating themselves. Once the client understands this, REBT strives to give the client insight that only through *hard work and practice* will these irrational self-defeating beliefs be corrected—and remain corrected. Only repeated rethinking and actions will extinguish the irrational beliefs. Ellis's view of REBT is nicely capsulized in the following quote.

> REBT practitioners often employ a fairly rapid-fire active-directive-persuasive-philosophic methodology. In most instances, they quickly pin clients down to a few basic dysfunctional beliefs. They challenge them to try to defend these ideas; show that they contain illogical premises that cannot be substantiated logically; analyze these ideas and actively dispute them; vigorously show how they cannot work and why they will almost inevitably lead to more disturbance; reduce these ideas to absurdity, sometimes in a humorous manner; explain how they can be replaced with more rational philosophies; and teach clients how to think scientifically, so they can observe, logically parse, and minimize any subsequent irrational ideas and illogical deductions that lead to self-defeating feelings and behaviors (Ellis, 1995, p. 178).

The Cognitive Therapy of Aaron T. Beck

Aaron Beck, like Albert Ellis, was originally trained in psychoanalysis. In the early 1960s he investigated Freud's theory of depression as "anger turned on the self," but found that the data he gathered did not support the theory. Instead, Beck found that the basic problem in depression was in how patients processed information—their cognitive processing. Based on this research, Beck (1967) developed a cognitive theory of depression and subsequently a cognitive therapy for depression as well as other disorders (Beck, 1976). A recent overview of this cognitive therapy is provided by Beck and Weishaar (1995).

Cognitive therapy is a brief (typically 12–16 sessions) present-centered, active, directive, and problem-oriented approach to counseling. In these ways it resembles REBT. Beck notes these similarities as well as Ellis's influence on the development of cognitive and behavioral therapies in general (Beck & Weishaar, 1995). Cognitive therapy differs from REBT, however, in aspects of its theory of personality and maladaptive behavior, and in the manner in which the therapist works with the client. Unlike REBT, cognitive therapy does not assume that the troubled person has "irrational beliefs" and that the disorder will be corrected by modifying these beliefs through persuasion. Rather, the therapist and client work collaboratively to find and understand the "dysfunctional" cognitive thoughts and underlying assumptions that are contributing to the client's problems. Also in contrast to REBT, Beck theorized that each psychological disorder has its own unique cognitive content. For example, people suffering from panic disorders show different cognitive content from those experiencing depression, obsessive–compulsive disorders, and paranoid problems. Each disorder requires a different approach to treatment.

Cognitive therapy uses a learning model to conceptualize how personality develops and how dysfunctional cognitive thoughts and assumptions form. Beck has delineated several kinds of systematic errors in reasoning (cognitive distortions) that appear when people are in distress. *Arbitrary inference* entails drawing conclusions in the absence of supporting evidence. An example of this might be the counselor who concludes after an especially difficult day with her clients, "I am an ineffectual counselor." *Selective abstraction* involves conceptualizing a situation on the basis of a detail taken out of context; for example, a man becomes jealous on seeing his fiancée lean toward another man to hear him at a noisy gathering. *Overgeneralization* means abstracting a general rule from a few instances and applying it too broadly. For example, based on the indifferent response of students in one undergraduate class to a few of his lectures, a college professor concludes, "All students are alike; my lectures will never be well received." *Magnification* and *minimization* involve perceiving something as far more or less significant than it is, for example: "If I don't do well on this date, that will be a disaster"; "This course will be a piece of cake for me" (think of the situations in which this form of minimization occurs). *Personalization* entails attributing blame for some event to oneself without any evidence, for example, when an acquaintance does not return a woman's hello from across a crowded room, the woman concludes that "I must have offended him." Finally, *dichotomous thinking* is rigid either/or thinking; for example, a man makes the cognitive assumption that "either women will reject and hate you or they will love you and give you everything you want."

Cognitive therapists, according to Beck and Weishaar (1995), are warm, empathic, and genuine as they try to understand how their clients experience the world and cognize their experiences. Unlike in Ellis's REBT, cognitive therapists do not persuasively confront their clients' irrational beliefs. Rather, they work together with their clients in what Beck calls *collaborative empiricism.* Therapists often help their clients frame their thoughts and assumptions into hypotheses. When these hypotheses represent cognitive distortions, therapists will seek to help clients see the faulty logic. At other times, counselors devise "behavioral experiments" that require clients to test their hypotheses outside of the counseling session. Beck conceptualizes the therapeutic process as one of *guided discovery,* rather than the therapist exhorting and cajoling the client to adopt a new set of beliefs. A major therapeutic technique used by cognitive therapists is *Socratic dialogue.* Thus therapists carefully develop a series of questions that they ask clients to promote learning. The purpose of this questioning is to help the client arrive at logical conclusions. Cognitive therapists do more than raise questions, though. They actively point out cognitive themes and underlying assumptions that appear to be working against their clients; they devise homework assignments aimed at helping clients see and correct dysfunctional thoughts, assumptions, and behavior; they use a wide range of both cognitive and behavioral procedures to correct faulty cognitions and behavior.

Four common specific cognitive techniques are decatastrophizing, reattribution, redefining, and decentering. *Decatastrophizing,* or "what if" hypothesizing, helps clients think through the outcomes they most fear and to make plans to cope with them. *Reattribution* moves clients toward considering alternative causes for events and reactions. This technique is especially helpful to clients who erroneously take responsibility for events and others' reactions. *Redefining* the problem seeks to make it more concrete and specific, and to state it in terms of the client's behavior. For example, the client who feels "nobody cares about me" may be led to redefine the problem to: "I need to reach out to people and show that I care about them." *Decentering* is a technique for treating anxious people who believe they are the constant focus of others' attention. After exploring in detail the logic of this belief, the cognitive therapist designs behavioral experiments that test it. Beck and Weishaar (1995) use the example of an anxious student who believed everyone was focusing on him. This student was instructed to observe others carefully, and he became aware that some were taking notes, some daydreaming, some watching the professor, and so forth. He concluded that his classmates had other concerns.

THE BEHAVIORAL AND COGNITIVE APPROACHES IN PERSPECTIVE

The Efficacy of Behavioral and Cognitive Therapies

Abundant research has been carried out on the effects of behavior therapy, cognitive therapy, and cognitive–behavioral therapy, on these therapies in general as well as on specific behavioral techniques and procedures. From their beginnings in the 1950s, the behavior therapies have been shown to have positive effects on clients, as have the cognitive therapies and cognitive–behavioral amalgamations in more recent times. In the overwhelming majority of studies, behavioral and cognitive procedures have demonstrated effectiveness well beyond what would be expected using a control group of nontreated clients or subjects. Also, in comparison to the psychoanalytic and humanistic therapies (see chapters 10 and 12), behavioral and cognitive approaches appear to fare *at least* as well. The typical finding is that all of the major approaches to counseling perform equally well. When differences have been found, however, between behavioral or cognitive therapies on the one hand, and psychoanalytic or humanistic therapies on the other, outcomes have usually favored the cognitive and behavioral therapies (see reviews of research by Emmelkamp [1994], Hollon and Beck [1994], Lambert and Bergin [1994], and Wampold, Mondin, Moody et al. [1997]). It is not now clear, however, whether the small differences in favor of the behavioral and cognitive approaches are valid or are due to methodological problems in the research to date (Lambert & Bergin, 1994).

The main, overarching question to which behavior therapy has addressed itself from its beginnings goes something like, "What techniques offered by which therapists work best when used with which clients possessing what kinds of problems?" (See Krumboltz, 1966; Paul, 1967.) Referred to as the *"who, what, when, and where"* question of counseling research, this formulation contains the numerous specific questions that counseling psychology researchers need to address (Gelso & Fassinger, 1990). Behavioral and cognitive counselors have probably done more to address these multifaceted issues than anyone else in the applied psychology fields. Answers are elusive, however, and the overwhelming majority of studies comparing, for example, one cognitive or behavioral technique to another, tend to show no differences. Although some answers are now emerging (see Emmelkamp, 1994), just how to match clients to treatments remains one of the most challenging research questions in behavioral and cognitive therapy.

In concluding this section, one further issue in behavior therapy presents itself. One early and potentially devastating criticism of behavior therapy by, for example, psychoanalysts was that when one treats a symptom, even if the treatment is successful, the underlying problem will just appear in another form. Unless the underlying problem is treated, the resolution of one symptom will be followed by the emergence of yet another symptom. Because this *symptom substitution* could be so damning to behavior therapy, the early behavior therapy researchers were sure to examine carefully whether empirical evidence existed to suggest such a phenomenon. In fact, of the numerous studies on this topic, none supports symptom substitution in behavior therapy. If anything, the hard data seem to suggest that successful treatment of a specific symptom or behavior in behavior therapy is likely to positively affect the person in other ways. For example, if a client with speech anxiety is successfully treated with systematic desensitization (see Paul's classic study and follow-up in Paul [1966, 1967]), the client is also likely to experience overall reduced anxiety and improved self-concept.

Counseling Psychology and the Behavioral and Cognitive Approaches

Most likely, behavioral and cognitive approaches are a major force in counseling psychology today because of their basic compatibility. In terms of counseling psychology's defining features, it can be seen that the cognitive and behavioral approaches also focus very clearly on clients' strengths or assets. In contrast to classical psychoanalysis, where it seems as if everything is a defense against something and pathology is latent in every behavior (we exaggerate to make the point), behavior therapy, since its inception, has been adroit in uncovering the client's strengths and building on those.

A second defining feature of counseling psychology that has made for an excellent fit with the cognitive and behavioral approaches is its emphasis on brevity in treatments. Although both counseling psychology and these learning-based approaches can permit, and are not opposed to, long-term treatments, the norm is brief treatment. Translated into duration of individual counseling or therapy, the behavioral and cognitive approaches are typically completed well within 6 months; probably the usual number of sessions is 10–12 (2–3 months of counseling).

Finally, one of the principal defining features of counseling psychology has been attention to both the person and the environment (the person–environment interaction) in determining behavior. Yet it has seemed that in counseling psychology research and practice, the environmental part of the equation has often been left out. Of all the approaches to counseling, though, the learning-based ones do pay very close attention to the environment, in terms of what originally caused behavior, what currently serves to control it, and how to modify it. Emphasis on environment or external factors has been especially strong in the behavior therapies.

Despite these ways in which counseling psychology and the learning-based approaches are highly compatible, the behavior therapies did not become a major force in counseling psychology until cognitive processes began to be addressed. In the earlier days of behavior therapy, when only external events and limited aspects of the person's internal life (e.g., autonomically based conditioned anxiety) were considered and treated, it seemed as though the center of the person was being left out of the equation. To many counseling psychologists, behavior therapy, true to its behaviorist roots, placed too little value on the worth and dignity of humans, viewing them instead as no more than conditioned reactions, albeit complex ones. With the advent of social–cognitive theory and the cognitive–behavioral approaches, however, this has changed. The human's interior is amply attended to in the dominant forms of learning-based approaches, and the individual is seen as an active agent in the learning process of living, rather than as a passive recipient of stimuli.

Summary

In present-day counseling psychology, the behavioral and the cognitive perspectives rely heavily on each other, and nearly all practitioners who lean toward cognitive and behavioral theories mix the two. Such theoretical orientation is called *cognitive–behavioral counseling*.

Of the two approaches to counseling, the behavioral developed first, growing out of the *behaviorism movement* that began in the early part of the twentieth century as well as out of the experimental research on the *psychology of learning* that had begun around the turn of that century. Principles of classical conditioning (as in Pavlov's experiments) and operant conditioning (as in the work of B. F. Skinner) were formulated. Behavior therapy itself was born in the 1950s, its most important early book, Joseph Wolpe's *Psychotherapy by Reciprocal Inhibition,* appearing in 1958. In the 1960s, behavior therapy began to pay attention to internal cognitive processes such as expectancies, values, and beliefs. Albert Ellis, Albert Bandura, and Aaron Beck, each of whom stressed cognition in one way or another, contributed significantly to the cognitive revolution that deeply affected behavioral and cognitive counseling.

Nine basic assumptions of the cognitive and behavioral perspectives were discussed: (1) attention to overt processes; (2) the belief that behavior is learned, with a focus on classical, operant, and imitative learning; (3) the melding of cognitive and behavioral approaches in today's practice of counseling psychology; (4) the prepotency of the present in the conduct of counseling; (5) the fact that the client's presenting problem is taken very seriously by these approaches; (6) the great importance of specific and clearly defined goals in treatment; (7) the value placed on an active, directive, and prescriptive approach during counseling; (8) the view of the counselor–client relationship as important but not sufficient; and (9) the central value of controlled, scientific research in the practice of counseling.

A wide range of behavioral and cognitive procedures was described, from *operant conditioning* as it may be used in counseling, to *desensitization,* to the more cognitive procedure of *cognitive restructuring.* The two most prominent cognitively oriented therapies are Ellis's *rational emotive behavior therapy* (REBT) and Beck's *cognitive therapy.* The research on the effectiveness of behavioral and cognitive therapies, and their combination, shows them to be *at least as effective,* and often somewhat more effective, than other therapies. Further supporting the efficacy of cognitive–behavioral counseling, the available evidence clearly refutes the criticism that *symptom substitution* diminishes the effectiveness of these therapies.

The cognitive and behavioral approaches are a major force in counseling psychology today because they are highly compatible with counseling psychology's emphasis on human beings' assets, on treatment brevity, and on the person–environment interaction. The behavioral and cognitive approaches have become even more attractive to counseling psychologists in recent times because of the attention given to the internal life of the person.

REFERENCES

Bandura, A. (1969). *Principles of behavior modification.* New York: Holt, Rinehart & Winston.

Bandura, A. (1977). *Social learning theory.* Englewood Cliffs, NJ: Prentice-Hall.

Bandura, A. (1986). *Social foundations of thought and action: A social cognitive theory.* Englewood Cliffs, NJ: Prentice-Hall.

Bandura, A. (1997). *Self-efficacy: The exercise of control.* New York: Freeman.

Beck, A. T. (1967). *Depression: Clinical, experimental, and theoretical aspects.* New York: Hoeber.

Beck, A. T. (1976). *Cognitive therapy and the emotional disorders.* New York: International Universities Press.

Beck, A. T., & Weishaar, M. E. (1995). Cognitive therapy. In R. Corsini and D. Wedding (Eds.). *Current psychotherapies* (5th ed., pp. 229–261). Itasca, IL: Peacock.

Beidel, D. C., & Turner, S. M. (1998). *Shy children, phobic adults.* Washington, DC: American Psychological Association.

Brady, J. P. (1980). Some views on effective principles of psychotherapy. *Cognitive Therapy and Research, 4,* 271–306.

Deffenbacher, J. L., & Suinn, R. M. (1988). Systematic desensitization and the reduction of anxiety. *The Counseling Psychologist, 16,* 9–30.

Ellis, A. (1962). *Reason and emotion in psychotherapy.* New York: Lyle Stuart.

Ellis, A. (1995). Rational emotive behavior therapy. In R. Corsini and D. Wedding (Eds.), *Current psychotherapies* (5th ed., pp. 162–196) Itasca, IL: Peacock.

Emmelkamp, P. M. G. (1994). Behavior therapy with adults. In A. Bergin and S. Garfield (Eds.), *Handbook of psychotherapy and behavior change* (4th ed., pp. 379–427). New York: John Wiley & Sons.

Eysenck, H. J. (1952). The effects of psychotherapy: An evaluation. *Journal of Consulting Psychology, 16,* 319–324.

Eysenck, H. J. (1959). Learning theory and behavior threrapy. *British Journal of Medical Science, 105,* 61–75.

Eysenck, H. J. (Ed.). (1960). *Behavior therapy and the neurosis.* Oxford: Pergamon Press.

Gelso, C. J., & Fassinger, R. E. (1990). Counseling Psychology: Theory and research on interventions. *Annual Review of Psychology, 41,* 355–386.

Glass, C. R., & Arnkoff, D. B. (1992). Behavior therapy. In S. Freedheim (Ed.), *History of psychotherapy: A century of change* (pp. 587–628). Washington, DC: American Psychological Association.

Goldfried, M. R. (1988). Application of rational restructuring to anxiety disorders. *The Counseling Psychologist, 16,* 50–68.

Goldfried, M. R., & Davison, G. C. (1994). *Clinical behavior therapy* (2nd ed.). New York: Wiley Interscience.

Hollon, S. D., & Beck, A. T. (1994). Cognitive and cognitive–behavioral therapies. In A. Bergin and S. Garfield (Eds.), *Handbook of psychotherapy and behavior change* (4th ed., pp. 428–466). New York: John Wiley & Sons.

Jacobson, E. (1938). *Progressive relaxation.* New York: Brunner/Mazel.

Johnson, M. E., & Brems, C. (1991). Comparing theoretical orientation of counseling and clinical psychologists: An objective approach. *Professional Psychology: Research and Practice, 22,* 133–137.

Kanfer, F. H. (1977). The many faces of self-control, or behavior modification changes its focus. In R. Stuart (Ed.), *Behavioral self-management.* New York: Brunner/Mazel.

Kazdin, A. E. (1994). *Behavior modification in applied settings.* Pacific Grove, CA: Brooks/Cole.

Krumboltz, J. D. (Ed.). (1966). *Revolution in counseling: Implications of behavioral science.* Boston, MA: Houghton Mifflin.

Lambert, M. J., & Bergin, A. E. (1994). The effectiveness of psychotherapy. In A. Bergin & S. Garfield (Eds.), *Handbook of psychotherapy and behavior change* (4th ed., pp 143–189). New York: John Wiley & Sons.

Lent, R. W., Brown, S. D., & Hackett, G. (1994). Toward a unifying social cognitive theory of career and academic interest, choice, and performance. *Journal of Vocational Behavior, 45,* 79–122.

Meichenbaum, D. (1977). *Cognitive behavior modification.* New York: Plenum.

Meichenbaum, D., & Deffenbacher, J. L. (1988). Stress inoculation training. *The Counseling Psychologist, 16,* 69–90.

Norcross, J. C., Sayette, M. A., Mayne, T. J., Karg, R. S., & Turkson, M. A. (1998). Selecting a doctoral program in professional psychology: Some comparisons among Ph.D. counseling, Ph.D. clinical, and Psy.D. clinical psychology programs. *Professional Psychology: Research and Practice, 29,* 609–614.

Paul, G. L. (1966). *Insight versus desensitization in psychotherapy.* Stanford, CA: Stanford University Press.

Paul, G. L. (1967). Strategy of outcome research in psychotherapy. *Journal of Consulting Psychology, 31,* 104–118.

Rimm, D. C., & Cunningham, H. M. (1985). Behavior therapies. In S. Lynn and J. Garske (Eds.), *Contemporary psychotherapies: Models and methods* (pp. 221–259). Columbus, OH: Merrill.

Rimm, D. C., & Masters, J. C. (1979). *Behavior therapy: Techniques and empirical findings.* New York: Academic Press.

Sundel, M., & Sundel, S. S. (1999). *Behavior change in the human services* (4th ed). Thousand Oaks, CA: Sage Publications.

Ullmann, L. P., & Krasner, L. (1965). *Case studies in behavior modification.* New York: Holt, Rinehart, & Winston.

Wampold, B. E., Mondin, G. W., Moody, M., Stich, F., Benson, K., & Ahn, H. (1997). A meta-analysis of outcome studies comparing bonafide psychotherapies: Empirically, "all must have prizes." *Psychological Bulletin, 122,* 203–215.

Watkins, C. E., Lopez, F. G., Campbell, V. L., & Himmell, C. D. (1986). Contemporary counseling psychology: The results of a national survey. *Journal of Counseling Psychology, 33,* 301–309.

Wilson, G. T. (1995). Behavior therapy. In R. Corsini and D. Wedding (Eds.), *Current psychotherapies* (5th ed., pp. 197–228). Itasca, IL: Peacock.

Wolpe, J. (1958). *Psychotherapy by reciprocal inhibition.* Stanford, CA: Stanford University Press.

Zook, A., & Walton, J. M. (1989). Theoretical orientations and work settings of clinical and counseling psychologists: A current perspective. *Professional Psychology: Research and Practice, 20,* 23–31.

THE THIRD FORCE: THE HUMANISTIC– EXPERIENTIAL APPROACH

The humanistic–experiential approach includes an array of therapies such as client-centered, or person-centered; existential; gestalt; and experiential. These approaches are often combined under the rubric *third force* because they reached prominence later than the two dominant forces in American psychology during the first half of the twentieth century, psychoanalysis and behaviorism.

The humanistic–experiential approach (referred to hereafter as humanistic) not only followed psychoanalysis and behaviorism chronologically, as Belkin (1980) points out, in both the United States and Europe, humanistic psychotherapy evolved as a reaction to the determinism of Freudian psychoanalysis and to the mechanism of the behavioristic approaches to studying and treating disordered behavior. To many humanistic thinkers, the Freudian approach, which views all behavior as determined by intrapsychic forces outside the control and consciousness of the individual, does worse than miss the mark in terms of the creative, intangible, and often unpredictable aspects of the human personality and spirit. Rollo May (1967) quoted in Belkin (1980), one of the leading theoreticians within the third-force approach, offers this trenchant critique of Freudian determinism:

> The danger of the Freudian system of analysis arises when it is carried over into a deterministic interpretation of personality as a whole. The system can become simply a scheme of cause and effect: blocked instinctual urge equals repression equals psychic complex equals neurosis. . . . the danger lies in the influence of Freudian theory in setting up a mechanistic, deterministic view of personality in the minds of the partially informed public . . . *to imagine that the whole of the creative, of-*

tentimes unpredictable, certainly intangible aspects of the human mind can be reduced to cause-and-effect mechanistic principles is sheer folly. . . . If such a determinism is accepted, human responsibility is destroyed (pp. 48–49, italics added).

Indeed, the attacks on behaviorism by humanistic theorists and therapists are at least as strong as May's critique of psychoanalysis. What is found objectionable is not only the strict determinism of the behavioristic approach but also the exclusive focus on observable behavior (and nothing more) that had been so typical of American behaviorism in the past (see Chapter 11).

Because of these concerns about psychoanalysis and behaviorism, humanism flourished as a social movement within counseling and psychotherapy in the 1960s, synchronizing with the expansiveness and hopefulness of that decade and the early 1970s. Names often associated with the humanistic movement in this country include Gordon Allport, Sidney Jourard, Abraham Maslow, Rollo May, and Carl Rogers. American humanism was closely linked to the existential psychotherapy movement in Europe, and in fact the two are often seen as being highly similar if not the same, at least in terms of the practice of counseling and therapy. In Europe, the existential therapy movement aimed to integrate the insights of existentialism as a philosophy of human existence with the practice of psychiatry and psychotherapy. The major contributors to the European movement were Medford Boss, Ludwig Binswanger, Viktor Frankl, R. D. Laing, and Frederick Perls. Belkin (1980) notes that Rollo May was for many years the leading American spokesperson for existential psychotherapy.

Although the humanistic movement reached full bloom in the 1960s and 1970s in the United States, its seeds had been planted much earlier. Probably its most prominent proponent in counseling and psychotherapy was Carl Rogers, who completed his first major book on counseling in the early 1940s (Rogers, 1942) and whose seminal *Client-Centered Therapy* was published a decade later (Rogers, 1951). Also in the early 1950s, Fritz Perls produced his fundamental theoretical statement about gestalt therapy (Perls, Hefferline, & Goodman, 1951), an approach that fits clearly within the humanistic realm.

The humanistic perspective grew up with, or at least alongside, counseling psychology. The formal beginnings of counseling psychology can be traced to the Northwestern Conference of 1951, the same year as the publication of Rogers's and Perls's seminal books. More important than chronology, though, is the deep influence that the humanistic approach has always had on counseling psychology. As will be seen, the humanistic approach to studying and working with human beings is extremely compatible with some of the central defining features of counseling psychology as delineated in Chapter 1.

Today, in fact, the humanistic influence remains quite strong among counseling psychologists. In piecing together data on theoretical orientation (Norcross, Sayette, Mayne et al., 1998; Watkins, Lopez, Campbell, & Himmell, 1986; Zook & Walton, 1989), it appears that easily half of today's counseling psychology faculty and practitioners adhere to one or another of the humanistic approaches (e.g., person-centered, experiential), as either their primary or secondary theoretical orientation. Also, the humanistic perspective has been highly influential for many of the counseling psychologists who view themselves as theoretically eclectic.

HUMANISTIC ASSUMPTIONS ABOUT HUMAN BEINGS, COUNSELING, AND SCIENCE

Wide differences in technique separate practitioners adhering to theories within the humanistic perspective (Greenberg, Elliott, & Lietaer, 1994). For example, in the two approaches examined later in this chapter, person-centered and gestalt therapy, major differences exist in what might be called therapist activity, or directiveness. The gestalt therapist is, in a word, much more *active–directive* than the traditional person-centered therapist. At the same time, common assumptions about human beings, treatment, and science cut across all of the differing approaches under the humanistic–experiential umbrella. Six of these are especially applicable.

The Democratic Ideal

In Grummon's (1965) early and still apt description of client-centered counseling, "belief in the democratic ideal" is noted as a major assumption underlying Carl Rogers's theories. In fact, this belief is inherent in virtually all humanistic approaches. Although the democratic ideal is difficult to define, it can be summed up in terms of one of its most central tenets: *belief in the worth and dignity of each individual.* Another basic tenet is belief in the individual's right to his or her own opinions, thoughts, and interests. Further, each individual has the right and responsibility to control his or her own destiny. The democratic ideal is best served by a society and social institutions that encourage the individual to be independent and self-directing (Grummon, 1965).

The value placed on the individual and individual choice has been a key element of the philosophy of humanism from its beginnings. Although this value does not negate concern for others or for broader social institutions, it does bespeak a kind of individualism peculiar to the humanistic tradition (Lowe, 1969). This individualism is strikingly evident in Fritz Perls's (1969a) "Gestalt Prayer."

> *I do my thing, and you do your thing.*
> *I am not in this world to live up to your expectations*
> *And you are not in this world to live up to mine.*
> *You are you, and I am I.*
> *And if by chance, we find each other, it's beautiful.*
> *If not, it can't be helped.*

The Fundamental Predominance of the Subjective

Since the Renaissance, humanistic philosophers have placed a premium on humans' ability to reason. Within the counseling and psychotherapy community of humanists, however, equal value is placed on the subjective side of life. In fact, the humanistic therapist tends to see the subjective side of life as dominant in healthy functioning (e.g., Greenberg et al., 1994; Mahrer, 1996). Rogers elucidates this position thusly: "Man lives essentially in his own personal and subjective world, and even his most objective functioning, in science, mathematics, and the like, is the result of subjective purpose and subjective choice" (Rogers, 1959, p. 191). Gestalt therapists' investment in subjective experiencing and the awareness and living of one's inner subjective experiencing is unmistakable. On the other side of the ledger, equally clear is their view that to deny one's subjective experience by living in one's intellect is an indication of dysfunctioning.

The humanist's belief in the predominance of the subjective side is most powerfully stated by Rogers in the following passage:

> No matter how completely man comes to understand himself as a determined phenomenon, the products of past elements and forces, and the determined cause of future events and behaviors, he can never *live* as an object. He can only *live* subjectively. . . .
>
> The person who is developing his full potential is able to accept the subjective aspect of himself, and to *live* subjectively. When he is angry he is *angry*, not merely an exhibition of the effects of adrenalin. When he loves he is loving, not merely "cathected towards a love object." He moves in self-selected directions, he chooses responsibly, he is a person who thinks and feels and experiences; he is not merely an object in whom these events occur. He plays a part in a universe which may be determined, but he lives himself subjectively, thus fulfilling his own need to be a person (pp. 20–21).

Grummon (1965) notes that one of Rogers's major conceptions of humans is that they are "wiser than their intellects." Effective functioning is brought about by living one's full experiencing, of which our conscious thinking is only a fraction.

The Tendency Toward Growth and Actualization

"A musician must make music, an artist must paint, a poet must write if he is to be ultimately at peace with himself." Abraham Maslow (1954, p. 91) wrote this in his first major theoretical statement about the human tendency toward actualizing of one's basic nature. For Maslow and essentially all humanists, human motivation is guided by much more than the need for drive reduction, freedom from tension, and the elimination of undesirable states. Humans are active, initiating organisms possessing an inherent tendency toward and capacity for growth and self-actualization. The capacity may be latent because of negative upbringing or any of the myriad factors that suppress an individual's potential, but it exists nonetheless, and can be released under the right conditions—for example, through effective education or therapy. Rogers defines this actualizing tendency as the "inherent tendency of the organism to develop all its capacities in ways which serve to maintain or enhance the organism" (1959, p. 196). He views the actualizing tendency as the fundamental characteristic of all life, applying not only to human beings but also to one-celled protozoans, flowers, wild animals, and everything that lives.

What constitutes this process of self-actualization? The answer to this question is best seen in the work of Abraham Maslow. Over a period of several years,

Maslow studied self-actualized people and developed theories about human motivation and self-actualization. His writings continue to be a touchstone for humanistic counselors in this area.

Maslow defines the process as the

> . . . ongoing actualization of potentials, capacities and talents, as fulfillment of mission (or call, fate, destiny, or vocation), as a fuller knowledge of and acceptance of, the person's own intrinsic nature, as an unceasing trend toward unity, integration, or synergy with the person (1968, p. 25).

Maslow theorizes the existence of a "hierarchy of basic needs" common to all humans. One's more basic needs are at the bottom of the hierarchy—the physiological requirements for air, water, food, shelter, sleep, and sex. These are followed in ascending order by the needs for safety and security, for belongingness and love, and for self-esteem and respect. At the top of the hierarchy are the growth needs, such as those for self-actualization. As needs at one level of the hierarchy are taken care of, people then strive to satisfy those at a higher level. Thus one continually strives to move up the hierarchy toward self-actualization. Maslow believes all needs must be met if good mental health is to ensue. If they are not, a "deficiency condition" results, referred to as neurosis, personality disturbance, psychosis, and the like.

Because of his or her focus on growth and actualization, the humanistic counselor is often called a *growth psychologist*. Psychologists within this perspective view mental health in terms of growth, personal maturity, and actualization, rather than the absence of psychopathological symptoms (Greenberg, Rice, & Elliott, 1993). Formulations of the mature, actualizing individual (Maslow, 1970) or the fully functioning person (Raskin & Rogers, 1995) are used by the humanistic counselor as a gauge of mental health.

The Essential Trustworthiness of Persons

If we were to baldly categorize the humanistic, psychodynamic, and learning perspectives on the basic goodness or trustworthiness of human beings, the psychodynamic perspective would lean toward the bad or untrustworthy view. To exaggerate to make the point, humans in the psychodynamic model are at the core a bundle of instincts (the id) that must be tamed by later development (ego, superego) if society is to survive. We are essentially irrational and driven by irrational impulses. From the learning (e.g., behavioristic) perspective, humans are at the core *tabulae rasae*—clean slates. We have no basic nature but rather learn to be what we are through conditioning and imitating.

In contrast to the psychodynamic and learning perspectives, the humanistic perspective has always taken a positive stance, believing human beings' basic rationality is an aspect of their trustworthiness. As Lowe (1969) states: "The first humanistic value is that man is a rational being. If man is valued as a creature who above all else is good, then the rationality which sets him apart from the animal is his crowning glory" (p. 99).

Words such as *trustworthy, good, reliable,* and *constructive* are seen over and over in the writings of Rogers and other humanists. These humanists are by no means naive about the evil and untrustworthiness of many human acts, but tend to see them as a function of defensiveness that people learn as an unhappy consequence of their environmental backgrounds. This essentially positive view of human nature is stated eloquently by Rogers (1961):

> I have little sympathy with the rather prevalent concept that man is basically ir-rational, and that his impulses, if not controlled, will lead to destruction of others and self. Man's behavior is exquisitely rational, moving with subtle and ordered complexity toward the goals his organism is endeavoring to achieve. The tragedy for most of us is that our defenses keep us from being aware of this rationality, so that consciously we are moving in one direction, while organismi-cally we are moving in another. But in the person who is living the process of the good life, there would be a decreasing number of such barriers, and he would be increasingly a participant in the rationality of his organism. The only control of impulses which would exist, or which would prove necessary, is the natural and internal balancing of one need against another, and the discovery of behaviors which follow the vector most closely approximating the satisfaction of all needs (pp. 299–300).

We should add that not all third-force counselors advocate this positive view of human nature. To the gestalt therapist, human nature is more a mixture of the good with the bad, and humans have equivalent potentialities for both. Even some person-centered theorists (e.g., Levant & Shlien, 1984) promote this mixed view. Yet there is no doubt that the legacy left to us by the humanist perspective over the years is one of optimism about human nature and its possibilities.

The Value of an Authentic Human Encounter in the Present

Each and every humanistic approach promotes the counselor's being "real," being involved in a person-to-person encounter, and focusing on the here and now in that encounter. Although early client-centered therapy tended to inhibit the role of the counselor and limit his or her responses to paraphrasing, significant changes have occurred over the years. A major aspect of these changes has been the increased im-plied permission granted to counselors to be genuine in the therapeutic encounter.

Whereas this focus on authenticity developed in the later person-centered ap-proach, it has always been a basic feature of other humanistic approaches. For ex-ample, in gestalt therapy, therapist authenticity occurs through an I–thou relationship between counselor and client (Greenberg, 1985). In the I–thou (as op-posed to I–it) relationship the therapist is fully present in the moment, and both participants are open to each other. The therapist cannot force the client to be open, but can be open himself or herself while maintaining the belief that the client will eventually enter the I–thou relationship.

Humanistic therapists do not suggest that the counseling relationship be fully rec-iprocal. After all, the client is the one seeking help and exploring his or her feelings, thoughts, and experiences. However active, the therapist attempts to put himself or herself aside and enter the world of the client, albeit in a partial and temporary fashion. The I–thou relationship advocated by gestalt therapists and virtually all others within the humanistic perspective is not a strictly mutual one wherein the therapist is equally acknowledged and confirmed by the client (Greenberg, 1985). The therapist participates in the relationship with an I–thou attitude but does not seek confirmation from the client. Thus, the therapist's full presence in the moment, unreserved communication, and abiding involvement with another human being are what define his or her contribution to the "I–thouness" of the relationship.

Greenberg (1983) gives some good examples from the gestalt perspective of the kinds of responses the therapist makes that reflect this authentic open I–thou encounter. These examples are broadly applicable to all humanistic approaches.

> To engage at the level of I–thou, without the demand that the other confirm one, is the essence of the therapist's attitude when he or she enters into an I–thou dialogue. The therapist might share with the client what he or she feels in the first moment of their contact, "I feel eager to meet you and find out what it is you want," or later in the encounter might say, "When I hear you say that, I feel sad and I wonder how you feel." As the encounter intensifies, the therapist might give the client some feedback by saying, "My heart is pounding as I say this to you but I want to tell you that I find myself pulling away from you when you are like that" or "I am aware that I am not listening to you and I'm wondering if you're feeling involved in what you're saying." The therapist must also accept and share his or her own sense of self in the encounter: "I felt defensive when you didn't want to do what I asked and I found myself trying to force you to do it" or "I feel frustrated with your deadness and I realize I'm expecting you to be lively so I'll feel good about myself." Another important moment for the therapist to share is when he or she is feeling lost and doesn't know where to go with the client. An essential feature of all encountering is that the therapist must express his or her feelings in an undemanding way and be willing to explore with the client what these feelings are about. In addition, the therapist must express all his or her feelings by saying not only "I am angry" but also "I am afraid that I may alienate you when I say this." In this way, the therapist shares his or her total humanness (p. 141).

Obviously, the above responses and the vision they reveal of the therapeutic encounter differ highly from those promoted by the psychoanalytic and learning perspectives.

The Necessity of Scientific Methods Accommodating the Human Experience

The humanistic movement in psychology has not focused on counseling and therapy alone. Of almost equal concern have been the scientific study of human behavior and the methods used for such study. Humanistic theoreticians and researchers over the years have been critical, though, of a scientific orthodoxy that equated science with a specific method and restricted its subject matter. Thus, the humanistic psychologist strongly advocated methods beyond the traditional psychological experiment, usually conducted in an antiseptic laboratory environment. Relatedly, the humanist has been critical of the belief that behavior could be dissected into miniscule parts and then studied in terms of those parts. Likewise, the humanist has always deeply opposed the behaviorist notion that only overt behavior is the proper subject matter of psychological science.

In contrast, humanistic psychologists have promoted scientific heterodoxy (Maslow, 1970). They believe that scientific methods should fit the subject matter being studied, ranging from rigorous experiments to less controlled qualitative methods. The *wholeness* of human behavior needs to be addressed scientifically, rather than the study of human nature being reduced to a narrow obsession with microscopic parts. In this same vein, the proper subject matter of psychology must be the complex human experience, including all of those internal processes and experiences so difficult to study neatly and simply. In research, humans are seen as active agents, capable of choice and of shaping their own destiny.

It will be recalled that in Chapter 3 we discussed alternative methodologies in scientific research in counseling psychology. Much of the attack on the "received view" and what is being called for by way of alternative methods has a clear connection to the humanistic tradition in psychology. Unfortunately this connection all too frequently goes unrecognized by advocates of alternative methodologies. Yet the roots of scientific heterodoxy are deeply embedded in counseling psychology because of humanistic influence.

Table 12.1 summarizes the six humanistic–experiential assumptions we have been describing.

We shall now look at the two humanistic approaches to counseling that have been the most prominent in counseling psychology: Carl Rogers's person-centered approach, and gestalt therapy, which was originated by Fritz Perls but modified in significant ways over the years. Throughout the discussion we shall be mindful of the relationship of the two theories to counseling psychology and its practice.

THE PERSON-CENTERED THERAPY OF CARL ROGERS

Theories of counseling and therapy are to an important extent a reflection of the lives, needs, and personalities of their creators (Corsini & Wedding, 1995; Dolliver, 1981a). Nowhere is this clearer than in the two humanistic approaches that we shall discuss. In this section, we offer a glimpse of the life and professional accomplishments of Carl Rogers, the founder and intellectual leader of person-centered therapy. We shall look at Rogers's background in some detail because, in our view, he is probably the most influential scientist–practitioner in the history of counseling. Rogers's effect on counseling psychology has been so pervasive that many of his ideas now seem like self-evident truths. They have become so ingrained in counseling that many counselors forget they ever came from Rogers!

Carl R. Rogers (1902–1987) was one of six children raised in a fundamentalist religious atmosphere. He attended grade school in a wealthy Chicago suburb before

TABLE 12.1.   **Fundamental Assumptions and Propositions of Humanistic–Experiential Theories.**

1. Each individual possesses worth and dignity.
2. Life should be lived subjectively.
3. All humans have an inherent tendency toward self-actualization.
4. People are fundamentally rational and trustworthy.
5. Effective counseling involves an authentic, I–thou encounter.
6. Science needs to study subjective meaning of whole persons construed as active agents.

the family moved to a Wisconsin farm, where his engineer father applied scientific techniques to farming. Rogers (1973) had this to say about his family and early years:

> I knew my parents loved me, but it would never have occurred to me to share with them any of my personal or private thoughts or feelings because I knew these would have been judged and found wanting. . . . I could sum up these boyhood years by saying that anything I would today regard as a close and communicative interpersonal relationship with another was completely lacking during that period. My attitude toward others outside the home was characterized by the distance and the aloofness which I had taken over from my parents. I attended the same elementary school for seven years. From this point on, until I finished graduate work, I never attended any school for longer than two years, a fact which undoubtedly had its effects on me. Beginning with high school, I believe my hunger for companionship came a little more into my awareness. But any satisfaction of that hunger was blocked first by the already mentioned attitudes of my parents, and second by circumstances (pp. 3–4).

It is easy to see how the counseling theory Rogers developed—focusing on a close, accepting nonjudgmental relationship between counselor and client—reflects the unmet needs of Rogers's childhood. The flexibility in Rogers's theory, as well as its ability to embrace new concepts, is also a reflection of his style and personality. Note, for example, these observations about Rogers, presented as a preface to Prochaska and Norcross's (1999) extensive discussion of person-centered therapy.

> The air and aura about him were warm and gentle though his words were strong and poignant. He was willing to field any question and respond to even the most critical comments. When asked how he as a therapist could be both genuine and nondisclosing, he surprised us with his candor. He said that over the past several years of working first with psychiatric clients and then with growth-oriented groups, he had come to see that his model of a therapist as reflective and nondirective had been very comfortable for a person like him. For most of his life he had been rather shy and therefore nondisclosing. In the sunny climate of California with its emphasis on openness in groups, he had come to recognize that too much of his former style was a convenient role that had protected him from having to reveal much of himself. Right until his death, Rogers was realizing more fully in psychotherapy, as in his life, the genuineness he had always valued but never fully realized (p. 136).

After his years on the farm, Rogers majored in agriculture and then history at the University of Wisconsin. (Rogers is one on a long list of prominent psychologists whose undergraduate major was not psychology.) Breaking with his fundamentalist background, he then entered the very liberal Union Seminary in Manhattan to prepare for the ministry. After 2 years, Rogers again changed, this time to his lasting vocation, psychology.

Rogers completed his Ph.D. in clinical and educational psychology at Columbia University in 1931. Significantly, the theoretical emphasis during his graduate training was Freudian; Rogers's subsequent theory was in many ways a reaction to the orthodox psychoanalytic perspective.

Rogers's Path to the Person-Centered Approach

After receiving his doctorate, Rogers spent 12 years as an intern and then psychologist at a child guidance clinic in Rochester, NY. There he developed theories of intervention based on his own personal experience. During this time, Rogers was influenced by the work of Otto Rank, a prominent psychoanalyst who had developed views about personality and therapy markedly different from those of orthodox psychoanalysis. Rogers was especially affected by Rank's views on human will and the prime importance of the relationship in therapy (as opposed to techniques).

In 1939 Rogers published his first book, *The Clinical Treatment of the Problem Child*. In it one can see the seeds of what eventually became his person-centered approach. In 1940, Rogers moved to Ohio State University so that he could be more involved in training psychologists to do counseling. In this stimulating environment, with a coterie of graduate students to help further his thinking, Rogers published the controversial *Counseling and Psychotherapy* (1942). In this book, Rogers stressed the importance of the counselor's being warmly receptive to the client and establishing a permissive atmosphere. Counseling was seen as essentially nondirective, with the client taking the lead in its progress. Thus the basic nondirectiveness of therapy was established. Rogers also emphasized his antidiagnostic views, which were almost heretical for that time. Diagnosing the client, Rogers argued, was nontherapeutic at best, taking the counselor away from his or her primary focus, that of understanding the client's internal frame of reference and helping the client move in the direction that was best for that individual.

At Ohio State, Rogers also began what became a lifelong pursuit—scientific study of the counseling process. He and his students conducted a series of studies of nondirective counseling. Rogers and Francis P. Robinson organized separate but related research programs that made use of newly developed tape recorders to study counseling sessions. Audiotapes allowed researchers to witness for the first time what went on in counseling. The use of such tapes brought about major scientific breakthroughs in the study of counseling.

In 1945 Rogers moved to the University of Chicago to head that university's counseling center. He continued his vigorous research program, and in 1951 published what many consider his most significant book, *Client-Centered Therapy* (Rogers, 1951). The change in the name of his theory, from *nondirective* to *client-centered* therapy, reflected key modifications in Rogers's approach. Whereas the use of techniques had still been emphasized in *Counseling and Psychotherapy,* in the new book the therapist's attitudes toward the client became the focus—one that has remained and even been strengthened over the years. Also new in *Client-Centered Therapy* was the stress on counselor attention to the client's unstated and underlying feelings, rather than his or her words and explicit feelings.

The 1950s was a period of great productivity for Rogers and his colleagues and students. In fact, nearly all of the fundamental ideas about therapy formulated by this group were published or written during that decade. The book *Psychotherapy and Personality Change,* based on research on client-centered therapy, was published in 1954 (Rogers & Dymond, 1954). In 1957 Rogers presented his famous paper on "necessary and sufficient conditions" (Rogers, 1957) discussed in Chapter 5. Few if any articles in the history of counseling and psychotherapy have promoted so much research. At the end of the 1950s, Rogers presented his full view of the process of client-centered therapy, along with his theory of personality and interpersonal relationships (Rogers, 1959). His next book, *On Becoming a Person* (Rogers, 1961), presented a wonderful array of articles on therapy, science, education, and life. It is lucidly and interestingly written for the lay audience as well as the professional, and remains as relevant today as when it was first published in 1961.

In 1957 Rogers moved back to his home state. There, at the University of Wisconsin, he continued research on the "necessary and sufficient conditions," and sought to test his theories with one of the most difficult populations possible—hospitalized schizophrenics. The 5-year study he organized may be the largest therapy study ever done, even to this day. The results provided only partial support for the effectiveness of client-centered therapy and the necessary and sufficient conditions, when applied to hospitalized schizophrenics (Rogers, 1967). Rogers and his collaborators had set themselves an extremely difficult task: They compared subjects of client-centered therapy *not* to an equivalent group of nontreated patients but to patients receiving the hospital's regular treatment program (including, for example, group therapy).

In any event, this work with schizophrenic patients brought about more changes in client-centered theory. The movement toward greater therapist openness and authenticity, already under way for several years, was further energized by the individual therapy experience with these difficult patients. Eugene Gendlin, one of the principal researchers in this project, was moved to comment:

> It is already certain that the patients did a great deal to us. I might say that our improvement has been remarkable. . . . Thus, for example, genuineness has changed for us from the mere absence of a false front, to a very active, self-expressive mode of making an interaction (Gendlin, 1970, p. 284).

In 1964 Rogers left the university environment, moving to the Western Behavioral Sciences Institute in La Jolla, California, to work with normal individuals and groups. In 1968, he helped to found the Center for the Study of the Person in La Jolla. There he worked to apply his theories to a wide range of situations, especially in relation to education, groups, and couples. The move away from therapy techniques and toward relationship attitudes reached fulfillment in 1974, with the

Rogers's Major Propositions About Personality Development.   TABLE 12.2.

1. Each individual exists in a continually changing world of experience of which he or she is the center.

2. The organism reacts to the field as it is experienced and perceived. This perceptual field is, for the individual, "reality."

3. Behavior is basically the goal-directed attempt of the organism to satisfy its need as experienced, in the field as perceived.

4. The organism reacts as an organized whole to this phenomenal field.

5. The best vantage point for understanding behavior is from the internal frame of reference of the individual himself or herself.

6. A portion of the total perceptual field gradually becomes differentiated as the self.

7. Most of the ways of behaving that are adopted by the organism are those that are consistent with the concept of *self*.

change from *client*-centered to *person*-centered therapy. This second change was again not simply in name, but reflected what, over the years, had become an attitude toward life and being. Rogers noted in 1980:

> The old concept of "client-centered therapy" has been transformed into the "person-centered approach." In other words, I am no longer talking simply about psychotherapy, but about a point of view, a philosophy, an approach to life, a way of being, which fits any situation in which *growth*—of a person, a group, or a community—is part of the goal (Rogers, 1980, p. ix).

Theory of Personality: Growth and Maladjustment

Rogers was always more concerned with the conditions for change and growth than with the roots of personality development. Because of this interest, his ideas about intervention came *before* his statements on personality. Yet he did offer formal conceptions of personality, its development and unfolding. Rogers's key formulations on this topic were published in his *Client-Centered Therapy* (1951, pp. 481–533) and later in a major chapter (Rogers, 1959). In his 1951 work he presented 19 propositions about personality development. Seven of these propositions seem to capture a major part of the theory and are presented in Table 12.2.

Inspection of Table 12.2 suggests the key elements of Rogers's personality theory. First, the theory is based on *phenomenology*. That is, it is the person's subjective perceptions of self and environment, his or her subjective experience and reality, that guide behavior. Second, and relatedly, each individual has his or her own private world, and to understand this individual we must enter this private world and seek to comprehend the individual from his or her internal frame of reference. "External" understanding—the kind that involves, for example, diagnosis by an expert—often leads us away from the internal frame of reference. Third, all persons develop a self-concept or self-structure. For Rogers, this self-concept contains the person's perceptions of himself or herself alone and interactively with his or her environment as well as the values attached to those perceptions. This self-structure is fluid and changing, but, once formed, serves to guide one's behavior and perceptions. Finally, persons' reactions are based on the whole of their self-structures and perceptions of themselves and their world, rather than on specific portions of their perceptions, as other theories might maintain.

Incongruence, Congruence, and the Fully Functioning Person

If all individuals are basically trustworthy and have a tendency toward self-actualization, why is there so much unhappiness in the world? What goes wrong so as to interfere with and often cripple people's actualizing tendencies? In several of his early papers, Rogers developed the client-centered (now person-centered) theory of maladjustment, in which *incongruence* is the key concept.

Maladjustment occurs when an incongruence or rift exists between one's self-concept and his or her organismic experiencing; that is, between the person's image of self and his or her inner experiencing. Why and how does this happen? As children develop, so does their inherent need for *positive regard* and *positive self-regard.* As experiences with the world (mostly family and primary caretakers) unfold, children also develop a self-concept. If children experience enough love, especially love *without* conditions, they develop a positive self-concept and, just as important, do not develop *conditions of worth* (conditions under which they feel worthwhile). If, on the other hand, parents are too restrictive or conditional (e.g., telling the child "We love you if you're a good boy or girl in the ways we define it"), the child develops these conditions of worth.

If our self-concept includes too many conditions of worth, it becomes rigid or "frozen," so that we lack a sense of positive self-regard. Thus, too many of our inwardly felt experiences (called "organismic experiencing") must be distorted or blocked from awareness, and we experience a sense of incongruence. Individuals in this situation are at odds with themselves because their self-concept and organismic experiencing are not unified; they are in conflict.

When such incongruence occurs—and Rogers would add that it occurs ever so frequently in modern Western civilization—individuals are at cross-purposes and are vulnerable to psychological maladjustment. They can no longer live as integrated whole persons. If such individuals were to perceive accurately what was being experienced at the feeling level, their self-concept would be threatened. This threat causes anxiety, which the individual defends against by either denying inner experience or misperceiving experience.

If, however, the child develops in an environment in which there are no or minimal conditions of worth, the self-concept is more flexible, and the person may thus acknowledge his or her organismic experiencing without feeling a threat to the self-concept. This congruence permits the actualizing tendency to do its work and helps the individual to become what Rogers calls a *fully functioning person.* The qualities of the fully functioning person reflect the humanistic assumptions discussed earlier as well as those of the person-centered theory of development as examined above. Fully functioning persons are increasingly (a) open to their experience, (b) accepting of their feelings, (c) capable of living in the present without preoccupation with past or future, (d) free to make choices that are best for them and to act on those choices spontaneously, (e) trusting of self and of human nature, (f) capable of balanced and realistic expressions of both aggression and affection, and (g) creative and nonconforming (see Burke, 1989; Prochaska & Norcross, 1999).

Counseling and Therapy Using a Person-Centered Approach

The person-centered view of counseling flows directly and logically from the humanistic assumptions discussed earlier and from the above-mentioned formulations about personality development, incongruence, and full functioning. The counselor seeks to gently enter the client's subjective world, to understand this client from his or her internal frame of reference, and to provide an experience in which the person is accepted and cared about *without* conditions of worth. As Prochaska & Norcross (1999) note, whether the client seeks counseling because of inadequate functioning tied to perceptual distortion, because defensive symptoms are causing too much emotional pain, or because of a wish for greater self-actualization, the goals of therapy are the same: to increase the congruence between self-concept and organismic experience. The therapeutic relationship, especially its personal and emotional components, is the primary vehicle for this reintegration of self and experience. In fact, it is this relationship, in and of itself, that produces growth in the client. Rogers (1951, p. 172) makes this point decisively: "The process of therapy is seen as being synonymous with the experiential relationship between client and therapist."

Lest the reader get the impression that any kind of positive relationship will promote change, we hasten to add that, according to person-centered theory, it is only when certain relationship conditions predominate that constructive change occurs. To begin with, Rogers says, "I launch myself into the therapeutic relationship having a hypothesis, or a faith, that my liking, my confidence, and my understanding of the other person's inner world, will lead to a significant process of becoming" (1951, p. 267). This statement effectively summarizes relationship conditions that Rogers believes "necessary and sufficient" for constructive change to occur. Briefly, they are as follows:

1. Two persons, the client and counselor, are in psychological contact.

2. The client is in a state of incongruence, being vulnerable or anxious.

3. The counselor is congruent or integrated in the relationship.

4. The counselor experiences unconditional positive regard for the client.

5. The counselor experiences empathic understanding of the client's internal frame of reference.

6. The counselor succeeds in communicating conditions 4 and 5 to the client; the client perceives these conditions.

As discussed in Chapter 8, the conditions that have been given the greatest attention in person-centered therapy are 3, 4, and 5, which are the counselor's contributions to the relationship: congruence, unconditional positive regard, and empathy. It is crucial that the counselor enter the therapeutic relationship with these attitudes, and counseling techniques are simply the way of *implementing* these attitudes. Without these attitudes, all the polished techniques in the world will not produce effective therapy.

Rogers (1980) described empathy as a way of being that is powerfully curative because: (a) the nonevaluative and accepting quality of the empathic climate facilitates clients taking a prizing, caring attitude toward themselves; (b) being listened to by an understanding other allows clients to listen more accurately to themselves, with greater empathy for their own organismic experiencing, their own vaguely felt experiences; and (c) clients' greater understanding and prizing of themselves opens them up to inner experiences that, in turn, become part of a more accurately based self-concept.

In discussing the profound impact of the therapist's empathic way of being with clients, Rogers notes a paradox: As clients change during counseling due to the therapist's empathy, positive regard, and congruence, these clients become more empathic, positively regarding, and congruent toward and with themselves. Thus, as one experiences the empathic way of being from another (e.g., a counselor), one develops attitudes toward oneself that enable one to become an effective therapist—for one's self. (For an in-depth examination of this process, see Barrett-Lennard, 1997.) Although Rogers (1980) focused mostly on the empathic way of being, he also reiterated the person-centered view of the primacy of all three facilitative conditions. In comparing the influence of the three conditions, he notes that in ordinary life interactions (between members of a couple, teacher and student, colleagues, friends) congruence is probably the most important element. Since congruence or genuineness involves your letting the other person know your emotional state, Rogers believed it was the basis for living together in a climate of realness. In other situations, though, caring or prizing (i.e., unconditional positive regard) may be most important. For example, such positive regard may be of great importance in nonverbal relationships such as those between therapist and profoundly disturbed client, between parent and infant, and between physician and very ill patient. Finally, Rogers believes that empathy may be the most important of the three conditions when "the other person is hurting, confused, troubled, anxious, alienated, terrified, or when he or she is doubtful of self-worth, uncertain as to identity" (1980, p. 160). For Rogers, the gentle and sensitive companionship provided by an empathic person helps to clarify and heal. As Rogers talks about this sensitively empathic person, it appears that empathy merges with the other conditions, and we are back to the trio operating in a creatively interactive way.

We have focused mostly on what the person-centered therapist is and does with clients. As a final comment, we add that there are as many "do not's" as "do's" in this approach. Thus person-centered therapists avoid with the client any expression that has an evaluative connotation. Nonevaluativeness is essential to their approach. Person-centered counselors also do not interpret meanings to clients, do not question them in a probing manner, and do not diagnose, reassure, criticize, judge, praise, or describe them. These "do not's" are crucial. A common misunderstanding is that the person-centered therapist provides a great deal of praise and reassurance. Not so. The therapist prizes the client as a person, but his or her unconditional regard and empathy do not translate into continual positive evaluation or reassurance (see Bozarth, 1997; Raskin & Rogers, 1995).

The Person-Centered Approach in Perspective

Just what does the person-centered therapist do in a session? Despite the emphasis on attitudes and relationship rather than techniques, are there techniques that are favored by the person-centered approach? What differentiates the person-centered therapist from therapists of other persuasions?

In fact, everything we have seen (case presentations, examples of client–counselor interactions) indicates that the person-centered counselor responds to clients in a distinctive manner. His or her responses are, for example, "following" rather than "leading" responses. That is, the client's expressions are followed by the therapist, and paraphrasing responses are the most commonly used. Reflection of feeling is a predominant technique, as can be seen in virtually all of the cases Rogers himself presented in the literature. At the same time, it would be inaccurate to equate the person-centered approach and the empathic way of being with one or a few techniques (e.g., reflection of feeling). Reflection is used because it fits well with person-centered theory and philosophy. Over the years an increasingly broad range of techniques has been permitted. The bottom line theoretically is that the techniques be in sync with person–centered theory and philosophy (Bozarth, 1997).

Person-centered therapy, from its beginnings, has always been a nondirective approach, even though the term *nondirective therapy* has now fallen into disfavor. Advocates of the person-centered approach believe that the term has come to connote a much narrower range of responses to clients than is desirable and seems to put the emphasis in the wrong place—on techniques. At the same time, it is clear that a very deep nondirectiveness is a fundamental part of person-centered therapy (Bozarth, 1990, 1997; Raskin & Rogers, 1995). Bozarth (1990) states that the implications of this nondirective attitude "are staggering" and tells us that the therapist must have no other intentions than the following:

> The therapist goes with the client—goes at the client's pace—goes with the client in his/her own ways of thinking, of experiencing, of processing. The therapist can not be up to other things, have other intentions without violating the essence of CC/PC [client-centered/person-centered] therapy. To be up to other things—whatever they may be—is a "yes but" reaction to the essence of the approach (p. 63).

We have noted that from early in his career Rogers was deeply invested in the empirical study of his theories. What can in fact be said about the empirically demonstrated efficacy of the person-centered approach? Put simply, does it work? As with all approaches to counseling and therapy, the response to this simple question must be an unsatisfying "It depends." We always need to look beyond the simple "Does it work?" question, and focus on the more probing question, "How effective is this treatment, with which clients, under what conditions, as applied by which counselors?" Be that as it may, the person-centered approach has been studied extensively over the years, and the results of controlled studies have been largely positive, especially when the facilitative conditions are present to a high degree. When we piece together several extensive analyses of the huge research literature on the topic, there is ample support for the proposition that the three facilitative conditions, especially empathic understanding, are important therapeutic factors in a wide range of treatments. The findings are especially positive when the facilitative conditions are assessed from the client's perspective, which is the perspective that Rogers believed was most appropriate. (See reviews by Beutler, Machado, & Neufeldt, 1994; Greenberg, Elliott, & Lietaer, 1994; Orlinsky, Grawe, & Parks, 1994; Orlinsky & Howard, 1986.)

The person-centered approach and the field of counseling psychology have always been highly compatible. The person-centered therapist's belief in human beings' inherent potential for growth and self-actualization is deeply ingrained within counseling psychology and is in keeping with the unifying themes of the specialty as discussed in Chapter 1; specifically, that of the focus on intact personalities and on assets or strengths. Also, because of belief in the inherent human tendency toward actualization, the person-centered approach has favored briefer treatments (the third unifying theme of counseling psychology discussed in Chapter 1) over extended treatment. Overall, throughout its development from nondirective counseling to client-centered therapy to person-centered therapy, this approach to life and intervention has had a profound impact on counseling psychology and its practitioners.

For more extensive and highly readable discussions, including case materials, the reader is referred to chapters by Bozarth (1997), Prochaska and Norcross (1999), Raskin and Rogers (1995), and Sharf (1996). The edited book by Lietaer, Rombauts, & Van Balen (1990) provides an extensive, in-depth look at the person-centered approach and its application to a wide range of treatments. Finally, Rogers's (1980) *A Way of Being* is a wonderfully rich, interesting, and still very relevant statement of issues and directions in the person-centered therapy movement.

FRITZ PERLS AND GESTALT THERAPY

Just as the development of person-centered therapy is inextricably tied to the personhood and writings of Carl Rogers, the beginnings and early advancement of gestalt therapy are a consequence of the personality and work of Fritz Perls. Although Rogers and Perls belong to the same camp—the humanistic, third-force, growth-oriented therapies—and share several basic assumptions about personality and therapy, it would be hard to find two people whose outward personalities differed more. If Carl Rogers, for example, was the prototypical warm, kindly, gentle minister (or grandfather in his advanced years), Fritz Perls can be seen as a sort of flamboyant, creative, and somewhat eccentric movie director.

Prochaska and Norcross (1999) note that as a person Fritz was much like his writings—both vital and perplexing. In his writings, and especially in his gestalt therapy workshops, Perls was keenly perceptive, provocative, manipulative, evocative, hostile, and inspiring. His great charisma, as well as his effectiveness, created an almost cultlike following, particularly among professionals who participated in his workshops and who spread the gestalt therapy gospel. Consider how Carl Rogers's gentle and modest presentation of himself contrasts with Fritz's statement:

> I believe that I am the best therapist for any type of neurosis in the States, maybe in the world. How is that for megalomania. At the same time I have to admit that I cannot work successfully with everybody (Perls, 1969b, unnumbered page).

If it was a gentle, soft-spoken grandfatherliness that people were looking for from Perls, they came away from encounters with him disappointed and frustrated; if it was a stimulating, lively, spontaneous, and genuine encounter his workshop participants wanted, they came away feeling enriched and enlightened (see Prochaska & Norcross, 1999).

Frederich S. Perls (1893–1970) began his therapy career as a psychoanalyst. After obtaining his M.D. degree in 1920 from Frederich Wilhelm University, he studied at the Berlin and Vienna Institutes of Psychoanalysis. Within the psychoanalytic framework, he was strongly influenced by Karen Horney, Otto Rank, and especially Wilhelm Reich, who was Perls's psychoanalyst in the early 1930s. Although Perls practiced analysis throughout much of the first half of his career, it is hard to see him using an analytic approach or attitude. His irrepressible, spontaneous, outgoing, and aggressive character seems to us to run counter to the restraint and control required in effective analysis.

Along with his training in analysis, Perls knew and was heavily influenced by the leading gestalt psychologists of the time, for example, Kohler, Wertheimer, Lewin; and in 1926 he became an assistant to the eminent gestalt psychologist Kurt Goldstein at Goldstein's Institute for Brain-Damaged Soldiers. While at Goldstein's institute, Perls met his wife to be, Laura Posner. Many (e.g., Simkin & Yontef, 1984) view Laura Perls as the cofounder of the gestalt movement. She received her D.Sc. in 1932 from the University of Frankfurt. She was well-versed in general and gestalt psychology. Although Laura wrote little, within the gestalt movement she is considered a leader.

By the time of Perls's first book (*Ego, Hunger and Aggression,* 1947), he had moved away from Freudian theory, but it was not until 1951 that he took his dramatic departure from psychoanalysis. At that time, he published (with Ralph Hefferline and Paul Goodman) *Gestalt Therapy: Excitement and Growth in Personality.*

Fritz and Laura had fled Hitler's Germany for South Africa in 1934; soon afterward he organized the South African Institute for Psychoanalysis. Then, with apartheid on the rise, the Perlses moved to New York in 1946. In 1952 they, along with the American psychologist Paul Goodman, formed the New York Institute for Gestalt Therapy. Run in the Perlses' apartment, the institute became the prototype for many gestalt therapy centers that sprang up around the country in the 1950s and 1960s. In 1960 Perls moved to California and in 1964 accepted an appointment at the Esalen Institute, where he held many of his training workshops and seminars along with gestalt leaders James Simkin, Walter Kempler, Irma Shepherd, and John Enright. It was during this time that Perls wrote two of his most interesting books. *Gestalt Therapy Verbatim* (1969a) is an engaging firsthand account of gestalt therapy and is generally considered Perls's best presentation of his approach. *In and Out of the Garbage Pail* (1969b) is a fascinating autobiography of one of the most creative and unusual personalities psychology has known. Perls spent the final year of his life, 1970, on Vancouver Island, where he was in the process of building a gestalt commune at the time of his death.

The gestalt therapy movement grew slowly at first and did not reach full force until the 1960s. The emotional climate of the 1960s, with its emphasis on self-expression in the here and now, seemed the ideal setting for gestalt therapy to take hold. And take hold it did. Belkin (1980) notes that no approach to therapy received more rapid popularity in a short time period than did gestalt therapy in the late 1960s and 1970s. It is hard to convey in writing the climate and the excitement of the gestalt therapy movement. Burke (1989) gets close with the following characterization:

> It is the late 1960s, and you are one of the lucky ones to attend a "human potential" seminar at the Esalen Institute, a center for workshops and training programs nestled between the mountains and the Pacific Ocean at Big Sur, California. You walk into a large room jammed with people, some seated on chairs, some sitting cross-legged on the floor, some standing along the sides. Every type of person imaginable appears to be here. There are young people, denim-clad, some a bit seedy. There are professional types, casually dressed, engaging in lively debate. There is even a psychoanalyst in the group, bearded, smoking a pipe, and looking more than a trifle uncomfortable in these environs. As a grandfatherly man walks into the room, the hum of conversations becomes a hush punctuated by cries of "Fritz, Fritz." Fritz is wearing a dashiki, and his round, smiling face peers out from an abundant white beard. What follows is a miracle to behold. One by one, like children before a Santa, members of the group volunteer to join Fritz at one end of the room on a "stage" set with three chairs, one for Fritz, one for the volunteer, and one empty. Fritz seems to know each person's soul, if not their names. One by one, he cajoles them, picks on them, intimidates them, surprises them. In response, they cry, laugh, scream, hug, and, from most reports, heal (p. 252).

Burke (1989) points out that although the setting he has tried to capture seemed, 20 years later, to be an unlikely one for training in therapy (and it seems even more unlikely as we write this chapter), it indeed was one in which many bright, young practitioners learned to become gestalt therapists. Scenes like the above were repeated over and over in the 1960s, and to many at the time (professional therapists as well as laypersons) Fritz Perls was a sort of guru, a one-man liberator of human potential (Burke, 1989).

Theory of Personality: Growth and Maladjustment

Neither Fritz Perls nor other gestalt therapists have developed a systematic theory of personality or psychopathology. Also, although many principles and procedures of counseling have been enunciated over the years, no comprehensive or definitive work is available. Perhaps this deficiency is related to Perls's view (a view widely endorsed in the gestalt arena) that gestalt therapy needs to be lived—writing about it misses its essence. The creation of comprehensive theories and definitive positions ignores the reality that the gestalt approach to therapy, like any living organism, is in a continual process of change and evolution.

The theory of personality that does exist is more a cluster of loosely connected ideas that have evolved from the clinical experience of gestalt practitioners, rather than an overall theory of personality. Careful examination of the gestalt literature, though, does suggest several themes related to personality development and to healthy versus unhealthy functioning. It must be underscored that gestalt therapy is not synonymous with gestalt psychology. Although Perls and other gestalt therapists drew some ideas from gestalt psychology, the personality theory of gestalt therapy is really a loose and unique mixture of psychoanalysis, phenomenology, existentialism, gestalt psychology, Eastern religions, humanistic philosophy, and even behavioral psychology. Below we list and briefly discuss what appear to be central themes.

1. Humans are unified organisms and always function as *wholes*. Behavior is guided by the whole person; the whole determines the part.

2. The individual is continually faced with factors that disturb his or her balance and is continually seeking to restore balance or achieve equilibrium by satisfying his or her physical and organismic needs. The unmet need is the *incomplete gestalt* that demands completion.

3. Personality consists of many *polarities*, or opposites (e.g., strength and weakness, activity and passivity); in healthy functioning these polarities are integrated such that they work in harmony: the person is *centered*. In unhealthy functioning the polarities develop into splits, or dichotomies, throwing the person into a state of conflict.

4. The principle of *ecological interdependence* suggests that persons exist by differentiating self and other as well as by connecting self and other. The boundary between self and environment or other must be kept permeable to allow exchanges (*contact*); at the same time, the boundary must be firm enough for organismic autonomy.

5. Human regulation is, to varying degrees, based on acknowledgment of *what is* (organismic) or on arbitrary imposition of what the person believes *should be* ("shouldistic"). The former reflects and leads to healthy functioning, the latter to neurosis.

6. *Awareness*—of what one is feeling, sensing, experiencing in the present, the *here and now*—is the key to healthy development and change, and is the immediate goal of gestalt therapy.

What ties these diverse propositions together? Perls and other leading gestalt therapists are more concerned about healthy and unhealthy development than personality development per se. The healthy individual is responsible for himself or herself and seeks to be that self. As Perls (1969a, p. 70) asserts: "[R]esponsibility means simply to be willing to say 'I am I' and 'I am what I am'." If the individual seeks to be aware of his or her organismic needs, rather than living by "shoulds" or by some image of what is good, emotional health results. When this self-acceptance occurs, the polarities referred to above are accepted—for example, we accept our aggressive side as well as our gentle side; thus the sides are integrated rather than being at war with each other.

As implied, the mature person lives in the present, in the so-called here and now. This does not mean that the individual is a hedonist who is concerned only with his or her own ego needs. It does mean that preoccupation with the past and the future is largely given up, so that one lives one's experience in the now. Values and standards are part of the immediate experience. The gestalt therapist understands the need for values; what is unhealthy is the all-too-frequent tendency to be driven by internalized "shoulds" at the expense of who one basically is and what one needs. When taking the responsibility to be oneself and to live in the present, one follows Perls's suggestion to live and review every second afresh. In doing this the joy, excitement, and creative potential in our lives may be actualized.

Growth Gone Awry: The Layers of Neurosis

What happens to interfere with the process of growth and with the actualizing tendency in all of us? Why is it that so many people become stuck in the deadness of living out social roles, in childish dependency, and in functioning more like computers than humans? Although Perls did not develop a formal theory of the causes of what he called growth disorders, he did point to some childhood factors (Perls 1969a, 1970). To address the question of what goes wrong, we first have to look at Perls's concept of maturation. For Perls, "maturing is the transcendence from environmental support to self-support" (1969a, p. 30). Parents can impede this process by undersupporting the child, so that needed support is pulled away before the developing child is ready for independence. More common is the critical, imposing parent who knows what is best for the child. The child either follows these unemphatic parents' dictates or runs the risk of losing love and approval. The child thus becomes fearful of independent behavior and becomes what he or she is "supposed" to become. The third and most common impediment to maturity is the parents' spoiling of the child. Parents, out of their own unmet needs, all too often give the developing child everything they did not have. The parents are afraid to frustrate the child's wishes, and yet such frustration is needed if the child is to move forward and develop his or her own self-support. If the home environment is so secure and gratifying that the child's every need is met, that child will not move forward but become stuck.

Whichever of these impediments occurs, the result is the same. Instead of learning to stand on his or her own two feet, "the child—or the childish neurotic—will use his or her potential not for self-support but to act out phony roles. These phony roles are meant to mobilize the environment for support instead of mobilizing one's own potential. We manipulate the environment by being helpless, by playing stupid, asking questions, wheedling, flattering" (Perls, 1970, pp. 17–18).

Perls and other gestalt therapists never developed a systematic or formal theory of neurosis (or *growth disorders,* as Perls liked to call them); but Perls did formulate an interesting concept of what he called the "layers of neurosis." These layers can be seen as the defensive shields that the person must work through to grow from neurosis to health. Because Perls placed no premium on consistency, the actual layers are somewhat different in two works published only a year apart (Perls 1969a, 1970).

There are five layers of neurosis that form what Perls views as the structure of neurosis. In combining Perls's publications on these layers, the first layer can be seen as the *phony,* or *synthetic,* level. The neurotic spends most of his or her time at this level, a level in which one plays roles and games, and tries to act out an ideal self-concept rather than being authentic. Perls describes this layer colorfully as follows:

> We behave *as if* we are big shots, *as if* we are nincompoops, *as if* we are pupils, *as if* we are ladies, *as if* we are bitches, etc. [Thus the neurotic has] . . . given up living for his self in a way that would actualize himself. He wants to live instead for a concept . . . like an elephant who had rather be a rose bush, and a rose bush that tries to be a kangaroo. We don't want to be ourselves; we don't want to be what we are. We want to be something else, and the existential basis for being something else is the experience of dissatisfaction. We are dissatisfied with what we do, or parents are dissatisfied with what their child is doing. He should be different, he shouldn't be what he is; he should be something else (1970, p. 20).

Once the person gets through the phony layer, she or he must then pass through the *phobic, impasse,* and *implosive* layers. Although the distinctions between these layers are very murky in Perls's writing, the key issue is that as persons become more real, they encounter the internal objections to being authentic—all of the "should nots" in their psyche. Beyond this is a sense of being stuck and of deadness. At this implosive layer persons contract and compress themselves. To move beyond this they must get into contact with the deadness involved in their imploding. When they do that, the next layer is entered. Implosion becomes explosion, as the *explosive* layer is experienced. The person comes to life, as this explosion is "the link-up with the authentic person who is capable of experiencing and expressing his emotions" (Perls, 1969a, p. 60).

The emerging healthy individual may explode into *grief* if he or she needs to work through loss experiences that had not been assimilated; *orgasm* if he or she is sexually blocked; *anger* if this feeling has been denied; and/or *joy* when there previously had been none. In fact, to be truly well functioning, the individual must be capable of all four of these explosions or experiences. In response to questions about the dangers involved in the explosion layer, Perls notes that the one way the danger is diminished is through the process of "melting." When in therapy the client becomes moved, he or she begins to melt, to feel soft, or to cry, which is a kind of melting that buffers against a dangerous explosion. Yet, at the same time, "basically one has to be willing to take risks" (Perls, 1970, p. 23).

The Practices and Procedures of Gestalt Therapy: Exercises and Experiments

What do gestalt therapists actually do? No other major theory of counseling presents as wide an array of interesting and evocative techniques and procedures as does gestalt therapy. To begin with, in the response modes sense (see Chapter 9), the main verbal technique is *confrontation.* The gestalt therapist vigorously confronts discrepancies in the client's presentation of himself or herself and challenges the client to express what he or she truly is and feels in the moment.

> "You are telling me you're sad, but you are smiling."
> "You say you're relaxed, but I see your feet are fidgeting."
> "You say you'd like to be strong but that's hard to believe right now because my fantasy is that you're a little baby."

These are the kinds of confrontations gestalt therapists often make. Discrepancies in the moment are noted, highlighting contradictions in what the client says, in what the client does, and between what the client says or does and what the counselor fantasizes about him or her.

Another response mode that typifies the gestalt therapist is *direct guidance*. The gestalt therapist often instructs the client about exercises (see below) and other behaviors that are desired in the moment. In addition, the gestalt therapist is probably more self-disclosing than any other kind of therapist, and *self-involving disclosures* about what is being experienced in the here and now with the client are the preferred kinds. On the negative side, the one response type that is clearly taboo in gestalt therapy is *interpretation*. This response mode seeks to get at the "whys" of behavior, whereas the gestaltists are more interested in "hows" and "whats." Interpretations more often than not lead to intellectualized responses that do not reflect immediate experiencing. To Perls, the search for underlying causes is useless at best. It takes the client away from where she or he needs to be.

Before discussing gestalt exercises and experiments, it is necessary to talk about how material from the client's past is to be dealt with in the gestalt approach. The focus on here-and-now experiencing, with the aim of developing awareness, does not preclude the exploration of past experiences. The critical thing is that those past experiences be explored in a way that is alive in the present. Thus, the client isn't to simply talk about the past; she or he is to experience the past in the now. Gestalt therapists will often encourage this process by asking clients to be themselves during the past time being examined: for example, "Be the 7-year-old of your memories right now, and tell me what is going on for you."

Although Perls and other gestalt therapists have repeatedly cautioned against overreliance on techniques in the form of exercises, gestaltists do use a range of these strategies. We discuss some of these exercises and experiments here, both because they are valuable procedures in gestalt work and as a way of clarifying some of the major elements of gestalt counseling. It should be noted that the therapist is not to preplan the use of techniques. Following the rule of working with the present experience (the therapist's as well as the client's), the gestalt counselor uses exercises as they are felt to fit the moment.

The basic purpose of exercises and experiments in gestalt therapy is to enhance the client's *awareness*, especially awareness of inner experiencing and feelings in the here and now. *Exercises* are techniques that are used in individual or group counseling. *Experiments* are innovations that therapists use when client awareness and progress are blocked. These terms are often used simultaneously; the term *game* is also often used by gestaltists. Below we give a sampling of some key gestalt tech-

niques. The reader is referred to Levitsky and Perls (1970), Passons (1975), and more currently Greenberg et al. (1993) for a thorough exploration of gestalt exercises and experiments.

Games of Dialogue

As discussed earlier, gestalt therapy views personality as consisting of many polarities or opposites, for example, passive and aggressive, weak and strong, masculine and feminine, controlled and impulsive. In healthy functioning, these opposites are integrated—they coexist in a harmonious way and in fact support each other—for example, the dominant and submissive poles in us can each be given expression, and each helps the other become less extreme. The individual is *centered* when these polarities have been integrated. Often, however, there exists a split between the polarities, causing a state of conflict.

Games of dialogue are especially suited to situations in which such splits occur, and the aim of these games is to create full awareness of the split in the client. Awareness leads to resolution so that the person may become centered. In games of dialogue, the client is asked to stage a dialogue between the two parts of himself or herself. With the counselor's guidance, each part is acted out and the dialogue goes on until it feels appropriate to stop. Often this dialogue is carried out with a "two-chair technique," whereby the client sits in one chair representing one side of the split and talks to the other side. Then, when he or she feels it is time to respond as the other side, the client switches chairs, and the dialogue continues.

Although, as we have noted, there exists a wide range of polarities in all of us, the one that has been given the greatest attention by gestaltists is called the *top-dog* and *under-dog split*. The top-dog is that side of personality that moralizes and lives in a world of "shoulds." Top-dog tends to be bossy and condemning. On the other side, under-dog tends to be childlike, impulsive, and irresponsible—this side makes excuses and resists responsibility passively. You can see how easy it would be for a split to exist between these two sides (note their similarity to the superego and id in psychoanalytic theory), and in fact it may help clarify the concept to consider how this polarity might exist in yourself. In any event, given the prevalence of the top-dog versus under-dog split, many gestalt dialogue games focus on it.

Unfinished Business

"Unfinished business" is a form of "incomplete gestalt" in gestalt psychology. Whenever unfinished business is detected in gestalt therapy (usually in the form of unresolved feelings), the client is asked to finish it. Clearly, any person will have a wide array of unfinished business in the interpersonal arena, for example, with parents, siblings, and spouses. In Perls's opinion, resentments are the most common and significant type of unfinished business.

"I Take Responsibility"

In gestalt therapy a premium is placed on the person's taking responsibility for his or her feelings and actions. The client is asked to say "I won't" rather than "I can't,"

and is also asked to say "and I take responsibility for it" as an addendum to his or her perceptions, feelings, and actions. Thus, "I am aware that I am smiling when I talk about this painful feeling—and I take responsibility for it." Or, "I don't know what to say—and I take responsibility for it." Although this may seem like a foolish and mechanical game, it does eventually drive home the point that responsibility resides in the person for all behaviors and that we constantly make choices about what we do and feel.

Playing the Projection

Probably the major defense mechanism according to gestalt therapists is projection, and whenever the gestalt therapist sees signs of projections, the client is asked to play the projection, as a way of becoming aware of the parts of himself or herself that are being projected onto others. Thus, for example, if the client feels the therapist is being critical, the client is asked to play the critical therapist. Often a two-chair dialogue may be used to highlight the split occurring along with this projection.

Nowhere is playing the projection seen more vividly in gestalt therapy than in work on dreams. Such dream analysis is vastly different than in psychoanalysis. Whereas in psychoanalysis, the client is to free-associate to segments of the dream, in gestalt therapy the client is asked to actually *be* each and every object in the dream. Imagine, for example, a dream as follows (one actually reported by a client of one of the authors):

> "I was in the attic and a monster was looking at me hatefully. A little baby was sitting near the monster and was very frightened. The attic door slammed shut; I ran out and tripped over a cinder block."

In a gestalt analysis, the client was asked to play the role of the monster, the baby, the cinder block, and the door that slammed shut. Each was eventually experienced as a warring part of herself, and the awareness that resulted took this client a step toward resolving these splits.

Reversals

As an example of a particular kind of split, the client's behavior is often seen as a reversal of underlying impulses. To bring about awareness of the hidden side, the gestaltist asks the client to play the opposite of what is being expressed. For example, the client who is expressing excessive timidity is asked to play an exhibitionist; the client who is hostile and critical is asked to be receptive and nonjudgmental; the client who is overly sweet is asked to play one who is unreceptive and attacking.

Exaggeration and Repetition

Exaggeration is aimed at helping clients understand body language. When unwitting gestures or movements seem to be significant communications (e.g., a wave of the arm, tapping of the foot), clients are asked to exaggerate the movement repeatedly so as to become more aware of its meaning. This attention to nonverbal be-

Examples of Some Gestalt Therapy Exercises and Experiments.   **TABLE 12.3.**

Exercise	How It's Done and Why
Two-chair technique	When the therapist sees conflict in client, he or she has the client enact both sides by engaging in a dialogue where one side is enacted when the client sits in one chair, then the other side is enacted when the client sits in the second chair. This helps the client resolve internal splits or polarities.
Empty-chair technique	The therapist asks the client to place into an empty chair the visual image of a person with whom the client has present conflicts. This is an excellent technique to resolve unfinished business.
"I take responsibility"	The client is asked to say, for example, "I won't" or "I don't want to," rather than "I can't."
Playing the projection	The client is invited to *be* the person he or she is projecting feelings or reactions onto. This helps the client own projections.
Reversals	The therapist asks the client to play the *opposite* of what the client is expressing. This helps to get at hidden reactions.
Exaggeration	The client is instructed to exaggerate gestures or body movements that reflect and help the client get in touch with his or her hidden feelings.
Repetition	The therapist asks the client to repeat—over and over and louder and louder—statements that reflect hidden feelings. This helps the client really see what was being glossed over.
"I see"	Members of a couple share perceptions of how they perceive each other. This helps them to understand and communicate what each sees in the other.

havior forms a significant part of gestalt treatment. In fact, probably no other theoretical persuasion is as attentive to nonverbal behavior. Gestaltists believe that the body is used as a crucial vehicle for communicating messages of which the client is unaware. Thus attention to nonverbals aids greatly in the effort to enhance awareness. Earlier we noted confrontation as the major response mode used in gestalt therapy. Many such confrontations attend to discrepancies between verbal and nonverbal expressions.

The verbal counterpart of the exaggeration game is called "repetition." Here the gestalt therapist asks the client to repeat a statement over and over, and often in a louder and louder voice. This is done when the therapist suspects that the client is not hearing himself or herself or is emotionally glossing over verbalizations that are significant. The repetition and the increased loudness help the client really hear rather than just form words.

Marriage Counseling Games

Gestaltists use several exercises when working with couples. For example, the therapist may have partners face each other and take turns beginning sentences with "I resent you for . . ." This work may be followed by beginning sentences with "I appreciate you for . . ." Other games reflective of important relationship themes are "I spite you by . . ."; "I am compliant by . . ."; and "I see." This last preface, "I see," aims at helping discover what members of a couple see in each other. Perls felt that a major problem in marriages is that partners are in love with a concept rather than an individual. The "I see" game seeks to help the partners see each other as they really are.

When involved in the exercises we have just described, the gestalt therapist seeks to have the client follow some "rules." The most common rules are to (a) stay in the here and now; (b) communicate with the other person, the "thou," rather than an "it"; (c) use "I" language rather than "it" language (e.g., "*I* feel bad" rather than "*It* is a bad feeling").

Throughout all of the exercises and in fact throughout all of gestalt therapy there is one overriding goal, rule, and exercise: to make use of the awareness continuum. That is, the therapist seeks to facilitate the client's awareness—of bodily sensations, perceptions, and emotions. The therapist often asks the client to "stay with this feeling" as a way of heightening awareness. As noted earlier, if there is a key to health in gestalt therapy, it resides in being aware. As Fritz Perls urged: "Lose your mind and come to your senses."

The Gestalt Approach in Perspective

Just as there is a lack of clarity in person-centered therapy as to the role of therapist techniques, in gestalt therapy the role of the counselor–client relationship has been inconsistently and unclearly articulated, at least until recent times. Although Fritz Perls was fond of the expression, "here and now, I and thou," in his own counseling it never seemed that Perls developed "I-thou" relationships. Dolliver (1981b), for example, points out how the interpersonal quality that is necessary for an I-thou encounter was missing in Perls's work with clients and workshop participants. His exclusive focus seemed to be on the client and on exercises to promote awareness, and the "I" was missing from his interactions. In fact, Laura Perls commented that "what was problematic in Fritz's approach was that he was not interested in the person as such but in what he could do with her" (in Friedman, 1983, p. 89).

Other gestalt therapists have noted this deficiency and have sought to strengthen the relationship component of gestalt therapy (e.g., Hycner & Jacobs, 1995; Polster & Polster, 1973; Simkin & Yontef, 1984). For example, whereas Perls seemed never to examine or reveal his own feelings and biases in his work, Shepherd (1970) asserts that, "[t]he therapist needs to listen carefully and admit, 'what you say is true of me' if it fits, rather than dealing with this as the patient's fantasy, and implying inaccuracy or distortion of perception [as Perls so often did]" (p. 237).

In fact, the apparent inconsistency and lack of clarity that mark the role of relationship in gestalt therapy appear to stem from its two distinct lines of thought on the role and importance of the relationship. Greenberg (1983) highlights this split when he notes that some gestalt therapists, in the Perls tradition, focus on the role of "therapist as teacher of the method," whereas others key in on the relationship. Those who take the role of teacher use techniques and exercises to help clients learn to focus attention on experiencing in the moment. For these counselors, I-thou relating is engaged in only as a means of teaching clients the significance of I-thou relationships. For the relationship-oriented gestalt therapists, however, the role of the authentic human encounter in the present is the key to change. These therapists seek to share themselves as part of the work and deemphasize the role of techniques and exercises.

It is clear that gestalt therapy as it is currently practiced is far more relationship-oriented than during Perls's time. Gestalt therapists now tend to use techniques as an extension of the kind of relationship that has been developed with the client (Gelso & Hayes, 1998). Hycner and Jacobs (1995) reflect this trend when they note that emotional *contact* between therapist and client (the relationship part) is essential for full *awareness*. These authors summarize this position nicely: "Therapy composed solely of awareness techniques, without contact engagement of the therapist/person with the patient/person, paradoxically limits the awareness possibilities for the patient and interrupts the becoming of both people" (Hycner & Jacobs, 1995, p. 84).

Gestalt Therapy Now

What is the current status of gestalt therapy in counseling psychology? As a system of intervention, its creativity and confrontiveness (often aggressiveness when practiced by some gestaltists) fit beautifully with the turbulence of the late 1960s and early 1970s. The focus on the self, on "doing your own thing," seemed to capture the *Zeitgeist*. However, as the 1960s and 1970s have faded from the field's consciousness, the immense popularity of gestalt therapy has clearly waned. By the 1980s, few counseling psychologists claimed gestalt therapy as either their primary or secondary theoretical orientation (Watkins et al., 1986; Zook & Walton, 1989).

In part, the decline in popularity of gestalt therapy is due to its lack of a research base. Few outcome studies have been conducted to support its effectiveness, partly because of the indifference among gestaltists to scientific study (Greenberg et al., 1994). Perhaps the deemphasis of intellect in gestalt therapy was inappropriately applied to research. If we should "lose our minds and come to our senses," perhaps scientific study is unnecessary. It should be noted that some empirical research has accumulated in the 1980s and 1990s on the effectiveness of gestalt techniques and the process of gestalt therapy (see summary by Sharf, 1996), but more is needed.

Although few counseling psychologists are now gestalt therapists, the gestalt approach has had an enormous influence on the practice of counseling psychology. Many of the techniques and exercises created by Perls and others are often used by therapists in their day-to-day practice (e.g., requesting first-person pronouns, staying in the here and now, bringing out internal dialogues). As Burke (1989) notes, a technique such as the two-chair technique and its variations is immensely versatile in its applications. Interestingly, this technique is exceptional in the gestalt therapy literature in that a solid line of research does exist supporting its positive effects on clients' awareness and behavior change (Greenberg et al., 1993; Greenberg et al., 1994).

Not only have the techniques been influential, the concept of an authentic "I–thou" relationship has become a central part of the work of many counseling psychologists. No other theory has so powerfully articulated the importance of an I–thou relationship in counseling. The belief in its value in therapy is even stronger today than when Perls was alive (see Gelso & Hayes, 1998; Greenberg et al., 1993; Hycner & Jacobs, 1995).

Finally, the influence of gestalt therapy is also evidenced in approaches that seek to integrate gestalt principles and techniques with other theories. Such integrative efforts are perhaps more notable in what is called process–experiential therapy (Greenberg et al., 1993) than in any other writing. Greenberg and colleagues have successfully blended the empathic approach of person-centered therapy with the more active techniques of gestalt therapy. Such thoughtful integrations lead us to believe that gestalt therapy and person-centered therapy are indeed alive and well in the practice of counseling psychology, although not in pure form.

As with person-centered therapy, we have offered only a glimpse of the main ingredients of gestalt therapy. For more detailed discussions, we suggest chapters by Prochaska and Norcross (1999), Simkin and Yontef (1984), Sharf (1996), and Burke (1989). Perls's (1969a) *Gestalt Therapy Verbatim,* in tandem with Polster and Polster's (1973) lucid and interesting book, remain the classic works. *Gestalt Therapy Now* (Fagan & Shepherd, 1970), more than 30 years after its publication, remains a valuable book of readings. Hycner and Jacobs's (1995) book reflects some of the most exciting developments in the gestalt therapy scene, especially in its focus on the therapeutic relationship and in its attempts to integrate gestalt therapy with psychoanalytic self psychology (Chapter 10). The ways in which gestalt therapy can be integrated effectively with other approaches, in fact, may represent the growing edge of this theory of therapy and its influence in counseling psychology.

SUMMARY

Although the philosophy of humanism is rooted in much earlier times, humanistic approaches to counseling are a product of the mid-twentieth century. These approaches developed as a reaction to both psychoanalysis and behaviorism. As a group, they are aptly labeled the "third force" in psychology and counseling.

Although the different humanistic approaches vary in their specifics, they share several assumptions about human beings, counseling, and science, regarding the democratic ideal as an essential value, the fundamental predominance of subjective experience, the inherent tendency of humans toward growth and self-actualization, the essential trustworthiness of people, the value of authentic human encounters in the present as a powerful way of helping clients grow and develop, and the necessity for scientific methods to fit the human experience if they are to enlighten us.

The two humanistic approaches that have had the greatest impact on counseling psychologists are Carl Rogers's person-centered therapy and Fritz Perls's gestalt therapy. Although Rogers's approach to counseling came before any theory of personality, he did develop a set of clear and consistent theoretical statements about personality development. His emphasis was phenomenological, emphasizing the need to understand the private world of the individual and the whole person, rather than isolated parts. The self and self-concept are key components in Rogers's personality theory. In his effort to delineate healthy and unhealthy development, he focused on the actualizing tendency, how it goes awry, and how it may be facilitated. Difficulties caused by the formation of *conditions of worth* are pivotal in humans' estrangement from themselves, whereas in healthy functioning congruence exists between inner experiencing and behavior.

To Rogers, the key to successful counseling lies not in techniques or in accurate diagnosis, but in the therapeutic relationship. In fact, the kind of relationship that is both necessary and sufficient for client change is marked, on the person-centered counselor's side, by empathic understanding, unconditional positive regard, and congruence.

Although techniques are deemphasized in person-centered therapy, counselors of this persuasion mainly use paraphrasing techniques, especially reflection of feeling. Clearly the person-centered approach to life and therapy is one of nondirectiveness.

Largely because of Rogers's own self-actualization as a scientist as well as a practitioner, his ideas have been subjected to careful and thorough scientific scrutiny. Many ideas have been supported, some not; but in the main, client-centered therapy and now person-centered therapy have received empirical support for their effectiveness, at least with clients who are not severely disturbed. Rogers and his approach to treatment have had a profound effect on counseling psychology.

The gestalt approach of Fritz Perls also emphasized intervention more than personality development. Perls's theoretical statements about personality were unsystematic, although they were related to gestalt therapy formulations about treatment. Regarding neurosis, or growth disorders, Perls speculated that there are five layers to the neurosis—the synthetic, phobic, impasse, implosive, and explosive layers—each of which must be worked through if a person is to become mature.

In terms of verbal techniques or response modes, the gestalt therapist uses primarily confrontation, direct guidance, and self-involving disclosures. A hallmark of the gestalt approach is the use of exercises or games during counseling. Revealing key issues, these exercises include dialogues, "unfinished business," "I take responsibility," "playing the projection," role-playing reversals, exaggeration and repetition, and marriage counseling games. The overriding goal in gestalt therapy, whether approached through exercises or the counselor–client relationship, is the creation of awareness in the here and now of one's subjective experiencing.

Regarding the counselor–client relationship, there has long been a division in gestalt therapy between those who emphasize their roles as teacher of the method and those who focus on the I–thou relationship. Current gestalt theory emphasizes the importance of the I–thou relationship as a precondition for the development of client awareness.

Although the popularity of gestalt therapy has clearly declined since its heyday in the late 1960s and early 1970s, many of its techniques and ideas continue to appeal, and have been incorporated by practitioners.

REFERENCES

Barrett-Lennard, G. T. (1997). The recovery of empathy toward others and self. In A. C. Bohart and L. S. Greenberg (Eds.), *Empathy reconsidered—new directions in psychotherapy* (pp. 103–121). Washington, DC: American Psychological Association.

Belkin, G. S. (1980). *Contemporary psychotherapies*. Chicago, IL: Rand McNally.

Beutler, L. E., Machado, P. P. P., & Neufeldt, S. A. (1994). Therapist variables. In A. Bergin and S. Garfield (Eds.), *Handbook of psychotherapy and behavior change* (4th ed., pp. 229–269). New York: John Wiley & Sons.

Bozarth, J. D. (1990). The essence of client-centered therapy. In G. Lietaer, J. Rombouts, and R. Van Balen (Eds.), *Client-centered and experiential psychotherapy in the nineties* (pp. 59–64). Leuven, Belgium: Leuven University Press.

Bozarth, J. D. (1997). Empathy from the framework of client-centered theory and the Rogerian Hypothesis. In A. C. Bohart and L. S. Greenberg (Eds.), *Empathy reconsidered—new directions in psychotherapy* (pp. 81–100). Washington, DC: American Psychological Association.

Burke, J. F. (1989). *Contemporary approaches to psychotherapy and counseling: The self regulation and maturity model.* Pacific Grove, CA: Brooks/Cole.

Corsini, R. J., & Wedding, D. (1995). *Current psychotherapies* (5th ed.). Itasca, Ill: Peacock.

Dolliver, R. (1981a). Personal sources for theories of psychotherapy. *Journal of Contemporary Psychotherapy, 12,* 53–59.

Dolliver, R. H. (1981b). Some limitations of Perls' gestalt therapy. *Psychotherapy: Theory, Research, and Practice, 18,* 38–45.

Fagan, J., & Shepherd, I. L. (Eds.). (1970). *Gestalt therapy now.* New York: Harper & Row.

Friedman, M. (1983). *The healing dialogue in psychotherapy.* New York: Jason Aronson.

Gelso, C. J., & Hayes, J. A. (1998). *The psychotherapy relationship: Theory, research, and practice.* New York: John Wiley & Sons.

Gendlin, E. T. (1970). Research in psychotherapy with schizophrenic patients and the nature of that "illness." In J. T. Hart and T. M. Tomlinson (Eds.), *New directions in client-centered therapy* (pp. 280–291). Boston: Houghton Mifflin.

Greenberg, L. S. (1983). The relationship in gestalt therapy. In M. Lambert (Ed.), *Psychotherapy and patient relationships* (pp. 126–153). Homewood, IL: Dow Jones–Irwin.

Greenberg, L. S. (1985). An integrative approach to the relationship in counseling and psychotherapy. *The Counseling Psychologist, 13,* 251–260.

Greenberg, L. S., Elliott, R. K., & Lietaer, G. (1994). Research on experiential psychotherapies. In A. Bergin and S. Garfield (Eds.), *Handbook of psychotherapy and behavior change* (4th ed., pp. 509–539). New York: John Wiley & Sons.

Greenberg, L. S., Rice, L. N., & Elliott, R. (1993). *Facilitating emotional change: The moment-by-moment process.* New York: Guilford Press.

Grummon, D. L. (1965). Client-centered theory. In B. Stefflre (Ed.), *Theories of counseling* (pp. 30–90). New York: McGraw-Hill.

Hycner, R., & Jacobs, L. (1995). *The healing relationship in gestalt therapy.* Highland, NY: Gestalt Journal Press.

Levant, R., & Shlien, J. (Eds.). (1984). *Client-centered therapy and the person-centered approach.* New York: Praeger.

Levitsky, A., & Perls, F. S. (1970). The rules and games of gestalt therapy. In J. Fagan & I. L. Shepherd (Eds.), *Gestalt therapy now* (pp. 140–149). New York: Harper & Row.

Lietaer, G., Rombauts, J., & Van Balen, R. (Eds.) (1990). *Client-centered and experiential psychotherapy in the nineties.* Leuven, Belgium: Leuven University Press.

Lowe, C. M. (1969). *Value orientations in counseling and psychotherapy: The meanings of mental health.* San Francisco: Chandler Publishing.

Mahrer, A. R. (1996). *The complete guide to experiential psychotherapy.* New York: John Wiley & Sons.

Maslow, A. H. (1954). *Motivation and personality.* New York: Harper & Row.

Maslow, A. H. (1968). *Toward a psychology of being* (2nd ed.). New York: Van Nostrand Reinhold.

Maslow, A. H. (1970). *Motivation and personality* (rev. ed.). New York: Harper & Row.

May, R. (1967). *Psychology and the human dilemma.* New York: Van Nostrand Reinhold.

Norcross, J. C., Sayette, M. A., Mayne, T. J., Karg, R. S., & Turkson, M. A. (1998). Selecting a doctoral program in professional psychology: Some comparisons among Ph.D. counseling, Ph.D. clinical, and Psy.D. clinical Psychology programs. *Professional Psychology: Research and Practice, 29,* 609–614.

Orlinsky, D. E., Grawe, K., & Parks, B. K. (1994). Process and outcome in psychotherapy—*Noch Einmal.* In A. Bergin and S. Garfield (1994), *Handbook of psychotherapy and behavior change* (4th ed., pp. 270–376). New York: John Wiley & Sons.

Orlinsky, D., & Howard, K. (1986). Process and outcome in psychotherapy. In S. Garfield and A. Bergin (Eds.), *Handbook of psychotherapy and behavior change* (3rd ed., pp. 311–381). New York: John Wiley & Sons.

Passons, W. R. (1975). *Gestalt approaches to counseling.* New York: Holt, Rinehart, & Winston.

Perls, F. S. (1947). *Ego, hunger, and aggression.* New York: Random House.

Perls, F. S. (1969a). *Gestalt therapy verbatim.* New York: Bantam.

Perls, F. S. (1969b). *In and out of the garbage pail.* Lafayette, CA: Real People Press.

Perls, F. S. (1970). *Four lectures.* In J. Fagan and I. L. Shepherd (Eds.), *Gestalt therapy now* (pp. 14–38). New York: Harper & Row.

Perls, F. S., Hefferline, R., & Goodman, P. (1951). *Gestalt therapy: Excitement and growth in personality.* New York: Dell.

Polster, E., & Polster, M. (1973). *Gestalt therapy integrated: Contours of theory and practice.* New York: Vintage Books.

Prochaska, J. O. (1979). *Systems of psychotherapy: A transtheoretical analysis.* Homewood, IL: Dorsey.

Prochaska, J. O., & Norcross, J. C. (1999). *Systems of psychotherapy: A transtheoretical analysis* (4th ed.). Pacific Grove, CA: Brooks/Cole.

Raskin, N. J., & Rogers, C. R. (1995). Person-centered therapy. In R. J. Corsini and D. Wedding (Eds.), *Current psychotherapies* (5th ed., pp. 128–161). Itasca, IL: Peacock.

Rogers, C. R. (1939). *The clinical treatment of the problem child.* Boston: Houghton Mifflin.

Rogers, C. R. (1942). *Counseling and psychotherapy.* Boston: Houghton Mifflin.

Rogers, C. R. (1951). *Client-centered therapy.* Boston: Houghton Mifflin.

Rogers, C. R. (1957). The necessary and sufficient conditions for therapeutic personality change. *Journal of Consulting Psychology, 21,* 95–103.

Rogers, C. R. (1959). A theory of therapy, personality, and interpersonal relationships, as developed in the client-centered framework. In S. Koch (Ed.), *Psychology: A study of science* (Vol. III). New York: McGraw-Hill.

Rogers, C. R. (1961). *On becoming a person.* Boston: Houghton Mifflin.

Rogers, C. R. (Ed.). (1967). *The therapeutic relationship and its impact: A study of psychotherapy with schizophrenics.* Madison: University of Wisconsin Press.

Rogers, C. R. (1973). My philosophy of interpersonal relationships and how it grew. *Journal of Humanistic Psychology, 13,* 3–15.

Rogers, C. R. (1980). *A way of being.* Boston: Houghton Mifflin.

Rogers, C. R., & Dymond, R. (1954). *Psychotherapy and personality change.* Chicago: University of Chicago Press.

Sharf, R. S. (1996). *Theories of psychotherapy and counseling: Concepts and cases.* Pacific Grove, CA: Brooks/Cole.

Shepherd, I. L. (1970). Limitations and cautions in the gestalt approach. In J. Fagan and I. L. Shepherd (Eds.), *Gestalt therapy now* (pp. 234–238). New York: Harper & Row.

Simkin, J. S., & Yontef, G. M. (1984). Gestalt therapy. In R. Corsini (Ed.), *Current psychotherapies* (3rd ed., pp. 279–319). Itasca, IL: Peacock.

Watkins, C. E., Lopez, F. G., Campbell, V. L., & Himmell, C. D. (1986). Contemporary counseling psychology: The results of a national survey. *Journal of Counseling Psychology, 33,* 301–309.

Zook, A., & Walton, J. M. (1989). Theoretical orientations and work settings of clinical and counseling psychologists: A current perspective. *Professional Psychology: Research and Practice, 20,* 23–31.

CHAPTER 13

SCIENCE AND PRACTICE OF ASSESSMENT IN THE NEW ERA

The psychological test was the invention that revolutionized psychological science, comparable in its impact to the telescope in physics and the microscope in biology . . . In terms of practical application, the psychological test is the technological innovation from psychology that has had the greatest effect on society (Dawis, 1992, p. 10).

Critics argue that psychological assessment is time-consuming, expensive, and not useful in the context of current patterns of care. . . . The profession's lack of advocacy in encouraging, collecting, and disseminating research that demonstrates the efficacy and utility of psychological assessment has compounded the problem (Eisman, Dies, Finn et al., 1998, p. 2).

The contrasting messages in the preceding quotes are an all-too-clear signal that assessment in psychology is at a pivotal point. In this chapter we will first explain why assessment is at such a pivotal point in its existence in the profession of psychology. We will then describe the concepts, tests, and skills that counseling psychologists need to be competent in psychological assessment in this age of industrialized health care with an increasingly diverse society.

ASSESSMENT: PSYCHOLOGY'S DODO BIRD OR PHOENIX?

In today's world, the primary cognitive association most of the public has with a psychologist is that of "a shrink"; that is, a mental health practitioner (who may well be analyzing you at this very moment). Even other health practitioners will typically view psychologists primarily as therapists for mental problems. Given these perspectives, it may be difficult to comprehend that until the 1960s psychologists were viewed *primarily* (if not exclusively) as professionals who developed, administered, and interpreted psychological tests in hospitals, clinics, counseling centers, and employment bureaus.

That our professional roles in those years were so focused on psychological assessment was a direct outgrowth of successful development, in the first half of the twentieth century, of ability, then personality, then interest measures. There was strong governmental support for the development and use of such tests first in World War I, then in the Great Depression. These advances were so highly regarded that they led to the development of the U.S. Employment Service, the precursor to the agency that today produces such documents as the Dictionary of Occupational Titles and the General Aptitude Test Battery.

During this same time period, the development of both objective and projective (a distinction that will be explained later in this chapter) personality tests became the foundation for psychologists having a unique role in the what were then called mental hospitals. All states had one or more hospitals that focused on severe and chronically mentally ill patients; psychologists were called on to use their testing skills to differentiate organic from nonorganic mental illness, schizophrenia from depression, psychosis from neurosis, and so forth. The psychological test information was typically combined with information from psychiatric interviews (psychologists were almost always supervised by psychiatrists in these hospitals), and observations from nurses and attendants in order to make a final diagnosis, treatment plan, prognosis, and posthospitalization treatment plan. At the end of World War II, the Veterans Administration (VA) developed training programs for psychologists primarily for these assessment functions. At that time, psychologists were rarely involved in providing psychotherapy for the veterans.

Moreover, also during the post–World War II era and continuing until the 1960s, counseling psychologists in most university and college counseling centers were also heavily involved in psychological testing. Indeed, in those times, students were expected to complete at least one or more personality and interest measures, possibly ability measures as well, before seeing a counselor. The counselor would then be expected to study all that information, along with any intake interview information, before beginning counseling.

The definitions of the specialties of counseling, school, and clinical psychology that were developed in the 1940s explicitly emphasized psychologists' roles in assessment; the revisions of these definitions over the years, through to those definitions archived in 1998 by the American Psychological Association (APA), continue to emphasize the role of assessment. Yet, in surveys conducted in recent decades, counseling psychologists typically spent only about 10% of their time on testing, plus or minus 5% depending on their work setting. Psychological testing had changed from a primary role to a distant subsidiary role.

What happened? Two major developments of the 1960s brought about the decline of psychological testing in many settings. The first was the increasing role of psychologists in providing psychotherapy and counseling. The development of client-centered therapy most especially affected counseling psychology. Rogers's (1951) emphasis on facilitative conditions, regardless of the presenting problem (see Chapter 8), arguably eliminated the need for formal diagnosis. How could one justify the routine practice of testing all individuals before counseling if the intervention strategy to be used was the same whatever the result of the testing? The absence of any empirical data showing that diagnostic information yielded by psychological testing related in any way to which kind of therapy was provided or what outcome could be expected led to increasing criticism of routine testing of clients. The best way to know what kind of treatment a client would be provided in the middle of the twentieth century was not to know what his or her problem/diagnosis was, but rather to know the theoretical predilection of the counselor.

A second factor in the decline of psychological testing was the emergence of evidence, beginning in the 1960s, of the adverse impact of many psychological test results on the employment opportunities and educational placements of women and racial and ethnic minorities. Walsh and Betz (1995) provide a concise summary of some of the issues of race and gender bias that appeared in test content and in test usage prior to the 1980s. Some members of the U.S. Congress, as well as some psychologists, called for a moratorium on the use of psychological test results in admitting students to educational programs or in selecting employees. In that era of strident critiques of psychological testing, many graduate students became quite cynical about whatever training in psychological testing they were still required to complete and many universities reduced required courses in psychological assessment.

Yet there were at least two positive developments from these critical challenges to psychological assessment. The first was the shift from using a "shotgun" to a "rifle" in diagnostic testing. (The terms in quotes may be offensive to many in today's more violent world, but these were the words used in the 1960s and 1970s.) This analogy refers to a shift from giving a battery of tests to every patient or student who was referred for assessment to a more focused selection of tests, specifically designed to provide the kind of information needed for the diagnosis or placement decision to be made. In the former tradition, a comprehensive picture of the patient or student was developed by integrating the results of the battery of tests. That picture may or may not have specifically answered the question in the referral. In the more focused model of assessment, less time is needed and extraneous material is eliminated. Forensic psychology today still relies heavily on focused test results in determining psychological functioning for legal cases involving disability, discrimination, custody, and emotional injury (Boccaccini & Brodsky, 1999).

The other positive development was, with the aid of knowledgeable consultants, the development of psychological tests that were less culturally biased in content, norms, and usage. While the search for "culture free" tests proved to be an impossible goal, the development of somewhat more culturally fair tests proved attainable. As was already noted in Chapter 6, and will be further discussed below in the section on "Standards for All Assessments," a culturally competent counseling psychologist can use psychological testing in ways that will be truly helpful to culturally diverse clients. Almost all the major tests reviewed later in this chapter have been revised to be more useful with a wide range of clientele.

While the two criticisms discussed above threatened to make assessment the dodo bird of psychology, the positive developments, along with the earlier successful history of assessment in the profession of psychology, limited the damage, we might say, to "clipped wings." To stay with this analogy, assessment was limping along until the 1990s when, to add insult to injury, managed health care organizations took the position, regarding assessment, "this bird won't fly!" Meyer, Finn, Eyde et al. (1998) and Eisman et al. (1998) provide survey summaries of over 400 psychologists in managed care, indicating the emergence of extreme restrictions on the amount of psychological assessment that could be authorized for diagnostic and treatment processes for clients in managed care. Ambrose (1997) finds that while therapists often tried to justify the expense of conducting psychological assessments on the basis that it would help choose the shortest effective treatment and improve outcomes, "there is no conclusive, unequivocal research that demonstrates . . . assessment does any of the above" (p. 66). As Meyer and colleagues (1998) ruefully note, "Most psychological assessment research has been psychometrically focused on demonstrating the theoretical validity of test scales, rather than practically focused on demonstrating the day-to-day utility of those scales" (p. 6).

Perhaps somewhat ironically, this managed care assessment "crisis" may be just the impetus the profession of psychology needs to attend to issues it should have attended to more seriously several decades ago. What evidence can we develop showing that the use of psychological testing will improve treatment processes and outcomes? Psychological testing has thrived in educational and employment settings because of the continued production of significant (even if not as large as hoped for) empirical relationships between psychological test results and examinees' success in educational and employment programs. Moreland, Fowler, and Honaker (1994) note that psychological assessment will be viewed positively by industrialized health care only when it can be demonstrated that it will help contain health care costs. They describe how, in the treatment of alcoholics, assessment has been used effectively to identify whether outpatient care (as compared to inpatient care) will be a sufficient and effective treatment. From a managed care viewpoint, such evidence will be very convincing for increased authorization of psychological testing; inpatient treatment is the most expensive way to treat behavioral problems.

If the current and next generation of counseling psychologists can meet these challenges from managed care, then psychological assessment may once again be "the technological innovation from psychology that has had the greatest effect on society" (Dawis, 1992, p. 10). Our research in the coming decades will help decide whether psychological assessment is our dodo bird or a phoenix rising from the "ashes" of the critiques of recent decades.

ASSESSMENT: MORE THAN PSYCHOLOGICAL TESTS

In the opening section of this chapter, the terms *assessment* and *psychological test* have been used interchangeably. Until the 1960s, with the emergence of the critiques of the substance and use of psychological tests, such interchangeability was both conceptually and practically sound. In those times, use of assessment in practice and research—whether for diagnosis, treatment, or for evaluating the results of counseling—relied primarily on published psychological tests rather than specially designed measures. However, in more recent decades, the public's criticisms and misunderstandings about psychological *tests* have led many psychologists to desire a distinction be made between *assessment* and *testing*. For example, psychologists concerned with how managed care looks at assessment take the position that in assessment, in contrast to psychological testing,

> [T]he focus is on taking a variety of test-derived pieces of information, obtained from multiple methods of assessment, and placing the data in the context of historical information, referral information, and behavioral observations made during the testing and interview process, in order to generate a cohesive and comprehensive understanding of the person being evaluated (Meyer et al., 1998, p. 8).

There is no clear consensus in the profession of psychology about what constitutes psychological tests as compared to assessment. Some psychologists narrowly limit the use of the word *tests* to those achievement and ability measures that have right and wrong answers. They use the word *inventories* for those measures of interest and personality that have no right or wrong answers but rather compare an individual's answers to those of a norm group. They use the word *scales* (or checklists) for lists of behaviors, symptoms, problems, and so forth that are frequently used in diagnostic and therapeutic progress research.

The critical issue for whatever is called "assessment" is the degree to which the assessment process meets acceptable standards (described in the next section). However, before moving on to a discussion of standards, it may be useful to ask seemingly obvious questions: Why are assessment measures even necessary? Why does a person need to be psychologically measured? At a fundamental level, assessment is the psychologist's way of communicating. Although each person is unique in some ways, each is similar in many ways to other persons. Without ways to identify and communicate similarities and differences within and among individuals, psychologists cannot make accurate predictions beyond a chance level of accuracy. Means must exist to determine, for example, what kind of persons will be most satisfied in people-oriented compared to data-oriented occupations. As another example, knowing that counseling strategies should differ for a client whose problem is depression compared to dependency is useless information unless there is some way of assessing whether the client is depressed or dependent (or possibly both). Thus assessment is central to both the science and practice of counseling psychology.

Why not just ask persons in which ways they are unique, or whether their problem is depression or dependence? After all, one often hears, "No one can know us better than ourselves." But how well does each of us know ourselves? Most of us do not know ourselves very well with regard to the "normative" aspects of our feelings and behaviors. How often do other persons feel depressed compared to me and am I depressed enough that I should seek help? If I feel that my verbal skills are relatively poor compared to others', should I try to avoid all jobs requiring verbal skills? Certainly in making career decisions, it is just as important to have an understanding of one's abilities and interests *compared to others* as it is to realize their place within one's own range of strengths, weaknesses, preferences and dislikes. Therefore, psychologists can proceed in practice or research only when they have some way of making assessments.

STANDARDS FOR ALL ASSESSMENT TECHNIQUES

For readers who have not had prior coursework in the basics of psychological assessment, we recommend a reading of "A Primer of Testing" (Green, 1981) before proceeding. His 11-page article, written for the general public, concisely describes the constructs and considerations that underlie much of the material and recommendations in this section. Ethical use of assessment by counseling psychologists fundamentally requires an understanding of the topics covered by Green (1981).

Decisions about just how extensive standards for assessment should be, and how rigorously they should be applied, have been major sources of controversy for psychologists for nearly 50 years. When the 1999 version of the Standards for Educational and Psychological Testing (American Educational Research Association, American Psychological Association, and National Council of Measurement in Education, 1999 [hereafter cited as AAN]) were being prepared, a draft was sent to all members of the participating organizations. Over 8,000 pages of comments were received! Most of these comments reflected two overarching concerns: first, when is it acceptable to use a psychological assessment as compared to some other form of assessment, for example, high school diploma as the only requirement for acceptance into a training program for nursing compared to using some measure of the applicant's emotional stability and/or attention to detail? Second, should the level of rigor of application of the standards vary according to how the measure will be used? For example, does one have to observe established assessment standards as fully and rigorously when developing a scale for evaluation of a teacher as when developing a scale for selecting security employees for a nuclear energy facility? If it were possible to easily meet all assessment standards, this issue would not exist. However, meeting high levels of assessment standards is costly both in terms of time and dollars. Let us now look more closely at both of these issues.

With rare exceptions, all psychological assessments have limited effectiveness in making predictions; the critical issue is whether there is anything else such as past school or job performance, or recommendations, and so forth, that can result in more effective predictions than psychological assessments. Since many readers might recently have taken, or will soon be taking, the Graduate Record Examination (GRE), a poignant illustration of this issue may be found in nine strenuous objections, in the May 1998, issue of *The American Psychologist,* to an article by Sternberg and Williams (1997). Their article outlined some major concerns in the use of the GRE for selecting graduate students for doctoral programs in psychology. The nine objections were packed with substantive criticisms of the authors' conclusions, as well as passion for not being too quick to judge the GRE as ineffective. These objections call to mind the saying that, "yes, democracy is a flawed political system, it's just that we've never found any better system of government." Yes, psychological assessments are flawed, but for many situations in which we are trying to make diagnoses and interventions to help people improve their mental and physical health, and/or their options in life, we have not found, all things considered, any fairer or better predictor of performance.

Arguments about how rigorously to apply the standards are no less easily resolved than the issue of when to use psychological assessment as compared to other data about persons. In the 1985 version of the Standards for Educational and Psychological Testing, each standard was labeled as primary (necessary for all assessments), secondary (desirable), or conditional (importance varies with application). In preparing the 1999 standards, the panel of experts reviewed numerous passionate and theoretically justified disagreements about whether standards regarding issues like internal consistency (see below) or testing fairness should be primary or secondary. Their final decision was to eliminate the categories cited above and substitute commentary for each standard as to how and when it should be applied.

In short, the current standards are a carefully constructed consensus that should be part of the fundamental training in assessment. An ideal exercise in a course on psychological assessment is to have each student evaluate a published assessment measure according to the Standards for Educational and Psychological Testing (AAN, 1999). In making such an evaluation, the introduction to the current standards is most important to consider:

> Evaluating the acceptability of a test or a test application does not rest on the literal satisfaction of every standard in this document, and acceptability cannot be determined by using a checklist. Specific circumstances affect the importance of individual standards. Individual standards should not be considered in isolation. Therefore, evaluating acceptability involves (a) professional judgment that is based on a knowledge of behavioral science, psychometrics, and the professional field to which the tests apply; (b) the degree to which the intent of the standard has been satisfied by the test developer and user; (c) the alternatives that are readily available; and (d) research and experiential evidence regarding feasibility of meeting the standard (AAN, 1999, p. 1).

The next three sections are based on the three major sections of these standards; we identify some key problem areas for counseling psychologists as both scientists and practitioners and make recommendations for how to proceed when using assessments in both practice and research.

Evaluating and Constructing Assessments

The words in the heading of this section may seem reversed—*evaluating* before *constructing?* Our choice of order is deliberate. As noted, if an existing assessment instrument can be evaluated as appropriate, that is what should be used in either practice or research settings. However, for some problems for which counseling psychologists wish to make assessments, there may be few if any measures that have adequate psychometric support or evidence of fairness and usefulness. In these situations, we encourage counseling psychologists to develop appropriate assessment instruments. Before computers became readily available to almost every graduate student and professional counseling psychologist, development of assessment measures of any sophistication was beyond most psychologists' capabilities. That situation has changed radically. Now what were once considered complex analyses, such as measures of internal consistency, factor analyses, or discriminant analyses, can be executed on personal computers. Thus, the scientist–practitioner counseling psychologist is now able to quite easily obtain basic psychometric data on any newly developed measure or, for existing tests, psychometric data for unique samples (e.g., a culturally diverse population).

Of the major concerns in evaluating assessments, as Green (1981) makes clear, *reliability* and *validity* are the linchpins of adequate assessment. *Reliability* refers to the consistency with which one measures something. Without consistency, one cannot develop validity; that is, predictable and useful relationships with other variables that are important to us, such as clients' mental health, employees' career adjustment, or adolescents' self-esteem. Our one recommendation regarding reliability is that measures need to be evaluated for both *temporal consistency* and *internal consistency*. The former is most easily illustrated by considering test–retest reliability. One asks, "If a test is given this week and the same test is given 2 weeks later, how well do the second set of scores for examinees correlate with their first scores?" The higher the correlation, the more reliable, or consistent, the results are said to be.

Internal consistency refers to the homogeneity of the items on a test. Whereas there are a number of theoretical arguments about the importance of homogeneity in a test, both Green (1981) and Nunnally (1978) have argued persuasively: "A test gains its reliability and its power by adding up a large number of homogeneous items" (Green, 1981, p. 1005). Homogeneous items are found by inspecting the intercorrelations of all items in a measure with each other. While this was once a very difficult process to compute, now computer software statistical packages exist that determine "coefficient alpha," the key measure of internal consistency. Nunnally notes that trying to demonstrate validity of measures with alphas below .70 is almost fruitless. He describes several ways for improving internal consistency, thereby permitting a new measure to become more useful in predicting and understanding human behavior.

Turning to the issue of *validity* of assessment measures, there are two basic recommendations to be considered. Among the many kinds of validity (see Green, 1981), the validity question that should take precedence is: "What evidence is there that the use of this test in the past has been useful in answering questions like the one I'm asking now?" For example, if one is trying to assess depression in a deaf client, is there any evidence that the measure of depression being considered produces useful results with deaf clients? If no such evidence exists, then one has to consider whether (1) to find another measure that has established usefulness for deaf persons; or, if no such measure exists, (2) consider the development of a scale that might become useful for such assessments. While the second option seems almost overwhelming to students, for counseling psychologist practitioners who work extensively with a specific population like deaf clients, they may well begin the development of more useful assessment tools. For researchers, development of unique scales has become widely practiced; simply consult any recent issue of the *Journal of Counseling Psychology* to see how researchers have developed unique measures, assessing both reliability and validity.

Whenever new measures are developed, a second major validity consideration is that of *convergent* and *discriminant validity* (Campbell & Fiske, 1959). *Convergent validity* refers to finding significant relationships with other indices of the trait or behavior being measured. For example, we would expect persons who score high on a measure of extroversion to prefer being with people compared to being alone. *Discriminant validity* is the opposite; that is, finding only minimal relationships between variables we think are very different, for example, extroversion and anxiety. Unless a test has discriminant validity, it can add little to what is already known from other measures. Additionally, if tests measure similar constructs but have different names, both the public and users can become confused. Researchers in the areas of self-efficacy and competence face this problem: Are these two different constructs with different relationships or simply two different names for essentially the same human characteristic? Reaching a conclusive answer to such questions is difficult, but an essential step in meeting high standards of assessment.

Fairness in Assessments and Testing

As discussed above, a major positive development from the extensive criticisms of psychological tests in the 1960s was a greatly increased sensitivity to bias in the construction and use of tests. Over the past few decades there has been a great deal of attention to reducing bias in the substance and norming of tests. There is agreement that all assessment instruments should have evidence of fairness with respect to absence of bias in content and in providing equitable treatment of all examinees in the testing process. For counseling psychologists, Fouad and Chan (1999) provide a concise review of the psychometric issues in using psychological assessments with women and ethnic minorities as well as a review of how cultural status affects both counselor and client use of assessment results.

More controversial are those issues that relate to equality of testing outcomes of examinee subgroups (e.g., ethnicity, gender). Is the issue one of unfair tests or unequal opportunities to learn pertinent knowledge and skills? This issue is especially critical for educational and industrial/organizational (I/O) psychologists who use tests for placement in various programs. While there is a ready consensus among psychologists that all persons should have equal opportunity to learn the material covered in selection and placement tests, providing that opportunity is the ethical responsibility of all educators and psychologists alike, not the primary responsibility of those who develop tests. Moreover, in current assessment standards, the idea that fairness requires all subgroups to have comparable passing rates is not supported *as a standard for the assessment instrument itself.* However, once again, because there is consensus among psychologists that persons who are equivalent, except for cultural group membership, should have equal opportunity for being chosen for competitive programs, assessment strategies need to attend carefully to situations where lack of equivalence on a test seems determined primarily by cultural status. A variety of assessment methods and complex statistical techniques have been developed over the years to better understand how to achieve fairness in the use of psychological assessments (Gottfredson, 1994; Sackett & Wilk, 1994).

Applications of Assessments

For counseling psychologists, standards for applications of assessment relate primarily to using tests with our increasingly diverse clientele (see Chapter 6 for additional discussion of multicultural assessment). Fortunately, in recent years several comprehensive books have been published that address the issues that counseling psychologists need to attend to in meeting acceptable standards in the application of psychological assessments (Dana, 1993, 1997; Paniagua, 1998; Suzuki, Meller, & Ponterotto, 1996). Care must be taken by counseling psychologists that they not make either of two frequent errors, errors that may be just as harmful as using psychological tests without consideration of clients' culture. The first of these errors is simply to eliminate the use of any psychological assessments because they have all been developed largely with Anglo middle-class Americans. As Dana (1997) points out, when test results are appropriately interpreted with consideration for culture, the results can be every bit as valuable for culturally diverse clients as for Anglo middle-class Americans. Several of the 21 chapters in the book edited by Suzuki and colleagues (1996) are devoted specifically to making appropriate multicultural usage of many of the tests reviewed later in this chapter.

The second error to avoid is assuming that all persons of a given subgroup (e.g., Native American or African American) are similar in their ways of looking at the world and in cultural background and immediately "adjusting" assessment results for a member of a given group. As explained in Chapter 6, such adjustments lead to over- or underdiagnosing of critical psychological phenomena. Ridley, Li, and Hill (1998) provide all counseling psychologists with an excellent conceptualization of how to improve attention to cultural concerns in all parts of the assessment process, from a choice of measures to interpretations of results. Space constraints here do not permit a full description of their Multicultural Assessment Procedure (MAP), but training in assessment for all counseling psychologists should now include training in the use of such a model. As Spengler (1998) notes, their recommended procedures are built upon established principles derived from psychologists' knowledge of behavior, decision making and information processing.

PSYCHOLOGICAL TESTS

There are now hundreds of published psychological tests, many of which have been revised and updated to comply more fully with the kinds of standards just reviewed. In addition, each year new tests appear to help investigators and practitioners make more effective assessments. In this section we describe the major categories of tests most used by counseling psychologists and, within each of those categories, we provide brief descriptions of the particular tests most often used. Many texts now exist (e.g., Walsh & Betz, 1995; Watkins & Campbell, 1990) that provide greater detail on each of these tests, as well as on categories of tests that we do not cover, such as achievement tests, since these are used mostly by educational and school psychologists.

About two-thirds of all counseling psychologists regularly use some sort of psychological tests (Fitzgerald & Osipow, 1986; Watkins, Campbell, & McGregor, 1988), even though spending only about 10% of their time in using these tests. However, both figures, as averages, are somewhat misleading. Since over one-third of counseling psychologists never use tests, obviously their time spent on such assessment is 0%. Some counseling psychologists may use more than 20 tests a week; others have never used a test since completing their doctoral studies. Watkins and colleagues have published a series of studies since the late 1980s showing which tests are most used varies significantly among settings such as counseling centers compared to hospitals and clinics, and varies somewhat according to the theoretical orientation of the psychologist (Watkins et al., 1988; Watkins, Campbell, Nieberding, & Hallmark, 1996). Therefore, the amount of use any one counseling psychologist makes of any one of the following tests will vary greatly as one moves into various positions in internships, residencies, and subsequent career positions.

Interest Measures

Considering all the types of psychological assessments, counseling psychologists have been most visibly involved with the development of interest measures. Because counseling psychology has been the specialty most centrally involved in career development and career counseling, almost every key person in the history of interest measurement has also been a key figure in the leadership and scholarship in counseling psychology. A bit of history: By the 1920s, early psychologists began to see major limits to the usefulness of considering only abilities as predictors of occupational success. Increasing attention was therefore given to the role of interests in understanding occupational success and adjustment. The work of E. K. Strong (1943), started in the late 1920s, laid the foundation for the development of the most widely used measure of interests throughout much of the twentieth century, the Strong Interest Inventory (SII) (Harmon, Hansen, Borgen, & Hammer, 1994).

The reasonable skeptic may ask, Why does one need a *measure* of interests? Why not simply ask the person to state his or her interests? The SII manual concisely reviews the decades of data showing how *expressed interests* and *measured interests* often disagree and examines the various hypotheses that have been put forward to explain why. These data, along with the extensive literature on the significant contributions of measured interests in predicting who will stay in a position and find success in it, have led not only to several revisions of the SII but also to the developments of several other well-developed measures of interests, especially the Kuder Occupational Interest Survey (KOIS) (Kuder & Zytowski, 1991) and the Self-Directed Search (SDS) (Holland, 1998; Reardon & Lenz, 1998). Although these two latter measures have somewhat different formats and conceptual histories than the SII, all have entered the counseling psychology mainstream as useful and adequately validated instruments in assisting clients in exploring and choosing satisfying and successful careers (see Donnay & Borgen, 1994; Holland, 1997; Zytowski, 1992).

Of the three measures, the SII provides the widest range of information as well as having the most extensive empirical history. Beginning in 1974, the SII included the six occupational themes of Holland's SDS (see next paragraph), as well as 25 basic interest areas (sales, teaching, medical sciences) and 207 occupational scales (e.g., audiologist, forester, police officer, psychologist), all grouped within Holland's six occupational themes. Norms for both males and females in each of these areas are provided except in those few occupations where there are either too few females or too few males to develop a separate norm. Both the manual for the newest form of the SII (Harmon et al., 1994) and the later research of Lattimore and Borgen (1999) provide evidence of the validity and usefulness of the current SII for the major racial and ethnic groups in the United States.

By the 1990s the SDS became more popular than the SII as an interest measure, primarily because of its self-scoring system and shorter administration time. Now in its fourth edition (Holland, 1998), it provides updated items and expanded norms, plus a large range of supplemental interpretive materials and software, almost all of which can be used by the test-takers themselves. There are also French, Spanish, and Vietnamese language versions of the SDS. Reardon and Lenz (1998) provide a comprehensive review of the practical applications of the SDS and its underlying theory of six personality types related to six work environments. (see Chapter 14).

The current KOIS is the latest development of what was once the most widely used interest measure in schools. The precursor to the KOIS, in the 1930s through the 1950s, simply required students to use a pin to punch holes in an answer sheet and then score it themselves (or have teachers score the measure for younger students). The homogeneous scales of that early form still serve as the basis for the KOIS designed for youngsters in middle school and junior high. The KOIS form for high school students and adults has now come to include scales for college majors and various occupations. Since these scales require comparisons to normative groups, the KOIS must now be machine scored. Zytowski (1992) very concisely describes the history of developments in, and usefulness of, the family of Kuder interest measures.

All three interest measures noted above are widely used in schools and universities to assist students in extensive exploration of career options both for those who have no idea which career they want to enter as well as for those who seek to confirm their interests. Moreover, counseling psychologists in independent practice whose clients' problems are related to career concerns also find the measures immensely valuable in opening new horizons for these clients.

The research uses of the interest inventories are also extensive. Almost every issue of *Career Development Quarterly, Journal of Vocational Behavior,* and *Journal of Career Assessment* contain one or more research reports in which an interest inventory has been a major assessment technique. In addition, both books and journals for psychologists in general, compared to those prepared specifically for counseling psychologists, have increasingly reported the results of investigations of interests. These investigations have ranged from testing theoretically based models on the relationships of interests to personality (Tracey & Rounds, 1997) to the universality of vocational interest structure among racial and ethnic minorities (Day & Rounds, 1998).

Personality Measures

Although the history of the development of psychometrically based personality tests coincides chronologically with the development of interest measures, the diversity of personality measures far exceeds that of interest measures. The multiplicity of personality theories in the first half of the twentieth century resulted in very different *kinds* of tests (e.g., some tests asked written questions, others showed inkblots or pictures, others asked for drawings), yet all were called "personality" tests. While the Minnesota Multiphasic Personality Inventory (MMPI) is currently far and away the most widely used personality test, there are nearly a dozen other personality measures used frequently by counseling psychologists. These include the Sixteen Personality Factor Questionnaire, the California Psychological Inventory, the Edwards Personal Preference Schedule, the Myers–Briggs Type Indicator, the Thematic Apperception Test and the Rorschach. Descriptions of each of these tests and their uses in practice and research may be found in any of the major textbooks on psychological tests (e.g., Walsh & Betz, 1995; Watkins & Campbell, 1990).

With the exception of the last two measures just listed, all of the others could be described as objective personality tests, whereas the last two are what are called projective personality tests. Objective personality tests typically include lists of questions or statements to which one responds with true or false, agree or disagree, like or dislike. (As we shall explain later in this section, these objective tests have also been most useful to counseling psychologists whenever the focus is on identifying strengths, as compared to psychopathology.) Projective tests involve the presentation of an ambiguous stimulus such as a vague picture or an inkblot; subjects "project" themselves into their open-ended responses to the presented stimulus. Projective tests were developed by adherents of the psychoanalytic approach as a way of assessing the unconscious experience. By definition, one cannot get direct access to unconscious experience through client self-report because the client is not aware of what is in the unconscious. For many years, the only way of interpreting projective techniques was through a clinician's judgment regarding dominant themes apparent in the clients' responses. There were significant problems in both reliability of scoring and in establishing validity of test results for making diagnoses or prognoses. In the past few decades, Exner and Weiner (1996) developed a comprehensive scoring system for the Rorschach that has addressed many of these problems of reliability and validity. The key variables, clusters and constellations derived from Exner's system are now becoming more widely used in both the diagnostic and treatment aspects of practice and in a variety of research projects. While counseling psychologists have traditionally not been trained in the use of projective techniques for both theoretical and practical reasons, as Watkins, Campbell, Hollifield, and Duckworth (1989) make clear, there may be a need to reexamine such traditions. This reexamination may be especially pertinent since counseling psychologists now more frequently work with distressed clients in counseling centers (Pledge, Lapan, Heppner et al., 1998) and with a wide range of emotional disturbances in clientele in industrialized health care settings.

By far the most exhaustively researched personality assessment instrument of any type is the MMPI, which is specifically designed to identify different types of psychopathology. Over the past five decades, literally thousands of studies have been completed on its clinical and validity scales. Now in its second edition, and with a separate edition for adolescents, its use in practice and research is unparalleled. From true/false responses to over 500 items, scores are provided on 10 clinical scales (e.g., depression, paranoia, social introversion), four validity scales (e.g., lie, defensiveness), and 15 content scales (e.g., anxiety, obsessiveness, bizarre mentation, low self-esteem). Even the earliest research with the MMPI indicated that a high score on any one scale meant very little; it is the configuration of scores that has been most valuable. Over the years many code books have been produced for various types of clientele. The most recent and most valuable books for counseling psychologists using the MMPI-II (the second and current edition of the MMPI) are those by Duckworth and Anderson (1995) and Butcher and Williams (1992). These books help counseling psychologists identify patterns of MMPI responses that are useful both in making diagnoses and in exploring personal and career concerns. Even with the help of such resources, however, the strong psychopathological focus of the MMPI makes it a difficult personality assessment measure to use beyond diagnosis; that is, in interpreting results to clients and having them use personality assessment information as part of the process of counseling. For such uses, counseling psychologists have long preferred other personality measures that focus more on strengths and assets.

Prior to the 1980s, the personality tests most often used by counseling psychologists were the California Psychological Inventory, the Edwards Personal Preference Schedule and the 16PF. While all of these tests are still used by some counselors, and have updated reliability and validity data available, counseling psychologists who wish to incorporate personality assessment as part of counseling now more often use the Myers–Briggs Type Indicator. Although this measure was originally developed primarily to assess four key dimensions of Jung's personality theory (Myers & McCaulley, 1985), it has proved to be very useful in a wide variety of personal and career counseling. The measure has what is called high "face validity"; that is, persons who complete the 126 two-choice items find both the questions and their results meaningful and logical. Four preference scores (extroverted vs. introverted, sensing vs. intuitive, thinking vs. feeling, and judging vs. perceiving) are combined into one of 16 personality types. Each type has been related to compatibility in various careers. Moreover, because descriptions of these types explain how persons differ in their information-processing and decision-making styles, learning about one's own type, as it contrasts to others' types, has often proved useful to clients in understanding conflicts with management styles and in interpersonal and marital relationships. Bayne (1995) provides both a critical review and practical guide to the range of uses of the MBTI.

Aptitude and Intelligence Tests

Of all the categories of tests reviewed in this chapter, it is in this category of aptitude and intelligence tests that the role of counseling psychologists has changed most drastically. To understand that change, a few sentences of history about the development and use of aptitude and intelligence tests are essential. Intelligence tests date back to the beginning of the twentieth century with the work of Binet. His carefully developed individually administered battery of subtests was increasingly used in schools both as a way of assessing potential and for understanding students' learning difficulties. Later, the desire of military leaders to assess both intellectual potential and specific aptitudes in World War I and World War II had a major impact on the development of group-administered tests so that large numbers of persons could be quickly tested. The development of group-administered intelligence tests for the military was the forerunner of tests now known to every college student, such as the Scholastic Aptitude Test (SAT) or the American College Test (ACT). Less well known are group tests such as the Differential Aptitude Tests and the General Aptitude Test Battery, which had their impetus from work conducted during and between the two world wars to address *aptitudes* beyond the kinds of intelligence measured by Binet. It was assumed that an identification of specific aptitudes could help select those who were most apt to be successful in skilled jobs like airplane mechanic, radio operator.

Recall that counseling psychology, along with the other applied specialties, emerged immediately after World War II. Given the relatively successful development and use of intelligence and aptitude tests in World War II, it is not surprising that counseling psychologists made extensive use of such tests in their work with the millions of returning veterans who were making a delayed entry into the labor force or going on to higher education with financial assistance from the GI Bill. Counseling psychology texts of the 1950s discussed the most effective ways to use a variety of intelligence and aptitude tests in counseling.

However, currently, with the two exceptions discussed below, counseling psychologists are much less involved in the development and use of intelligence and aptitude tests. What happened? Two major concomitant changes: first, ever since World War II the workforce in the United States has increasingly moved from a "blue-collar" skilled and semiskilled manufacturing work force to a "white-collar" service workforce. Formal education and what is often called "general intelligence," such as verbal and numerical skills, have become far more important for job success than specialized aptitudes like mechanical reasoning, manual dexterity, and coding speed.

Concomitant with this change has been a continual increase in the percent of young people attending some form of college. Less than 10% of the population attended college prior to World War II; by the end of the twentieth century that figure was over 70%. Counselors in the 1960s quickly learned that students who had sufficient educational background and intelligence to enter college did not really need any further assessment of their intelligence as part of their career planning. Within most professions, the amount of general intelligence necessary to be successful does not differ much from that needed to succeed in college. For example, there are successful nuclear engineers whose general intelligence is no greater than that of average college students. Interests, persistence, and other motivational factors may bring distinguished success to those with slightly above average intelligence while their more brilliant colleagues stumble. The routine administration of a measure of intelligence as part of the process of college counseling therefore quickly died out in the 1960s.

Having noted these decreases in use of aptitude and intelligence testing in general, there are two areas where some counseling psychologists continue to have significant involvement with such tests. The area most clearly related to the profession's history is that of the use of specialized aptitude tests. Counseling psychologists working with the military, with Job Corps type programs, or with corrections facilities will still find the use of specialized aptitude tests quite useful. Clients in those settings will typically be beginning their work careers at the very lowest of entry-level jobs. Such clients also typically know very little about their own aptitudes and can benefit immensely from any counseling that will direct them into training or positions in which they are likely to find success. For clients such as enrollees in Job Corps programs, having an early successful job experience is perhaps the most critical factor in their developing a sense of competence and becoming integrated into the workforce and into society. Counseling psychologists working with such populations need to develop a full awareness of the range of available aptitude tests and how the results of such tests can become an integral part of the counseling.

The second area of continued involvement of counseling psychologists with respect to this category of tests concerns the use of individually administered intelligence tests. While school and clinical psychologists have been the primary users of such tests, counseling psychologists who work in either general or psychiatric hospitals will find that individual intelligence tests are widely used as part of the diagnostic evaluation of patients who have a wide range of medical and/or psychiatric problems. Why are individually administered intelligence tests particularly useful in such settings? Does one really need to know the patient's IQ? No, not really. If only an IQ were desired, than a group-administered intelligence test would be far more efficient. There are two factors that make individually administered intelligence tests particularly useful in hospital settings. Such tests allow for determining whether there are specific areas of perceptual and/or cognitive dysfunctions, both of which may be related to brain injuries, substance abuse, or psychiatric problems such as depression. We will further explain how intelligence tests may be used in this connection after providing a brief description of the most widely used family of individualized intelligence tests.

Since the beginning of the 1950s, Wechsler and colleagues have developed and revised individually administered intelligence tests for all ages, from preschool through adulthood. All of the tests have essentially the same structure: a verbal scale containing five or six subtests and a performance scale containing five or six subtests. Three areas of IQ are computed: a Verbal IQ, a Performance IQ, and a Full Scale IQ. Since counseling psychologists are generally most likely to be working with an adult-age population, we describe here the most recent edition of the Wechsler Adult Intelligence Scale, the WAIS-III (Wechsler, 1998).

The WAIS-III Verbal subtests include vocabulary, similarities, arithmetic, digit span, information, and comprehension. Performance subtests include picture completion, digit symbol coding, block design, picture arrangement, and object assembly. Three new subtests have been added for the WAIS-III: matrix reasoning, symbol search, and letter–number sequencing. These new subtests are especially helpful in addressing cognitive concerns of patients beyond simply determining an IQ. This most recent version of the WAIS now provides, in addition to IQs, indexes on verbal comprehension, perceptual organization, working memory, and processing speed— all valuable assessment indexes in assessing cognitive functioning among the elderly.

Simply reviewing the diversity in the names of the subtests listed above should give some hint of the diagnostic value of the WAIS-III for determining types of perceptual and/or cognitive dysfunctions. In normal intellectual functioning, the examinee earns approximately the same level of score for each subtest of the WAIS. Therefore, whenever there are significant deviations (e.g., a very poor digit span performance compared to other verbal tests), the psychologist would certainly want to check for the cause of that interference in concentration. Although the intelligence test result cannot say what is causing the problem, it does indicate an area of dysfunction that needs further assessment, probably neurological (see the next section on neuropsychological tests) as well as psychological.

A second diagnostic value of an individually administered intelligence test derives from the extensive observations made on how the examinee approaches each test. For example, when the client encounters difficulties in one of the subtests, is it a lack of perseverance? slowness? carelessness? Is the examinee too depressed to respond to many items, or made particularly anxious by some of the subtests? All of these observations can be highly useful in making diagnostic formulations about any cognitive problems the patient is having as a result of either psychiatric problems such as depression or alcoholism, or medical problems such as cardiovascular dysfunction, chronic diabetes, or head injuries. Whereas training in individually administered intelligence testing has more typically been part of clinical as compared to counseling psychology training programs, in recent decades, more and more counseling psychology training programs have arranged for doctoral-level students to obtain training and supervised experience in administering at least the adult version of the Wechsler scales. Once training in administering such tests is completed, guidance in how to use individualized intelligence tests in making diagnoses and in treatment planning may be found in Sprandel (1995) and, for the children's form of the Wechsler Intelligence scales, Cooper (1995).

Neuropsychological Tests

When discussing individually administered intelligence tests, we pointed out that observations of behavior during the testing and/or significant variations in levels of scores obtained on the subtests could indicate the need for neuropsychological testing. Since the 1960s, psychologists have developed greatly improved neuropsychological tests. These tests remain essential even today since, while CAT-scans and MRIs can indicate the location and extent of brain damage, they cannot provide information on how the patient can perform. Learning to administer and make careful use of the results of these batteries has proven to require both extensive and intensive training. A less than fully trained person using these measures can make serious diagnostic errors; therefore, training in these techniques is usually now undertaken primarily in internships and postdoctoral residencies. Ryan, Lopez, and Lichtenberg (1999) find that although there is now less predoctoral training in neuropsychological testing than in earlier decades, the number of board-certified diplomates (see Chapter 7) in neuropsychology, whose predoctoral training was in counseling psychology, continues to increase. Counseling psychologists who have an interest in neuropsychology do need to choose both internships and postdoctoral residencies (see Chapter 4) that focus on neuropsychology. A valuable resource for learning about both training and practice issues in neuropsychology may be found in eight special articles in the October 1992, issue of *The Counseling Psychologist*.

Behavioral and Symptom Checklists

Since the 1970s there have been numerous inventories and checklists developed that are designed to be sensitive to small changes in behaviors (Cauteda, 1977; Nelson, 1987), affect (Beck, 1987, 1990; Zuckerman, 1977) and symptoms (Derogatis, 1977). Such measures, in contrast to global personality inventories, are especially useful for demonstrating significant relationships between diagnoses, therapeutic progress, and eventual outcomes. As noted both in Chapter 4, and again in this chapter, establishing such empirical relationships is the key to having industrialized health care provide more authorization for the use of assessment in behavioral health care.

The emergence of behavioral approaches to counseling (see Chapter 11) greatly enhanced development of such measures. That theoretical emphasis requires therapists, external observers, and clients themselves to learn how to record behaviors in reliable ways (Drummond, 1996). Such measures are often initially administered as part of the diagnostic stage to establish what behaviorists call "baseline" behaviors (or levels of affect or symptoms). These measures can then be readministered periodically throughout therapy since many of them are relatively brief (as few as 15–30 items) and can be completed in just a few minutes.

Both Burlingame and Lambert, longtime contributors to the literature in counseling psychology, are currently developing a variety of measures suitable for assessing small changes in ongoing psychotherapy (Burlingame, Lambert, Reisinger et al., 1995; Tingey, Lambert, Burlingame, & Hansen, 1996). By employing such measures, with just a few minutes of clients' and therapists' time after each session, or at least every few sessions, information can be immediately available on whether the client is experiencing any changes in behavior, affect, beliefs, or symptoms. Just as importantly, the counselor obtains information on the normative aspects of the client's level in each of these areas. The client may be making some measurable gains in psychotherapy but still be several standard deviations below what one would call adjusted; such information then establishes the need for continued counseling.

Career Development and Decision-Making Measures

As noted earlier in this chapter, and as further discussed in Chapter 15, the earliest forms of career counseling relied heavily on the use of interest and aptitude measures. Next most frequently used were personality inventories. For many, or even most clients, these assessments, appropriately integrated into the counseling process, provided the assistance they needed in reaching a satisfactory resolution to their career-related issues. However, there have always been a notable number of clients for whom such assessments, even with extensive counseling, have not led to satisfactory outcomes. Over the past few decades a number of different kinds of measures have been developed to better understand and counsel such clients. In this section we identify four kinds of such measures with brief references to their theoretical and empirical origins.

From careful study of those clients for whom traditional counseling proved unsatisfactory both Holland, Johnston, and Sasama (1993) and Osipow, Carney, Winer et al. (1976), from quite different theoretical perspectives (see Chapter 14), developed measures of *indecisiveness*. Over the years these measures have proved very useful in diagnosing those for whom traditional or self-directed career interventions would likely be insufficient for obtaining satisfactory counseling outcomes. Those with low scores on Holland and colleagues' 18-item Vocational Identity Scale (1993) or high scores on Osipow and colleagues' 18-item Career Decision Scale (1976) are most likely those who will need at least several sessions of counseling, along with appropriate interest and/or personality assessments, in order to make progress on career decision making. These measures are also quite useful in indicating areas where clients feel blocked or conflicted, for example, conflicts with parents or significant others about career choice, value conflicts, and so forth.

The theoretical and empirical work of Super and colleagues focuses on determining when and how effective career decisions are made (see Chapter 14). This work led to the development of measures of *career development* (Super, Thompson, Lindeman et al., 1981) and *career maturity* (Crites, 1981). These measures focus on whether individuals have mastered the tasks essential for effective career decision making, for example, self-appraisal, occupational information, goal selection, planning, problem solving. Having scaled scores in these several domains can make clear to counselors where and how to focus the counseling process for clients who have difficulty reaching career decisions.

Krumboltz and others working from a behavioral perspective have shown that career indecision and career problems are often related to clients' irrational beliefs about the world of work: women never become successful architects; one can't become a software programmer without passing calculus (see Chapter 14 for other examples of irrational beliefs). Krumboltz developed the Career Beliefs Inventory (1988) to assess the types and pervasiveness of such beliefs. Sampson, Peterson,

Lenz, et al. (1996) have further developed this concept of beliefs into both a diagnostic and treatment modality. Through factor analyses they find dysfunctional beliefs derive primarily from (1) confusion about how to make effective decisions, (2) commitment anxiety, and (3) external conflicts (e.g., parental vs. own choices, perceived discrimination). Sampson and colleagues' Career Thoughts Inventory is accompanied by a workbook designed to assist individuals in identifying, challenging, and altering their negative career thoughts and follow up with appropriate action.

The fourth and final type of career assessment measure to be reviewed here is that of values. While there has long been some attention to the assessment of values as part of career counseling (Weiss, Dawis, Lofquist et al., 1975), attempts to help both indecisive and culturally diverse clients have resulted in increased attention to the role values play in making career decisions. Culturally diverse clients especially may well experience strong value conflicts between, for example, need to achieve and need for security, or need for social service and need for high compensation (conflicting needs in the U.S. culture). Measures such as the Minnesota Importance Questionnaire (Weiss et al., 1975) and Super's (1973) Work Values Inventory and Super and Nevill's (1986) Values Scale may help identify conflicts clients are experiencing that lead to avoidance of the career decision-making process.

The development of all of these measures in recent decades has clearly helped in the development of more cost-effective services for career counseling clients; by using these kinds of measures as screening assessments, it is possible to identify many clients who can use self-administered measures like the Self-Directed Search and Career Thoughts Inventory to work through their career concerns largely on their own or with only minimal assistance from a counselor. For those who need individualized counseling, use of the kinds of measures described in this section will help the counselor quickly and effectively focus on the clients' most troublesome areas. Despite these very real practical gains, there remain many theoretical and empirical questions about the independence of the four types of measures described. They have different labels primarily because each was developed within different theoretical frameworks. Are they separate and complementary measures, or actually competing ones, such that it would be redundant to use more than one of them? As Betz (1992) notes, counseling psychologists would do well to focus their research on determining the convergent and discriminant validity (see prior section in this chapter) of existing career measures rather than continuing to develop new ones.

Environmental Measures

In keeping with counseling psychology's emphasis on person–environment interactions, comprehensive assessments of an individual ideally need to include a consideration of those environmental factors that can facilitate ones' adjustment and development. Holland (1997) developed much of his model of career assessment and counseling by directly incorporating environmental assessment in his measures (see Chapter 14). While other counseling psychologists have made some use of environmental measures, it has been primarily in consultation and organizational development (see chapters 18 and 19) rather than in individual assessment. Yet the nature of the environment can often be the key factor to the unhappiness of an individual in a work or interpersonal relationship; change the environment and the problem goes away. Consider, for example, how unhappy a number of physicians have become with their work, and have even left the profession, when they found that they could no longer maintain an economically viable practice unless they became part of managed care. When they entered into such an environment, they discovered they had to deal with significantly diminished autonomy, seemingly mindless rules and regulations, and were treated punitively if they did not fully comply. Patients had not changed; the physicians had not changed; it was the changed work environment that caused the problem.

The measures described in the next paragraph can be used only with groups of participants, determining how they themselves perceive their environments. Therefore, although these measures are ideal for counseling psychologists' consultation with organizations, they are not well adapted for use with individuals *unless* a client comes from an environment where measures of the environmental climate are already available. If such data are available, an individual client can be asked to also complete the environmental measure, then the "fit" between the client and the prevailing environment can be quickly determined. Otherwise, environmental assessment in individualized counseling must be made mostly through interviewing to determine which aspects of clients' work and/or interpersonal environments are most troublesome to them. Such an assessment is particularly crucial when working with ethnically diverse clients who often have quite different experiences of an environment that the counselor thinks he or she knows. Pertinent examples range from the client experiencing overt discrimination to more subtle patterns like not being called on in class as often as other students, being asked to meet with potential new employees only if they are ethnic minorities, and so forth.

Walsh and Betz (1995) provide an excellent chapter on the theoretical and empirical development of a wide range of environmental measures. Counseling psychologists made somewhat frequent use, starting in the 1960s, of the Stern indexes such as the College Characteristics Index (Stern, 1970) and later Pace's (1987) College Student Experiences Questionnaire. These measures assessed how students perceived the dominant "pressures" in their college environment, for example, for socializing, for achieving, for competing, and so forth. The assumption of studying environments was that students who "fit" their environment would perform better. Equally academically talented students might perform quite differentially if there were poor fits; for example, an extroverted academically talented student in a highly individualistic, competitive environment might not perform well and/or like the environment and therefore want to transfer to another college. A recent interesting application of this concept of fit is found in the development of residence halls devoted to specific kinds of majors or programs, for example, foreign languages, natural sciences, and so forth. While there are pros and cons to homogeneous housing, students who can feel both a personal and intellectual colleagueship with their residence hall companions often have fewer roommate conflicts and fewer academic problems and concerns.

Moos (1987) developed numerous social climate scales on the same premise as Stern and colleagues. Moos developed specific scales for settings like the military, prisons, hospital wards, and so forth. These scales, with their more recent development and data than the Stern indexes, have largely replaced the latter and are quite widely used by community psychologists, I/O psychologists, and counseling psychologists consulting with agencies that are having difficulties such as high employee turnover, high levels of client complaints, or problems getting staff to meet performance standards, for example, those imposed by various accrediting agencies in educational or health service settings. Understanding how the employees as a group perceive their environment typically provides critical cues for what organizational changes might be necessary to address the company's or agency's concern.

USING ASSESSMENT: MEETING THE CHALLENGES OF INDUSTRIALIZED HEALTH CARE

> The assessment process is, ideally, a collaboration between counselor and client in which both gain in knowledge and understanding while their working relationship is developed and helpful interventions are identified and implemented (Seligman, 1996, p. 85).

> It is no wonder that psychological testing went through a period of disfavor in the 1960s and 1970s. Psychologists felt that testing was an antiquated enterprise that had little bearing on the real work of modern clinical psychology. The empirical foundations of testing were questioned by behaviorists and others trained in the experimental traditions of academic psychology, whereas analytic psychologists felt that the results of assessments rarely contributed to the treatment effort. In large part, this attitude reflected the bankruptcy of the entire diagnostic enterprise. There was little agreement about the meaning of diagnostic terminology or the relationship between diagnosis and treatment (Smith, 1998, p. 229).

The second quote makes clear that the ideal, specified in the first quote, has not been achieved in recent decades. In this section, we will describe some of the factors that made diagnosis almost a "dirty word" for some years and what changes have occurred both within and outside of the profession that now brings renewed attention to the diagnostic process. In subsequent parts of this section we review the emerging use of assessment, not only for diagnosis, but also for treatment planning, for treatment (using tests as part of the counseling process) and for evaluating the effectiveness of counseling.

Making Diagnoses: A Necessary, But Insufficient Step

In the earliest years of the profession of counseling psychology, every text had major sections on making diagnoses (e.g., Pepinsky & Pepinsky, 1954). Some of the first studies published in the *Journal of Counseling Psychology* focused on the diagnostic process. Part of the reasons for those studies was the fact that making agreed upon psychological diagnoses, compared to medical diagnoses, was far more difficult. Cases of pneumonia share far more symptoms in common than do cases of depression. Moreover, psychological symptoms are displayed less consistently than are symptoms of physical illness. Compounding these problems were notable variations in what factors psychologists attended to when making diagnoses. Analytically oriented psychologists tended to emphasize dynamics, whereas behaviorists emphasized overt behaviors. Given all of the above, it is not surprising that there were often alarming differences in diagnoses made on the *same* patient but by *different* psychologists.

Concerns about diagnoses in psychology quickly accelerated throughout the 1950s for two more reasons beyond the lack of consistency just described. First was the growing evidence of the lack of significant relationships between diagnosis and treatment activity, as already reviewed in the beginning of this chapter. Second was the growing concern of the stigma of diagnoses both for how the counselor viewed the client and how clients viewed themselves if they became aware of the diagnosis assigned to them. Rogers (1951), in fact, came to believe that traditional diagnoses were in many ways inimical to facilitating client growth and development. In his view, since diagnosis in the medical tradition is very focused on deficits and problems, the very act of diagnosis served to reduce the attention paid to possibilities for growth and development, a tendency of particular concern to counseling psychologists. Rogers also believes making diagnoses forces psychologists to focus on similarities rather than unique differences and individuality. Finally, the labeling of persons was of concern to Rogers in how it would affect not only clients' views of their own potential but also how significant others would treat them. He quite properly anticipated later disturbing empirical evidence: Stewart (1970) took a group of people who were functioning quite normally in their everyday lives, then had them, as part of an experiment, hospitalized on the basis of psychiatric diagnoses. He found the participants were treated like "crazy" people by hospital staff even though the subjects ("patients") did not behave any differently than they did in everyday life. Given all these concerns about making diagnoses, it should not be too surprising to learn that diagnosis practically disappeared as a major topic in many counseling psychology texts in the last half of the twentieth century, at least until the 1990s.

Then why was there renewed interest in diagnosis in the 1990s (Barron, 1998)? The simplest and most concise answer is: the industrialization of health care, through its authorization of treatment only after a diagnosis is provided. The increasing use of practice guidelines, as described in Chapter 4, specifying the kind of therapy that should be used with particular kinds of problems, obviously also requires that a diagnosis be made. How can one know what treatment guidelines apply if there is no differential diagnosis? Thus the industrialization of health care has actually helped psychology focus on the need for diagnoses and the need to relate these diagnoses to treatment plans. By the late 1990s, new texts were emerging focused on the use of psychological assessment both in making diagnoses and treatment planning (e.g., Beutler & Berren, 1995; Maruish, 1999; Quirk, Strosahl, Kreilkamp, & Erdberg, 1995).

What is now involved in making a diagnosis and what kinds of assessment need to be made? The next section focuses specifically on what most psychologists associate with diagnosis: the DSM-IV; that is, the current diagnostic manual of the American Psychiatric Association (American Psychiatric Association, 1994).

DSM-IV

Attempts to provide a manual that would assist mental health practitioners in making reliable and useful diagnoses, even in the face of the problems with diagnoses outlined above, go back to 1952 when the first edition of the *Diagnostic and Statistical Manual of Mental Disorders* was developed. Nathan (1998), one of many psychologists involved in the preparation of the fourth edition (no psychologists were involved in preparing the first edition, and only one psychologist in preparing the second edition) provides an excellent and concise history of the development of all editions of the manual. He describes the criticisms of earlier editions that were addressed as much as possible in each subsequent edition. The fourth edition is now more "user friendly" as well as built on more reliable and culturally sensitive data. Nathan acknowledges the validity of the criticism that the *DSM-IV* is still very medically oriented in its terminology. Also of concern is the fact that, by adding to the number of diagnostic conditions (now over 300), it has potentially stigmatized as "mental illness," seemingly everyday problems such as insomnia and bearing grudges. Psychoanalytically oriented therapists have outlined numerous other concerns about inadequacies in the *DSM-IV* in attending to various developmental and system issues in making diagnoses (see Barron, 1998). Notwithstanding these criticisms, the *DSM-IV* is, without question, the foundation for decision making by managed care companies as to what behavioral health care will be covered for their subscribers. If a problem cannot be given a *DSM-IV* diagnosis, it is likely that no treatment will be authorized by a managed care company. Clients will then have to pay, entirely from their own resources, if they wish to have counseling for their problems.

An important advance in the development of the *DSM-III*, now retained in the fourth version, was the introduction of the multiaxial system. Recognizing that understanding a person's distress required far more than reviewing their symptoms, a five-axis system was introduced calling for separate assessments of the following: Clinical Disorders and Other Conditions That May Be a Focus of Clinical Attention (Axis I); Personality Disorders and Mental Retardation (Axis II); General Medical Conditions (Axis III); Psychosocial and Environmental Problems (Axis IV), and Global Assessment of Functioning (Axis V). Axis V is actually a scale of 1–100 on which a therapist rates a client's current level of functioning. Calling for this rating recognizes that several clients, even though having the same symptoms and environmental problems, could still be functioning quite differently, perhaps one almost incapacitated, but another, even if painfully, meeting current work and family obligations. Counseling psychologists especially appreciate this attention to assets in functioning, even in the presence of significant psychological problems.

While the Axis I is typically the one that is considered most important in establishing the need for treatment, the others all become critical components in deciding which type(s) of treatment may be needed for the client, as well as for perhaps a spouse and/or family, depending on the environmental aspects of the client's problems. Several useful handbooks are now available to help beginning, as well as

TABLE 13.1.   **DSM-IV Diagnostic Classification: An Example.**

Axis	Conditions Listed on Axis	Example
I	clinical disorder	Generalized Anxiety Disorder
II	long-standing problems that would complicate clinical disorder	Dependent Personality Disorder
III	relevant general medical conditions	Asthma
IV	psychosocial or environmental stressors	family violence
V	global assessment of functioning	60 (moderate symptoms, or moderate difficulty in social, occupational, or school functioning)

established professionals, become skilled in making diagnoses using the *DSM-IV* (First, Frances, & Pincus, 1995; Frances & Ross, 1996). Both of these handbooks just cited help the reader by providing useful tables and decision trees for choosing one diagnosis over another when the presenting symptoms may be quite similar, for example, narcissistic personality disorder versus borderline personality disorder. What these references do not cover is how psychological assessment is to be integrated into that decision making. To help in this way, the Millon inventories (Millon, 1997) are designed to provide results that directly translate into the DSM system. Even more helpful is the work of Beutler and Berren (1995) who provide very specific methodologies for using assessments in making DSM diagnoses and then in treatment planning. Mastering the use of such materials is essential for meeting the demands for diagnoses and treatment planning now required by industrialized health care.

Using Assessment in Treatment Planning

Industrialized health care has had much the same impact on treatment planning that it has had on diagnosis: whereas there was little attention to treatment planning in earlier decades, since the 1990s it has received far more attention. It may be important to again point out that the first several generations of counseling psychologists trained to do counseling and psychotherapy were rarely trained in treatment planning, but rather how to provide the core facilitative conditions or working alliance that would allow a client to improve. Changes should now be taking place in the training of counseling psychologists that make treatment planning a part of all training practice. There are new and useful books on how to use psychological assessment for the development of treatment plans (Beutler & Berren, 1995;

Seligman, 1996). The authors in the first of these texts provide not only clear conceptual bases but also workbook style tables and illustrative cases. These authors and Westen (1998) describe some of the areas that need to be assessed, *in addition to* the five axes of the *DSM-IV*, in order to develop an effective treatment plan. For example, Westen (1998) lists four questions that need to be considered: (1) What are the person's motives for being in psychotherapy? (2) What psychological resources does the client have, such as effective defenses, ego strength? (3) How does the client experience himself or herself and interpersonal relationships? (4) What is the developmental level (maturity) of the client's personality?

What is yet to be developed is a system that directly integrates assessment information with agreed upon practice guidelines. Until the publication of such "user friendly" systems, current graduate students in counseling psychology should ensure that they receive explicit training, as well as supervised experience, in preparing treatment plans that can be justified on the basis of psychological assessments and established clinical practice guidelines.

Using Assessment As a Treatment Modality

Counseling psychologists have, since the formal beginnings of the profession in the 1940s, incorporated the use of test results in to the process of counseling (Goldman, 1961; Zunker, 1990). Counseling psychologists in those earlier times, compared to clinical psychologists, typically worked with college students compared to hospitalized psychiatric patients. Consequently, the counselors could consider sharing directly with the client the results of the extensive psychological assessments that were often, as described earlier in this chapter, a routine part of being seen at a clinic or counseling center. Ever since the 1940s there has been a steady flow of research examining how best to have clients involved in the selection and interpretation of psychological assessments so that they, the clients, obtain the maximum benefits of psychological assessment. Goodyear (1990), who summarizes much of the first 40 years of such research, finds that "clients who receive test interpretations—regardless of format or of the particular outcome criteria employed—do experience greater gains than do those in control conditions" (p. 242).

Unfortunately, the criteria in most of these studies has focused primarily on clients' accurate recall and understanding of the results and/or satisfaction. To give full consideration to the value of psychological assessment as a treatment modality, more attention must be paid to criteria such as lasting changes in self-perceptions, enduring reductions in symptoms of distress, improved problem solving and decision making (Claiborn & Hanson, 1999; Duckworth, 1990). Finn and Tonsager (1992) moved in that direction, encouraging clinical psychologists as well as counseling psychologists to incorporate test results as part of the treatment process.

> Clients . . . who hear their MMPI-II test results reported a significant increase in their self-esteem immediately following the feedback session, an increase that continued to grow over the 2-week follow-up period. In addition, after hearing their MMPI-II test results, clients showed a significant decrease in their symptomatic

> distress, and distress continued to decline during the subsequent 2-week
> period . . . clients . . . showed more hopefulness about their problems immedi-
> ately following the feedback session, and this persisted at the final follow-up
> (Finn & Tonsager, 1992, p. 284).

The earliest research on the effects of using tests as part of the counseling
process focused on whether clients who were actively involved in selecting the tests
they would take would then make more effective use of the results in dealing with
their personal problems (Bordin & Bixler, 1946). Brammer and Shostrom (1977)
reviewed the positive effects of such client participation if (a) the counselor and
client discussed the kinds of data that were needed to help solve the client's problem, and (b) the counselor described the tests that could provide such information.
Based on the findings of Gustad and Tuma (1957), some counselors also ask clients
to make predictions after taking the tests, but before receiving their results, what
the results will be. This strategy allows the counselor to assess whether the client
understands the kinds of data a given test can provide and increases the client's
commitment to finding out what the test can tell him or her.

An even larger research literature concerns ways in which test interpretation
might be varied to improve clients' learning from test results. As Goodyear (1990)
notes, variation in individual versus group interpretation, computer-provided versus counselor-provided, or using versus not using actual test profiles as part of the
interpretations does not seem to matter much. Much more potent is simply the comparison of using test results versus not using them: Using test results as part of counseling yields significant gains for clients. More recently, Hanson, Claiborn, and Kerr
(1997) again focus on differential styles of test interpretation and find that when
the counselor used a more collaborative compared to "expert" style of interpretation, there were no differences in cognitive gains for students; however, students
who participated in the more collaborative process felt their sessions had more
depth and that their counselors were more expert, trustworthy, and attractive.
Counseling psychologists have long been more comfortable with the collaborative,
compared to expert style; the Hanson and colleagues' (1997) research is nicely reassuring that playing the expert is actually perceived as less expert than being a collaborative participant with the client in conducting the feedback. It is important
that such research now be replicated with more clinical populations, as compared
to college students, to see if similar effects can be found to result from collaborative
interpretations when the outcome criteria include changes in affect and behavior as
well as changes in cognitions.

Both Healy (1990) and Tinsley and Bradley (1986) describe strategies allowing
for greater integration of test interpretation in the process of counseling, with the
counselor more as a collaborator than an expert. Tinsley and Bradley articulate two
fundamental principles underlying all their recommendations for test interpretation.

> First, test interpretation must not be viewed as a discrete activity but conceptual-
> ized as part of the ongoing counseling process . . . counselors who take "time
> out" from being sensitive, warm, empathic and caring individuals while conduct-
> ing test interpretations engage in a practice detrimental to the overall counseling

process . . . Second, it seems useful to think of tests as structured interviews designed to provide information about clients in an efficient manner. They should not be deified or thought of as magically providing answers (p. 462).

Several of Tinsley and Bradley's recommendations regarding test interpretation are often overlooked by beginning counselors. We strongly urge any counseling psychologists who provide test interpretations to be thoroughly familiar with *all* their recommendations before engaging in the use of psychological tests as a treatment modality.

Using Assessment to Measure Treatment Progress and Outcomes: Turning Potential Into Reality

As described in Chapter 4, in the section on provider profiling, until the 1990s, very few psychologists in independent practice made any regular use of assessment instruments when evaluating their clients' progress during or at the end of counseling and psychotherapy. In some counseling centers and clinics, psychologists were asked to provide some ratings and/or summaries of progress as part of closing a case file; however, even in those instances, it was rare to find that clients had been asked to complete any well-established assessment instrument that could be used to determine both the progress they had made as well as their end-of-counseling level of functioning. Usually such assessments have been made only for a research study focused on a particular kind of counseling. In these studies, clients, as part of their agreement to receive counseling, agree to complete fairly extensive assessments before and after counseling, and possibly even after every few sessions, as a way of assessing progress during counseling. The *Journal of Counseling Psychology* and *Journal of Consulting and Clinical Psychology* frequently publish such studies (see Wampold and Poulin [1992] for an overview and commentary on studies of counseling and psychotherapy).

Just as the industrialization of health care created a resurgence of interest in diagnosis and treatment planning, there is now increasing interest on the part of practitioners in finding assessment measures that may be relatively nonintrusive and efficiently completed by clients, and possibly themselves as the counselors, as a way of providing evidence of therapeutic effectiveness. By the mid-1990s, articles and books began to appear devoted specifically to the use of psychological testing in both treatment planning and outcome assessment (Maruish, 1999; Tingey et al., 1996). The 23 articles in Maruish's edited volume cover both psychological measures that might be used, as well as the principles and procedures one should consider when assessing counseling process and outcome. Many of the measures discussed in the Maruish volume are those described earlier in this chapter, for example, the Rorschach, the MMPI-II, and standardized behavioral and symptom checklists. For examples of newer, brief measures that can show small changes in clients, see Tingey et al. (1996).

A careful reading of such material can aid a counseling psychologist, even if working solely on his or her own, in the design of a program of process and outcome assessment for his or her clients. Such an assessment then provides informative feedback not only for the counseling psychologist as a practitioner, but also for third-party payers or managed care companies desiring information on the practitioner's effectiveness. As noted earlier in this chapter, several software programs have now been developed which include brief measures for the client and counselor to complete after each session as well as at the end of therapy (Lambert & Anderson, 1996).

CLINICAL JUDGMENT IN PSYCHOLOGICAL ASSESSMENT

With the many years of experience psychologists now have in using psychological assessments, how accurate are they in making predictions and judgments about clients? Are some psychologists better than others in making more accurate assessments? From the very beginnings of the specialties of applied psychology such as counseling, clinical, and school, there have been studies of both the processes and outcomes of psychological assessment. In the next section we review some of these results; in the subsequent section, we describe the significant progress that has been made in determining how to improve judgment accuracy. This progress has been made primarily by counseling psychologists and is widely recognized by a broad range of authorities in assessment: "These (judgment) processes help refine the final conclusions and treatment recommendations and ultimately increase the accuracy and clinical utility of the assessment (Meyer et al., 1998, p. 48).

Is the Computer the Winner?

In those times before there were computers in psychologists' offices (less than 20 years ago), the heading for this section would have been clinical versus statistical prediction (Holt, 1970; Meehl, 1954). *Statistical prediction* refers to the use of actuarial tables to make predictions of behavior and relying on test scores alone to make diagnostic and prognostic decisions. (Today, many major tests are packaged with software that when downloaded to a computer will, once a client's test results are entered, generate a number of diagnoses and predictions, e.g., *DSM-IV* diagnosis, client probability to be a substance abuser, commit suicide, and so forth.) In contrast to statistical prediction, *clinical prediction* refers to the process of the psychologist making diagnoses and predictions based on interviews with a client or a combination of interview data with his or her interpretations of results from tests such as the Rorschach or MMPI-II. From an outcome perspective, the question has always been: Are statistical or computer-generated classifications and predictions as good as those made by psychologists who incorporate a wide variety of data in making their assessments? The controversy is not one of idle curiosity—if computerized testing can generate as accurate diagnoses and prognoses as psychologists (who require several interview and assessment sessions to generate their diagnoses), then managed care companies will certainly be willing to authorize only computerized assessments!

In 1954, Meehl published the first large set of such comparisons. He found that while there were often no significant differences in accuracy of straightforward, test-based statistical predictions compared to clinical judgments, whenever one was better than the other, it was almost always the statistical-based procedure that was superior. These results have generated decades of controversy (see Holt, 1970). Fortunately, there have been three quite useful outcomes of this controversy. Those who felt that psychologists' judgments had been unfairly impugned devoted significant empirical effort into determining (1) whether there were some psychologists who were more accurate than others in making assessment judgments, and if so, what were their strategies (see next section for useful outcomes of these investigations); (2) whether there were some situations, especially quite unique ones, in which the judgment of a psychologist would almost always be better than statistical prediction. The short answer to this second question is "yes"; see Holt (1970) for some of the key factors that determine when clinical judgment will generally be more accurate than statistical prediction. The third positive outcome of the comparisons of clinical versus statistical prediction was psychologists' increased respect for the comparative power of psychological tests. Contemporary psychologists who are called upon to testify in court when dealing with custody cases, prerelease assessments, discrimination cases, and so forth, will almost always include formal psychological assessments and be aware of the predictions made by statistical prediction rules and automated assessment reports generated by a published tests' software. Any predictions or recommendations a psychologist makes that disagree with test-based predictions must be extraordinarily well justified. Garb (1994) provides an excellent set of basic assessment considerations that should be consulted by any psychologist who is called upon to give testimony in court.

Improving Judgment Accuracy

Concern with understanding and improving the accuracy of psychologists' judgment began even before Meehl's (1954) controversial results. At the same time Meehl's work was published, the very first volume of the *Journal of Counseling Psychology* included McArthur's (1954) article on "Analyzing the Clinical Process." In that same year the Pepinskys published their text on counseling psychology (Pepinsky & Pepinsky, 1954), which outlined a model of the counselor judgment process, a model that even today serves as the foundation for the contemporary work of Spengler, Strohmer, Dixon, and Shivy (1995). This latter work is a frequently cited comprehensive summary of pertinent research and relevant training, research and practice recommendations regarding how to improve judgment accuracy. The brief summary of their major points in the next paragraph should only be the starting point for all psychologists who want to use assessment effectively in service of both their research and clients.

Spengler and colleagues (1995) find many studies indicating that there is substantial variability in the accuracy of psychologists' judgments. Some psychologists are not very accurate at all; others are quite expert, even though they may not have many years of experience or recognition as national leaders in the profession. The processes used in making judgments turn out to be far more critical than demographics (e.g., experience, age, gender) or theoretical orientation (e.g., behavioral, analytic). From years of study of how accurate assessment judgments are made, and synthesizing these findings with research in social cognition, Spengler et al. (1995) generated a model they describe as a self-correcting "reciprocal interaction between assessment and intervention decisions or judgments" (p. 517). In other words, accuracy improves when a psychologist (1) carefully checks the outcome of each assessment-based prediction in terms of actual outcomes, then (2) using such data, adjusts for subsequent clients his or her assessment interpretations and predictions.

While the brief description of this model may seem simply a statement of the way scientist–practitioner psychologists should operate, Spengler and colleagues (1995) find numerous impediments to such functioning. It is beyond the scope of this chapter to describe the four types of common judgment errors they found, all supported by extensive research. What needs to be noted most critically is that the assessment training of all psychologists should now include explicit exposure to the types of errors and strategies for how to reduce their impact on judgment accuracy. As Spengler et al. (1995) note, their work is relevant not only to assessment procedure per se, but also to the entire process of effective counseling and psychotherapy. They lament that supervisors all too rarely require students to engage in the reciprocal process of building, then testing, and then reformulating hypotheses about their clients. For counseling psychologists to attain increased accuracy and effectiveness, as Belar and Perry (1992) note: "The process of critical thinking, hypothesis-testing, and other elements of the scientific method should be engendered and integrated into *all* experiential activities throughout the training process" (italics added, p. 72) whether the topic is assessment, counseling, or research.

Communicating Assessment Results

Preparing Written Reports

Thus far in this chapter, when we discussed communicating assessment results, we focused primarily on communicating results to clients or to health care managers in order to justify requests for services for clients. Yet, traditionally in applied psychology, especially school and clinical psychology, assessments were completed most frequently in response to a referral for a "psychological evaluation." The referral request might come from a general practice physician (Is the client's sexual dysfunction psychologically based?), a teacher (Does the student have a learning disability?), an attorney (Has the client been harmed psychologically by forced early retirement?), a court (Is the client a danger to himself or others?), and so forth. In hospitals and clinics, referrals may be made by other mental health professionals, none of whom have the specialized training in assessment that psychologists have. These latter type of referrals are usually made in order to obtain information that can be used in diagnosing and planning the treatment for a patient. Or, if the referral is made near the end of treatment, the request is usually for an assessment of the patient's prognosis for functioning without further inpatient treatment. If the patient is not ready for fully independent functioning, what kinds of outpatient services need to be provided?

For each of the referrals just described, the expectation has always been that the psychologist would provide a written report that provides an answer to the re-

ferral question, with clear specification of the assessment results that underlie that answer. Almost every text on assessment includes major points to consider in writing such reports, as well as examples of various kinds of reports. In the next sections, we highlight just two of the major points that need to be considered when writing assessment reports. For extensive and excellent advice on report writing, readers should consult texts by Fischer (1985) and Tallent (1988).

What Is the Purpose?

This question actually should pervade every aspect of a psychologist's response to a referral from another professional, from establishing a clear understanding with the referring professional as to why the request for psychological assessment is being made, to the selection of assessments to use, to the psychologist's own interpretation of the results obtained and, finally, to considerations of how to frame the written report. Does the referring professional want an answer as straightforward as possible, or would a more comprehensive description of functioning be most helpful? Consider two examples from the kinds of possible referrals listed above: Is the client's sexual dysfunction psychologically based? and Does the student have a learning disability? For the first example, the physician probably wants a concise straightforward answer, yes or no; in the second example, especially if there is no evidence of a learning disorder, the teacher will want as much assistance as possible in understanding the academic performance problems of the student. Obviously, very different reports would be written in the first as compared to the second example. In either case, the report needs to contain clear and precise information as to what kinds of assessment were completed and how those results support the response to the referral question.

Who Is the Audience?

The second major question to consider when writing a psychological report is to whom it is addressed. Consider the examples of referrals given above, made by those outside of the mental health professions. Such persons may have little understanding about the kinds of tests available and the tests' various strengths and weaknesses. Yet, as counseling psychologists, our primary training in writing reports may have been in writing for other psychologists, whether writing research reports or case presentations to our peers and supervisors in practice settings. We learn to write in very technical terms, with assumptions that we do not need to explain such terms as ego strength, self-efficacy, narcissistic injury, construct validity, predictive validity, and so forth. Obviously, such language will leave many professionals who make referrals to psychologists, frustrated at not having received a comprehensible answer to the question asked. Before writing any report, counseling psychologists need to think carefully about the professional person(s) who will be reading their report and attend to minimizing professional jargon, yet clearly and comprehensibly explaining the strengths and weaknesses of the assessment procedures and results. In addition to avoiding jargon, reports need to attend to the fundamental guidelines in effective writing (Harvey, 1997) that can make for more easily understood reports. The impetus for Harvey's article was the finding that many of the psychological reports she reviewed were written using highly technical language (jargon and acronyms) that were difficult to understand (long, complex sentences and paragraphs).

ETHICAL ISSUES: THE COMPUTER DOESN'T MAKE YOU DO IT!

In the past two decades, the emergence of, and ease of using, computer-generated psychological test reports has led some psychologists to give less than full ethical attention to three areas: informed choice of tests, confidentiality of results, and attention to multicultural concerns. Sampson (1990) points out the "seductiveness" of tests that come packaged with software that can generate written reports as soon as a client's scale scores are entered via computer. He was aware that counselors might choose a test *not* because they had been trained in its use and/or studied its adequacy as an assessment device, but simply because it would make the assessment process much simpler and quicker. Of even greater concern was Sampson's finding that results from a given test, when entered into different software packages, yielded quite different results for the same client! Were these differences merely a reminder that any one set of test results is only one sample of the "truth," or was one of these interpretations a more accurate judgment than the other? Should such discrepancies affect choice of tests and software used? Psychologists need to carefully review assessment results themselves and form their own judgments before relying on a computer-generated report. The results in such a report, to the extent that they differ from the psychologist's own formulation, need to be carefully considered in preparing a final report. Under the best of circumstances, a computer-generated report may provide a good first draft of a psychological report; in other cases, such reports become a stimulus for a psychologist's careful evaluation of conflicting findings in accord with Spengler and colleagues' (1995) reciprocal interaction model for improving judgment accuracy.

As illustrated in one of the ethical violations included in Chapter 5, it is all too easy to unwittingly violate the confidentiality of tests or test results. While counseling psychologists are usually very concerned and careful about assuring that the content of counseling sessions is not inappropriately shared with even other professionals, the fact that such content is not typically written up and distributed makes such confidentiality a bit easier to maintain. When written reports are prepared, there needs to be assurance that the client agrees to the release of results to any professionals who have requested the results and that those professionals understand they are not to share the report with others without the specific consent of the client. A somewhat tangential confidentiality issue has also arisen with the ease of "home computer" scoring and interpretations—a psychologist's friends and family, or even a "satisfied" client's friends, may well, out of curiosity, want to "take the test" to see what it's like and what they can learn from it. While it may always be difficult for a counseling psychologist to "just say no," it is professionally required that tests be used and interpreted only after the examinee understands fully that test results must be considered in the context of a wide range of information and ideally only when there is an opportunity to discuss with results with a trained professional.

Computerized assessment has also led to some lapses in attending to cultural sensitivity in preparing test interpretations and psychological reports. Computer-generated reports are typically insensitive to clients' culture, mostly because it is nearly impossible to consider, within the software development, all of the permutations that might apply. As reviewed in Chapter 6, there are many different racial/ethnic variables to consider as well as varying levels of client acculturation. How might the worldview of the client affect the test results obtained? For example, is the high level of dependence indicated in the computerized report for a particular client, while well beyond the test's published norms, abnormal for the client's culture? Will such dependence be as detrimental to the person's mature functioning in his or her life situation as it might be for a client raised in a typical Anglo middle-class home? Again, the counseling psychologist will always need to review the cultural background of the client before using a computerized report, and consider alternative hypotheses to those generated by standard norms. As Ridley et al. (1998) make clear in their MAP procedure cited earlier in this chapter, testing alternative hypotheses is the key point. Simply dismissing test results because there are no norms specific to the client's culture can be just as harmful to the client as using test results without considering the effects of culture.

The final four sections of this chapter have repeatedly demonstrated the importance of the scientist–practitioner approach is using psychological assessment. Therefore counseling psychologists have been, and can continue to be, the leaders in keeping psychological assessment a valued keystone in the contributions of psychology to the well-being of our society.

SUMMARY

In the first half of the twentieth century, the development of psychological tests and assessment techniques was regarded as psychology's major contribution to society. Yet by the second half of that century, there emerged two major challenges to the use of psychological tests. In the first third of this chapter, we reviewed how those challenges resulted in a significant decline in use of tests as psychologists shifted from assessment/testing roles to more therapeutic roles as evidence accumulated showing the adverse impact of some tests on women and racial/ethnic minorities. We described how, fortunately, some counseling psychologists have been among the leaders in attending to these issues in constructive ways, rather than simply abandoning psychological tests and using what are often even more biased and inaccurate strategies. Their contributions to standards for all kinds of psychological assessments were reviewed in our sections on evaluating and constructing assessments, fairness in multicultural assessment, and standards in applying assessments.

The middle third of this chapter was devoted to an exploration of seven types of psychological tests frequently used by counseling psychologists. For each type we described the most well-known tests of that type and how counseling psychologists use them in both practice and research. The training of counseling psychologists ideally includes coursework and supervised practice in the use of each of these types of tests.

The last third of this chapter focused on issues in, and strategies for, more effective use of psychological assessment. The emergence of industrialized health care has clearly provided new challenges to psychologists' use of assessment. Fortunately, these challenges have helped psychologists develop new strategies for using assessment in diagnosis, in treatment planning, as a treatment modality (using tests in counseling), and in evaluating the outcomes of psychotherapy. In addition to identifying these strategies, we also described how counseling psychologists have conducted the most useful research on improving the accuracy of clinical judgment when using psychological assessment. The final sections of the chapter identified two key points in effective communication of test results to other professionals and then three unique ethical problems that have been generated by the increasing use of computerized psychological assessment.

REFERENCES

Ambrose, P. A. Jr. (1997). Challenges for mental health service providers: The perspective of managed care organizations. In J. N. Butcher (Ed.), *Personality assessment in managed health care* (pp. 61–72). New York: Oxford University Press.

American Educational Research Association, American Psychological Association and National Council of Measurement in Education [AAN]. (1999). *Standards for educational and psychological testing.* Washington, DC: American Psychological Association.

American Psychiatric Association. (1994). *Diagnostic and statistical manual of mental disorders* (4th ed.). Washington, DC: Author.

Barron, J. W. (1998). *Making diagnosis meaningful.* Washington, DC: American Psychological Association.

Bayne, R. (1995). *Myers–Briggs type indicator: A critical review and practical guide.* San Diego, CA: Singular Publishing.

Beck, A. T. (1987). *Depression inventory.* San Antonio, TX: Psychological Corporation.

Beck, A. T. (1990). *Anxiety inventory.* San Antonio, TX: Psychological Corporation.

Belar, C. D., & Perry, N. W. (1992). National conference on scientist–practitioner education and training for the professional practice of psychology. *American Psychologist, 47,* 71–75.

Betz, N. E. (1992). Career assessment: A review of critical issues. In S. D. Brown and R. W. Lent (Eds.), *Handbook of counseling psychology* (pp. 453–484). New York: John Wiley & Sons.

Beutler, L. E., & Berren, M. R. (Eds.). (1995). *Integrative assessment of adult personality.* New York: Guilford Press.

Boccaccini, M. T., & Brodsky, S. L. (1999). Diagnostic test usage by forensic psychologists in emotional injury cases. *Professional Psychology: Research and Practice, 30,* 253–259.

Bordin, E. S., & Bixler, R. S. (1946). Test selection: A process of counseling. *Educational and Psychological Measurement, 6,* 361–373.

Brammer, L. M., & Shostrom, E. L. (1977). *Therapeutic psychology* (3rd ed.). Englewood Cliffs, NJ: Prentice-Hall.

Burlingame, G. M., Lambert, M. J., Reisinger, C. W., Neff, W. L., & Mosier, J. (1995). Pragmatics of tracking mental health outcomes in a managed care setting. *Journal of Mental Health Administration, 22*(3), 226–236.

Butcher, J. N., & Williams, C. L. (1992). *Essentials of MMPI-2 and MMPI-A interpretation.* Odessa, FL: Psychological Assessment Resources.

Campbell, D. T., & Fiske, D. W. (1959). Convergent and discriminant validation by the multitrait–multimethod matrix. *Psychological Bulletin, 56,* 81–105.

Cauteda, J. R. (1977). *Behavior-analysis forms for clinical intervention.* Champaign, IL: Research Press.

Claiborn, C. D., & Hanson, W. E. (1999). Test interpretation: A social influence perspective. In J. W. Lichtenberg and R. K. Goodyear (Eds.), *Scientist–practitioner perspectives on test interpretation* (pp. 151–166). Needham Heights, MA: Allyn & Bacon.

Cooper, S. (1995). *The clinical use and interpretation of the Wechsler Intelligence Scale for Children—third edition.* Springfield, IL: Charles C. Thomas.

Crites, J. O. (1981). *Career Maturity Inventory: Theory and research handbook* (2nd ed.). Monterey, CA: CTB McGraw-Hill.

Dana, R. H. (1993). *Multicultural assessment perspectives for professional psychology.* Boston, MA: Allyn & Bacon.

Dana, R. H. (1997). *Understanding cultural identity in assessment and intervention.* Thousand Oaks, CA: Sage Publications.

Dawis, R. V. (1992). The individual difference tradition in counseling psychology. *Journal of Counseling Psychology, 39,* 7–19.

Day, S. X., & Rounds, J. (1998). Universality of vocational interest structure among racial and ethnic minorities. *American Psychologist, 53,* 728–736.

Derogatis, L. (1977). *SCL-90: Administration, scoring and procedures manual for the revised version.* Baltimore, MD: Clinical Psychometric Research.

Donnay, D. A. C., & Borgen, F. H. (1994). Validity, structure, and content of the 1994 Strong Interest Inventory. *Journal of Counseling Psychology, 43,* 275–291.

Drummond, R. J. (1996). Appraisal procedures for counselors and helping professionals (3rd ed.). Englewood Cliffs, NJ: Merrill.

Duckworth, J. (1990). The counseling approach to the use of testing. *The Counseling Psychologist, 18,* 198–204.

Duckworth, J. C., & Anderson, W. P. (1995). *MMPI & MMPI-2: Interpretation manual for counselors and clinicians* (4th ed.). Odessa, FL: Psychological Assessment Resources.

Eisman, E. J., Dies, R. R., Finn, S. E., Eyde, L. D., Kay, G. G., Kubiszyn, T. W., Meter, G. J., & Moreland, K. L. (1998). *Problems and limitations in the use of psychological assessment in contemporary health care delivery: Report of the Board of Professional Affairs Psychological Assessment Work Group, Part II.* Washington, DC: American Psychological Association.

Exner, J. E. Jr., & Weiner, I. B. (1996). *The Rorschach: A comprehensive system* (3rd ed.). Odessa, FL: Psychological Assessment Resources.

Finn, S. E., & Tonsager, M. (1992). Therapeutic effects of providing MMPI-2 test feedback to college students awaiting therapy. *Psychological Assessment, 4,* 278–287.

First, M. B., Frances, A., & Pincus, H. A. (1995). *DSM-IV handbook of differential diagnoses.* Washington, DC: American Psychiatric Press.

Fischer, C. G. (1985). *Individualizing psychological assessment.* Monterey, CA: Brooks/Cole.

Fitzgerald, L. M., & Osipow, S. H. (1986). An occupational analysis of counseling psychology: How special is the specialty? *American Psychologist, 41,* 535–544.

Fouad, N. A., & Chan, P. M. (1999). Gender and ethnicity: Influence on test interpretation and reception. In J. W. Lichtenberg and R. K. Goodyear (Eds.), *Scientist–practitioner perspectives on test interpretation* (pp. 31–58). Needham Heights, MA: Allyn & Bacon.

Frances, A., & Ross, R. (1996). *DSM-IV case studies.* Washington, DC: American Psychiatric Press.

Garb, H. N. (1994). Judgment research: Implications for clinical practice and testimony in court. *Applied & Preventive Psychology, 3,* 173–183.

Goldman, L. (1961). *Using tests in counseling.* New York: Appleton-Century-Crofts.

Goodyear, R. K. (1990). Research on the effects of test interpretation. *The Counseling Psychologist, 18,* 240–257.

Gottfredson, L. S. (1994). The science and politics of race-norming. *American Psychologist, 49,* 955–963.

Green, B. F. (1981). A primer of testing. *American Psychologist, 36,* 1001–1011.

Gustad, J. W., & Tuma, A. H. (1957). The effects of different methods of test introduction and interpretation on client learning and counseling. *Journal of Counseling Psychology, 4,* 313–317.

Harmon, L. W., Hansen, J. C., Borgen, F. H., & Hammer, A. L. (1994). *Strong Interest Inventory applications and technical guide.* Palo Alto, CA: Consulting Psychologists Press.

Harvey, V. S. (1997). Improving readability of psychological reports. *Professional Psychology: Research and Practice, 28,* 271–274.

Healy, C. C. (1990). Reforming career appraisals to meet the needs of clients in the 1990s. *The Counseling Psychologist, 18,* 214–226.

Holland, J. L. (1997). *Making vocational choices* (3rd ed.). Odessa, FL: Psychological Assessment Resources.

Holland, J. L. (1998). *Self-directed Search Form R* (4th edition). Odessa, FL: Psychological Assessment Resources.

Holland, J. L., Johnston, J. A., & Sasama, N. G. (1993). The Vocational Identity Scale: A diagnostic and treatment tool. *Journal of Career Assessment, 1,* 1–12.

Holt, R. R. (1970). Yet another look at clinical and statistical prediction: Or, is clinical psychology worthwhile? *American Psychologist, 25,* 337–349.

Krumboltz, J. D. (1988). *Career Beliefs Inventory.* Palo Alto, CA: Consulting Psychologists Press.

Kuder, G. F., & Zytowski, D. G. (1991). *Kuder Occupational Interest Survey Form DD, general manual.* Monterey, CA: California Testing Bureau.

Lambert, M. J., & Anderson, E. M. (1996). Data-based management for tracking outcome in private practice. *Clinical Psychology: Science and Practice, 3,* 172–178.

Lattimore, R. R., & Borgen, F. H. (1999). Validity of the 1994 Strong Interest Inventory with racial and ethnic groups in the United States. *Journal of Counseling Psychology, 46,* 185–195.

Lichtenberg, J. W., & Goodyear, R. K. (Eds.). (1999). *Scientist–practitioner perspectives on test interpretation.* Needham Heights, MA: Allyn & Bacon.

Maruish, M. E. (1999). *The use of psychological testing for treatment planning and outcome assessment.* Hillsdale, NJ: Lawrence Erlbaum.

McArthur, C. (1954). Analyzing the clinical process. *Journal of Counseling Psychology, 1,* 203–208.

Meehl, P. E. (1954). *Clinical versus statistical prediction.* Minneapolis: University of Minnesota Press.

Meyer, G. J., Finn, S. E., Eyde, L., Kay, G. G., Kubiszyn, T., Moreland, K., Eisman, E., & Dies, R. (1998). *Benefits and costs of psychological assessment in health care delivery: Report of the Board of Professional Affairs Psychological Assessment Work Group, Part I.* Washington, DC: American Psychological Association.

Millon, T. (1997). *The Millon inventories: Clinical and personality assessment.* Odessa, FL: Psychological Assessment Resources.

Moos, R. H. (1987). *The social climate scales: A user's guide.* Palo Alto, CA: Consulting Psychologists Press.

Moreland, K. L., Fowler, R. D., & Honaker, L. M. (1994). Future directions in the use of psychological assessment for treatment planning and outcome assessment: Predictions and recommendations. In M. E. Maruish (Ed.), *The use of psychological testing for treatment planning and outcome assessment* (pp. 581–601). Hillsdale, NJ: Lawrence Erlbaum.

Myers, I., & McCaulley, M. (1985). *Manual: A guide to the development and use of the Myers–Briggs Type Indicator.* Palo Alto, CA: Consulting Psychologists Press.

Nathan, P. E. (1998). The *DSM-IV* and its antecedents: Enhancing syndromal diagnosis. In J. W. Barron (Ed.), *Making diagnosis meaningful* (pp. 3–28). Washington, DC: American Psychological Association.

Nelson, R. O. (1987). *DSM-III* and behavioral assessment. In C. G. Last and N. Hersen (Eds.), *Issues in diagnostic research* (pp. 303–327). New York: Plenum Press.

Nunnally, J. (1978). *Psychometric theory* (2nd ed.) New York: McGraw-Hill.

Osipow, S. H., Carney, C. C., Winer, J. L., Yanico, B., & Koschier, M. (1976). *The Career Decision Scale* (3rd rev.). Columbus, OH: Marathon Consulting Press.

Pace, C. R. (1987). *CSEQ: Test manual and norms.* Los Angeles: Center for the Study of Evaluations, University of California.

Paniagua, F. A. (1998). *Assessing and treating culturally diverse clients* (2nd ed.). Thousand Oaks, CA: Sage Publications.

Pepinsky, H. B., & Pepinsky, P. N. (1954). *Counseling: Theory and practice.* New York: Ronald.

Pledge, D. S., Lapan, R. T., Heppner, P. P., Kivlighan, D., & Roehlke, H. J. (1998). Stability and severity of presenting problems at a university counseling center: A 6-year analysis. *Professional Psychology: Research and Practice, 29,* 386–389.

Quirk, M. P., Strosahl, K., Kreilkamp, T., & Erdberg, P. (1995). Personality feedback consultation to families in a managed mental health care practice. *Professional Psychology: Research and Practice, 26,* 27–32.

Reardon, R. C., & Lenz, J. G. (1998). *The Self-directed Search and related Holland career materials: Practitioner's guide.* Odessa, FL: Psychological Assessment Resources.

Ridley, C. R., Li, L. C., & Hill, C. L. (1998). Multicultural assessment: Reexamination, reconceptualization, and practical application. *The Counseling Psychologist, 26,* 827–910.

Rogers, C. R. (1951). *Client-centered therapy.* Boston, MA: Houghton Mifflin.

Ryan, J., Lopez, S. J., & Lichtenberg, J. W. (1999). Neuropsychological training in APA-accredited counseling psychology programs. *The Counseling Psychologist, 27,* 435–442.

Sackett, P. R., & Wilk, S. L. (1994). Within-group norming and other forms of score adjustment in preemployment testing. *American Psychologist, 49,* 929–954.

Sampson, J. P. (1990). Computer assisted testing and the goals of counseling psychology. *The Counseling Psychologist, 18,* 227–239.

Sampson, J. P. Jr., Peterson, G. W., Lenz, J. G., Reardon, R. C., Saunders, D. E. (1996). *Career Thoughts Inventory.* Odessa, FL: Psychological Assessment Resources.

Seligman, L. (1996). *Diagnosis and treatment planning in counseling* (2nd ed.). New York: Plenum Press.

Smith, B. L. (1998). Psychological testing, psychodiagnosis, and psychotherapy. In J. W. Barron (Ed.), *Making diagnosis meaningful* (pp. 227–246). Washington, DC: American Psychological Association.

Spengler, P. M. (1998). Multicultural assessment and a scientist–practitioner model of psychological assessment. *The Counseling Psychologist, 26,* 930–938.

Spengler, P. M., Strohmer, D. C., Dixon, D. N., & Shivy, V. A. (1995). A scientist–practitioner model of psychological assessment. *The Counseling Psychologist, 23,* 506–534.

Sprandel, H. Z. (1995). *The psychoeducational use and interpretation of the Wechsler Adult Intelligence Scale—revised* (2nd ed.). Springfield, IL: Charles C. Thomas.

Stern, G. G. (1970). *People in context.* New York: John Wiley & Sons.

Sternberg, R. J., & Williams, W. M. (1997). Does the Graduate Record Examination predict meaningful success in the graduate training of psychologists? A case study. *American Psychologist, 52,* 630–641.

Stewart, R. B. (1970). *Trick or treatment*. Champaign, IL: Research Press.

Strong, E. K. (1943). *Vocational interests of men and women*. Palo Alto, CA: Stanford University Press.

Super, D. E. (1973). The Work Values Inventory. In D. G. Zytowski (Ed.), *Contemporary approaches to interest measurement* (pp. 189–205). Minneapolis: University of Minnesota Press.

Super, D. E., & Nevill, D. D. (1986). *The Values Scale*. Palo Alto, CA: Consulting Psychologists Press.

Super, D. E., Thompson, A. S., Lindemen, R. H., Jordan, J. P., & Myers, R. A. (1981). *Career Development Inventory*. Palo Alto, CA: Consulting Psychologists Press.

Suzuki, L. A., Meller, P. J., & Ponterotto, J. G. (Eds.). (1996). *Handbook of multicultural assessment*. San Francisco: Jossey Bass.

Tallent, N. (1988). *Psychological report writing* (3rd ed.). Englewood Cliffs, NJ: Prentice-Hall.

Tingey, R., Lambert, M., Burlingame, G., & Hansen, N. (1996). Clinically significant change: Practical indicators for evaluating psychotherapy outcome. *Psychotherapy Research, 6*(2), 144–153.

Tinsley, H. E. A., & Bradley, R. W. (1986). Test interpretation. *Journal of Counseling and Development, 64*, 462–466.

Tracey, T. J. G., & Rounds, J. (1997). Circular structure of vocational interests. In R. Plutchik and H. Conte (Eds.), *Circumplex models of personality and emotions* (pp. 183–203). Washington, DC: American Psychological Association.

Walsh, W. B., & Betz, N. E. (1995). Tests and assessment (3rd ed.). Englewood Cliffs, NJ: Prentice-Hall.

Wampold, B. E., & Poulin, K. L. (1992). Counseling research methods: Art and artifact. In S. D. Brown and R. W. Lent (Eds.), *Handbook of counseling psychology* (2nd ed.), (pp. 71–109). New York: John Wiley & Sons.

Watkins, C. E. Jr., & Campbell, V. L. (Eds.). (1990). *Testing in counseling practice*. Hillsdale, NJ: Lawrence Erlbaum.

Watkins, C. E. Jr., Campbell, V. L., Hollifield, J., & Duckworth, J. (1989). Projective techniques: Do they have a place in counseling psychology training? *The Counseling Psychologist, 17*, 511–513.

Watkins, C. E. Jr., Campbell, V. L., & McGregor, P. (1988). Counseling psychologists' uses of and opinions about psychological tests. *The Counseling Psychologist, 16*, 476–486.

Watkins, C. E. Jr., Campbell, V. L., Nieberding, R., & Hallmark, R. (1996). On Hunsley, harangue, and hoopla. *Professional Psychology: Research and Practice, 27*, 316–318.

Wechsler, D. (1998). *Wechsler Adult Intelligence Scale* (3rd ed.). San Antonio, TX: Psychological Corporation.

Weiss, D. J., Dawis, R. V., Lofquist, L. V., Gay, E., & Hendel, D. D. (1975). *The Minnesota Importance Questionnaire*. Minneapolis: University of Minnesota, Department of Psychology, Work Adjustment Project.

Westen, D. (1998). Case formulation and personality diagnosis: Two processes or one? In J. W. Barron (Ed.), *Making diagnosis meaningful* (pp. 111–138). Washington, DC: American Psychological Association.

Zuckerman, M. (1977). Development of a situation-specific trait-state test for the prediction and measurement of affective responses. *Journal of Consulting and Clinical Psychology, 45*, 513–523.

Zunker, V. G. (1990). *Using assessment results for career development* (3rd ed.). Pacific Grove, CA: Brooks/Cole.

Zytowski, D. (1992). Three generations: The continuing evolution of Frederic Kuder's interest inventories. *Journal of Counseling & Development, 71*, 245–248.

CAREER PSYCHOLOGY: MILESTONES AND NEW FRONTIERS

[V]ocational research and intervention continue to represent some of the strongest and most vigorous areas of endeavor in counseling psychology (Gelso & Fassinger, 1992, p. 279).

[A]nnual production of articles related to vocational behavior is about 700 (Borgen, 1991, p. 263).

Research and intervention in vocational behavior is not only extremely vigorous and productive, it is also the oldest and most distinctive area of research endeavor associated with counseling psychology. As described in Chapter 2, the origins of formal study of vocational behavior and counseling go back to 1909 with Parsons's development of a "vocations bureau."

While programs of research and counseling related to vocational behavior are located primarily in counseling psychology programs, this unique location does not, however, signify that counseling psychologists are the only professionals attending to career development. Whereas the topics presented in the last few chapters have overlapped mostly with clinical psychology, career psychology shares common endeavors mostly with industrial/organizational (I/O) psychology. Further, the study of vocational behavior brings counseling psychologists into interdisciplinary contact with sociologists and economists. These professions often focus also on "world-of-work" problems, using approaches and methodologies common to their own specialties.

Throughout the history of counseling psychology, there has been ongoing attention to both the "normal" developmental, as well as the "dysfunctional" aspects of vocational behavior. How and why do people follow particular vocational paths? The focus of this chapter will be on the theoretical developments that address this question. Chapter 15 will then focus on the various strategies that counseling psychologists utilize for both prevention and remediation of problems that arise in clients' work lives. We must make very clear at this point that theories of career choice and development are not per se theories of career counseling and interventions. The study of the "what, how, when, and why" of career choice and development is as much a part of the basic psychological study of personality and development as it is a foundation for the development of intervention strategies.

The first half of this chapter is devoted to an overview of developments in three different approaches to the study of vocational choice and development. As will be evident in that exploration, theorists and researchers have called on various traditions within psychology—for example, personality, development, cognitive processes—to explain the "what, how, when, and why" of people's patterns of vocational behavior. Our grouping of numerous theories into three approaches is just one of many possible groupings. Some textbooks list nearly a dozen approaches, others as few as two to four. Within the three approaches we have chosen, we review a total of eight theories. For each theory, we briefly describe its historical roots, key concepts, key measures, then theoretical and practical strengths and limitations of each. Our purpose is to acquaint readers with the basics so that they may have an overview of both the diverse accomplishments and remaining gaps in our understanding of vocational behavior. More extensive presentations of these and other theories may be found in texts such as those by Brown and Brooks (1996) and Osipow and

Fitzgerald (1996). More extensive literature reviews and critiques of the theories we review may be found in Hackett and Lent (1992) and Walsh and Osipow (1995).

The second half of this chapter explores the exciting developments that seem to be emerging from what we view as expansions and shifts in the paradigms that have previously been employed in the study of vocational behavior. These changes have occurred as researchers articulated and reflected on the inadequacies of the theoretical developments reviewed in the first half of this chapter. As described in that section, these new developments hold great potential for advances in both the theory and practice of career psychology, helping us address some ongoing and some new important social and individual problems related to the world of work and our personal lives.

Before proceeding any further, we must clarify the use of the many terms used by researchers and practitioners related to vocational behavior. Over the years, changing terms reflect changing perspectives about what needs to be studied. Although there is much overlap and interchangeability among the terms we explore, there are good reasons why variations have emerged. In the next few paragraphs, we describe the origins and unique meaning of the terms vocational choice, vocational guidance, vocational psychology, career development, career psychology, career counseling, educational development, and educational counseling.

Vocational choice is, in one sense, a behavioral term. In our society, there is a clear expectation that everyone will seek gainful employment. To the extent that someone chooses to find something more than just a paying job—that is, some kind of work that is appealing and satisfying—we speak of making a vocational choice. Studies of the antecedents, correlates, and consequences of such choices constitute the major portion of the literature in the study of vocational behavior. (*Vocational choice* and *occupational choice* are essentially interchangeable terms. Sociologists and economists tend to prefer the word *occupational*, whereas psychologists tend to prefer the word *vocational*.) *Vocational guidance* is the term applied to the processes developed to help individuals with the assessments and reasoning needed to make wise career choices. Perhaps the most encompassing term is *vocational psychology*, defined by Crites (1969) as the study of vocational behavior and development. *Vocational behavior* is defined as including "all responses the individual makes in choosing and adjusting to an occupation" (p. 16); *vocational development* is defined as that "which is inferred from the systematic changes that can be observed in vocational behavior over time" (p. 17).

The terms *career development, career counseling,* and *career psychology* all evolved from theoretical and research developments in vocational psychology in the 1950s and 1960s. Much of the research in those decades turned to developmental psychology to understand the processes of vocational choice and development. Noting that most persons engage in several related vocations during their lives, Super (1957) promoted use of the word *career* to cover the sequence of major positions held by a person throughout his or her preoccupational (student) years, working years, and retirement years. *Career,* compared to *vocational,* has become the preferred word to use when theorizing and researching vocational behaviors and development.

The terms *educational development* and *educational counseling* may, at first reading, seem particularly out of place in this and the next chapters. However, if one considers education as part of career development (and in contemporary technological society, education becomes more and more a critical factor in setting the range of career possibilities), then it can be seen that choices of degree programs, and performance in those programs, are inextricably involved with career psychology. Consequently, since the earliest days of the profession, there have been counseling psychologists who focused on issues related to selecting, adjusting to, and performing satisfactorily in college settings. Russell and Petrie (1992) provide one of the more recent comprehensive reviews of the research contributions to and issues in the study of academic adjustment and success.

EVOLUTION IN CAREER CHOICE AND DEVELOPMENT THEORIES

Before reviewing the evolution in career choice and development theories, we need to ask how it is that we can account for nearly 100 years of almost uninterrupted attention to career related behaviors and why there are currently at least three professional journals (*Journal of Vocational Behavior, Career Development Quarterly, Journal of Career Assessment*) devoted exclusively to theoretical and practical issues related to vocational behavior. From one perspective, career choices are simply a few of the many choices made in everyone's life—whether to marry, to buy a house, to take a vacation, and so forth. On the other hand, according to Erikson (1950), Freud wrote explicitly about the positive relationship of one's mental health to the ability to love *and to work*. The last half of the twentieth century yielded an impressive accumulation of empirical evidence in support of Freud's observation. Loftquist and Dawis (1984) cite some of the classic studies of the impact of work on both life satisfaction and mental health. Perhaps most intriguing is the study by Palmore (1969) who found that work satisfaction was a better predictor of how long one lives than physicians' ratings, use of tobacco, or genetic factors.

Socially and economically, there are yet other driving forces for a focus on career psychology. Recall from earlier chapters the role of both world wars in advancing the vocational guidance movement (Chapter 2) and development of assessment techniques (Chapter 13). Using human resources effectively was, and continues to be, the major impetus for governmental support of the development of occupational classification, selection, and promotion procedures. Some jobs demand specific talents; placing employees in positions who do not possess these talents is at best economically wasteful and in wartime potentially catastrophic. On a less dramatic basis, everyday issues like absenteeism and job turnover are two of the highest, most preventable costs businesses incur. Each year, millions of dollars are invested in research to find out what steps can be taken to increase workers' satisfaction, a factor directly linked to absenteeism and job turnover (Loftquist & Dawis, 1984).

From the societal compared to the economic viewpoint, a well-functioning society is one in which there are low levels of social alienation; that is, one in which few persons are found who are not contributing to, or possibly are acting out against, society as a community. Worker dissatisfaction has long been a major component of social alienation when it occurs. It is not difficult to recall how much social unrest has occurred in times of high unemployment and/or when groups of individuals are systematically denied the opportunity to enter and succeed in valued careers. As we will explore further in the last half of this chapter, continued issues of unemployment, underemployment, and inequalities in pay and advancement opportunities, all as related to gender, ethnicity, and culture, are major factors in paradigmatic shifts in what and how to study career choice and development.

During the first half of the twentieth century, psychologists working in areas of vocational behavior were focused primarily on the development and use of assessment techniques. It was not until the 1950s that theories began to address just how persons go about implementing the "true reasoning" of Parsons's (1909) pioneering model. Parsons postulated that wise vocational choices were a matter of "true reasoning" about the relationships between knowledge of self and knowledge of the world of work. In the first half of the twentieth century, assessments were created to develop the two types of knowledge, but how was "true reasoning" to be ensured?

The three approaches reviewed in this chapter reflect historical developments not only from Parsons's fundamental concepts, but also from research emphases in the discipline of psychology at large. The first approach we review is most commonly referred to as "trait oriented," building on the measurement accomplishments of the first half of the twentieth century. The second approach, referred to as developmental, was built upon the growing literature in developmental psychology during the middle of the twentieth century. The third approach, social learning and cognition, is distinctively a product of psychology of the 1960s and subsequent decades, when cognitive behavioral viewpoints became the preeminent explanatory concepts in developmental and personality psychology. Within each of the approaches we review, there have been early (i.e., 1950s and 1960s) significant developments, as well as later ones (i.e., 1970s and 1980s). The review of each approach begins with an early theory and then moves on to more recently developed theory related to that approach.

Trait-Oriented Theories

Holland's Theory of Vocational Personalities and Work Environments

Historical Roots.   In their earliest form, trait-oriented approaches were known as trait and factor approaches. The essence of this approach is that the "counselor" measures the traits of the person, finds out the requirements of a job, and then counsels the person into a job that provides a match between person traits and job factors. During the first half of the twentieth century, several studies indicated that as much as one-third of the information needed to predict occupational success could be obtained simply by knowing the measured ability of workers (Brown, Brooks, & Associates, 1990). Yet, what about the two-thirds of remaining variance? Many persons have the required abilities for particular jobs, for example, teaching, engineering, but for personal reasons do not wish to enter that profession. External factors such as discrimination, low income potential, undesirable job environment, peer and parental influences all keep many persons from selecting a profession that is a good match between their measured abilities and job requirements. Additionally, internal factors such as interests and personality style may also lead to persons not choosing jobs for which they have all the requisite abilities.

On the job side of the coin, there are an equally large number of reasons for inadequacies in a simple matching approach. A primary reason is the immense variety of activities subsumed under any one job title, even though there are over 20,000 different job titles listed in the United States. Consider what seems to be a relatively narrow occupation, that of oceanographer. Some oceanographers focus their work on alternative energy resources; others are involved in movements of the ocean that affect weather; still others are concerned largely with the biology of life in the oceans. Even within each of these categories, some oceanographers may be involved in research, others in applied design technology, others in sales of an innovative process for using ocean resources.

John Holland, based on experiences early in his career in military and educational settings, became astutely aware of the limitations of a simple matching of persons' traits and job requirements. In perhaps one of the finest manifestations of the value of the scientist–practitioner model, he drew upon these experiences as a counselor and researcher to develop a theoretical model that addresses some of the limitations of the basic trait and factor matching approach.

Key Concepts.   The basic premise Holland derived from his early experiences as a counselor was that people choose occupations as an expression of their personalities. Nearly 50 years after Holland began his work on this premise, it is impossible to overstate the impact he has had on the theory and research in career development and the practice of career counseling. In one sense, his premise created a major new way of looking at career choice and development; that is, a paradigmatic shift (see later section in this chapter for discussion of paradigms and shifts). Instead of focusing on a match of abilities and possibly other traits, to job requirements, Holland's work shifted attention to persons' *perceptions of themselves;* perceptions that could be assessed by examining persons' perceptions of various jobs (Holland, 1997).

Persons who find work environments that are congruent with their personalities will flourish in their work. "Lack of congruence between personality and environment leads to dissatisfaction, unstable career paths, and lowered performance" (Holland, 1996, p. 397). To study such congruence, Holland needed a way to assess both personality and environment related to vocational behavior. While a few of the measures he and his colleagues developed are outlined in the next section, what must be noted here is the resulting structure that evolved from those assessments, the now well-known RIASEC model. Each letter in the acronym RIASEC stands for one of six types of personality, each with a corresponding type of environment. To illustrate as well as to identify each of the six different types, typical occupations are listed here for each.

1. <u>R</u>ealistic: mechanic and air traffic controller
2. <u>I</u>nvestigative: economist and biologist

The RIASEC Model. A hexagonal model for defining the psychological resemblances among types and environments and their interactions.   **FIGURE 14.1.**

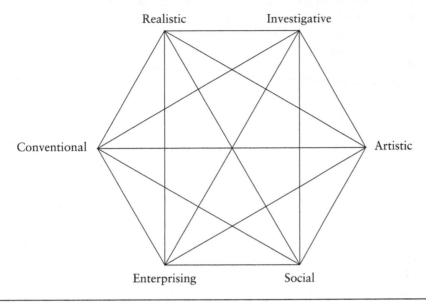

3. <u>A</u>rtistic: editor and photographer
4. <u>S</u>ocial: athletic coach and minister
5. <u>E</u>nterprising: real estate sales agent and radio/tv announcer
6. <u>C</u>onventional: receptionist and accountant.

The key concepts to be used in conjunction with this model are *congruence, consistency, differentiation,* and *identity. Congruence* is the fit between an individual's type and the environment in which he or she works. For a person whose primary type is artistic and who works in an artistic environment, a fully congruent match has been made. The match of an artistic person to a conventional environment is totally incongruent (Conventional is opposite Artistic on the RIASEC hexagon as shown in Figure 14.1) and one would predict that such a person is unlikely to remain in such a position, at least with any degree of satisfaction. *Consistency* for an individual can be determined by looking at his or her highest two or three scores on the six different types and examining the positions of these types on the RIASEC model. A person who has primarily realistic interests but also strong social interests is less consistent (opposing types in Figure 14.1), compared to one whose strongest interests are realistic and investigative (adjacent types in Figure 14.1). For Holland, the principle of consistency is that the more consistent persons are in their types, the more predictable they are as to the occupation in which they will find success and satisfaction. The concept of *differentiation* is assessed by looking at the *size* of the differences in the highest versus lowest of the six type scores. The greater the magnitude of the difference, the more likely one can make an accurate prediction of what career choice a person will find satisfactory. Conversely, the person who has a "flat profile"—that is, relatively similar scores for all types—is one for whom no serious gambler would bet a lot of money in predicting that person's eventual career choice. Persons with flat profiles might find satisfaction in a very wide range of careers or just as likely not find satisfaction in any career.

Identity refers to the clarity of one's goals, interests, and talents and is measured by a separate scale on either the Vocational Preference Inventory or the Self-Directed Search; both measures are described in the next section. The concept of identity and Holland's development of the Vocational Identity Scale (Holland, Johnston, & Asama, 1993) will be more fully discussed in Chapter 15 in the section on vocational indecisiveness.

Key Measures.   The earliest measure developed by Holland was the Vocational Preference Inventory (VPI), now in its seventh revision (Holland, 1985). Extensive analyses of thousands of students' and adults' scores on this measure yielded the six personality types that form the foundation of Holland's RIASEC model. While the VPI is still useful to researchers studying the structure and interrelationships of the six types to other psychological dimensions, in the practice of career counseling, the VPI has essentially been replaced by the Self-Directed Search (SDS) (Holland, 1994). As already described in Chapter 13, this measure, now in its fourth edition, is extensively used by millions of individuals from early teens to retirement years. It is designed to be self-administered and self-scoring. The measure includes a variety of questions about self-assessments of abilities, interests, and preferences. From these responses, scores are obtained on each of the six RIASEC types. These scores, when examined in connection with auxiliary materials such as an Occupations Finder, Educational Opportunities Finder, or Leisure Activities Finder, help the examinee determine where the best fits occur between himself or herself and the environment (occupation, education, or leisure) being searched for.

Theoretical and Practical Strengths.   Holland's theory with its broad array of practice applications is now regarded as the strongest of all theories of career choice and development. That statement does not mean to imply that all the research is fully supportive of all the key concepts (see next section). What cannot be challenged, however, is the value of the theory in generating important research and new kinds of career interventions. Borgen (1991) finds that citations and publication of studies related to Holland's theory are more than six times greater than for any other career choice and development theory. The strongest research support is for the six RIASEC types of persons and environments. Workers in differing environments not only perform different work, they also have differing social skills and person preferences (Wampold, Ankavlo, Mondin et al., 1995). Moreover, there is both convergent and discriminant validity (see Chapter 13 for the importance of these kinds of validity) for Holland's six types compared to other measures of personality (Gottfredson, Jones, & Holland, 1993).

From the practice perspective, there is no real competitor in terms of numbers of persons who use the SDS as compared to any other measure of interests. It has been incorporated into self-help books such as *What Color Is Your Parachute*

(Bolles, 1998), into thousands of high school guidance programs, and countless other career intervention programs. "Consumer satisfaction" in use of the measure has always been high compared to that of other measures. The SDS has truly become, with all the revisions made over the years, a "user friendly" measure that is cost effective both in terms of the time of the person taking the SDS and in terms of counselor or administrative staff time. In fact, there may be essentially no staff time required if the person taking the measure has no questions during the self-administered and self-interpretation phases.

Theoretical and Practical Limitations.　Holland is the first to admit that the research evidence supporting the key concepts of congruence, consistency, differentiation, and identity has been less impressive than he would wish. Holland (1996) is beginning to look at persons' attitudes and strategies regarding careers as one way of possibly improving predictions about who will be satisfied and stable in careers. His new developments may converge nicely with some of the developments in cognitive and constructivist approaches to career theory reviewed later in this chapter.

Relative to a general paucity of vocational behavior research with culturally diverse populations, Holland's RIASEC model has been tested with individuals from widely diverse ethnic, socioeconomic, and international backgrounds. The fact that the SDS has now been translated to many languages speaks in part to the practical usefulness that has been found for it around the world. More rigorous research investigations on the structure of interests has yielded mixed data, some finding that ethnicity does not significantly affect structure (Ryan, Tracey, & Rounds, 1996), others finding that structure does vary when more international samples are compared (Rounds & Tracey, 1996). As described in Chapter 13, while care must be taken when using assessments with culturally diverse populations, there is at least a reasonable amount of empirical support to consider careful use of Holland's theory and assessments with culturally diverse populations.

Dawis's Theory of Work Adjustment

Historical Roots.　The theory of work adjustment grew out of research begun in 1959 that investigated the work adjustment of vocational rehabilitation clients. That focus on rehabilitation clients led to a greater emphasis on longer-range issues of *adjustment* compared to a shorter-term focus on vocational *choice*.

Key Concepts.　Based on results from their initial studies, Dawis, England, and Lofquist (1964) present a theory that has as its primary focus the proposition that tenure (length of stay on a job) will be predicted by a combination of satisfaction (worker's self-reported job satisfaction) and satisfactoriness (e.g., supervisor's ratings of employee as performing satisfactorily) and, most important, how the two interacted: greater job satisfaction would lead to higher ratings of satisfactoriness, and higher ratings of satisfactoriness would lead to greater job satisfaction. Note that, as in Holland's theory, which was being developed independently at the same time, Dawis and colleagues shifted the focus from simply looking at person–worker characteristics to an *interaction* of the person and the work environment.

By 1978, Dawis and colleagues felt they had sufficient data regarding the proposed interactions and their effects to redefine work adjustment "as a symmetric, circular process in which both person and environment attempt to achieve and maintain an acceptable level of satisfaction" (Dawis, 1996, p. 79). In this statement, then, achieving and maintaining some correspondence becomes a driving force *causing changes in environments as well as individual workers*. Paying attention to how, when, and why work environments change is a unique aspect of this theory and, as will be explored later in this chapter, a critical component of emerging new conceptualizations of reciprocity of person–environment interactions.

Key Measures.   The theory propounded by Dawis et al. makes extensive use of many existing measures of abilities, for example, General Aptitude Test Battery (GATB) (see Chapter 13), to assess the individual side of the person–environment fit. Examination of limits in much of their initial data led the theory's authors to go beyond an assessment of abilities and include an assessment of what they sometimes call needs, other times, using the learning terminology that had emerged in the 1960s, "reinforcer requirements." Dawis and colleagues developed the Minnesota Importance Questionnaire (Weiss, Dawis, Lofquist et al., 1975) in which 20 classes of "reinforcer requirements" cluster around six values: achievement, comfort (freedom from stress), status, altruism, safety, and autonomy. While the measure has not been used extensively outside of its use in testing work adjustment theory, it has withstood several years of empirical investigation supporting its factor structure and validity in understanding what workers deem important.

On the environmental side of the equation, Dawis, Dohm, Lofquist et al., (1987) developed the Minnesota Occupational Classification System. The classifications of that system have been incorporated into a computerized software program that after data entry, examines an individual's abilities and values and generates a list of the occupations that yield "correspondence" between the individual and the job. Recall that this correspondence is the key to tenure in a job.

Theoretical and Practical Strengths.   The theory of work adjustment contains some of the most explicitly stated testable hypotheses of any of the vocational theories. Although this theory has not attracted nearly as many researchers as Holland's, partly because of the need for more extensive assessments of individuals and environments than Holland's SDS, it is, however, an attractive theory for I/O psychologists and for counseling psychologists working in industry. Empirical data from industrial settings do support the importance of fit between the person and the environment for achieving both satisfaction and satisfactoriness. There is also a growing body of research results supporting their proposition that as a worker remains longer on a particular job, that worker will change in ways that are more correspondant (congruent) with that work environment (Dawis, 1996).

One of the major contributions the theory could make to both career counseling practice and the societal issue of job dissatisfaction still often found in our society, is an explication of the ways that work environments might be changed to provide for increased correspondence of workers and work environment. To accomplish this goal, more attention must be given to the assessment of job environments.

Dawis (1996) is clear in stating that (a) culturally diverse groups have not been a focus of the research but that (b) the theoretical propositions clearly would be less supportable to the extent that any cultural factor leads to a restriction in the preparation for and/or entry into any jobs that would provide for correspondence.

Theoretical and Practical Limitations.   Much of the research regarding the theory has been reported only in University of Minnesota reports rather than in refereed journals and has therefore received less critical peer review than the research on many of the other career theories. Many of the propositions of the theory have yet to be empirically tested. Hackett and Lent (1992) outline a number of strategies that could enhance the empirical and practical contributions of work adjustment theory. As long as the theory remains focused on the "what" of adjustment, rather than on the "how" (that is, the process by which clients can attain adjustment), use of the theory by counselors will be comparatively limited. Finally, the range of persons studied has been relatively restricted, especially compared to the cultural diversity now characterizing the workforce of the United States.

As a closing statement to this review of two trait-oriented approaches to career choice and development, it must be noted that these theories have sometimes been harshly criticized for supposedly making an oversimplification of the matchmaking process and giving inadequate attention to person–environmental interactions. Swanson (1996) provides an excellent response to these criticisms by giving both researchers and career counselors more up-to-date understanding of the many contributions of trait-oriented approaches to an understanding of and potential interventions for satisfactory career choice and adjustment.

Developmental Theories

Super's Approach: Stage Theory to Life Span, Life Space Perspective

Historical Roots.   During the early years of his career, while working as an employment counselor in the 1930s, Super became acutely aware of some of the deficiencies of the trait and factor model as it was then practiced; that is, assessing clients' abilities and finding a job for them that matched their abilities. The concept of making a "once and for all" supposedly satisfactory career choice struck Super as missing much of importance. Even by 1942, Super (1942) was proposing to theorists and practitioners that vocational adjustment was more a matter of dynamic unfolding than a one-time-choice event with static consequences. Concisely, he regarded career development as a process, one that occurs throughout the life span.

Key Concepts.   In Super's writing career of over 50 years of seminal, innovative (Borgen, 1991) thinking, there were at least three key conceptual developments, each leading to new kinds of assessment measures and researchable hypotheses. By 1953, Super had incorporated several developmental concepts from both psychologists and sociologists who were increasingly, in the 1930s and 1940s, focusing on development in the adult years compared to earlier emphases that were pretty much restricted to the years of childhood and adolescence. Super (1953) outlines five stages of growth: childhood, exploration during adolescence, establishment during young adulthood, maintenance during middle adulthood, and decline during old age. Within each of these age periods, the critical question, according to Super, is: "What are the appropriate vocational behaviors that should be occurring, for someone in this age group, in order eventually to attain career adjustment?" For each age, there are then developmentally appropriate tasks that a person needs to negotiate to achieve career maturity. As each age is successfully handled, the person moves on to the tasks of the next age. (See Figure 14.2.)

Perhaps the most critical research finding to emerge from all of Super's decades of theorizing and research was the key result of his 30-year longitudinal study of career success. Before examining that result, keep in mind that during the first 60 years of the twentieth century, the prevailing view was that the sooner persons made realistic career decisions, the more likely they were to become successful—they would have more streamlined preparation, earlier career entry, and opportunities for success. When Super and colleagues assessed students longitudinally from ninth grade through their mid-20s, collecting a wide variety of biosocial, environmental, vocational, personality, and achievement related data, they found that ninth graders who had already decided what they wanted to become had often made poorly grounded unstable choices. The best predictor of later vocational adjustment was *not* having reached a decision by ninth grade, but rather simply being actively oriented toward gathering career-relevant information. The tremendous effects of this finding on subsequent educational policy were summarized by Osipow (1983):

> Super suggested, based on such data, that the school curriculum should "foster planfulness" aimed at helping youngsters become aware of their level of occupational aspirations and the general amount of education required to achieve that level. This self-knowledge could be developed without specifically deciding on an occupational goal, which would be premature in the ninth grade. In fact, rather than restrict occupational choice possibilities at that age, the school should exert its efforts to broaden occupational perspectives and to teach the student to use available resources for exploration effectively. In this statement lie the roots of the Career Education movement (p. 163).

By 1963, Super had incorporated much of Rogers's thinking about self-concept as a way of explaining the process aspects of how career development unfolds. Briefly, Super postulates that we make career choices, and possibly career changes, in accordance with developments and changes in our self-concepts. Like Holland, Super uses the idea of congruence, but the congruence is not between personality and environment, it is rather between how persons perceive a job, or occupation, or career, fitting their self-concepts.

Super's focus on self-concept led him to look at the many different roles individuals have in their lives; career is just one of many roles a person might have and each role has an impact on self-concept. The more he studied multiple roles among people in our culture as well as in international cultures (Super, Sverko, & Super, 1995), the more he saw shifting emphases and recycling developmental phenomena in roles such as worker, student, housewife, leisurite, and so forth, throughout the

Cycling and Recycling of Developmental Tasks Throughout the Life Span. **FIGURE 14.2.**

	Age			
	Adolescence 14–25	Early Adulthood 25–45	Middle Adulthood 45–65	Late Adulthood 65 and over
Decline Developmental tasks at each age	Giving less time to hobbies	Reducing sports participation	Focusing on essentials	Reducing working hours
Maintenance Tasks at each age	Verifying current occupational choice	Making occupational position secure	Holding one's own against competition	Keeping what one enjoys
Establishment Tasks at each age	Getting started in a chosen field	Settling down in a suitable position	Developing new skills	Doing things one has wanted to do
Exploration Tasks at each age	Learning more about more opportunities	Finding desired opportunity	Identifying new tasks to work on	Finding a good retirement place
Growth Tasks at each age	Developing a realistic self-concept	Learning to relate to others	Accepting one's own limitations	Developing and valuing nonoccupational roles

Life Stage (vertical label at left)

life span. A concise overview of how these studies led Super to develop first a Life-Career Rainbow (see Figure 14.3) and then an Archway of Career Determinants may be found in one of Super's last major papers (Super, 1994), published in the year of his death. While it is beyond the scope of this overview to delineate all the details of these developments, his writings continue to keep career psychologists attending to both multiple roles and issues of vocational behavior throughout the life span. In fact, while Super's work was first identified as a developmental stage theory, then as a self-concept implementation theory, in the final years Super preferred the label a "life-span, life space perspective."

Key Measures. Super's theoretical propositions led to the development of two kinds of new measures. The Super, Thompson, Lindeman, and colleagues' (1981) Career Development Inventory is just one of several measures that Super's work engendered to assess what kinds of career planning and career explorations people were engaged in at different developmental stages. This measure, and others like it,

FIGURE 14.3. The Life–Career Rainbow: Six Life Roles in Schematic Life Space.

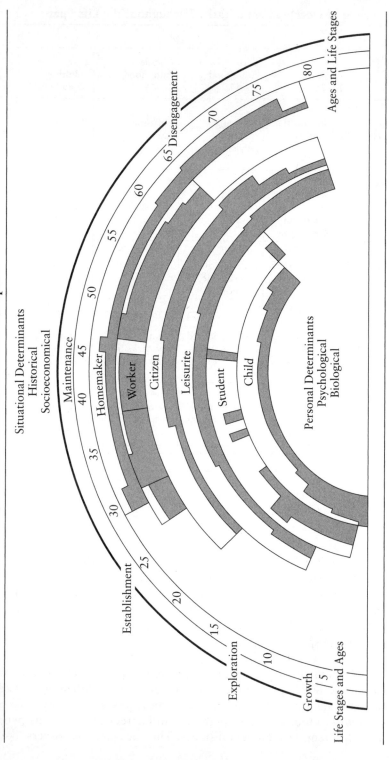

have come to be called career maturity measures since individuals' scores on these measures indicate whether or not they are engaging, or have engaged, in those age appropriate career-related tasks. Westbrook (1983) provides one of the best comparative reviews of the uses and values of the major measures of career maturity. Perhaps the greatest contribution of these measures is that, in identifying "immature" attitudes and competencies, counselors have been better able to focus intervention programs to address these "developmental deficiencies" whether they are in 7-year-old females' socially induced restrictive career stereotypes or in 70-year-olds' abandonment of hope for fulfillment in life.

The other key measure stimulated by Super's work was that of work salience (Nevill & Super, 1986). As Super worked with colleagues around the world, he found that individuals, in various roles and life stages, differed greatly in the importance they assigned to work/career as part of their lives. Super was one of first to see the need to assess this variable if one is ever to be able to make reasonably accurate predictions about career choice and development. While the measures of salience have not yet been widely used outside of those working specifically with Super's concepts, they should receive increased attention as career psychologists attend to some of the issues described in the last half of this chapter regarding expanding and shifting paradigms for vocational behavior research.

Theoretical and Practical Strengths.   The impact of Super's 50 years of theory and research has been tremendous for both the scientific and practical components of counseling psychology. By being among the first to bring a developmental emphasis to the study of vocational behavior, he provided the foundation for looking at *how* people make career choices, rather than just the content of the choice and its consequences. His delineation of stages, and later expansion to life span considerations, has affected the content and timing of career education and career interventions for all ages. Super's work proved especially adaptable to the computer technology that emerged in the past few decades; the extremely successful computerized career guidance system DISCOVER (see Chapter 15) was developed specifically within his developmental task framework. His increasing attention to the multiple roles we all hold, in what he called "life space," foreshadowed the need for more attention to contextualism, a "frontier" described later in this chapter.

Super often described himself as an eclectic, even when eclecticism was a "dirty word" in psychology (Borgen, 1991), and that his theory, in later years, was clearly a segmental one. The different parts hang together only loosely. The positive side of that eclecticism and looseness is its breadth of attractiveness to theorists and practitioners. Without doubt, Super's theorizing has been more comprehensive than any others'; at least some parts of his theory can be readily integrated with any other theory of vocational behavior, making it an attractive framework for many researchers to consider.

Theoretical and Practical Limitations.   Comprehensive theory often has the loosest connections between parts and the least specifiable hypotheses. Thus, the same factor that makes Super's theory very attractive to many theorists and practitioners, limits the possibilities for clear testing by researchers. Although there is much data to support many parts of Super's theory, it would be extremely difficult to lay out a set of specific propositions that have been sufficiently confirmed to allow a confident level of prediction for any one individual. Moreover, Super's work lends itself more readily toward understanding broad concepts of career choice and development and their educational implications for any age, less so toward understanding how to intervene with an individual's work adjustment issues.

Super began his work in an era when the workforce consisted of mainly male Anglos; much of the research regarding his theory reflects that population. Somewhat ironically, while Super's later theoretical "segments" give much attention to the social context of career development, there are very few studies (with studies of career maturity being an exception) within the United States that have looked at how ethnicity might affect his proposed developmental relationships.

Gottfredson's Theory of Circumscription and Compromise

Historical Roots.   Gottfredson was trained as a sociologist, but did her dissertation work in Holland's research center. From this different disciplinary background she brought new perspectives to the early developmental processes that affect career choice.

> [The] theory grew from my efforts to solve an apparent puzzle: why do people of both sexes and of different races and social classes tend to differ, even in childhood, in the kind and quality of jobs they wish for? . . . The most puzzling question in vocational psychology, for me, was this: if having interests that are congruent with those required by one's job is as central to successful career development as the field assumes, then why is congruence such a weak predictor of job satisfaction? Also, why do so many people seek occupations and enter college majors that do not match their assessed interests? Another obvious issue was that vocational psychology seemed to ignore the external barriers that might stunt people's goals and opportunities (Gottfredson, 1996, pp. 179–180).

Key Concepts.   We will focus on just five key concepts from among the many concepts and principles presented by Gottfredson (1981). The first three are essential to attend to carefully because they represent a clear shift in focus from most other career choice and development theories. Her first key concept is that of self-concept; in Gottfredson's theory, self-concept refers to the social self.

> The theory therefore emphasizes the most public, social aspects of self (gender, social class, intelligence) rather than the more private, personal elements (values, personality, plans for family) that are the principle focus of other theories. The more private and personal attributes are indeed important, as other theories argue, but their influence is circumscribed by efforts to implement or protect desired social identities. . . . [A]n individual's vocational preferences are conceptualized and measured as a *range* of preferences, not as a single point . . . [N]aturally occurring occupational choice proceeds largely by *eliminating the negative* rather than selecting the most positive (Gottfredson, 1996, pp. 181, 182; italics added).

Building upon those three basic propositions, the titular concepts of Gottfredson's theory emerge.

> *Circumscription* [is the] progressive elimination of unacceptable alternatives to create a social space (zone of acceptable alternatives). Choosing one particular occupation is but the end of a long process in which youngsters have greatly constrained that final choice. *Compromise* is the process by which youngsters begin to relinquish their most preferred alternatives for less compatible but more accessible ones . . . Compromise can occur either in anticipation of external barriers (anticipatory compromise) or after they are encountered (experiential compromise) (Gottfredson, 1996, pp. 187–188).

Four principles of circumscription are spelled out as they occur in four stages from (1) orientation to size and power (age 3–5), (2) orientation to sex roles (age 6–8), (3) orientation to social valuation (age 9–13), and (4) orientation to the internal, unique self (age 14+).

Key Measures.   In one sense, there are no key measures that have been stimulated by Gottfredson's theory. Her propositions can be tested by obtaining youngsters' occupational aspirations and/or ratings of occupations along various dimensions, for example, prestige, sex appropriateness. These ratings can then be examined in conjunction with respondents' demographic characteristics and/or measured abilities and interests. The latter are measured by the same kinds of measures used in the trait-oriented theories reviewed earlier in this chapter.

Theoretical and Practical Strengths.   The incorporation of a sociological perspective into career choice and development has been provocative and seminal. While the theory is among the youngest in this chapter, the empirical evidence is rapidly accumulating. The evidence is mixed; empirical data do support the propositions that the processes of circumscription and compromise regularly occur at an early age; however, the particular effects of gender, class, ethnicity that were expected have not always been confirmed (Leung, 1993). In short, circumscription and compromise are processes that need the attention of career psychologists. Much is yet to be learned about how and when they occur and how to overcome their limiting effects.

A potential practical strength of the theory is the specification of what needs to occur in career education of very young children. In recent years considerable attention has been given to programs to overcome the circumscription and compromise in career choices of adolescent females and ethnic minorities; Gottfredson's theory and research clearly indicate that our focus must begin in much earlier years. According to results obtained by Lapan and Jingeleski (1992), interventions must begin well before junior high school years if we are to maximize the range of career choices of female students.

Theoretical and Practical Limitations.   With a focus on the very young years of childhood, Gottfredson's theory obviously leaves unaddressed issues of career choice and adjustment in adult years—years in which compromise certainly continues.

Future researchers may want to expand testing of her compromise principles to adult populations.

Some criticisms of Gottfredson's theory are at least, implicitly, like the proverbial "killing the messenger." Because her work focuses on the kinds of stereotypes that occur in very young children, there is some fear that counselors could treat these stereotypes as "a reality to be recognized" rather than something to be confronted and challenged. If the former, then the stereotypes become self-fulfilling prophecies and students consider a far more limited range of careers. On the other hand, if these stereotypes are challenged and students are helped to overcome what they have learned about occupations that "women don't enter," "African Americans have no chance at," or "only rich people get to do," then counselors have made the best uses of the data Gottfredson is presenting. It may not be surprising that, compared to other vocational choice and development theories, a higher proportion of the data collected regarding Gottfredson's theory comes from intentional samples and from ethnic groups within the United States. Mainstream middle-class Anglo America often has a more difficult time facing up to the pervasive effects of social class than do most other societies. In our culture, it is the cultural minorities who know all too well that society imposes limitations on occupational choices based on visible racial features, visible religious affiliation (clothing and/or hairstyles of some Moslems, Orthodox Jews, and Hindus), visible physical disabilities and identifiable gay or lesbian sexual orientation.

Bordin's Ego Psychological Model

Historical Roots.   To some, it may seem inappropriate to include a psychoanalytic type model within a group of developmental theories. Moreover, while this theory is being presented last within the developmental group, historically, its roots preceded all others. In older texts on career development, this type of theory was referred to as "personality-oriented theory"; in some more recent texts, this approach has been eliminated because of a comparative lack of empirically supportive data and unclear practical implications. From early in his career as a counselor, Bordin (1990) held a dynamic perspective about career choice and development. Yet it was not until he began collaboration with some very psychoanalytically oriented colleagues at the University of Michigan in the 1950s that he began to articulate a clearly psychodynamic career theory. His desire to develop such a theory grew out of what he viewed as some serious problems in college students' career indecisions that were simply not addressed by either trait-oriented or self-concept-oriented theories.

> [My theory speaks] to both the decision processes through which this search for vocation is pursued and to the ways of construing the occupational world that are the target of the search. Finally, the theory will address the question of the *developmental* sources of individual differences in the kinds and styles of satisfactions sought (Bordin, 1990, p. 104, italics added).

Thus, Bordin's will be the last of the developmental theories we present, even though its roots are clearly in the pre-twentieth century pioneering personality development theory of Freud.

Key Concepts.　　While, on the one hand, one would expect an analytic theory to focus primarily on the individual, Bordin was keenly aware that in the arena of vocational behavior, one had to be able to define how occupational environments would allow for intrinsic satisfaction of an individual's dynamics. Thus, the first step was the development of a framework for mapping occupations, identifying the intrinsic work requirements of each that "give the individual a way of being that is consonant with the dynamics and structure of his or her personality" (Bordin, 1990, p. 104). Occupations were initially mapped in terms of how occupations could nurture, feed, and foster; or, for other occupations, how they provided for aggressive acts such as biting, cutting, and devouring (Bordin, Nachman, & Segal, 1963). In later decades, incorporating more recent ego-analytic concepts (compared to orthodox analytical concepts), Bordin classified occupations into one of six categories, each providing different kinds of intrinsic satisfaction: precision (neatness and control), nurturance, curiosity, power (tractor drivers as well as lawyers and writers), aesthetic expression, and ethics and concern with right and wrong.

Returning to a focus on the individual, the last three of seven propositions he developed (Bordin 1990) state:

> The roots of the personal aspects of career development are to be found throughout the early development of the individual, sometimes in the earliest years. . . . Each individual seeks to build a personal identity that incorporates aspects of father and mother yet retains elements unique to the self. . . . One source of perplexity and paralysis at career decision points will be found in doubts in and dissatisfactions with current resolutions of self (pp. 116–117).

Key Measures.　　There are no key measures that have been developed for theoretical or applied use in Bordin's psychodynamic approach. Occupations have been classified into psychodynamic categories by Bordin and colleagues; individuals' dynamics are appraised largely through interviews, projective techniques, and/or retrospective reports on early childhood memories and descriptions of family relationships. Some family relationship inventories were developed in the 1960s for testing some of the parent–child relationships in Roe's related approach (Roe & Lunneborg, 1990); however, the lack of predicted results with such measures eventually led to their being abandoned.

Theoretical and Practical Strengths.　　Bordin (1990) describes a number of studies from a broad array of developmental, personality, and sociological studies that give at least indirect support to each of his propositions. However, when it comes to attaining confirmation of specific effects of parents, identity formation, and the like, on career choice and adjustment, the results of several decades of studies have been inconclusive. While different kinds of relationships with ones' parents have been found to have limited statistically significant relationships with later career decisions, the nature of those relationships varies greatly by sex of respondent, cultural background, family structure (e.g., one- or two-parent family), and even the era of the study. For example, there have been rapid changes in the past few decades in how both mothers and fathers relate to daughters in terms of what are desirable career options. On the other hand, the work of Bluestein, Walbridge, Friedlander, and Palladino (1991) well illustrates the significance—yet complexity—of the effects of psychological separation and parental attachment on the career development process.

As we will further illustrate in Chapter 15, we believe that even within the present theoretical limitations of the psychodynamic approach, there is great practical value. This value is most apparent for clients who seem "stuck" when trying to make a career decision, even though they might be reasonably decisive in other parts of their lives, or are clients who are just pervasively indecisive. For either type of client, dynamic linkages between their personal styles/issues and their career difficulties are almost surely present. Cohen, Chartrand, and Jowdy (1995) give some of the more recent data indicating that various degrees of career indecision are significantly related to ego identity development. They relate their results to different kinds of career interventions for groups of clients who have identifiably different psychological dynamics underlying their problems with career decisions.

Theoretical and Practical Limitations.   Like all psychodynamic theories, the research related to Bordin's approach suffers from the fact that one must often use less precise measures than that used for other theories. Early childhood data on relationships with parents is usually from retrospective reports and is subject to all the distortions of long-term memory. The failure of many studies to obtain statistically significant relationships, or relationships that can be replicated in another study, has caused most researchers to pay little attention to psychodynamic principles in their studies. Practicing counselors have probably had the best opportunity to provide some informative evaluations of the impact of utilizing psychodynamic approaches in counseling; however, once again, most studies have focused on using more precise and widely used measures such as Holland and colleagues' (1993) Vocational Identity Scale and various career maturity and career belief inventories both for diagnosing and treatment planning for career indecision.

Social Learning and Cognition Theories

Krumboltz's Social Learning Theory

Historical Roots.   By the early 1960s, the principles of Skinner's (1938) behaviorism and other learning models were increasingly being applied to a broad range of human behaviors. Krumboltz and colleagues were the first counseling psychologists to incorporate principles of social learning (Bandura, 1986) in a comprehensive approach to understanding the factors that influence people to pursue various lines of work, as well as the impediments to their making and implementing choices (Krumboltz, Mitchell, & Jones, 1976; Mitchell & Krumboltz, 1996).

Key Concepts.   Four categories of factors are postulated as influencing career decisions: (1) genetic endowment and special abilities; (2) environmental conditions and events, such as number and nature of job opportunities; (3) learning experiences, and (4) task-approach skills. In this social learning approach, three major types of learning are described as they apply to career decisions. The first two are similar to the instrumental (operant) and associative (classical) conditioning models taught in introductory psychology. *Instrumental* learning experiences are identified as those that occur when one experiences a positive outcome for a behavior. For example, if one successfully completes a science project that receives an award, or receives compliments for writing an essay, these behaviors are far more likely to be repeated. *Associative* learning is used to describe the associations developed between a neutral event or stimulus with an emotionally laden one, such as the classical conditioning of salivation to a bell in Pavlov's dogs. For a career-related example, if a youngster's only experience with plush furnishings comes from waiting in a dentist's office, he or she may decide that being a dentist is the best way to achieve a comfortable lifestyle. This example may seem like an oversimplification; however, Krumboltz and colleagues (1976) documented numerous examples of pervasive generalizations that resulted from the effect of a single stimulus or event. It is a well-established fact that enrollments in particular kinds of career or skill training programs are temporarily affected by the appearance of any new "hero" in the media, for example, lawyers, figure skaters, fighter pilots. The third kind of learning that is critical to career development is *vicarious* learning. New behaviors and skills can be learned merely by observing the behaviors of others via the media or direct observation. Think of how one dance after another has spread throughout the country because of its display on television. More specific to career development, Krumboltz and colleagues (1976) show that students can learn how to obtain useful occupational information simply by observing someone (ideally, a role model of the students) go through the process.

By incorporating social learning theory with these basic types of learning, this approach specifies three components of successful career development (Mitchell & Krumboltz, 1996). The first component, *self-observation generalizations,* are statements persons make to themselves based on their own experiences. The experiences each person has lead to generalizations about whether or not he or she can do something (task efficacy); these generalizations are then extended to what one thinks are his or her interests and values. Someone unskilled at fixing a bike, compared to a friend who is adept at it, might well conclude that he or she has neither mechanical skills nor interests.

Moreover, based on the various kinds of learning outlined above, each person forms views about the world around him or her and its characteristics. These views are referred to as *worldview generalizations.* Television shows have a tremendous impact, for example, in determining which stereotypes the public holds about what gender and ethnicity occupations "are"; for example, until recently, TV shows portrayed all nurses as females, most cleaning personnel as African American, and so forth. The fact that such stereotypes on television have become widely discussed and reported as social issues speaks to their importance as a source of vicarious learning in the shaping of young people's worldviews about careers.

To shape these various kinds of learning and resultant self and worldview generalizations into career decisions and actions, individuals must learn and engage in *task approach skills.* The most important of these skills for career decision making are clarifying values, goal setting, predicting future events, generating alternatives, seeking information, and planning and generalizing (Krumboltz & Baker, 1973). "People will be more likely to learn these task approach skills if they (1) have been positively reinforced for demonstrating or attempting these skills or (2) have observed models being positively reinforced for demonstrating these skills" (Mitchell & Krumboltz, 1996, p. 267). In their 1984 presentation of the theory, Mitchell and Krumboltz (1984) provided six excellent examples of how distortions in these processes lead to inappropriate career choices, or even more often, to avoidance of making a decision that could lead to more satisfying results:

> (1) drawing faulty generalizations ("I'm the only person in my class who is afraid of public speaking"), (2) making self-comparisons with a single standard ("I'm not as warm as Carl Rogers, so I could never be a counselor"), (3) exaggerating the estimates of the emotional impact of an outcome ("If I don't succeed in business school I just couldn't stand it"), (4) drawing false causal relationships ("To get ahead, you just have to be in the right place at the right time"), (5) being ignorant of relevant facts ("High school English teachers spend their day helping eager students to appreciate the finer points of literature") and (6) giving undue weight to low probability events ("I wouldn't accept a job in California because it's going to fall into the ocean during the next earthquake") (p. 266).

These distortions underlie the development of the major assessment device related to this theory and described in the next section: the Career Beliefs Inventory (Krumboltz, 1991). Of great value to career counselors are articles by Keller, Biggs, and Gysbers (1982), Nevo (1987), and Corbishley and Yost (1989), which outline specific interventions for these kinds of beliefs that seriously impede effective career decision making.

In the latest iteration of this theory, Mitchell and Krumboltz (1996) take the interesting position that we should be attending less to indecision (see Chapter 15) and congruence (a key factor in Holland's, Dawis's, and Super's theories) and more attention to the following three questions:

1. How successful have my interventions been in stimulating new learning on the part of my clients?

2. How well have my interventions helped my clients to cope with a constantly changing work world?

3. How much progress are my clients making in creating a satisfying life for themselves (Mitchell & Krumboltz, 1996, p. 264)?

Key Measures.   The Career Beliefs Inventory (Krumboltz, 1991) was developed to help clients understand some of their beliefs that could be blocking them from achieving their career goals. The measure has five major scales and 25 subscales, providing counselors and clients with examples of irrational beliefs and overgeneralizations that impede the decision-making process. There is also a workbook (Levin, Krumboltz, & Krumboltz, 1995) that facilitates clients' examination of their responses in conjunction with their results on the Strong Interest Inventory and the Myers–Briggs Type Indicator.

Theoretical and Practical Strengths.   By bringing together new psychological principles and knowledge from learning and cognition with what is known, and needed to be known, about career behavior, Krumboltz has provided a model of the kind of disciplinary collaboration that can best advance the science and profession. His thoughtful integrations of social learning models and vocational behavior directly stimulated the development of the next two approaches reviewed in this chapter, both of which have moved on to higher levels of specificity in addressing important issues in vocational behavior. This model has also stimulated the development of some novel approaches to encouraging information seeking and career planning. In fact, the most supportive research regarding the social learning theory of career decision making is found in the results of studies showing that either direct reinforcement of career-seeking behavior (instrumental learning) or presentations by models (vicarious learning) can lead to students making more informed and rational career decisions. Moreover, the theory's articulation of problematic career beliefs and the development of relevant cognitive interventions provides important new strategies for career counselors.

Theoretical and Practical Limitations.   Although Krumboltz's initial theoretical presentation included many testable propositions, only those related to clients' seeking occupational information have received much attention. Without research on most of the other propositions, no significant refinement of the theory has been accomplished. Also, while the theory could easily be extended to vocational behavior issues throughout the life span, and to culturally diverse groups, no research programs have been developed for these populations.

Social Cognition Theory

Historical Roots.   "[T]he cognitive revolution has quietly overtaken vocational psychology" (Borgen, 1991, p. 279). "Accompanying this quiet cognitive revolution has been an equally important trend toward viewing people as active agents in, or shapers of, their career development" (Lent, Brown, & Hackett, 1996, p. 373). Building upon both the social learning theory of Krumboltz and the self-efficacy research on women's career development (Hackett & Betz, 1981), Lent and colleagues (1996) recently developed a reasonably comprehensive model of career development that addresses interest development, vocational choice, and vocational performance.

Key Concepts.   Central to their theory are the three central variables from general social cognitive theory: self-efficacy (Can I do this?), outcome expectations (If I do this, what will happen?) and personal goals. "By setting personal goals, people help to organize, guide, and sustain their own behavior. . . . Though environmental events and personal history undoubtedly help shape behavior . . . it is also motivated or animated, in part, by people's self-directed goals" (Lent et al., 1996, pp. 381–382). Their model also incorporates Bandura's (1986) triadic reciprocity; that is, fully bidirectional causal relationships between personal attributes, external environmental factors, and overt behavior. To illustrate this reciprocity, consider Lent and colleagues' model of how interests develop: When an individual believes he or she is interested in something, some intention is made to select and practice that activity. The actual performance attainment when the interest is tried out then affects the person

FIGURE 14.4. How Basic Career Interests Develop Over Time.

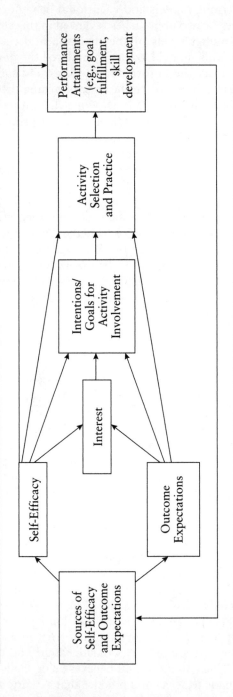

This model highlights cognitive and behavioral influences during childhood and adolescence. Copyright 1993 by R. W. Lent, S. D. Brown, and G. Hackett. Reprinted by permission.

not only in the traditional learning model reinforcement way, but perhaps of much greater importance, what "generalized conclusion" the person tells himself or herself. "Whether new interest emerge depends less on simple exposure and past reinforcement experiences than on how people read their competence (self-efficacy) at the activity and on their prospective expectations about obtaining prized versus non-valued outcomes" (Lent et al., 1996, p. 385). In their models of choice and performance, like their model on interest development, a key component is always the feedback loop of not only what happens, but also what conclusions the person draws from what happens. (See Figure 14.4.) The "conclusions" from what happens when these concepts are applied to vocational behavior appear in the next few paragraphs.

Key Measure.   The key new measure needed to test the propositions of this theory is a measure of self-efficacy. Early on in the study of self-efficacy and its effects in women's career development, the Career Decision-Making Self-Efficacy Scale was developed by Taylor and Betz (1983). Fifty items covering five areas, for example, accurate self-appraisal, goal section, problem solving, are responded to with a 10-point confidence scale. The measure has been shown to have very good reliability and validity when used with college students.

Theoretical and Practical Strengths.   The specificity of the model, combined with statistical modeling techniques that can identify bidirectional causality, allow for more sophisticated hypotheses about the development of vocational behavior than any of the other models we have reviewed. Hackett and Lent (1992) reviewed the research that clearly supports the proposition that self-efficacy has had unique and additive statistical power, over that of abilities and interests, in explaining variance in both development of interests and job performance. For example, if persons of lower levels of aptitude for a particular task are divided into groups of those who have higher versus lower perceptions of self-efficacy, those who possess higher levels will be found to perform better, even though their aptitude is no greater than the other group. For counselors, most important data is that self-efficacy can be improved with "self-regulatory skills training programs" that provide both ways of attaining better performance outcomes and drawing more appropriate conclusions from those performances. When self-efficacy is improved, job performance improves. Examples of such effects may be found in the results of training programs designed for young women to increase their interest and performance in math and science. Lent and colleagues (1996) describe and illustrate a number of individual and group approaches for developing and modifying self-efficacy precepts; Chartrand (1996) also provides a very informative case illustration of what she calls the Sociocognitive Interactional Model for Career Counseling. As Brown and colleagues (1996) note, this approach probably has the best potential for remediating and overcoming the limitations in options and opportunities that gender and ethnicity have created for decades among what is actually the majority of our population.

Theoretical and Practical Limitations.   The complexities of triadic, bidirectional interactions make it extremely difficult to create a generalized model that can predict the particular direction any one individual—or even group of individuals—will take in choosing or changing their vocational behavior. Moreover, non–Anglos with long histories of realistic conclusions about discrimination may not respond to programs to increase self-efficacy nearly as quickly as Anglos. On the other side of the coin, persons who develop inflated senses of self-efficacy may create problems for themselves and/or others if they "get in over their heads."

The relationships of the various cognitive constructs such as self-efficacy to career status and vocational behaviors have not been clearly established in research studies (e.g., Solberg, Good, Fischer et al., 1995). There is much yet to be learned about the best educational and counseling strategies for modifying self-efficacy in efficient and effective ways that will enhance career choice and development. Yet, of all the theories reviewed in this chapter, there seems to be the greatest potential from this approach for more "giant steps forward" in career education and career interventions.

Cognitive Information and Decision-Making Theory

Historical Roots.   Recall that Parsons's (1909) model of career guidance had three steps: knowledge of self, knowledge of the world of work, and "true reasoning" of these two domains. Cognitive information and decision-making theory, as applied to vocational behavior by Peterson, Sampson, and Reardon (1991) focuses more specifically and extensively on the "true reasoning" step than any of the other career choice and development theories. Their work has been greatly enriched by the incorporation of the principles of cognitive information processing that were extensively developed by psychologists during the 1970s. The authors of such models (e.g., Newell & Simon, 1972) were focused largely on decision making in general; it remained for Peterson and colleagues (1991) to "translate" these principles into a coherent and useful set of strategies to assist individuals in career decision making.

Key Concepts.   The theory begins with four key assumptions:

> First, career problem solving and decision making involve affective as well as cognitive processes. . . . Second, the capability for career problem solving depends on the availability of cognitive operations as well as knowledge. . . . Third, career development involves continual growth and change in knowledge structures . . . Since both the occupational world and individuals are ever changing, the need to develop and integrate these domains never ceases. . . . Fourth, the development of career problem-solving and decision-making skills is accomplished through the enhancement of information-processing capabilities (Peterson, Sampson, Reardon, & Lenz, 1996, pp. 429–430).

The key components of the theory then focus on five steps in decision-making skills and three steps in the metacognition, or executive processing domain. They spell out a feedback loop of communication (identifying a gap), analysis (interrelating problem components), synthesis (creating likely alternatives), valuing (prioritizing), and execution (forming means–ends strategies). The metacognition, executive processing domain includes the following.

[S]*elf-talk* . . . Negative self-talk is often associated with chronic indecisiveness . . . whereas positive self-talk not only creates positive expectations . . . but also reinforces effective problem-solving behavior as well. *Self-awareness* . . . enables a problem solver to recognize such executive processes as the existence of debilitating negative self-talk, the need for more information, one's state in the problem-solving process, or the concurrent affective states that accelerate, retard, or confound the process. . . . *Monitoring and control* . . . Good problem solvers and decision makers sense when a sufficient amount of information has been acquired to move through each phase . . . They also sense when each phase is sufficiently completed to progress to the next phase or when one should backtrack to a preceding phase for a more thorough consideration (Peterson et al., 1996, pp. 438–439).

While all these key concepts may seem quite alien to the usual focus of career choice and development, it is precisely this unique focus that has allowed the writers to provide a seven-step generic process for counseling individuals or groups or in providing psycho–educational outreach programs (see Chapter 18). Their model is very user friendly for counselors and provides specifics for developing individualized learning plans for each situation.

Key Measures.   Keeping with the user friendly concept, the authors have developed the Career Thoughts Inventory (Sampson, Peterson, Lenz et al., 1996). There is also an accompanying workbook that can be totally self-administered—from high school through adulthood—including scoring, interpretation, and the completion of exercises to address negative thoughts, decision-making confusion, commitment anxiety, and external conflict.

Theoretical and Practical Strengths.   Given the young history of this most recently developed model, its strengths are more potential than actual. While it is still too soon to assess its empirical status, numerous hypotheses can be inferred from their flowchart types of thinking, which are all testable with computer models. Such testing may also yield important linkages with cognitive psychology as well as more fully explain career kinds of thinking. Its practical strength is found in the workbooks provided for clients that are quite adaptable for many age groups. It also seems likely that online versions of workbooks will soon be developed allowing for more self-administered programmed instruction in career development.

Theoretical and Practical Limitations.   As noted above, it is still too soon to assess the empirical status of the theory; that will become more evident in coming years. From a practical viewpoint, implementing the model's strategies for helping clients places counselors more in didactic and coaching roles than they usually prefer; some research will have to focus on how well counselors adapt to using the model. Finally, given that some of the ethnically diverse cultures in this country do not share a passion for rational decision making, some unique research and practice issues may be encountered when the model is used with ethnic populations who are not highly acculturated in the majority culture.

TWENTY-FIRST CENTURY-FRONTIERS: PARADIGMATIC SHIFTS AND/OR EXPANSIONS

While it is often risky to assess the historical significance of a decade when it has barely come to a close, we are willing to say that when the centennial history of counseling psychology is written in the late 2040s, the 1990s will be identified as a time of beginnings of expansions, and shifts in, paradigms used for the study of vocational behavior and career development. In this section we describe two major shifts that are occurring as many of the shortcomings of current theories and research, noted in the preceding sections, are more fully understood.

Before proceeding to an exploration of these shifts, it is important to explain what is meant by *paradigm* and the what, how, and why of paradigmatic shifts. Borgen (1992) provides an excellent description of the broader scientific issues in identifying paradigms and their impact. Citing Kuhn as the originator of the importance of paradigms, Borgen quotes Kuhn's (1970) definition of paradigms: "These I take to be universally recognized scientific achievements that for a time provide model problems and solutions to a community of practitioners" (p. viii). Kuhn notes that when there is a realization that things have gone wrong, or at least that there are some seemingly unremediable deficiencies in present models, then scientists begin to "shift" to other sets of models or viewpoints to see if better predictions and understandings can be obtained. Borgen (1992) chose to speak of expanding paradigms since he felt that many counseling psychologists were not abandoning traditional models but rather were using new theories and statistical techniques to make new analyses of old problems. Our next section on person–environment reciprocity is a good example where a paradigm is probably more in need of expansion than replacement. On the other hand, in the section on contextualism we will see there is a growing consensus that a paradigmatic shift is needed—indeed, that an expansion of present paradigms will not suffice. While only time will tell whether expanded or shifted paradigms will be more productive, for the time being the easy conclusion is that theorists and researchers need to expand and/or shift. Merely conducting further traditional tests of present models of career choice and development seems destined to be of questionable scientific and practical value.

Person–Environment Reciprocity Effects

Walsh and Chartrand (1994) have captured the essence of the need for an expansion of the person–environment interaction paradigm. "The theories of career choice and development tend to say a great deal about selection or occupational fit, but very little about evoking, cognitively restructuring, and manipulating processes" (Walsh & Chartrand, 1994, p. 193). While those who adhered to trait-oriented theories were among the first to recognize that there were interactions between persons and environments, the focus has long been simply on how one can use that interaction to achieve better fits between persons and jobs. What is needed is greater attention to the fact that, as we explored in Dawis's work adjustment theory, in numerous instances, work environments often change because of the natures of the individuals who have entered them. And, probably just as often, individuals change because they learn new things about themselves as they seek to adjust to a work environment that is not a natural fit for them. In short, persons affect environments, just as environments affect persons. A good fit at any given time may well become less of a good fit if *either* the person or the environment changes.

As examples of the last sentence, consider what would happen to a traditional "realistic" (using Holland's terms) environment if suddenly there was an influx of social types who were respected by the "realistic" employees. It is possible that there would be increased interactions between individuals, a greater willingness to be self-disclosing, a greater tolerance for at least a little less preciseness. (Yes, we know, some readers are saying it would never happen, but it has; university administrations often have "realistic" types who have "evolved," as they rose higher and higher in the university, into more "people-oriented" leaders.) If the "realistic" environment changes in that way, then if a new traditional "realistic" person enters that environment, the fit will not be as good as that in the prior environment. On the other side of the coin is how persons change. An example from managed care: Some psychologists who are very high on "social" and "investigative" scales on interest inventories, and would describe themselves as "not having an enterprising bone in my body" have found themselves reluctantly choosing some administrative roles in order to bring some humaneness to the managed care companies in which they work. Some of these psychologists have found that they are good administrators, valued by both their superiors and their colleagues, and they have then greatly increased their enterprising activities. It could reasonably be predicted that they, like others who have become administrators, may in later years of life, show greatly increased enterprising scores on interest measures. In short, their work environment changed their pattern of interests even many years into their careers.

We have used the word *reciprocity* in the heading for this section to recognize that these changes are bidirectional. There is at least a growing appreciation of this reciprocal influence apparent in the more recent presentations of many career development theories (Savickas & Lent, 1994) in which there are a number of figures indicating causal affects going both ways between sets of variables. These figures reflect the results from use of newer statistical modeling techniques. We are now beginning to understand that making predictions about vocational behavior requires an understanding of ongoing dynamic changes in both individuals and environments, each affecting the other. While we even now may be able to achieve reasonably good predictions for a group of individuals, the dynamics of reciprocity will mean that making predictions about any given individual will always be less than perfect. Moreover, whatever degree of accuracy a prediction has for a given time may have little to say about the accuracy of such a prediction for a future time.

The last sentence is especially critical for career counselors to be cognizant of when working with individuals. While achieving a good fit for a client at a given time may make the client satisfied with counseling, unless she or he has learned something about how individuals can shape environments, and vice versa, the good fit satisfaction may not be as enduring as both the client and counselor would like.

Constructivism and Contextualism

Throughout the first two-thirds of the twentieth century, social sciences, including psychology, relied primarily on the scientific paradigm of logical positivism; the paradigm that has so well served the physical sciences such as physics and chemistry: Develop theories with logical proofs, then collect empirical data and determine whether the data support or refute the theory. However, in the social sciences there is general agreement that logical positivism has not resulted in theories that are nearly as productive and supportable as those in the physical sciences. During the last third of the twentieth century, those social scientists who studied the philosophy of science and reviewed alternative paradigms, increasingly turned to constructivism. While numerous monographs and books have been published in recent decades describing and illustrating constructivism, Brown and colleagues (1996) concisely summarize the major propositions:

1. All aspects of the universe are interconnected; it is impossible to separate figure from ground, subject from object, people from their environments.

2. There are no absolutes; thus human functioning cannot be reduced to laws or principles, and cause and effect cannot be inferred.

3. Human behavior can only be understood in the context in which it occurs.

4. The subjective frame of reference of human beings is the only legitimate source of knowledge. Events occur outside human beings. As individuals understand their environments and participate in these events, they define themselves and their environments (p. 10).

A careful reading of these propositions, considered along with the limitations noted earlier in this chapter for each of the theories discussed, makes evident the attractiveness of a constructivist approach to the study of career choice and development. In one sense, constructivism is an elaboration and broad expansion of Rogers's (see Chapter 12) phenomenological views; that is, persons' subjective perspectives of self and environment guide behavior. Vondracek, Lerner, and Schulenberg (1986) and more recently Young, Valach, and Collin (1996) provide what they call a contextual approach to career, focusing on the context of any given career-relevant actions of an individual. While those authors elaborate a large number of constructs, most germane to the concerns discussed in the next two sections of this chapter is Young and colleagues' (1996) focus on three perspectives on action: manifest behavior, internal processes, and social meaning. To illustrate: One might observe two persons sitting next to each other reading this very paragraph (manifest behavior). Yet while the manifest behaviors of both are identical, one reader might be truly focused on the words and meanings, the other may be thinking primarily about getting lunch, and barely attending to these words (internal processes). One reader may be thinking that this material will clearly be on the next exam and therefore must be memorized if he or she is ever to receive a Ph.D. The other reader may be thinking this is like something he heard Bob talking about last week and would be interesting to discuss with Bob (social meaning). Obviously, despite equivalence of observable behavior, the eventual understanding and use each reader makes of this material might be extremely different!

In the next two sections, we focus on two factors that are known to radically affect the internal processes and social meanings related to career relevant behaviors. We then close the chapter with a brief discussion of the research and policy implications of including constructivist perspectives in the paradigms used to study vocational behavior.

Work: A Location in People's Lives

The heading for this section is taken from Richardson's (1993) provocative and insightful article. She provides four reasons why she objects to the word *career* compared to *work* and how we have hurt our own explorations of vocational behavior by ignoring so many other aspects of people's lives. Richardson argues that *career* is a concept that at best might be useful for understanding the vocational behavior of middle-class Anglo males, that it ignores *work* in the home and in caring for others, that it truncates what we can learn about what is truly important in people's lives, and finally, that "The concept of career is embedded in an ethos of self-centered individualism and in an ethnocentric conception of self. . . . that may contribute to undermining the social fabric of society and culture" (Richardson, 1993, p. 428). She is particularly distressed that counseling psychologists, who have worked with such a wide range of clients' concerns from eating disorders to identity development, from learning disabilities to self-actualization in retirement years, would try to understand vocational behavior using such a narrow focus as represented by the key concepts and measures in all of the theories discussed in the first half of this chapter. Obviously, Richardson believes we will not make significant advances in any further understanding of vocational behavior unless we shift our paradigm from career as central to people's lives to a paradigm that considers it as just one of many interacting roles.

In less dramatic fashion, both Super and Bordin, in their contributions to the Savickas and Lent (1994) volume, also argue that career theorists have neglected other major life roles. Moreover, empirical studies of women's career development have also clearly identified multiple roles, and the dilemmas they present women in our culture, as significant components in understanding the career development of women (Hackett, 1997; Weitzman, 1994).

The time has clearly come for more attention to the context provided by multiple roles in life, it may therefore be important to realize that the initial narrow focus of career theory that emerged in the 1950s, and held sway for many decades, was indeed a reflection of the zeitgeist of the time. In that era, men's identity, and perceived worth by themselves and others, was largely determined by their job. Their wives' and children's perceived worth were also greatly affected by the husband's–father's job. For a better appreciation of that perspective of the 1950s, read two of the very popular books of the era: *The Organization Man* (Whyte, 1956) and *The Man in the Gray Flannel Suit* (Wilson, 1955). One of the consequences of that perspective was that those workers who faced retirement in the last quarter of the twentieth century were often extremely reluctant to retire. Their reluctance was not so much because they loved their work, but because they at least vaguely felt they would lose a great deal of status and perceived worth once they were no longer working.

Culture: Attending to Previously Ignored Realities

Fitzgerald and Betz (1994) provide one of the most comprehensive overviews of current theoretical and empirical inadequacies in the literature on vocational behavior due to neglect of the influencing factors of gender, race, class, and sexual orientation. Moreover, Helms (1994) and Meyers, Haggins, and Speight (1994) describe numerous ways in which the salience of different worldviews and race have not been given adequate attention in theories of career choice and development. Fassinger (1995, 1996), Prince (1995), and Chung (1995) provide reviews of the effects of homophobia stigma on career identity, choice, and adjustment for gays and lesbians. All these authors provide numerous reasons for why career development is often not a meaningful concept for the *majority* of the population. Discrimination and oppression often limit both the real and *self-perceived* opportunities in the occupational structure; therefore, significant advancement and personal fulfillment in careers are often not viable options for women, ethnic minorities, lower socioeconomic class individuals, and lesbians and gays.

As Fitzgerald and Betz (1994), Leong (1995), and others have made clear, ethnic minorities have been tremendously underrepresented in the research on vocational behavior. It may be possible that the current theories can actually be somewhat useful.

> [T]here is no intrinsic reason to assume a priori that constructs such as congruence, career stages, and so forth are necessarily less applicable to non-white or working-class individuals. The point is that we simply do not know, mainly because we have not asked (Fitzgerald & Betz, 1994, p. 105).

These authors report that the increased study of women's vocational behavior suggest that available career theories may be useful for women who have surmounted the effects of traditional gender bias. They suggest, as corollary to this finding, that concepts such as racial identity and acculturation (see Chapter 6) may well be useful expansions of traditional paradigms for studying vocational behavior. Empirical evidence is now beginning to accumulate regarding how cultural influences are a significant component in causal models of career development of minority women (McWhirter, Hackett, & Bandalos, 1998) and therefore might be incorporated in expanded paradigms.

An alternative position, more evident in the writings of Richardson (1993) and Leung (1995), is that a paradigmatic shift is more essential than an expansion of paradigms. Leung (1995) argues that the differences in worldviews of ethnic minorities, along with all the issues about discrimination and oppression outlined by Fitzgerald and Betz (1994), and the issues of meaning of career noted by Richardson (1993), require that we seek to develop new models based on the inclusion of far more contextual data. Further, Leung (1995) notes that there are significant divergences among the four major ethnic groups in this country that may make it difficult to develop a single model, for example, "nontraditional" careers for African Americans (science, engineering) are in fact the "traditional" careers of the Asian American minority. All these authors agree that a shift to explicit and focused attention on these diverse cultures is essential if we are to develop theories about vocational behavior that will be valid for more than just middle-class Anglo males. Osipow and Littlejohn (1995) establish a foundation for a multicultural theory of career development. Richardson (1993) is willing to postulate that multicultural studies of work will also enhance our understanding of the career development and personal adjustment of Anglo males, as well as allow us, for the first time, to address, for all members of our society, long neglected social issues related to our occupational structure.

Research and Policy Implications

The paradigmatic shifts and expansions described above all have implications not only for those whom we study, but also for how and on what constructs and variables we collect data, then how we analyze and use the data. The new "whoms" we need to include in research were just described in the preceding paragraphs. While studies of the career psychology of women have rapidly increased in the past few decades (see special review section in the *Journal of Counseling Psychology* [1997], pp. 123–188), career relevant studies including ethnic minorities, gays, and lesbians are only now beginning to appear (e.g., Leong [1995] edited a volume on "Career Development and Vocational Behavior of Racial and Ethnic Minorities"; the special issue of the *Career Development Quarterly* [December 1995], on gay/lesbian career development; and Fassinger [1996]). Still extremely rare are studies of the lowest socioeconomic classes regardless of cultural background. Moreover, if the study of vocational behavior is to be put into the broader life contexts proposed above by Super, Bordin, and Richardson, then some studies must focus on young children, as Gottfredson's theory does, where many of the key elements of perceptions about self and the world of work begin to develop. At the other end of the chronological scale, retirement clearly includes an adjustment to changed vocational behavior roles and needs greater attention (Tinsley & Schwendener-Holt, 1992). Finally, the study of any one of these new groups needs to attend to the various demographic roles of a person. One is never just a woman, or just a child, or just a lower socioeconomic class subject. The multiple demographic roles one holds may well be critical parts of the interweavings of meaning that are critical to analyze. Such analyses can be made only if those collecting data ensure that full demographic data is obtained on each research participant.

The "how" and on "what" we collect data present two quite different sets of issues. Considering first the "what" part, as already described in Chapter 13, care must be taken when using any existing assessment instruments with culturally diverse populations not included in standardization samples. Further, studies of specific worldviews of various ethnic minority cultures (Leong, 1995) may suggest the need for some assessments for which there are no standardized measures. Variations in worldviews may also mean that choices of outcomes to study might include other than traditional measures of work satisfaction. While actually enjoying one's work might be seen as a desirable characteristic in the Anglo majority culture, for many minorities, pleasing one's family or making a clear contribution to one's community may far outweigh the importance of enjoying one's work when defining job satisfaction.

These considerations of what we collect data on lead nicely to a consideration of how we collect that data. To the extent that one sees expanding our paradigms as the most desirable route for enhancing the study of vocational behavior, then data will continue to be collected in many of the current ways, simply expanding the kinds of assessments made. On the other hand, to the extent that a clear paradigmatic shift is seen as essential, then, others argue, we need to incorporate qualitative constructivist approaches. Both Howard (1991, 1992) and Young et al. (1996) describe the importance of obtaining research participants' "coherent narratives" of work–life development. Using established qualitative techniques may provide researchers with their best opportunities to find totally new and unexpected variables to investigate in relation to vocational development and behaviors.

Regarding how we analyze such data, fortunately, in recent years, a variety of new statistical modeling techniques have emerged that allow for studying a wide range of variables and their sequential causal relationships with one another; a vital set of techniques for determining how person–environment reciprocity affect career behaviors. Also, as already made clear in Chapter 6, what we have learned about individual differences, within any given culturally diverse group, requires that our analyses include explicit attention to both between- and within-group differences. For example, Helms and Piper (1994) find significant variations in vocational perceptions and behaviors related to racial identity. Lastly, regarding how we analyze new data, just as we described the value of qualitative techniques in *collecting* data, we expect to see greater use of qualitative techniques in *analyses* of career data.

Finally, we come to the uses of the kinds of new data and analyses we have just described. If indeed there are both expansions of current paradigms as well as some paradigmatic shifts, then there is a clear potential for the study of vocational behavior to make far more significant contributions to our society at large, as well as to our individual clients. Harmon (1994) provides some thoughtful beginnings of such contributions in a subsection of her article titled "Can Theory Influence Practice and Policy?" Her short answer is yes; her longer answer is reflected in the overall title of her article, "Frustrations, Daydreams, and Realities of Theoretical Convergence" (Harmon, 1994). In Chapter 15 we will explore some of the emerging career interventions designed to address some long-enduring social problems such as persistent unemployment and underemployment, both of which are closely intertwined with major social problems such as interpersonal violence, drug abuse, and AIDs.

Just as importantly, we should keep within our range of focus the need to address quality of life issues even for those who are more fully integrated into the current occupational structure. Consider first consistently employed but unskilled workers. In the past two decades they have seen an actual decrease in spendable income, even after several increases in state and federal minimum wage laws. This loss of income has been exacerbated by losing various health and paid leave benefits as well. Combining this loss of benefits with loss of spending power leaves the unskilled making less than a fifth of the average income of the top 10% of wage earners, whereas that ratio was about one-fourth a little over 10 years ago. A different set of issues concerns all workers, but most especially managerial and professional positions. Consider the fact that 20-some years ago it was predicted that technological advances would result in significantly reduced workweeks for everyone. Yet in the past 20 years, the number of days typical employees take off from work has decreased from 21 to 16. More and more employees, as well as the self-employed, are engaged in increasing amounts of "overdoing." By this we mean more but less-defined workdays—computers, cell phones, and the like all add to this liability by allowing work to be done at home, in cars, even in health clubs while working out! Studies of occupationally related stress were essentially nonexistent in counseling psychologists' studies until the 1980s. Borgen (1991) was one of the first to note the emergence of a body of research in this area. Annual reviews of career research that appear quite regularly in journals such as the *Journal of Vocational Behavior* and the *Career Development Quarterly* now frequently include the small but growing number of studies on this topic.

What we have learned about vocational behavior in the past 50 years has brought us to new frontiers. The current vigor and productivity of career psychology combined with a growing willingness to expand our present paradigms, as well as shift to some new ones, will lead to an expansion of the contributions of counseling psychologists to a society that may be economically thriving but is increasingly full of hassles and frustrations for all.

SUMMARY

Career psychology is one of the oldest and most central components of counseling psychology. The most distinctive theoretical and empirical contributions counseling psychology has made to the discipline of psychology are in the area of career development. We described how the robustness of career psychology as a field of research and practice, for nearly 100 years, is no doubt related to the implications of career psychology for both individual and societal well-being. Decades of research have shown that career adjustment is vital for both the mental and physical health of individuals as well as for the economic and social health of a society.

The major part of this chapter was devoted to the presentation of three diverse approaches to the study of career psychology. We explored how each of these approaches is rooted in, and now contributes to, mainstream psychological research emphases. Two or three theories were described to illustrate the developments within each approach.

Trait-oriented theories began to develop in the early part of the nineteenth century when much psychological research was focused on measurement. Early theories were known as trait and factor and emphasized matching individual abilities to job requirements. The later theoretical developments of this type that we explored included Holland's theory of vocational personalities and work environments and Dawis's theory of work adjustment. Holland's RIASEC model has proved extraordinarily valuable in generating new research and innovative career counseling interventions that attend more to a congruence of persons' assessment of themselves and job environments than to a matching of persons' abilities and job requirements. The work of Dawis and colleagues has focused more on adults in the work world than on career choice. Their theory and research about how *both* individuals and work environments reciprocally change each other, as workers remain in positions for long time periods, has great potential for both industrial–organizational psychologists and counseling psychologists. Our clients as well as our society all benefit when we can facilitate high levels of worker satisfaction as well as organizational productivity.

Developmental theories of career development emerged largely in the middle of the twentieth century just as psychology as a discipline was attending much more to developmental processes. These theories focus highly on "how" career choices are made compared to "what" choices are made. Donald Super's lifetime of work in developing a life span stage theory of career development has stimulated a great deal of innovative research and new psychological assessments (e.g., work salience). His research findings radically altered the nature of career guidance for young adolescents. The more recent developmental work of Gottfredson has focused on how very young children circumscribe their career choices and goals based on societal stereotypes about gender, social class, and intelligence. Counseling psychologists can learn a great deal from her research about how we need to help our society understand, and then make the necessary changes to reduce, the severely limiting effects of the stereotypes being conveyed in the media and in our communities. The last developmental theory we presented was Bordin's ego psychological model. His theory is particularly useful in explaining why clients often seem "stuck" when trying to make a career choice and/or keep repeating behaviors that are dysfunctional for their careers.

Social learning and cognition theories of career choice and development have been the most recent to develop, reflecting again the emphases in psychology at large; cognitive learning theories emerged largely after 1960. Krumboltz and colleagues were the first to incorporate basic principles of learning and generalization to help us understand what goes on in the minds of individuals as they make career choices. How do individuals come to believe what they do about both themselves and the world of work? This model has been especially useful in examining how various mistaken beliefs lead to unsatisfactory vocational choices. The specificity of the model has been particularly helpful in devising new kinds of career assessments and interventions to rectify individuals' inappropriate beliefs about themselves and the world of work. The recent social cognitive theory of Lent, Brown, and Hackett was built on self-efficacy research results. Here the focus is on people as active agents in shaping their career choices and development. With research that shows that persons' perceptions of their own self-efficacy do add significantly to the predictability of satisfactory career choice, more attention is now being given to the development of preventive-oriented "self-regulatory skills training programs." Whether participants are math students or computer salespeople, when self-efficacy improves, so do classroom or job performance. The most recent of the social learning and cognitive theories is the cognitive information and decision-making theory of Peterson, Sampson, and Reardon. Building on recent advances generated by computer models, they are attempting to "translate" these models into a coherent and useful set of strategies for career decision making. Their model focuses almost exclusively on the "true meaning" reasoning part of Parsons's original model, adding greatly increased specification to "how" that reasoning can best be guided, through specified feedback loops, to arrive at an efficient, qualitatively good decision. While Parsons, from 1909, might find their seven-step true reasoning process a bit mind-boggling, today's Internet users may find the work of Peterson, Sampson, and Reardon truly user friendly for working through career decisions and career dilemmas.

In our final section of this chapter, we showed how that, concurrent with the advances reviewed, there was a growing awareness of significant shortcomings in the applicability of much career theory and research to the diversity of workers in contemporary society. By the beginning of the twenty-first century, innovative thinkers and researchers in career psychology had established the foundations for expanding traditional strategies as well as incorporating shifts to new ways of looking at the world of work. We described how and why strategies to study person–environment interactions need to be expanded, paying greater attention to how we can change work environments as well as to how work environments change people. Totally new strategies for career theory and research have emerged from the more qualitative approaches of constructivism and contextualism. These new models will permit greater attention to both (a) the multiple roles in all our lives, of which work is only one; and (b) the effects of culture on the choices people make about work and its meanings in their lives. We concluded by showing how counseling psychologists, by combining the advances from the past 50 years with these new and expanded paradigms, will be well poised to address both societal and individual issues in the world of work in the twenty-first century.

REFERENCES

Bandura, A. (1986). *Social foundations of thought and action: A social cognitive theory.* Englewood Cliffs, NJ: Prentice-Hall.

Bluestein, D. L., Walbridge, M. M., Friedlander, M. L., & Palladino, D. E. (1991). Contributions of psychological separation and parental attachment to the career development process. *Journal of Counseling Psychology, 38,* 39–50.

Bolles, R. N. (1998). *What color is your parachute?* Berkeley, CA: Ten Speed Press.

Bordin, E. S. (1990). Psychodynamic model of career choice and satisfaction. In D. Brown, L. Brooks, & Associates (Eds.), *Career choice and development* (2nd ed., pp. 102–144). San Francisco: Jossey-Bass.

Bordin, E. S., Nachman, B., & Segal, S. J. (1963). An articulated framework for vocational development. *Journal of Counseling Psychology, 10,* 107–116.

Borgen, F. H. (1991). Megatrends and milestones in vocational behavior: A 20-year counseling psychology retrospective. *Journal of Vocational Behavior, 39,* 263–290.

Borgen, F. H. (1992). Expanding scientific paradigms in counseling psychology. In S. D. Brown and R. W. Lent (Eds.), *Handbook of counseling psychology* (pp. 111–140). New York: John Wiley & Sons.

Brown, D., Brooks, L., & Associates (1990). *Career choice and development* (2nd ed.) San Francisco: Jossey-Bass.

Brown, D., Brooks, L., & Associates (1996). *Career choice and development* (3rd ed.). San Francisco: Jossey-Bass.

Chartrand, J. M. (1996). Linking theory with practice: A sociocognitive interactional model for career counseling. In M. L. Savickas and W. B. Walsh (Eds.), *Handbook of career counseling theory and practice* (pp. 121–134). Palo Alto, CA: Davies-Black Publishing.

Chung, Y. B. (1995). Career decision making of lesbian, gay, and bisexual individuals. *The Career Development Quarterly, 44,* 178–190.

Cohen, C. R., Chartrand, J. M., & Jowdy, D. P. (1995). Relationships between career indecision subtypes and ego identity development. *Journal of Counseling Psychology, 42,* 440–447.

Corbishley, M. A., & Yost, E. B. (1989). Assessment and treatment of dysfunctional cognitions in career counseling. *Career Planning and Adult Development Journal, 5,* 20–26.

Crites, J. O. (1969). *Vocational psychology.* New York: McGraw-Hill.

Dawis, R. V. (1996). The theory of work adjustment and person–environment–correspondence counseling. In D. Brown, L. Brooks, & Associates (Eds.), *Career choice and development* (3rd ed., pp. 75–120). San Francisco: Jossey-Bass.

Dawis, R. V., Dohm, T. E., Lofquist, L. H., Chartrand, J. M., & Due, A. M. (1987). *Minnesota Occupational Classification System III.* Minneapolis: Vocational Psychology Research, Department of Psychology, University of Minnesota.

Dawis, R. V., England, G. W., & Lofquist, L. H. (1964). A theory of work adjustment. *Minnesota Studies in Vocational Rehabilitation, No. XV,* 1–27.

Dawis, R. V., & Lofquist, L. H. (1978). A note on the dynamics of work adjustment. *Journal of Vocational Behavior, 12,* 76–79.

Erikson, E. (1950). *Childhood and society.* New York: Norton.

Fassinger, R. E. (1995). From invisibility to integration: Lesbian identity in the workplace. *The Career Development Quarterly, 44,* 148–167.

Fassinger, R. E. (1996). Notes from the margins: Integrating lesbian experience into the vocational psychology of women. *Journal of Vocational Behavior, 48,* 160–175.

Fitzgerald, L. F., & Betz, N. E. (1994). Career development in cultural context: The role of gender, race, class, and sexual orientation. In M. L. Savickas and R. W. Lent (Eds.), *Convergence in career development theories* (pp. 103–118). Palo Alto, CA: CPP Books.

Gelso, C. J., & Fassinger, R. E. (1992). Personality, development, and counseling psychology: Depth, ambivalence, and actualization. *Journal of Counseling Psychology, 39,* 275–298.

Gottfredson, G. D., Jones, E. M., & Holland, J. L. (1993). Personality and vocational interests: The relation of Holland's six interest dimensions to five robust dimensions of personality. *Journal of Counseling Psychology, 40,* 518–524.

Gottfredson, L. S. (1981). Circumscription and compromise: A developmental theory of occupational aspirations. *Journal of Counseling Psychology, 28,* 545–579.

Gottfredson, L. S. (1996). Gottfredson's theory of circumscription and compromise. In D. Brown, L. Brooks, & Associates (Eds.), *Career choice and development* (3rd ed., pp. 179–232). San Francisco: Jossey-Bass.

Hackett, G. (1997). Promise and problems in theory and research on women's career development. *Journal of Counseling Psychology, 44,* 184–188.

Hackett, G., & Betz, N. E. (1981). A self-efficacy approach to the career development of women. *Journal of Vocational Behavior, 18,* 326–336.

Hackett, G., & Lent, R. W. (1992). Theoretical advances and current inquiry in career psychology. In S. D. Brown and R. W. Lent (Eds.), *Handbook of counseling psychology* (pp. 419–452). New York: John Wiley & Sons.

Harmon, L. (1994). Frustrations, daydreams, and realities of theoretical convergence. In M. L. Savickas and R. W. Lent (Eds.), *Convergence in career development theories* (pp. 225–234). Palo Alto, CA: CPP Books.

Helms, J. (1994). Racial identity and career assessment. *Journal of Career Assessment, 2,* 199–209.

Helms, J. E., & Piper, R. E. (1994). Implications of racial identity theory for vocational psychology. *Journal of Vocational Behavior, 44,* 124–138.

Holland, J. L. (1985). *The Vocational Preference Inventory.* Odessa, FL: Psychological Assessment Resources.

Holland, J. L. (1994). *Self-directed Search Form R* (4th ed.). Odessa, FL: Psychological Assessment Resources.

Holland, J. L. (1996). Exploring careers with a typology: What we have learned and some new directions. *American Psychologist, 51,* 397–406.

Holland, J. L. (1997). *Making vocational choices* (3rd ed.). Odessa, FL: Psychological Assessment Resources.

Holland, J. L., Johnston, J. A., & Asama, N. F. (1993). The Vocational Identity Scale: A diagnostic and treatment tool. *Journal of Career Assessment, 1,* 1–12.

Howard, G. S. (1991). Culture tales: Narrative approach to thinking, cross-cultural psychology, and psychotherapy. *American Psychologist, 46,* 187–197.

Howard, G. S. (1992). Behold our creation! What counseling psychology has become and might yet become. *Journal of Counseling Psychology, 39,* 419–442.

Keller, K. E., Biggs, D. S., & Gysbers, N. C. (1982). Career counseling from a cognitive perspective. *Personnel and Guidance Journal, 60,* 367–370.

Krumboltz, J. D. (1991). *Manual for the Career Beliefs Inventory.* Palo Alto, CA: Consulting Psychologists Press.

Krumboltz, J. D., & Baker, R. D. (1973). Behavioral counseling for vocational decision. In H. Borow (Ed.), *Career guidance for a new age* (pp. 143–186). Boston: Houghton Mifflin.

Krumboltz, J. D., Mitchell, A. M., & Jones, G. B. (1976). A social learning theory of career selection. *The Counseling Psychologist, 6*(1), 71–80.

Kuhn, T. S. (1970). *The structure of scientific revolutions.* Chicago: University of Chicago Press.

Lapan, R. T., & Jingeleski, J. (1992). Circumscribing vocational aspirations in junior high school. *Journal of Counseling Psychology, 39,* 81–90.

Lent, R. W., Brown, S. D., & Hackett, G. (1996). Career development for a social cognitive perspective. In D. Brown, L. Brooks, & Associates (Eds.), *Career choice and development* (3rd ed., pp. 373–421). San Francisco: Jossey-Bass.

Leong, F. T. L. (1995). *Career development and vocational behavior of racial and ethnic minorities.* Mahwah, NJ: Lawrence Erlbaum.

Leung, S. A. (1993). Circumscription and compromise: A replication study with Asian Americans. *Journal of Counseling Psychology, 40,* 188–193.

Leung, S. A. (1995). Career development and counseling: A multicultural perspective. In J. G. Ponterotto, J. M. Casas, L. A. Suzuki, and C. M. Alexander (Eds.), *Handbook of multicultural counseling* (pp. 549–566). Thousand Oaks, CA: Sage Publications.

Levin, A. S., Krumboltz, J. D., & Krumboltz, B. L. (1995). *Exploring your career beliefs: A workbook for the Career Beliefs Inventory with techniques for integrating your Strong and MBTI results.* Palo Alto, CA: Consulting Psychologists Press.

Loftquist, L. H., & Dawis, R. V. (1984). Research on work adjustment and satisfaction: Implications for career counseling. In S. D. Brown and R. W. Lent (Eds.), *Handbook of counseling psychology* (pp. 216–237). New York: John Wiley & Sons.

McWhirter, E. H., Hackett, G., & Bandalos, D. L. (1998). A causal model of the educational plans and career expectations of Mexican American high school girls. *Journal of Counseling Psychology, 45,* 166–181.

Meyers, L. J., Haggins, K. L., & Speight, S. (1994). Optimal theory and career assessment: Toward an inclusive, global perspective. *Journal of Career Assessment, 2,* 289–303.

Mitchell, L. K., & Krumboltz, J. D. (1984). Social learning approaches to career decision making. In D. Brown, L. Brooks, & Associates (Eds.), *Career choice and development* (pp. 235–280). San Francisco: Jossey-Bass.

Mitchell, L. K., & Krumboltz, J. D. (1996). Krumboltz's learning theory of career choice and counseling. In D. Brown, L. Brooks, & Associates (Eds.), *Career choice and development* (3rd ed., pp. 233–280). San Francisco: Jossey-Bass.

Nevill, D. D., & Super, D. E. (1986). *The Salience Inventory manual: Theory, application, and research.* Palo Alto, CA: Consulting Psychologists Press.

Nevo, O. (1987). Irrational expectations in career counseling and their confronting arguments. *Career Development Quarterly, 35,* 239–250.

Newell, A., & Simon, H. (1972). *Human problem solving.* Englewood Cliffs, NJ: Prentice-Hall.

Osipow, S. H. (1983). *Theories of career development* (3rd ed.). Englewood Cliffs, NJ: Prentice-Hall.

Osipow, S. H., & Fitzgerald, L. (1996). *Theories of career development* (4th ed.). Needham Heights, MA: Allyn & Bacon.

Osipow, S. H., & Littlejohn, E. M. (1995). Toward a multicultural theory of career development. In F. T. L. Leong (Ed.), *Career development and vocational behavior of racial and ethnic minorities* (pp. 251–262). Mahwah, NJ: Lawrence Erlbaum.

Palmore, E. (1969). Predicting longevity. *The Gerontologist, 9,* 247–250.

Parsons, F. (1909). Choosing a vocation. Boston: Houghton Mifflin.

Peterson, G. W., Sampson, J. P., & Reardon, R. C. (1991). *Career development and services: A cognitive approach.* Pacific Grove, CA: Brooks/Cole.

Peterson, G. W., Sampson, J. P., Reardon, R. C., & Lenz, J. G. (1996). A cognitive information processing approach to career problem solving and decision making. In D. Brown, L. Brooks, & Associates (Eds.), *Career choice and development* (3rd ed., pp. 423–475). San Francisco: Jossey-Bass.

Prince, J. P. (1995). Influences on the career development of gay men. *The Career Development Quarterly, 44,* 168–177.

Richardson, M. S. (1993). Work in people's lives: A location for counseling psychologists. *Journal of Counseling Psychology, 40,* 425–433.

Roe, A., & Lunneborg, P. W. (1990). Personality development and career choice. In D. Brown, L. Brooks, & Associates (Eds.), *Career choice and development* (2nd ed., pp. 68–102). San Francisco: Jossey-Bass.

Rounds, J., & Tracey, T. J. (1996). Cross-cultural structural equivalence of RIASEC models and measures. *Journal of Counseling Psychology, 43,* 310–329.

Russell, R. K., & Petrie, T. A. (1992). Academic adjustment of college students: Assessment and counseling. In S. D. Brown and R. W. Lent (Eds.), *Handbook of counseling psychology* (pp. 485–512). New York: John Wiley & Sons.

Ryan, J. M., Tracey, T. J. G., & Rounds, J. (1996). Generalizability of Holland's structure of vocational interests across ethnicity, gender, and socioeconomic status. *Journal of Counseling Psychology, 43,* 330–337.

Sampson, J. P. Jr., Peterson, G. W., Lenz, J. G., Reardon, R. C., & Saunders, D. E. (1996). *Career Thoughts Inventory.* Odessa, FL: Psychological Assessment Resources.

Savickas, M. L., & Lent, R. W. (1994). *Convergence in career development theories.* Palo Alto, CA: CPP Books.

Skinner, B. F. (1938). *The behavior of organisms: An experimental analysis.* New York: Appleton.

Solberg, V. S., Good, G. E., Fischer, A. R., Brown, S. D., & Nord, D. (1995). Career decision making and career search activities: Relative effects of career search self-efficacy and human agency. *Journal of Counseling Psychology, 42,* 448–455.

Super, D. E. (1942). *The dynamics of vocational adjustment.* New York: HarperCollins.

Super, D. E. (1953). A theory of vocational development. *American Psychologist, 8,* 185–190.

Super, D. E. (1957). *The psychology of careers.* New York: Harper & Row.

Super, D. E. (1963). Self-concepts in vocational development. In D. E. Super, R. Starishevsky, N. Matlin, and J. P. Jordaan (Eds.), *Career development: Self-concept theory* (pp. 17–32). New York: College Entrance Examination Board.

Super, D. E. (1994). A life span, life space perspective on convergence. In M. L. Savickas and R. W. Lent (Eds.), *Convergence in career development theories* (pp. 63–74). Palo Alto, CA: CPP Books.

Super, D. E., Sverko, B., & Super, C. M. (Eds.). (1995). *Life roles, values, and careers: International findings of the Work Importance Study.* San Francisco: Jossey-Bass.

Super, D. E., Thompson, A. S., Lindeman, R. H., Jordaan, J. P., & Myers, R. A. (1981). *Career Development Inventory.* Palo Alto, CA: Consulting Psychologists Press.

Swanson, J. L. (1996). The theory is the practice: Trait-and-factor/person-environment fit counseling. In M. L. Savickas and W. B. Walsh (Eds.), *Handbook of career counseling theory and practice* (pp. 93–108). Palo Alto, CA: Davies-Black Publishing.

Taylor, K. M., & Betz, N. E. (1983). Applications of self-efficacy theory to the understanding and treatment of career indecision. *Journal of Vocational Behavior, 22,* 63–81.

Tinsley, D. J., & Schwendener-Holt, M. J. (1992). Retirement and leisure. In S. D. Brown and R. W. Lent (Eds.), *Handbook of counseling psychology* (pp. 627–664). New York: John Wiley & Sons.

Vondracek, F. W., Lerner, R. M., & Schulenberg, J. E. (1986). *A life-span contextual approach to career development.* Hillsdale, NJ: Lawrence Erlbaum.

Walsh, W. B., & Chartrand, J. M. (1994). Emerging directions of person–environment fit. In M. L. Savickas and R. W. Lent (Eds.), *Convergence in career development theories* (pp. 187–195). Palo Alto, CA: CPP Books.

Walsh, W. B., & Osipow, S. H. (1995). *Handbook of vocational psychology: Theory, research, and practice* (2nd ed.). Mahwah, NJ: Lawrence Erlbaum.

Wampold, B. E., Ankarlo, G., Mondin, G., Trinidad-Carillo, M., Baumler, B., & Prater, K. (1995). Social skills of and social environments produced by different Holland types: A social perspective on person–environment fit models. *Journal of Counseling Psychology, 42,* 365–379.

Weiss, D. J., Dawis, R. V., Lofquist, L. V., Gay, E., & Hendel, D. D. (1975). *The Minnesota Importance Questionnaire.* Minneapolis: University of Minnesota, Department of Psychology, Work Adjustment Project.

Weitzman, L. M. (1994). Multiple-role realism: A theoretical framework for the process of planning to combine career and family roles. *Applied & Preventive Psychology, 3,* 15–25.

Westbrook, B. W. (1983). Career maturity: The concept, the instrument, and the research. In W. B. Walsh and S. H. Osipow (Eds.), *Handbook of vocational psychology. Vol. 1* (pp. 263–303). Hillsdale, NJ: Lawrence Erlbaum.

Whyte, W. (1956). *The organization man.* New York: Simon & Schuster.

Wilson, S. (1955). *The man in the gray flannel suit.* New York: Simon & Schuster.

Young, R. A., Valach, L., & Collin, A. (1996). A contextual explanation of career. In D. Brown, L. Brooks, & Associates (Eds.), *Career choice and development* (pp. 477–512, 3rd ed.). San Francisco: Jossey-Bass.

CAREER COUNSELING AND CAREER INTERVENTIONS

The title of this chapter includes the two slightly different terms of career counseling and career interventions for a specific reason. For much of the public, and even the profession of psychology, career counseling connotes an individual counselor administering some tests to a client who has not decided which job/career to pursue, then telling the client what to decide. As early as 1991, Spokane (1991) described that particular perception of career counseling as already 30 years out of date. Since the 1960s, there has been a steady increase in development of new interventions, built upon the theories and research described in Chapter 14, that addresses both individual problems with, and social concerns about, the world of work. These interventions range from highly structured classroom activities, to computer-assisted interventions, to job clubs, to individualized relationships that are essentially indistinguishable from personal counseling. Because all but the latter type of these interventions are quite different from most people's conceptions of career counseling, we use *career interventions* as the encompassing term. Like Spokane (1991), we define *career interventions* as "Any activity (treatment or effort) designed to enhance a person's career development or to enable that person to make more effective career decisions" (p. 22).

The primary goal of this chapter is to acquaint the reader with the very broad range of career and world-of-work interventions that have been, and continue to be, developed by counseling psychologists. Following an initial section that identifies some contemporary world-of-work issues concerning the continued use of the word *career* compared to words like *work* and *occupation,* the very broad range of contemporary career interventions is presented within five different dimensions. We then provide examples of three quite diverse interventions, illustrating all the different dimensions.

Following these examples is an overview of studies of the processes and outcomes of career interventions. These studies have provided very favorable results for a broad range of career interventions but, as we review, there is much to be learned about what it is in these interventions that can most efficiently and effectively lead to positive outcomes. Moreover, there has clearly been one small group of clients who have not easily benefited from career interventions. These indecisive clients, as they have come to be called, provide the ultimate challenge for career counselors. From attempts to enhance services for them, counseling psychologists have learned a great deal about the values of differential diagnosis, treatment planning, and the relationships of psychotherapy to career counseling: are all reviewed in the section on indecisive clients.

The last major sections of this chapter describe, first, the evolving markets and new frontiers in career interventions and, second, the current issues that must be addressed in contemporary training programs to ensure that counseling psychologists are prepared to provide effective career interventions in these new settings.

Are Reports of the Death of Career Greatly Exaggerated?

The world of work at the beginning of the twenty-first century is indeed a quite different place from the world of work in the middle of the twentieth century. As Herr (1996) spells out quite clearly, the globalization of the world economy, a world oversupply of labor (except for highly computer-literate positions), and the establishment of "contingent"—that is, temporary workforces—all have affected earlier patterns of career stability. Today's clients may have grandparents who worked for the same employer for most of their adult working years, but it is unlikely that their parents did so. Even if their parents kept working in the same position, the chances are that mergers or acquisitions meant a change in employer, even if the job did not change. Others were "downsized" out of their positions after 20 or 30 years of highly rated work performance. While experts differ on the exact number of positions an adult can now be expected to hold during the 30–40 working years, the number 7 is frequently cited. Not the one, two, or three positions of past generations, but now 5–10 or more, not counting the odd jobs of adolescence or part-time work during college years. Herr (1996) raises questions about whether we need new theories to take these kinds of changes into account in our career counseling; Meara (1996) argues that we at least need to make our assumptions explicit to our clients and ourselves. That is, we, as counseling psychologists, still believe being future-oriented and rationally planful is the best way to cope with the vicissitudes of the contemporary world of work and that we hold those beliefs even though, for many workers in contemporary society, such beliefs seem to offer less promise for success than they did in the twentieth century.

The concept of career as Super used the word (see Chapter 14), referring to a pattern of related employment and activities throughout the life span, may certainly appear challenged by current world-of-work trends. Yet, in one sense, his underlying concept becomes even more critical as a worker is forced to seek multiple jobs. Every approach reviewed in Chapter 14 confirmed the need for individuals to understand that job satisfaction and satisfactory performance were related to some fit between person characteristics and the work environment. No longer will it be a one-time fit; now a career will truly span a variety of "fits." The remainder of this chapter should be read with the perspective that career interventions must help individuals perceive that there are always a wide range of possible fits that can be discovered with extended effort and that one can indeed learn useful strategies for finding satisfactory fits. Krumboltz (1996) astutely states that the goal of career counseling in today's world should be

> . . . to facilitate the learning of skills, interests, beliefs, values, work habits, and personal qualities that enable each client to create a satisfying life within a constantly changing work environment. The task of career counselors is to promote client learning. Thus, career counselors can be seen as coaches, educators and mentors—not simply matchmakers (p. 61).

INTERVENTION DIVERSITY

The incredible array of career interventions now being offered by counseling psychologists can perhaps best be comprehended by looking at how interventions vary along at least five different dimensions: questions asked, populations, strategic goals, theoretical orientation, and techniques. Our choice of these five dimensions has been determined by our review of the growing literature on types of career interventions. While the dimensions are certainly not mutually exclusive, nor the components within each dimension, each dimension does lead to a somewhat different emphasis and format for career interventions. For each of the components within these dimensions there is at least some literature describing how to conduct a pertinent career intervention. Many citations will be provided here; additional information regarding career interventions may be found in texts such as those by Spokane (1991), Sharf (1992), and Gysbers, Heppner, and Johnston (1997). For an exploration of underlying concepts and issues in the appropriate *use* of this variety of interventions, compared to descriptions of strategies, the 1996 handbook by Savickas and Walsh is an excellent resource.

Questions Addressed

Savickas (1996), in articulating his framework for career interventions, identifies six different questions that career clients ask. Each of these questions calls for different kinds of interventions, often offered by different kinds of agencies. The six questions are: (1) How do I get a job? (2) What shall I choose? (3) Who am I? (4) How do I shape my career? (5) How can work help me grow as a person? and (6) How can I do better? While well-trained counseling psychologists might be prepared to offer services to address each of these career related questions, it is usually true that, depending on the question they have, students, workers, or clients will go to different agencies. For example, to get help with the first question, one might go to a job placement service; whereas for the third question one would most likely seek personal counseling; for the last question a worker might well go to the human resources services of his or her present employer.

Populations

There are three important subdimensions of the populations dimension to which career interventions are offered: age, gender, and cultural diversity. Counseling psychologists are continuing to learn about needed variations in career interventions when the population of participants is very different from the middle-class Anglo males who were the initial focus of most of the early theory and research on career interventions.

Looking first at age, it is important to note that career interventions now truly cover the life span, even though the primary focus of career counseling theory and research has often been the adolescent and young adult years. An example of one of the youngest age groups for career interventions is the preschool children who were provided with cognitive restructuring exercises in order to expand their interests (Barak, Shiloh, & Haushner, 1992). The positive results they obtained for both males and females suggest that much of the stereotyping and narrowing of interests found in children of young ages (see review of Gottfredson's theory in Chapter 14) can be overcome by interventions at the preschool level. At the other end of the age span, career counseling has been modified to suit the needs of retirees, all of whom are facing new life role decisions that will impact both their psychological and physical health (Fretz & Merikangas, 1992; Tinsley & Schwendener-Holt, 1992).

There is an accumulation of over three decades of literature on special issues in interventions designed to enhance women's career development. For career counselors, the single best resource regarding the critical components in a broad range of effective career interventions for women may be found in the diverse articles in *Career Counseling with Women* edited by Walsh and Osipow (1994).

It was not until the 1990s that significant numbers of published literature began to appear regarding issues in and strategies for career counseling with racial and ethnic minorities. Arbona (1996), Bingham and Ward (1996), Fouad and Bingham (1995), and Leong (1993) all provide excellent resources and practical aids for career counselors working with ethnic minorities. Bingham and Ward's (1996) Multicultural Career Counseling Checklist, carefully used, will greatly enhance all counselors' abilities to be sensitive to unique issues in career counseling with ethnic minorities. Gays and lesbians is another cultural minority for which specific guidelines regarding career counseling has emerged. Pope (1995) identified 15 articles with special recommendations for career counseling with gays and lesbians. The focus of these recommendations, each with a supporting rationale, ranged from counselors' examination of their own biases and learning about lesbian identity development to how to help clients come out in the workplace and how to work with partners of gay and lesbian clients regarding dual-career couple issues. Unlike a few decades ago, there is now pertinent literature to guide career counselors working with culturally diverse populations.

Strategic Objectives

Although career counseling is stereotypically regarded as a "remedial" intervention to address some career-related decision making or work dysfunction, the actual objective of an increasing array of career interventions is to fulfill the developmental and/or preventive roles of counseling psychologists outlined in Chapter 1 of this text. It may be useful to repeat Jordaan, Myers, Layton, and Morgan's (1968) brief definitions of the developmental, preventive, and remedial roles; illustrations of career interventions matching those descriptions are then provided for each.

The developmental role is to "help individuals to plan, obtain, and derive maximum benefits from the kinds of experiences which will enable them to discover and develop their potentialities" (Jordaan et al., 1968, p. 1). Recall how the research on Super's developmental approach, as reviewed in Chapter 14, became the basis for career education programs for junior and senior high school students. All students take part in such programs, but the programs are not a "fix" for some dysfunction. Spokane (1991) provides a brief overview of a range of developmentally oriented career education programs. Moreover, in large industries and governmental agencies there may now be career development centers. One of the key functions of such centers is to help employees learn more about ways in which they can advance their careers. Employers know that many employees see such centers as a valuable benefit, thereby enhancing employees' morale and perceptions of their employer. Employers also know that some of their most talented and motivated employees will become better prepared for advancement within the company if they take part in the various programs offered in a career development center. Lea and Leibowitz (1992) and Gerstein and Shullman (1992) provide useful information regarding the nature of industry-based career development programs.

The preventive role is to "anticipate, circumvent, and, if possible, forestall difficulties that may arise in the future" (Jordaan et al., 1968, p. 1). Recall the example of the work of Barak and colleagues (1992) cited in the section above on age, regarding an intervention with preschool children to overcome narrow perspectives on interests. Such an intervention is indeed designed to forestall difficulties that may arise because of overly circumscribed interests. Fuller, Blinne, and Johnston (1994) administered Holland's "My Vocational Situation" to all first-year college students in their institution as an outreach program to identify those students most in need of career planning. They then provided these students with career intervention opportunities so that their career-choice problems did not reach crisis level. Outplacement counseling, a concept that has grown rapidly as many companies "downsize"— that is, dismiss many satisfactory employees—is most often seen by the dismissed employees as a way of helping them get another job. In one sense that is the purpose of outplacement, but the more important reason for having the "dismissing" company provide the outplacement counseling is to prevent the significant personal and family dysfunction that comes with unemployment (Mallinckrodt & Fretz, 1988).

The remedial role is used when something is awry, needs to be "fixed." This role is, of course, the role most people assume is being served by career counseling: a client can't seem to find a satisfactory choice or has a work adjustment problem that needs to be addressed. To help make the distinction of remedial career counseling from other kinds of career interventions, Lowman (1993) uses the phrase "counseling of work dysfunction" and has chapters on topics such as work-related anxiety and depression, overcommitment to work, and so forth.

Theoretical Orientations

Almost every career intervention—no matter which question is being addressed, for whatever population, with whichever strategic objective—will typically be framed primarily within one of the theoretical orientations reviewed in Chapter 14. A rereading of that material would clearly lead to the realization that some fits between theory and certain questions to be addressed, or between theory and a chosen strategic objective, will be more "natural." Developmental theory leads quite naturally to interventions with a developmental strategic objective, perhaps addressed to the question "How can work help me grow as a person?" A social learning theory approach is a most natural fit for remedial interventions for a client "stuck" on the question of "What shall I choose?" Trait-oriented approaches play a key role in outplacement counseling, helping the person see a new and larger array of opportunities than were considered while satisfactorily employed, thereby preventing some of the stress and despair of just throwing oneself on the job market looking for any paying job. Sharf (1992) is the single best resource for seeing how each of the major theories of career development can be "translated" into career counseling practice.

Techniques

The dimension of techniques differs qualitatively from the first four dimensions just reviewed. While each career intervention typically has a primary focus on one question, with one population, with one strategic goal, offered primarily within one theoretical framework, when it comes to techniques, the choices are typically eclectic and multiple for each intervention. The techniques of career counseling fall into two large categories: (1) assessment strategies for learning about oneself, the world of work, and putting the two together; and (2) job finding, getting, and holding skills. Many of the strategies in this first group were reviewed in the "key measures" section for each theory reviewed in Chapter 14; Spokane (1991) provides helpful overviews of 13 classes of such measures, all with evidence of use in career counseling. For an understanding of the range and good illustrations of techniques for job finding and getting, the single best resource is the "Job Club Counselor's Manual" (Azrin & Basalel, 1980). The Job Club concept has been used effectively both in assisting welfare recipients find satisfactory employment, as well as in "outplacement" services set up to help soon-to-be-terminated employees (due to mergers, downsizing, and so forth) find compatible new positions.

CAREER INTERVENTIONS: THREE DIVERSE EXAMPLES

All of the dimensions just reviewed could be used to create a multidimensional matrix to encompass an extraordinarily broad array of career interventions. In this section, we have provided three examples that differ from one another on every one of the dimensions: questions addressed, population, strategic objective, theoretical orientation, and techniques. At the beginning of each of the three examples, we identify the specific aspect of each dimension that is illustrated. Each of these examples could easily be modified to present an intervention that was offered to a different population, or for a different strategic objective, or from a different theoretical orientation than those in our examples. A large comprehensive university counseling service, serving both college-age and older adult populations, might offer all the kinds of services illustrated. On the other hand, a counseling psychologist in a small group practice might have a full practice by offering only two or three of the services from the matrix. Ideally, all counseling psychologists, as part of their training, receive supervised experience in a broad range of interventions. Note that by obtaining experience in just three career interventions, like those described in this chapter, one has been exposed to variations in every one of the major dimensions of diversity in career interventions. (The relevant dimensions appear in parentheses as each example is introduced.)

DISCOVER: A Computerized Career Guidance System

This career intervention utilizes a computer-assisted guidance system (technique) with 18- to 22-year-old college students (population) to address "Who am I?" and "What shall I choose?" (questions addressed). This particular computer-assisted system was developed by Super and colleagues (American College Testing Program, 1987) in accordance with Super's developmental approach (theoretical orientation); it is presented here as a developmental intervention (strategic objective) even though DISCOVER can certainly also be used for preventive or remedial purposes.

In the early 1960s, even while computers were in their infancy, at least in the public's eye, some career counselors foresaw their immense value in addressing all three components of career counseling: gaining information about oneself, gaining information about the world of work, and putting these two together in making some decision. Especially valuable was the computer's huge memory base for dealing with information on the world of work. Filled with books on the various occupations, counselors' libraries still do not provide much detailed information on the more than 20,000 careers available in today's society. Computers could also assist individuals in using information about themselves (e.g., abilities and interests) to identify which of these careers are suitable. Able to sort multiple parameters in just milliseconds, computers can handle the almost limitless number of permutations produced through combinations of interests, abilities, values, and experience. The computer career guidance systems such as DISCOVER incorporate both self-assessment and interactive sections that help students and clients increase and organize information about themselves and at the same time teach them strategies for using that information in identifying occupations to consider.

Like all the computerized career guidance systems, DISCOVER is a program that can be used almost totally on one's own or in conjunction with the help of a counselor. Career counselors can have the program available on a personal computer to be used on a "sign-up" basis just as one might use the PC-ROM unit in a college library for computerized bibliographic searches. Most counseling psychologists prefer to have some initial contact with career clients to ensure that they have concerns appropriate for the use of computer-assisted career guidance. For example, an individual who comes in knowing that he very much wants to be an artist but whose parents want him to be a physician is not going to find much help in a computerized approach. On the other hand, the client who has no firm ideas about which careers might be attractive is an ideal candidate for using the DISCOVER program as a way to identify and explore alternatives. Once a set of alternatives has been identified, the counselor can help the client plan strategies for further exploration and decision making.

DISCOVER now includes nine modules for college students: (1) beginning the career journey, (2) learning about the world of work, (3) learning about yourself (knowledge of self), (4) finding occupations, (5) learning about occupations (knowledge of the world of work), (6) making educational choices, (7) planning next steps (decision making), (8) planning the career, and (9) making transitions. (Note that the three common components of career interventions are well covered.)

While the first two modules are primarily for orientation to and information about the world of work, the third is designed to help the client develop more information about himself or herself in terms of interests, abilities, values, and experiences. The program includes inventories for each of these areas, all of which can be completed at the computer. Alternatively, instead of using the briefer, less standardized measures, one can enter a client's results from major standardized inventories and tests such as Holland's Self-Directed Search (SDS), the Strong Interest Inventory (SII), the Differential Aptitude Tests, or the Armed Services Vocational Aptitude Battery. For whatever scores one enters, a summary of results is provided. This summary can be printed for later review. (In fact, clients can print any page of the display in the entire program, including the units designed to teach about the work classification system and later modules providing comparisons of jobs related to clients' specific skills, interests, values, and so forth. In other words, each client can create his or her own personalized information packet.)

Based, then, on Super's concept that one makes the best career choices when one can implement one's self-concept in terms of interests, abilities, values, and experiences, the computer generates a list of options that fit the client's particular pattern. The program also allows more emphasis to be given to any one of these areas if the client feels, for example, that interests should be more important than experiences in deciding on career choices. An intriguing feature of this particular module is the "why not" section. If jobs the client thought might be interesting do not appear on the list, he or she can ask the computer, "Why not?" The computer will show what that job requires in the way of interests, abilities, and values and how it does not fit with the client's. At that point, this feature invites the client to of course consider whether he or she wants to reexamine some of his or her values or interests in making a career choice. Thus, does one change one's career choice to fit current values, interests, and so forth, or does one reconsider the importance of these relative to career choice? This step is the clearest manifestation of the concept of career choice as an implementation of the self-concept.

Module 5 provides the opportunity to examine detailed information on 15 different topics, such as work tasks, ways to get training, employee outlook, and so forth, for the occupations corresponding to a client's particular self-assessment. In addition to the occupations that come up on a client's list according to self-assessment, one can inquire about any of 400 different occupations on which one would like the latest information.

The sixth module, on making educational choices, focuses on choosing different kinds of training in terms of education and majors. The seventh (planning) module is for those who are ready to take specific steps toward further education such as graduate school or toward developing job-seeking skills. The eighth module, on planning a career, incorporates Super's concept of the "career rainbow"; that is, looking at how, over the life span, one's work role will interact with other roles, such as those of parent, citizen, homemaker, spouse/friend. The final module, on making transitions, is designed especially for those who have returned to school after being in other roles and/or who find themselves in a "career crisis," such as that caused by beginning graduate school and wondering if that is the right decision. Based on the work of Schlossberg (1981) regarding transitional factors that create significant adjustment problems, the program helps determine "the temperature" of a transition and then, using cognitively oriented stress-management skills, explains how to reduce the temperature of the transition by coping with the various stresses and problems the transition is causing.

Obviously, some of these modules are more important for some persons than others; one always has the choice of not even starting a module or starting it and, seeing that it is not really helpful, simply "signing off." At the completion of the use of DISCOVER and after getting the printout of all parts of the program wanted for further reference, the client can save the information in a computer file so as to come back and use it again or, if completely finished, erase all responses. At completion, all clients or students are asked to provide an evaluation of the helpfulness of the various modules; in this way the developers continually receive feedback about how to make the program more useful and user friendly.

As an example of how a counselor might typically use this program in a university counseling center, the following procedures might be followed. After completing a standard interview, a counselor could describe the various modules to the client, explaining what kinds of information they provide and then assist the client in choosing the modules that are most helpful. The client's "homework" would be to complete one or more selected modules before the next counseling session. The following counseling session would be devoted to exploring what the client had gained. This step helps the client more clearly articulate what has been learned and allows the counselor to determine if appropriate understandings have been acquired. Client and counselor then examine which further modules need to be completed and/or decision-making steps to complete.

Computer-assisted programs such as DISCOVER can also be uniquely useful to researchers in their study of career decision-making processes. As Gati (1996) concisely describes, computers not only lead participants through a step-by-step process, they also record what each participant does at each step. For example, how does a participant weigh skills versus interests or other life roles? If the program advises the participant that he or she is overly constraining career options early in the process, what does the participant do, if anything, to expand options? If, when participants sign on, information is gathered about their demographics (e.g., gender, ethnicity, age) and environmental situations (e.g., about to become unemployed, single parent, bored in job), then researchers can easily determine not only the content and outcomes of choices but also decision-making processes and any significant relationships such processes have to demographic and/or situational variables. Such information can be extremely useful to counselors in learning more about any systematic effects of diversity on the content and processes of career decision making.

Outplacement Group Counseling

This career intervention is illustrated as it would be presented to a group of 40- to 50-year-old union workers and salespersons (population) who have recently been given notice that their employment is soon to be terminated due to a merger of their employer with another company. It is a small group (technique), trait-oriented (theoretical orientation) intervention designed to prevent (strategic objective) floundering in the job market and possible negative mental health consequences of unemployment (Mallinckrodt & Fretz, 1988). Participants will receive help in answering "What shall I do?" and "How do I get a job?" (questions addressed).

We provide here a brief overview of a 12-hour outplacement program offered in six 2-hour sessions. The opening 2 hours are the least structured and most like a typical therapeutic group counseling session, providing opportunity for a catharsis of participants' feelings of frustration, rejection, and loss of control over their lives. Although the content of the session may seem strikingly depressing, under skillful group leaders the employees will show some of the benefits that Yalom (1985) has so often shown accompanies effective group work, for example, the realization that other people have the same concerns and a sense that somebody cares enough to listen. Many workers, for example, may not have talked about their problems with anyone else and so felt alone in their feelings of rejection, anger, or depression. If unattended, these feelings may well keep employees from engaging in an active search to find new kinds of employment. Failure to find new employment after 5–6 months can result in significant mental health and physical health problems for both employees and their families (Mallinckrodt & Fretz, 1988).

The second 2 hours are devoted to countering the passivity and negativity often shown in the first 2 hours. As further described in Chapter 16, a large number of structured counseling programs have been developed to address issues of low self-esteem, as well as other relevant job-search topics such as communication skills and assertiveness training. Choosing from a variety of structured exercises as described in, for example, Drum and Knott (1977) and Danish and D'Augelli (1983), the group leader can begin to help the employees find that they do have other strengths they can call upon, that they still have areas in their lives over which they have control, and that they have coping skills they have used in other situations to get them out of tough times. In short, the goal of the second 2 hours is to mobilize and activate the employees' coping resources.

The third and fourth 2-hour components of the program are designed to increase employees' career options. It is here that the Self-Directed Search (SDS) is used. While those familiar with the SDS may be surprised to see it used with adults who have already been in the job market (since it is often seen as a preferred instrument for high school students and those who have not yet entered the job market), with blue-collar employees, as in the present example, it is precisely the kind of instrument needed to help employees look at a variety of options they have not previously considered. Many blue-collar employees, especially those in jobs not requiring high-level skills, entered a position, not because of any special training or interests but simply because it was a well-paying job that was available after they finished high school or left their previous job. The most typical reaction of unskilled blue-collar employees is to first look for any other job in the area that pays about the same or to look for the same kind of job available in another company, preferably nearby. There may be few if any of the same kinds of jobs available in that community and, of course, all of the dismissed employees will probably be competing for whatever few slots might be available. Using the SDS helps overcome this narrowness of options.

After the workers have taken and scored the SDS, with a chance for individuals to get clarifications from the counselor, many of their basic questions about the instrument can be answered from a booklet called "You and Your Career" (Holland, 1985). It explains a great deal about the Holland person–environment model described in Chapter 14 but in a way that is directly related to SDS results and helps persons see how to use their SDS scores for exploring alternative occupations. Repeatedly, the SDS has been shown to yield increases in self-understanding and the number of vocational alternatives considered (Holland, 1994).

Following the 2-hour section in which the SDS is completed and associated materials reviewed, the next session of the program focuses on group exploration of these results. The group now examines the relevance of their occupational aspirations to their obtained codes and begins, with the assistance of both other group members and the counselor, to identify the kinds of skills they have obtained in their present position that might be utilized in the various jobs identified in their personal SDS codes. Other members of the group serve as immediate resources, oftentimes having some knowledge if not actual experience in some of the jobs that appear on other employees' lists. Thus group members help each other see various possibilities.

The last two sessions of the outplacement program focus on job-getting skills. First is résumé writing, helping participants see how best to present the various skills learned in their previous jobs. Next comes training in job-interviewing skills. (Because this session especially requires a lot of individual monitoring, and because of the value of giving everybody a chance to take part in group discussions, each group should be limited to no more than 10 or 12 persons. A company with many layoffs may need to run several groups.)

To the extent that more time can be made available in this phase, workers would, after receiving basic instruction on preparing résumés, bring them back for review and critique by each other in order to learn how best to present themselves. More important, with additional available time, they will role-play job interviewing and begin to set specific goals in applying for jobs. Azrin and Basalel (1980) developed highly effective job club programs that include these components, especially designed for those without high levels of education. For those who are sufficiently motivated and have at least a high school reading level, the popular self-help book *What Color Is Your Parachute?* (Bolles, 1998) covers many of these same areas in a most humorous and effective manner.

In summary, the outplacement program added the component of "therapeutic" group counseling to the knowledge-of-self component of career counseling with specific attention to how past experiences/skills can be incorporated into self-knowledge. The use of the SDS expands the workers' knowledge of related areas in the world of work. The third component of career counseling, decision making, is achieved in this program by a focus on tailoring job-getting skills to workers' choices.

Individual Career Counseling: An Eclectic Combination of Psychodynamic and Social Learning Approaches

In one sense, this final illustration comes closest to the usual perception of career counseling; that is, a counselor meets individually with a client who has significant career concerns. Yet, in another sense, it is quite different from the stereotype of career counseling in that it utilizes no interest inventories or aptitude tests. Rather, the focus that develops is a therapeutic exploration of both career and personal issues to help Sheila, a 35-year-old female, first-generation American (population), remediate (strategic goal) both her current career difficulties as well as other troublesome issues in her life. While individual counseling focused on career concerns could easily occur in any one of the theoretical approaches reviewed in Chapter 14, this illustration is an eclectic combination of psychodynamic and social learning approach interventions (theoretical orientations). The counselor focuses on (techniques) helping Sheila (1) develop insights into the interface of her career and personal issues and, after having her assess her career beliefs, (2) make at least some first steps in taking more active responsibility for addressing her concerns such as "How do I shape my career?" "How can work help me grow as a person?" and "How can I do better?" (questions addressed).

Given the individualized nature of this particular case, it is probably easiest to begin by looking first at the intake notes; that is, the notes made when the client first came to the counselor. Following these will be some of the weekly case notes of the counselor, revealing the topics of the various sessions and the progress being made. After each set of notes we have added some commentary of our own, showing how this case exemplifies some of Bordin's (1968) concepts of psychodynamic career counseling and the counselor's use of techniques based on Krumboltz's (1996) learning theory approach to career counseling. (All case notes have been appropriately altered to protect confidentiality.)

Intake Note: Sheila is a 35-year-old administrative assistant who came for career counseling to get out of a rut she has been in for 10 years. She began full-time work at age 20 as a legal secretary following 2 years of community college. In both high school and while attending community college, she took mostly business courses. The attorney she worked for initially joined others in a large firm; she has had several promotions during her 15 years with them and has been the "office manager" (in her words), though she lists her title as administrative assistant, for 4 years. There is no opportunity for further promotion or new positions within the firm. Sheila feels that the money and benefits are good for someone with her education, however she is increasingly bored with her job and wants to change but has no idea what to consider. Both of Sheila's parents were born in India; soon after their family-arranged marriage, her father received funding for graduate work in the United States. Sheila was born in this country and has never been to India. She feels her parents were always "more Indian than American." There was far greater support for her brother to attend college than for her to do so. She says her parents always expected her to marry an "Indian professional"—a doctor or scientist. Her mother stopped nagging Sheila about her unwillingness to marry anyone after Sheila moved in with her, following the death of her father 10 years ago. Wow, what a bunch of issues here!

Relatively low self-esteem is readily apparent, but she reports no other signs of depression. Says she has numerous minor physical ailments—"I'm a hypochondriac." Talks readily though not with any psychological sophistication. She has no prior experience in psychotherapy. Minimal probing of sensitive areas (e.g., family and cultural issues, interpersonal relationships) yields much defensiveness. Trying to discuss relationships of her career and personal life during counseling may be quite threatening.

Diagnosis: Bordin and Kopplin (1973) developed a diagnostic system of five major categories for dynamic understanding of vocational development problems: synthetic difficulties (minimum psychopathology, problem is in overcoming realistic obstacles and/or integrating diverse interests), identity problems, gratification conflicts (approach–avoidance conflicts with a given choice), overt psychopathology, and change orientation (the client is dissatisfied and wants to change himself or herself by changing vocational choice). Since the counselor did not see overt psychopathology in this client but did find some lack of satisfaction with other roles in life as well as work, it seems quite likely that the change-orientation diagnosis is particularly relevant in this case. The counselor, at this point, had too little information about identity (including racial identity) formation to know if these kinds of problems were present. Gratification conflicts are also probably part of the problem given that she gets some important need satisfied by her present job, yet other needs, like challenge, are totally unmet.

The next set of notes was made after Sheila's first regular counseling session.

Session One Notes: Sheila seemed more agitated in this session. She is feeling some urgency for doing something, anything, to get out of the present work situation. I tried to check out particular areas on the job that might have created a sense of urgency but got nothing. She reports feeling trapped in her routine. No stimulation from work, or home, or friends. No close friends, bowls once a week with friends from high school days. She is the only one without a husband or serious boyfriend. I have a strong sense that her routine, while frustrating to her as she "takes stock" at age 35, has been a major source of security. The possibility of change is probably at least as frightening as it is attractive. Sheila does not acknowledge any limitation in her life from her responsibilities for her mother or from her cultural background.

A Psychodynamic Model for Vocational Counseling: Bordin (1968) sees the career counselor's task as "how to go about facilitating an optimal self-confrontation under conditions of minimal anxiety. . . . The major problem is to avoid either overly superficial, abortive self-examination or seduction into an equally abortive psychotherapy" (p. 429). The first important component is to explore how the client seeks gratification; that is, gains satisfaction from various aspects of life, including not only job but also home and social life. The counselor has obviously begun in this first session to explore these various areas, and will want to continue to do so during the next couple of sessions. The counselor will also expect Sheila to become somewhat impatient with these explorations of areas other than her job situation because she came for "career counseling." The counselor will need to help Sheila understand that the best career choices are made by gaining an understanding about how to find sources of gratification in one's life. Getting the client to make relevant self-confrontations yet keeping the focus of the counseling on the career problem is "a fine line" (p. 430) that Bordin recognizes career counselors must face.

In the later sessions the counselor will use a great many comparisons as a way of facilitating self-confrontation. For example, "On the one hand, you feel very competent in your job but, on the other hand, have no idea what those competencies are. Therefore, you can't think of any alternative career choices," and, "On the one hand, the responsibility of taking care of your mother has made you feel helpful and appreciated yet, on the other hand, this greatly limits what job options you might consider."

Sheila's cultural identity seems to be at the least mature levels: conformity/obliviousness to socioracial concerns, or dissonance/repression of anxiety-provoking racial information (see Chapter 6). The counselor will need to facilitate self-confrontation on socioracial issues that affect Sheila's real and perceived career options.

Session Four Notes: (Sessions two and three are not discussed here; however, it must be noted that, since Sheila was quite insistent on taking some "test" to help her with her career concerns, the counselor had her take the Career Beliefs Inventory (Krumboltz, 1991) between the second and third counseling sessions. On 13 of the 25 scales in this measure, Sheila obtained scores indicating beliefs that were blocking her progress. Her four lowest (i.e., most blocking) beliefs were: career path is influenced by others, expert help can determine the best career choice, would not move for a better job, and the right job is impossible to find. In discussing these results in the third session, the counselor worked with Sheila to develop her interpretations (see Chapter 13 for techniques for involving clients in test interpretation; strategies developed largely within psychodynamic frameworks). While the counselor was struck by the passive dependency in the results, Sheila began to focus more and more on the risks of making changes.)

Today's theme was security. Sheila has clearly grasped the security she gets from her routines and how that makes any change scary. She is also beginning to see that she has a very limited view about her competencies both on the job and socially. Her family seems to have stimulated that sense of inadequacy in ways she has not yet really described, in fact, I am not sure she has really been able to admit them to awareness. The combination of security in present routine and a limited sense of competence severely limits availability of options that could be considered. I plan to focus on understanding the dynamics of the need for so much security in hope of helping her take a risk or make some minor change in some part of her life. This seems more workable to me, in our time-limited relationship (Sheila was seen in an agency with a 12-session limit for individual counseling) than trying to significantly expand her limited sense of competence.

Comment: The counselor has followed one of Mann's (1973) suggestions here for working in time-limited therapy, that is where the client is seen for a limited number of sessions, say, 7 to 20. In dynamically oriented time-limited counseling, the counselor tries to focus on *one* of the major themes in the person's lifestyle that may be an impediment to having more gratification. While all of the different areas that the client has brought up could potentially be worked on in psychotherapeutic relationships, this could require months of counseling. The counselor chose the theme of security as the one where progress might be made most rapidly for helping the client understand its pervasiveness and implications and to make some small steps to change its hold on her life.

Session Seven Notes: (Sessions five and six are not discussed here.) Excitement! Sheila has decided to enroll in an evening program for older students who want to earn a bachelor's degree. She told me, in a very didactic way, that this was a good decision for her since it did not change any other routines that were satisfying to her yet it gave her a new challenge. She is not sure that she meets her own standard of "what it takes to get a college degree," but feels she is at least as bright, if not brighter, than any of the persons she supervises who have college degrees. She criticized me for not being more enthusiastic about what she called her "big step." She was right in one sense, but I was considering whether this was an action that would prematurely end our exploration of her security needs and other possible options that she might consider.

I am angry at myself also for missing this opportunity to reinforce independent action on her part. This was a great chance to begin developing her sense of self-efficacy. Reminder: ATTEND TO THIS IN NEXT SESSION.

Comment: The counselor has quite legitimate concerns about a possible "abortive self-examination" (Bordin, 1968, p. 429) or what others might call "flight into health" (seizing on the very first option that makes one feel somewhat better). Notice, however, how Sheila is beginning to think about herself in a more purposeful, psychological way. While she initially came to counseling saying implicitly, "You get me out of this rut," she has now, on her own, taken a step that brings some change into her life and provides gratification where she had none before. She had reached what Bordin calls the stage of critical decision in the struggle for growth and change. Now look at what happens three sessions later after Sheila had the opportunity to work on changes with the counselor's gentle confrontations and strong reinforcement of autonomous steps.

Session Ten Notes: Sheila seems confident about her choice and has already completed enrollment for a composition course next semester. The security—or more precisely, play-it-safe style, originated in her earliest years—both her parents led their lives that way and she was always taught that "a bird in the hand is worth two in the bush." She sees the course she will be taking as not only a new challenge, but also as a new way to get out of the house and meet new friends, other changes she has been wanting to take. She feels no need for further counseling at this time; feels it has been very helpful to look at herself. She asks if she could return after taking some courses to consider "what then." For now, "I can easily tolerate my job if there is something challenging somewhere in my life."

Comments: Although this outcome is hardly typical of career counseling—that is, Sheila made no change in her job—those who counsel "mid-life" clients will not at all be surprised with the result. One can achieve life satisfaction in many ways, sometimes through changes in jobs, but just as often through changes in other aspects of one's life. When one weighs both the advantages and disadvantages of a current job situation, current marital situation, or current social life, the conclusion might well be that the risk of change in one area, such as work, may outweigh the benefits of a change and that more gratification might be achieved by changes in another aspect of life, such as one's social life. (Conversely, marriage counselors know that many marriages suffer because of job problems and that changes in the job situation can be a critical component in improving a marital relationship.) Sheila made a small change and (recall the concepts explored in the last chapter regarding social learning theory) to the extent that she experiences the challenges of the college courses as successful ones, she will be more willing to risk other changes in life.

While the counselor felt Sheila had made a good initial step, there remained extensive issues about sense of competence (self-efficacy) and unverbalized family and cultural issues, all which could make additional steps difficult. Yet, two years after the end of counseling, Sheila saw her counselor in a shopping mall parking lot and said she was still taking courses and had recently moved away from her mother's home to share an apartment downtown with a friend she met at work. She had stayed in the same job, becoming more and more convinced that it paid better and was as tolerable as most of the jobs her fellow classmates held. For now she was taking a variety of classes, not even worried about getting a degree and stated, "I might come back to see you if I ever have to decide what I want to do when I grow up."

PROCESS AND OUTCOME STUDIES OF CAREER INTERVENTIONS

Accomplishments and Challenges

Now that we have described and illustrated the diversity of career interventions, in this section we provide an overview of the results of studies of the processes and outcomes of career interventions. Two major meta-analytic reviews on the outcomes of career interventions have been published, encompassing the results of studies from 1950 to 1995 (Oliver & Spokane, 1988; Whiston, Sexton, & Lasoff, 1998). Meta-analysis is a set of statistical procedures that can be applied to the results across a collection of empirical studies. In each of the two meta-analytic investigations discussed here, the focus was on studies of "treatment" effects of career interventions; these treatment effects are typically referred to as the outcomes of counseling. Both meta-analytic investigations yielded significant positive effects for a wide range of types of interventions, from career development classes to self-guided use of computer-based career guidance systems to individual career counseling. Positive results were obtained from treatments as short at 45 minutes of self-administered activities to those as long as 64 hours of classroom activities. Whether participants were high-school- or college-age students, whether they were "clients" or simply students electing a program or class related to career decisions, overall, career interventions had positive effects. The size of these positive effects from career interventions has been at least as great, if not greater than, those obtained in meta-analytic studies of the outcomes of psychotherapy.

The meta-analytic findings parallel those found in more traditional qualitative reviews ranging from Fretz (1981) to Swanson (1995), all of which report many positive results, yet many still-to-be-answered questions exist about how to achieve those outcomes. In the next few paragraphs we describe four improvements that are needed in research on career interventions to help us learn how to obtain the most efficient and effective outcomes. Many of these improvements can be made quite simply; it is our hope that some readers will incorporate such improvements in the theses and dissertations they might undertake while graduate students.

Whiston and colleagues (1998) note that 106 of the 152 career intervention outcome studies from the period 1983–1995 could not be used in their meta-analysis for one of two easily correctable reasons. First, many studies had no comparison group of participants to which to compare the results of the career intervention; that is, neither a no-treatment control group, nor a group of participants who completed some type of psychological or educational treatment program other than a career intervention. Second, many studies failed to report basic statistical data such as means and standard deviations on each measure used; such data are essential for determining treatment effect size, a statistic that is needed both for meta-analyses and for comparing the strengths of different kinds of treatments.

A third needed, easily accomplished improvement relates to the populations studied. Very few studies reviewed reported inclusion of significant numbers of ethnically diverse clients or students. There is thus no way of confirming whether the very positive effects obtained would apply equally well to a diverse clientele. Future studies need to attend to direct comparisons of treatment effects for culturally diverse groups. Whereas no one study can include many types of diversity, small studies comparing effects for just two diverse groups would bring significant advances to an understanding of the generalizability of outcomes. The fourth change needed also comes from the conclusions of Whiston and colleagues (1998) who found current studies too often looked at very different outcomes, for example, client satisfaction, career maturity, congruence. Even when looking at the same outcome, quite different measures were sometimes used. Consider, for example, the very different kinds of measures for congruence developed by Holland, Dawis, and Bordin (see Chapter 14). Whiston et al. (1998) recommend that career researchers agree on a standard battery of outcome assessments to be used in all career intervention outcome studies, batteries that can of course be expanded to address any investigators' special concerns, yet the standard battery will yield a dataset with indexes that can be compared across many outcome studies.

The remaining issues that need to be addressed in improving career intervention outcome studies are a bit more difficult to achieve, yet perhaps just as essential as those improvements just reviewed, if the profession is to make major, as compared to minor, gains in understanding how to provide the most efficient and effective career interventions. It is remarkable not only that such a large array of career interventions provide significant positive gains, but also that most of those gains occur within the first 2.5 hours (Whiston et al., 1998). What is it in the diversity of treatments that causes those most immediate effects despite great variations in overall length of career interventions?

To address this concern, Rounds and Tinsley (1984) provide a useful conceptualization they called "dismantling and constructive" strategies. For example, two treatments could be compared in which one treatment excludes one of the four components outlined by Holland, Magoon, and Spokane (1981). Does the deletion of the component reduce the effectiveness of the treatment? The constructive effort simply does the reverse; a program would be offered with perhaps only two of the components, then another offered with three components, a method that would allow determination of the incremental role of the third component in relation to the other two. As an example, there are now some studies that have looked at the values of adding individual or group counseling to the use of computer-assisted career programs. As Whiston and colleagues (1998) report, computer-assisted career counseling is the least expensive of all interventions; adding individual career counseling helps clients achieve much greater results, but at a far more expensive cost.

In addition to increased analyses of the effective components of career interactions, there is a need to determine whether various client characteristics affect the effectiveness of any of the components of career interventions. For example, do students with more rational decision-making styles find working with the SDS more helpful and satisfying? Do students with lower general levels of anxiety benefit more from computer-assisted career counseling? We already know that students who have interpersonal or environmental complexities that lead to persistent indecision do *not* benefit much from most of the usual career interventions (see later section on indecisiveness); how can the career issues of such clients be effectively addressed? A study of how these client attributes affect the outcomes of counseling are referred to as attribute–treatment interactions.

Clients also vary with respect to the environmental constraints and barriers they are experiencing. Harmon (1994) astutely reminds counseling psychologists that many contemporary career problems are beyond individuals' control and are embedded in a context of other problems of living in contemporary society (Richardson, 1996). An assessment of how these problems affect the outcomes of career interventions has thus far been largely neglected; the concept of client attributes is much in need of being conceptually expanded to include dimensions of client environment as well as intrapersonal factors. Even though Fretz (1981) long ago called for increased attention to client attribute—treatment interactions (like those noted in the preceding paragraph) as a way of helping select the most effective and efficient treatments for clients, Whiston et al. (1998) find that only a few such studies had been conducted between 1981 and 1998. Swanson (1995) provides the most recent detailed review of the results of studies of interactions of client attributes and treatment effectiveness. More attention to these interactions should be a high priority for career intervention outcome researchers.

Now, given the almost infinite number of comparisons that might be considered in looking at all the kinds and components of career interventions, along with a wide range of clients' personal and environmental situations that might affect outcomes, how is the researcher to choose one or two comparisons that hold promise for yielding significant meaningful information? One of the most cost effective informative sources for deciding on such comparisons may well be found in process research. In such studies, there is careful attention in each session paid to factors like what clients found most helpful and what specific techniques counselors were using at the time the client felt helped. Although there has been an impressive growth in sophisticated process research in general psychotherapy, very few such studies focused on career counseling. Swanson (1995) provides a very thorough review of the effective strategies for career counseling process studies as well as the results of those few that had been completed prior to 1995. The process studies of career counseling have yielded the somewhat expected greater attention to information-giving compared to traditional psychotherapy techniques such as confrontation and interpretation (e.g., Kirschner, Hoffman, & Hill, 1994). Somewhat more surprising has been career clients' high ratings of the importance of their counselors' use of techniques such as developing insight, challenging, and building a working alliance (e.g., Heppner & Hendricks, 1995). In short, at least in these initial process studies of individual career counseling, traditional therapeutic elements, such as building a working alliance, are just as critical as counselors providing information for achieving those powerful effects found by Whiston and colleagues (1998) for individualized career counseling.

INDECISIVENESS: THE ULTIMATE CHALLENGE

As reviewed in the last section, most participants in career counseling and career interventions experience measurable positive gains. However, it has long been evident that there is a *small* group of career counseling clients who never reach any satisfactory decisions and remain unhappy with their counseling experience. In most cases, the counselors of these clients have been as unhappy, or even more unhappy than their clients, with the experience and outcomes of working with these indecisive clients. In this section, we provide an overview of the conceptual and empirical results of the work of counseling psychologists, as scientist–practitioners, addressing the problems presented by this most challenging group of clients. Three questions have been addressed, each question having emerged based on developments regarding the prior question. First: Are there reliable and meaningfully different types of indecisive clients? Second: If such types exist, are there different treatments that should be employed when providing career counseling for them? Third: If a different treatment is needed, should it be some variation of career interventions or some version of psychotherapy?

The Return of Diagnosis

Crites (1981) has concisely reviewed some of the issues and problems with career-related diagnostic systems developed in the early years of the profession of counseling psychology. As discussed in Chapter 13, one of the major problems with such systems was that they were never closely tied to providing different kinds of career interventions. Career counseling strategies were based more on the theoretical predilections of the counselor than on any differential diagnosis of the client. Yet even within a given theoretical framework such as trait-oriented ones, Holland and Holland (1977) note that there were clearly some career counseling clients who had concerns about being undecided, but simply did not respond favorably to traditional interventions that emphasized learning information about oneself and the world of work and then how to find and choose satisfactory options.

Over the past few decades there have been numerous theoretical and empirical studies to understand more about these clients. In the earliest phases of that research, the focus was on how to separate those clients who were simply undecided from those who were called indecisive, and the different treatments needed for each (Fuqua & Hartman, 1983; Holland & Holland, 1977; Salamone, 1982). Undecided clients were those individuals who had not made career decisions but generally responded quickly and well to a variety of career interventions, even self-administered ones like the SDS; their undecided state may have been simply a normal developmental phase or a temporary reaction to the need to consider other career options, either because of dissatisfaction with a current career or because of involuntary dismissal from previous employment. On the other hand, studies of those labeled indecisive—that is, those who did not respond well to many career interventions—

showed that such clients typically had high levels of anxiety and often inadequate decision-making and coping skills. Over the years it also became evident that "indecisive" clients were themselves not a homogeneous group. Some indecisive clients seemed immobilized by anxiety, others perceived what they considered insurmountable barriers, others were simply poor and ineffectual decisionmakers. In some cases, clients possessed all three types of problems.

Various measures have been developed to help make differential diagnoses related to these types of indecisiveness. Clearly the two most widely used have been the Career Decision Scale (CDS) (Osipow, Carney, Winer et al., 1980) and My Vocational Situation (MVS) (Holland, Daiger, & Power, 1980; Holland, Johnston, & Asama, 1993). Both these measures have been used with many age groups and studied for their factor structure, reliability, and validity. These measures have yielded the clearest distinctions between "undecided" and "indecisiveness." There is much less clarity about whether indecisiveness is a unidimensional or multidimensional construct (Lucas, 1993). Spokane (1991) despairs of the lack of clarity from such an extensive literature; he does make an important contribution to understanding the complexities of indecisiveness by pointing out the potential bidirectional effects of such factors as anxiety and identity in relationship to career indecision. That is, having to make a career decision may increase anxiety or identity concerns, which in turn make the decision making a more difficult process. Peterson, Sampson, Reardon, and Lenz (1996), using their cognitive information approach (described in Chapter 14), focus on what they call problems in the "executive processing" of indecisive individuals. Just how to make the most effective diagnoses about these hard-to-help career counseling clients is not yet conclusively evident; there will no doubt continue to be further developments of assessment techniques in the coming years. If counseling psychologists follow the good advice of Phillips (1992), there will also be increased attention to tying the results of assessments to differential treatments in order to determine what works best with different types of indecisive clients. Such differential treatment planning is the focus of the next section.

Treatment Planning

Even as early as the late 1970s, Holland could conclude from his research (Holland & Holland, 1977) that those who were identified simply as "undecided" compared to those labeled "indecisive" could be provided much less intensive, even self-administered career interventions like the SDS (Holland, 1994). The tremendous cost savings in professional time that arise from simply knowing who can benefit from essentially self-help treatments, like the SDS or computer-assisted counseling, makes the use of even present forms of diagnostic instruments such as the CDS or MVS extremely useful as treatment-planning devices.

For those clients who cannot benefit effectively from such self-directed interventions, investigators have suggested a variety of more therapeutic intervention strategies for career counselors to employ, focused on issues like anxiety, decision-making deficiencies, inability to confront barriers, and so forth (Fuqua & Hartman, 1983; Salamone, 1982; Savickas, 1989; Spokane, 1991). Heppner and Hendricks (1995) provide one of the first process and outcome studies comparing treatment of an un-decided client to an indecisive client. Their findings are quite illuminating regarding the complexities in treating indecisiveness. Congruent with the kinds of outcome findings reported above, they find that the *undecided* client made the most and fastest progress and had the greatest satisfaction. Moreover, they find that the *undecided* client rated the counseling *relationship* (not just a rating of the counselor) even more highly than did the *indecisive* client who had been working with the counselor on more personal issues. The limited outcomes and poor ratings of counseling from their indecisive client no doubt elicited responses of "I told you so" from those coun-seling psychologists who have consistently stated that some "career clients" really need to be referred for "personal counseling" before their career problems are ad-dressed (e.g., Dawis, 1996). The provocative and engaging ongoing discussions about the relationships of career counseling and personal counseling are the basis for the final section on meeting the challenge of the indecisive client.

Career Counseling and Psychotherapy: Fusion, Diffusion, and Confusion

Given the kinds of difficulties just described for counseling indecisive clients, it is not surprising that almost all counseling psychologists agree that, for some clients, some *fusion* of personal and career counseling is necessary. Just what the nature of that fusion should be was the subject of numerous articles in the 1990s; a special 1993 issue of the *Career Development Quarterly* (volume 42, pp. 129–173) in-cluded a variety of views about, and examples of the need for, more fusion of career counseling and personal counseling/psychotherapy. Hackett (1993) spells out what she believes to be numerous false dichotomies between career and personal counsel-ing that get perpetuated by graduate programs offering separate courses and prac-tica in the two areas as well as many counseling centers offering separately labeled services in career counseling and personal counseling. How to overcome these di-chotomies will be explored later in this section.

Just as it is clear that for some clients, some fusion of career counseling and psy-chotherapy is necessary, it is also clear that for some career interventions, no fusion is necessary or reasonably possible. Some career interventions involve almost no per-sonal interactions with counselors, for example, a computer-assisted guidance pro-gram or self-administration of the SDS. Some career education classes, career development workshops, and preretirement programs are offered to groups of 30–100 persons. With these types of interventions, many conducted outside of any interper-sonal relationship with a counselor, there is clearly a *diffusion* of activities with little or no relationship to psychotherapy. This is not to say that a person who completes one of these kinds of interventions may not at a later time request a counseling relationship to deal with concerns raised by the intervention; however, there would still be, at least initially, separate phases of the career- and personal-focused counseling activities.

When it comes to looking at those individual or small group counseling situa-tions where career concerns are taken up in the context of a relationship with a coun-selor, there is an immense array of opinions (Swanson, 1995), one could even say *confusion,* about the nature of any fusion between career counseling and personal counseling/psychotherapy. Are career counseling and psychotherapy basically separate "sets" that have limited intersections, or overlap only in times of stress (Spokane, 1991)? Or is career counseling just one of many subsets of psychotherapy? To illustrate the separate sets notion, there are some counselors who feel that a person with pervasive anxiety, depression, and so forth cannot benefit from consideration of career concerns until those symptoms are treated. This position is often taken by those counselors who work primarily with trait-oriented approaches and expect the client to be able to engage in active exploration of self and environmental assessment and then engage in a rational decision-making process—all steps that may prove extremely difficult for a highly anxious or depressed client to undertake.

The "subset" position is illustrated by person-centered counselors, who see a client with career concerns as really no different from one with sexual dysfunction concerns, or substance abuse concerns; "[I]t is only required . . . that the practitioner accurately understands the client's need, addresses that need in counseling, and correctly guides the client to appropriate sources of information outside of the counseling setting" (Lent, 1996, p. 112). Krumboltz and Coon (1995), from their social learning perspective, have a similar view that career concerns are simply just one of many possible unique sets of concerns, like deciding whether to enter into a long-term relationship, or dealing with a phobia; for each unique set of concerns a client brings, the key issue is: Which interventions will promote diverse learning outcomes? These authors, along with Richardson (1996), all articulate ways of fusing career counseling and psychotherapy in ways in which career problems simply become one of many sets of concerns a client might bring to counseling. In fact, some clients bring more than one set of concerns simultaneously, for example, career concerns, along with family planning concerns, and/or substance abuse concerns.

Blustein and Spengler (1995) provide a succinct analysis of the extensive overlap of psychotherapy and career counseling even as presently practiced, identifying several shared change processes as well as evidence of some personal therapeutic gains for clients who complete "career counseling" as well as some career development and satisfaction gains for clients who complete "personal counseling." They prefer the term "domain-sensitive approach," rather than career counseling, when working with clients with career concerns. In such an approach, the counselor–client relationship, manifested in a working alliance (Meara & Patton, 1994) is, as in any therapeutic counseling, a key component of achieving positive outcomes. Blustein and Spengler (1995) quite rightly suggest that training programs must give far more attention to training and supervised experiences in integrating career concerns with psychotherapy, a topic explored at the end of this chapter.

EVOLVING MARKETS AND NEW FRONTIERS FOR CAREER INTERVENTIONS

In the first draft of this section, the heading used the term emerging, as compared to evolving, markets. *Emerging* seemed correct, in one sense, because some counseling psychologists specializing in career interventions are now working in very different contexts than in past years. However, a closer examination of these new contexts suggested continuities with the history of the profession that were more indicative of *evolution* than the *emergence* of truly new roles.

In the past 20 years, in both workplaces and school settings, there have been two important changes in how the work of counseling psychologists is regarded and utilized. The first of these changes has been driven by the same economic forces reviewed in Chapter 4 that are affecting the delivery of health care in this country. The effects of global competition in both the workplace and in public education have caused a significant constriction in providing *institutionally based* services that have been deemed less essential to productivity. While counseling psychologists will certainly not like having career education or career adjustment and development described as "frills," many such services along with, for example, art and music in public schools, lunch rooms and training programs in industry, have been reduced or eliminated because they do not contribute significantly to the primary goals and/or profits of the institution or business. The term institutionally based is italicized above to emphasize that in many cases programs like career education and career development have not been totally ignored, but rather that in many companies and school systems, there are no longer departments with full-time psychologists offering such services. The kinds of services described in the remainder of this section are now often provided through "outsourcing"; that is, a contract is made between a company or a school system and a counseling psychologist to provide a career development or career intervention service on a periodic, or in most cases, an as-needed basis. Because the counseling psychologist in such arrangements is typically functioning as a consultant, all of the material covered in Chapter 19 is a critical part of the perspective needed to function most effectively in these new contexts for career interventions.

A second contextual change shared by work settings and school systems is an increased understanding that career development and adjustment do not occur in isolation from other life roles. For example, workers who have become responsible for caring for aging parents in a distant city might suddenly be faced with urgent conflicts in meeting their job responsibilities, leaving them with both less time for their work as well as emotionally upset. Another example: Divorce proceedings have long been known to affect not only the work performance of each spouse, but also often the academic performance of the children. All of the frontiers explored later in this section can be described as encompassing a more holistic perspective on an integration of career and personal psychology.

Changing Focuses for Career Interventions in the Workplace

At the very beginnings of career psychology, with Parsons in 1909, the focus of counselors' work with industries was to *select* appropriately skilled workers. After World War II, counseling psychologists, along with industrial/organizational (I/O) psychologists, became increasingly involved with industry and business in studying and intervening to improve levels of worker satisfaction and adjustment. I/O psychologists focused largely on *organizations* and how to get them to change in ways that would make employees more productive and satisfied. Counseling psychologists, on the other hand, focused more on *employees* to empower them to make changes in their worklife that suited each of their own complex of roles and needs (Gerstein & Shullman, 1992).

Beginning in the 1960s, several changes in society and the workforce brought greatly expanded roles for counseling psychologists in the workplace. The workforce at that time shifted from primarily a blue-collar skilled labor force to primarily a white-collar professionalized workforce. Moreover, with an expanding economy but limited expansion in the workforce (the demographic bubble of "baby boomers" were still in school and college), companies increasingly turned to psychologists for assistance in selecting and training managers and executives. Committing errors in such selections is extremely costly and the established role of psychologists in improving selection processes during World War II made them attractive to leaders of industry when faced with selection problems.

Counseling psychologists therefore gained roles in executive screening and coaching; from these beginnings the first career development centers emerged in some larger industries as places where employees could both complete assessments of themselves as well as participate in leadership development workshops that would prepare them for advancement. While some employees might use such training to move to better positions in other companies, many companies felt that the in-house career development opportunities provided both employer and employee a better opportunity to determine advancement potential of employees and was therefore cost effective. By the 1990s, however, as globalization of the economy required some severe cutbacks in services, as noted above, in-house career development services were largely abandoned and replaced with outsourcing. A goodly number of counseling psychologists who were once employed in industry-based career development centers simply shifted to an individual, or small partnership, consulting practice. Today, there are numerous small partnerships across the country, each with a variety of ongoing and developing contracts with six or more companies, offering a variety of services as the company needs them, ranging from executive development to managing human relations to stress management resulting from mergers and acquisitions—what some psychologists have called "marriage counseling" for businesses.

The civil rights movement of the 1960s (described in Chapter 6) also brought new roles for counseling psychologists in the workplace. The "old-boy network" way of hiring and promoting no longer was acceptable. Psychologists were first called on for their assessment skills in designing and implementing equal employment opportunity programs. Now industries more often seek the help of psychologists in designing and implementing human relations management programs that can help both employees and employers cope more effectively with issues of discrimination, harassment, and other forms of grievances.

Yet other roles for counseling psychologists in workplace settings emerged with the development in the 1970s of outplacement programs and employee assistance programs. Each of these developments evolved quite differently. Outplacement programs, and their "close relative" preretirement programs, were initially a result of the combination of a sudden downturn in the economy in the early 1970s, along with extreme cutbacks in the aerospace and defense industries after the Vietnam War came to a close and men had landed on the moon. Suddenly, thousands of America's best and brightest engineers and the like, who had been hired by defense and aerospace industries directly out of college, and who, had therefore never even really applied for a job, were facing unemployment in an economy that had few jobs for persons whose only career experience was in aerospace or defense. Many governmental agencies and large aerospace companies then developed programs to assist these employees in developing effective career plans and strategies to "translate" their prior work experience into résumés that would help them obtain new employment. Such programs had to deal not only with the realities of helping these persons make self-assessments and implement job-getting skills, but also with how to incorporate strategies for dealing with the psychological consequences of becoming unemployed (Mallinckrodt & Fretz, 1988). Pickman (1994) has the most complete guide to the history, development, and offering of outplacement programs. Such programs have proved popular with soon-to-be-terminated employees as a kind of reasonable "good-faith" effort by the terminating employer. Since, in good economic times, such programs are not needed, most companies now outsource such services, using them only in times when the economy and/or mergers require downsizing and its consequent dismissal of many long-term employees. Most counseling psychologists who practice as a consultant to business and industry are able to offer individual and/or group outplacement counseling.

Preretirement programs are a "close relative" of outplacement in that they often were supported by companies in order to encourage early retirement of current employees. "Early out" retirement options remain one of the most attractive ways companies have for reducing their workforce. Today, such programs are seldom company run; rather, when a company, for whatever reason, needs to reduce the number of employees, it may offer older workers early retirement. To accomplish this, it contracts with consultants, such as counseling psychologists, who design and offer preretirement programs. Tinsley and Schwendener-Holt (1992) review many of the conceptual and research issues in counseling psychologists' work with retirement; Fretz and Merikangas (1992) identify the key components of effective preretirement programs and provide a description of a model program.

The development and evolution of employee assistance programs (EAPs) has been quite different from that of outplacement. EAPs emerged largely in the 1970s as company-run programs to reduce the direct and indirect costs of treating alcohol and substance abusers. Not only is it expensive to pay for such treatment in hospital or outpatient programs, but also the employee has even more frequent absenteeism from work than that caused directly by substance abuse. Although severe cases still have to be referred to hospital-based programs, many prevention, remedial, and follow-up services to hospital-based programs can be offered in the work setting. The employee can then achieve better attendance and also have a ready place to turn for help at any time of the workday, but also the perception that the workplace does care about his or her situation. This immediate accessibility to, and perception of, support are key components of psychological services for anyone struggling with substance addiction.

The fact that employers perceived a value to the treatment of a problem in the workplace setting, even when the problem was not totally related to the work environment, was a major "breakthrough." Now workplace treatment went beyond simply emergency care for workplace injuries. Whereas most of the types of services described in this section have not been evaluated empirically, at least in published studies, the effects of EAPs are supported by a reasonable body of literature of significant results for both employees (better psychological functioning) and employers (lower direct and indirect costs for care of and performance by employees who are substance abusers) (Myers & Cairo, 1992).

While many employee assistance programs initially employed primarily master's-level substance abuse counselors, as services have expanded in some EAPs, there have been increased opportunities for doctoral-level psychologists providing a wide range of assessment and counseling services. Somewhat ironically, in this age of industrialized managed health care, Seppa (1997) reports that psychologists may have more administrative power over coverage and treatment decisions in EAPs than in managed care settings!

In some cases employers have been quite ambivalent about a continued expansion of EAPs into "comprehensive mental health" facilities for reasons of both cost and company image. On the other hand, employers are far more enthusiastic about an interesting evolution in the past decade—the emergence of occupational health psychology with its more narrow focus on job-related stress. There is clear evidence that such stress leads to increased absenteeism, turnover, and injuries (Keita & Hurrell, 1994). New training programs in occupational health psychology have been developed as a direct outcome of collaboration between the National Institute for Occupational Safety and Health (NIOSH) and the American Psychological Association (APA). Three universities have been funded to offer graduate-level curricula on the application of psychology to improving the quality of worklife and protecting and promoting the safety, health, and well-being of workers. Of the three programs, the one most closely integrated with counseling psychology will be at the University of Minnesota. Students in the University of Minnesota counseling psychology program will be able to minor in occupational health psychology and take courses and training in collaboration with the Industrial Relations Center of the Carlson School of Management, the School of Kinesiology and Leisure Studies, and the Center for Research on Girls and Women in Sport. Further description of the rationale for and the development of occupational health psychology training and service programs may be found in a special section of the journal, *Professional Psychology: Research and Practice* (volume 30, pp. 117–142).

Counseling psychologists in other settings have already begun research programs related to the components of programs for preventing stress in the workplace (Kagan, Kagan, & Watson, 1995; Roberts & Geller, 1995) as well as developmental programs for improved coping with occupational stress (Bowman & Stern, 1995). Such efforts, along with the remedial interventions for stress (Lowman, 1993; Murphy, Hurrell, Sauter, & Keita, 1995) clearly suggest that counseling psychologists who have been trained in understanding how to intervene in career settings to reduce occupational stress will have many new opportunities in the coming years.

The School-to-Work Transition Movement: Frontiers for Career Interventions

Counseling psychologists have had a long, even if more recently declining, role in schools. As described in Chapter 14, the work of Super and colleagues was key in the development of career education programs. Such programs were expanded rapidly in the 1960s as one way of responding to the challenge of the Russians being the first in space with their successful launching of *Sputnik*. America felt challenged to identify and channel its best students into greater achievement. The "Great Society" concepts of then President Lyndon Johnson also included helping all students identify and realize their potential. Numerous counseling psychologists were involved in the design, implementation, and evaluation of career education programs throughout the 1960s and 1970s. Then, as noted earlier in this section, the narrowing of focus in public education to basic academic skills (that is, the reduction or elimination of art, music, career education, and so forth) resulted in significant restrictions in the continuation and development of such programs. Gysbers (1997) provides a review of the smaller but significant continuation of such concepts in some ongoing comprehensive guidance programs.

One of the long extant criticisms of career education programs has been their focus on college-bound youths. The very concept of "career" hardly applies to the experience of most students who move from high school years, often even before finishing high school, into the workforce. As the workforce became more technological and service-oriented, and fewer jobs were available in unskilled or semiskilled manufacturing plants, students who were not college bound were increasingly found to be unemployed, floundering in whatever jobs they did get, switching jobs frequently, and rarely finding chances for advancement. The discrepancies in pay for college graduates compared to high school graduates has steadily widened in recent years; when current pay rates are adjusted for inflation, contemporary high school graduates actually make less than high school graduates of their parents' generation. Concerns with these potentially costly social trends—costly to individuals in terms of their mental health, to society in terms of unemployment, and welfare payments—led the federal government to pass, in 1994, the School-to-Work Opportunities Act. The purpose of this act was to support the development of partnerships between industries and schools so that high school students would receive more coursework and experience directly related to the kinds of work they might enter after graduating from high school. Ideally, such programs will result in students receiving, at graduation, a "skill certificate verifying that they have mastered occupational skills . . . [to] be used in any state to obtain employment" (Worthington & Juntunen, 1997, p. 331).

There are significant challenges for counseling psychologists who work with these work-bound, as compared to college-bound youths. Modest changes in career education programs are *not* going to address the issues of this culturally diverse, often discouraged and poorly educated population. As Fouad (1997) describes, many of the participants in such programs are irregular in their school attendance and continue that pattern of irregular attendance in the workplace. Blustein, Phillips, Jobin-Davis et al. (1997) completed a comprehensive qualitative study of such youth and had three strong recommendations to offer regarding new concepts that must be considered when working with the school-to-work population. First, accept these students' need to rely on counselors and instructors to help them make decisions. Expecting them, based on their own life experiences, to achieve highly autonomous rational career decision-making styles, is unrealistic. Second, understand that for most of these students, "career" will be an emergent process (more like a "set of happenings") rather than a planful process. Only as such students begin to accumulate positive job experiences will they be able to see the value of planning future steps. Finally, their results point to complexities in who can provide effective support as these young people struggle with life and career transitions. Strong support from certain individuals, like counselors, mentors, and supervisors at work, often prove to be the most significant components of success and satisfaction in jobs for these youths. Ironically, the involvement of these youths' family members, although often well intentioned, may actually have a negative impact. These findings by Blustein and colleagues (1997) regarding the often negative effects of family members trying to provide support, parallel findings reviewed by Mallinckrodt and Fretz (1988) regarding the experiences of recently unemployed professionals.

While counseling psychologists and other professionals are only in the first stages of implementing school-to-work programs, the new opportunities are certainly broad in scope and professionally challenging. This is a frontier that encompasses the preventive, developmental, and remedial roles of counseling psychologists on every one of the five unifying themes of the profession: focus on intact individuals, focus on assets and strengths, focus on brief interventions, focus on person–environmental interactions (a very pervasive and powerful environment for these individuals), and focus on educational and career development.

TRAINING COUNSELING PSYCHOLOGISTS AS CAREER INTERVENTIONISTS

There has been a striking paradox in counseling psychology for the past 30 years regarding the training of counseling psychologists as career interventionists. Though we, the authors, believe this paradox is shrinking, we must acknowledge that we have yet to see empirical, as compared to anecdotal, evidence of this change. We hope that the emerging literature and patterns we identify and support in this section will soon bring this paradox to an end so that it becomes no more than a historical footnote in the history of counseling psychology.

What is the paradox? Recall from Chapter 1 that an emphasis on career development and vocational environments was presented as the fifth unifying theme of the profession of counseling psychology. In Chapter 14, Borgen (1991) and Gelso and Fassigner (1992) were cited as using words like *vitality* and *vigorous* to describe vocational research and intervention. On the other hand, Heppner, O'Brien, Hinkelman, and Flores (1996) provide evidence of continuation of a pattern, well documented by Fitzgerald and Osipow (1988), that counseling psychology trainees perceive themselves as having less interest and less ability in career vocational counseling than in social emotional counseling. Heppner and colleagues (1996) also find that less attention and creative teaching are given to career, as compared to personal, counseling coursework. Spokane (1991) and Krumboltz and Coon (1995) lament the comparative lack of attention in the published literature to the quantity and quality of supervision of practicum training in career interventions. Swanson (1995) reviews several studies showing "that some counseling psychologists hold negative attitudes toward career counseling . . . these attitudes may be communicated to clients and reflected in the quality of counseling" (p. 228). Perhaps most painful are the responses from the trainees surveyed by Heppner et al. (1996): "trainees' most negative experiences were disparaging remarks about career counseling from faculty and supervisors . . ." (p. 105).

Moreover, while the profession holds to the scientist–professional model as the ideal for counseling psychologists, in the area of vocational behavior and interventions, there has at best been uneven interactions between theory and practice. A special conference was held in the 1990s devoted to the lack of utility of contemporary theories of vocational behavior for career interventions appropriate for today's world of work (Savickas & Walsh, 1996). The fact that this text has two separate chapters on career development and career interventions also reflects that disconcerting separation. Thus, the paradox: A key historical root of the profession that still manifests vitality and vigor in research has been comparatively marginalized in the practice portions of many counseling psychology training programs.

Fortunately for the profession, the "negative" side of this paradox is increasingly being countered by contemporary experiences of trainees and by proposed new developments in training and supervision for career interventions and an integration of psychotherapy and career counseling. The preceding paragraph described only the negative experiences of Heppner and colleagues' (1996) respondents; on the other hand, trainees reported having very positive results from their actual experiences in providing career counseling. Not only did they like conducting career counseling, they also found themselves fascinated by areas like the match between work environment and personality style and the need to be able to integrate career and personal counseling. Another positive development is found in Krumboltz and Coon's (1995) description of an innovative training program that integrates preparation for career interventions with preparation for multicultural counseling. Their program is conceptually well articulated in terms of bringing contextual factors into interpersonal relationships in counseling focused on career concerns; as such, it responds to long unmet critical needs to provide potentially more effective career interventions for culturally diverse populations. Additional advances in conceptualizations for more appropriate training in career interventions may be found in Gerstein and Shullman (1992) who provide a detailed outline of the coursework, practica, and postdoctoral experiences needed to become an effective counseling psychologist in business and organizational settings. All these articles are important references for readers to consult to understand what *should* be the nature of coursework training and supervised experience for competent functioning in career interventions.

Although several authors have described the importance of a fusion of psychotherapy and career counseling (described in a preceding section), there have as yet been no published models for such training. How can we effectively and efficiently encompass preparation for a broad range of career interventions, such as career education and outplacement counseling, as well as for the more psychotherapeutically oriented interventions needed by indecisive clients? As one way of having trainees and supervisors better understand the kinds of developments needed to become effective providers of career interventions, O'Brien, Heppner, Flores, and Bikos (1997) developed a career counseling self-efficacy scale for *counselors*. This measure may prove quite useful not only for trainees for their own self-assessments, but also for training programs to use as a "needs assessment" tool. Knowing how students see their own self-efficacy as career interventionists can provide critical information for developing courses and practica that will enable trainees to become more competent providers of a full range of career interventions, from preventive and developmental, to remedial psychotherapeutic interventions.

The development of occupational health psychology programs, such as described earlier in this chapter in the section on evolving markets in the workplace, may well incorporate many of the training and supervised experience recommendations of Gerstein and Shullman (1992); if so, these programs will provide a much-needed increase in breadth of experience in career intervention practica. The new millennium thus begins with key conceptual components in place to restore training in the practice of career interventions to a place as vital and vigorous as the productivity of the researchers in vocational behavior and career development.

SUMMARY

Concomitant with changing meanings of the word *career* in recent decades, there have been new research and service program developments yielding an extraordinarily broad array of career interventions. These interventions range from classroom activities to self-administered computerized programs to individualized relationships that are essentially indistinguishable from personal counseling. We described five dimensions on which this diversity of interventions can be compared: clients' questions, populations served, strategic objectives, theoretical orientation, techniques used. We then provided three extensive illustrations of career interventions that encompassed variations on each of the five dimensions. All of the interventions illustrated could be offered by a counseling psychologist as an independent practitioner or as part of the services of a counseling service in a school, university, or work setting.

Given the variety of interventions, an important question is whether some are more helpful than others. In the past two decades, a wide variety of reviews and meta-analyses have documented the impact of career interventions on the career development and adjustment of diverse groups of students, workers, and clients. The average effects of career counseling are slightly greater than those typically obtained in meta-analyses of psychotherapy. However, for career interventions, measurements have been largely on more immediate outcomes such as gains in occupational information and self-knowledge. Ultimately, the profession needs to demonstrate that career counseling has an impact on persons obtaining and retaining jobs in which they are more productive and satisfied. We described four needed changes in research on career interventions that can be made quite easily, yet will greatly improve the quality of our research findings. By following such recommendations, we can learn much more about what works best for whom in career interventions: Are there some personal or cultural characteristics of clients that affect the quality of outcomes? Are some particular components of career interventions more helpful than other components?

The persisting difficulties presented to career counselors by a small group of clients known as "indecisive" clients provided an opportunity to explore the values of diagnosis and treatment planning in individualized career counseling. When working with such clients, there is great overlap between traditional psychotherapy and career counseling. We explored the wide array of opinions about this overlap using the words *fusion, diffusion,* and *confusion.* There are indeed many important shared change processes in psychotherapy and career counseling that are beneficial for counseling psychologists to explore.

In our section on evolving markets and new frontiers for career interventions, we described new opportunities for counseling psychologists in the workplace and in schools. In workplace settings, there are a wide range of opportunities ranging from career development offices to employee assistance programs to newly funded training and service programs in occupational health psychology. In schools, recent federal legislation supporting the development of school-to-work transition programs provides counseling psychologists with a unique opportunity to combine the five unifying themes of our profession in much-needed innovations to serve those high school students who will be entering directly into the world of work.

The final section of the chapter, on training counseling psychologists as career interventionists, reviewed a remarkable paradox regarding the training of many graduate students in past decades: Despite the vigor and vitality of *research* in career psychology, *training* in career counseling and career interventions has often been marginalized in counseling psychology graduate programs. We reviewed some evidence that these image and training issues are now being attended to. Indeed, it is only when students, faculty, and practicum/intern supervisors address these issues that all counseling psychologists will be prepared to serve as effective practitioners of career interventions for the world of work in the twenty-first century.

REFERENCES

American College Testing Program. (1987). *DISCOVER.* Iowa City: Author.

Arbona, C. (1996). Career theory and practice in a multicultural context. In M. L. Savickas and W. B. Walsh (Eds.), *Handbook of career counseling theory and practice* (pp. 45–54). Palo Alto, CA: Davies-Black Publishing.

Azrin, N. H., & Basalel, V. A. (1980). *Job club counselors manual: A behavioral approach to vocational counseling.* Baltimore: University Park Press.

Barak, A., Shiloh, S., & Haushner, O. (1992). Modification of interests through cognitive restructuring: Test of a theoretical model in preschool children. *Journal of Counseling Psychology, 39,* 490–497.

Bingham, R. P., & Ward, C. M. (1996). Practical applications of career counseling with ethnic minority women. In M. L. Savickas and W. B. Walsh (Eds.), *Handbook of career counseling theory and practice* (pp. 291–314). Palo Alto, CA: Davies-Black Publishing.

Blustein, D. L., Phillips, S. D., Jobin-Davis, K., Finkelberg, S. L., & Roarke, A. E. (1997). A theory-building investigation of the school-to-work transition. *The Counseling Psychologist, 25,* 364–402.

Blustein, D. L., & Spengler, P. M. (1995). Personal adjustment: Career counseling and psychotherapy. In W. B. Walsh and S. H. Osipow (Eds.), *Handbook of vocational psychology* (2nd ed., pp. 295–329). Hillsdale, NJ: Lawrence Erlbaum.

Bolles, R. N. (1998). *What color is your parachute?* Berkeley, CA: Ten Speed Press.

Bordin, E. S. (1968). *Psychological counseling* (2nd ed.). New York: Appleton-Century-Crofts.

Bordin, E. S., & Kopplin, D. A. (1973). Motivational conflict and vocational development. *Journal of Counseling Psychology, 20,* 154–161.

Borgen, F. H. (1991). Megatrends and milestones in vocational behavior: A 20-year counseling psychology retrospective. *Journal of Vocational Behavior, 39,* 263–290.

Bowman, G. D., & Stern, M. (1995). Adjustment to occupational stress: The relationship of perceived control to effectiveness of coping strategies. *Journal of Counseling Psychology, 42,* 294–303.

Crites, J. O. (1981). *Career counseling: Models, methods, and materials.* New York: McGraw-Hill.

Danish, S. J., & D'Augelli, A. R. (1983). *Helping skills II. Life development interventions.* New York: Human Sciences Press.

Dawis, R. V. (1996). The theory of work adjustment and person–environment–correspondence counseling. In D. Brown, L. Brooks, & Associates (Eds.), *Career choice and development* (3rd ed., pp. 75–120). San Francisco, CA: Jossey-Bass.

Drum, D. J., & Knott, E. F. (1977). *Structured groups for facilitating development.* New York: Human Sciences Press.

Fitzgerald, L. F., & Osipow, S. H. (1988). We have seen the future, but is it us? The vocational aspirations of graduate students in counseling psychology. *Professional Psychology: Research and Practice, 19,* 575–583.

Fouad, N. A. (1997). School-to-work transition: Voice from an implementer. *The Counseling Psychologist, 25,* 403–412.

Fouad, N. A., & Bingham, R. B. (1995). Career counseling with racial and ethnic minorities. In W. B. Walsh and S. H. Osipow (Eds.), *Handbook of vocational psychology* (2nd ed., pp. 331–366). Hillsdale, NJ: Lawrence Erlbaum.

Fretz, B. R. (1981). Evaluating the effectiveness of career interventions. *Journal of Counseling Psychology, 28,* 77–89.

Fretz, B. R., & Merikangas, M. W. (1992). Preretirement programming: Needs and responses. In D. Lea and Z. Leibowitz (Eds.), *Adult career development* (2nd ed., pp. 269–294). Alexandria, VA: National Career Development Association.

Fuller, B. E., Blinne, W. R., & Johnston, J. A. (1994). First year student early intervention project: The applications of "My Vocational Situation" in outreach career planning programming. *Journal of Career Development, 21,* 149–154.

Fuqua, D. R., & Hartman, B. W. (1983). Differential diagnosis and treatment of career indecision. *Personnel and Guidance Journal, 62,* 27–29.

Gati, I. (1996). Computer-assisted career counseling: Challenges and prospects. In M. L. Savickas and W. B. Walsh (Eds.), *Handbook of career counseling theory and practice* (pp. 169–190). Palo Alto, CA: Davies-Black Publishing.

Gelso, C. J., & Fassinger, R. E. (1992). Personality, development, and counseling psychology: Depth, ambivalence, and actualization. *Journal of Counseling Psychology, 39,* 275–298.

Gerstein, L. H., & Shullman, S. L. (1992). Counseling psychology and the workplace: The emergence of organizational counseling psychology. In S. D. Brown and R. W. Lent (Eds.), *Handbook of counseling psychology* (2nd ed., pp. 581–626). New York: John Wiley & Sons.

Gysbers, N. C. (1997). Involving counseling psychology in the school-to-work movement. *The Counseling Psychologist, 25,* 413–427.

Gysbers, N. C., Heppner, M. J., & Johnston, J. A. (1997). *Career counseling: Process, issues, and techniques.* Boston: Allyn & Bacon.

Hackett, G. (1993). Career counseling and psychotherapy: False dichotomies and recommended remedies. *Journal of Career Assessment, 1,* 105–117.

Harmon, L. W. (1994). A moving target: The widening gap between theory and practice. In M. L. Savickas and W. B. Walsh (Eds.), *Handbook of career counseling theory and practice* (pp. 37–44). Palo Alto, CA: Davies-Black Publishing.

Heppner, M. J., & Hendricks, F. (1995). A process and outcome study examining career indecision and indecisiveness. *Journal of Counseling and Development, 73,* 426–437.

Heppner, M. J., O'Brien, K. M., Hinkelman, J. M., & Flores, L. Y. (1996). Training counseling psychologists in career development: Are we our own worst enemies? *The Counseling Psychologist, 24,* 105–125.

Herr, E. L. (1996). Toward the convergence of career theory and practice. In M. L. Savickas and W. B. Walsh (Eds.), *Handbook of career counseling theory and practice* (pp. 13–36). Palo Alto, CA: Davies-Black Publishing.

Holland, J. L. (1985). *You and your career.* Odessa, FL: Psychological Assessment Resources.

Holland, J. L. (1994). *Self-Directed Search Form R* (4th ed.). Odessa, FL: Psychological Assessment Resources.

Holland, J. L., Daiger, D. C., & Power, P. G. (1980). *My Vocational Situation.* Palo Alto, CA: Consulting Psychologists Press.

Holland, J. L., & Holland, J. E. (1977). Vocational indecision: More evidence and speculation. *Journal of Counseling Psychology, 24,* 404–415.

Holland, J. L., Johnston, J. A., & Asama, N. G. (1993). The Vocational Identity Scale: A diagnostic and treatment tool. *Journal of Career Assessment, 1,* 1–12.

Holland, J. L., Magoon, T. M., & Spokane, A. R. (1981). Counseling psychology: Career interventions, research and theory. *Annual Review of Psychology, 32,* 279–305.

Jordaan, J. E., Myers, R. A., Layton, W. C., & Morgan, H. H. (1968). *The counseling psychologist.* Washington, DC: American Psychological Association.

Kagan, N. I., Kagan, H., & Watson, M. G. (1995). Stress reduction in the workplace: The effectiveness of psychoeducational programs. *Journal of Counseling Psychology, 42,* 71–78.

Keita, G. P., & Hurrell, J. J. (Eds.). (1994). *Job stress in a changing workforce: Investigating gender, diversity, and family issues.* Washington, DC: American Psychological Association.

Kirschner, T., Hoffman, M. A., & Hill, C. E. (1994). Case study of the process and outcome of career counseling. *Journal of Counseling Psychology, 41,* 216–226.

Krumboltz, J. D. (1991). *Manual for the Career Beliefs Inventory.* Palo Alto, CA: Consulting Psychologists Press.

Krumboltz, J. D. (1996). Learning theory of career counseling. In M. L. Savickas and W. B. Walsh (Eds.), *Handbook of career counseling theory and practice* (pp. 55–80). Palo Alto, CA: Davies-Black Publishing.

Krumboltz, J. D., & Coon, D. W. (1995). Current professional issues in vocational psychology. In W. B. Walsh and S. H. Osipow (Eds.), *Handbook of vocational psychology* (2nd ed., pp. 391–426). Mahwah, NJ: Lawrence Erlbaum.

Lea, D., & Leibowitz, Z. (Eds.). (1992). *Adult career development* (2nd ed.). Alexandria, VA: National Career Development Association.

Lent, E. B. (1996). The person focus in career theory and practice. In M. L. Savickas and W. B. Walsh (Eds.), *Handbook of career counseling theory and practice* (pp. 109–120). Palo Alto, CA: Davies-Black Publishing.

Leong, F. T. L. (1993). The career counseling process with racial/ethnic minorities: The case of Asian Americans. *Career Development Quarterly, 42,* 26–40.

Lowman, R. (1993). *Counseling and psychotherapy of work dysfunctions.* Washington, DC: American Psychological Association.

Lucas, M. S. (1993). A validation of types of career indecision at a counseling center. *Journal of Counseling Psychology, 40,* 440–446.

Mallinckrodt, B., & Fretz, B. R. (1988). Social support and the impact of job loss on older professionals. *Journal of Counseling Psychology, 35,* 281–286.

Mann, J. (1973). *Time limited psychotherapy.* Cambridge, MA: Harvard University Press.

Meara, N. M. (1996). Prudence and career assessment: Making our implicit assumptions explicit. In M. L. Savickas and W. B. Walsh (Eds.), *Handbook of career counseling theory and practice* (pp. 315–330). Palo Alto, CA: Davies-Black Publishing.

Meara, N. M., & Patton, M. J. (1994). Contribution of the working alliance in the practice of career counseling. *Career Development Quarterly, 43,* 161–178.

Murphy, L. R., Hurrell, J. J., Sauter, S. L., & Keita, G. P. (1995). *Job stress interventions.* Washington, DC: American Psychological Association.

Myers, R. A., & Cairo, P. C. (1992). Counseling and career adjustment. In S. D. Brown and R. W. Lent (Eds.), *Handbook of counseling psychology* (2nd ed., pp. 549–580). New York: John Wiley & Sons.

O'Brien, K. M., Heppner, M. J., Flores, L. Y, & Bikos, L. H. (1997). The Career Counseling Self-efficacy Scale: Instrument development and training applications. *Journal of Counseling Psychology, 44,* 20–31.

Oliver, L. W., & Spokane, A. R. (1988). Career-intervention outcome: What contributes to client gain? *Journal of Counseling Psychology, 35,* 447–462.

Osipow, S. H., Carney, C. C., Winer, J. L., Yanico, B., & Koschier, M. (1980). *The Career Decision Scale* (3rd rev. ed.). Columbus, OH: Marathon Consulting Press.

Peterson, G. W., Sampson, J. P., Reardon, R. C., & Lenz, J. G. (1996). A cognitive information processing approach to career problem solving and decision making. In D. Brown, L. Brooks, & Associates (Eds.), *Career choice and development* (3rd ed., pp. 423–476). San Francisco, CA: Jossey-Bass.

Phillips, S. D. (1992). Career counseling: Choice and implementation. In S. D. Brown and R. W. Lent (Eds.), *Handbook of counseling psychology* (2nd ed., pp. 513–548). New York: John Wiley & Sons.

Pickman, A. J. (1994). *The complete guide to outplacement counseling.* Hillsdale, NJ: Lawrence Erlbaum.

Pope, M. (1995). Career interventions for gay and lesbian clients: A synopsis of practice knowledge and research needs. *The Career Development Quarterly, 44,* 191–203.

Richardson, M. S. (1996). From career counseling to counseling/psychotherapy and work, jobs, and career. In M. L. Savickas and W. B. Walsh (Eds.), *Handbook of career counseling theory and practice* (pp. 347–360). Palo Alto, CA: Davies-Black Publishing.

Roberts, D. S., & Geller, E. S. (1995). An "actively caring" model for occupational safety: A field test. *Applied & Preventive Psychology, 4,* 53–59.

Rounds, J. B., & Tinsley, H. E. (1984). Diagnosis and treatment of vocational problems. In S. D. Brown and R. W. Lent (Eds.), *Handbook of counseling psychology* (pp. 137–177). New York: John Wiley & Sons.

Salamone, P. R. (1982). Difficult cases in career counseling: II. The indecisive client. *Personnel and Guidance Journal, 60,* 496–500.

Savickas, M. L. (1989). Annual review: Practice and research in career counseling and development, 1988. *Career Development Quarterly, 38,* 100–134.

Savickas, M. L. (1996). A framework for linking career theory and practice. In M. L. Savickas and W. B. Walsh (Eds.), *Handbook of career counseling theory and practice* (pp. 191–208). Palo Alto, CA: Davies-Black Publishing.

Savickas, M. L., & Walsh, W. B. (Eds.). (1996). *Handbook of career counseling theory and practice.* Palo Alto, CA: Davies-Black Publishing.

Schlossberg, N. K. (1981). A model for analyzing human adaptation to transition. *The Counseling Psychologist, 9*(2), 2–18.

Seppa, N. (1997, March). Psychology's interest in EAPs grows. *APA Monitor,* p. 32.

Sharf, R. S. (1992). *Applying career development theory to counseling.* Pacific Grove, CA: Brooks/Cole.

Spokane, A. R. (1991). *Career intervention.* Englewood Cliffs, NJ: Prentice-Hall.

Swanson, J. L. (1995). The process and outcome of career counseling. In W. B. Walsh and S. H. Osipow (Eds.), *Handbook of vocational psychology* (2nd ed., pp. 217–259). Hillsdale, NJ: Lawrence Erlbaum.

Tinsley, D. J. & Schwendener-Holt, M. J. (1992). Retirement and leisure. In S. D. Brown and R. W. Lent (Eds.), *Handbook of counseling psychology* (2nd ed., pp. 627–663). New York: John Wiley & Sons.

Walsh, W. B., & Osipow, S. H. (Eds.) (1994). *Career counseling with women.* Hillsdale, NJ: Lawrence Erlbaum.

Walsh, W. B., & Osipow, S. H. (Eds.) (1995). *Handbook of vocational psychology* (2nd ed.). Hillsdale, NJ: Lawrence Erlbaum.

Whiston, S. C., Sexton, T. L., & Lasoff, D. L. (1998). Career-intervention outcome: A replication and extension of Oliver and Spokane (1988). *Journal of Counseling Psychology, 45,* 150–165.

Worthington, R. L., & Juntunen, C. L. (1997). The vocational development of non-college bound youth. *The Counseling Psychologist, 25,* 323–363.

Yalom, I. (1985). *Theory and practice of group psychotherapy* (3rd ed.). New York: Basic Books.

C H A P T E R 16

THERAPEUTIC GROUP WORK: AN ESTABLISHED FORMAT

Stages of Therapeutic Groups

Exploratory Stage

Transition Stage

Working Stage

Termination Stage

Therapeutic Factors in Group Work

Ethical Issues in Therapeutic Group Work

Informed Consent

Confidentiality

Involuntary Membership

Training in Therapeutic Group Work

Therapeutic Group Work in Perspective

An Established Format

Some Research Findings and Issues

Summary

References

Both research and practice have now clearly demonstrated that individual counseling or therapy is effective for a variety of client concerns. Also, clients who seek counseling typically want individual help. Why then should counseling psychologists bother with group treatments such as group counseling and psychotherapy? Why not simply assign all clients to individual counseling? Doing so would certainly simplify the training of counseling psychologists, for then they could be trained only in individual interventions. Assigning all clients to individual treatments would also simplify agency practices, since counseling agencies would no longer need to worry about whom to assign to what interventions. Neither would agencies need to grapple with logistical problems such as how to arrange for group meeting times.

In devising our answer to the above questions, we must first say that what is the simplest practice is often not the *most effective*. To begin with, group procedures allow for an efficient use of the counseling psychologist's time, as a number of individuals may be worked with simultaneously in a group format. More important than this efficiency, however, is the fact that group interventions such as group therapy, just like individual counseling, have been shown to be especially helpful for a range of concerns (Kivlighan, Coleman, & Anderson, 2000).

ADVANTAGES AND LIMITATIONS

Are there unique advantages to group interventions such as group counseling or therapy? Although the research evidence is as yet unclear about this, the major advantages of group treatment are generally seen as *interpersonal*. Thus, the client in group therapy learns by observing other group members, receiving feedback from others, giving feedback and being helpful to other group members, becoming part of a cohesive group and, moreover, participating in the sharing and the give and take of this very personal form of interpersonal interaction.

It follows that clients who will profit most from group interventions are those whose difficulties are in the interpersonal arena. For example, clients who suffer from interpersonal anxiety, who are unsure of their relationship skills, who desire close relationships but for one reason or another shy away from them—all are prime candidates for group therapy. Group therapy also can be particularly effective in less obvious cases. For example, the client whose family dynamics breed secrecy and shame may experience enormous growth from a group experience in which his or her inner feelings are shared and accepted by other members. Likewise, the client whose major problem itself breeds secrecy and shame may find group therapy strikingly helpful. An example of this latter type might be the female incest survivor who participates in group therapy as a way of coming to grips with her sense of shame and self-blame about her incestuous experiences. Recent literature on women who have experienced the trauma of incest supports the idea that group treatments can be especially effective for these clients (Courtois, 1999). The unique efficacy of group therapy for the incest survivor has been stated in a particularly convincing way by one therapist who has worked with this client group in both individual and group formats:

> I can't tell you how many times I have worked with individual clients who were incest survivors on the "shame and blame" syndrome common to incest survivors, and no matter what I say or do as a therapist, I'm only one countervoice to years of self-blame and humiliation. Progress is often relatively slow. Put the same client into an incest survivor's group—she shares her horrible secret—and other people communicate their common experience, and she sees clearly that she is not to blame. The change in group therapy is so much more dramatic than in individual, it is a truly astounding experience for some. The relief often happens even after only one or two sessions. There is something about *universality* and *consensual validation* [see later discussion of these two factors] that occurs in group treatment that makes it extremely effective with incest survivors (Dr. Ruth E. Fassinger, Department of Counseling and Personnel Services, University of Maryland, personal communication, June 12, 1990).

The major advantages of therapeutic groups, as discussed by Corey and Corey (1997), are as follows.

1. Participants can explore their style of relating to others and learn more effective social skills.

2. The group situation offers support for new behaviors and encourages experimentation. Members can try out new behaviors and decide whether they want to incorporate them into their repertoire outside the group.

3. More than in individual counseling, there is a re-creation of the everyday world in many groups, especially if the membership is diverse with respect to interest, age, background, culture, socioeconomic status, and problem type. When groups are heterogeneous in this way, members are able to contact a wide range of personalities, and receive rich and diverse feedback.

4. Members are able to learn about themselves through the experience of others; to experience emotional closeness and caring, which encourages meaningful self-disclosure; and to identify with the struggles of others.

5. The group setting optimally helps participants discover how they affect others. Members can effectively learn what they may be doing interpersonally to create some of their problems, e.g., loneliness, isolation. And members also learn to change unhelpful patterns.

Despite the many advantages of group interventions and the consistent evidence of the overall effectiveness of therapeutic groups (Bednar & Kaul, 1994; Kivlighan et al., 2000), groups are certainly not cure-alls and, just as certainly, groups are not for everyone. In fact, some clients can be emotionally damaged by participating in certain groups. For example, in virtually all forms of group work, there is often a subtle pressure to conform to the group's norms and expectations; and some members may be especially vulnerable to such pressures, taking in these expectations without questioning. As Corey and Corey (1997) note, some clients are too suspicious, too hostile, or too fragile to benefit from group treatment. Persons suffering from certain personality disorders (e.g., borderline personality, narcissistic personality, or sociopathy) may also be ill suited for group therapy (Dykeman & Appleton, 1998; Yalom, 1995). Before a person is accepted into a group, it is important that both counselor and client weigh the advantages and limitations of whatever type of group is being considered for that person. The counseling psychologist needs to assess how likely the client is to profit from the group, as well as how the client's presence will impact on that group.

We would like now to take a step back and examine just what is meant by therapeutic groups and describe some of the major types of such groups as well as the backgrounds of these interventions. Then, in the remainder of the chapter, we explore leadership factors in group work, the stages of groups, the ingredients of effective groups, and some ethical issues in group work. We conclude the chapter with a discussion of the place of group work in counseling psychology, the research issues involved in group treatment, and findings in this area.

Differing Types of Therapeutic Groups.   **TABLE 16.1.**

Type of Group	Focus	Characteristics
Group counseling	Interpersonal Vocational Intrapersonal	Clients within normal range; educational setting; short term; growth-oriented
Group therapy	Interpersonal Intrapersonal	Clients more troubled; clinic or medical setting; longer term; personality change
Training or sensitivity group	Interpersonal Leadership	Clients in normal range; business setting; short term; growth-oriented
Growth groups	Interpersonal	Well-functioning clients; educational setting; short term; self-actualization
Structured groups	Single theme	Varied settings and client disturbance levels; treatment manual; short term; problem solving
Self-help groups	Common problem	Varied settings and client disturbance levels; short term; support and motivation; led by lay person

THERAPEUTIC GROUP WORK: DEFINITION, TYPES, AND BACKGROUND

To begin with, it is possible to define a *group* as "any aggregate of individuals among which some degree of interdependence exists." A *therapeutic group* may be defined as an "aggregate of interdependent individuals whose interaction is in pursuit of some shared goal or goals." The therapeutic group is always more than the sum of its individual parts because the group itself takes on its own life, its own psyche so to speak, and its own personality.

Therapeutic groups can include a wide range of interventions such as group psychotherapy, group counseling, encounter and growth groups, training or T groups, structured groups, and self-help groups. Below we describe each of these types of groups, in particular, group counseling/therapy, and briefly note the background of their development in counseling psychology. The focus and characteristics of each of these types of groups are summarized in Table 16.1.

Group Counseling and Group Psychotherapy

Group counseling tends to be more oriented toward prevention (vs. remediation) than group psychotherapy. Also, group counseling is more likely to focus on the conscious concerns of the client, to include attention to educational and vocational issues as well as personal issues, to occur in educational settings (in contrast to medical or clinical settings), and to be used with clients within the normal range rather than with severely troubled persons. Group counseling is, on the whole, briefer than group therapy, with generally an upper limit of about 20–25 sessions. Group therapy, on the other hand, may continue for several years and is more likely than counseling to seek deep personality change in clients.

Although we have described the typical distinctions between group counseling and therapy, it should be emphasized that the differences are more of degree than kind. There is considerable overlap between the two, just as there is much overlap between the words *counseling* and *therapy* (see definitions in Chapter 1). In fact, except at the extreme ends of the continuum, the differences become blurred or eliminated with most groups in counseling practice. Corey and Corey's (1997) description of group counseling really applies to both group counseling and therapy. According to these authors, participants in group counseling or therapy often have problems of an interpersonal nature, which are well suited to the group format. Clients are able to see a reenactment of their everyday struggles and problems unfold before them in the group. In the group, however, the client is able to work on and through these problems, with the feedback and help of group members. In this way the group provides a slice of reality to the client as well as a vehicle for change. Members are encouraged to get feedback from others about how they are seen, as well as to give such feedback. They also have the chance to reexperience early conflicts with significant others, and in the process of reliving, to work through old issues. The empathy and support of the group also allow members to identify what and how they want to change and to try out new behaviors. Clients can learn to respect individual and cultural differences and, at the same time, discover that on a deep level they are more alike than different. Life situations differ, but their pain and struggles are universal.

Despite the similarities and overlap between group counseling and therapy, the two have differing historical backgrounds. Group counseling, for example, has its roots in education and guidance; its beginnings may be traced to the vocational guidance movement in the early part of the twentieth century. Early guidance groups were mostly in the form of classes and the methods used in these classes were largely instructional (Gazda, 1984). The group psychotherapy movement can also be traced to the early part of the twentieth century, but is usually seen as beginning with the work of Boston internist Joseph Hersey Pratt and his publication in 1906 of "The Home Sanitorium Treatment of Consumption." Like the early group guidance workers, Pratt's group procedures with his tuberculosis patients were largely inspirational and instructional. During this time period also, early psychoanalysts (Freud, Adler, Driekurs, and Furrow) were writing about group analytic work.

Although therapeutic group work was practiced throughout the early part of the twentieth century, it was not until the 1930s that it experienced a major growth spurt. The term *group counseling* may have been first used in 1931 by Dr. Richard D. Allen within a school setting, whereas in the same year J. L. Moreno first used the term *group therapy*. Moreno, an actor turned group therapist, is often seen as the father of group therapy and of the related fields of psychodrama and sociometry. He began experimenting with group therapy early in the twentieth century, and as a medical student in Vienna he organized and led group sessions for Viennese prostitutes. Before emigrating to the United States in 1925, Moreno established "The Theatre of Spontaneous Man," which attempted to represent the dramas of life for therapeutic staging. Moreno also developed the first group therapy journal, *Impromptu,* in 1931.

Other individuals who had a major role in the mushrooming of group therapeutic procedures during this time period were Louis Wender, Paul Schilder, Lauretta Bender, Alexander Wolf, and Samuel Slavson. Slavson's work is of particular note. Ettin (1989) states that Slavson was a prominent proselytizer, prolific writer, and vigilant watchdog in the field of group therapy for more than half of his 91 years. Slavson founded the American Group Psychotherapy Association in 1943 and originated the *International Journal of Group Psychotherapy* in 1951. Many consider Slavson, rather than Moreno, to be the father of group therapy.

Training (T) Groups and Sensitivity Training Groups

The concept of T group (*T* for *training*) or what has come to be its synonym, sensitivity group, grew out of the work of Kurt Lewin. Lewin is considered by many to be the major researcher and theoretician of democracy in psychology (Schmuck & Schmuck, 1979), and the basic mission of the T group was to train democratic managers and administrators in business and industry. These training groups began with the birth of the National Training Laboratories (NTL) in 1947 at Bethel, Maine. NTL tried to create an environment where change could occur, especially interpersonal change, through laboratory training.

In the standard NTL-type T group, participants find themselves in an unstructured situation, in which it is their task to build out of their interaction a group that can help them meet their needs for support, feedback, and learning. The behaviors enacted by members as they participate in the group provide the material for analysis and learning. Thus, T group members have the chance to learn about how their behavior is seen by others, the roles they and others tend to play, ways of being more sensitive to others, and methods for understanding group dynamics. All of this is aimed at translating behavior into more effective democratic leadership. Time is usually provided for trainees to plan how they will apply their knowledge after the laboratory (Eddy & Lubin, 1971). T groups are oriented toward the here and now and are developmental and growth-oriented in nature, rather than remedial or even preventive. They may range from a 1-day workshop to an ongoing group, although the typical T group may entail two or so weeks of intensive training.

Encounter and Growth Groups

Just as the 1930s witnessed a mushrooming of interest in group therapy, the 1960s saw heightened involvement in new kinds of therapeutic groups. Undergirding these new groups was a social–psychological movement, called the "human potential movement." In psychology, this movement was spearheaded by humanistic therapists such as Carl Rogers, Abraham Maslow, Herbert Otto, Jack Gibb, and William Schutz. The essential theme of this movement was that humans tend to actualize only a tiny fraction of their potential and that psychological interventions of a developmental nature can help them move toward self-actualization. Many of these interventions took the form of groups, the most prominent groups of the times were called "encounter," or "growth," groups.

Thus, the encounter or growth group grew out of individuals' needs to become more fully functioning. These groups aimed to help already well-functioning persons relate more effectively and intimately with others, reduce feelings of alienation, and become more aware of their feelings and direct experiencing rather than only their cognitive functioning. Encounter groups tend to promote such norms as openness, honesty, release of inhibitions, sharing, being on a feeling level, risking new behaviors, and being in the here and now (Peterson & Nisenholz, 1987). Such groups are usually emotionally intensive experiences, and the leader tends to take a more active and directive role than in most therapeutic groups. In the 1960s and early 1970s encounter groups often contained physical interaction among participants, and there was a good bit of experimenting with dance, art, massage, and nudity. In today's more conservative climate, there is much less of this sort of experimentation, and group leadership tends to be less active and aggressive. Although growth groups are not as popular as they once were, there is clearly still a place for them in counseling psychology, particularly given their focus on human potential and growth.

Finally, one additional type of growth group deserves note. The *marathon growth group* also grew out of the 1960s, and it, too, aimed at enhancing interpersonal openness, sensitivity, and intimacy. The distinguishing feature of the marathon group was its continuation over many hours or even days with only minimal breaks. The typical marathon group, for example, might occur over a weekend, with breaks only for eating and sleeping. The idea behind this procedure is that when interaction among participants occurs without the usual interruptions, people are more likely to take off their social masks and become genuine with one another. Although not now as popular as in the 1960s and 1970s, marathons are still conducted, usually as part of ongoing group therapy. Thus, the typical marathon group is held at some point during the ongoing life of a therapy group, with enough regular group therapy time after the marathon to work through issues that emerged during the intensity of the extended sessions. Marathons conducted in this way can be powerful adjuncts to group counseling or therapy.

Structured Groups

Just as the encounter group was a child of the 1960s, the structured group grew out of the social–psychological climate of the 1970s, with its emphasis on accountability of services and the need to provide efficient as well as effective treatments. These groups are increasingly used by agencies, schools, and college counseling centers (Corey & Corey, 1997). The structured group is oriented toward a single theme, and from this theme emerges the goals of treatment. For example, the theme might be assertiveness training, and the goals consequently would revolve around improving participants' assertiveness skills. Structured groups tend to be brief, for example, 4–15 weekly sessions, lasting 1.5–2 hours. Typically, the leader follows a predeveloped treatment manual in which the tasks for each session are spelled out. In terms of the developmental–preventive–remedial continuum, structured groups tend to be preventive. Over the years, the themes of such groups have emerged from issues that were reflected in the broader society. Examples of popular structured group themes are: stress management, adult children of alcoholics, assertion training, support for incest survivors, managing relationships, ending relationships, overcoming perfectionism, women in transition, and eating disorders (e.g., bulimia).

Self-Help Groups

The final type of therapeutic group that we shall describe is often ignored in discussions of group work. Self-help groups, however, fulfill a critical need for many people that is not met by mental health workers. Self-help groups are composed of people with common interests and problems. They give participants a crucial support system, providing motivation to help them begin changing their lives. Self-help groups stress a common identity based on a common life situation far more than any other type of group. Typically open (new members may enter the group at any time), these groups offer inspiration, hope, encouragement, and support, often to people who feel little hope to begin with. Examples of self-help groups are Alcoholics Anonymous, Weight-Watchers, Mended Hearts, and Recovery. These groups are led by persons who struggle with the same problems as members (e.g., the recovering alcoholic in AA), rather than being professionally led. During the 1990s, it was estimated that somewhere between 10 and 15 million persons were members of self-help groups (Conyne, Wilson, & Ward, 1997).

GROUP LEADERSHIP: APPROACHES, TASKS, AND QUALITIES

The Leader's Focus

Over the years, there has been considerable controversy over whether the group leader ought to focus his or her observations on the group as a whole or on the individuals within the group. A third possibility is to focus on the interactions between and among members.

Group-Centered Approach
The method of focusing on the group as a whole originated and received its strongest voice at the Tavistock Clinic in England (e.g., Bion, 1961). This approach is based on the idea that the group is an entity in itself and that individuals learn most by understanding this entity, how they fit into it, and how they contribute to it. In the extreme, the therapist's comments when following this method are rarely aimed at individuals but rather seek to clarify the underlying meanings and processes in the group as a whole.

Individual-Centered Approach
Examples of the individual-centered approach are psychoanalytic groups and certain gestalt therapy groups. In some gestalt groups, for example, the individual

participant is placed into the "hot seat" and the counselor devotes his or her thera-peutic energies for a period of time to that client and the issues he or she is experi-encing at the moment. Other participants presumably learn through observing and identifying, although their comments are sought at times. Individual members take turns in the hot seat.

Interpersonally Centered Approach

In this third approach the main attention of the leader is given to the interactions between and among members. The focus tends to be how the members affect and experience one another.

As a way of clarifying the three approaches, imagine a group therapy client, Jane, en-tering her group for a given session, expressing that "I feel angry today—I've had this sense of irritation since yesterday, and today it has just gotten bigger and bigger. I feel so abusive toward this group, but don't know why." Consider the three therapist re-sponses given below, and decide which of the three approaches they fit.

1. "I notice the group has responded with silence, like last week when Jim ex-pressed irritation. Actually it feels more like silent irritation. I wonder what is happening in the group right now."

2. "Jane, could you share with us what these feelings are like [about] for you right now?"

3. "Jane, you looked at Jim when you said that, and now he's looking very respon-sive. Jim, what are you feeling right now about Jane's experience?"

Toward an Integrated Approach

Perhaps most group leaders attempt to integrate the group and individual ap-proaches (the interpersonal approach fits well with both), as theory and research have suggested that neither extreme is very helpful (Horwitz, 1986). Basically, two types of attempts at such integration have occurred. The first might be called the *al-ternation view*. There are certain points in the life of a group when the total mem-bership is affected, for example, beginning phases, entry of new members, therapist's absence. At these points, group interpretations are most appropriate, since group behavior is best understood in terms of the dynamics of the entire group. When the group is functioning cohesively, however, work on individual (and interpersonal) issues is most effective.

The second integrative approach is the *common group tension* approach, ex-emplified by the work of Horwitz (1986). Within this approach it is theorized that a common group theme is always operative in the functioning of the group and that individual needs are always interacting with this underlying theme. Horwitz's ap-proach is to offer interpretations and other comments to individuals, and after working with a few individuals, to detect the underlying group theme that begins to emerge. As this common group "tension" becomes clearer to the therapist, she or he then makes a group observation or interpretation. As an example of this ap-proach, Horwitz describes a group in which, following a vacation by the therapist, virtually all members expressed often confused and confusing feelings of abandonment as well as guilt over such feelings. As these feelings were expressed in various ways by the individual members, the therapist focused on each individual's specific issues. As it became clear that the theme of abandonment was common to each member's concerns, the therapist made several interpretations about this and how it was affecting the life of the group.

The Leader's Tasks

In virtually all types of therapeutic groups, but especially in the less structured, more interactional ones such as group counseling/therapy and growth groups, there are common tasks in which the leader must engage. Although one could think of numerous leader tasks in therapeutic group work, Yalom (1995) has convincingly proposed that there are three fundamental tasks: (1) the creation and maintenance of the group, (2) group culture building, and (3) activation and illumination of the here and now.

Creation and Maintenance of the Group

The therapist's first crucial task is to create and convene the group. The importance of selecting and preparing members cannot be overemphasized. Research and clinical experience generally support the observation that certain types of individuals tend to do poorly in therapeutic groups. It is probably wise not to include persons who are paranoid, hypochondriacal, sociopathic, brain damaged, acutely psychotic, or addicted to drugs or alcohol (unless the group is explicitly aimed at the drug-dependent person). Also, Yalom (1995) suggests that persons who have extreme difficulties with intimacy are not good group candidates (with the emphasis on the extreme), and those in an acute life crisis may need more individual attention than can be given in the group format. Finally, Yalom (1995) discusses at length the group "deviant," who should not be placed into an interactional group. What is meant by *deviant* is someone who cannot or will not examine himself or herself and his or her relationship with others in the group.

On the positive side, it is wise to select members who fit well with the group and to form groups with a reasonable balance of interpersonal styles. Try for a "reasonable diversity," while avoiding potential scapegoats and "misfits" (Dies, 1987). Considerable clinical skill is required to "screen in" suitable members and "screen out" those who will not do well in the group. Often more than one individual interview is required to perform this selection.

During the process of selection and during the early phase of the group's life, it is important that members be well informed about what groups are like, what can be expected of them, and what they can expect from others. Indeed, people have many misconceptions about what group therapy is like, and much of this misinformation is negative—for example, groups are unpredictable and will force individuals to reveal what they do not want to (Corey & Corey, 1997). Correcting these misconceptions is a valuable beginning.

Once the group begins, the therapist's job is to deter anything that threatens the group's cohesiveness. Thus, the therapist works to prevent dropouts because these, more than perhaps anything else, will threaten the group's existence. Continued tardiness, absences, the formation of cliques within the group, certain kinds of socializing between members outside the group, and scapegoating all threaten the integrity of the group and require the therapist's intervention. The creation and maintenance of the group is so important in the early stages that at times the pressing needs of the individual must be put aside. Yalom uses the example of a group containing four core members who were male and who had trouble keeping female members. During two new female members' first group meeting, they were ignored. One of the male members entered the group late and immediately began discussing a problem he was having without acknowledging the new members' presence or existence. After a half hour, Yalom interrupted the client with the question, "Mike, I wonder what hunches you have about how our two new members are feeling in the group today?" This question turned the members' attention to how they had ignored the two new members and helped Mike begin to work on his tendency to ignore the needs of others.

Group Culture Building

Once the group becomes a physical reality, the counselor's main job is to develop it into a therapeutic social system. In seeking to do this, the counselor works to establish a code of behavioral rules (often unstated), or norms, that guide the interactions of the group members. This norm building is more complicated in group than in individual counseling. In individual counseling, the counselor is the only agent of change, but in group therapy other group members serve as perhaps the most potent agents of change. The therapist's task is to create a group culture that facilitates therapeutic interaction among members.

This therapeutic culture, as we said, contains the norms that guide client behavior. Just which norms are we talking about? Active involvement, self-disclosure of immediate feelings, nonjudgmental acceptance of other members, spontaneity of expression, desire for self-understanding, dissatisfaction with at least some of one's present behavioral patterns, and the desire for change—these are the main norms (or values or "oughts") that the group leader works toward establishing.

Both group theory and research support the notion that the therapist facilitates the building of therapeutic norms through two roles: that of a *technical expert* and that of a *model-setting participant* (Dies, 1987; Yalom, 1995). The therapist functions as a technical expert when instructing the client about the rules of the group prior to the group's beginning and during the early stages. Such instruction is reinforced by the weight of the therapist's authority and experience and by the fact that the rationale presented by the therapist for these rules makes good, clear sense to the client.

During the early stages of the group, the counselor as technical expert can use a variety of means to help shape norms. Yalom (1995) provides examples of the methods available. If the therapist wants to create an interactional network in which the members freely interact rather than directing all comments to the therapist then:

> . . . therapists may implicitly instruct members in their pre-group interviews or
> in the first group sessions; they may, repeatedly during the meetings, ask for all

members' reactions to another member or toward a group issue; they may wonder why conversation is invariably directed toward the therapist; they may refuse to answer questions or may even close their eyes when . . . addressed; they may ask the group to engage in exercises that teach patients to interact—for example, asking each member of the group, in turn, to give his or her first impressions of every other member; or therapists may, in a much less obtrusive manner, shape behavior by rewarding members who address one another—therapists may smile or nod at them, address them warmly, or shift their posture into a more receptive position. Exactly the same approaches may be applied to the myriad of other norms the therapist wishes to inculcate: self-disclosure, open expression of emotions, promptness, self-exploration, and so on (p. 113).

The therapist also shapes norms through serving as a model-setting participant. For example, by offering a model of nonjudgmental acceptance and appreciation of members' strengths along with their problem areas, the leader helps shape a group that is health-oriented. The therapist also models honesty, spontaneity, and human fallibility. This does not imply, however, that the counselor freely expresses all feelings. Clients' needs must take preeminence, as in any form of therapy; and the effective therapist models responsibility and restraint, as well as honesty and openness. Integrating such qualities as restraint and openness is no easy task, even for the seasoned counselor.

Activation and Illumination of the Here and Now

Some group counselors, depending on their theoretical orientation, will focus on material in the client's past, whereas others will attend only to the present. Whether the counselor's focus is primarily on the past or present, however, group members live their group lives in the present, in the here and now. Thus, even when past material is being explored, it may be done so in a way that is fresh and alive in the present. To this extent, we agree with Yalom's (1995) suggestion that the activation and illumination of the here and now is one of the three primary tasks of group therapy.

According to Yalom, if the here-and-now focus is to be effective, it must consist of two interrelated tiers. The first tier is the "experiencing" one. The members must *live* with each other in the present. They develop strong feelings toward each other, toward the therapist, and toward the group. These here-and-now feelings need to be expressed, and indeed form the main interactions in the group. As vital as this here-and-now experiencing (called "activation of the here and now") is, it is not enough. If all that group members do is express immediate feelings, they would have a powerful experience that would be soon forgotten, without behavior change taking place.

If clients are to change, the counselor must also *illuminate the here-and-now process*. Thus the effective counselor helps members to observe and think about what is happening in their interactions and what the meanings are of those interactions. This is the cognitive component, the observing and thinking about one's experience; and, just as in individual therapy, it is critical to effective change in groups. Whereas the group members, with the aid of the counselor, are responsible for activation of the here and now, only the therapist is responsible for commenting on the process, for directing the client's attention to the meaning of what is happening in the group. We should also note that if only this second tier is actualized in the group, that too would not be effective. The interactions would be emotionally sterile.

The counselor has many techniques at his or her disposal in the effort to activate and illuminate the here and now. The bottom line, however, is noted nicely by Yalom (1995), when he suggests that counselors "think here-and-now." He further states:

> When you grow accustomed to thinking of the here-and-now, you automatically steer the group into the here-and-now. Sometimes I feel like a shepherd herding a flock into an ever-tightening circle. I head off errant strays—forays into personal historical material, discussions of current life situations, intellectualisms—and guide them back into the circle. Whenever an issue is raised in the group, I think, "how can I relate this to the group's primary task? How can I make it come to life in the here-and-now? *I am relentless in this effort, and I begin it in the very first meeting of the group*" (p. 143).

The Leader's Personal Qualities

Just as in individual counseling, the personal qualities of the group leader or counselor are of utmost importance. Also, as in individual counseling, the ability to offer a good relationship may be the most important of these. Thus, the group counselor's ability to experience and communicate (a) empathic understanding; (b) positive regard, warmth, and respect; and (c) genuineness or congruence, forms the groundwork of effective therapeutic group work. In group interventions, however, the relationship task is more complicated than in individual work. The leader not only must be effective in developing therapeutic relationships with his or her clients, the leader must also facilitate therapeutic relationships among the members of his or her groups.

In line with the above relationship qualities, Corey and Corey (1997) discuss 15 personal characteristics of effective group leaders: courage, willingness to model, presence, goodwill and caring, belief in group process, openness, becoming aware of your own culture, nondefensiveness in coping with attacks, personal power, stamina, willingness to seek new experiences, self-awareness, sense of humor, inventiveness, and personal dedication and commitment. This list should be studied and integrated by the beginning group counselor. Let us elaborate on a few of these qualities.

Courage
Courage is a personal quality that is all too infrequently addressed in both the individual and group intervention literature. It is probably an important trait for both counselors and clients. It may take courage as well as other ingredients for clients to take the risks involved in opening up in counseling and making the changes that need to be made. For group leaders, Corey and Corey (1997) believe that courage is reflected in their willingness to (1) be vulnerable, admitting to mistakes and taking the same risks that are expected of group members; (2) confront members even when they are not sure that they are right; (3) act on their beliefs and hunches;

(4) be emotionally touched by their group members; (5) continually examine themselves and strive for a depth of awareness; (6) be direct and honest with members; and (7) express to the group their expectations (including fears) about the group process.

Becoming Aware of Your Own Culture

Leaders' self-insight into how their own culture influences decisions and behavior provides a frame of reference for understanding the worldview of others who may differ from them. The most effective group leader, in our view, embraces diversity in its many forms, ranging from cultural to individual (and their interaction); and cultural and individual self-awareness is a fundamentally important starting point.

Belief in Group Process

As a scientist-practitioner, the counseling psychologist who leads therapeutic groups must balance an appropriate scientific skepticism and thoughtful clinical judgment with a belief in the value of group treatment and the therapeutic forces in groups. The leader need not accept group efficacy on faith, for there is plenty of research evidence (as well as clinical evidence) that group treatment is effective (Kivlighan et al., 2000). The belief in the efficacy of groups and of group process is especially important since what the counselor believes is bound to influence his or her behavior. In other words, the counselor who believes in the effectiveness of group process will behave in a way that actualizes that belief. On the other side of the ledger, Corey and Corey (1997) note that some therapists lead groups despite the belief that group work does not effect significant client change. Some lead groups mainly for money or power or because the agencies at which they work require them to lead groups. To do so is clinically unsound at best, for negative beliefs will tend to result in lessened effectiveness—a self-fulfilling prophecy of sorts. Indeed, leading groups while doubting their effectiveness is unethical.

Inventiveness

Inventiveness is another leader quality that is underemphasized. Corey and Corey (1997) assert:

> The capacity to be spontaneously creative, approaching each group with fresh ideas, is a most important characteristic. Freshness may not be easy to maintain, particularly if you lead groups frequently. You must somehow avoid becoming trapped in ritualized techniques or a programmed presentation of self that has lost all life (pp. 67–68).

The ability to think up new techniques and new ways of approaching a group prevents group-leader burnout. As a way of staying fresh and reducing burnout, many group experts recommend co-leadership. Having a co-leader takes some of the strain off the leader; it also provides fresh interpersonal and technical input. One may also reduce the number of groups one leads when energy and enthusiasm are diminished.

Nondefensiveness

Criticism and other negative reactions toward the group leader occur in virtually all groups of any duration. The group counselor will be seen as structuring too much, structuring too little, not caring enough or caring too selectively, being too critical or demanding, and so forth. One reason for this is that the leader cannot be what everyone wants at all times. Second, many of the members will have issues related to authority, parenting, and helping; often when helping and authority are combined, as in the role of the group leader, reactions are inevitable. At the same time, the spirit of openness and sharing that must exist in groups encourages members to express and reflect upon whatever negative reactions they have. Some of the negative reactions will be earned, as the leader inevitably makes mistakes that produce them. Many of the negative reactions will be expressions of distorted perceptions (e.g., transferences) related to the leader–helper role. All of this is to say that when leading therapeutic groups, the counselor must not only expect some reactions but must also be able to facilitate their expression and examination. Counselors who are easily threatened, who must have group approval, or who are hypersensitive to negative feedback are going to have a difficult time with leading groups.

THE LEADER'S THEORETICAL ORIENTATION TO GROUP WORK

There are as many theoretical orientations and approaches to therapeutic group work as there are to individual counseling and therapy. As a starter for the beginning group counselor, we provide a brief summary of the major group theoretical approaches that fit the individual approaches discussed in chapters 10, 11, and 12. Thus, the summaries below relate to group approaches that are psychoanalytic, behavioral, rational–emotive, person-centered, and gestalt. Note how the approaches to group work connect to their individual counseling counterparts in the earlier chapters.

Psychoanalytic group counseling or therapy has very clear resemblances to psychoanalytic therapy as discussed in Chapter 10. Many view this form of treatment as individual therapy done in a group rather than as group therapy. The analytic group therapist usually focuses on individual members and on interpersonal interactions among them rather than on the group as a whole.

A key feature of psychoanalytic group therapy is viewing the group as a symbolic representation of each client's original family. Within the group setting, the member's interactions with other members and the leader reflect many of the unresolved issues that related to earlier times and places, with parents, siblings, and other significant persons. As clients' issues get relived in the present, the therapist seeks to help the client gain insight into these issues and work them through in the present. Transferences to the group leader and members are central phenomena that need to be understood and resolved. This working through of interpersonal issues from the past in the context of present relationships results in personality change, the goal of psychoanalytic groups.

Personal Qualities of the Good Group Leader.   **TABLE 16.2.**

Quality	Examples
Courage	Examines and faces own motives and issues Takes risks and shares feelings with members appropriately
Cultural awareness	Has insight into how own and members' cultural beliefs affect process
Belief in the group process	Believes firmly that groups are effective interventions
Inventiveness	Approaches group issues with freshness and creativity
Nondefensiveness	Faces negative reactions from members openly Is not easily threatened personally

Behavioral group interventions most often take the form of short-term structured groups as discussed in Chapter 18, for example, assertiveness, anxiety management, and stress reduction groups. Since such groups are considered to be a type of education, group leaders do a great deal of teaching. They take an active and directive (not dominating) stance in such work, the main goal being to apply behavioral principles to the group. The focus is on the individuals in the group rather than the group as a whole. The behavioral group tends to be structured, and a portion of most sessions may be taken up with leader instruction around some common theme (e.g., assertiveness). The group format has the advantage of allowing clients to practice new behaviors and receive reinforcement for appropriate changes. Homework assignments related to the behaviors being modified are usually key elements of behavioral group counseling. The leader applies a wide range of behavioral techniques, depending on the behaviors being modified. As in individual therapy, in the behavioral group focus is placed on overt and specific behaviors, the statement of precise goals, the formulation of a treatment plan, the application of behavioral action-oriented methods, and the evaluation of outcomes.

Ellis's (1992) *rational emotive behavior therapy in groups,* like its behavioral cousin, is seen as a type of education, or more aptly reeducation. The therapist's main task is to help clients become aware of their irrational beliefs, see how these beliefs impede their happiness, and importantly substitute rational, healthy beliefs for the irrational ones. The ultimate aim is to help clients internalize a rational philosophy of life. Ellis contends that rational emotive behavior therapy (REBT) works well in very large groups (e.g., 50–100 "clients") or small groups (10–13 members). The therapist in this treatment uses a range of active–directive cognitive and behavioral techniques to accomplish the main tasks. Techniques include persuading, teaching, informing, disputing, role-playing, modeling, self-reinforcing, feedback, and skill training. Homework assignments are an almost inherent part of REBT, and Ellis believes that they are even more effectively used in group than individual counseling.

As may be evident, the focus of REBT in groups is the individual, and much of the interactions are between the therapist and individual clients. The dynamics of the group as a whole are seen as largely beside the point. Group intervention is often seen as the preferred mode by REBT therapists, however, because it is efficient and because group members can be powerful allies of the therapist in changing others' irrational self-defeating thinking. Thus, group members contribute comments, suggestions, and hypotheses; they also reinforce interventions offered by the therapist.

The *person-centered* approach to therapeutic group work grew out of Carl Rogers's work, initially his client-centered therapy with individuals, and subsequently (1960s and 1970s) his focus on encounter and growth groups. In the person-centered approach, the leader is more aptly called a "facilitator," as he or she seeks to enable the group and the individuals within it to develop itself and themselves (its and their own goals, directions, and procedures) rather than to lead the group in any traditional leader-oriented way. The facilitator in many ways participates as a member in this approach and in the process relinquishes the role and power of the expert. The leader's task is to create group conditions that will allow for self-actualization within the capacity of group members. The leader's attitudes, rather than techniques, are what matters most; the relationship attitudes of empathy, unconditional positive regard, and congruence are fundamental.

The person-centered facilitator has a deep trust in the ability of the group to develop its potential and to move in the direction of awareness and spontaneous expression of immediate experiencing, looking inward for answers, tolerance for ambiguity, openness to outside reality, and openness and expressiveness with others. These changes occur at the group level as well as at an individual level within the group. As you might suppose, the person-centered approach is highly unstructured; it is the group's responsibility to create its own structure. Because of the lack of leader direction, such groups tend to flounder quite a bit in their early stages. But as the leader's attitudes of acceptance and understanding are internalized by the members, and as the members' actualizing tendencies emerge, person-centered groups develop into cohesive, self-directing organisms.

The *gestalt* therapy approach to therapeutic group work has as its goals enhancing the self-awareness of the individuals. Self-awareness is developed through consistent attention to immediate experiencing of rather than talking about feelings and thoughts. There are actually two gestalt therapy approaches to groups. The first, developed by Fritz Perls in the 1960s, is in reality individual therapy done in a group. Individuals take turns in the "hot seat," a situation in which the therapist works with one member. As this is going on, other members are encouraged to observe and process and then to offer feedback and personal reactions to what has occurred. The second approach, which probably emanates from the work of Irving and Miriam Polster, is much more process- and interaction-oriented. The focus is still on awareness and experiencing, but the leader also seeks to foster spontaneous interaction among members as well as a group culture. Thus, the focus of the leader is on the group as a whole and the interactions of participants, as well as the individual.

Highly active, the gestalt leader facilitates awareness, experiencing, and spontaneous interaction through the use of a range of techniques, exercises, and experiments (see Chapter 12). At the same time, gestaltists are careful to emphasize the leader's person over techniques. Techniques should emerge spontaneously from the therapist as a person. The therapist must stay in close touch with his or her own experiencing in the group.

As summarized from the five theoretical perspectives above, *none* of the approaches to therapeutic group work resembles very closely group counseling or psychotherapy as it is typically practiced. By "typical," we refer to relatively unstructured groups that have about 6–10 members, are held once or twice a week for 1.5–2 hours, continue for anywhere from 6 months to several years, and are closed in the sense that new members are added only on occasion. The focal points of the typical therapy group tend to be at all three levels: the individual, the group, and interaction among members. Immediate experiencing is of fundamental importance but so is the need to cognitively understand this experiencing of the group and its individuals. The leader is not highly directive, but neither is she or he nearly as nondirective as the person-centered therapist. This leader does assume the role of expert but uses this expertise to maintain the group, develop the group culture, and help the group focus on the present (see the previous section). She or he is not nearly as dominant or knowing as, for example, the rational–emotive group leader.

It is safe to say that the leader of group counseling/therapy as typically practiced is a combination of the above theoretical orientations and more. Yet some orientations have been more influential than others. The typical leader represents some amalgamation of psychodynamic (not strictly psychoanalytic—see the distinction in Chapter 10) and humanistic approaches to thinking about and leading groups. Within the humanistic approach, both gestalt and person-centered views have been a powerful influence on group work.

STAGES OF THERAPEUTIC GROUPS

Now that we have examined aspects of leader behavior in therapeutic groups, it is time to look at aspects of the group itself; namely, how the group unfolds or develops. An extensive literature has accumulated on group development, and there is general agreement within this research and clinical literature that therapeutic groups progress through different stages or phases of development (Capuzzi & Gross, 1998). Tuckman (1965) appears to be the first to summarize the literature on stages, labeling them as "forming," "storming," "norming," and "performing" (to which others later added "adjourning"). Although different authors propose differing numbers of stages, considerable similarities exist in the way these stages are described and their sequencing. Below we describe a sequence of four stages: exploratory, transition, working, and termination. This is probably the most commonly presented sequence in the literature.

First, it should be pointed out that all formulations of stages apply in a clear way only to groups in which membership is more or less closed. The closed group maintains the same or nearly the same membership throughout the life of the group, adding new members only on occasion. The open group, on the other hand, continually adds new members as members leave the group. Particularly in groups in which there is a frequent turnover of membership, the concept of stages becomes confounded. Stages may mark each member's development within the group, but no clear stagewise progression occurs for the group itself.

We also note that, just as there is general agreement that therapeutic groups progress in stages or phases, group therapy authors are unanimous in their agreement that these stages do not unfold in a discrete and orderly way. George and Dustin (1988) state this nicely:

> The stages described do not occur in discrete and neatly separated points in the life of a real group. There is considerable overlap between the stages, as groups move from one stage to the other in a somewhat jerky, hesitant manner . . . there may be some movement toward the next stage and then regression to the previous stage (p. 102).

Exploratory Stage

During this beginning stage, members introduce themselves, tell why they are in the group and what they hope to get out of it. Some basic ground rules of the group are established early on. The interaction of group members tends to be on the superficial side. Issues of inclusion and influence are primary in this first stage. Members wonder if they will fit in and be liked and listened to and, as a result, try to present themselves in a way that is acceptable to others. There is also the question in each member's mind, however framed, of how much influence he or she will have in the group. In fact, as Bonney (1969) notes, the group does consciously and unconsciously assign varying degrees of power and influence to each member.

There are often periods of silence and awkwardness in the early meetings, as members seek to find direction and wonder what the group really will be about, *really*. In the exploratory stage, members also wonder if the group is a safe place in which to share their inner feelings. Beginning efforts at self-disclosure are made, partly as a way of testing the waters. If members are able to express themselves, a beginning sense of group cohesion emerges. It is essential that a sense of trust be built up during this stage.

During this crucial and delicate stage, as discussed in the section on leadership, the group counselor helps to establish therapeutic norms through both a sensitive use of instruction and through his or her behavior. Thus he or she functions both as the technical expert and as the participant–model. The primary mission of this stage is simply to maintain the group and to build a solid foundation.

Transition Stage

As the group moves beyond the exploratory stage, members will seek to disclose a bit more deeply. They go beyond talking about their background and presenting their beginning stories. This movement is not without ambivalence, however, as anxiety and defense also become heightened during the transition stage. Thus, there is the urge to move forward into deeper explorations and also the counterpoint, the flight away from more personal (and thus dangerous) ways of being.

As members move beyond superficial expressions, aggression seems to enter the scene. (Note that the word *storming* has been used for this stage.) Members will often alternate between "fight and flight," between aggressiveness and avoidance of emotions. Power and influence become even more central in the transition stage than they were during the exploratory stage. The leader is frequently the object of aggressive reactions, and at this stage such aggressiveness is often related to the leader's structuring and controlling too much or too little. Some members will seek to wrestle power from the leader, others will be sure to find the leader's shortcomings.

The major challenge to the leader in the transition stage is to intervene in a sensitive and timely way. The leader must offer both encouragement and challenge in helping clients face their resistances, which are tied to anxiety. These same leader ingredients must be used to help the group work with the conflict and negative feelings that are emerging in this stage. It is particularly important that the leader not be defensive or hostile in response to challenges or downright attacks from group members. The leader must at once be open about his or her feelings and maintain a therapeutic stance of helping the group explore itself. During this period, the leader also has to reinforce growth-enhancing behaviors such as acceptance and respect, constructively expressed feedback, nondestructive expression of disagreements, and deeper self-explorations and self-disclosures.

Working Stage

During the next stage, the group has already worked through many of its doubts and anxieties. Those who were not able to commit to the group or who should not have been there to begin with have already left. The group has a deeper sense of trust and cohesion, and members are able to express themselves deeply as well as give and receive feedback without great defensiveness. When confrontation occurs, it is done in a way that does not attack or judge the person being confronted. The leader is seen more realistically, and the individual is more ready to explore the transferences and other distortions that do occur. Leadership functions are more readily shared by members, without the power struggles characteristic of the transition stage. Members during the working stage feel accepted and supported in a deeper way than earlier and are consequently willing to risk new behavior. This support–risk sequence forms a spiral such that support leads to greater risks and more openness, which leads to greater support and acceptance.

The working stage may be the most exciting one for the leader. The initial resistances and defensiveness have been worked through, therapeutic norms have been established, and members are able to live in the here and now. The leader can focus energies on facilitating continued and deepened exploration of the interpersonal and intrapersonal issues in the group. A crucial leader function during the working stage is to help members translate their understandings into constructive action, certainly within the group, but also outside the group. The leader of course continues to function as the participant–model, who confronts in a caring way and appropriately discloses ongoing reactions to the group.

Termination Stage

In the final stage of group development—ending, or termination—becomes the central issue. The duration of this stage will depend on the length of time it has been a group, with longer-term groups having longer termination stages. The major tasks of the group during this stage are looking back at what has been accomplished, looking forward in terms of members' plans and hopes for the future, and saying good-bye. It is fairly common for clients to initiate a "going around" procedure in which feedback is solicited from all other members. The group experience itself is usually evaluated as part of ending. Naturally, members tend to experience some sadness and anxiety about ending the group and the relationships that have been developed, although this is usually overshadowed by the sense of growth and accomplishment that has been evidenced during the life of the group. Self-disclosures tend to taper off in the final stage, as members are reluctant to open up new issues with the end of the group in close sight.

The group leader's main task during the ending phase is to help members face termination and deal directly with termination issues such as separation and loss, and with positive feelings as well. The leader provides a structure in which members can clarify the meaning of the group experience to them and think actively about how their learning may be generalized and continued after the experience ends. Positive development and behavior of clients are reinforced by the leader. In structured groups, the leader often helps members formulate specific contracts and homework assignments aimed at fortifying changes. The four stages we have been describing are summarized with a counseling example in Table 16.3.

Now it is time to take a look at what makes for positive change in group interventions. This is discussed in the following section.

THERAPEUTIC FACTORS IN GROUP WORK

At the beginning of this chapter, we noted that research evidence clearly indicates that group interventions, on the whole, do foster change and growth in participants. What is it about these groups that helps people? What goes on in, for example, group therapy that facilitates the client's changing in a desirable way? Are there certain ingredients of group therapy and other therapeutic groups that allow for such change? In an extremely thoughtful formulation by one of the masters of group therapy and group therapy research, Irving Yalom (1985, 1995) proposes that there are 11 therapeutic factors that are either mechanisms of change or conditions for change to take place in group therapy and other therapy-like interventions. Yalom derived these factors both from his experience leading groups and from research findings, and his formulation has been a potent guide to theory and research on group work in recent years. As we define and discuss the 11 therapeutic factors, the reader should keep in mind that these are not independent of one another. Rather, they work together, interdependently, in a very complex way. Additionally, they operate in different ways for differing types of groups (discussed below). The 11 factors, along with brief definitions and discussion, are as follows.

1. *Instillation of hope.* Clients often begin therapy feeling demoralized. If therapy is to be effective, clients need to begin feeling a sense of hopefulness—that they

Stages of Therapeutic Groups.   TABLE 16.3.

Stage	Counseling Example
Exploratory	Jane wonders if she belongs and how she will fit into the group; she also wonders if she will be able to affect other members. After sharing what brought her to the group, she finds herself holding back at times, wondering if the group is safe for her.
Transition	Jane gradually explores her conflicts more deeply, but also backs off and hides emotionally. She finds herself at times being very polite, while at other times getting angry at other members, and even at the leaders, Dr. Medvin and Dr. Collens (or Arnie and Ann, as they prefer to be called).
Working	The group has become a place for Jane that is both emotionally safe and trustworthy, at least to a large extent. She can count on members to give her honest feedback and be genuinely concerned; she also enjoys the fact that she can be open and direct with members, a first for Jane. She can have a range of feelings toward members and leaders, but mostly she has positive feelings. She is surprised at how much of what happens in the group actually exemplifies each member's issues outside the group.
Termination	As the group enters the last month of its year-long experience, Jane finds herself pleased with what she has come to understand about herself and her relationships, how she has changed; she is also sad about ending such a positive experience and leaving relationships that have mattered to her. She and other members, at the leaders' urging, share what the group has meant to them, their future plans and hopes, and in the last meeting they say good-bye, some sharing affectionate hugs, others warm handshakes. Jane senses that she can take this experience with her emotionally for a long time.

can change as a result of the treatment. Observing others in the group change is a major impetus to hope.

2. *Universality.* Many people enter counseling feeling isolated and alone in their problems, as if they are different from the rest of the human race in the conflicts that they experience. Universality, experienced early in the group, is the sense that we all have problems, that we are all alike in this way, and that others can understand and share our concerns.

3. *Imparting information.* Included here is instruction, given by therapists about mental health and illness and general psychodynamics, along with advice, suggestions, and direct guidance offered by the counselor and other group members. Instruction is especially pertinent in certain kinds of groups (e.g., structured groups) and therapies (e.g., rational–emotive therapy). Although direct advice may not itself help, the interest and caring it implies may do so.

4. *Altruism.* The desire experienced by group members to help others is a key factor, since clients receive through giving. Not only does giving stimulate others to return the giving, but giving in itself often enhances one's sense of effectiveness and self-esteem. Clients can be enormously helpful to one another, for example, through support, suggestions, shared insights, and experiences.

5. *The corrective recapitulation of the primary family group.* The ongoing group comes to resemble the client's original family, and the client tends to interact

with the group in the way he or she did with the family. As early family experiences are relived with the help of the therapist and other members, the client comes to resolve many central issues and change fixed patterns tied to unresolved issues.

6. *Development of socializing techniques.* Social learning or the development of social/interpersonal skills is fostered in all therapeutic groups, although the types of skills taught and how directly they are taught varies tremendously from group to group. Some groups train social interpersonal skills directly, others do so implicitly, mainly through feedback from members and leaders.

7. *Imitative behavior.* Clients learn in groups by identifying with leaders and other members. Although blind imitation may reflect unresolved problems, there is a healthy kind of learning through observing and identifying that occurs in therapeutic groups. Such learning may occur at a conscious level, but is more often than not unconscious.

8. *Interpersonal learning.* This is a particularly powerful factor. As a group unfolds (particularly a less structured one), it evolves into a social microcosm—a miniature representative of the individuals' social worlds. At the same time, the client becomes more open about the self and is able to display his or her interpersonal issues and problems. As this occurs, and with the help of feedback as well as self-observation, the client gains insight into his or her impact on others, maladaptive behavior with others, distortions in interpersonal relationships (e.g., transference), and his or her responsibility for relationships and the responses he or she gets from others.

9. *Group cohesiveness.* This is the parallel of the client–therapist working alliance in individual counseling. In groups, it includes the client's relationship to the therapist, other group members, and the group as a whole. This has been an extremely elusive factor to define over the years, although it is seen as crucial by virtually all theoreticians of therapeutic groups, especially in less-structured groups, and has been the subject of numerous studies. One may simply define it as the attractiveness of a group for its members, keeping in mind that there is a difference between group cohesiveness and individual member cohesiveness (the individual's attraction to the group). Groups with a greater sense of solidarity, bonding, or "we-ness" are high on cohesion. In cohesive groups, members are accepted, approved of, and have a sense of being "taken in." Group cohesiveness is not in itself a mechanism of change, but is rather a precondition for group therapy to be effective in helping clients.

10. *Catharsis.* The release of emotions, the open expression of affect, is a necessary factor in group work, but by itself is not sufficient. For change to occur, the feelings that are released need to be understood, processed, and dealt with. Catharsis also helps through its interaction with other therapeutic factors. For example, members' catharsis enhances group cohesiveness, allows for interpersonal learning, and deepens members' sense of universality.

11. *Existential factors.* This factor is actually a constellation of factors revolving around one's basic and ultimate responsibility for his or her life and actions, one's

basic aloneness, the recognition of one's mortality, and the inevitability of some human problems and pain. Although this factor was included by Yalom almost as an afterthought, some of the items within it have been rated by group therapy clients as extremely important in what they got out of their group experience.

We noted at the beginning of this section that the 11 therapeutic factors would be expected to operate differently for different types of groups. Research findings suggest that in personal growth groups and outpatient groups, for example, interpersonal learning (including self-understanding) and catharsis are seen as most important by clients, whereas clients in inpatient groups place more importance on instillation of hope, universality, and existential factors ("assumption of ultimate responsibility for my own life," Kivlighan et al., 2000; Yalom, 1995). In addition to type of group or setting, Yalom proposes that the factors operate differently according to the stage of group development, as discussed in the preceding section. For instance, early in the group life, instillation of hope, universality, and imparting of information are seen as relatively more important. Factors such as altruism and cohesion are important throughout the life of the group, but their nature changes as the group matures. Early in therapy, altruism often takes the form of offering suggestions and asking help-oriented questions, whereas later on it may appear as a deeper caring and "being with." Cohesiveness first operates as a therapeutic factor through support, acceptance, and facilitation of attendance. It has its later effect, however, through the kind of deeper self-disclosure, confrontation, and conflict that are an inherent part of the interpersonal learning factor. Early–late differences such as these have been at least partially supported by research studies (see the extensive review by Kivlighan et al. [2000]). Research has tended to look at highly global group development in relation to the therapeutic factors (e.g., early vs. late). For a systematic theoretical discussion of how the factors operate across distinct stages of counseling, the reader is referred to MacDevitt (1987).

ETHICAL ISSUES IN THERAPEUTIC GROUP WORK

Professional ethics have been discussed already in depth in Chapter 5. Because there are some special ethical issues in therapeutic group work, however, we shall offer additional discussion below. Before doing so, we should note that ethical codes do exist that are focused specifically on group work, and these codes should be studied carefully by anyone who plans to work with groups. For counseling psychologists, the most relevant documents, in addition to those discussed in Chapter 5, are the *Ethical Guidelines for Group Counselors* (1990, 1996) developed by the Association for Specialists in Group Work. This code of ethics has been integrated into the more general *Code of Ethics and Standards of Practice* (1995), published by the American Counseling Association. Also, Corey, Corey, and Callahan (1992) have written a useful book on the topic of issues and ethics, many of which pertain to group counseling.

Four issues deserve special note: those of informed consent, confidentiality, involuntary membership, and training.

Informed Consent

Potential group members or clients have a right to know what they are getting into. Although this applies to individual as well as group treatments, it needs to be emphasized here because group work is often poorly understood or misunderstood by the public. People seem to have less accurate information about group treatment than individual treatment.

Clearly informing potential members about the group should begin as soon as the leader or agency decides to recruit members. Announcements aimed at recruitment should include an explicit statement of the purpose, time length, and size of the group; the leader's qualifications; and the financial cost of the intervention. Claims should not be made unless they can be supported by scientific evidence.

The matter of informed consent is related to leaders' making members aware of their rights and responsibilities as group participants. Those who join a group have a right to expect *at least:*

- a clear statement regarding the purpose of the group, procedures to be used, and the leader's policies and ground rules;
- respect for member privacy;
- freedom from undue group pressure or coercion from either members or leaders to participate in exercises or to disclose matters they are unwilling to discuss;
- notice of any research involving the group, any observations of the group through one-way mirrors, or any audio- or videotaping of group sessions; and
- full discussion on the limitations of confidentiality (see below).

Confidentiality

The principles of confidentiality discussed in Chapter 5 apply to group interventions as well as other interventions. In groups, however, confidentiality becomes a more complicated matter than in individual treatment because the leader must be concerned about other members in addition to the leader himself or herself maintaining confidentiality. This is no easy task because group members naturally want to talk about their group experiences with significant others in their lives.

The counselor needs to underscore the importance of confidentiality from the first contact with potential clients, for example, when members are being recruited and when groups are advertised. Confidentiality should also be discussed in the counselor's initial individual meeting with each member before the group, during the first group meeting, and at appropriate times during the group's evolution. It is the leader's job to note to members that confidences are usually broken by simple carelessness, and without any ill intent. Corey and Corey (1997) suggest that members will not violate confidentiality if they talk about *what* they learned in the group rather than *how* they gained insight or what they *did* in the group. For example, the male client who learns for the first time how he protects himself from fear of rejection by acting aggressively toward his intimates may share that he learned this in the group. However, he does not need to be specific about what went on in the group that sparked this insight. Cautions such as these are always important, but they are vital when members have contact with each other and with each other's friends and acquaintances outside the group, as in school settings.

The importance of confidentiality in group treatment cannot be overemphasized, for it is hard to imagine groups functioning as they must without a sense of trust that what members share will not be revealed outside the group. Because of this, some group leaders ask members to sign a contract agreeing not to discuss anything that goes on in sessions and not to reveal the identity of other members.

Involuntary Membership

Much of the theory and practice of therapeutic group work as discussed throughout this chapter hinges on voluntary membership. Participants seek out a group experience because of what they hope to learn. At times, though, group work is required. This may occur in psychiatric hospitals or prison settings, or in outpatient clinics as a court-mandated procedure (e.g., for someone charged with spouse abuse, delinquency, or substance abuse). Required groups for sex offenders is a fairly common practice in many inpatient settings. In other settings, potential clients are pressured into joining groups. One of the authors, for example, worked at a university agency in which, because of a very long waiting list, students seeking counseling had to wait for several weeks before being seen. To provide some service while students waited for individual counseling, the agency offered "transitional groups." This was a fine idea, except that students were often pushed to join these groups rather than remain on the waiting lists. A study of this procedure (Collins, Gelso, Kimball, & Sedlacek, 1972) reveals that the drop-out rates from such groups were exceedingly high, and significantly higher than when students simply waited for the treatment they preferred. Unless there are legal or moral issues that dictate requiring group experiences, it is at best unwise to make such requirements; at worst, it is unethical.

When it is appropriate to require a group experience, this still creates problems for the leader and the group. In such cases, the leader should at least facilitate the client's expression of feelings around this requirement. Also, it is appropriate for the leader to make clear that although participation is involuntary, members still have the right to discuss or hold back as they wish. On the other hand, it is the leader's job to facilitate members' opening up, so this represents a dilemma for both the leader and the involuntary member.

There are times when it is unclear whether or not group experience ought to be required. An example of this gray area is whether groups ought to be required for graduate students who plan to lead therapeutic groups in the future. Certainly participation in some form of experiential group is desirable, as unique learning occurs in this way; learning that differs from the more didactic, theoretical learning in formal courses. Also, one must wonder about the motivations and even competence of students who would choose not to participate while planning to lead groups. At the same time, many see mandatory therapy as a contradiction. In any event, Corey and Corey (1997) offer some sensible guidelines for when group experience is required of students. First, if the program requires group therapy, for example, that program ought to be sure it is available, either free of charge or at rates that students can manage. Second, it is unethical for graduate faculty to require counseling for a fee and then to encourage students to become the faculty's own clients. Referral should be made to professionals who have no evaluative responsibility for the student.

Training in Therapeutic Group Work

Therapeutic group work has had a shaky history in counseling psychology and other psychological specialties. On the one hand, there is much empirical evidence to suggest that group experiences tend to be effective in helping participants change in desirable directions, and this evidence has been around for a long time. On the other hand, unfortunate abuses have occurred in this area of psychological intervention. Some of these abuses are tied to the extreme practices in which some leaders engaged during the 1960s and early 1970s as part of the encounter group movement. Highly confrontational and aggressive leaders at times sought to push participants of encounter and marathon groups to do more and more emoting, seemingly for its own sake, and some clients were psychologically harmed by such aggressive pushing (Lieberman, Yalom, & Miles, 1973). Reports of nude marathons including a great deal of sexuality certainly did not help much, either in the eyes of the public or of well-trained professionals.

Fortunately, the excesses of that period are behind us. At the same time, therapeutic groups have become an established part of the psychological practice of counseling psychologists. Part of the problem of the 1960s and early 1970s, though, remains with us. In the group area perhaps more than any area, people with inadequate credentials and training seem to be willing to call themselves expert leaders.

The issue of training is further complicated by graduate training programs that expect students to lead groups after training only in individual counseling and therapy (Yalom, 1995). Fortunately, the attitude that training in individual counseling and therapy is sufficient for the practice of any form of intervention (e.g., group therapy) is changing; however, more than traces of that attitude can be found today.

What is the proper training for individuals who wish to lead therapeutic groups? Unfortunately, there is no clear-cut answer to this question, as different types of groups require different types of training. Yet some general guidelines are possible. In terms of academic training, in addition to basic coursework in individual counseling and assessment received in a counseling psychology program, potential group leaders should take a minimum of one course in the theory and practice of therapeutic groups. In addition, the Association for Specialists in Group Work (ASGW) (1983) has long recommended the following types of experience in group work:

- critiquing of group tapes;
- observing group counseling sessions;
- participating as a member in a group;
- co-leading groups with supervision;
- practicum experience—leading groups alone with critical self-analysis of performance along with a supervisor's feedback; and
- internship—further work in leading groups under supervision.

The ASGW also suggests specific knowledge competencies and skill competencies for group counselors. These guidelines should be consulted by students and training programs involved in therapeutic group work.

THERAPEUTIC GROUP WORK IN PERSPECTIVE

In this final section we address two key questions about therapeutic groups. (1) What is the place of therapeutic groups in counseling psychology? (2) What are some of the major research findings and issues in this area?

An Established Format

As we noted in the section above, group interventions have not had a stable history in professional psychology. The excesses of the 1960s and 1970s were part of this problem. Additionally, the group field was slow to develop a solid research base. Without such a base, any area in psychology suffers diminished respectability and, more important, is at the mercy of passing fads and fancies. Finally, for many years group work was seen as desirable only if the personpower did not exist to treat all clients with individual counseling. Groups existed as fill-ins of sorts, to be used when demand for service clearly exceeded an agency's supply of providers. The group field was thus an undernourished stepchild of individual counseling and therapy.

Views have slowly but surely changed over the years, as it has become clearer and clearer that therapeutic groups are a viable and effective treatment for a large percentage of clients and as the excesses of past decades have given way to a more thoughtful approach to group treatment. Of course, we should add that some very positive things came out of the 1960s, and it would be extremely unfortunate if the group field became so cautious and conservative that the experimentation and spontaneity of group work were greatly diminished.

The change in attitude toward therapeutic group work has progressed to the point that counseling and therapy groups, growth groups, and structured theme-oriented groups have become established modes in the counseling psychologist's repertoire. In fact, by 1990, Fuhriman and Burlingame were able to view the practice and investigation of group treatment as integral parts of the counseling psychologist's identity. A decade later, in their survey of the group counseling literature, Kivlighan and colleagues (2000) proposed group treatment to be a fundamental element of the work of counseling psychologists. Virtually all surveys that have been conducted in recent years on the work and training of counseling psychologists point to the centrality of therapeutic group work in the specialty.

Some Research Findings and Issues

By now the research literature on the outcomes of group interventions is very extensive. In fact, Kivlighan and colleagues (2000) have located eight meta-analyses of research on the effects of various group treatments published in the 1990s. (Recall that meta-analysis is a quantitative approach to studying the treatment effects summed over several studies.) In the eight meta-analyses summarized by Kivlighan et al., many dozens of studies were reviewed.

The overall conclusion from these reviews is that a wide array of group interventions in wide-ranging settings on broad client populations produce positive results (see, also, the review by Bednar & Kaul [1994]). It is very clear that group counseling and related treatments are more effective than control or placebo treatments, and are equal in effectiveness to individual counseling and therapy and to other recognized educational and psychosocial interventions. Beyond the statement that group treatment is effective on the whole, there is fairly solid research support for *some* of the factors that may underlie these positive effects. For example, it is clear that group cohesiveness—the group equivalent to the working alliance in individual counseling—promotes positive group processes and outcomes. Additionally, leader factors like warmth and ability in structuring groups are related to the development of cohesion. Other therapeutic factors from Yalom's (1995) list have received strong empirical support: interpersonal learning (e.g., through feedback), self-understanding, and catharsis appear to stand out in their desirable effects (Bednar & Kaul, 1994). Still other of Yalom's factors have received support in some settings but not in others. The reader is referred to the extensive reviews by Kivlighan and colleagues (2000), and Bednar and Kaul (1994) for further research findings. Yalom's (1995) theoretical discussion of the role of the 11 therapeutic factors as presented earlier is an extremely useful guide to the variables that can be studied in relation to the process and outcomes of group interventions.

On the negative side, research progress in group therapy has occurred at a slow pace. Perhaps this is inevitable, given the enormous complexity that occurs when any given study will usually examine several groups, each with several members and one or more leaders. Thus the already daunting complexity of individual counseling is compounded in the group situation (see Bednar & Kaul, 1994). These complexities suggest that progress in studying group work will continue to be gradual. The most important facts, though, are that progress has indeed occurred over the years and that research on therapeutic groups is a firmly embedded feature of the group movement in counseling psychology and other help-giving fields.

In this chapter, we have tried to highlight some of the key elements of therapeutic group work. For more in-depth coverage of this topic, the reader is referred to Yalom's (1995) *Theory and Practice of Group Psychotherapy*. Throughout its four editions, Yalom's book has probably been the most influential work in the group therapy area. It is relevant to beginning students and seasoned practitioners alike. Books by Corey and Corey (1997) and Gladding (1999) provide excellent overall treatments of therapeutic groups for beginning students. Corey (1995) offers an equally excellent review of different theoretical approaches to group counseling. Capuzzi and Gross (1998) give an especially informative overview of professional issues (e.g., multicultural group counseling), group work with varying populations (clients with addictions, the elderly, gay and lesbian clients, etc.), and theme-focused groups (e.g., career groups, loss groups). The January 1990 (Vol. 18, No. 1) issue of *The Counseling Psychologist* provides valuable reviews on the topics of theme-oriented group therapy, career group counseling, time-limited group counseling, and a comparison of individual and group therapy.

SUMMARY

The advantages of therapeutic groups are seen largely in the *interpersonal* area. Groups are particularly helpful to participants who have difficulties in this area, and groups help most with interpersonal issues. The disadvantages of therapeutic groups include the pressure to conform, the tendency of some clients to get hooked on groups and to try to use them as a place to ventilate their miseries rather than change, and the fact that groups are not suited to everyone. We defined the therapeutic group as "an aggregate of interdependent individuals whose interaction is in pursuit of some shared goal(s)." The background and characteristics of five kinds of therapeutic groups were given: (1) group counseling and group therapy; (2) growth, or encounter groups; (3) T groups; (4) structured theme-oriented groups; and (5) self-help groups. Of the differing kinds of groups, this chapter was particularly concerned with group counseling or therapy. These two terms were differentiated in the same way as the terms *counseling* and *therapy* were differentiated at the beginning of the book. In counseling practice the two terms and processes are usually melded.

There tends to be three different approaches to leading groups: (1) the group-centered approach in which the leader focuses on the group as a whole; (2) the individual-centered approach in which the leader focuses on the individuals in the group; and (3) the interpersonally centered approach in which the leader focuses on the interactions between and among individuals in the group. Integration of these three kinds of focus is seen as desirable.

The leader was seen as having three main tasks: (1) creating and maintaining the group, (2) facilitating the building of a group culture, and (3) activating and illuminating the here and now. Once the group becomes a physical reality, the leader's main job is to develop it into a therapeutic social system. To do this, the leader must actively shape the desired norms in the group. His or her role as a *technical expert* and a *model* were examined as potent vehicles for norm shaping. The personal qualities of the leader may be more important than the particular techniques that are used. Especially important among these personal qualities are courage, willingness to model, belief in group process, inventiveness, and nondefensiveness.

The leader's behavior is guided by his or her theoretical orientation. In the chapter, five orientations to group work were summarized to coincide with the five theoretical orientations discussed in chapters 10, 11, and 12: psychoanalytic, behavioral, cognitive, person-centered, and gestalt.

There is general agreement that stages exist in the development of closed groups, although the exact number of stages that are posited varies from theorist to theorist. We discussed and described four stages. In the *exploratory* stage, members get acquainted, and begin self-disclosing. Members wonder if they will be accepted and if the group will be safe. Cohesion begins to develop. In the *transition* stage, participants move toward deeper exploration and at the same time resist this deepening.

Issues of power and influence are central, and aggression usually is evident, often toward the leader. In the *working* stage, cohesion is high, and members have moved toward deep self-exploration and feedback. Then, in the *termination* stage, clients pull back somewhat as they face issues of separation. They look back, look ahead, and say good-bye.

Irving Yalom proposed 11 therapeutic factors that contribute significantly to group effectiveness. These factors operate differently according to type of group (e.g., college student growth group, inpatient therapy group, outpatient group) and stage of group development.

Four main ethical issues in group work were discussed: (1) informed consent, (2) confidentiality, (3) involuntary membership, and (4) training. We also noted that, although group work has had a shaky history in counseling psychology, it is currently an established format in the field and forms an integral part of the counseling psychologist's identity. Research has clearly supported the effectiveness of a wide range of group interventions; it appears that groups are as effective as individual treatment. The complexities of group research are numerous.

REFERENCES

American Counseling Association (1995). *Code of ethics and standards of practice*. Alexandria, VA: Author.

Association for Specialists in Group Work. (1983). *Professional standards for training of group counselors*. Alexandria, VA: American Personnel and Guidance Association.

Association for Specialists in Group Work (1989). *Ethical guidelines for group counselors*. Alexandria, VA: Author.

Association for Specialists in Group Work. (1990). *Ethical guidelines for group counselors*. Washington, DC: American Personnel and Guidance Association.

Bednar, R. L., & Kaul, T. (1994). Experiential group research. In A. Bergin and S. Garfield (Eds.), *Handbook of psychotherapy and behavior change* (4th ed., pp. 631–663). New York: John Wiley & Sons.

Bion, W. R. (1961). *Experiences in groups*. New York: Basic Books.

Bonney, W. C. (1969). Group counseling and developmental processes. In G. Gazda (Ed.), *Theories and methods of group counseling in the schools*. Springfield, IL: Charles C. Thomas.

Capuzzi, D., & Gross, D. R. (1998). *Introduction to group counseling* (2nd ed.). Denver, CO: Love Publishing.

Collins, A., Gelso, C., Kimball, R., & Sedlacek, W. (1972). Evaluation of a counseling center innovation. *Journal of College Student Personnel*, 141–145.

Conyne, R. K., Wilson, F. R., & Ward, D. E. (1997). *Comprehensive group work*. Alexandria, VA: American Counseling Association.

Corey, G. (1995). *Theory and practice of group counseling* (4th ed.). Pacific Grove, CA: Brooks/Cole.

Corey, G., Corey, M. S., & Callahan, P. (1992). *Issues and ethics in the helping professions* (4th ed.). Pacific Grove, CA: Brooks/Cole.

Corey, M. S., & Corey, G. (1997). *Groups: Process and practice* (5th ed.). Pacific Grove, CA: Brooks/Cole.

Courtois, C. A. (1999). *Recollections of sexual abuse: Treatment, principles, and guidelines*. New York: Norton.

Dies, R. R. (1987). Clinical implications of research on leadership in short-term group psychotherapy. *International Journal of Group Psychotherapy, 37*, 27–78.

Dykeman, C., & Appleton, V. E. (1998). Group counseling: The efficacy of group work. In D. Capuzzi and D. R. Gross (Eds.), *Introduction to group counseling* (2nd ed., pp. 101–130). Denver, CO: Love Publishing.

Eddy, W. B., & Lubin, B. (1971). Laboratory training and encounter groups. *Personnel and Guidance Journal, 49,* 625–635.

Ellis, A. (1992). Group rational–emotive and cognitive–behavioral therapy. *International Journal of Group Psychotherapy, 42,* 63–80.

Ettin, M. F. (1989). "Come on Jack, tell us about yourself": The growth spurt in group psychotherapy. *International Journal of Group Psychotherapy, 39,* 35–57.

Fuhriman, A., & Burlingame, G. M. (1990). Group therapy: Introduction. *The Counseling Psychologist, 18,* 5.

Gazda, G. M. (1984). *Group counseling: A developmental approach* (3rd ed.). Boston, MA: Allyn & Bacon.

George, R. L., & Dustin, D. (1988). *Group counseling: Theory and practice.* Englewood Cliffs, NJ: Prentice-Hall.

Gladding, S. T. (1999). *Group work: A counseling specialty* (3rd ed.). Columbus, OH: Prentice-Hall.

Horwitz, L. (1986). An integrated, group-centered approach. In *Psychotherapist's casebook.* San Francisco, CA: Jossey-Bass.

Kivlighan, D. M., Coleman, M. N., & Anderson, D. C. (2000). Process, outcome, and methodology in group counseling research. In S. Brown and R. Lent (Eds.), *Handbook of counseling psychology* (3rd ed., pp. 767–796). New York: John Wiley & Sons.

Lieberman, M., Yalom, I., & Miles, M. (1973). *Encounter groups: First facts.* New York: Basic Books.

MacDevitt, J. W. (1987). Conceptualizing therapeutic components of group counseling. *Journal for Specialists in Group Work,* 76–84.

Peterson, J. V., & Nisenholz, B. (1987). *Orientation to Counseling.* Boston, MA: Allyn & Bacon.

Schmuck, R. A., & Schmuck, P. A. (1979). *Group processes in the classroom* (3rd ed.). Dubuque, IA: W. C. Brown.

Tuckman, B. W. (1965). Developmental sequence in small groups. *Psychological Bulletin, 63,* 384–399.

Yalom, I. D. (1985). *The theory and practice of group psychotherapy* (3rd ed.). New York: Basic Books.

Yalom, I. D. (1995). *The theory and practice of group psychotherapy* (4th ed.). New York: Basic Books.

CHAPTER 17

SYSTEMS IN ACTION: FAMILY AND COUPLES INTERVENTIONS

Consider the following case example, and in doing so also think about these questions: Who is the client to be counseled? Which treatment format would be used? How would the causes of the client's problems be conceptualized?

> Parents seek psychological help for their 15-year-old son. In recent months he has been increasingly angry and belligerent at home and has been unwilling to help out around the house. His grades in school have dropped, and the parents are worried that he has been drinking and possibly involved in drugs. Because of his behavior, the boy has been upsetting his younger brother and sister. The parents say that they can no longer reach the boy, although they have tried everything.

Based on what you have read in the preceding chapters, your answers to the three questions we have posed would be relatively straightforward. Traditionally, the adolescent boy, who is seen as the "identified patient" in family therapy terms, would be the client. He would probably be seen in individual counseling, with the aim of facilitating greater responsibility, self-control, and adjustment; and of controlling and eliminating alcohol and drug involvement, respectively. The causes of the client's problems would be seen as residing in the client's psyche and related to underlying conflicts and complexes by the psychoanalytically or humanistically oriented counselor. Alternatively, the behavioral counselor might conceptualize the client's problems as being tied to environmental contingencies that serve to control this adolescent's behavior.

In the present chapter, though, we present a different way of thinking about and treating human problems. The approach is called the *family therapy perspective*. From such a perspective, the answers to the three questions we have raised would be very different from those presented using the traditional, individual counseling perspective. For one, the troubled adolescent would probably not be seen as the client who is to receive treatment. The client to be treated would be the entire family and/or subunits within the family. Second, the treatment mode would probably not be individual counseling for the adolescent, but rather family counseling for the entire family or subunits, including for example, the parents. Finally, as to the causes of the adolescent's problems, they would be seen as residing in the family *system*—the system of interactions that have been established in the nuclear family, and possibly even the extended family.

To continue with our example, the family therapist might hypothesize that the boy's problems are a symptom of distress in the family (rather than simply a cause of such distress). A closer look at this family might reveal that the father behaves in a critical, dominating manner with the boy. The mother, who seems to passively submit to the father's authority, actually undermines his authority in numerous, often nonverbal ways. She might send the boy to the father for discipline but then passively disagree with the rules he establishes. The parents themselves may have many conflicts with each other, but these have gone underground, and attention to the teenager's rebelliousness helps the parents to avoid their own problems. The other children unconsciously seek to maintain their roles as the "good kids," and thus have some investment in their brother's being the "bad kid." In such a situation, individual treatment of the adolescent would probably not be very effective because the family system itself is the problem. Much of this chapter will serve to elaborate and clarify the observations just made and in doing so will seek to give the reader the fundamentals of the family therapy perspective.

The treatment of families and couples (married or unmarried) and conceptualization of problems in terms of systems rather than individuals are among the most recent phenomena in professional psychology. This way of conceptualizing and helping originated in the 1950s, and it is only in recent years that the family therapy approach has become popular among professional psychologists. For example, it has been suggested that only in the 1980s did this approach really become prominent in counseling psychology (Gelso & Fassinger, 1990).

The remainder of the chapter begins with a brief description of the origins of the family therapy movement (including work with couples). The focus will be on the individuals and groups who originated working with families. We then present some of the key assumptions and concepts that appear to undergird most, if not all, approaches to family interventions. Following the presentation of key assumptions and concepts, we review what might be called the six classic theoretical approaches to family interventions: psychoanalytic, experiential, behavioral, family systems, strategic, and structural. Perhaps more than any intervention approach, that of couples and family therapy has witnessed dramatic changes during the past decade, and some of these changes pertain to the very core of what family and couples treatments ought to be about. We therefore provide an overview of the major shifts in the couples/family counseling scene. The chapter concludes with a discussion of the role of family and couples' work in counseling psychology, and a presentation of key research findings about this approach.

In presenting the key assumptions and concepts that underlie family interventions, we shall underscore the main features of what is called *general systems theory,* a theoretical stance that cuts across most of the different approaches to treatment. Finally, the six classic approaches to working with family problems are reviewed in favor of a presentation of general principles of family interventions. This is so because general principles do not appear to exist in this young field. Thus we believe that if family treatments are to be presented clearly, it must be through the review of major theoretical approaches.

THE BEGINNINGS OF FAMILY INTERVENTIONS

Throughout the history of professional psychology, the importance of the family in shaping the psyche and behavior of the individual has been recognized. Sigmund Freud, for example, was acutely aware of the role of the client's family background in this respect. Freud, and virtually all other therapists in the first half of the twentieth century, however, sought to isolate the family from the individual client's treatment. The aim was to free the client from the unhealthy influence of the family. In contrast, the aim of family therapists is to assist the family and the individual through work on and with the family.

According to Foster and Gurman (1985), the earliest forerunners of family therapy interventions were the child-guidance and marriage counseling movements in the United States and England during the first half of the twentieth century. Child-guidance and marital counselors developed treatment models that involved concurrent treatment of two or more family members, despite the prevailing view that dictated that the individual be understood and treated.

The family therapy movement, which began in the 1950s, originated from two directions. One of these was the study of families in which one or more of the offspring became severely disturbed psychologically; that is, schizophrenic. As will be discussed below, a number of important family treatments stemmed from this original aim of understanding troubled families. The second source of family therapy was the independent work of several creative clinicians who began in the 1950s to experiment with family-based treatment. Let us look at some of the key figures in this movement.

The Palo Alto Group: Schizophrenia and Family Communications

According to Nichols and Schwartz (1998), one of the groups with the strongest claims to starting family therapy was Gregory Bateson's schizophrenia project in

Palo Alto, California. Bateson was an anthropologist interested in studying communication in general. In the mid-1950s he formed the Palo Alto group, consisting of himself, Jay Haley, Don Jackson, John Weakland, and William Fry. Although the members of this group studied various topics related to communication, they joined together in studying communication within families as it might help explain the nature and causes of schizophrenia.

Among the many creative concepts about family communication developed by the Palo Alto group was that of the *double-bind*. Based on their observations of families in which one of the children suffered from schizophrenia, the Palo Alto group (Bateson, Jackson, Haley, & Weakland, 1956) hypothesized that schizophrenia resulted from the person's having to cope with confused and confusing communication within the family, usually from parent to child. Communications involving double-binds were a central part of such parent–child interactions. In such communication, the recipient (i.e., the child) repeatedly receives two related but contradictory messages of different levels (e.g., verbal vs. nonverbal) from the parent but finds it difficult or impossible to comment on the inconsistency. A classic example of this double-bind communication was given in Bateson et al.'s (1956) original article: A young man recovering from a schizophrenic reaction was visited in the hospital by his mother. When he embraced her, she stiffened. In response to this, he withdrew. She commented, "Don't you love me anymore?" His face reddened, and the mother responded, "Dear, you must not be so easily embarrassed and afraid of your feelings." The young man was caught in a double-bind. After the mother left the hospital, he assaulted an aide and had to be placed in seclusion.

Although the findings of the Palo Alto group had implications for family therapy, treatment or treatment research was not the group's mission. A second group in Palo Alto was concerned about treatment. The Mental Research Institute (MRI) was established by Don Jackson in 1958 and actually contained many of the same members as Bateson's Palo Alto group. (In fact, Bateson, himself, was a consultant to the MRI.) Within MRI, Jackson and Haley developed and popularized a communications approach to the treatment of families (Nichols & Schwartz, 1998). Communications therapists are not concerned about *intra*psychic phenomena or about the childhood causes of clients' problems. Rather, the treatment of families (actually, usually married couples in the early days) was present-centered, directive, and sought to uncover the communication patterns and problems in the family.

Other Originators: Ackerman, Whitaker, and Bowen

Originally trained in psychoanalysis, Nathan Ackerman was a key figure in the early family therapy movement. As early as the 1930s he was writing about family dynamics, and in 1955 he organized and led the first session on family diagnosis at a meeting of the American Orthopsychiatric Association. In 1961 Ackerman, along with Jackson, founded the field's first professional journal, *Family Process*.

Whereas the communications therapists focused on overt communication, Ackerman was concerned about the intrapsychic effects of families on individuals (e.g., Ackerman, 1958). He conceptualized families as being emotionally separated into competing factions or dynamic coalitions, for example, mother and daughter or competing generations. Difficulties within families were seen in terms of "interlocking pathologies," since the problems of one person could not be understood separately from those of other family members. Although Ackerman focused a great deal on individuals' dynamics within the family, he was one of the first therapists to recommend that all members in the same household participate in all family therapy sessions. He also suggested that certain members be counseled individually as well as in the family group. As a therapist, he was far from the stereotype of the silent analyst. He believed the family therapist should be spontaneous and lively—at times she or he should provoke emotional reactions, at times siding with one member and at other times serving as a referee. The therapist should be deeply involved emotionally in the families she or he treats.

Carl Whitaker was among the first therapists to treat entire families, having worked with families even in the late 1940s. Whitaker was considered by many to be the dean of *experiential* family therapy (Nichols & Schwartz, 1998). This approach is closely related to gestalt therapy (see Chapter 12), and employs some of the same confrontational and experiential techniques. Like Fritz Perls, Whitaker was an extremely colorful man who was often irreverent, iconoclastic, and even outrageous.

The problem with families, said Whitaker, was that they are emotionally deadened. They have become rigidified into stereotyped routines, and what they need to free themselves is an emotionally alive therapist, who behaves spontaneously and presents them with an authentic human encounter. Whitaker was one of the first to promote the benefits of co-therapy (two therapists working together with couples and families). When practicing such a spontaneous, no-holds-barred approach, a co-therapist can be invaluable in helping the therapist detect and modulate countertransference reactions.

During the late 1970s and 1980s, Whitaker seemed to mellow and to add a greater understanding of family dynamics to his spontaneous, shoot-from-the-hip approach. As this happened, "the former wild man of family therapy became one of the elder statesmen of the movement. Whitaker's death in April 1995 left the field with a piece of its heart missing" (Nichols & Schwartz, 1998, p. 51).

The final "co-originator" of the field of family therapy has had perhaps the most profound influence of all; an influence that is just as powerful today as it was when the field began. Murray Bowen, who like so many of the early leaders came from a psychoanalytic background, began treating families while he directed a research project on schizophrenic families. He first treated family members individually, but by the mid-1950s came to see the family as the unit of disorder and shifted to working with the entire family. Although he began family work by being nondirective, he soon shifted to a structured and directive approach, believing that this was needed to stimulate movement in families entrenched in their problems. At the same time, from the beginning Bowen viewed it as essential that the family therapist remain objective and detached, lest he or she become embroiled in the family's pathology. His approach in this way is in stark contrast to that of Ackerman and Whitaker, whom we have just described. Bowen's family systems therapy will be reviewed later in this chapter.

Bowen eventually became dissatisfied with his results when treating the entire family and, in the early 1960s, shifted to working with just the parents of troubled children. He believed it to be more helpful to all involved to have the parents work through their own relationship issues. Bowen and his followers have maintained this couples focus over the years.

We have given only a brief synopsis of the approaches taken by some of the main figures of the family therapy movement. There were many other early leaders. For thoughtful and interesting reviews of the history and beginning years of the family therapy movement, the reader is referred to Becvar and Becvar (1993) and Nichols and Schwartz (1998).

KEY ASSUMPTIONS AND CONCEPTS OF FAMILY AND COUPLES THERAPY: SYSTEMS THEORY

The field of family therapy may be described as "a diverse set of perspectives having in common a *systems perspective of behavior*" (Foster & Gurman, 1985, p. 413, italics added). This systems perspective contains several concepts that most if not all family-oriented practitioners tend to share.

Before describing the concepts and assumptions, it should be noted that systems theory in family work draws heavily from what is called *general systems theory*. As a twentieth-century phenomenon, systems theory has been applied widely to physical systems, and also extended to social and biological systems (P. Minuchin, 1985). VonBertalanffy's (1968, 1974) writing on general systems theory is generally credited with having a profound effect on the family therapy movement, although family therapists have drawn at least as heavily from theoreticians in the field who have applied basic principles of systems theory to living systems such as families. Members of the Palo Alto group, as described earlier, have been leaders in the application of general systems principles (e.g., Bateson, 1972, 1979; Watzlawick, Beavin, & Jackson, 1967).

What are some of the basic assumptions and concepts of systems theory as applied to families? Following Patricia Minuchin's (1985) discussion, we describe the five most basic concepts below. This description is summarized in Table 17.1.

Wholeness and Interdependence

Perhaps the most fundamental assumption of systems theory is that *systems are organized wholes, and elements within a system are necessarily interdependent* (P. Minuchin, 1985). When we talk about a system being an organized whole, we imply that this whole is greater than the sum of its parts. Thus a family is more than the sum of the individuals in it. It also includes all of the interactions between and among these individuals and the unique ways in which these individuals interrelate. The concept of interdependence implies that the behavior of each part (e.g., each member of a family) is dependent to some extent on the behavior of every other part.

Basic Assumptions and Concepts of Systems Theory Applied to Families. TABLE 17.1.

Concept	Definition
Wholeness and interdependence	Systems organized as wholes; all elements are interdependent
Circular causality	Members of system mutually influence one another
Equifinality	One does not need to go to origins in order to solve problems; start anywhere to solve problem
Homeostasis and change	Families seek equilibrium *and* they also strive to meet new challenges effectively
Systems, subsystems, triangles	Family systems consist of subsystems and interlocking triangles
Boundaries	Subsystems within families separated by boundaries; unspoken rules for interactions across boundaries

Family therapists are interested in the interactional patterns developed over time among family members and how these patterns regulate the behavior of members within this system. From the systems perspective, with the concepts of wholeness and interdependence in mind, it is most effective to study or treat a member of a family as part of an organized system because that member can best be understood in context.

Circular Causality and Equifinality

Psychologists typically conceptualize behavior in terms of linear causality. Thus A (e.g., mother's rejection) is assumed to cause B (e.g., child's low self-esteem). According to systems theory, thinking in terms of linear causality does not yield a valid picture of reality. The problem goes beyond the simplistic nature of our example. Point A may be extended so that it includes many causes (e.g., the father's behavior, the mother and father's interaction, etc.), but this is still linear causality, with A and its subparts causing B.

A more valid way of thinking about causality, say the systems theorists, is what is called *circular causality*. Here A may cause B, which in turn causes A1, which in turn causes B1, and so forth. In other words, A and B mutually influence each other. Consider, for example, the domineering father, who stimulates dependency in his son, and when the son behaves dependently, the father increases his dominance. This in turn further robs the son of his self-confidence and he becomes more passive. The father reacts by taking over. In this example, father and son are involved in a causal pattern, with each affecting and reinforcing the behaviors of the other.

When working with a family system or subsystem, this circular causality shows itself consistently and powerfully to the counselor. It takes only minimal experience with couples, for example, to see that neither is the cause of the other's behavior, but rather that each influences the other in a circular way. As P. Minuchin notes, "the irreducible unit is the cycle of interaction" (p. 290).

A central concept that stems from the assumption of circular causality is that of *equifinality*. This concept implies that any family problem—regardless of its original causes—may be solved if modifications are made at any point in time in the system. Open systems are not governed by their initial conditions, and systems have no memories. Because of these features, the concept of equifinality suggests that the family therapist need not explore the past. The therapist may focus on the present and get the job done just as effectively and certainly more efficiently as when original causes are explored.

Most family therapists, even those who are psychoanalytically oriented, focus much of their energies on the present interactions within the family and believe that it is the current interaction within the system that perpetuates, if not causes, the problem. Foley (1989) uses the example of the man who began drinking heavily 20 years ago because of unresolved problems with his mother but drinks now because of unresolved problems in his present relationship with his wife. Following the principle of equifinality, the therapist may focus on the husband–wife interaction, and not the mother–son relationship, with just as positive an outcome.

Homeostasis and Change

Since Jackson (1957) of the Palo Alto group first theorized about *family homeostasis,* this concept has been crucial for family therapists. Just as a thermostat serves to maintain room temperature, family mechanisms serve to regulate the patterns of interaction within the family unit. Homeostasis maintains a constancy of functioning within the family. This does not mean that the family is rigid. As discussed by Nichols and Schwartz (1998), family homeostasis is seen as a nonstatic, dynamic state—a state of equilibrium in which the family may be at point A on one day and point B on another day. Although families seek to maintain the status quo, the result is not rigid invariance in behavior. Rather, the result may be stable variance; the family may vary from one day to the next, but the pattern of variability is stable.

Homeostatic processes in the family, on the whole, are adaptive. They allow the family to maintain a state of equilibrium. In disturbed families, however, the processes that serve to maintain homeostasis may also incorporate symptoms and maladaptive behavior as necessary parts of the system. Here, as P. Minuchin (1985) notes, the need to maintain established patterns makes the family rigid and inhibits needed changes. Resistance to change in therapy, for example, is seen as a homeostatic process.

An example of how psychological symptoms may serve a "positive" function—for example, to maintain the family balance—was offered by Jackson and Weakland (1959). They note the case of a young woman who was diagnosed as schizophrenic, with one of her major symptoms being a deep and pervasive indecisiveness. Curiously, though, when she behaved decisively, her parents fell apart emotionally. The mother acted helpless, and the father became sexually impotent. Because of this, the parents had a difficult time even being aware of instances when the daughter was decisive. Here we can see vividly how the daughter's seemingly pathological indecisiveness served to protect the parents from facing their own issues. As long as the parents focused on their daughter's deficits, their own could be avoided and homeostasis in the family maintained.

The literature of family therapy is virtually filled with examples of how symptoms serve a function in families and thus also serve to maintain balance. In fact, the concept of family homeostasis has been so powerful in family therapy that it took a long time to develop the companion concept of *morphogenesis,* or change (P. Minuchin, 1985). Just as systems seek to maintain homeostasis, they also strive to meet new challenges and circumstances in effective ways. As a family develops, it inevitably faces many challenges, and it must periodically reorganize (e.g., when an offspring leaves home for college).

Family theorists have described typical stages families go through as the family develops. For example, Carter and McGoldrick (1999) developed a six-stage model with the following order: (1) the unattached young adult, (2) joining of families through marriage, (3) family with young children, (4) family with adolescents, (5) launching children and moving on, and (6) the family in later life. Whatever the particulars of these stages, the point is that each stage contains its own crises and demands for change. The family must be able to meet these demands if it is to continue to function in a healthy way. When families cannot handle transitions, then family therapists may be needed to help the family see that its established patterns no longer suffice, to mobilize the family's resources for change, and finally to consolidate new, more adaptive patterns.

Systems, Subsystems, and Triangles

Another assumption of systems theory is that complex systems are made up of subsystems. Although the individual may be considered a subsystem, family therapists pay attention to larger subsystems within the family, for example, the parent subsystem (more complex than just the spouses in divorced or blended families), the sibling subsystem, the parent(s)–child(ren) subsystem, the grandparent subsystem, and so forth.

A kind of subsystem that has particular importance for family therapists is called the *triangle.* As theorized by Bowen (1976), triangles are viewed as the building blocks of all interpersonal systems, including families. Families may be seen as consisting of a series of interlocking triangles. Such triangles occur when tension arises in two-person subsystems. Thus a third person or thing is triangulated into the relationship. For example, two lovers may have a stable relationship as long as the tension between them is low. When stress occurs, however, one of the lovers may feel the need to triangulate in a third person or thing, such as alcohol, a friend, or a psychotherapist. Unfortunately, common examples of triangulation are husbands in a troubled marriage resorting to drinking heavily or affairs, and wives in such situations becoming overinvolved with the children, clubs, the family, and so forth. The classic example of triangulation in families exists when husband and wife are experiencing tension in their relationship, and as a means of avoiding it, focus on the children. Instead of fighting with each other, the parents concentrate on the kids. If the unresolved issues between parents are too great, one of the parents is likely to become overattached to one or more of the children, with the regrettable consequence that the child may develop emotional problems.

Family therapists typically pay close attention to the triangles that exist in the family system. One of the major tasks in most family interventions is to work with triangles so that unhealthy triangulations are modified. In the classic example above, the therapist would work with the couple, with the aim of helping them resolve their issues and reducing their triangulation with the children.

Boundaries, Rules, and Patterns

Most family therapists would subscribe to the systems theory concept that subsystems within the family are separated by psychological boundaries. Further, a systems view suggests that family interactions across these boundaries are governed by unspoken rules and patterns (P. Minuchin, 1985).

The concept of emotional boundaries between subsystems of a family, one of the major theoretical advances in family interventions, was first proposed by Salvador Minuchin (Minuchin, 1974). More will be said about the concept of boundaries and rules when we discuss Minuchin's structural family therapy in the next section. For now, suffice it to say that boundaries are seen by S. Minuchin as invisible barriers surrounding individuals and subsystems. These boundaries regulate the amount and kind of contact with others, and serve to protect the separateness and independence of the family and its subsystems. When young children can interrupt their parents' conversation whenever they wish, the boundary between the parent and child subsystems in the family is seen as too "soft," or *diffuse*. Likewise, if parents rush in to protect their children whenever they experience some threat, the boundaries are diffuse. Diffuse boundaries tend to inhibit healthy development, especially in the area of autonomy. They lead to *enmeshment* between members of different subsystems.

On the other hand, boundaries may be *rigid*, which allows for little emotional contact between subsystems, resulting in *disengagement*. Using the example of parent and child subsystems, rigid boundaries and lack of emotional contact between these two subsystems allow for plenty of independence but also lead to emotional isolation.

CLASSIC THEORETICAL APPROACHES TO FAMILY AND COUPLES TREATMENT

As noted at the beginning of this chapter, apart from the assumptions and concepts of general systems theory as just described, there are few general principles or techniques of family/couples treatment that cut across the different theoretical perspectives. There is no "family therapy approach" to assessment and intervention. Rather, there are clusters of theories that differ from one another in terms of the conceptual framework used to understand families: who is actually seen in treat-

Major Theories of Family and Couples Counseling.   TABLE 17.2.

Theory	Originator(s)	Key concepts
	Classic Theories	
Psychoanalytic–object relations	Ronald Fairbairn Melanie Klein John Bowlby	Internal representation, projective identification (see Chapter 10)
Experiential	Carl Whitaker Virginia Satir	Emotional experience, awareness, genuine expression
Family systems	Murray Bowen	Triangles, differentiation of self, family projection, multigenerational transmission
Strategic	Jay Haley Cloe Madanes	Circular sequences, triangles, first- and second-order change, directives and paradoxical techniques
Structural	Salvador Minuchin	Family structure, subsystems, boundaries
Cognitive–behavioral	Gerald Patterson Robert Liberman Neil Jacobson	Parent and couple training, behavioral techniques, cognitive restructuring
	Newer Approaches	
Narrative	Michael White David Epson	Organizing stories, empathy and questioning, externalizing the problem
Solution-focused	Michael de Shazer Insoo Berg	Solutions and goals, exception questions, language

ment, the dimensions attended to in the assessment, and the treatment techniques used (Foster & Gurman, 1985).

The six approaches briefly reviewed below are: psychoanalytic, experiential, behavioral, family systems, strategic, and structural. These six classic approaches, as well as two more recent theories, are summarized in Table 17.2. Although space considerations permit us only to present the essential ingredients of each perspective, it must be kept in mind that there is often much variability in viewpoints *within* a given perspective as well as overlap between perspectives. For an extensive, thoughtful, and highly readable review of these systems and others, the reader is referred to Nichols and Schwartz (1998).

The Psychoanalytic Approach

Although psychoanalysis has traditionally been concerned with intrapsychic functioning of individuals, a number of theories have developed during the past few decades that focus more attention on relationships and human beings' inherent relatedness. Within the couples and family therapy domain, the major current theory of this nature is called *object relations theory*. Much of the present section will focus on this interesting brand of psychoanalytic theory.

In contrast to classic Freudian psychoanalysis, which focuses on biologically based drives revolving around sex and aggression, object relations theorists posit an innate human need for relationships (see Chapter 10). In fact, object relations theory may be defined as "the psychoanalytic study of the origin and nature of interpersonal relationships, and of the intrapsychic structures that grew out of past relationships and remain to influence present interpersonal relations" (Nichols, 1984, p. 183). The word *object,* as used by object relations theorists and indeed all psychoanalytic theorists, refers primarily to people and usually to people other than the self.

From birth on, the human being seeks sustaining relationships with significant others, especially of course with mother and father in early life. Like all psychoanalytic theories, object relations theory posits developmental stages, but these are quite different in many ways from the psychosexual stages posited by Freud (oral, anal, phallic, etc.). Rather, the stages generally revolve around the child's relationship with primary caretakers. The earliest stage, for example, involves profound dependency on the primary caretaker, usually mother. Subsequent stages focus on the differentiation of a self separate from caretakers and individuation of that self while maintaining connection to others. Parents need to respond to the growing child's needs during each of these stages. All parents will of course make mistakes, and most of us make many of them. What is needed is not perfection, but rather "good enough parenting"—for the parents who are able to respond appropriately, on the whole, to the child's needs. As supposed in all analytic theories, if the child's needs are too frustrated during the early stages, they will go underground but then show up later. What is of greatest interest to couples/family therapists is that these needs show themselves in the choice of and behavior toward love objects, and in terms of one's strengths and weaknesses as a parent.

In addition to a particular kind of theory about development as just summarized, the heart of object relations theory is how early relationships are "taken in" (internalized) by the person, and carried with him or her in subsequent relationships. In essence, the person forms internalized representations of early love objects such as parents, and these representations serve as a blueprint of sorts for subsequent relationships. The internal object representations profoundly affect the choice of subsequent love objects, behavior toward those persons, and perceptions of the objects. It must be understood that the internal representations only partly correspond to reality. They are always affected by the child's existing needs and drives.

Although object relations therapists do work with entire families and various family subsystems, it is safe to say that most analytic work involves the couple subsystem. Some of the most fascinating object relations theory focuses on how marital partners choose each other and respond to each other in a way that matches the internal representations of early objects, such as mother and father (see Scarf, 1987).

The concept of *projective identification* is used by most object relations therapists as a key to the troubled interactions of members of a couple and of a family. When using this defense, the person unconsciously projects hidden feelings and ideas (which in turn reflect hidden object representations from childhood) onto the spouse or other significant objects. The person not only projects hidden parts of the self onto others but then identifies with those parts because these are, after all, parts of the self. In couples and family interactions, projective identification, ordinarily a complex concept, is even more complicated. The object (e.g., spouse) takes on these projections and then acts them out. For example, in his earliest years a husband has internalized the bad mother, represented as a hostile rejecting object who will not provide him nurturance. He then sees rejection and hostility in his wife, even when it is not present in reality. Significantly, the wife "takes in" this projection, and acts out the role of the hostile rejecting object. To carry this example further, the wife, too, has her internal object representations, for example, the cool, distancing father introject. She may project these into her husband, and he may in turn act them out. Thus, in the systems theory sense, we have a true system in operation, with definite circular causality. The cure, from an object relations perspective, is for each to learn to acknowledge and accept his and her own repressed parts (object representations) and, just as significantly, not to accept the projections of the other (Scarf, 1987).

Even when the "identified patient" is a child, in the object relations perspective the child is often seen as the carrier of the split-off (from consciousness) and unacceptable impulses of other family members. For example, in the case of the delinquent child, the parents are able to avoid facing certain of their own impulses, experience vicarious gratification of these impulses through the child, and still punish the child for expression of the impulses. The parents can act as the superego while punishing the child for acting out the impulses of the parents' id. Nichols and Schwartz (1998, p. 215) use the following telling example of this phenomenon:

> The J. family sought help controlling 15-year-old Paul's delinquent behavior. Arrested several times for vandalism, Paul seemed neither ashamed of nor able to understand his compulsion to strike out against authority. As therapy progressed, it became clear that Paul's father harbored a deep but unexpressed resentment of the social conditions which made him work long hours for low wages in a factory, while the "fat cats didn't do shit, but still drove around in Cadillacs." Once the therapists became aware of Mr. J.'s strong but suppressed hatred of authority, they also began to notice that he smiled slightly when Mrs. J. described Paul's latest exploits.

The psychoanalytic family therapist assesses his or her cases in terms of both the dynamics of the individuals in the family and the dynamics of the family system and subsystems (Nichols & Schwartz, 1998). During the initial assessment, most analytic therapists would meet with the family as a whole (cf. Ackerman, 1961; Skynner, 1981). The aim of the initial work is to understand dynamics of the family as a whole as well as those of the individuals and subgroups within the family. Following this initial phase, a decision is made as to which members of the family should be worked with. Although modern psychoanalytic family therapists work with all imaginable combinations of family members, work with the couple dyad is the norm.

Although the psychoanalytic family therapist tends to be more active and directive than the psychoanalytic individual therapist (see Chapter 10), this treatment is clearly nondirective in comparison to other family/couples approaches. The therapist listens a great deal, and although this listening is very active, he or she is relatively quiet. Interpretation is the primary technique in most analytic approaches, and rarely would a therapist offer more than two or three interpretations in a session

(Nichols & Schwartz, 1998). As in virtually all psychoanalytic approaches, great emphasis is placed on the client's transference, although in the case of couple and family therapies, this transference gets even more complicated than in individual treatment. Thus in evidence are transferences to the therapist from each of the family members as well as transferences between and among family members themselves. As Boszormenyi-Nagy (1972) points out, transference specifically to the therapist is less intense than in individual therapy. Both the real and transference reactions between and among other family members divert some of the energy ordinarily invested in the individual therapist.

The psychoanalytic family therapist usually prefers to work with families in a longer-term format than other approaches. The goal is personality change in individual members of the family. The object relations perspective clearly defines how that change is conceptualized. Terms such as *separation–individuation* (Katz, 1981) and *differentiation* (Skynner, 1981) are often used. In other words, the goal is for individuals to differentiate themselves (from other family members, e.g., parents), while at the same time maintaining and improving the quality of relationships with family. The overarching goal of psychoanalytic family therapy is to "free family members of unconscious restrictions so that they'll be able to interact with one another as whole, healthy persons on the basis of current realities rather than unconscious images of the past" (Nichols & Schwartz, 1998).

The Experiential Approach

Experiential family therapy grew out of the humanistic psychology movement of the 1960s, and because of this it bears a close resemblance to the humanistic counseling perspective described in Chapter 12. The essential problem with families, just as with individuals, is that they are emotionally frozen and stuck; the job of therapists is to help the family and its members to become unstuck. This process entails learning to experience one's underlying feelings and to express what is experienced. Through such experiencing and expressing, members of the family both get in touch with themselves and are enabled to touch each other emotionally.

As we have mentioned, Carl Whitaker was considered the dean of experiential family therapy, for he was probably the first within this perspective to work with families and write about this work. Virginia Satir (1967), who was known for her work in family communication as well as experiential therapy, was also a charismatic leader of the experiential movement. Experiential family therapy differs from most systems-oriented family work in its focus on expanding immediate personal experience, and in the early days of this approach, attention was directed far more to the individuals in a family than to the family system. To be sure, there was great stress on sharing among individuals in the family, but the individual emphasis was unmistakable. Also, unlike the systems therapists to be discussed later but similar to psychoanalytic family therapists, experiential therapists work to help members of the family get in touch with feelings that are hidden from awareness—the awareness of the individual as well as the awareness of other family members. In more recent years, experiential therapists have focused to a greater extent on the family as a system, on the interconnectedness of the family. As Nichols and Schwartz (1998) point out in their analysis of the experiential approach, experientialists now see the family as a team in which none of the players can perform effectively without the unity and wholeness of the group. Thus, individual problems are broadened to include the involvement of other family members, and members are invited to consider their own part in maintaining the behavior of other members with which they are unhappy.

As part of this movement toward the family and couples system, experiential family therapists increasingly worked with the entire family. Whitaker (1976), for example, believed the therapist should have at least a few meetings with the entire family, including three generations. He also believed that children should always be part of the work. Whitaker often invited extended family members to early meetings as consultants rather than clients. Inviting grandparents as consultants, for example, helps reduce their resistance to attendance, facilitates their support of the treatment aims, and also gives a fuller picture of the family's dynamics.

Given the goals of emotionally unfreezing the family, the experiential therapists, like their cousins the gestalt therapists (Chapter 12) and encounter group therapists (Chapter 16), stress the importance of being open, not wearing a professional mask, and sharing immediate experience with family members. The spontaneous expression of the therapist is placed at a premium. An adherence to theory is often seen as a hindrance to the therapeutic process rather than an aid. Theory can provide a cover for the therapist, getting in the way of his or her spontaneous experience and expression. (Of course, this is a theoretical statement in itself!)

Just as theory is deemphasized by the experientialists, the use of cookbook techniques is eschewed. It is the person of the therapist, not a set of techniques, that is curative. Kempler (1973) underscores this point when he states that experiential therapy has no techniques, only people. To further the experiential process, these therapists are quite active and directive. They involve themselves deeply and often provoke clients to do likewise. "Look at each other when you talk"; "Say that again, only this time let your feelings be part of what you say"; "You are whining—tell him to get off your back, but this time *mean it!*" These are the kinds of directives often used by experientialists.

The confrontational and provocative nature of experiential family therapy is made clear in a case example presented by Nichols and Schwartz (1998). After an information-gathering session, the L. family was discussing Tommy's misbehavior. Mrs. L. and Tommy's sister were listing the "terrible things" Tommy did around the house. The therapist noticed how uninvolved Mr. L. seemed to be as he passively nodded in response to his wife's complaints. When the therapist asked about what he felt, he responded minimally, and it seemed that in fact little was on his mind, at least consciously. The therapist did not know why this was, but she did know that she felt annoyed by the lack of involvement, and decided to express this:

> *Therapist to Mr. L.:* You know what, you piss me off.
> *Mr. L.:* What? [He was shocked; people he knew didn't speak that way.]
> *Therapist:* I said, you piss me off. Here your wife is concerned and upset about Tommy, and you just sit there like a lump on a log. You're about as much a part of this family as that lamp in the corner.

Mr. L.: You have no right to talk to me that way [getting angrier by the minute]. I work very hard for this family. Who do you think puts bread on the table? I get up six days a week and drive a delivery truck all over town. All day long I have to listen to customers bitching about this, and that. Then I come home and what do I get? "Tommy did this. Tommy did that." I'm sick of it.
Therapist: Say that again, louder.
Mr. L.: I'm sick of it! I'm sick of it!

This interchange dramatically transformed the atmosphere in the session. Suddenly the reason for Mr. L.'s disinterest became clear. He was furious at his wife for nagging and complaining about Tommy. She, in turn, was displacing much of her feeling for her husband onto Tommy, as a result of Mr. L.'s emotional unavailability. In subsequent sessions, Mr. and Mrs. L. spent more time talking about their relationship, less and less was heard about Tommy's misbehavior (Nichols & Schwartz, 1998, pp. 188–189).

The experiential family therapy movement, like the gestalt therapy movement with which it shares much in common, was at its peak of popularity in the late 1960s and 1970s. The focus on emotional expression and spontaneity fit those times beautifully, but did not seem as suited to family therapy as did approaches that inherently focus on systems and action. Yet, as Nichols and Schwartz (1998) indicate, the experiential focus on unblocking honest emotional expression in families is important, and is a useful counterweight to the reductionistic cognitive emphasis of currently popular approaches (see later discussion of solution-focused therapy). Modern experientialists teach and practice expressive techniques that any family or couples therapist will find useful. Also, the research-based experiential approach to couples therapy practiced by Greenberg and Johnson (1988) and Johnson and Greenberg (1991) appears to be revitalizing the experiential family and couples therapy.

The Family Systems Approach

A school of family therapy that strongly adheres to the main tenets of general systems theory is the family systems approach. Although a number of creative therapists have been involved in the refinement of this perspective, the creator and prime mover over many years was Murray Bowen. He not only originated family systems therapy, but was responsible for the training of many of its leading spokespersons.

Bowen was always more interested in developing theories of how families operate than in creating techniques of treatment because effective theories serve as guides to the treatment of family systems (Bowen, 1966, 1976). Bowen was originally trained as a psychoanalyst, and his family systems theory is decidedly psychodynamic, with many psychoanalytic elements. It is one of the most powerful, comprehensive, and widely used theories of families and family interventions.

Bowen began theorizing about families in the 1950s, and although his theory has evolved, the most fundamental constructs have revolved around two sets of opposing forces: One set pulls the person into the family and makes for family togetherness; the other set pushes the person toward individuality. The key assumption of the theory is that excessive and conflictual emotional attachments to one's family need to be resolved, rather than accepted passively or reacted against, if one is to differentiate into a mature personality and become a well-functioning parent (Becvar & Becvar, 1993; Bowen, 1976, 1978).

Five interrelated concepts serve as the nucleus of Bowen's rich and far-reaching theory. We shall briefly summarize each of these.

Emotional Triangles

The notion of triangulation is a significant part of Bowen's theory. As discussed earlier, family systems therapists pay close attention to triangles in troubled families and work actively at helping their clients detriangulate. Couples, for example, are helped to work directly with their issues and to avoid triangulating a third person or object into their situation.

Differentiation of Self

Perhaps the most fundamental construct in family systems theory is differentiation, both as it occurs within a person and between persons. Undifferentiation, or fusion, occurs when people do not separate feelings from intellect but instead are flooded by their feelings. At an interpersonal level, the undifferentiated person tends to either absorb others' feelings or react against others. Such intra- and interpersonal undifferentiation is passed on from one generation to the next in families, and a central aim of all family systems therapy is to help clients learn to become differentiated within themselves and from other members of their nuclear and extended families. Helping an individual within the family or a couple become differentiated has a healthy effect on the entire family system.

Nuclear Family Emotional System

This concept refers to emotional entanglements that become transmitted from one generation to the next in families and that form unhealthy patterns. When lack of differentiation exists in the family of origin, the person is either emotionally fused with his or her parents or cut off emotionally from them. The consequence, though, is lack of differentiation within the person. Persons then unconsciously seek out mates with about an equal level of undifferentiation, and the two people form a new fused relationship. This will produce any of the following: (1) a defensive distancing between spouses, (2) overt conflict in the relationship, (3) psychological or even physical dysfunction in one of the spouses, or (4) projection of the problem onto one or more of the children.

Family Projection Process

Parents transmit their own lack of differentiation to their children through a kind of projection. As just noted, undifferentiation causes stress in the marital situation. Because of this, one or more of the children often get unconsciously triangulated into the process. A common scenario is for the husband to withdraw from his wife, and for the wife to project her needs into the children, such that she becomes fused with one of them. The husband unconsciously supports this entanglement because it relieves him of the stress of the relationship. The wife is also enabled to avoid the marital situation. The child, however, does not develop healthy differentiation and often becomes emotionally crippled. The parents then have to invest even more concern in the child, and the family pattern becomes deeply embedded.

Multigenerational Transmission Process

Not only do parents transmit their lack of differentiation to their children, but this transmission process goes on for several generations. Thus, in family systems theory the constructs of differentiation and fusion are applied to individuals, nuclear family systems, and the extended family system. In each family, the children who are most affected by the family's fusion will go on to create families in which there is lack of differentiation, and the cycle continues. Along the way, some spouses and some children develop symptoms of emotional disorder, for which treatment is sought. These individuals become the "identified patient," but the problem of undifferentiation is an inherent part of the system.

Although problems inhere in the family system, Bowenians aim to help individuals differentiate, which in turn affects the system. Family systems therapists work with all combinations of family members, including individuals (Kerr, 1981), but it is the marital dyad they most often treat. In striking contrast to some of the family therapists described earlier (e.g., Ackerman, 1958; Whitaker, 1976), Bowenians believe it is crucial for the therapist to maintain an unemotional and rational stance with patients. If the therapist gets too emotionally involved, she or he will become triangulated, and be less effective.

In working with couples, family systems therapists do not encourage interaction between the members. These therapists invite each member to take turns interacting with the therapist, while the other member observes and tries to empathize. Clients are discouraged from becoming too emotional, since it is through the use of reason and intellect that one learns to be differentiated. This "deemotionalizing" is a distinctive feature of family systems therapy.

Bowen (1978) states that the therapist's functions are fourfold: (1) defining and clarifying the relationship between spouses, (2) keeping the self detriangulated from the family emotional system, (3) teaching the functioning of emotional systems, and (4) demonstrating differentiation by taking the "I position." Regarding this last function, the therapist must acknowledge his or her views and ideas and state them calmly. This serves as a model of differentiation to the couple.

Two other elements are vital in Bowenian therapy. First, if the treatment is long term (e.g., beyond 6 months), family systems therapists will tend to include didactic methods, teaching clients about family systems and recommending that they attend relevant seminars. Second, as part of long-term treatment, family systems therapists encourage members of the couple to return home for visits so that they can further the process of differentiation in their extended families. During this phase, the treatment often resembles "coaching" (Bowen, 1976), and the time gap between sessions is widened, for example, to one meeting a month. Clients who are not differentiated often separate from their parents by emotionally cutting off the relationships. Family systems therapists want their clients to return to the system and form healthier relationships, where a sense of togetherness can exist within the context of differentiation.

One key shortcoming of the family systems approach, as noted by Nichols and Schwartz (1998), is that it neglects the power of working directly with the nuclear family. Stated simply, sometimes it is preferable to work directly with families rather than with couples or individuals, as do Bowenians. Also, as we gain increasing awareness of cultural differences among peoples, questions arise about how constructs like differentiation operate in, for example, collectivist cultures, in contrast to individualist cultures that have predominated in the United States. At the same time, the family systems approach originated by Bowen has maintained its great appeal to practitioners over the years, and has been refined and revised by many clinicians and theorists trained in the Bowenian tradition (e.g., Carter & McGoldrick, 1999).

The Strategic Family Therapy (SFT) Approach

Strategic family therapy (SFT) is actually a cluster of approaches with a common systems orientation to family problems and some shared conceptions of how treatment is best performed. Also called problem-solving therapy and systemic therapy, SFT is typically a short-term treatment in which the therapist is highly active and directive. The treatment is aimed at modifying overt behavior in the form of family members' communications with one another. SFT represents a controversial approach to treatment, as the therapist takes control of the interactions with his or her clients and actively manipulates clients into behaving more constructively. Virtually all strategic therapists agree on one point: Insight is of no help and may in fact serve to deepen clients' resistance to change. What helps is behavior change, actively instigated by the therapist's directives.

There are many leading figures in SFT, although recently, several leaders have moved on to other approaches (Nichols & Schwartz, 1998). Probably the most towering figures within this approach are Jay Haley and Cloe Madanes, each having made vital and creative contributions to theory and practice (e.g., Haley, 1976; Madanes, 1981). The Brief Therapy Center of the Mental Research Institute in Palo Alto, California, has also been the home of many creative insights (e.g., Fisch, Weakland, & Segal, 1982). The Milan (Italy) Group, lead by Mara Selvini Palazzoli (Selvini Palazzoli, Boscolo, Cecchin, & Prata, 1978) was a major force in the SFT movement during the 1970s and 1980s, but therapists from this group have essentially given up on SFT and sought to develop other treatments.

On the whole, strategic therapists, like their behavioral cousins, focus treatment on the primary symptom presented by the family, usually in the form of maladaptive behaviors exhibited by the identified patient. These symptoms, however, are seen as originating in the family system and are treated within that system. Thus the identified patient (often a misbehaving child in the family) is usually not isolated for treatment. He or she may be treated as part of family treatment, or the marital dyad may be worked with in an effort to resolve the child's symptom.

True to its systems theory roots, SFT conceptualizes the symptom in terms of circular sequences in the family. In addition, strategic therapists, borrowing Bowen's concept of triangles, view these circular sequences as usually involving three persons. A common sequence, noted by Haley (1976), is as follows: (a) Father becomes unhappy and withdraws; (b) child misbehaves; (c) mother deals with the misbehavior ineffectively; (d) father moves toward involvement with mother and child; (e) child behaves more appropriately; (f) mother becomes more effective, and expects more from the father and the child; (g) father becomes unhappy and withdraws.

Selvini Palazzoli and colleagues (Selvini Palazzoli et al., 1978) view troubled families as playing games that serve to maintain homeostasis in the family. Healthy systems balance homeostasis and change, and they do change when transitions in the family require it (e.g., when a first child enters the family, a child leaves the family, or a parent's vocational situation changes). Pathological families, however, seem to maintain the status quo at all costs.

A key distinction in SFT is that between first-order change and second-order change (Watzlawick et al., 1967). First-order change involves "more of the same," as the family seeks change without changing the system. Such change is ineffective. Second-order change alters the system itself and is more likely to be effective. Troubled families only employ first-order change. Nichols (1984) notes, for example, that parents of a clinging, dependent child might change from telling the child to stay home to telling the child to go out and play as a way of facilitating independence. This does not work, however, because it does not alter the basic system pattern—dominant parents dictating to a dependent child.

In terms of interventions, strategic therapists work with any combination of family members, and some even include the entire family and the extended family. Most common, however, is work with either the marital dyad or the parents along with one of the children, usually the identified patient. Unlike the experiential and family systems approaches, SFT usually does not entail the use of co-therapists, although strategic therapists do typically use consultation in the unique way. For example, consultants will often observe the therapy through a one-way mirror and even enter the therapy session to make active suggestions. As noted, SFT is symptom-oriented, and tends to be brief because of this. Strategic therapists at Palo Alto's Mental Research Institute, for example, typically implement a treatment that continues for only 10 sessions.

The most frequent technique used by strategic therapists is the directive. Clients are given directives for in-session behavior, but most often directives are given in the form of homework assignments. These directives may entail straightforward suggestions, or may be in the form of paradoxical interventions, as described below.

Perhaps the most distinctive feature of SFT is the use of active therapist manipulations aimed at dramatically changing behavioral sequences in the family system. The most frequently used manipulations are those called *paradoxical interventions*. Dowd and Milne (1986) offer an extensive discussion of such interventions in counseling psychology and family work. One of the most common forms of paradox is *symptom prescription*. Here the therapist instructs the client to actually engage in the behavior that the client seeks to eliminate. An example given by Watzlawick, Weakland, and Fisch (1974) took place in a family in which the mother rationalized her son's frequent misbehavior by stating, "It's all the result of psychological problems." Her strategic therapist directed the child to misbehave even more during the coming week, and the mother was to forgive him with even greater amounts of understanding. Here the mother can comply with the therapist's directive and come to see the problem as controllable. Alternatively, she could rebel against the directive, in which case a big step is taken toward solving the problem. The dynamics of such paradoxical interventions involve the client's being placed in a therapeutic double-bind, in which a positive outcome is accomplished, regardless of what the client does. Strategic therapists view this as a "no-lose" situation, in contrast to the pathological double-bind discussed early in this chapter, which involves a "no-win" situation.

Other paradoxical interventions involve symptom scheduling, restraining, and positioning. In *symptom scheduling*, the counselor directs the client to set aside a certain time to engage in the symptom. For example, a therapist might instruct the client who has problems with obsessive thinking to spend 1 hour a day, from 4:00 to 5:00 P.M., engaging completely in obsessive thinking. A *restraining strategy* involves cautioning the client against changing too rapidly and is often helpful with oppositional clients who may oppose the counselor and undergo rapid change. *Positioning* occurs when the therapist agrees with the client's negative self-view, and may even exaggerate it.

Therapists are often uncomfortable with the confrontational quality of paradoxical interventions. Madanes (1981) uses *pretend techniques* as a way to insert a sense of playfulness into what might otherwise be an antagonistic process. She might, for example, invite a child to pretend to have the symptoms that everybody has been trying to get the child to abandon. Madanes here would also ask the parents to pretend to help the child have these symptoms. As a consequence of making it into something playful, the child often gives up the actual symptom.

Strategic therapists use paradox and straightforward directives very thoughtfully. They often meet with the entire family, and carefully observe the family's interactions with the therapist, with each other, with the identified patient in the family, across generational lines, and so forth. The therapist then decides on a treatment strategy, including the kinds of directives to use, to fit the problem or symptom. The therapist pays very close attention to the system factors that serve to maintain the presenting problem and that might also be the vehicle through which the problem is solved.

SFT reached its heyday during the 1980s, as the family therapy field was charmed by the clever techniques and approaches, as well as reports of dramatically effective outcomes. Around the mid-1980s, however, reactions set in (Nichols & Schwartz, 1998). Family therapists became critical of the manipulative and calculating aspects of SFT, as well as the lack of attention to the development of a caring, empathic, therapeutic relationship. Also rejected by family therapists was the "mechanistic view of families, as though they were puppets of a system they were too blind to see, and a hierarchical view of therapy, as though only an oh-so-clever therapist could pull the strings" (Nichols & Schwartz, 1998, p. 378).

Although current SFT is still technique-oriented, it is less "gimmicky" than in the past. More attention is being paid to the development of a respectful caring relationship between therapists and clients (Cade & O'Hanlon, 1993). Also, more attention is now paid to *collaboration* between therapist and clients, rather than the therapist pulling all the strings. Thus, while its initial glitter has worn off, SFT continues to develop, and it ought to maintain its status as one of the main approaches to treating family and couple problems.

The Structural Approach

The structural approach entered the family therapy scene in full force in the 1970s and has remained one of the most popular and influential approaches to family intervention (Becvar & Becvar, 1993; Nichols & Schwartz, 1998). Structural theory is deeply embedded in systems theory, holding similar conceptions of how families operate and how to intervene with troubled families. It is an appealing theory in several ways. Structural theory offers ideas about the structure or underlying organization of families that make a great deal of sense to the practicing counselor. The theory of how families operate and how they go emotionally awry also has clear implications for assessment and treatment. Finally, a number of clear counseling techniques are suggested by the theory.

The founder and leader of the structural approach is Salvador Minuchin, whose ideas about family intervention took shape when he worked with multiproblem, economically impoverished families of delinquent children in the 1960s. Some of the most important and useful works on the structural approach are as follows: Minuchin's definitive work (1974), Minuchin and Fishman (1981), Minuchin, Lee, and Simon (1996), and Minuchin and Nichols (1993).

Three concepts form the nucleus of the structural theory of family functioning: structure, subsystems, and boundaries.

Family Structure

The concept of family structure may be defined as the organized pattern in which family members interact. All families have predictable patterns of interaction, and such patterns reveal the who, when, and how of family members' interactions. Patterns that are repeated develop into psychological structures. For example, a father may play the role of distant disciplinarian, whereas the mother may be affectionate but unable to set limits. This pattern may be manifested in numerous interactions between the spouses and their children when affection and discipline are at issue. These parental roles are a clear, even if implicit, part of the family's structure.

Part of the family's structure involves a number of unspoken rules about how members are to interact within and outside the family. Examples of such rules are that mother spends time with the children while father works, the children act up whenever the parents seem to have a conflict, father plans and orchestrates the family trips, family members do not share their feelings directly. Rules, patterns, and structure in families, once established, are highly resistant to change.

Subsystems

As noted in the earlier discussion of key assumptions in systems theory, all complex systems are divided into subsystems. Such subsystems may contain any number of people within the family, and subsystem groupings may be determined by age, generation, gender, interests, and so forth. Thus, there is usually a parent subsystem and a children subsystem, as well as less obvious ones—for example, the mother aligned with the male children, and the father forming another subsystem with the female child. Subsystems may be fluid in the sense that any individual within the family may belong to more than one subsystem. The mother in a particular family may be part of the spousal subsystem in certain ways, of the female subsystem in other ways, and the athletic subsystem in still other ways.

Boundaries

In all families there are invisible barriers that surround and to an extent insulate all individuals and subsystems, and Minuchin's notions about the characteristics of these boundaries are among the most interesting and significant concepts within structural theory.

Boundaries serve to control the amount of contact with those outside the boundary. As noted earlier, these boundaries range from being rigid to diffuse, with the boundary labeled "clear" being at the midpoint on the continuum. Neither of the extremes (rigid or diffuse) is healthy. Rigid boundaries permit little emotional contact with individuals or systems outside of the boundary, and this results in what Minuchin calls *disengagement*. Diffuse boundaries, on the other hand, are not solid enough, and foster too much emotional connection with outside individuals or systems. This results in *enmeshment*.

Disengaged individuals or subsystems tend to be isolated. Although this isolation permits independence and at times mastery, there is a cost. Disengagement also limits warmth, affection, and a sense of support. On the other side of the continuum, enmeshment allows for plenty of support and affection across subsystems. Enmeshed parents provide an abundance of love and affection, but, at the same time, their children are not given room to develop themselves as independent effective individuals.

Structural therapists pay close attention to boundaries in families. If enmeshment exists (e.g., between any of the combinations of parent and child subsystems), structural therapists seek to solidify boundaries. If individuals or subsystems are disengaged, on the other hand, the therapist works to soften boundaries and open communication.

As regards interventions, structural therapists, like strategic therapists described in the previous section, are very active, directive, and at times manipulative. Unlike the strategic group, however, structuralists do not work directly on presenting symptoms. Instead, they seek to modify structure because the best and longest-lasting way to change problem behavior is to change the family patterns (structure) that maintain it. Structuralists typically work with families in which a child or adolescent is the identified patient, and may work with any combination of family members, at times dealing with individuals and at times with different subsystems within the family. The therapist, for example, may meet with the entire family for a while. Then, feeling that the parent subsystem needs clearer boundaries from the child subsystem, the therapist may meet with the parents alone. In this same family, it may be clear that the father and son need their boundaries softened, and the therapist may also meet with this pair.

In his most thorough statement of treatment, Minuchin (1974) describes steps and techniques of structural therapy. During the first session or two the therapist seeks to "join" the family—to demonstrate respect for it and each of its members. At the same time, he or she is carefully observing structure, subsystems, and boundary issues. The therapist may have family members enact problem sequences. For example, if the husband complains that his wife is not communicating with him, the therapist may ask the husband and wife to talk this over in the session. As the therapist observes sequences and directs enactments, he or she is also making a diagnosis, not a traditional psychiatric diagnosis but a structural one. The diagnosis includes *all* family members. It is not enough, for example, to know that a husband and daughter are enmeshed. The therapist must also learn the ways in which the wife is involved with both. She may also be enmeshed with the daughter, disengaged from the husband, or close to him. These patterns all call for different diagnoses and interventions.

After joining the family, observing interactions, and diagnosing the problem, structural therapists seek to change family patterns and boundaries. When Minuchin and other structural therapists intervene in these patterns, they do so in intense, forceful, and at times dramatic ways. Family patterns are usually entrenched, and it requires intensity and forcefulness to modify them. Structuralists pay particular attention to systems of circular causality in the family. The husband withdraws from the wife because she is emotionally demanding; the wife is emotionally demanding because the husband withdraws from her. The therapist intervenes in these circles, actively and forcefully points them out, and seeks to promote change.

Nichols and Schwartz (1998) give a case example from Nichols' own work of how affective intensity is used to modify entrenched patterns and boundaries. A mother and daughter, a 29-year-old woman suffering from anorexia, were enmeshed in a rigidly structured family. The father, the only one who would express anger openly, was excluded from that subsystem. The mother had covertly taught the daughter to be fearful of the father's anger because of her own issues in dealing with it. During one session, the father expressed how isolated he felt from his daughter. He and the daughter both felt it was because of his anger, for which the daughter blamed him. Nichols asked the mother what she felt, and she expressed that it wasn't the father's fault, it was no one's fault. In an effort to get the mother's attention and begin to cut into the rigid system, Nichols exclaimed, "Like hell it isn't!" She asked what he meant, and Nichols replied, "It's *your* fault!" Nichols notes that the content—who was really afraid of anger—was not as important as the structural goal of reducing the destructive enmeshment between mother and daughter. Softening the father–daughter boundaries and strengthening the mother–father subsystem would also be important in this case. Given the intensity of such interventions, structural therapists emphasize the importance of timing and having a sound diagnosis of the system and individuals prior to intervening.

In the early part of the twenty-first century, the structural approach is as popular to family therapists as it ever was. The appeal of this approach rests on its simplicity, inclusiveness, and practicality. Its basic concepts are easy for practitioners to grasp and apply. They pay attention to the individual, the family, and culture; and they provide a cohesive framework for understanding and counseling families. The appeal of structural family therapy is further enhanced by the sound empirical support for its effectiveness garnered over the years (Nichols & Schwartz, 1998).

Cognitive–Behavioral Approaches

Of all the approaches to family intervention discussed in this chapter, the cognitive–behavioral approach most often incorporates the results of empirical research into the development of treatment guidelines. Although there is more evidence on the effectiveness of behavioral interventions than on other family therapies, this approach is often not even included in discussions of family therapy. This is so because the behavioral approach is generally not considered to be family therapy treatment in the sense that there is little attention to systems theory or the family as a system. The focus in behavioral treatment has tended, for example, to be on two-person situations. The marital couple and parent–child dyads have been given almost exclusive attention. The triad and the entire family system, so often the focus of family therapists, have tended to be ignored.

The behavioral approach is also unlike the other, more systems-oriented family therapies in that it most often conceptualizes family problems in terms of linear causality rather than circular causality. The behavioral family counselor seeks to isolate specific and concrete problem behaviors, identify what in the (usually) interpersonal environment is controlling them, and use behavioral techniques to reduce the problem behaviors while increasing positive behaviors. In recent years, cognitive concepts have been added to behavior therapy. Just as is the case for individual counseling, most behaviorally oriented family counselors today are actually cognitive–behavioral family counselors. As part of the cognitive element, heavy emphasis is placed on the clients' *schema* (or core beliefs) about their families, and how these family schemata influence and are influenced by family members' interactions (Datillo, 1993, 1997). Be that as it may, there is still a strong emphasis on isolating and treating specific and concrete problems, as well as a tendency among cognitive–behavioral family/couple therapists to conceptualize clients' problems in terms of linear rather than circular causality (Nichols & Schwartz, 1998).

Foster & Gurman (1985) note that this specificity of the behavioral approach (now the cognitive–behavioral approach) is both a strength and a deficiency. It is a deficiency in that being highly specific about the enormously complex interactions that seem inherent in dysfunctional families is notoriously difficult. Without a framework for understanding the interactions in the family as a whole, identifying specific behaviors (or cognitions) to be changed may be very limiting.

Cognitive–behavioral family interventions rely on the same principles of learning discussed in Chapter 11, and on many of the same intervention techniques, as well. The learning model most often used in the family area is social–cognitive theory, with particular attention to principles of operant conditioning in terms of what maintains undesirable behavior and what is needed to increase desirable behavior in couple and parent–child interactions. As indicated, more attention has been given in recent years to the role of cognitive factors in behavioral marital and parent–child interventions.

Like most family therapists, cognitive–behavioral counselors tend to be active and directive, and emphasize their clients' active involvement in the treatment, as well. These counselors often serve as educators, teaching their family clients to apply learning and cognitive principles and techniques to develop and reinforce desired behaviors in their clients. Cognitive–behavioral family counselors have worked primarily in two general areas: couples counseling (which may itself focus on a range of issues, e.g., communication, sexual problems) and parent training. In both these areas, treatment is preceded by a careful assessment to determine which behaviors and cognitions are to be modified. A range of assessment techniques are used (discussed in Chapter 11). The goal is to pinpoint target behaviors and cognitions (those to be changed) and get a baseline on these. Great pains are taken to reduce presenting problems to specific cognitive and behavioral terms.

Numerous behavioral and cognitive techniques and programs have been presented in the literature, in both the couples counseling and parent training areas (Foster & Gurman, 1985; Jacobsen & Christensen 1996). Only a general flavor of these procedures will be given here. In couples counseling, the therapist helps each member of the couple identify behaviors in the other that are desirable and to communicate what is wanted. The therapist also develops a behaviorally oriented treatment plan aimed at increasing the desired behaviors. Focus is more on increasing the positive than decreasing the negative. Various types of contingency contracting are frequently used. Here positive behavior of one member is made dependent upon positive behavior of another. For example, Charlie agrees to spend a half hour with the children each night before bedtime if Jane does the dishes. Such a contingency is usually also balanced; for example, Jane goes on weekly hiking trips with Charlie if Charlie vacuums twice a week. In such contracting, it is important that none of the behaviors be objectionable to either member. Also, for problems that are too conflictual to be dealt with by simple contingency contracting methods, the behavioral counselor uses structured problem-solving techniques. The couple is taught to clearly define problems, discuss one problem at a time, listen to and paraphrase what the other has said, avoid verbal abuse, and state what they want in positive terms rather than deficiencies, for example: "I like the way you do . . . ," and "I would like it if you did . . ."

In behavioral parent training, behavioral and cognitive principles are used to modify the behavior and cognitions of the parent(s) and child, and the parent–child interactions. But if the child is brought for help as the identified patient, the cognitive–behavioral counselor tends to accept that. At times, though, the problem the family seeks help with may not be the one the therapist judges to be appropriate for the first phase of treatment. For example, a family seeks help because the children seem to be fighting all the time. On observation, the therapist notices that the children fight with each other especially when the parents argue, which is often. The therapist is likely to judge that marital counseling is the best first step; that is, before working directly on modifying the children's behavior.

As a first step in parent training, the parent(s) is (are) taught to specify the problem behavior in the child or adolescent, record its frequency, and note the events that accompanied the problem behavior. The last step is aimed at determining what events might be the stimuli or reinforcers for the problem behavior. The parents are then taught to intervene systematically, using behavioral techniques. The most common techniques involve operant conditioning, whereby desirable behaviors are positively reinforced and undesirable ones are either ignored or punished (see Chapter 11). Care is taken in selecting effective reinforcers, as children vary greatly in what is reinforcing to them. The Premack Principle is a long-standing one followed in parent training. Thus a high-frequency behavior is used as a reinforcer for a low-frequency but highly desired (by the parents) behavior. For example, let us say that the parents of Johnny, a 5-year-old boy, are driven to distraction by his constant refusal to eat reasonably balanced meals (rather than just sweets). We find that Johnny's favorite activities are riding his tricycle and playing with his buddy, Stan, in the backyard. The Premack Principle would involve making Johnny's favored (high-frequency) behaviors contingent on his eating properly while reducing complaining behavior. This program might be implemented in steps, so that reinforcers would be given as desired behaviors approximate the end goals.

Time-out procedures (as noted in Chapter 8) are also often used in parent training in an effort to extinguish unwanted behavior. Here the child is usually taken to a place where the usual reinforcers are lacking (e.g., a room without TV, when she or he misbehaves). It is important, though, that appropriate behaviors be reinforced positively.

Despite their tendency to ignore systems, cognitive–behavioral counselors have devised an arsenal of techniques that appear to modify behavior and cognitions effectively in couple and parent–child interactions. From a systems perspective, what may be learned from these behavioral technologists is that changes in any part of the system have effects on other parts; recall the concept of equifinality discussed in the early part of this chapter. Even though a given behavior may be tied to numerous elements of the family structure, system, and subsystem, that behavior may be modified without directly altering the system; the resulting change may be long-lasting and, in itself, have a positive effect on the system.

FAMILY AND COUPLES THERAPY IN PERSPECTIVE

In this final section we discuss the current status of family therapy and its relationship to counseling psychology. We conclude by examining some of the major research findings in the family therapy field.

Current Status of Family and Couples Therapy

The 1970s and 1980s have been described as the Golden Age of family and couples therapy (Nichols & Schwartz, 1998). The growth of this field was astounding, by almost any yardstick (Gurman, Kniskern, & Pinsoff, 1986). The numbers of new journals and books coming out during this time period were remarkable, as was the growth in membership in professional organizations. For example, the American Association for Marriage and Family Therapy grew from 973 members in 1970 to almost 13,000 members by 1985 (Gurman et al., 1986). The growth and excitement during this period are nicely conveyed by Nichols and Schwartz (1998) as follows:

Training centers sprouted up all over the country, workshops were packed, and the leaders of the movement were as celebrated as rock stars. Active and forceful interveners, their self-assurance was infectious. Minuchin, Whitaker, Haley, Madanes, Selvini Palazzoli—they seemed to rise above the limitations of ordinary forms of talk therapy. Young therapists needed inspiration, and they found it. They learned from the masters, and they legendized them (p. 59).

However, somewhere in the mid-1980s a reaction began to set in. The intense excitement over the new ways of helping people that epitomized the family therapy movement began to wane. Rather than being brilliant and clever, some of the approaches seemed manipulative and bossy. The major systems-oriented approaches all too often appeared to forget that the family system is composed of feeling and thinking individuals, *a reality that must not be ignored*. For example, Minuchin and collaborators (Minuchin, Rosman, & Baker, 1978, p. 91) worried about the danger in "denying the individual while enthroning the family."

As part of this reaction against the established approaches and ways of thinking about family therapy, some of the great successes appearing in family therapy literature now seemed tied to the individual effectiveness of the leaders (e.g., Haley, Madanes, Whitaker, Minuchin) rather than the theories that were promoted. As the 1990s unfolded, it appeared that the influence of the major schools of family therapy was waning. Nichols and Schwartz (1998) state it this way:

> What once seemed heroic now seemed aggressive and overbearing. A series of challenges—feminist and postmodern critiques, the reemergence of analytic and biological models, the magic bullet Prozac, the success of recovery programs like Alcoholics Anonymous, the ugly facts of wife beating and child abuse that challenged the notion that domestic problems were always a product of relationship—all shook our confidence in the models we knew to be true, knew would work (pp. 59–60).

The family that was studied and treated by the classical theories was largely a two-parent nuclear family system, and next to no attention was given to other variations (e.g., blended families, single-parent families). Little attention was also paid to race, ethnicity, culture, sexual orientation, or power imbalances between men and women in families. The family therapist's role was to take charge and unfreeze the family's homeostatic tendencies. The therapist was very active and technique-oriented. As noted, the role of the individual was often lost in the systems approaches. To boot, the impact of larger systems like schools, social agencies, and institutions and, more broadly, culture was also essentially ignored.

Recent Family Therapy Developments in a Postmodern World

The changes that were building throughout the 1990s in family and couples therapy actually were part and parcel of a broader philosophical movement that reflected changes in how we think about knowledge, reality, and truth. Such philosophical shifts were themselves part of broader cultural changes during the decade. We shall briefly point to these shifts and refer the reader to more in-depth coverages.

A profound change in how scholars and counselors considered truth, reality, and knowledge has been termed *postmodernism*. Unlike the modernism that came before it (and began around the turn of the twentieth century), postmodernism reflects the assumption that absolute truth cannot be known and that reality is a construction of the observer (or a co-construction of counselor and client). Whereas modernism reflected the belief that truth and, in fact, universal principles could be uncovered by science—which itself was seen as objective—postmodernism suggested that neither truth nor universal principles were there to be uncovered. Science can only produce useful information about differing viewpoints. The postmodernist does not try to determine which family therapy theory has the greatest truth value. Theories are but different perspectives, useful guides.

The philosophies underpinning postmodern thought are called *constructivism* and *social constructionism*. Although there are subtle differences between these philosophies, they share in common the fundamental view that reality is a construction of the observer. As a constructivist, the family counselor does not ask "What are the actual interaction patterns in this family?" Instead, the key question is "What assumptions do the family members have about the problem?" Rather than seeking truth, the constructivist therapist seeks to find what meaning the problem has for each family member.

A constructivist society entertains a plurality of views. As part and parcel of this pluralism, attention to issues of race, ethnicity, gender, sexual orientation and, more broadly, culture have permeated the family therapy movement and are a key part of it in the twenty-first century. Lack of attention to cultural factors can render a treatment useless. Prochaska and Norcross (1999) present, as an example of the latter, the therapy experience of a family in the Netherlands. The eminent family therapist, Carl Whitaker, visited Europe and was invited to conduct live demonstration sessions with actual families. The family in question was one of those selected for this demonstration. Because of cultural differences, Whitaker's highly confrontive experiential approach totally missed the mark for this family. As reported by one of the family members, now a professional therapist himself:

> The validity of his [Whitaker's] assumptions were probably affirmed in his mind by the turmoil in our family. But the interpretations he gave, however true, we did not understand; the interventions he made, however adequate within his therapy system, only aroused fright and shock; the way he made contact with us, whatever he wanted to convey, was experienced as disrespectful. His therapy felt to us like a balancing act on the brink of chaos. From the point of view of a Dutch upper-middle-class family, there was no way that this session could have been helpful (Prochaska & Norcross, 1999, p. 400).

The present-day family therapist does not presume to have all the answers, as his or her predecessors seemed all too often to have. Nichols and Schwartz (1998) talk about how constructivism has fostered greater therapist humility in dealing with families. The family therapist is more often seen as a collaborator with the family rather than as an expert who can brilliantly undo family dysfunction. Just as the therapist does not have the answers, no theory represents the truth. Because of this belief, the present-day family therapist is far more likely to seek an integration of the different theories in his or her practice (see Prochaska & Norcross, 1999).

Much of the family and couples counseling that occurs today is within the framework of existing classical theories, and seeks to modify those theories to take into account the factors we have been discussing. However, two new approaches have emerged in recent times that deserve note: narrative therapy and solution-focused therapy.

Narrative Therapy

This approach is decisively postmodern and constructivist in its orientation. Narrative therapists are antirealists, in that for them no reality exists beyond the stories we create to understand our lives (Held, 1996). The two names most often associated with narrative family therapy are the Australian Michael White, and David Epston, a family therapist in New Zealand.

Narrative therapy is concerned most basically with how human experiences create expectations that become *organizing stories,* which in turn, deeply shape experience. Unlike the systems approaches, narrative therapy seeks to help individuals reexamine themselves rather than discuss family issues. This reexamination occurs almost exclusively via *questioning.* That is, the narrative therapist becomes an expert question-asker, one who seeks a nonimposing and respectful approach to whatever the client or family's story is (Freedman & Combs, 1996; White, 1995). The counselor also places a premium on *narrative empathy* (Omer, 1997), which sounds to us essentially the same as empathy from the perspective of person-centered therapists.

To an unusual extent, this approach seeks to keep clients blameless, and the major way accomplishing this is to *externalize* the problem. The problem thus becomes something outside the individual and the family; an external source of pain and grief, so to speak. As clients tell their "problem-saturated story," the narrative therapist separates the problem from the person. The problem becomes the "it" outside of the person or family that has ill effects. The therapist fosters this externalization by asking questions about how this "it" does its demonic work, for example, "How does the *anger* affect you?" "What does *anger* tell you?" "What does *anger* do to your relationship?" The problem is seen as not being possessed by the client, but rather as possessing the client.

A key to change in this therapy is the therapist's listening for "unique outcomes" or "sparkling events" in the client's life. Stated simply, these events and outcomes represent situations in which the client or family won a victory over the problem, and as such they are viewed as heroic episodes. By highlighting these with further questions, the narrative therapist helps the client bring success and ways of succeeding into the foreground. People can come to view themselves as courageous protagonists rather than powerless victims.

In keeping with its postmodern and constructivist roots, narrative therapy is highly sensitive to cultural issues, and it is also very political. As Nichols and Schwartz (1998) state,

> [Narrative therapists] aren't just interested in the effects of obviously toxic social narratives such as misogyny, racism, class bias, and heterosexism; they're also interested in more subtle pressures regarding such day-to-day issues as how much

money people believe they need to make, how perfect their children need to be, and how many cars they need to have (p. 403).

Solution-Focused Therapy

A second family therapy approach that is embedded in social constructionism hit the scene in the 1990s: Solution-focused therapy (SFT). The primary developers of this approach are Michael de Shazer and Insoo Berg (Berg & de Shazer, 1993; de Shazer, 1988, 1994). SFT actually grew out of strategic therapy (described earlier), and maintained the emphasis on very brief work (usually 2–5 sessions). However, SFT represents a significant departure from the strategic approach in that, rather than focusing on the client's problems, the almost exclusive focus is on solutions. Like their strategic cousins, practitioners of SFT rank high on cleverness. They have devised several ingenious strategies for helping clients solve problems in a short time.

Consistent with a counseling psychology orientation, SFT emphasizes clients' strengths and assets, and seeks to capitalize on them. Although SFT practitioners certainly listen to clients' problems and histories, what they seek most fundamentally is to address clients' goals and solutions to problems. For example, rather than delving deeply into a client's tendency toward depression and the roots of that depression, the SFT counselor asks, "When are the times you don't feel depressed?" The therapist uses the client's answers to devise strategies that avert depression. If the answer is, "When I am with friends, and when I am at prayer services," the SFT practitioner helps the client consider how to develop and expand these situations. In the process, the therapist is highly reinforcing of steps clients take in the right direction.

The focus on solutions and goals begins in the first session. Referred to as the *formula first task,* clients are asked to observe what happens in their life or relationships that they want to continue. Like the narrative therapist, the SFT counselor becomes an expert in asking the right questions; that is, questions focusing on goals and solutions. For example, the miracle question is "Suppose one night, while you were asleep, there was a miracle and this problem was solved. How would you know? What would be different? The *exception question* circumvents attention to the problem, and asks about times in the past or present when the client didn't experience the problem, when they otherwise would have. The couple is asked, "When did you manage to not blame each other?" or "When did you feel good with each other?" The couple's answers are used to build solutions.

Another class of questions are called *scaling questions:* "On a scale of 0 to 10, with 0 being how you felt in your marriage when you called me for couples' work, and 10 being how you felt the day after the 'miracle,' how do you feel in your relationship right now?" If the client says "3," the SLT counselor asks: "How did you achieve this improvement?" Or, in order to encourage and reinforce small steps, the therapist might ask, "What do you need to do to get to 4?" Alternatively, a client might be asked "On a scale of 1 to 10, how confident are you that you will not blame your wife for something this week?" And then, "What can you do to increase the chances that you won't blame her?" As Nichols and Schwartz (1998) note, scaling questions are clever ways of "anticipating and disarming resistance, and of encouraging commitment to change" (p. 387).

During SFT, counselor and client co-construct solutions through their conversations. Language is itself what needs to change because language to the SF counselor *is* reality, and nothing exists outside of language. Change problem-talk to solution-talk, says the SFT counselor, and you are most of the way to solving the problem.

Family Therapy and Counseling Psychology

Perhaps because so many counseling psychologists worked with college students, whose primary developmental tasks seemed to involve individuation and healthy independence from their families, counseling psychology was slow to become involved in family therapy. As both counseling psychology and family/couples counseling expanded, however, the two fields grew closer together. Thus, Gelso and Fassinger (1990) suggest that "In the 1980s, counseling psychology finally discovered the family" (p. 361). Training in couples/family counseling became more common in doctoral programs, and work with couples and families became seen as an integral part of the identity of counseling psychologists (Fitzgerald & Osipow, 1988; Schneider, Watkins, & Gelso, 1988). During the 1990s, training in couples and family interventions became a standard part of doctoral training (Kaczmarek & Riva, 1996; Murdock, Alcorn, Heesacker, & Stoltenberg, 1998).

Although counseling psychology has embraced couples and family interventions, our impression is that counseling psychologists still do far more couples therapy than family therapy. The gap between efforts devoted to couples versus family therapy is likely less than it was in several years ago (see Watkins, Lopez, Campbell, & Himmell, 1986), but because so many counseling psychologists continue to work in college counseling centers—where family therapy is still infrequently practiced—a gap is still likely to exist.

True to its history, the couples/family therapy field has shown great receptivity to new ideas and approaches. The newer approaches that are embedded in postmodernism and social constructionism (narrative therapy and solution-focused therapy), with their great attention to clients' strengths and to brief interventions, fit especially well with counseling psychology. Will these approaches maintain their attractiveness to practitioners? Will they withstand the test of time (and the scrutiny of empirical research)? Will they become practicing counselors' preferred approaches? The answers to these questions will be unfolding as we progress into the twenty-first century.

Research and Family Interventions

What does empirical research have to say about the effectiveness of family and couples interventions? Just as with all types of recognized interventions, the evidence suggests that family and couples counseling *on the whole* are effective forms of treatment in resolving a range of problems (Friedlander & Tuason, 2000). Beyond this global evaluation, family and couples researchers are beginning to accumulate findings about what has been referred to in Chapter 3 as the "who, what, when, and where" question of counseling effectiveness. In other words, family and couples researchers are now tackling the many complex questions embedded in the following general question: "With what kinds of clients are what kinds of family and couples interventions effective in which ways when offered by which kinds of counselors using what techniques?"

As with counseling research in general, we may divide research on family and couples counseling into two kinds: process and outcome (see Chapter 3). There has been far more research on outcome (Does it work?) over the years than on process (What leads to what within the session?), although process research has increased in recent years. What does research tell us about the effects of couples and family interventions? Based on large-scale reviews of existing research (Alexander, Holtzworth-Munroe, & Jameson, 1994; Friedlander & Tuason, 2000; Nichols & Schwartz, 1998; Pinsoff, Wynne, & Hambright, 1996), some conclusions are possible.

1. As noted above, the research evidence to date strongly supports the overall effectiveness of both family and couples therapy for a range of problems. These treatments clearly produce positive change, above and beyond that which occurs in nontreated control groups.

2. In comparisons of the efficacy of couples/family therapy to individual therapy, few if any substantial differences occur. Generally, couples/family therapies are equal in effectiveness to individual therapy.

3. Comparisons of differing approaches to couples/family therapy do not support one form over another. Thus, just as with individual counseling, the differing theoretical approaches seem to produce equal effectiveness. The growing edge of couples/family research, as with individual counseling research, is to find which approaches are best for what clients and what outcomes.

4. Couples therapy has been found to be effective with certain individual problems. In these cases, partner involvement is used to motivate clients to engage in counseling, change maladaptive habits, and maintain gains over time. Couples therapy has been found to be especially effective with individual problems of sexual dysfunction and alcoholism.

5. Strong evidence supports psychoeducational family treatments for individuals suffering from schizophrenia and bipolar depression. In a family context, such counseling includes training in coping skills, reducing blame, improving communication, and crisis intervention. Behaviorally oriented approaches such as these have been found to be highly cost effective and have prevented relapses effectively.

6. Parent management training (PMT) has been found to be very effective for children's problems like oppositional and conduct disorders, behavioral problems, delinquency, and attention-deficit hyperactivity disorder. PMT targets specific behaviors using modeling, role-playing, and home practice with parents.

7. The classic theories of couples/family therapy have received solid empirical support. The newer narrative and solution-focused therapies have to date been infrequently studied. Much more evidence is needed to determine their general effectiveness and efficacy for different problems.

8. The counseling process literature suggests that therapists are most effective if they focus actively on relationship dynamics in couples and families; take a dominant position with the family; explore hidden feelings and thoughts about family relations; and develop clear goals that each family member agrees on.

9. As in individual therapy, counselors' ability to foster a safe, warm, and trusting relationship appears to be an important ingredient of successful couples/family intervention.

Throughout this chapter, we have pointed to key readings, especially on the different approaches to couples/family treatment. In terms of general readings on family therapy, Nichols and Schwartz's (1998) book is a lively, thoughtful, and comprehensive treatment, perhaps the best overall work we have read. A clear, in-depth and comprehensive treatment of the family, including the many facets of what is called the *family life cycle,* is presented by Carter and McGoldrick (1999). Regarding research on couples and families, Nichols and Schwartz's chapter on research is well done and readable. Friedlander and Tuason's (2000) chapter in the *Handbook of Counseling Psychology* (Brown & Lent, 2000) is an extensive critical analysis of research findings and future directions.

SUMMARY

The family therapy movement, which began in the 1950s, originated from two sources: the Palo Alto studies of families in which one (or more) of the children was (were) schizophrenic and the independent work of several creative clinicians who began to experiment with family therapy. Besides the Palo Alto group and the Mental Research Institute, the work of three clinicians had a profound effect on the new field of family therapy: Nathan Ackerman, Carl Whitaker, and Murray Bowen.

Family therapy was described as a *diverse set of perspectives having in common a systems perspective of behavior.* Several basic assumptions of systems theory as applied to families include: (a) systems are organized wholes with interdependent parts; (b) causality is circular rather than linear, and one can effectively intervene at any point in a system; (c) systems seek to maintain homeostasis, but effective systems do change when needed; (d) systems contain subsystems, of which a major example is the triangle; (e) all systems have boundaries, rules, and patterns.

Six classic approaches to family and couples counseling were reviewed. The *psychoanalytic approach* most often uses object relations theory as a way to conceptualize couples and family dynamics. Attention is given to how objects are internalized and to their far-reaching effects on couples and families. *Projective identification* is a major defense in couples relationships. The *experiential approach* focuses on here-and-now feelings, therapist spontaneity, and confrontation to help expand couples' and families' immediate experience and to emotionally unfreeze the family. The *family systems* approach, originated by Murray Bowen, contains several major constructs about families: emotional triangles, differentiation of self, nuclear family emotional system, family projection process, and multigenerational transmission.

The family systems therapist takes a rational approach in helping clients develop differentiation within the self and between the self and other family members. The *strategic approach* is brief, active, and symptom-oriented. Strategic therapists treat specific behaviors within a systems context. They are directive and at times manipulative, using straightforward suggestions as well as *paradoxical interventions*. Minuchin's *structural approach* focuses on the constructs: (1) family structure, (2) subsystems, and (3) boundaries. Structuralists are active and directive, using affective intensity to unshake clients' embedded problems. They seek to influence the family's structure and to develop boundaries between subsystems that are neither rigid nor diffuse. The *behavioral approach* works most with couples or parent–child dyads in modifying specific behaviors through the use of behavioral techniques and principles. Of all the approaches it is *least* systems-oriented, but studies have shown behavioral couples counseling and parent training to be effective interventions.

The 1970s and 1980s were the Golden Age of family and couples therapy, with the field showing phenomenal growth. The great enthusiasm and optimism of that period, however, waned during the 1990s. The postmodernism of the 1990s stirred many questions about therapists who seemed to have all the answers, were too dominant, and even engaged in therapeutic trickery with their client/families. Newer approaches, often deriving from the classic models, emerged. Fitting both postmodern thinking and the economically driven mandate for brief treatment, approaches such as *narrative therapy* and *solution-focused therapy* gained increasing ascendancy during this period. These approaches are gentler, more explicitly attend to clients' strengths, and seem more "client-centered" rather than "therapist-centered." Only time, clinical experience, and rigorous research will tell whether or not these approaches will take their places along with classical schools of treatment in the couples/ family area.

Research strongly supports the efficacy of couples and family interventions. All indications are that they are clearly superior to no-treatment control groups and equal in effectiveness to individual approaches. Couples/family treatment is helpful for a range of individual problems, childhood difficulties, and family issues. The leading edge of research revolves around what family/couple problems are best treated by which approaches and techniques.

REFERENCES

Ackerman, N. (1958). *The psychodynamics of family life*. New York: Basic Books.

Ackerman, N. (1961). A dynamic frame for the clinical approach to family conflict. In N. Ackerman, F. Beatman, and S. Sherman (Eds.), *Exploring the base for family therapy*. New York: Family Services Association of America.

Alexander, J. F., Holtzworth-Munroe, A., & Jameson, P. (1994). The process and outcome of marital and family therapy: Research review and evaluation. In A. E. Bergin and S. L. Garfield (Eds.), *Handbook of psychotherapy and behavior change* (4th ed., pp. 595–630). New York: John Wiley & Sons.

Bateson, G. (1972). *Steps in an ecology of mind*. New York: Ballantine.

Bateson, G. (1979). *Mind and nature*. New York: Dutton.

Bateson, G., Jackson, D., Haley, J., & Weakland, J. (1956). Toward a theory of schizophrenia. *Behavioral Science, 1*, 251–264.

Becvar, D. S., & Becvar, R. S. (1993). *Family therapy: A systemic integration* (3rd ed.). Boston, MA: Allyn & Bacon.

Berg, I. K., & de Shazer, S. (1993). Making numbers talk: Language in therapy. In S. Friedman (Ed.), *The new language of change*. New York: Guilford Press.

Boszormenyi-Nagy, I. (1972). Loyalty implications of the transference model in psychotherapy. *Archives of General Psychiatry, 27,* 374–380.

Bowen, M. (1966). The use of family theory in clinical practice. *Comprehensive Psychiatry, 7,* 345–374.

Bowen, M. (1976). Theory in the practice of psychotherapy. In P. Guerin (Ed.), *Family therapy* (pp. 42–89). New York: Gardner Press.

Bowen, M. (1978). *Family therapy in clinical practice*. New York: Jason Aronson.

Brown, S., & Lent, R. (2000). *Handbook of counseling psychology* (3rd ed.). New York: John Wiley & Sons.

Cade, B., & O'Hanlon, W. (1993). *A brief guide to brief therapy*. New York: Norton.

Carter, B., & McGoldrick, M. (Eds.) (1999). *The expanded family life cycle* (3rd ed.). Needham Heights, MA: Allyn & Bacon.

Dattilio, F. M. (1993). Cognitive techniques with couples and families. *The Family Journal, 1,* 51–65.

Dattilio, F. M. (1997). *Integrative cases in couples and family therapy: A cognitive–behavioral perspective*. New York: Guilford Press.

de Shazer, S. (1988). *Clues: Investigating solutions in brief therapy*. New York: Norton.

de Shazer, S. (1994). *Words were originally magic*. New York: Norton.

Dowd, E., & Milne, C. (1986). Paradoxical interventions in counseling psychology. *The Counseling Psychologist, 14,* 237–282.

Fisch, R., Weakland, J., & Segal, L. (1982). *The tactics of change: Doing therapy briefly*. San Francisco, CA: Jossey-Bass.

Fitzgerald, L., & Osipow, S. (1988). We have seen the future, but is it us? The vocational aspirations of graduate students in counseling psychology. *Professional Psychology: Research and Practice, 19,* 575–583.

Foley, V. (1989). Family therapy. In R. Corsini and D. Wedding (Eds.), *Current psychotherapies* (4th ed., pp. 455–500). Itasca, IL: Peacock.

Foster, S., & Gurman, A. (1985). Family therapies. In S. Lynn and J. Garske (Eds.), *Contemporary psychotherapies: Models and methods* (pp. 377–418). Columbus, OH: Merrill.

Freedman, J., & Combs, G. (1996). *Narrative therapy: The social construction of preferred reality*. New York: Norton.

Friedlander, M. L., & Tuason, M. T. (2000). Processes and outcomes in couples and family therapy. In S. Brown and R. Lent (Eds.), *Handbook of counseling psychology* (3rd ed., pp. 797–824). New York: John Wiley & Sons.

Gelso, C., & Fassinger, R. (1990). Counseling psychology: Theory and research on interventions. *Annual Review of Psychology, 41,* 355–386.

Goldenberg, I., & Goldenberg, H. (1985). *Family therapy: An overview* (2nd ed.). Monterey, CA: Brooks/Cole.

Greenberg, L. A., & Johnson, S. M. (1988). *Emotionally focused therapy for couples*. New York: Guilford Press.

Gurman, A., Kniskern, D., & Pinsoff, W. (1986). Research on marital and family therapies. In S. Garfield and A. Bergin (Eds.), *Handbook of psychotherapy and behavior change* (3rd ed., pp. 565–623). New York: John Wiley & Sons.

Haley, J. (1976). *Problem-solving therapy*. San Francisco, CA: Jossey-Bass.

Held, B. (1996). Solution-focused therapy and the post-modern: A critical analysis. In S. Miller, M. Hubble, and B. Duncan (Eds.), *Handbook of solution-focused brief therapy*. San Francisco, CA: Jossey-Bass.

Jackson, D. (1957). The question of family homeostasis. *Psychiatric Quarterly Supplement, 31,* 79–90.

Jackson, D., & Weakland, J. (1959). Conjoint family therapy: Some considerations on theory, technique, and results. *Psychiatry, 24,* 30–45.

Jacobson, N. S., & Christensen, A. (1996). *Integrative couple therapy: Promoting acceptance and change.* New York: Norton.

Johnson, S. M., & Greenberg, L. A. (1991). There are more things in heaven and Earth than dreamed of in BMT: A response to Jacobson. *Journal of Family Psychology, 4,* 407–415.

Kaczmarek, P. G., & Riva, M. Y. (1996). Facilitating optimal adolescent development: Training considerations for counseling psychologists. *The Counseling Psychologist, 24,* 400–432.

Katz, B. (1981). Separation–individuation and marital therapy. *Psychotherapy: Theory, Research, and Practice, 18,* 195–203.

Kempler, W. (1973). *Principles of gestalt family therapy.* Oslo, Norway: Nordahls.

Kerr, M. (1981). Family systems theory and therapy. In A. Gurman and D. Kniskern (Eds.), *Handbook of family therapy* (pp. 226–264). New York: Brunner/Mazel.

Madanes, C. (1981). *Strategic family therapy.* San Francisco, CA: Jossey-Bass.

Minuchin, P. (1985). Families and individual development: Provocations from the field of family therapy. *Child Development, 56,* 289–302.

Minuchin, S. (1974). *Families and family therapy.* Cambridge, MA: Harvard University Press.

Minuchin, S., & Fishman, H. (1981). *Family therapy techniques.* Cambridge, MA: Harvard University Press.

Minuchin, S., Lee, W-Y., & Simon, G. M. (1996). *Mastering family therapy: Journeys of hope and transformation.* New York: John Wiley & Sons.

Minuchin, S., & Nichols, M. P. (1993). *Family healing: Tales of hope and renewal from family therapy.* New York: The Free Press.

Minuchin, S., Rosman, B., & Baker, L. (1978). *Psychosomatic families.* Cambridge, MA: Harvard University Press.

Murdock, N. L., Alcorn, J., Heesacker, M., & Stoltenberg, C. (1998). Model training program in counseling psychology. *The Counseling Psychologist, 26,* 658–672.

Nichols, M. (1984). *Family therapy: Concepts and methods.* New York: Gardner Press.

Nichols, M. P., & Schwartz, R. C. (1998). *Family therapy: Concepts and methods.* Boston, MA: Allyn & Bacon.

Omer, H. (1997). Narrative empathy. *Psychotherapy, 34,* 19–27.

Pinsoff, W. M., Wynne, L. C., & Hambright, A. B. (1996). The outcomes of couple and family therapy: Findings, conclusions, and recommendations. *Psychotherapy, 33,* 321–331.

Prochaska, J. O., & Norcross, J. C. (1999). *Systems of psychotherapy: A transtheoretical analysis* (4th ed.). Pacific Grove, CA: Brooks/Cole.

Satir, V. (1967). *Conjoint family therapy.* Palo Alto, CA: Science and Behavior Books.

Scarf, M. (1987). *Intimate Partners: Patterns in love and marriage.* New York: Random House.

Schneider, L., Watkins, C. E., & Gelso, C. (1988). Counseling psychology from 1971 to 1986: Perspective on and appraisal of current emphases. *Professional Psychology: Research and Practice, 19,* 584–588.

Selvini Palazzoli, M., Boscolo, L., Cecchin, G., & Prata, G. (1978). *Paradox and counterparadox.* New York: Jason Aronson.

Skynner, R. (1981). An open-systems, group-analytic approach to family therapy. In A. Gurman and D. Kniskern (Eds.), *Handbook of family therapy* (pp. 39–84). New York: Brunner/Mazel.

VonBertalanffy, L. (1968). *General systems theory: Formulations, development, applications.*

New York: George Braziller.

VonBertalanffy, L. (1974). General systems theory and psychiatry. In S. Arieti (Ed.), *American handbook of psychiatry* (Vol. 1, pp. 1095–1117). New York: Basic Books.

Watkins, C. E. Jr., Lopez, F. G., Campbell, V. L., & Himmell, C. D. (1986). Contemporary counseling psychology: Results of a national survey. *Journal of Counseling Psychology, 33,* 301–309.

Watzlawick, P., Beavin, J., & Jackson, D. (1967). *The pragmatics of communication.* New York: Norton.

Watzlawick, P., Weakland, J., & Fisch, R. (1974). *Change: Principles of problem formation and problem resolution.* New York: Norton.

Whitaker, C. (1976). The hindrance of theory in clinical work. In P. Guerin (Ed.), *Family therapy: Theory and practice.* New York: Gardner Press.

White, M. (1995). *Re-authoring lives: Interviews and essays.* Adelaide, South Australia: Dulwich Centre Publications.

18

PREVENTIVE AND EDUCATIONAL–DEVELOPMENTAL INTERVENTIONS

Summary

References

Read the following 10 article titles as if they were a test of your ability to find a common theme.

> *"Strategic Hope-Focused Relationship-Enrichment Counseling With Individual Couples"* (Worthington, Hight, Ripley, Perrone et al., 1997).
>
> *"Conjoint Monitoring of Symptoms of Premenstrual Syndrome: Impact on Marital Satisfaction"* (Frank, Dixon, & Grosz, 1993).
>
> *"Promoting Optimal Adolescent Development Through Conflict Resolution Education, Training, and Practice"* (VanSlyck, Stern, & Zak-Place, 1996).
>
> *"Enhancing a Sense of Agency Through Career Planning"* (Kush & Cochran, 1993).
>
> *"Comparison of Self-Help Books for Coping With Loss"* (Ogles, Lambert, & Craig, 1991).
>
> *"The Zuni Life Skills Development Curriculum: Description and Evaluation of a Suicide Prevention Program"* (LaFromboise & Howard-Pitney, 1995).
>
> *"Indirect Treatment of Children via Parent Training"* (Wright, Stroud, & Keenan, 1993).
>
> *"Changing the Rape-Supportive Attitudes of Traditional and Nontraditional Male and Female College Students"* (Rosenthal, Heesacker, & Neimeyer, 1995).
>
> *"A Model of the Effects of Protective Parent and Peer Factors on Young Adolescent Alcohol Refusal Skills"* (Spoth, Yoo, Kahn, & Redmond, 1996).
>
> *"Life Development Intervention for Athletes: Life Skills Through Sports"* (Danish, Petitpas, & Hale, 1993).

Despite the immense diversity of topics, settings, and populations encompassed by these articles, the programs they report all involve counseling psychologists in professional activities that have been described by terms such as *prevention, educational–developmental interventions, outreach,* and *psychoeducation.* Chapters on these topics are often not included in counseling psychology texts even though both preventive and educational–developmental roles are considered fundamental aspects of counseling psychology (see Chapter 1). To begin this chapter we first review the reasons why so many different terms have been used to describe the professional activities exemplified by the above-cited articles. Some counseling psychologists feel passionate about maintaining different terms; however, there is a growing consensus that the term *preventive interventions* can be used to encompass all these activities. We describe both traditional and newer definitions, from both educational and medical perspectives, along with the cautions that must be considered when using *prevention* as the encompassing word.

Counseling psychologists have been the major developers of two kinds of preventive interventions during the past few decades: structured groups and psychoeducation.

We describe each of these developments and identify some key illustrative contributions. As already explored in Chapter 4, current trends in the industrialization of health care are providing numerous new opportunities for counseling psychologists to become involved in more cost-effective health care services by addressing many deleterious behavioral and lifestyle issues through preventive and developmental interventions. (Many of the roles for counseling psychologists in medical settings also involve consultation, the topic of the final chapter in this book.)

The chapter concludes with sections on how to cope with some of the unique difficulties in implementing effective training, practice, and research related to preventive and educational–developmental interventions. As we describe, graduate students in counseling psychology oftentimes have been the best catalysts for development, implementation, and evaluation of preventive interventions.

Definitions of Overlapping Diverse Terms: Historical Contexts and Evolutions

Although the terms *preventive* and *educational–developmental* have long been listed as two of the three major roles of counseling psychologists, the professional services provided within the two roles have a high degree of overlap. In fact, distinctions between the terms derive more from different historical contexts than from any functional analysis. During the 1960s and 1970s, the words *outreach* and *psycho-education* came into popular usage to describe then new developments in preventive and educational–developmental interventions. Simultaneously, within the broader mental health arena, *prevention* was being elaborated into three parts: primary, secondary, and tertiary. Any one of the kinds of services provided in the listed articles could easily be categorized using at least two or more of the various terms, for example, conflict resolution programs could be called psychoeducation or primary prevention. This proliferation of terms was not entirely accidental. Passionate ideological feelings were, and continue to be, involved. In the following two sections we explore how and why different terms emerged in educational settings to describe new services that, in medical settings, were typically referred to as "preventive interventions." We also describe why new services were developed in educational settings during the late 1960s and on into the closing decades of the twentieth century. We then explore the evolving perspective on prevention that has allowed at least some counseling psychologists to feel more comfortable when using *prevention* as the word to encompass a broad range of activities in educational, work, and community settings as well as in medical settings.

The Educational Perspective

As noted in chapters 1 and 2, counseling psychology developed as a profession in educational rather than in medical settings. Many of the new services that were developed and promulgated in educational settings during the 1960s and beyond were identified as "outreach" or "psychoeducational programs," compared to being called "preventive interventions." Sometimes identical services, such as crisis intervention, might be labeled "outreach" when offered by a counseling center, but labeled "prevention" service when offered by a university hospital psychiatric service.

Why this difference in terminology? Over the past few decades, a number of psychologists have been, and continue to be, concerned that using the word *prevention* for psychological services will cause both professionals and their clients to take a more passive, dependent view of clients' psychological problems. To the extent that the word *prevention* connotes immunization processes, hygiene, and a vision of a client waiting passively and dependently for the "doctor" to do something, "prevention" is an undesirable label for most of what counseling psychologists want to accomplish in their preventive educational–developmental interventions. Sarbin (1997) succinctly states such a perspective:

> There is a serious moral issue here. As behavior scientists, we need to be cognizant of how our formulations affect social policy. The increasing medicalization of distress contributes directly to the belief that a person is not responsible for his or her actions . . . The very fabric of democratic society is endangered when its citizens are regarded as passive organisms rather than proactive agents who are responsible for the choices they make in defining their self-narratives (p. 242).

As prevention activities of psychologists have evolved in the age of industrialized health care, and with the emergence of occupational health psychology (see Chapter 15), both calling for participants to take more active roles in their own well-being, there are fewer concerns with using the word *prevention*. We will provide further evidence of this evolution of the word *prevention* in the next section; first, we here describe the kinds of, and reasons for, the development of the services originally identified as "outreach" and "psychoeducational services" of counseling psychologists.

As cogently described by Drum and Figler (1973), professional activities labeled "outreach" grew out of counseling psychologists' efforts to aid the psychological development of students they served; that is, moving beyond remediation. As may be recalled from Chapter 2, from the beginnings of counseling psychology, through at least the 1960s, most counseling psychologists worked in schools and colleges. *Outreach* initially referred to innovative services provided by counseling psychologists within schools or colleges that were provided *outside* of the offices in which they typically did one-to-one counseling or therapy.

Why were these "innovative" services developed and just what were they? There are at least three reasons for their development. The first, articulated by Warnath (1971), is frequently cited as one of the most incisive critics of college counseling centers' failure to respond to student needs in the 1960s.

> Every center is highly selective in the clientele who will seek its services, and unless the counselors reverse the process and seek out the problem areas which might use their attention, they will be unaware of many student needs they are neglecting. The pregnant girl, the potential draft resister, and the student hooked on drugs are unlikely to walk into a counseling center to ask for help from any counselor who may be available (Warnath, 1971, pp. 58–59).

To respond to such needs, Warnath believes that counselors must get out of their offices and develop innovative services, for example, setting up satellite locations for drop-in "anonymous" one-session counseling in residence halls or student activities buildings. Additionally, there was a call for what were then very innovative services such as developing audiotapes for self-help programs. Self-help audiotapes on study skills, choosing careers and majors, and managing test anxiety were all new outreach services that were designed to reduce the frequency or at least intensity of typical college student developmental problems.

A second reason for the development of outreach services was the greatly increased attention to mental health services in the 1960s as a result of the Community Mental Health Centers Act. With a sudden increase in demand for mental health services, there were immense shortages of professional-level counseling psychologists to staff college and student counseling centers and community mental health centers. Much of the rationale for outreach activities evident in Drum and Figler (1973) is based on responding to such shortages by providing innovative group-based services.

The third reason is the most theoretically based: life-span development theory. Given this theoretical foundation, it is not surprising that it is the primary basis upon which outreach activities have continued. The focus of developmental psychology has "aged" with the profession, with the strong emphasis on children beginning in the 1920s, to a rapidly emerging emphasis on aging in the 1980s. Throughout the 1940s and 1950s there was an ever-increasing amount of literature on adolescent and college student development: intellectual development, moral development, psychosocial development, and especially identity development. By the late 1960s a variety of innovative psychological programs were being developed, based on the work of developmental psychologists such as Piaget, Kohlberg, Perry, and Erikson, that were designed to facilitate and enhance students' progress through various developmental stages and tasks.

The term *deliberate psychological education* (Mosher & Sprinthall, 1971) was used to describe a model curriculum that could foster psychological development. The primary purpose was to reduce the occurrence of psychological stress and dysfunction. The coursework in this curriculum was extremely varied. A participant–observation methodology was used for the study of the psychology of work whereby junior high school students left the school premises to spend time at work settings. Another course taught the high school students to be "counselors" by studying

> . . . the generic processes of counseling and the general themes which adolescents bring to counseling. The course focuse[d] heavily on the processes of listening to another individual, listening for feeling and for ideas and learning to respond both to another person's feelings and his ideas (Mosher & Sprinthall, 1971, p. 14).

A study of the changes in psychological development of participants in these special programs found that, compared to control nonparticipants, they showed greater advances on both the Loevinger Ego Development Scale and Kohlberg Moral Judgment Scale.

Another area of developmental research, that of coping with life transitions, has also led to the emergence of new types of outreach services. Many transitions are expected to occur at certain times of life (e.g., graduating from school, having children, retiring). Other transitions are less predictable but have an equal impact on new challenges they create for us (e.g., infertility, reaching a plateau at work, having a child who never leaves home). Schlossberg (1989) notes that many transitions bring changes in our roles, relationships, routines, and our assumptions about ourselves. The more changes there are, the more likely we are to experience psychological distress when undergoing them. If effective interventions are designed to help one prepare for such transitions (e.g., orientation courses for new college students, preretirement planning programs), then the probability of psychological dysfunction is reduced.

Return to the opening list of titles. Note how each is focused on a population other than clients coming to a counseling center (that is, an outreach intervention), helping participants learn strategies for enhancing the quality of their lives (educational–developmental intervention), with at least the implicit, if not explicit goal of preventing (preventive intervention) later problems in interpersonal relationships, substance abuse, and so forth. These titles represent only a small sample of services and programs developed in recent decades, each reaching "nontraditional" client populations in cost-effective ways. In recent years, the reports of such programs have routinely come to include evidence of their effectiveness and their contributions to the prevention of problems such as substance abuse, marital discord, and interpersonal violence. Additional illustrations of two major categories of such programs— that is, structured groups and psychoeducational interventions—will be provided following an exploration of the evolution of the word *prevention* in behavioral health.

The Medical Perspective

The word *prevention* has a long history in physical medicine. Most significant historical breakthroughs in medicine are typically identified as the discovery of something that would *prevent* the spread of a major disease, for example, protecting against rat bites as a way of preventing the spread of the plague, spraying for mosquitoes as a way of preventing the spread of malaria, or practicing "safe sex" as a way of preventing the spread of AIDS. Specific attention to prevention in mental health has a more recent history (Caplan, 1964). As of 1978, prevention in mental health was still labeled a "new revolution":

> The new revolution will involve major societal efforts of preventing mental illness and emotional disturbance. It will apply the best available knowledge, derived from research and clinical experience, to prevent needless distress and psychological dysfunction. It will, in the best public health tradition, seek to build strength and increase competence and coping skills in populations and thereby reduce the incidence of later disturbance (Albee, Bloom, Broussard et al., 1978, p. 1827).

In light of our earlier mention regarding the interchangeability of "prevention" and "developmental services," notice even here the presence of developmental terms: "build strength," "increase coping skills."

Prevention in the mental health area has been most fully explicated by Caplan (1964). His terms are often found in the literature on prevention, outreach, and consultation and are therefore worthy of a brief review. When reviewing his terms one will quickly see that some usage of *prevention* seems to overlap with *remediation*. It is perhaps best to consider a continuum rather than discrete categories between "prevention" and "remediation" or even between types of prevention. Caplan uses the terms *primary, secondary,* and *tertiary prevention.* He defines *primary prevention* as those steps taken to prevent the occurrence of a mental illness or psychosocial dysfunction, with the prevention activities directed toward a total population rather than individuals *before* they experience any of the problems they are at risk of encountering. Primary prevention programs include, for example, communication skills training for parents of young adolescents, support group interventions for new mothers who are at risk for experiencing postpartum depression, and career education programs for undecided college students.

Secondary prevention involves the earliest possible identification and treatment of existing problems so as to reduce their intensity and duration. Crisis intervention counseling is a classic example of secondary prevention; providing frustrated employees with career counseling might also be viewed as secondary prevention to the extent that it prevents the development of higher levels of general anxiety and depressive disorders.

Tertiary prevention is a manner of treating those who experience problems in ways that the highest levels of functioning can be restored and the recurrence of the problems is minimized. Clearly, secondary and tertiary prevention have significant overlap with remediation roles. In fact, some would argue that differences in use of the words *counseling* and *psychotherapy* should reflect the differences between "prevention" and "remediation." The emphasis of counseling psychology on brief interventions, designed to utilize a client's assets and strengths, is directly oriented toward both secondary (reduce intensity and duration of stress) and tertiary prevention (treat so as to minimize recurrence of the problem). If psychotherapy, then, is seen as purely remedial with the goal being to restore the client to a previous level of functioning, then psychotherapy is categorized as tertiary prevention.

In the 1960s, large numbers of psychologists first began to pay attention to various kinds of prevention services, largely as a result of the report of the Joint Commission on Mental Illness and Health (1961) and the Community Mental Health Centers Act of 1963. This legislation facilitated the development of new programs of community-based research focused on prevention and providing innovative treatments, oftentimes reaching segments of our population who previously received few if any mental health services. Collaboration of psychologists with community leaders soon led to the development of the specialty of community psychology; many of the leaders in this new field soon became advocates of changes in the political and social structure of our society so that problems such as juvenile delinquency, teen pregnancy, and chronic unemployment could be addressed in ways that would reduce the occurrence of many of the mental health problems encountered in the previously underserved or ignored populations. Shore (1992) documents the rapid emergence of community psychology in the 1960s and 1970s, then the political and economic changes of the 1980s that led to the "death of community mental health practice" (p. 257). In his article titled "Community Mental Health: Corpse or Phoenix?" Shore (1992) accurately predicted that greater attention would be given to prevention in the twenty-first century especially because "the contributions of the community mental health movement have permeated the current service structure" (p. 257).

Indeed, it was just as community psychology seemed to be declining in vitality that counseling psychologists were greatly increasing their developments of the kinds of outreach and psychoeducation programs (described later in this chapter). The industrialization of health care of the 1990s (described in Chapter 4) has added further impetus for the development of preventive interventions. As Wright and colleagues (1993) note, a single hour of a professional psychologist working with parents in a well-designed parent training program "can be translated into 500–800 hours of different experiences for children during the weeks in which consultation is taking place" (p. 192). Hospitals and some of the newer health care corporations now employ psychologists to run wellness clinics, provide programs on eating disorders, smoking cessation, and so forth. Such prevention programs are supported primarily because of their cost effectiveness in reducing later, more expensive hospitalizations.

In the world of work, there have also been significant new developments in prevention. As described in Chapter 15, the emergence of occupational health psychology is based primarily on evidence regarding the effects of job-related stress on both worker productivity and workers' physical and mental health. Quick, Quick, Nelson, and Hurrell (1997) provide a comprehensive theoretical analysis of, and practical guide to, preventive stress management in work organizations. Building on the concept that person–environment "fits" in to the world of work yields the least stressful conditions (see chapters 14 and 15), they devote several of their chapters to strategies for changing and modifying (a) organizational and work environments (e.g., goal setting, team building, career development, diversity programs); and (b) "individuals' perceptions, attitudes, and behaviors to enhance individual health and well-being" (Quick et al., 1997, p. 207); for example, learned optimism, constructive self-talk, progressive relaxation, social support. Obviously, all of these strategies are well within the purview of counseling psychologists' intervention skills.

The evolution of the word *prevention* reached new levels of acceptability in the late 1990s when then-president of the APA, Martin Seligman, chose "prevention" as the theme for his special presidential project:

> We need massive research on human strength and virtue. We need practitioners to recognize that much of the best work they do is amplifying the strengths rather than repairing their patients' weaknesses. We need psychologists who work with families, schools, religious communities and corporations to emphasize their primary role of fostering strength (Seligman, 1998).

Seligman's focus on prevention clearly and emphatically transcended any remaining medical perspective that allowed clients/patients to be seen as passive organisms waiting for "doctors" to address issues of prevention. His proposals on fostering strength echo the recommendations of Gelso and Fassinger (1992) for counseling psychologists in the section of their review titled "An Unfulfilled Promise: Development of the Healthy or Effective Self."

Seligman cast prevention clearly in the terms of many of the major themes of counseling psychology outlined in Chapter 1: working with normal populations, emphasis on strengths, interactions of the person and the environment. Concurrent with these evolutional developments in prevention in the 1990s, Osipow, one of the major leaders and editors of the profession of counseling psychology, founded and became the first editor of the new journal *Applied and Preventive Psychology*. Counseling psychologists have become more frequent contributors of research in the *Journal of Primary Prevention;* a Special Interest Group on Prevention and Public Interest has been created within the Division of Counseling Psychology, providing a newsletter to its members as well as numerous opportunities at APA conventions for roundtable meetings and presentations of training, research, and practice programs focused on counseling psychologists' involvement in prevention. In short, prevention, by the 1990s, had become the most used encompassing word to describe services as outreach and educational/developmental.

In the next section, we describe the now-classic "cube" conceptualization of psychological services. This model was developed by counseling psychologists to assist mental health agencies in planning for a range of strength-building, educational–developmental, and preventive services, as well as remedial services. Such an array of services is essential to address the full range of mental health needs of the community an agency serves, whether that "community" be a university, subscribers of a managed care corporation, or employees of a large company that operates an employee assistance program.

THIRTY-SIX FACES OF COUNSELING: THE CLASSIC MODEL

Despite the plethora of new roles for counseling psychologists that emerged in the 1960s and 1970s under the many labels just reviewed, there was no systematic way to determine what balance was desirable and whether a psychological services center was being reasonably comprehensive in its offerings. Morrill, Oetting, and Hurst (1974) provide a three-dimensional cube (see Figure 18.1) to respond to this need for a systematic description of counselor functions. The cube has had seminal value not only in organizing what has been accomplished by the profession but also in pointing to what needs to be done in those "cells" of the cube where there are few if any existing services. Most counseling services continue to focus on just a few "faces" of the cube. Consequently, the well-prepared counseling psychologist uses the cube as a way to explore opportunities for prevention and outreach services in both current and emerging career settings.

One could argue that a truly comprehensive counseling service should have some available program for each of the 36 faces of counseling. It is probably easiest to conceptualize such a comprehensive set of services by choosing a method of intervention, such as media, and then asking what kind of media program is needed for each of the psychological *targets* of intervention with each of the different *purposes* (i.e., remediation, prevention, and development). To be fully comprehensive, one would need 12 media programs, whether written or audiovisual. Likewise, one could specify 12 sorts of consultation or training programs and 12 kinds of direct service.

It is certainly possible to see how some outreach might be done in every cell, whether it is simply moving direct service to a satellite center, for example, setting

FIGURE 18.1.   The Thirty-Six Faces of Counseling. Courtesy of Weston H. Morrill, Ph.D.

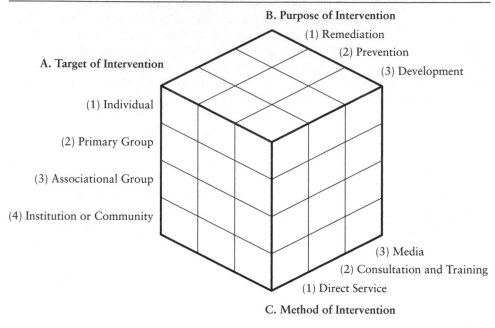

up an office in the student union to maximize initial interviews, or developing a preventive intervention for an international company in order to reduce the stresses of employee relocation. The frequent overlapping implications of a single outreach intervention for both development and prevention have already been described.

Atkinson, Kim, and Caldwell (1998) recently presented a modification of this cube to help counseling psychologists envision and plan for more multiculturally responsive psychological services (see Figure 6.1 in Chapter 6). Their modification changes the three dimensions to goal of helping (purpose of intervention in original model), locus of problem etiology—internal to external (variation of target of intervention in original model), and acculturation, a critical dimension to respond to individual differences in cultural diversity (see Chapter 6). In their modification, they include (as in the original cube), a variety of methods of intervention, from counselor to consultant to facilitator of indigenous healing methods, and add the unique aspects of working with multicultural populations. Their modification of the cube is especially useful for agencies that serve culturally diverse populations.

STRUCTURED GROUPS

Structured groups and psychoeducation interventions, as described in the next two sections, are the two types of preventive services most uniquely developed by counseling psychologists. We will provide separate sections on these two developments, even though in one sense structured groups are all actually a subset of psychoeducation interventions; all structured groups share with psychoeducation the goal of showing clients how to apply what they learn in the group to other problem situations that might arise. Yet structured groups remain a unique subset in both the extensiveness of their development and in their high degree of structure in design and implementation. Though such groups first came to prominence in counseling psychology in the 1970s as part of outreach, they actually foreshadowed the development of "manualized" approaches to dealing with psychological problems. As discussed in Chapter 4, the industrialization of health care has led to a demand for treatment guidelines and protocols for dealing with mental health problems such as depression and anxiety. This need for treatment protocols has greatly increased the call for manualized treatment procedures. Attempts to manualize any preventive, developmental, or remedial treatment will benefit greatly from careful attention to the well-articulated definitions, rationale, and developmental parameters for structured groups as described by Drum and Knott (1977). They define a structured group as

> a delimited learning situation with a predetermined goal, and a planned design to enable each group member to reach this identified goal with minimum frustration and maximum ability to transfer the new learning to a wide range of life events (p. 14).

Drum and Knott categorize the numerous kinds of structured groups that have been developed within three broad groupings: *lifeskills* (e.g., assertion training, decision making, parenting skills), *life theme groups* (e.g., clarifying personal values, raising self-esteem, developing gender awareness), and *life transition groups* (e.g., for separated and divorced persons resolving personal loss). As Drum and Knott cogently summarize, there are eight easily identifiable values inherent in the offering of structured groups. One, structured groups are "relatively non-threatening to participants and make the process of learning enjoyable. Through appropriately structured exercises they encourage people gently but firmly to increase their ability to try out new behaviors or examine issues they would normally avoid" (p. 24). Two, they take the mystery out of the process of self-discovery and self-enhancement, making it seem possible to change without undergoing intensive psychotherapy. Three, the implied contract in such groups is far more limited: "Each participant can enter into the group experience with a feeling of inner comfort that the group will stick to the stated goal and not attempt to restructure the whole personality" (p. 25). Four, structured groups, like all group treatment, have the advantage of helping the person realize that many others experience the same kind of problem situation. The sense of not being alone provides a reassurance to the participant. Five, there is less stigma associated with taking part in groups that focus on common developmental or transitional needs using an educational–experiential format than there is in entering remedial counseling or therapy. Six, the interactions within such groups encourage change and growth while also providing the chance for group members to practice skills with other persons who are sharing the same problem. Seven, there is the opportunity for both peer and professional feedback related to the trying out of skills.

Eight, structured groups, like all group interventions, provide an economical use of counselors' time. The needs and issues of many persons can be addressed in the same number of hours that one-to-one counseling would provide for only one person.

Recent examples of structured groups can be found in two of the articles cited at the beginning of this chapter: five structured sessions of "enrichment counseling" for couples as described in Worthington et al. (1997); and a five-session, 10-hour program called Preparing for the Drug Free Years, a family-skills training program designed for parents of young adolescents. Further examples, with yet other populations, may be found in Perrone (1989) and Holtzworth-Munroe, Markman, O'Leary et al. (1995). Perrone (1989) developed a 10-session program for adult children of alcoholics to help them address the kinds of problems their dysfunctional family has created: "Adult children of alcoholics have difficulty trusting others, have difficulty identifying and/or expressing feeling, and often cannot ask for what they need" (Perrone, 1989, p. 1). The structured group program therefore assists participants to label feelings and make requests of others in appropriate ways. Holtzworth-Munroe and colleagues (1995) provide full descriptions of two structured groups designed to (a) prevent marital violence and (b) stop anger and violence escalation. These cognitive–behaviorally oriented programs are often offered together. The first is a 12-hour program with the acronym PREP (Prevention and Relationship Enhancement Program); the second is a 4-hour structured psychoeducation workshop SAVE (Stop Anger and Violence Escalation) that was developed for military couples considered to be at high risk for marital violence. These examples illustrate the broad range of populations and topics that well-defined structured groups can address. Because structured groups have clearly articulated procedures, they can often be led by master's-level psychologists and/or graduate students in the advanced stages of doctoral work in counseling psychology.

PSYCHOEDUCATION

Another unique preventive contribution of counseling psychologists has been the development of psychoeducation interventions. These interventions, in contrast to the structured groups just described, are typically somewhat more comprehensive and focus on dissemination of knowledge, self-understanding, and attitude change as well as skill development. Whereas structured groups are more like a highly structured modification of group counseling, psychoeducation interventions are more like coursework with explicit attention to emotions and psychological functioning. Typically, more teaching and coaching occurs than in structured groups.

While such interventions were initially targeted primarily on school-age populations, as described in the work of Mosher and Sprinthall (1971), similar programs have now been extended to the full range of adult development. Before describing some of those programs, it is important to note that school-age programs in psychoeducation continue to be developed. One of the articles listed at the beginning of this chapter describes a conceptual model for introducing conflict resolution into the educational curriculum for adolescents, providing specific educational, training, and practice objectives. The school-to-work transition movement, described in Chapter 15, will also include psychoeducational components designed to help students become knowledgeable about the world of work and to develop effective work habits.

Two exemplary extensions of psychoeducation programs to adult populations may be found in the work of Danish and colleagues (1993) and of LaFromboise and Howard-Pitney (1995). The former focuses on life development intervention for professional athletes. Their article provides a richly detailed description of the strategies that are taught as part of this program. Since athletes are accustomed to receiving intensive coaching, this psychoeducation model incorporates active coaching for athletes' implementation of the strategies they learn about in the coursework part of the program. They are first taught how to develop and use goal ladders. Then they learn about the kinds of interventions that can assist their personal and skill development as they (a) anticipate normative events, (b) need social support during a critical event and, possibly, (c) need further coaching (counseling) for coping with unexpected events. Research has shown that athletes' recovery from either physical or "psychological" injury is enhanced by their understanding and use of such information and skills.

A multicultural application of psychoeducation is provided by LaFromboise and Howard-Pitney (1995). Responding to evidence of a suicide rate among some Native American adolescents that is 2.5 times greater than the already high rate for U.S. adolescents in general, they developed a program of seven major units that could be incorporated into the curriculum of the Zuni Public High School. These units include:

> (a) building self-esteem; (b) identifying emotions and stress; (c) increasing communication and problem-solving skills; (d) recognizing and eliminating self-destructive behaviors such as pessimistic thoughts or anger reactivity; (e) receiving suicide information; (f) receiving suicide intervention training; and (g) setting personal and community goals. . . . A unique feature and strength of the curriculum was that it was specifically tailored to be compatible with Zuni norms, values, beliefs, and attitudes; sense of self, space, and time; communication styles; and rewards and forms of recognition (LaFromboise & Howard-Pitney, 1995, p. 481).

Students who completed this program, compared to those who did not, showed less suicide probability and less hopelessness at the end of the program as well as increased problem-solving skills.

These few illustrative psychoeducational programs show how a broad range of adolescents and adults can be helped to build on their own strengths in order to reduce stress and enhance the quality of their lives. "Students" of psychoeducation may range from nursery school age to retirees who enroll in the kinds of retirement programs described in Chapter 15, and in the various courses offered to retirees by the Elderhostel program and the American Association of Retired Persons (AARP). Counseling psychologists have been key contributors to all these kinds of programs, adding their expertise on how to incorporate a full range of preventive and educational–developmental services.

HEALTH PSYCHOLOGY

One of the fastest growing areas of new career opportunities for counseling psychologists is *general medical* health care, as compared to *mental* health care (Haley, McDaniel, Bray et al., 1998). Dorken (1993) notes a more than 600% increase in the number of patients treated by psychologists in medical hospitals during the 1980s; the number of states that passed legislation enabling psychologists to have hospital privileges more than doubled in the 1990s. By the early 1990s, an entire issue of *The Counseling Psychologist* (July 1991) was devoted to counseling psychology and health applications; in 1992 Altmaier and Johnson provided, for the second edition of the *Handbook of Counseling Psychology,* a full chapter describing a broad variety of preventive, educational–developmental, and consultative roles established by counseling psychologists in health care settings.

The growing number of training and career opportunities for counseling psychologists in primary health care settings will be described in the next section. However, it is important to first become acquainted with how counseling psychologists in health care settings almost routinely combine preventive, educational–developmental, and consultative roles. In such settings, the remedial role is greatly reduced; it is the application of counseling psychology's strengths in developing and offering preventive and educational–developmental services that creates an increasing number of challenging career opportunities.

The single best way to understand the broad range of opportunities for counseling psychologists to make unique contributions to general medical practice may be found by reading Friedman, Sobel, Myers et al. (1995). While their article was prepared to present evidence on different ways psychologists' interventions lead to medical cost offset (see Chapter 4 for a description of, and the critical importance of, medical cost offset in contemporary health care), the six pathways they describe provide a framework for looking at both preventive and educational–developmental interventions. We divide their six pathways into two subsets. The first subset is more a primary prevention subset; the second, a secondary prevention subset. In the first subset are Friedman and colleagues' (1995) pathways of information and decision support, social support, and behavior change. In the first of these, the emphasis is on empowering patients in appropriate self-care; that is, developing the knowledge, skills, and confidence for self-management. They note that a variety of instructional materials, 1:1 teaching, and peer-led support groups all contribute to patients learning how to depend more on themselves and less on medical professionals for managing their health care situations. As patients depend more on themselves, there are, of course, reduced direct care costs. More important to counseling psychologists are the gains obtained in patients' feeling more in charge of their own lives and the potential for their coping more satisfactorily (by both their own and professionals' judgments) in future medical situations. Regarding Friedman and colleagues' (1995) dimension of social support, it should be noted that counseling psychologists have developed many interventions to create increased social support in a wide range of areas, from college students' coping with loneliness, to adding to the longevity of AIDS patients, to coping with unemployment. Friedman et al. (1995) provide similar evidence of the effectiveness of increasing social support for the recovery of cardiac and cesarean birth patients. Finally, their behavior change category includes the preventive services in which counseling psychologists have the longest history of direct involvement in general hospital settings (see Altmaier & Johnson, 1992): programs for smoking cessation, eating disorders, and managing Type A behaviors. Now, in the age of industrialized health care, some health care corporations are adding such services for their subscribers in order to reduce subscribers' later use of either outpatient or inpatient services.

The secondary prevention subset of Friedman and colleagues (1995) involves more direct service compared to the psychoeducational types of intervention just described. They have three pathways in this group, which they label psychophysiological, somatization, and undiagnosed psychiatric problem. In the first of these pathways, the emphasis is on the patient learning how to manage stress more effectively as part of their "medical" treatment. The focus may be on stress management in life in general, or specifically focused on a current medical crisis such as major surgery. Patients who effectively learn stress management not only show expected gains such as lower blood pressure, but also recover more quickly from surgery and show other psychoneuroimmunological gains (Kiecolt-Glaser, Page, Marucha et al., 1998). Counseling psychologists have well-established structured groups on stress management that can be offered to patients.

Regarding somatization, it has long been known that many physical problems such as ulcers, high blood pressure, soft tissue and muscle deterioration may all have significant emotional components. Counseling psychologists' contributions in such cases are largely through providing counseling to address the emotional needs of the patient in order to develop more effective coping skills so that less stress is somaticized (i.e., secondary prevention treatment of existing problems). When such counseling is successful, there is far less need for physician treatment and at least a stabilization of, or ideally improvement in, physical problems such as high blood pressure and ulcers. Finally, counseling psychologists address the issue of undiagnosed psychiatric problems by using their assessment skills. Many problems presented to physicians—such as heart pain, impotence, and panic attacks—all have emotional dysfunction as the root cause. With proper diagnosis, more effective treatment plans can be developed that will increase patient satisfaction and, in most cases, be less costly than physician care.

The one area of preventive interventions that Friedman et al.'s (1995) system does *not* encompass is the contributions of counseling psychologists to provider–patient relationships. Altmaier and Johnson (1992) provide concise descriptions of both (1) the training programs developed by counseling psychologists for physicians, to improve their interpersonal skills in dealing with patients; and (2) the development of methods of selection and evaluation that medical schools can use with interns and residents to assess the "noncognitive" components of physician functioning that are so critical to patient satisfaction. Altmaier and Johnson (1992) report that most of the critical problems that occur in provider–patient relationships are not because of the physician's inadequate knowledge of the medical aspects of the patients' problems, but rather because of interpersonal skills and communication styles.

In summary, these seven areas of interventions in medical settings all clearly call upon the strengths of counseling psychologists in providing a range of preventive and educational–developmental interventions as well as remedial counseling services.

Training and Career Opportunities in Medical Settings

Much of the controversial material about training opportunities in prevention discussed in the next section applies primarily to counseling psychologists preparing for roles in *mental* health settings, such as counseling centers, community mental health centers, and psychiatric services within VA and state-administered hospitals. The opportunities for training and practice in preventive interventions are quite different for counseling psychologists choosing to focus on practice in general medical services; therefore, special note is given here to those opportunities. All that follows in this section is equally applicable to training and career opportunities for consultation within general medical settings and should therefore be recalled when reading Chapter 19. In fact, in general medical settings, almost every day one functions as a consultant as well as a provider of preventive and educational–developmental services.

Because of this increased participation by counseling psychologists in the kinds of services described in the preceding section, some training programs in counseling psychology have developed specific courses and/or tracks of training and experience in general health care settings. Alcorn and McPhearson (1997), from their own experience in providing training for multidisciplinary health settings, provide several recommendations for graduate students in counseling psychology who seek health-related careers. Drotar (1998) similarly provides recommendations for those who wish to specialize in hospital work with children. Sheridan (1999) describes both the opportunities and training needed for expanded roles for psychologists in medical schools and academic health care centers. Since the APA approved "clinical health psychology" as a distinct specialty in 1998, it is likely that there will soon be a number of internships and postdoctoral residencies labeled "clinical health psychology." Graduates of counseling psychology programs will be eligible for such internships and residencies if their predoctoral work has included (1) attention to the kinds of preventive, educational–developmental, and consultative roles described above and in the next chapter; and (2) received some supervised experience in practica or externships in general medical settings—that is, primary care centers or medical hospitals. As described in Chapter 4, there are an increasing number of opportunities for psychologists in industrialized health care who complete such training. It must be noted, however, that for graduates of counseling psychology programs whose training and internship experiences have been limited to *mental health* settings, such as counseling centers, community mental health clinics, and psychiatric units, it will be difficult to be competitive for career opportunities in *primary health* care centers and general medical hospitals.

TRAINING IN COUNSELING PSYCHOLOGY FOR PREVENTIVE INTERVENTIONS

Rhetoric and Reality

What are the opportunities for training in preventive and educational–developmental interventions for graduate students in counseling psychology who are *not* preparing for careers in medical settings? The current reality is less than clear but appears to be more positive than that of the 1980s. In the first edition of this book, eight articles were cited that documented that, despite counseling psychology's long history of emphasizing its contributions to preventive and educational–development roles, as well as remedial roles, "prevention, unfortunately, continues to occupy last place in the hearts of counseling psychologists" (Krumboltz, Becker-Haven, & Burnett, 1979, p. 588). In the era before industrialized health care, when insurance payments for psychotherapy seemed almost unlimited, Osipow (1977) concisely formulated the dilemma in "Osipow's Law" that "remediation (in the form of psychotherapeutic interventions) drives out prevention in the form of counseling interventions where the two are present in the same agency" (p. 94). Within the past few years, no new surveys have been published indicating any changes in this gulf between the *rhetoric* of counseling psychology's endorsement of prevention and the *reality* of training opportunities in graduate programs and internships. Yet there are now certainly more opportunities for graduate students to find support for their interests in prevention through the Special Interest Group on Prevention and Public Policy in the Division of Counseling Psychology. Moreover, as well illustrated by Humphrey (1995), graduate students themselves may be the catalysts for designing, implementing, and evaluating prevention programs. She describes how graduate students at two different universities developed prevention programs: one devoted to sexual violence, the other to stress management. As already illustrated in prior sections of this chapter, there are opportunities for learning about preventive and educational–developmental interventions in the full array of training areas within counseling psychology—career, interpersonal communication, behavior modification, substance abuse, and so forth.

At the internship and postdoctoral residency level of training in psychology, the best opportunities for training in prevention are found in health psychology. Yet there are also a few counseling centers and community mental health centers that provide supervised experience in developing, implementing, and evaluating prevention programs. Sandler and Chassin (1993) developed a postdoctoral training program devoted primarily to prevention research. As described in the next and final section of this chapter, the 1990s clearly resulted in better articulations of frameworks for support of preventive interventions; these frameworks make clear the potential for a true scientist–practitioner model of functioning. Ideally, increased internship and postdoctoral residency opportunities for training in preventive interventions in counseling centers and public health clinics as well as in medical hospitals will soon follow.

SCIENTIST–PRACTITIONERS AND PREVENTIVE INTERVENTIONS

The 1990s brought valuable new attention to both the research and practice components of preventive interventions. Prior to that decade, much of the prevention research and practice had been seen as largely the domain of U.S. public health agencies, rather than as a mainstream part of psychology. As psychologists (1) gained a better understanding of some persisting social problems like violence in youth, substance abuse, and racial discrimination; and (2) found support for prevention in at least the stated purposes of industrialized health care (that is, reduce medical costs by improving wellness behaviors), greater attention was given in psychology publications to both research and practice in preventive interventions.

To see developments in the more purely *research* perspective on prevention, consider the titles of three articles published in the *American Psychologist* in the 1990s: "The Science of Prevention" (Coie, Watt, West et al., 1993); "A Framework for Health Promotion and Disease Prevention Programs" (Winett, 1995); and "National Research Agenda for Prevention Research" (Reiss & Price, 1996). Concomitantly, the establishment of the journal *Applied & Preventive Psychology* provided psychologists with a new venue for disseminating articles that integrate research and practice.

The development of models of prevention that attend to existing data about a given social problem area followed by the development, implementation, and evaluation of prevention interventions, is the scientist–practitioner at work! Instructive examples of scientists–practitioners working in prevention may be found in Blechman, Prinz, and Dumas (1995) and O'Hearn and Gatz (1996). The former developed a model of aggression prevention for young adolescents that depended on increases in coping skills and competence. Their model was built only after they had synthesized the research that demonstrated that such skills could reduce aggression. They designed a comprehensive psychoeducation program involving both the school and the community. The O'Hearn and Gatz project adapted, for middle school students, the goal-setting skills program developed by Danish and colleagues (1993) for athletes, and described in this chapter. They created an educational pyramid in which (a) psychology faculty supervised (b) psychology graduate students serving as (c) consultants to undergraduates who trained and supervised (d) high school students as the (e) "teachers and coaches" for middle school students as they learned about goal setting. They had built into the program several components of evaluation. These evaluations showed not only significant positive attitude and behavioral changes among the targeted group—that is, the middle school students—but also that some of these students began to "teach" their own family members about goal setting. Finally, both the high school students and undergraduate students involved as "consultants" and "teachers" showed increased levels of self-efficacy.

These are just two illustrations of how preventive interventions, developed within the scientist–practitioner approach, will yield multiplicative effects in behavioral, affective, and knowledge domains. Yet at the same time, conducting research on preventive interventions is one of the most difficult challenges facing psychologists, and even more so for graduate students in psychology. Looking at the two projects just described, one can see that there had to be multiyear efforts involving an extensive number of professionals and others—hardly a project for a graduate student to conduct for a dissertation! Obtaining the cooperation of the schools or agencies in which one conducts prevention interventions will almost always be far more difficult than obtaining clients' permission to participate in a research project. Convincing such agencies that there can be observable gains from preventive interventions is a major "marketing" issue for prevention researchers—an issue that is concisely addressed by Perla (1997) and that should be consulted in the early implementation stages of a preventive intervention in a new setting.

Given some of these inherent difficulties in implementing the research and practice components of preventive interventions, the very best opportunities for obtaining training for becoming a scientist–practitioner in preventive interventions will occur (1) where one or more faculty of a training program have an ongoing research and intervention program on prevention, or (2) in postdoctoral residencies that are funded by grants to ongoing prevention research and intervention programs. In either case, a graduate student in counseling psychology can become part of a team of scientists–practitioners who provide supervised experience both in implementing and evaluating preventive interventions. Such training will prepare counseling psychologists for using their professional strengths and skills to address society's most persistent problems.

SUMMARY

The first part of this chapter was devoted to describing how medical and educational perspectives have led to different terminology for "prevention" and "outreach" services. The words *outreach* and *psychoeducational* are derived from the educational perspective, especially as education is considered in a life-span view of human development. Counseling psychologists have preferred using these words compared to the word *prevention,* in order to avoid having participants functioning in passive, "wait for the doctor to do something," ways. During the past few years, as both industrialized health care and workplace prevention programs have been developed that call for participants taking more active roles in their own well-being, there has been a decrease in concerns about the use of the word *prevention.* We explained how the traditional tripartite medical categorization of prevention (primary, secondary, tertiary) can fit the roles of counseling psychologist in educational–developmental, preventive, and remedial roles.

The second major section of this chapter described the classic cube model of counselor functions for encompassing *purpose* of intervention (i.e., the three roles noted in preceding sentence); *targets* (i.e., individuals, groups, and institutions); and *methods of intervention* (i.e., direct service, consultation/training, and media). The model is especially helpful in designing the variety of services that should be provided in a comprehensive service setting. To be truly comprehensive, agencies must address, in addition to the clients who do seek help, the needs of those who might not voluntarily come to a clinic themselves but still need some sort of psychological service to cope with problems they are having in their homes, community, or workplace.

The development of both structured groups and psychoeducation interventions are counseling psychology's unique contributions in the domain of "prevention." Structured groups are limited learning situations designed to help participants reach an identified goal *and* to transfer their learning to a broader range of life events. Such groups may range from life skills (e.g., assertion training) to theme groups (clarifying personal values), to life transition groups (e.g., bereavement groups). Psychoeducation usually has a somewhat broader focus than structured groups and includes dissemination of knowledge, self-understanding, and attitude change.

Psychoeducation interventions, in one sense, are like coursework focused on psychological functioning, with the counselor taking more active teaching and coaching roles than in traditional counseling. We provided two examples of psychoeducation programs, one developed for athletes, the other for a Native American group.

Recent developments in industrialized health care have brought many new opportunities for counseling psychologists in preventive roles. While we were able, earlier in the chapter, to show an extraordinarily good fit of traditional counselor training with the needs for prevention activities in the workplace (e.g., cognitive restructuring, career development), working in health care settings often requires a bit more adaptation of traditional counselor roles. We used the six pathways of Friedman et al. (1995) to describe the diversity of prevention activities being developed in contemporary health care settings.

The final two sections of this chapter focused on the challenges of becoming trained for, and practicing preventive interventions. Critics say that counseling psychology has given more rhetorical support to prevention than to actual training and practice. It is true that there are often fewer courses and supervised training opportunities for preventive interventions than for any other area of practice included in this text. One of the key reasons for less availability is the fact that we do not have clients "waiting" for preventive services. Another key reason is that developing, implementing, and evaluating a prevention service is always more than a one-semester practicum. We described a number of ways for graduate students to obtain training in preventive interventions. The challenges of such interventions call precisely for the skills of counseling psychologists as scientist–practitioners. We provided two brief illustrations of interventions built upon a careful analysis of existing literature; interventions that had broad, multiplicative effects for a large number of individuals coping with critical social problems.

References

Albee, G. W., Bloom, B. L., Broussard, E., Cowen, E. L., Erlenmeyer, Kinmling, L., Gomez, E., Klein, D. C., Menninger, R., Pastor, V. S., Reilly, J., & Rubinger, V. (1978). Report of the task force on primary prevention. *President's commission on mental health.* Washington, DC: U.S. Government Printing Office.

Alcorn, J. D., & McPhearson, R. W. (1997). Counseling psychology in multidisciplinary health settings: Implications for future training. *The Counseling Psychologist, 25,* 637–653.

Altmaier, E. M., & Johnson, B. D. (1992). Health-related application of counseling psychology: Toward health promotion and disease prevention across the life span. In S. D. Brown and R. W. Lent (Eds.), *Handbook of counseling psychology* (2nd ed., pp. 315–348). New York: John Wiley & Sons.

Atkinson, D. R., Kim, B. S. K., & Caldwell, R. (1998). Ratings of helper roles by multi-cultural psychologists and Asian American students: Initial support for the three-dimensional model of multicultural counseling. *Journal of Counseling Psychology, 45,* 414–423.

Blechman, E. A., Prinz, R., & Dumas, J. E. (1995). Coping, competence, and aggression prevention. *Applied & Preventive Psychology, 4,* 211–232.

Caplan, G. (1964). *Principles of preventive psychiatry.* New York: Basic Books.

Coie, J. D., Watt, N. F., West, S. G., Hawkins, J. D., Asarnow, J. R., Markman, H. J., Ramey, S. L., Shure, M. B., & Long, B. (1993). The science of prevention: A conceptual framework and some directions for a national research program. *American Psychologist, 48,* 1013–1022.

Danish, S. J., D'Augelli, A. R., & Ginsberg, M. R. (1984). Life development intervention: Promotion of mental health through the development of competence. In S. D. Brown and R. W. Lent (Eds.), *Handbook of counseling psychology* (pp. 520–544). New York: John Wiley & Sons.

Danish, S. J., Petitpas, A. J., & Hale, B. D. (1993). Life development intervention for athletes: Life skills through sports. *The Counseling Psychologist, 21,* 352–385.

Dorken, H. (1993). The hospital private practice of psychology. *Professional Psychology: Research and Practice, 24,* 409–417.

Drotar, D. (1998). Training students for careers in medical settings: A graduate program in pediatric psychology. *Professional Psychology: Research and Practice, 29,* 402–404.

Drum, D. J., & Figler, H. E. (1973). *Outreach in counseling.* New York: Intext.

Drum, D. J., & Knott, J. E. (1977). *Structured groups for facilitating development.* New York: Human Sciences Press.

Frank, B., Dixon, D. N., & Grosz, H. J. (1993). Conjoint monitoring of symptoms of premenstrual syndrome: Impact on marital satisfaction. *Journal of Counseling Psychology, 40,* 109–114.

Friedman, R., Sobel, D., Myers, P., Caudill, M., & Benson, H. (1995). Behavioral medicine, clinical health psychology, and cost offset. *Health Psychology, 14,* 509–518.

Gelso, C. J., & Fassinger, R. E. (1992). Personality, development, and counseling psychology: Depth, ambivalence, and actualization. *Journal of Counseling Psychology, 39,* 275–298.

Haley, W. E., McDaniel, S. H., Bray, J. H., Frank, R. G., Heldring, M., Johnson, S. B., Lu, E. G., Reed, G. M., & Wiggins, J. G. (1998). Psychological practice in primary care settings. *Professional Psychology: Research and Practice, 29,* 237–244.

Holtzworth-Munroe, A., Markman, H., O'Leary, K. D., Neidig, P., Leber, D., Heyman, R. E., Hulbert, D., & Smutzler, N. (1995). The need for marital violence prevention efforts: A behavioral–cognitive secondary prevention program for engaged and newly married couples. *Applied & Preventive Psychology, 4,* 77–88.

Humphrey, C. F. (1995). *Graduate students can make a difference: Two student-initiated prevention programs.* Newsletter, APA Division 17 Prevention Special Interest Group, #2.

Joint Commission on Mental Illness and Health (1961). *Action for mental health.* New York: Basic Books.

Kiecolt-Glaser, J. K., Page, G. G., Marucha, P. T., MacCallum, R. C., & Glaser, R. (1998). Psychological influences on surgical recovery. *American Psychologist, 53,* 1209–1218.

Krumboltz, J. D., Becker-Haven, J. F., & Burnett, A. F. (1979). Counseling psychology. *Annual Review of Psychology, 30,* 555–602.

Kush, K., & Cochran, L. (1993). Enhancing a sense of agency through career planning. *Journal of Counseling Psychology, 40,* 434–439.

LaFromboise, T., & Howard-Pitney, B. (1995). The Zuni life skills development curriculum: Description and evaluation of a suicide prevention program. *Journal of Counseling Psychology, 42,* 479–486.

Morrill, W. H., Oetting, E. R., & Hurst, J. C. (1974). Dimensions of counselor functioning. *Personnel and Guidance Journal, 52,* 354–359.

Mosher, R. L., & Sprinthall, N. A. (1971). Psychological education: A means to promote personal development during adolescence. *The Counseling Psychologist, 2*(4), 3–82.

Ogles, B. M., Lambert, M. J., & Craig, D. E. (1991). Comparison of self-help books for coping with loss. *Journal of Counseling Psychology, 38,* 387–393.

O'Hearn, T. C., & Gatz, M. (1996). The educational pyramid: A model for community intervention. *Applied & Preventive Psychology, 5,* 127–134.

Osipow, S. H. (1977). Will the real counseling psychologist please stand up? *The Counseling Psychologist, 7(2)*, 93–94.

Perla, M. L. (1997). Public support for prevention. *American Psychologist, 52*, 1143.

Perone, J. (1989). *Adult children of alcoholics* (manual). College Park: University of Maryland Counseling Center.

Quick, J. C., Quick, J. D., Nelson, D. L., & Hurrell, J. J. (1997). *Preventive stress management in organizations*. Washington, DC: American Psychological Association.

Reiss, D., & Price, R. H. (1996). National research agenda for prevention research. *American Psychologist, 51*, 1109–1115.

Rosenthal, E. H., Heesacker, M., & Neimeyer, G. J. (1995). Changing the rape-supportive attitudes of traditional and nontraditional male and female college students. *Journal of Counseling Psychology, 42*, 171–177.

Sandler, I., & Chassin, L. (1993). From research to implementation in the teaching of prevention: A postdoctoral training program. *Teaching of Psychology, 20*, 144–148.

Sarbin, T. R. (1997). On the futility of psychiatric diagnostic manuals and the return of personal agency. *Applied & Preventive Psychology, 6*, 233–243.

Schlossberg, N. K. (1989). *Overwhelmed: Coping with life's ups and downs*. Lexington, MA: Lexington Books.

Seligman, M. E. P. (1998, January). Building human strength: Psychology's forgotten mission. *APA Monitor*, p. 2.

Sheridan, E. P. (1999). Psychology's future in medical school and academic health care centers. *American Psychologist, 54*, 267–271.

Shore, M. F. (1992). Community mental health: Corpse or phoenix? *Professional Psychology: Research and Practice, 23*, 257–262.

Spoth, R., Yoo, S., Kahn J. H., & Redmond, C. (1996). A model of the effects of protective parent and peer factors on young adolescent alcohol refusal skills. *Journal of Primary Prevention, 16*, 373–394.

VanSlyck, M., Stern, M., & Zak-Place, J. (1996). Promoting optimal adolescent development through conflict resolution education, training, and practice. *The Counseling Psychologist, 24*, 433–461.

Warnath, C. F. (1971). *New myths and old realities: College counseling in transition*. San Francisco: Jossey-Bass.

Winett, R. A. (1995). A framework for health promotion and disease prevention programs. *American Psychologist, 50*, 341–350.

Worthington, E. L., Hight, T. L., Ripley, J. S., Perrone, K. M., Kurusu, T. A., & Jones, D. R. (1997). Strategic hope-focused relationship-enrichment counseling with individual couples. *Journal of Counseling Psychology, 44*, 381–389.

Wright, L., Stroud, R., & Keenan, M. (1993). Indirect treatment of children via parent training. *Applied and Preventive Psychology, 2*, 191–200.

CONSULTATION:
EMPOWERING OTHERS

What do the following four situations have in common?

> A staff psychologist in a university counseling center notes that 60% of the fresh-men students seen in this past semester came from just one of the eight residence halls on campus.

> A counseling psychologist in independent practice was often asked to interview students who had been suspended or expelled from the school system for disruptive behavior. Four of the seven students referred to her in the past year were suspended because of creating serious disruptions in Mr. Watson's history classes.

> A counseling psychologist in an employee assistance program of a manufacturing company provided career counseling for workers who wished to consider transfers, promotions, or alternative careers. His records for the past year indicate that 75% of the requests for career counseling came from plant workers in just one of six work groups of relatively equal size.

> A department chairperson in a large university noted that most of the complaints she received were from graduate students in one of the four graduate programs in the department and that the withdrawal rate in that program had been about 70% for the past 5 years, whereas in the other three programs the withdrawal rate was approximately 25%.

In each of these examples one part of an organization is generating more problems than others. Counseling psychologists can simply keep counseling all of the referrals (the steady flow of clients is "good for business"). On the other hand, one may begin to wonder whether there is something that can be done to prevent so many "casualties." The ultimate goal of consultation is typically that of prevention and/or development as defined in Chapter 18. In contrast to some of the services discussed in that chapter, consultation achieves these goals by working with other persons who have responsibilities for students, clients, and workers. Exploring and illustrating the broad range of such work is the goal of this chapter.

The first sections of this chapter explore the unique nature and values of consultation. We then describe several different kinds of consultation, followed by four examples that vary in terms of setting and "clients." Within our exploration of eight typical stages in the process of consultation, we describe the characteristics and skills consultants employ in these stages—a description that makes evident the unique qualifications of counseling psychologists to serve as consultants. Despite the congruence of counseling psychologists' skills with those needed in consultation, there remain two groups of frustrating impediments to effective consultation that we then explore. We explain how, in addition to learning how to cope with these impediments, counseling psychologists as consultants also need to address several unique multicultural and ethical issues. Our exploration of these issues brings us to the final section of this chapter and this text, as we explain how consultation is an ideal synthesis of the diverse roles of counseling psychologists.

CONSULTATION DEFINED

We define *consultation* as a professional service that uses knowledge of human behavior, interpersonal relationships, and group and organizational processes to help others become more effective in their roles. Thus, consultation may encompass an extremely broad range of interventions, from consulting with parents having difficulty managing their children or teachers managing their students, to assisting in the design of staff development for a 12-person staff of a day-treatment center who are experiencing low morale and high turnover, to helping a university design an entirely new program of student services and campus living arrangements. Consultation is, therefore, often described as a triadic relationship: consultant–consultee–client. The "consultee" might be, for example, a physician or a parent or resident hall advisor; the "client(s)" might be one student or patient or a group of students or patients or employees, or an entire organization. Further, we have learned that consultation is most effective when the consultant and consultee develop an egalitarian collaborative working relationship; that is, the consultant is *not* the expert who fixes something. According to Brown, Pryzwansky, and Schulte (1998), this egalitarian collaboration underlies the contrasts they describe between consultation and other roles of counseling psychologists—such as therapist, teacher, and supervisor—even though a consultant might employ any or all of these roles as one part of a consultation intervention.

It is important to contrast consultation with both traditional counseling and the kinds of prevention and outreach activities described in Chapter 18. The concept that probably provides the greatest contrast is that of *indirect service,* which means, for example, helping the resident director, the history teacher, the supervisor, and the faculty of a program with high attrition become more skilled in their professional roles so that fewer of the persons they work with develop problems needing the help of counselors and/or that their program or organization will function more effectively. While the consultant does not directly see the employees, students, and so forth, in any of these situations, these persons benefit from the consultation services to the extent that the consultee (e.g., the resident director, teacher, supervisor, department chair) acquire new perspectives for working with their constituencies. Obviously, consultation provides some direct services to the directors, leaders, or supervisors, but the primary beneficiaries are the larger numbers of students, employees, and so forth, in these organizations.

The Values of Consultation

> [O]ur society is awakening to the realization that the potential of our young and old alike is constrained by practices that impair mental health in families, schools, work environments, and governmental agencies. Consultation is viewed as a viable method of removing these impediments to mental health and, perhaps more important, preventing them from occurring in the first place (Brown et al., 1998, p. 3).

This quote immediately extends the horizons of the values of consultation far beyond those stereotypically associated with professional consultation; that is, one professional offering his or her expertise to help another professional. This latter, more limited view of expert consultation has, Gallessich (1982) points out, existed at least since the thirteenth century when it was first cited in medicine. For a contemporary prevalent example of this limited type of consultation, a general practice physician consults with a neurologist when a patient's symptoms suggest brain involvement. Similarly, in the business world, consultants are often viewed as "experts" to hire for advice on a focused issue, for example, a company employs a psychologist for advice on developing more effective selection strategies with a culturally diverse pool of applicants. In the past few decades, however, the goals of consultation have moved far beyond this "expert" advisor role. The practice of consultation as described and illustrated in this chapter is focused more on interventions with the goals of enhancing human growth and development for the "clients" (patients, students, employees, children, etc.) of the "consultee." The greater values and more extensive results of this developmental perspective on consultation have now been well described by Burke (1994), Brown et al. (1998), Gallessich (1982), and Mannimo, Trickett, Shore, Kidder, and Levine (1986).

The consultation casebook of Conyne and O'Neil (1992) well illustrates the range of organizations that have sought out counseling psychologists to achieve broad goals: a nonprofit public funding board, a school system, a financial service company, a hospital, and a university coping with issues of institutional racism. Each of these consultations extended over many months, in some cases years, in order for the counseling psychology consultant to make needed assessments, interventions, and evaluations of how all the "clients" of these consultees could gain improved opportunities for effective functioning in their employment or educational setting. Brown and colleagues (1998) review the growing number of contributions since the 1970s, by community, school, and counseling psychologists to the theory and practice of consultation focused on human development. There are also now increasing opportunities for counseling psychologists as consultants with primary care physicians not only for expertise about specific cases but also for the design of services that can be more cost effective for delivery of both physical and psychological care (Pace, Chaney, Mullins, & Olson, 1995).

In recent years, increasing attention has been given to the value of consultation for not only increasing the effectiveness of executives and managers, but also for empowering their "clients."

> *Empowerment* refers to a sense of personal power, confidence, and positive self-esteem. Empowerment involves a process of change that can be achieved in relation to specific goals. . . . The end result may be a greater sense of confidence in fulfilling one's functions, that is, getting the best productivity from employees (Arredondo, 1996, p. 17).

When employees, or students, or participants in a managed care organization, feel they are listened to and respected, rather than treated bureaucratically, they are likely to feel more satisfied and to want to contribute to the well-being of their organization (Burke, 1994). Conyne and O'Neil state: "We think that empowerment represents a desirable overarching value system for consultation that would clarify and organize the specific processes of a consultation training program" (1992, p. 193).

Further, consultation is potentially one of the most cost-effective strategies for reducing the need for remedial services such as counseling and psychotherapy, and also for preventing many psychological and social dysfunctions. The typical triadic model of consultation has a counseling psychologist employed as the consultant, working with one or more consultees (executives, managers, teachers), each of whom affect the lives of tens or hundreds of others. As the consultees become more effective in their leadership roles, all of the persons they teach/supervise/manage ideally experience fewer stressful problems and find more opportunities for growth and development in their environment. While this description is indeed an idealized view, it is not impossible. As Brown and colleagues (1998) cogently state, while "[c]onsultation is not a panacea for all the ills of an ailing society" (p. 3), it is increasingly a preferred cost-effective strategy for achieving the goals of counseling psychology. We will return to this perspective at the end of this chapter.

TYPES OF CONSULTATION

The first thing to understand when reading about types of consultation is that there are about as many categorizations of consultation as there are writers of books on consultation. Perhaps the most often cited categorization is Caplan's (1970) four types of mental health consultation: client-centered case consultation, consultee-centered case consultation, program-centered administrative consultation, and consultee-centered administrative consultation. Brown et al. (1998) provide graphic descriptions of the various focuses, goals, and consultant's role and responsibilities for each of these types. Dustin and Blocher (1984) see the first two of these types as traditionally triadic; that is, an "expert" helps the consultee with his or her client or with his or her own professional functioning. The latter two types fall more within what is often called "process consultation" (Schein, 1987):

> [P]rocess consultation puts the emphasis on helping others to help themselves, not on solving their problems for them or giving them expert advice. The reasons for advocating the relevance of process consultation are both theoretical and practical. On the practical level, we have all had our share of disastrous experiences where our "expert" advice was refused, misunderstood or actually

sabotaged. On the theoretical level, process consultation is more developmental. If the person being helped just accepts expert advice he may solve his immediate problem but he may not learn anything about how to solve problems of this nature, skills that would enable him to solve a similar problem in the future. (Schein, 1987, pp. 8–9).

In the past few years, there has been increasing overlap—even interchangeability—between the terms *process consultation* and *organization development* (OD). In the view of an increasing number of OD experts, all effective OD requires process consultation: "Organization development is a planned process of change in an organization's culture through the utilization of behavioral science technologies, research, and theory" (Burke, 1994, p. 12).

We have chosen to provide four examples of consultation from our own and colleagues' experiences that illustrate the diversity within these various authors' categories of consultation. Our four choices (mental health consultation, behavioral consultation, process consultation—consultee-centered and process consultation—program-centered) will show that the models are not mutually exclusive. In fact, as consultation projects develop, the initial model chosen may well change, for example, from a focus on the organization to a focus on the consultee, or from triadic "expert" model to a process, organizationally focused model. Our illustrations also encompass a range of professionals as consultees—doctors and nurses, teachers, company administrators; and a range of clients—patients, students, employees. Following these four illustrations we will present some of the basic stages that are essential in almost all forms of consultation we describe in this section.

Mental Health Consultation

Before getting into our example of a mental health consultation, it must be noted that both the legal and medical professions have frequently used the term *psychological consultation* or *mental health consultation* in a manner that does *not* meet our stipulation of consultation as indirect service. For example, an attorney employed one of the authors as a consultant to make assessments of some individuals who had been mandatorily retired to determine whether or not their mental health had been significantly impaired, as was stipulated in a legal case. Physicians often ask psychologists for assessments of a person's psychological status, especially if there is insufficient organic evidence to explain the patient's symptoms. Surgeons and physicians also frequently ask psychologists to provide counseling to clients before or after surgery or after heart attacks, regarding adjustments and needed changes in lifestyles. In the examples just cited, the psychologist is providing direct assessment or direct service to the client and the other professional person learns nothing about how to provide services that would prevent future occurrences of such a need.

We firmly agree with Gallessich (1982) that "the goal of the mental health model [of consultation] is to expand consultees' knowledge and skill in preventing and remediating mental illness and promoting mental health" (p. 149). Consultees may be lacking in information, skill, or confidence in meeting the professional demands of their everyday life. Physicians, ministers, dormitory counselors, police officers, and teachers are all examples of groups that can benefit tremendously from having a better understanding of some of the mental health aspects of both the typical and atypical psychological problems faced by their patients, parishioners, clients, students, and so forth. In fact, mental health consultation developed primarily out of the recognition of the need for considering the mental health implications of various stress points in life. Ever since Lindemann's (1944) work on natural disasters, psychologists have been more aware of many of the psychological problems associated with various life stresses.

Our illustration of a mental health consultation *begins* with what Caplan (1970) would call an expanded client-centered case consultation, where the "client" was actually all the surgeon's pediatric patients. It was thus initially a triadic model: consultant (psychologist), consultee (pediatric surgeon), and clients (all pediatric patients). Following the assessment stages of this consultation, it became very clear to both the consultant and the consultee that much of the staff of the pediatric service needed to be involved in developing new policies and practices. Therefore, this client-centered mental health consultation appropriately evolved into a program-centered administrative consultation.

The "What will happen to me?" Project

To illustrate the mental health consultation approach, we have chosen a project that took place in a pediatric surgical unit of a major hospital. The problem for this consultation began with a surgeon's concern over how distraught she repeatedly found her young patients before they underwent what she considered relatively routine surgery such as tonsillectomies and appendectomies.

The pediatric surgeon sought out one of the hospital psychologists to find out if there was something she, as the surgeon, could do to reduce the children's anxiety. She was asking for a simple, brief "prescription" that she could obtain by spending 5 minutes with a psychologist and then go back to the wards and never have an anxious patient again! Fortunately, the psychologist was knowledgeable about a number of pertinent areas, including separation effects (Bowlby, 1988) and some of the fears and threats of the unknown that both children and adults experience when facing surgical procedures. He was also aware that many parents deliberately tried to keep the children from thinking about the surgery and hospital and gave them lots of reassurances without much information.

In an initial discussion with the psychologist, the surgeon quickly saw that there was no simple answer, and readily realized the psychologist was talking about a lot of behaviors and issues she had seen in her patients. She invited the psychologist to join her in meeting with some of her patients and becoming familiar with the services on the pediatric ward. In the following weeks, the psychologist spent an increasing amount of time observing both preoperative and postoperative contacts between the surgeon and the patients and their families. The psychologist also came to realize the critical role of the nurses in these cases and spent time getting acquainted with their roles. (The consultant was even invited to observe a surgical procedure but, remembering why he chose psychology rather than medicine, declined.)

Although the many hours the psychologist spent in this "observation phase" are somewhat atypical of mental health consultation, the fact that he did so allowed him to become readily accepted by the surgeon and nurses as a concerned and trustworthy person who saw what their harried professional lives were like. It is absolutely essential that a relationship be established between consultant and consultees whereby they believe the consultant understands the nature of their work if the eventual goal is to have the consultees change something in their styles.

The consultant recommended to the surgeon that the two of them needed to review a variety of possible procedural changes they might make to address the children's anxieties. Given that many of these interventions involved changes in the nurses' routines, he also suggested a subsequent meeting with the nurses to explore the range of possibilities and identify which ones they felt could most readily be incorporated into the hospital's procedures. By including the nurses in the remaining steps, this consultation shifted from a consultee-centered mental health consultation project (with the surgeon as the consultee) to a more program-centered administrative mental health consultation project focused on the pediatric service.

To provide a quick overview of the eventual decisions, the surgeon, interns, residents, and nurses seemed to readily understand how both separation anxiety and lack of information contributed to the children's inordinate anxiety. With the strong leadership of the surgeon, some changes were made in procedures that would allow parents to be with their children for far greater periods of time than before in both the presurgical and recovery periods. The consultant also became involved in preparing a videotape regarding a number of routine surgical procedures, appropriate parts of which could be viewed by children with their families. From the consultant's viewpoint, the most important outcome of his intervention was not those changes in procedures or the videotape, but rather the fact that the surgical team and the nurses were all now aware of the need to provide answers to the children's questions, as much as they could. Often they found the children did not really want many details; they were pleased just to have someone willing to give them some information rather than just dismiss their question with vague reassurances.

Because of a surgeon's request for assistance in dealing with anxious children, an entire team of medical personnel had developed skills in reducing the stress of surgery and helping patients become more involved in their own recovery. Similar kinds of mental health consultations can be used to help police officers deal with rape victims or to help teachers understand how to deal with the effects of a student suicide on the victim's classmates. In all these examples, counseling psychologists as consultants can make significant contributions to both the professional well-being of the consultees and, perhaps most important, to the well-being of the students, clients, patients, and citizens with whom their consultees interact.

Behavioral Consultation

Our next example of consultation is based on behavioral psychology. While the behavioral principles of Skinner (1938) are best known to the general public, the basic concepts underlying this type of response-contingent learning theory go back to Thorndike (1911). In recent decades, several excellent books have been published on the application of these principles to human problems, for example Kanfer and Goldstein (1986) and Kazdin (1994). Both of those books focus on the psychologist as the direct service provider; that is, the psychologist goes into the setting and works directly with the clients, students, or employees to change their behavior. In the behavioral consultation model, however, the consultants work with teachers or supervisors or managers, as consultees, to help them understand the basic behavioral principles pertinent to their situation and to help them design appropriate interventions and evaluation. There are two excellent texts on behavioral consultation: Bergan (1977) and Bergan and Kratochwill (1990).

Our behavioral example of consultation could also be considered a consultee-centered case consultation in that the teacher recognized that he needed to make some changes in his classroom-management strategies. It also illustrates the triadic nature of consultation in that changes are desired for both the consultee (teacher) and the clients (students). It is a behavioral consultation in that behavioral principles guided the nature of the intervention.

The Pizza Reading Project

A teacher assigned to teach a class of seventh-grade "slow learners" contacted the counseling psychology consultant for whatever help she could give him with his unruly class. For the first time, he had been assigned to teach the slow learners, and was finding them disruptive, uncooperative, and stubborn. In addition, the students were performing poorly in all academic areas. The teacher had heard from a colleague how the consultant had assisted another teacher in getting her students to be more attentive in class. This kind of request for consultation is fairly typical in that the consultee (the teacher) describes the problems in terms of internal states of the students; that is, they are stubborn, lazy, unruly, and so forth. The first task of the behavioral consultant is to help the consultee define the problem in terms of actions that can be easily seen and readily measured. Further, as explained in the study of experimental analysis of behavior, it is often easier to begin behavioral consultation projects designed to increase rather than decrease behaviors. Therefore, to help this teacher, the consultant's first interest was in helping the teacher define behaviors that he wanted to see increase in the classroom. The teacher named many such behaviors. However, when he was asked to decide which one was most important to begin with, he readily chose reading. The class's average reading level was at the fourth-grade level and reading was one of the most difficult tasks for many of these students to do for more than a couple of minutes at any one time. The teacher's own creativity had helped him find some other tasks and problem sets he could get the students to work on for as much as 15 to 20 minutes, but in his words, "On a good day, I might be able to have the class read 5 minutes before there are so many disruptions and conversations that further reading is impossible."

Unwittingly, the teacher had given the consultant important information for the next step in a behavioral consultation: identifying measures of behavior. He had standardized measures of the current reading level of each of the students and, although he had not recorded the actual time spent reading, his primary goal was an increase in the number of minutes spent reading. It was easily possible during the following weeks to have the teacher record, for each of the students, how many minutes they spent on a reading assignment before they became distracted and stopped. Such measures, taken at the very beginning of the project, served as baselines against which students' subsequent progress could be evaluated.

The third step for a behavioral consultation project involves establishing contingencies; that is, tying a behavior to a specific outcome that will hopefully change the behavior. The teacher needed to choose some reinforcement that the students would want to work for and that could be offered frequently enough; students should not have to work many days or weeks to earn the reinforcement. The teacher had the misfortune of having the students for the last period of the day. Therefore, his immediate thought was to provide early dismissal as a very potent reinforcement, but he quickly realized that this would create problems for other classes if his students were running around the halls. Early dismissal also was logically unacceptable—he wanted the students to be spending more time working in class, not getting out of class. The teacher felt that the other most powerful reinforcement would be some sort of snack food, noting that it had been a couple of hours since lunch and many of the students could not wait to get out of class to head for the school snack bar. Wanting to avoid the worst of junk foods, the teacher decided that making pizza available (the home economics teacher was willing to loan the microwave oven to the teacher) could meet the requirements of a readily available reinforcer.

For the beginning stages of the project, the plan was kept as simple as possible. The students were informed that for each 5-minute segment of the 15-minute reading period spent reading (or at least staying at their desks and engaging in no side conversations or distractions) they would receive a small sliver of pizza. The teacher could easily daily record the number of minutes each student read. Moreover, the plan benefited from those students who were especially hungry and did not want to be disrupted by other students. Thus, for the first time since the beginning of the year, the teacher had some of the students themselves interested in discouraging other students from disruptive behaviors.

While the project continued for several months and the contingencies were changed to help "phase in" other valuable reinforcers, such as feedback from improvement on tests and more smiles and verbal approval from the teacher, the principles that have been reviewed were not in any way changed. Time spent reading was tied to a specific contingency. By the end of the semester, the teacher was feeling much better about his skills in managing the class. Relative quiet was maintained for the full 20-minute reading period he now included. The students varied immensely, however, as to how much they actually read and understood. Some showed significant gains in reading, others did not but were at least not disrupting other students.

Several observations can be made about both the effectiveness and generalizability of these kinds of approaches. As Rimm and Masters (1979) find in their review, contingency management approaches to reading have frequently been investigated and found to be quite effective, although the results vary somewhat according to the ability level of the students. Moreover, as in this project, a typical side effect of these interventions is that classroom disruption significantly declines. This approach is best implemented in a situation where someone is in control of reinforcements, such as the teacher or, in a business setting, the supervisor or manager. O'Brien, Dickenson, and Rosow (1982) describe a large number of industrial settings where this kind of behavioral approach is directly applicable. Further, Glenwick and Jason (1980) show how this approach can also be useful in community settings where, although no supervisors may be present to observe behavior, outcomes such as saving money or responding to important social issues such as saving energy can be sufficient reinforcers for changing behaviors.

Looking at the project from the perspective of the consultant, it can be seen that the consultant in this situation functioned primarily as an expert, teaching the consultee the principles of behavior management. The consultee then in turn used these principles to enhance his performance in his role. It is probably clear that our example could have focused simply on one individual child in the classroom, which would have been the purest case of the triadic model: consultant, consultee, student. In our example, the third part of the triad was a class. It could have been a particular division of a production company, a sports team, or a nursing home staff. In all of these latter cases, one gains the cost–benefit effects of the pyramid nature of the triad. The consultee, with the expert help of the consultant, is able to affect many other persons in the performance of their roles.

Process Consultation: Consultee-Centered

Our next example illustrates a gradual shift from a focus on helping a director look at what he might do to address morale issues of his employees (consultee-centered administrative consultation) to a focus on the organization and policies of the agency (program-centered administrative consultation). This shift occurred as the process of consultation included the employees in the assessment phase; it became clear the morale issues were more a matter of institutional policies than the behaviors of the director.

He's a Nice Guy, BUT . . .

The young director of a small, residential center for disturbed children contacted us about some morale problems his staff was having. He had heard from one of his employees that we had helped a nursing home staff that had experienced similar problems. First, a bit of agency description. As a residential facility it had three shifts of personnel, largest for the daytime, smallest for night. Night-duty workers were typically college students with the primary responsibility of keeping things quiet between 11 P.M. and 7 A.M. The day shift consisted of one teacher, one social worker, and one recreational therapist, each of whom were assisted by one or two trainees in related university programs. The evening shift had no teachers but had one social worker and a counselor to coordinate various programs run by college student employees who typically were enrolled in majors like special education, recreation, and psychology. A long-standing problem, from the director's perspective, was that each shift felt it was left with residual problems that the previous shift should have handled, ranging from the evening shift faulting the teachers for lack of clarity in homework assignments, to the night shift saying that the evening shift did not have the kids settled down by 11 P.M. "as they were supposed to," to the day shift saying the night shift "didn't control" some of the most obstreperous kids.

Recently, these disagreements had escalated and several threats were being made between employees about getting them fired, filing charges about unethical behavior, and so forth. Over the past 6 months, 60% of the college student employees had quit, one of them saying he did not need "this kind of crap for what you're paying me." The director felt things were getting out of control.

We thought we needed a great deal more information about staff relationships, information we could get only by observing some of the staff at work. We explored the possibilities of having a consulting team member spend a couple of hours on each shift over a period of 4 weeks during which she would also have an opportunity to interview each employee for about 20 minutes. We also asked about whether staff meetings were held and if so, about the opportunity for our team member to sit in on these meetings. Obviously, this kind of preparation for consulting is very expensive, timewise. However, we believed it to be essential before we could know how to proceed to accomplish Schein's first stage of "unfreezing"; that is, providing an atmosphere in which staff member would feel psychologically safe enough to receive feedback about his or her own roles and how they might be changed. From the consultant's observation of staff roles and interviews, two things became clear. First, there was no sense of teamwork within or among the three shifts; within each shift all individuals described certain duties they had and those duties constituted the beginning and end of their jobs. Second, the director was seen as a "nice guy," but one who knew little about how to manage. Staff members were never sure where they stood with him and felt it useless to bring up staff problems since he usually ignored them or said, "Well, we'll have to work on that," and then nothing would happen. Staff meetings were rarely held and usually included only the daytime staff and one or two persons from the evening staff. The director would make announcements, tell staff about some problems he knew about and how he thought they should be handled. Memos were passed on to evening shift and night shift persons as the director thought appropriate.

We proposed to the director a "staff development project" in which there would be late afternoon weekly staff meetings involving the consultant plus most of the staff from all three shifts. A minimum number of staff, plus perhaps some temporary volunteers, could be assigned to cover the residents' programs for the 90 minutes that staff would meet each week. Workers from the day and night shifts would each receive comp time since the meeting was to be held outside of their regular work hours. A total of 16 persons would be at each staff meeting. The consultant outlined a program of problem-exploration strategies, including how to establish group goals and resolve conflicts as well as other team-building exercises (see Johnson & Johnson, 1987). The consultant would act as a "facilitator" for these staff development meetings. By this time in the project, employees had come to know the consultant and felt that she was "really a good listener" and that the proposed plan would probably work. In short, the consultant had established a working relationship that allowed the unfreezing process to occur.

Despite the consultant's worries about the first joint staff meeting being potentially explosive, the combination of team-building exercises and a chance for each staff member to describe "some problems that affect all the work shifts" ended with high positive feelings on the part of the staff. They became aware that more of their problems were shared than they realized (mostly as a result of the consultant asking them to focus on problems that concerned all the work shifts). Once a greater sense of teamwork was established, the staff members felt that they could begin to air some of their more individual concerns without alienating other staff members. Serendipitously, a few staff members also found they had interests and friends in common with other shift employees yet had not previously known this since they had had so little interaction.

Although not all subsequent staff meetings went so well, the eventual outcomes were quite positive. By the end of the 6 weeks of staff meetings, the staff had begun to make plans with the director to hold two staff meetings a month, using the same kind of arrangement they had had during the consultation, so that everyone could attend. Thirty minutes was to be devoted to a "case presentation" dealing with one of the current residents. Staff could then discuss some management issues as well as to try to better understand the causes of the child's behavioral problems. Remaining meeting time would be spent discussing the issues that had been put on the agenda during staff development meetings (a long list from "establishing goals" to "keeping the kitchen clean"). Task forces were to be set up, including representatives from two or more shifts, to address those problems that needed more discussion and planning time than was available at staff meetings. The director's lack of personnel management skills became less problematic as staff assumed responsibility for both identifying and working on problems. The director was also quite pleased because the arrangement freed him to do better what he already did well; that is, keep on top of finances, maintenance, and day-to-day operational details. Thus Schein's second step of changing through "cognitive restructuring" had occurred from the very first through the very last of the 6 weeks of meetings. Staff members had found it helpful to look at their roles and the work environment in different, more constructive ways.

As an interesting follow-up note, a year later the agency expanded their staff meeting agenda to include inservice training topics, bringing in specialists from the university and community to address relevant topics such as diagnosing dyslexia, building self-esteem, and managing self-destructive behavior. The group was also working on ways to have some staff rotate to different shifts so they could get a better feel for what some of the problems were on each shift. At this stage, it can be seen that the process consultation had accomplished Schein's third stage of "refreezing"—that is, integrating the new point of view into the consultees' view of their own roles and their relationships with significant others.

Process Consultation: Program-Centered

The primary goal of the consultation in our next illustration is to develop multiple changes in programs and policy rather than to focus on interpersonal relationships (even though these will be a necessary part of the consultation project). The term *organizational development* is often used for this kind of consultation. Many consultants see all process consultation as part of organizational development. As seen in the previous example, the process consultation that focused on staff relationships also resulted in policy changes. This distinction may at best be a matter of initial emphases. Moreover, it should be noted that organizational development (OD) is a broad term that encompasses far more than just consultation. OD specialists are increasingly full-time employees of large organizations.

Our example also illustrates the conception that the best beginning for OD is a diagnosis based on data collection from various members representing *all* parts of the organization (Baker & Gorman, 1976). To achieve this kind of databased diagnosis we utilized the concepts of environmental assessment. As Huebner and Corazzini (1984) explicate, the person–environment interaction focus of environmental assessment is most congruent with the emphases of counseling psychology. From this perspective, to make improvements in human functioning in any setting, one must assess not only the characteristics of individuals but also their perceptions of the environment in which they find themselves. The results of the environmental assessment are then shared with all divisions of the organization as a basis for planning possible changes in policies. Our illustration has a surprise ending—more on that later.

The Hospital Career Development Project

We were contacted by the personnel director of a large city hospital that specializes in some of the most difficult kinds of surgery and health care. The director was concerned about the high degree of employee turnover at the entry level in many of the technical fields, such as radiology, as well as in most of the service positions, for example, kitchen and custodial workers. Employees had complained about lack of advancement opportunities. The personnel director wanted us, as experts in the area of career development, to tell him how to help employees see more opportunity for advancement within the hospital system. The director spoke of the possibilities for creating a "career development center" to help advise employees as well as establishing some clear "mechanism" within their hiring policies to make clear that there were opportunities for career changes and advancement.

In our first phone discussions with the consultee, we described our need for a better understanding of the 1,000+ employees' concerns about their career development opportunities as well as other aspects of their work that were related to high rates of turnover. (As a side point, it is important to note that we had already done some quick, even if crude, comparisons of their turnover rate to some other major hospitals and found that they did indeed have a slightly higher turnover rate. This factor is an important one to check, for often an organization will talk about its high turnover rate when, because of the nature of the positions or setting, it may actually have a low turnover rate. For example, a nursing home with a yearly turnover rate of 40% would have a good record—many nursing homes have 80%–100% turnovers in staff in a given year!)

The director wanted to go with whatever would work best. We asked to meet with representatives of the workers' groups. The employee representatives were particularly enthusiastic about this strategy and helped us obtain random samples of the employees in each work category to complete the brief questionnaire we designed. The questionnaire focused on the employees' perceptions about opportunities for transfer and promotion within the hospital setting. We also utilized standardized measures of the work environment (Work Environment Scale: Moos, 1981) and job satisfaction (Job Description Index: Smith, Kendall, & Hulin, 1969). We were therefore able to provide the consultee with not only a fairly extensive report of employee concerns with limited opportunity for promotion or transfer but also a description of the employees' perception of an extremely rigid and authoritarian command structure from the top down; that is, from the hospital director through ward and section administration. While there was respect for the management's emphasis on efficiency and competency in this highly specialized hospital, these emphases seemed to preclude any attention to or caring for human needs, for example, some variation in job roles, occasional flexibility of workshifts, and inviting employee input on how to improve the environment. "Show up on time, never question the orders, and get out of here as soon as possible" was a typical employee description of their attitude toward the hospital.

As is our usual style, we sent our written statement to the consultee and set up a time to meet with him and the various employee group representatives after they had had a chance to read the report (a procedure we had all agreed to in the initial phase). The project then came to an abrupt end! After the consultee—that is, the personnel director—had read the report, he shared it with the hospital director. He informed him about our planned meeting in which we intended to look at what the results of the environmental assessment could tell us about possible policy changes that would address employee concerns. The hospital director was infuriated on two counts: First, it was his understanding that the personnel office was working with us to explore "the possibility of setting up a career development office, not to make a survey of employee morale." He did not want anyone in the hospital to know of the report's findings regarding morale. Second, the hospital director made clear—for the first time, in the view of the personnel director—that the two of them had very different views about potential possibilities for change in the organization. Whereas the personnel director was familiar with concepts such as job enrichment and the importance of opportunities for horizontal or vertical mobility, the hospital director's view was that this was a highly technical agency that required much specialized training; therefore, there would be few if any opportunities for horizontal mobility and "there [would be] ample opportunity for *good* people to move up within their own specialties." If high turnover was the price that had to be paid to have appropriately trained people, then so be it.

The personnel director had gotten caught in the same problem that many of the employees had—he was trying to do something beyond his immediate job description of simply keeping the personnel office running. In retrospect, we wondered whether we might be faulted for not having included contact with someone higher up in the administrative structure from the beginning of the project. However, we reminded ourselves that in the large organization we were working with, the director of the personnel office was only one step removed from the top and that (1) he genuinely believed that he had support of the director to proceed as we were and, (2) in large organizations it is unusual for consultants to work directly with the very top executive. While our project failed in "organizational development"—that is, no changes were made in formal policy—we include it for its usefulness in identifying both the public (in this case, concerns over lack of career mobility) and hidden (in this case, authoritarian structure and poor morale) agenda with which an organization must deal. Schein (1987) provides other examples where consultation results in information about the organization that is unanticipated and highly uncomfortable. Organizational development, as Schein uses the term, can take place only when administrators are open to recognizing both the positive and negative aspects of their organization.

Environmental assessment approaches to organizational development can have successful conclusions. In one example particularly relevant for counseling psychologists, Daher, Corazzini, and McKinnon (1977) were consultants to a residence hall where a large number of students had made complaints about the living conditions to the resident assistant, who in turn described the students as frustrating and belligerent. Using both standardized and specially developed environmental assessment measures, the consultants found significant concerns raised over the issues of privacy, noise, involvement, support, intellectuality, organization, and order. After the results were reported to the residents, there was a greater acknowledgment by them of some of these difficulties. They agreed among themselves to appoint committees to develop quiet hours and other programs to develop mutual respect. When the residents took part in completing questionnaires at a later time, significant improvements were noted on resident involvement, academic achievement, and support.

STAGES AND PROCESSES IN CONSULTATION

Brown and colleagues (1998) describe eight stages of consultation that must be considered in any consultation project. (See Table 19.1.) Whether it is a triadic- or process-oriented intervention, focused on cases or consultees or organizations, or based on behavioral or organizational principles, these eight stages (some consultants call them steps; Burke [1994] calls them "phases") provide a template for looking at consultant skills needed and issues to be addressed. The order in which we present the stages is the most typical order; however, in actual practice there may be considerable back-and-forth movement and redoing of any of stages two through eight. Moreover, at any given time, it is likely that the consultant will be working simultaneously on two or more adjacent stages. While Brown et al. (1998) devote a full chapter to defining and illustrating each of the eight stages, we provide only brief descriptions in order to capture the essence of the stage and, at least implicitly, indicate those skills and characteristics of counseling psychologists which enable them to serve as effective consultants.

Stage 1—Entry into the Organization: This stage is in many ways similar to the establishment of a relationship with a client. In addition to the necessary formal contractual steps (well-delineated by Galessich [1982]), there is a need for establishing a high degree of trust between the consultee and the consulting counseling psychologist. Obviously, counseling psychologists' listening skills, and willingness to develop a careful plan before rushing into action, are fundamental in this stage.

Stage 2—Initiation of a Consulting Relationship: This stage in consultation is similar to the development of a working alliance with an individual client.

Stages and Processes in Consultation. TABLE 19.1.

Stage	Goals
Entry Into the Organization	Establish trust, clarify contractual issues
Initiation of a Consulting Relationship	Developing a collaborative relationship, establishing confidentiality
Assessment	Assessment of client, consultee, and environmental characteristics
Problem Definition and Goal-Setting	Developing comprehensive definition of the problem, introduce problem-solving strategies
Strategy Selection	Collaborative selection of appropriate strategy, defining responsibilities within that strategy
Strategy Implementation	Maintain close communication, modify strategy as unforeseen developments occur
Evaluation	Conduct both formative evaluation (during strategy implementation) and summative evaluation (at completion of consulting contract)
Termination	Transfer of responsibilities, disengagement of consultant

However, in consultation, in addition to developing a working alliance, one ideally develops "an egalitarian relationship characterized by open communication between the consultant and consultee, collaboration between the consultant and consultee at each phase of consultation, and confidentiality of all communication" (Brown et al., 1998, p. 110). Further, this stage needs to allow for agreements to be reached not only for how the consultant and consultee will work together, but also for what will be expected of each throughout all the remaining stages. All too many consultation projects are terminated prematurely because the consultee—even though liking and trusting the consultant—lacked a clear understanding of his or her responsibilities for later stages of the project.

Stage 3—Assessment: Assessment in consultation goes far beyond identification of the problems of the consultees and/or their "clients." Brown and colleagues (1998) usefully list several pertinent questions for each of four separate and important domains of assessment for consultants: (a) client characteristics, (b) consultee characteristics, (c) environmental characteristics—immediate environment, and (d) environmental characteristics—larger environment. One addresses the first two largely in terms of behavioral and cognitive factors, the last two largely in terms of structural and cultural issues. For assessment in consultation, observational methods of assessment are more critical than use of standardized measures; an understanding of environmental assessment techniques (see Chapter 13) is also fundamental.

Stage 4—Problem Definition and Goal Setting: This step is really a matter of achieving an accurate, more comprehensive definition of the problem than the "presenting problem." The process in this stage is somewhat analogous to finding the problem that underlies a client's symptoms; that is, even after a diagnosis is made of a client's psychological problem, client and counselor need to develop a mutual understanding of what is causing the problem and how to proceed to address it.

Similarly, in consultation, the consultant must help the consultee understand problem-solving strategies (Heppner & Krauskopf, 1987). Brown et al. (1998) review the evidence that indicates that "short circuiting" this step—that is, moving immediately to "solve" the problem as the consultee initially defines it, in contrast to exploring a variety of perspectives on the problem and options for dealing with it—characterizes the work of those consultants who are rated as least skilled.

Stage 5—Strategy Selection: Just as any one problem in counseling can be treated with a variety of strategies, so too can any one problem in consultation. The critical issue for counseling psychologists as consultants is the emphasis on collaborative functioning; both consultant and consultee, after exploration of applicable strategies, need to agree on the appropriateness of a chosen strategy and the responsibilities that the choice creates for the consultee. Brown and colleagues (1998) review research showing how this agreement is often influenced by a variety of consultant, consultee, treatment, and client variables. All of these variables need to be considered in understanding how best to achieve a mutually satisfactory strategy selection. Once again, counseling psychologists' skills in exploration, listening, and patience in reaching a decision are all critical in this stage.

Stage 6—Strategy Implementation: As in counseling, implementation is the longest and most unpredictable stage of consultation. An added factor in consultation is that this stage is the first that moves beyond primarily consultant–consultee interactions. Now the "clients" (students, patients, employees, etc.) are all involved at some level, adding to the unpredictability. Consequently, even though the consultee may have a good understanding of how to implement the chosen strategy, unforeseen developments are bound to occur. Therefore, the counseling psychologist as consultant needs to maintain close communication with the consultee throughout implementation, always prepared to be a highly supportive, empathic listener, as well as advisor on how to modify, if necessary, any part of the chosen strategy.

Stage 7—Evaluation: Once again, just as a good counselor evaluates, with a client, progress both during and at the end of the relationship, so too do consultants conduct what Brown et al. (1998) call "formative" evaluation during implementation of a chosen strategy and "summative" evaluation at the completion of the consulting contract. Formative evaluation during the implementation could well result in a return to an earlier stage if, for example, some other kinds of assessment seem to be needed, or a different or additional strategy employed. Most critically, consultants must regularly initiate such formative evaluation since consultees will seldom initiate this unless the implementation is in a "crisis" state. Summative evaluation is in one sense the equivalent of an outcome evaluation in counseling. However, the difference in consulting is that outcomes are to be determined not only for the consultee, but also for the "clients" of the consultee. Consultees are often somewhat resistant to having their clients assessed; however, if the consultee is really to understand the *effects of*—not just his or her satisfaction with—the consultation, data must be obtained at least indirectly, if not directly, from "clients." All experienced consultants agree that the nature of the data to be collected from clients at all stages of the consultation, from assessment through summative evaluation, needs to be clearly specified at stages 2–4. Specific decisions need to be made during those early stages about which questionnaires or instruments might be used and/or behavioral observations made, and by whom, at all later stages. Brown and colleagues (1998) provide a description of nine different instruments that can be used, or at least readily modified, for almost any consultation project.

Stage 8—Termination: The following concise advice for termination of consultation is essentially identical to the steps in effective termination in counseling:

> First, consultants may gradually transfer responsibilities to the consultees. This transfer of responsibility signals the consultant's exit and also prevents an abrupt change upon departure of the consultant that can be disruptive to consultees. Second, consultants should openly discuss their impending departure, validate consultees' success, and encourage them to continue on their own. Third, a disengagement period where the consultant reduces his or her involvement on a trial basis may give consultees a chance to see if the problem is resolved or if he or she can make needed changes without consultant input. Lastly, rituals, such as a summary conference, a request that the consultee fill out an evaluation form, or a formal review of case, can help signal or remind consultees that the end of consultation is imminent (Brown et al., 1998, p. 122).

CONSULTANT CHARACTERISTICS AND SKILLS: QUINTESSENCE OF COUNSELING PSYCHOLOGISTS

In all of the eight stages of consultation just described, we noted many skills of counselors that are directly applicable. Effective listening skills and trust building are essential at every stage; effective use of empathy and support are critical for developing and maintaining a working alliance with the consultee throughout the assessment through termination stages. In short, the characteristics and skills of a well-trained counselor are the essential fundamentals for a consultant. While the literature on additional critical consultant characteristics and skills is based largely on the views of experts in organization development (Brown et al., 1998; Burke, 1994) compared to empirical research on successful consultants, there is ready agreement among such experts on the need also for multicultural sensitivity (see later section in this chapter) as well as one additional characteristic: self-efficacy.

Consultants, even more than counselors, need to be able to communicate a clear sense of their own self-efficacy as consultants, exhibiting a self-confidence that they can help the consultee take the risks to make any changes that are agreed on as needed. Consultees are typically (1) in less pain than clients (at least, pain they will acknowledge), and (2) less willing than clients to put themselves "in the hands" of a professional. Whereas counselors often have to work with clients to take on more responsibility themselves and depend less on the counselor, consultants often have to build a consultee's trust to work collaboratively with the consultant, rather than merely receiving advice and running with it. Consultants who can communicate both a knowledge of what is needed and a confidence that consultant–consultee collaboration can be productive is a key characteristic that counseling psychologists need for effective consulting relationships.

IMPEDIMENTS TO EFFECTIVE CONSULTATION

Ever since the late 1970s, various authors have lamented the limited number of consultation services offered by most counseling psychologists (Conyne & O'Neil, 1992; Kandell, 1988; Magoon & McDermott, 1979). The first authors do note that there has been a significant increase in the amount of literature on consultation, but no new empirical evidence of increased levels of consultation activity by *most* counseling psychologists, even though there are now a number of recent leaders of the profession of counseling psychology who have developed full-time consulting practices (e.g., Arredondo, 1996). Why the lag between recommendations and actual practice? There are at least two major factors: (1) some inherent characteristics in the process of consultation, and (2) a long-standing and remaining gap between the necessary versus actual kinds of training in consultation typically provided in counseling psychology training programs.

Inherent Characteristics of Consultation

Conyne and O'Neil (1992) provide the most concise list of barriers to effectiveness inherent in the process of consultation: consultee resistance, complex circumstances, and professional isolation. In addition to all the factors that lead to client resistance in traditional counseling, consultees often have to deal with not only their own resistance (threats of change, threats to their own self-efficacy as managers), but also with the resistance of their "clients"; that is, the students, employees, patients, and so on, for whom they are responsible. Some clients may well try to sabotage new interventions by the consultee, increasing threats to the self-efficacy of the consultee. Additionally, the executive to whom the consultee reports (e.g., the president, CEO) might withhold support for the changes that the consultant and consultee have agreed are needed. In short, consultees have to deal not only with resistance from their own personal dynamics, but also possibly resistance from their "clients" and "bosses." Both Arredondo (1996) and Brown et al. (1998) provide an extensive array of strategies for coping with various sources of resistance in consultation.

Because the broader kinds of consultation we have discussed in this chapter involve "clients" as well as the consultee and his or her superiors, there are greatly increased complexities to deal with compared to individual counseling. Consultation is aimed at changing an environment, not just an individual; therefore, there are many more variables to confront. Moreover, implementing change in environments typically requires many more months of time than individual counseling and therefore greatly increases the likelihood of unpredictable events. As noted in the discussion of the stages of consultation, the consultant must always be ready to move back and forth between stages, oftentimes redoing entire stages because of the development of new events.

Consultants usually work alone; this factor leads to even greater threats of professional isolation than for the counselor in independent practice for two reasons. Because consultation interventions develop very slowly there is often very little positive feedback during the initial stages and the consultant may well question whether he or she can be successful. There may also be the discomforting contrast that the consultee, and possibly some of the "clients," see the consultant as a "savior" whereas other "clients" see the consultant as an intruder: welcomed and shunned in the same setting! Both of these factors can lead to a heightened sense of professional isolation. Although the expense of having two consultants work on the same project is often prohibitive, co-consulting is an excellent way to address these issues. In training programs, experienced consultants can often have advanced-level trainees as their co-consultant as a way of not increasing expenses yet providing both the senior consultant with a colleague and the junior consultant with valuable experience.

Gap Between Necessary and Actual Consultation Training and Practice

Conyne and O'Neil (1992) devote an entire chapter to the long-standing gap between the kinds of training that should be provided, versus what is typically provided, for preparing counseling psychologists as effective consultants. They support their concerns with extensive citations from surveys of training practices. We believe their concerns can be captured in two major points. First, the knowledge bases that are typically provided in counseling psychology programs compared to those that are needed for effective consultation; second, the extensiveness and intensiveness of supervised training experience.

Although there are great overlaps between the skills needed for counseling and those needed for consulting, there are also some unique bases of knowledge needed for effective consulting that are often not included in the curriculum for individual counseling. Personality theory, for example, is far less important for consulting than is the theory of organizational development (Schein, 1987, 1990). Environmental assessment (see Chapter 13) is also a key component for consultation yet is at best often only minimally covered in many training programs. Effective consulting also requires a broader knowledge of problem-solving strategies (Heppner & Krauskopf, 1987) than does traditional individual counseling. Burke (1994) provides an excellent description of the kinds of courses one needs to achieve competence as an organization development consultant. While much of what he recommends can be found in many counseling psychology programs, in some universities the relevant courses can be found only in business colleges. In sum, the knowledge bases that are needed are well known; what is required is that counseling psychology students have the opportunity to supplement their traditional counselor training with appropriate coursework electives to prepare for effectiveness as consultants.

Regarding the second concern—that of extensiveness and intensiveness of supervised experience—surveys of counselor training indicate quite minimal expectations for supervised training in consultation (Conyne & O'Neil, 1992). Thus most new doctoral-level counseling psychologists enter the profession with neither intensive nor extensive supervised experience in consultation despite the fact that the chief administrators of many psychological service agencies see the need for greater amounts of such services. These deficiencies in supervised training are particularly ironic since consultation provides perhaps the greatest threats to perceived self-efficacy of counseling psychologists; yet, as described in our section on essential characteristics, a high degree of self-efficacy is critical for effective functioning as a consultant. While many counseling psychologists in training perceive threats to their self-efficacy as they move from individual to, for example, group or career counseling, the move to consulting involves greater changes and complexity than either group or career counseling. Our consultation supervisees tell us that in consultation these threats are more pervasive and longer lasting. Conyne and O'Neil rightly conclude,

> Ideally, practicum and internship experiences in consultation should be accorded the same status enjoyed by the "bread and butter" delivery systems of counseling and psychotherapy or of testing and assessment. Consultation competencies learned in training must be exercised in real settings with real cases, under watchful and qualified on-site and university supervision (Conyne & O'Neil, 1992, p. 6).

MULTICULTURAL COMPETENCE IN CONSULTING

All of the kinds of value and worldview differences discussed in Chapter 6 come into play in consultation in even more extensive ways than in individual counseling. In the 1980s, several authors (e.g., Gibbs, 1980; Pinto, 1981) explored the kinds of culturally insensitive strategies that oftentimes led to failure even when both consultant and consultee had good intentions. There are two major areas where problems frequently occur: establishing trust between consultant and consultee, and value differences between the consultant and the "clients" of the consultee.

Consultees who differ in cultural background from the consultant may well enter the relationship with increased tentativeness. Does the consultant, even though an expert, interact in condescending and subordinating ways with the consultee? While such a relationship is never desirable in the egalitarian view of consultation, it is even more damaging in a cross-cultural situation, preventing the development of both trust and true collaboration. Is the consultant interested in how the culture of the consultee might affect the options to be considered and strategies to be implemented? Once again, if the consultee does not perceive the consultant as culturally empathic, no matter how many good ideas the consultant has, there may be very limited collaboration from the consultee.

Even if there are few value differences between the consultant and the consultee, there may well be extensive value differences between the consultee and his or her "clients." When trying to implement changes in organizational policies and programs, a major problem often occurs in deciding which incentives will be necessary for "clients" to change. The Eurocentric thinking that prevails in much of our educational system may well lead to faulty assumptions about what will motivate change. Arredondo (1996) spells out some of the problems caused by the dominating influences of competition and individuality in U.S. organizations. In some cultures, individuals are socialized to promote a collective orientation for the community; the last "reward" a person from such a culture wants is to be named as "employee of the month." Such a "reward" to them may denigrate their coworkers. As Arredondo (1996) points out, managing diversity in the contemporary workplace often means greater attention to teamwork and cooperation than to competitive individuality.

By the 1990s several excellent books and articles appeared to guide both the theory and practice of multicultural consultation (Arredondo, 1996; Sue, 1995; Sue, Carter, Casas et al., 1998). These authors address not only the fundamental strategies for being a culturally empathic consultant, but also the importance of, and strategies for, assessing the culture of the environment in which one is consulting, no matter what the degree of cultural difference between the consultant and the "client" environment (Schein, 1990).

UNIQUE ETHICAL PROBLEMS IN CONSULTING

While Gallessich (1982), Robinson and Gross (1985), Newman (1993), and Brown et al. (1998) all have outlined a large number of ethical concerns regarding consultation activities, we agree with Lowman (1985) that, with a few exceptions, these issues are largely extensions of many of the ethical issues already reviewed in Chapter 5. The consultation situation, by virtue of the numbers of persons involved and the complexities of the interactions with so many different levels of the organization, may increase the *probability* of ethical conflicts but most are not substantively different. For example, in both individual counseling and consultation, the counseling psychologist may be forced to deal with issues of radically different value orientations. In individual counseling, how does the counselor proceed in working with a client who has radically different views about abortion than the counselor? Analogously, how does the consultant proceed when asked to work with an organization where the management is seen as far more coercive and authoritarian than the consultant believes essential or with an organization that has a long record of being insensitive to minorities? A consultant may become aware of ethical or illegal activities on the part of some of the employees or perhaps even the consultee. Again, the choices and issues are essentially no different than when learning about illegal or unethical behavior on the part of a client in individual counseling. Similarly, consultants may receive inappropriate requests from a consultee to "shade" the data to support a particular viewpoint; individual counselors have certainly had clients ask for similar "shadings" when written reports have to be prepared and sent to an agency administrator.

There are, however, at least three issues that are arguably qualitatively different in consulting. Even beginning consultants should be aware of these unique ethical dilemmas so that the potential problems they present may be prevented or at least minimized. The first of these is most succinctly worded as "Who is the client?" This question needs to be asked in terms of ethical principles regarding rights of the client, including confidentiality. While the easy immediate answer is that the consultee is the client, the problem quickly becomes evident when two related questions are considered. First, who has to give consent for providing interviews or completing questionnaires or surveys as part of the data collection? An individual client responds only for himself or herself and can give full consent. However, in consultation, is it appropriate for the consultee to give consent for his or her students or employees or supervisees to allow the consultant access to employee or student records? How do laws regarding invasion of privacy affect the relationship between the consultant and the employees or students? Second, who owns the information and data that are collected? The consultee who is paying the consultant may feel that he or she has the right to ask for either any questionnaires or surveys that employees filled out or for any notes taken in interviews. How does the consultant protect the confidentiality of the people interviewed or surveyed even though they are not clients? Obviously, these issues must be addressed as part of the contract negotiation for consultation; unfortunately, unless consultants are aware of such issues, they may not address them in initial negotiations and later find themselves in difficult dilemmas in trying to protect the "hidden clients" in the consultation situation.

Newman (1993) identifies a second unique issue: power differentials. By that she means that the ability to influence others is not evenly distributed among members of an organization. Ideally, this issue is not any misuse of power by the consultant, who may have at least implicit, if not explicit, greater power than the consultee. The concerns are more with consultees' abuse or misuse of power they have over their "clients"; that is, employees, students, patients. Care must be taken so that even well-intentioned consultees do not use their status and power to ignore the rights of their "clients" for the "good of the organization." Newman (1993) makes the case for focusing on empowerment as perhaps the best strategy for reducing potential power abuses.

A final ethical concern seems somewhat less significant but can be equally troublesome and deserves careful thought. In the examples at the beginning of this chapter, certain teachers or supervisors or residence halls were generating a significant number of problems. It seems obvious that one might suggest that they invite a consultant to help them. Unlike most counseling where the clients request services, in suggesting a consultation project to a person or agency, it can be construed as solicitation; that is, trying to get them to buy services. Clearly, in the interest of developing prevention compared to remedial services, counseling psychologists want to *inform* persons of the possibilities of some relevant consultation activities; however, care must be taken to ensure that presentations stay more on the informing side than on the solicitation side no matter how strongly one feels about the appropriateness and importance of a consultation intervention.

CONSULTING AS THE PREFERRED INTERVENTION

In this closing section of our introductory text on counseling psychology, we explore how arguments for consulting as the *preferred* psychological intervention are challenged by the sobering empirical realities of research on consultation. We then describe how these consultation research realities provide exciting, even if difficult challenges for counseling psychologists as scientist–practitioners.

As discussed earlier in this chapter, administrators of clinics and counseling centers have long argued for greatly increased consultation and outreach services. Ideally, they propose, such services both enhance the quality of life in the communities they serve as well as reduce the need for costly remedial services. In this cost-conscious era of industrialized health care, many "wellness" programs are being developed to address better psychological, as well as physical, health. Counseling psychologists serve largely as consultants in the development of such "wellness" programs. The programs are typically then conducted by master's-level or paraprofessional health care professionals. Administrative leaders also suggest that highly effective consulting and preventive interventions should be the *primary* services of psychologists. Just as the effects of dentists' cavity-prevention programs have greatly reduced the need for costly dental services in recent years, effective psychological "wellness" programs should greatly reduce the need for extensive counseling and psychotherapy.

While the logic of consultation as the preferred intervention of counseling psychologists has good face validity, there is little empirical data to support such a position. What is readily available is much evidence of consultees' satisfaction with consultation as well as reasonable amounts of evidence that organizational procedures and policies have changed in accordance with the recommendations developed in consultation projects (Conyne & O'Neil, 1992; Dustin & Blocher, 1984; Mannimo & Shore, 1975). Such results are of course often quite satisfying to the administrators who paid for the consultation and lead to increased business for consultants. However, there have been no large-scale studies conducted to show that, in the years following consultation projects, there is less need for remedial services. Note that it is not a matter of negative evidence that the consulting did not work, but rather that consulting projects have simply typically not included any kind of long-term follow-up of "clients" and their needs for psychological services. Unfortunately, as repeatedly noted by Brown and colleagues (1998), all too few of the excellent consultation research recommendations of Meade, Hamilton, and Yuen (1982) have been implemented.

Counseling psychologists, as scientists–practitioners, might be considered the ideal professionals to conduct the critical research needed regarding the purported more extensive and longer lasting effects of consultation. There are two types of research that psychologists have already conducted in other areas of psychological interventions that now need to be applied to a study of the effects of consultation. "Medical offset" research (see Chapter 4) is closely related to the need for demonstrating the cost effectiveness of consultation. In traditional medical offset research, the goal is to demonstrate that psychological intervention reduces the need for seeing physicians and that the savings from lower physician costs more than pays for the costs of psychological intervention. In the case of consultation, the question that needs to be addressed is whether, in the months and years following a consultation project that, for example, addresses employee stress and morale, there are fewer absences from work, turnover, and fewer referrals for psychological services. Do the savings from these changes in employees' behavior save as much money as the consultation cost; that is, do the savings offset the consultation costs?

Size effect determinations of both personal counseling and career counseling (see Chapter 15) are a second example of the kind of research that is needed regarding the effects of consultation. What is the size effect of consulting interventions? None have yet been published. Both offset and size effect studies of consultation will, granted, be more difficult to conduct than those completed on more traditional interventions. Most consultants agree that it may be extremely difficult to have a consulting contract accepted that requires repeated assessment from the "clients" of the consultee. However, in some cases, offset research could be completed by simply tracking institutional data on numbers of persons seeking treatment subsequent to a consultation project. For example, if a consultation project is conducted with freshmen in one large university resident hall, with the intervention focused on improving interpersonal communication, time and stress management, and conflict reduction, a comparison can be made over the next 4 years of residents in this hall, compared to those in other university residence halls, as to their requests for roommate changes, their academic performance, their involvement in any university disciplinary actions, their requests for counseling, and so forth. All such data could be collected from institutional records and allow for at least an approximation of savings to both professional services on the campus as well as to students if they move more efficiently toward graduation and therefore have to be enrolled for fewer semesters.

An example of how data might be obtained that could contribute to the size effect literature may be found in the hospital career development project we described earlier in this chapter. Even though the project was never completed because of the hospital director's concerns, it did initially include data collection from large numbers of employees at the beginning of the project, regarding their work environment and personal concerns. If the project could have been carried to completion, pre–post data from the employees could have been computed, contributing to size effect literature on the results of consultation. Additionally, data from the personnel office on employee turnover would have allowed an assessment of cost–offset. Unfortunately, very few consultation projects include both pre- and postdata from "clients" of a consultee; even readily available institutional data are seldom tracked to compute offset costs.

There is one factor to be noted that may make it difficult to obtain significant offset and size effect results. Consultation projects often extend over months or even years (see examples in Conyne & O'Neil [1992]). Much occurs in the lives of "clients" outside the setting of the consultation project, all factors that may affect the amount of any change related to the consultation intervention. Needless to say, conducting the needed evaluations of consultation presents perhaps the most difficult challenge we have described for counseling psychologists as scientists–practitioners; difficult, yes; impossible, no.

We now come of the end of our exploration of the profession of counseling psychology. Just within this chapter on consultation we have seen the enormous potential of the profession for addressing major social and organizational issues as well as personal problems; we have reviewed both accomplishments and ongoing challenges for counseling psychologists as scientist–professionals in their development of a wide range of developmental, preventive, and remedial intervention strategies. Consultation may be viewed as both a preferred intervention and as a synthesis of all the key roles of counseling psychologists as scientist–practitioners.

SUMMARY

Consultation is one of counseling psychology's most cost-effective strategies for implementing preventive, remedial, and developmental services. With a focus on helping others become more effective in their service roles in all types of organizations from families to hospitals to businesses, consultants assist not only their consultees but, more important, potentially all those for whom the consultees have responsibility. Consultation is most congruent with counseling psychology's theme of working with intact persons' assets and strengths with special attention to person–environment interactions.

From among the numerous kinds of consultation that have been described four major types were illustrated in this chapter. What are often called triadic models involving a consultant, consultee, and "client" were illustrated by one based on behavioral principles and another based on mental health consultation. In both illustrations, instead of one person as a client, the "client" was a group of individuals (i.e., a class or pediatric surgery patients), illustrating the unique cost–benefit aspects of consultation.

Two examples of process consultation (now often called organization development) were provided. The first was initially focused on improving relationships between a director and his staff (consultee-centered); the second was designed to help a hospital develop new agency policies on career development (program-centered). In contrast to the first two examples of consultation in this chapter, which were both more in the traditional triadic mode where the consultant worked primarily with the consultee, in our process consultation examples, the consultants worked extensively with employees from many parts of the organization.

Whatever the type of consultation, the skills of counseling psychologists provide a basic foundation for each of eight stages we describe that are typically involved in any type of consultation. These skills, such as empathy, building trust, supporting and nurturing, must be supplemented as well by multicultural sensitivity and high levels of consultant self-efficacy.

We described three inherent characteristics of consultation that often make it far more challenging than individual counseling: multifaceted sources of resistance, unpredictable events from complex circumstances, and professional isolation. In order to be prepared to cope with these three challenges, as well as how to practice the kinds of skills identified in the previous paragraph, counseling psychology students must develop a knowledge base in organizational dynamics as well as receive supervised experiential training in consultation.

In recent years, as our country has become more culturally diverse, consultants have come to realize the importance of perceived power differences, worldview differences, and the components of culturally sensitive assessments. Counseling psychologists have been the most prominent writers to address the cultural sensitivities in consultation. Consultation also presents some unique ethical dilemmas: Who is the "client" of the consultant—the consultee, or his or her clients (employees, students, patients)? his or her supervisor? Who all must give "informed consent" before completing needs assessment measures? A second ethical issue relates to power differentials: What is the consultant to do if the consultee, even with good intentions, wants to implement procedures that override the rights of employees? Finally, consultants often have the opportunity to observe dysfunctional aspects of organizations for which no help is being requested. How does the counseling psychologist proceed in such situations? Fortunately, experienced counseling psychology consultants have provided valuable guidelines to deal with such issues.

Our final section described how the challenges of conducting and evaluating consultation call for a synthesis of the highest level of the scientist and practitioner aspects of counseling psychology. Going beyond simply evaluating the immediate consultation impact on an organization, counseling psychologists serving as consultants in the twenty-first century have the unique opportunity of evaluating the cost "offset" and "size effects" of consultation interventions.

REFERENCES

Arredondo, P. (1996). *Successful diversity management initiatives*. Thousand Oaks, CA: Sage Publications.

Baker, H. K., & Gorman, R. H. (1976). Diagnosis: Key to O.D. effectiveness. *Personnel Journal, 55,* 506–510.

Bergan, J. R. & Kratochwill, T. R. (1990). *Behavioral consultation and therapy*. New York: Plenum Press.

Bowlby, J. (1973). *Attachments and loss. Vol. 2. Separation, anxiety and anger.* New York: Basic Books.

Bowlby, J. (1988). *A secure base: Parent–child attachments and healthy human development.* New York: Basic Books.

Brown, D., Pryzwansky, W. B., & Schulte, A. C. (1998). *Psychological consultation* (4th ed.). Boston: Allyn & Bacon.

Burke, W. W. (1994). *Organization development* (2nd ed.). Reading, MA: Addison-Wesley.

Caplan, G. (1970). *The theory and practice of mental health consultation.* New York: Basic Books.

Conyne, R. K., & O'Neil, J. M. (Eds.). (1992). *Organizational consultation: A casebook.* Thousand Oaks, CA: Sage Publications.

Daher, D. M., Corazzini, J. G., & McKinnon, R. D. (1977). An environmental redesign for residence halls. *Journal of College Student Personnel, 18*(1), 11–15.

Dustin, D., & Blocher, D. H. (1984). Theories and models of consultation. In S. D. Brown and R. W. Lent (Eds.), *Handbook of counseling psychology* (pp. 751–781). New York: John Wiley & Sons.

Gallessich, J. (1982). *The profession and practice of consultation.* San Francisco: Jossey-Bass.

Gibbs, J. T. (1980). The interpersonal orientation in mental health consultation: Toward a model of ethnic variation in consultations. *Journal of Community Psychology, 8,* 195–207.

Glenwick, D., & Jason, L. (Eds.). (1980). *Behavioral community psychology.* New York: Praeger.

Heppner, P. P., & Krauskopf, C. J. (1987). An information-processing approach to personal problem solving. *The Counseling Psychologist, 15,* 371–447.

Huebner, L. A., & Corazzini, J. G. (1984). Environmental assessment and intervention: In S. D. Brown and R. W. Lent (Eds.), *Handbook of counseling psychology* (pp. 579–621). New York: John Wiley & Sons.

Johnson, D. W., & Johnson, F. P. (1987). *Joining together* (3rd ed.). Englewood Cliffs, NJ: Prentice-Hall.

Kandell, J. (1988). *Availability and desirability of candidates' skills for doctoral level counseling center positions: Ten year comparison.* Unpublished master's thesis, University of Maryland, College Park.

Kanfer, F. H., & Goldstein, A. P. (Eds.). (1986). *Helping people change* (3rd ed.). New York: Pergamon Press.

Kazdin, A. E. (1994). *Behavior modification in applied settings* (5th ed.). Monterey, CA: Brooks-Cole.

Lindemann, E. (1944). Symptomatology and management of acute grief. *American Journal of Psychology, 101,* 141–149.

Lowman, R. L. (1985). Ethical practice of psychological consultation. *The Counseling Psychologist, 13,* 466–472.

Magoon, T., & McDermott, M. (1979). Availability and desirability of various skills and candidates for positions in counseling centers: A replication. *Journal of Counseling Psychology, 26,* 169–172.

Mannimo, E. V., Trickett, E. J., Shore, M. F., Kidder, M. G., & Levine, G. (Eds.). (1986). *Handbook of mental health consultation.* Washington, DC: U.S. Government Printing Office. (DHHS Publication No. ADM 86-1446)

Mannimo, F. P., & Shore, M. F. (1975). The effects of consultation: A review of empirical studies. *American Journal of Community Psychology, 3,* 1–21.

Meade, C. J., Hamilton, M. K., & Yuen, R. (1982). Consultation research: The time has come, the walrus said. *The Counseling Psychologist, 10*(4), 39–51.

Moos, R. H. (1981). *Work Environment Scale.* Palo Alto, CA: Counseling Psychologists Press.

Newman, J. L. (1993). Ethical issues in consultation. *Journal of Counseling and Development, 72,* 148–156.

O'Brien, R. M., Dickenson, A. M., & Rosow, M. (Eds.). (1982). *Industrial modification: A learning based approach to industrial organization problems.* New York: Pergamon Press.

Pace, T. M., Chaney, J. M., Mullins, L. L., & Olson, R. A. (1995). Psychological consultation with primary care physicians: Obstacles and opportunities in the medical setting. *Professional Psychology: Research and Practice, 26,* 123–131.

Pinto, R. F. (1981). Consultant orientations and client system perceptions: Styles of cross-cultural consultation. In R. Lippitt and G. Lippitt (Eds.), *Systems thinking: A resource for organization diagnosis and intervention.* (pp. 159–178) Washington, DC: International Consultants Foundation.

Rimm, D.C., & Masters, J.C. (1979). *Behavior therapy.* New York: Academic Press.

Robinson, S. E., & Gross, D. R. (1985). Ethics of consultation: The Canterville Ghost. *The Counseling Psychologist, 13,* 444–465.

Schein, E. H. (1987). *Process consultation.* Vol. 2. Reading, MA: Addison-Wesley.

Schein, E. H. (1990). Organizational culture. *American Psychologist, 45,* 109–119.

Skinner, B. F. (1938). *The behavior of organisms: An experimental analysis.* New York: Appleton.

Smith, P. C., Kendall, L. M., & Hulin, C. I. (1969). *The measurement of satisfaction in work and retirement.* Chicago: Rand McNally.

Sue, D. W. (1995). Multicultural organization development: Implications for the counseling profession. In J. G. Ponterotto, J. M. Casas, L. A. Suzuki, and C. M. Alexander (Eds.), *Handbook of multicultural counseling* (pp. 474–492). Thousand Oaks, CA: Sage Publications.

Sue, D. W., Carter, R., Casas, J., Fouad, N., Ivey, A., Jensen, M., LaFromboise, T., Manese, J., Ponterotto, J., & Vasquez-Nuttal, E. (1998). *Multicultural competencies: Individual and organizational development.* Thousand Oaks, CA: Sage Publications.

Thorndike, E. L. (1911). *Animal intelligence.* New York: Macmillan.

CREDITS

Figure 14.1, p. 441, Reproduced by special permission of the Publisher, Psychological Assessment Resources, Inc., from *Making Vocational Choices, Third Edition,* copyright 1973, 1985, 1992, 1997 by Psychological Assessment Resources, Inc. All rights reserved.

Figure 14.2, p. 447, From "A Life-Span, Life-Space Approach to Career Development" by D.E. Super, 1990, *Career Choice and Development: Applying Contemporary Theories to* Practice, p. 216, Copyright 1990 by Jossey-Bass. Reprinted by permission of Jossey-Bass, Inc., a subsidiary of John Wiley and Sons, Inc.

Figure 14.3, p. 448, From "The Life-Span, Life-Space Approach to Careers" by D.E. Super, M.L. Savickas & C.M. Super, 1996, *Career Choice and Development* (3rd ed.), p. 127. Copyright 1996 by Jossey-Bass. Reprinted by permission of Jossey-Bass, Inc., a subsidiary of John Wiley & Sons, Inc.

Figure 14.4, p. 458, copyright R.W. Lent, S.D. Brown, G. Hackett. Reprinted by permission.

Figure 18.1, p. 594, Courtesy of Weston H. Morrill, Ph.D.

NAME INDEX

SUBJECT INDEX